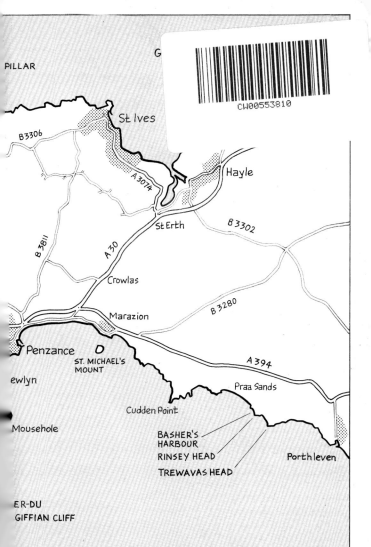

Unnamed route at Cripps Cove, Logan Rock
Climber: Shane Ohly   Photo: Norman Lomax

Climbers' Club Guides

Edited by Nigel Coe

West Cornwall

by

**John Hooper, Nick Hancock, Shane Ohly,
Pete O'Sullivan, Andy March, Sam Salmon,
Chris Craggs, Mike Raine, Martin Dunning,
Paul Bolton, David Hope, Des Hannigan**

Artwork by **Don Sargeant**

Front Cover: A Swift Flight of Fancy (E3), Sennen
Climbers: Nick Hancock and Sylvan Rondeau
Photo: Roger Ashby

Rear Cover: The Dream (E3), The Great Zawn
Climber: Egbert Dozekal
Photo: David Simmonite

Rear Cover Insert: Pre-Marital Tension (E8), Cribba Head
Climber: Ken Palmer
Photo: Rich Mayfield

Frontispiece Book One: Sennen
Frontispiece Book Two: Pordenack Point
Drawings: Pete O'Sullivan

Published by The Climbers' Club

Cornwall 1950
by A W Andrews and E C Pyatt

Cornwall Volume 2 1966
by V N Stevenson

Cornwall Volume 1 1968
by P H Biven and M B McDermott

Chair Ladder and the South Coast 1975
by R D Moulton and T D Thompson

Bosigran and the North Coast 1978
by E R Hart

Cornwall – West Penwith 1984
by P O'Sullivan

Bosigran and the North Coast 1991
by D Hannigan

Chair Ladder and the South Coast 1992
by D Hannigan

West Cornwall 2000
by John Hooper et al.

© The Climbers' Club 2000

Hooper, John   West Cornwall   (Climbers' Club Guides)

British Library Cataloguing in Publication Data

A catalogue record of this book is available from the British Library

796.552

ISBN 0-901601-69-1

Typeset by John Willson
Printed by Hi-Tec Print, North Anston, Sheffield
Distributed by Cordee, 3a De Montfort Street, Leicester, LE1 7HD

Contents

Book One

Book Two

Maps and Diagrams

Book One

Book Two

Climbers' Club Guides

The Climbers' Club
The publisher of this guidebook is The Climbers' Club, which was founded in 1898 from origins in Snowdonia and is now one of the foremost mountaineering clubs in Great Britain. Its objects are to encourage mountaineering and rock-climbing, and to promote the general interest of mountaineers and the mountain environment.

It is a truly national club with widespread membership, and currently owns huts in Cornwall, Pembrokeshire, Derbyshire, and Snowdonia. Besides managing six huts, The Climbers' Club produces an annual Journal and runs a full programme of climbing meets, dinners, and social events. Club members may also use the huts of other clubs through reciprocal arrangements. The Club publishes climbing guidebooks (currently 18 in number) to cover most of Wales and Southern England. The Club is a founder-member of, and is affiliated to, the British Mountaineering Council; it makes annual contributions to the BMC's Access Fund, as well as to volunteer cliff and mountain rescue organizations. In 1999, the Climbers' Club Colin Kirkus Guidebook Fund was established as a means of distributing some of the profits earned from guidebooks to assist climbing-related projects that are in keeping with the aims of the Club, though they need not be confined to the Club's guidebook areas.

Membership fluctuates around 1,000, and at present there are no limits on growth. Members of two years' standing may propose a competent candidate for membership and, provided that adequate support is obtained from other members, the Committee may elect him or her to full membership; there is no probationary period.

Climbing Style
The following policy statement on climbing style was agreed in principle at The Climbers' Club Annual General Meeting on 25th February 1990:

The Climbers' Club supports the tradition of using natural protection and is opposed to actions which are against the best interest of climbers and users of the crags. This applies particularly to irreversible acts which could affect the crags and their environs.

Such acts could include: the placing of bolts on mountain and natural crags; retrospective placing of bolts; chiselling, hammering, or altering the rock appearance or structure; excessive removal of vegetation and interference with trees, flowers, and fauna.

The Climbers' Club policy is that guidebooks are written to reflect the best style matched to the ethos and traditions of British Climbing.

Carn Galver mine stacks and
The Count House, Bosigran. D.J.S. 2000

Guidebook Disclaimer

This guide attempts to provide a definitive record of all existing climbs and is compiled from information from a variety of sources. The inclusion of any route does not imply that it remains in the condition described. Climbs can change unpredictably: rock can deteriorate and the existence and condition of *in-situ* protection can alter. All climbers must rely on their own ability and experience to gauge the difficulty and seriousness of any climb. Climbing is an inherently dangerous activity.

Neither The Climbers' Club nor the authors and editor of this guidebook accept any liability whatsoever for any injury or damage caused to climbers, third parties, or property arising from the use of it. Whilst the content of the guide is believed to be accurate, no responsibility is accepted for any error, omission, or mis-statement. Users must rely on their own judgement and are recommended to insure against injury to person and property and third party risks.

The inclusion in this guidebook of a crag or routes upon it does not mean that any member of the public has a right of access to the crag or the right to climb upon it. Before climbing on any crag in this guidebook, please read the access notes on page 17.

Acknowledgements

For the first time the West Penwith guidebooks have been produced by a group of authors rather than a single individual, each tackling a particular stretch of coast. All have been helped by a large number of climbers, to whom we express our gratitude. In particular, the authors and editor would like to thank:

The authors of all previous guidebooks covering West Penwith and The Lizard.

John Cox, Martin Crocker, Bob Moulton, and Scott Titt for checking the main text.

Mike Vetterlein for proof-reading the entire guidebook.

Hugh Alexander, Bob Banaster, Dave Birkett, Peter Brown, Barnaby Carver, Toni Carver, Alan and Wendy Cocker, Rick Collings, Mick Crayton, Tim Dennell, Steve Elliott, Ali Fewell, Justin Ford, Andy Grieve, Mike Hammill, Gill Heys and members of the Oread Mountaineering Club, Mark Hounslea, Gordon Jenkin, Ginny March, Roger Mitchell, Bob Mott, Harvey Mullen, Phil Oak, Ken Palmer, Luke Pavey, Graham Robinson, Robin Shail, Barrie Simpson, Gavin Slade, Raj Tewson, Simon Tong, Ken Vickers, Roger Wilkinson, John Willson, and Ken Wilson for volunteering information, checking routes, or helping in other ways.

Rowland Edwards and Mark Edwards for providing details of their new routes and information on others.

Jeremy Clitherow of English Nature and Jon Brookes of The National Trust for commenting on the environmental information, and Edward Davies of HM Coastguard for checking the accident procedure notes.

All who submitted photos.

The Society for the Promotion of Christian Knowledge for permission to quote from A Week at The Lizard by The Revd Charles Johns.

The editor would especially like to thank Bob Moulton for cross-checking the first ascent list and John Willson for typesetting the guide, and both of them for helping and guiding him through his first editing task.

NAC Autumn 2000

Introduction

West Cornwall belongs to the Atlantic. Its cliffs are the hard-faced survivors of the sea's grinding influence on masses of igneous and metamorphic rock. The main rock types of interest to the climber are the granite, greenstone, and 'killas' slate of West Penwith. The cliffs of the Lizard peninsula are included in this guide for the first time. While the Lizard is renowned for its 'soapstone', a rock of variable reputation, almost all the development has been on the more reliable schists, the quality of which should tempt climbers away from more traditional Penwithian haunts.

Most of the area's cliffs rise from sea-level and are thus affected by tide, wave, and swell with their attendant excitement and added danger. Yet West Penwith is famed for major crags like Bosigran, set well above the sea, and numerous other crags are affected by the tide only partly or not at all.

The area holds great appeal as a holiday venue for climbers, and because of this the guide is aimed chiefly at those whose time is precious. The following notes are therefore meant to help visitors get the best out of the area's astonishing and varied climbing opportunities without too many complications or missed chances.

Crag Overview
Godrevy Point   Fine evening bouldering at low tide.
Wicca Pillar   Short, pleasant routes in superb surroundings. Far from the madding crowd.
Zennor Cliff   A handful of good, steep routes on the non-tidal upper cliff. More atmospheric outings in the zawn below.
Carnelloe   A gentle, traditional crag situated off the breaten track.
Boswednack   Secluded. A couple of historic climbs set amidst tough modern fare.
Gurnard's Head   Very popular on account of the classic Hard Severe *Right Angle* and some fine harder additions. Mostly tidal, and atmospheric. A good evening crag.
Pedn Kei area   Not often visited due to some looseness, wetness, and nesting seabirds, but there are some worthwhile pitches, especially at Pedn Kei West, which is excellent on summer evenings.
Zawn Duel/Carn Gloose   Impressive situations. A few easy routes now eclipsed by harder additions on the main crag. *The Adversary* is a classic of the zawn climbing genre and *Astral Stroll* is a must-do.
Wenven Cove   A few easy routes. Bird sensitive.
Robin's Rocks   The greenstone essence. A handful of minor classics.
Windy Zawn   One of those nice little out-of-the-way places with some good, steep climbing. Superb geology!

Halldrine Cove   Quiet and friendly. A fistful of Diffs make this a beginner's delight.

Bosigran   The first of the big three – *the* classic Cornish cliff with something of stature for everyone. Multi-pitch routes, most of which start well above the sea.

Bosigran Ridge   A long, classic outing, rain or shine, but with a tidal first pitch.

Great Zawn   Adventure climbing at its best. Impressive atmosphere with a collection of great routes. All approaches require abseils and a high degree of commitment, adding to the serious nature of the place. The ledges below *Variety Show* are particularly dangerous when there is any swell.

Rosemergy Cove   Tidal and secluded. Most finishes require care.

Rosemergy Ridge area   A group of generally secluded crags. Monolith Slab has a handful of stiff little pitches.

Rosemergy Towers   A great evening crag with a pleasant atmosphere and low to middle grade routes. Easy access.

Whirl Pool Buttress   Hard routes in impressive surroundings. Tidal, with access especially difficult if the sand is missing! A couple of potentially classic E2s.

Great Moor Zawn   Remote and spectacular, but only for devotees of the damp and desperate. And with just the one route – unrepeated since 1976.

Trevowhan Cliff area   Adventurous. Tidal, swell-affected and (perhaps unsurprisingly) rarely crowded. If you like damp cracks, it's the place for you.

Carn Clough   Pleasant routes and a pleasant beach.

Pendeen Cliffs   Back on the slate (well, killas). Entertaining routes with easy, though tidal access.

Trewellard area   A succession of zawns and buttresses in a post-industrial setting. Good, generally short, routes abound.

Carn Vellan   A big, brooding cliff with steep, hard (some way-hard) routes and an 'entertaining' VS.

Botallack Head Zawn   Hidden gems.

Freedom Zawn   Big, steep adventure routes.

Crowns Mine Cliff   Mostly VSs here.

Evening Slabs   Evening is the best time, and an evening may be enough time, for the four routes here.

Kenidjack Cliffs   Killas classics on steep slabs, from *Seadreams* to *Saxon*, in the heart of tin country. The main cliff gets very busy at peak times.

Carn Glooze area   Esoteric.

Porth Nanven   Small but perfectly formed.

Aire Point   A superb outlook and some enjoyable routes. Close to one of West Cornwall's premier surfing beaches.

Sennen (Pedn-mên-du)   The shortest of the great West Penwith triumvirate. Ease of access, a delightful setting, and a variety of minor classics make this a very popular crag. Something for everyone, but surprisingly steep and strenuous in places.

Land's End area   A jumble of zawns and buttresses with sometimes difficult approaches and finishes, much of which is subject to the tourists' gaze. Some routes are worth the effort though; *Atlantic Ocean Wall* is a great challenge while *Land's End Long Climb* is an all-weather classic. Don't miss the low-tide walk through the arches beneath Dr Syntax's Head.

Pordenack Point   What a difference a kilometre makes. Take a stroll and leave the hordes behind. Your effort will be rewarded by a good mix of grades on mainly excellent rock. Non-tidal on the upper crags.

Carn Boel area   An interesting little headland with some worthwhile easy routes and a couple of 'Immaculate' classics.

Carn Lês Boel/Bosistow area   Well worth a visit. A rather enigmatic area where pre-war easies rub shoulders with modern desperates. Most of the more substantial routes are tidal and many require abseil approaches. The quality of the rock can be variable, especially in Bosistow Zawn. *Excalibur* is a hidden classic.

Pendower Coves   A generally friable area of granite with one or two solid bits.

Zawn Kellys   A small buttress of generally sound granite. Worth the walk for *American Dream*.

Carn Barra   Once a quiet place to get away from the Bank Holiday crowds, this crag is now much more popular, thanks to a sustained bout of E-grade activity during the early 80s. Mostly tidal, except for the excellent Central Wall.

Dutchman's Zawn   A handful of tidal extremes.

Folly Cove   Tidal climbs on sometimes friable granite.

Fox Promontory   Despite some good, mainly low to middle grade climbs, this can still be a quiet location. Watch the sea though.

Black Carn South   Now, if you want to really get away from the crowds...

Porth Loe/Pellitras area   This quiet, pleasant area is often passed by on the way to other things.

Carn Guthensbrâs   A good little crag, overshadowed by its mighty neighbour, yet with its own strong identity. Some pleasant, short pitches at all grades.

Chair Ladder   The third of West Penwith's big three requires more thought and care than the other two in terms of access, but the rewards repay the effort. Excellent multi-pitch routes of all grades, but it can get very crowded on those ledges.

Porthgwarra Buttress and Hella Point   A quieter alternative, with good routes (mostly low grades) and superb granite.

Levan's Wall/Pedn-mên-an-mere   Worth seeking out. A collection of climbs which includes a couple of treasures.

Porthcurno/Logan Rock area   This stretch of coast has it all: good beaches, isolated zawns, nude sunbathers, and a decent pub. Shoehorned in are a few half-decent rock climbs and some very good bouldering.

Cribba Head area   Once a sandbagger's delight, this isolated little buttress has rather more to offer nowadays. Non-tidal and with a sheltered east face.

Penberth/Porthguarnon   Quiet. Mostly easy routes in pleasant surroundings.

Coffin Cove   A delightful and remote spot.

St Loy   Has gained in popularity over recent years. One of the few completely non-tidal crags in the area, with some of the boldest pitches.

Tregiffian   Off the beaten track, but deserves to become popular, especially with slab enthusiasts.

Tater-du   The black stuff. A greenstone island in a sea of granite, with a classic VS and more besides. Don't come here in poor visibility as the nearby foghorn rattles teeth and holds alike.

Basher's Harbour/Trewavas   Penwithian outliers. Trewavas, in particular, is a delightful area with a superb outlook towards the Lizard. Little treasures, much prized by locals. Mostly low to middle grades.

Predannack Head   A rather complex area with mostly low to middle grade routes, though further possibilities abound.

Vellan Head   The Hidden Buttress is well worth seeking out. Big multi-pitch routes of true quality in an isolated area.

Soap Rock to Kynance Cove   A great deal of rock, but it tends to be of poor quality.

Lizard Point area   A good selection of routes, often steep, on Britain's most southerly point. Access is generally amenable. Tower Buttress and The Hollywood Walls are the main attractions.

Housel Bay to Bass Point   Although somewhat smaller in stature, Bass Point vies with Hidden Buttress for the title of the Lizard's premier crag. *The Cull* is a must-do for those who can-do. Pen Olver provides a worthwhile selection of short routes in the Difficult to Very Severe range.

Black Head   Some good climbs on unusual rock.

Isles of Scilly   A few scattered routes and plenty of bouldering in a superb setting.

Rock Types

Individual cliffs have their rock types identified throughout the guide.

Granite. West Penwith is famous for its granite, a hard, 'friendly', igneous rock of great structural beauty. The Land's End Granite, which gives form to the peninsula, contains three main joint-systems created as the granite magma cooled. The jointing forms planes of weakness which are attacked by weathering and erosion, giving the area's characteristic climbing features of deep horizontal breaks and vertical cracks. The rock is well supplied with flakes, jugs, edges, crystals, pockets, and erratic veins of minerals like quartz and tourmaline. Belay ledges are usually excellent. West Penwith granite is generally sound, although the Land's End area and parts of the south coast have small areas of altered (kaolinised) granite which are of weaker substance than the solid, wind-polished rock of Bosigran, Chair Ladder, or Sennen's main cliff. Climbing on granite is often steep and can be gymnastic, although there are many easy-angled pitches. There is marvellous variety available, from low-to-middle-grade climbs on virtually every crag, through multi-pitch extremes, to highly technical ultra-extremes. Protection possibilities are generally very good and varied so that a mixed rack is sufficient. There are some routes with poor protection, however.

Greenstone is a name applied to several kinds of metamorphosed basaltic igneous rocks. It is a dark hard rock with a 'greenish' tint and it forms dramatic features like Gurnard's Head. Greenstone cliffs are steep, although some easier-angled features exist. They are generally sound but minor looseness may occur. The rock offers fewer 'friendly' holds than granite and there are a lot of square-cut fingerholds and slots. Climbing on greenstone is delightful and often very atmospheric. Greenstone is compact and protection is not so varied as on granite. Small wires are useful.

Killas is a Cornish mining term for slate, a metamorphosed sedimentary rock, and is applied generally to cliffs like Kenidjack that are composed of greenstones and slates. Killas cliffs have a chaotic appearance and are dark-coloured and variegated. They have fewer defined features than granite cliffs and, although excellent independent lines are the norm, several routes have something of a 'climb anywhere' element. Killas is the least stable of the area's rock; occasional 'crunchiness' may be encountered. Although technically described as slate, the rocks have a completely different character to those in North Wales and are much more receptive to natural protection placements. However, protection is often not so deep-seated as on granite and can be sketchy on some routes. Small wires are useful.

The Lizard Complex is made up of rocks which are completely different to any found in West Penwith. For many years the subject of much debate among geologists, it is now recognised that the Lizard Complex represents a section of oceanic crust. During the tectonic closure of the ocean, huge compressional forces moved the rocks to their present position along a series of thrust planes, or low-angle faults. The Lizard Complex consists of four predominant rock types: peridotite, schist, amphibolite, and gabbro. The gabbro forms no cliffs on The Lizard that are of interest to climbers. Peridotite is an igneous rock formed at great depths, in the earth's mantle, and is not commonly seen at the surface. After formation, the peridotite was affected by metamorphism and hydrothermal processes, resulting in the complete alteration of the original minerals in the rock. This process is referred to as 'serpentinisation' and produces the serpentine, for which the peninsula is famous. Unfortunately for climbers, the alteration process has a profound effect on the integrity of the rock, which can vary enormously over relatively small distances, from solid to extremely loose, with frictional properties admirably described by the term 'soapstone'. The schists of the Lizard are highly deformed and metamorphosed ocean-floor sediments, while the amphibolites are metamorphosed lavas and gabbroic intrusions. Both form much more reliably solid cliffs which are often steep and juggy, and where the protection is generally good.

Weather Conditions

Most Penwith cliffs have a generally southerly to westerly outlook, although there are a few cliffs or cliff sections facing north or east. The guide gives the outlook of each crag. This allows individual judgement on wind direction and sunshine, relevant even in hot, dry conditions when cool shade may be welcomed. Even in dry summers, early mist and sea fog can cause dampness and 'greasy' rock, especially on granite. This soon vanishes on dry, sunny days.

West Penwith is usually first in line for whatever the Atlantic throws at Britain. However, the Peninsula's southerly position can mean milder temperatures, and so climbing in Penwith is definitely an all-year-round option. Throughout the winter, the area's south-facing cliffs especially can offer magnificent climbing on dry rock and in quasi-summer conditions. From late autumn through to spring, however, dampness on the cliffs is more common as the water-tables rise, drainage and seepage occur, and humidity increases. Most granite dries very quickly, and the nature of the rock, particularly the granite, means that wet conditions do not necessarily preclude doing a route.

The Lizard's cliffs also face south and west and are afforded a slight degree of shelter from westerly gales by the bulk of the Penwith peninsula (although you might not believe it on some days). Dampness can also be a problem, particularly on the serpentine crags.

Tides

At the head of each cliff section in the guide there is information about the overall tidal regime. Tide-tables can be bought cheaply at most local newsagents and give clear guidance to times of high and low water for the current year only. Tables for major sea-cliffs can also be viewed on the Climbers' Club website at www.climbers-club.co.uk.

There are two tidal cycles: springs and neaps. Spring-tides rise the highest but also go out the furthest. They give the best access to sea-level cliffs either side of low water. **While spring-tides give much better access at their low-water point they flood rapidly two or three hours after low water.** Neap-tides have less of a rise and fall.

The tidal cycle runs through an approximate seven days of spring-tides, increasing in rise and fall up to the middle day, and decreasing thereafter to merge into a following seven days of neap-tides. Neap-tides follow the same pattern until they again merge into the next run of spring-tides.

The daily routine of tides has its own cycle based on a six-hour flood to high water followed by a six-hour ebb to low water. Low water of a spring-tide is usually within three hours either side of midday and midnight. Low water of a neap-tide is usually within three hours either side of six a.m. and six p.m. Access to the base of most tidal cliffs is at its best from two to three hours before low water until two to three hours after low water. The times of low and high water shift ahead by an average of 40 minutes each day of the cycle, so that they occur slightly later each day.

Sea Conditions

Over the years, many people, climbers among them, have died needlessly on the Cornish coast due to ignorance of, or disregard for, the dangers of rough seas. Perfect tidal conditions can mean nothing if a big swell or a heavy sea is running. Stormy weather is obvious, but in West Penwith and The Lizard swell is deceptive. Substantial swells can run into the cliffs even in windless conditions with an apparently calm sea. Swell is often present in fine weather and is caused by low-pressure areas far out in the Atlantic. The sea can look smooth offshore yet at the base of a tidal cliff it may be boiling white with a vicious rise half-way up the face. Dangerous swell can also arise suddenly with a changing tide. **If in any doubt, do not go to the foot of the cliffs.** In any case, always belay when close to the sea.

Coastguard Identity

Each cliff has a 'Coastguard Identity'. This may seem unnecessary in many cases. However, several climbing venues have acquired names known only to the climbing fraternity while some traditional names are duplicated around the coast. The list of Coastguard Identities in the guide has been agreed with HM Coastguard and Air-Sea Rescue authorities and will be used by them as a location guide. Climbers are advised to use these precise names when giving details of an emergency.

Access

There are no major problems of access to the cliffs of West Penwith and surrounding areas, although one or two venues are sensitive. The National Trust owns many of the main cliff areas and maintains a policy of free access for individuals, subject to conservation needs. West Penwith is internationally important for its rock-climbing and most of its coastline is also covered by a number of overlapping protective designations. These range from the Ministry of Agriculture, Fisheries, and Food's Environmentally Sensitive Area scheme, through Government-designated 'Areas of Outstanding Natural Beauty', to English Nature's Sites of Special Scientific Interest (SSSIs). The coastal mining areas within Penwith are viewed as having potential for inclusion on the United Nations' list of World Heritage Sites.

One area in West Penwith has been identified by The National Trust as a sanctuary area: Porthmoina Island at Bosigran. The West Cornwall Environmental Liaison Group, which includes representatives from the British Mountaineering Council (BMC) and the Land's End Climbing Club supports this voluntary designation. It is hoped that this arrangement will be kept under review.

The climbing areas of The Lizard are as valuable and sensitive as those of West Penwith. The geology of the peninsula is reflected in the chemistry of the soils and this in turn gives rise to unusual and rare plant communities. Of particular importance is the stretch of coast between Mullion Harbour and Vellan Head. The cliffs extending for about a kilometre south of the harbour are The Lizard National Nature Reserve and climbing is prohibited.

There can be no doubt as to the area's genuine environmental importance. Climbers are asked to apply their normal good practice and care to the cliff environments of West Penwith and The Lizard. There are several venues which are especially vulnerable in terms of flora and fauna. These are mentioned where relevant, as are those few cliffs where land ownership may pose difficulties.

The Crag Environment

The coastline of Cornwall, which includes the crags described in this guide, is inhabited by a remarkable variety of flora and fauna which form part of a complex and inter-related eco-system possessing great natural beauty. This leaves responsible climbers facing awkward dilemmas. Our desire to climb can lead to some degree of damage. The overwhelming majority will want to see this kept to a minimum. A few years ago, in response to concerns being expressed by a number of bodies, representatives of the BMC, the National Trust, English Nature and the Land's End Climbing Club set up the West Cornwall Access and Conservation Liaison Group. The aim of the group is to identify environmental problems which climbing may create, and to propose ways in which they may be dealt with sensibly and positively. As a result of their investigations the Group published *The Green Guide* (much of which is now incorporated into this guide) with a view to promoting good environmental practice among those who wish to climb in the area. The Group also proposed a *Climbers Code for Cornwall*, which is reproduced below. Many of the crags in West Penwith and The Lizard lie within SSSIs. All SSSIs are protected by the provisions of the Wildlife and Countryside Act, under which offences include *damage to plant and animal life and to the fabric of the rock*. Climbers should be aware that all areas covered by the climbing guide are vulnerable. Those areas identified as giving particular cause for concern are identified in the text, together with local guidelines on access and conservation.

A Climbers Code for Cornwall

Respect land ownership. Continuing access depends on co-existence.

Tread lightly on the approach as well as on the face. Please avoid wearing heavy walking boots when descending vegetated slopes and gullies. Where possible, follow existing access paths. Do not create new paths, or shortcuts on existing paths. Try to avoid going to cliffs in large groups. Base your changing area on bare rock where possible. Keep noise to a minimum. Leave no litter.

Do not 'garden' vegetation or lichen on new or established routes, at any time of the year. Cracks and seams in the rock are often crucial habitats for insect life. Stripping of live vegetation is against the law.

Avoid entering biologically vulnerable areas, especially during the sensitive bird breeding and plant growth season of March to July. Keep up to date with agreed, published restrictions and respect these.

Respond constructively if approached by National Trust staff or by officers of English Nature, or by Countryside Officers of local and regional authorities. Avoid negative confrontation with other cliff users, and with farmers, private landowners, or their employees. Please report any problems to the local BMC Access Representative or the BMC Access Officer.

Consider seeking advice from National Trust staff if planning new routes, especially in underdeveloped areas.

For further access and environmental information, climbers can contact the following organisations:
Jon Brookes, National Trust Countryside Manager (West Penwith) 01736 796993;
Alastair Cameron, National Trust Countryside Manager (The Lizard) 01326 561407;
Ray Lawman, Site Manager, The Lizard National Nature Reserve 01326 240808;
English Nature 01872 865261;
The Access Officer, British Mountaineering Council 0161 445 4747.

Birds

Large numbers of birds nest along the West Cornwall coast. Some stay faithful to the same sites year after year, while others periodically switch cliffs. The principal sites are mentioned in the text, but climbers should use their judgement regarding the possible impact of their sports plan on nesting birds. The nesting season for the majority of birds stretches from the beginning of March to the end of June.

West Cornwall's cliff-dwelling sea-bird population has decreased for a number of reasons. These include pollution and a definite move of habitat to seaside towns and villages where the living is easy and where the massive intake of discarded junk food is increasing sea-bird aggression. Herring Gulls and Fulmars can be aggressive and may draw blood during the nesting season, and are best avoided for obvious reasons.

Peregrine Falcons are nesting at several locations on the West Penwith coast after years of serious decline. However, they are still a schedule 1 listed species (ie. threatened) and are particularly vulnerable during the nesting season. If the female Peregrine is scared off the nest for even a short period, the eggs may chill irretrievably and, at worst, the female may abandon the nest. Warnings of the proximity of protected species are included in the text. There are no statutory 'bird bans' in West Penwith but legislation relating to the 'disturbance' of nesting Peregrines holds good and heavy penalties can be imposed for cases of proven disturbance. This definition of disturbance is a grey area, but fair play and good sense are encouraged on the basis that while the principle of right of access should be defended, climbers have a choice of hundreds of climbs. The Peregrine's nest is its *only* chance.

Route Descriptions and Grades

The cliffs are described in an anti-clockwise direction around the coast of the peninsula. Descent routes are described with the terms 'left' and right' relating to the climber facing out unless otherwise stated. From its base each cliff is described from left to right, facing in, without exceptions. Pegs mentioned in the text are for runners unless explicitly described as being used for aid.

West Penwith grading remains traditional without being archaic: the established adjectival system is used, that is, in order of difficulty, Moderate, Difficult, Very Difficult, Severe, Hard Severe, Very Severe, Hard Very Severe, E1, E2, etc. Numerical (technical) grades are given for pitches of 4a and above.

Climbs in West Penwith are often felt by visiting climbers to be tough or undergraded, although this may reflect first impressions of a strange area made more intimidating by the sea. A large number of grade revisions were included in both the previous and this edition of the guide, the result of intensive consultation with dozens of climbers of all abilities. A number of 'sandbags' were dealt with and it is now felt that most grading idiosyncrasies have been removed without unduly altering the overall 'feel' of the area. Climbers should bear in mind that West Penwith is a traditional adventure climbing area. Common sense, good judgement and climbing craft should be employed in good measure at all times and on all crags.

However, some routes have not had objective, independent second ascents, and some of the more technical pitches have left even top climbers bewildered as to their status. Climbs which are not known to have had reasonably successful on-the-lead second ascents are marked with a dagger sign: †. Some older established routes on remote cliffs may not have had ascents for a number of years and may have changed. If a route has suffered a rockfall which may have affected its grade or description and the route has not been reclimbed, it is marked with ††. Bolted and chipped routes are indented in the text.

Stars

The star system has been used as a guide to the quality of selected routes of all grades. The publishers believe that stars should be awarded only by consensus and that the practice of first ascensionists 'starring' their own routes is inevitably suspect. Stars given by first ascensionists to their own new routes are included in the form of hollow stars, pending confirmatory ascents.

The star system in this guide is based on a jaundiced view of climbers' superlatives. Thus ★★★ should mean exceptional, ★★ extremely good, and ★ very good. This should indicate that there are many non-starred 'good' climbs and where possible a verbal opinion of such quality is included. Routes under 10 metres in length are not starred as a policy, although recognition of their quality may again be noted.

Equipment

West Penwith climbing accommodates virtually every type of on-the-lead placement. The revolution in camming devices has improved protection possibilities, especially on granite. Standard rope lengths are more than adequate, with few pitches exceeding 45 metres. Abseil ropes are essential for several cliffs and optional on others, although the majority of cliffs are accessible by walking, scrambling, or easy down-climbing. Salt water and sea air may adversely affect ropes and gear after only a short time. It is advisable to wash ropes and equipment after such use in warm fresh water, and then lightly oil their metal moving parts.

Pegs

There are still a number of pegs on the West Penwith cliffs. The standard warning about their uncertainty and susceptibility to corrosion as a result of salt assault is stressed. All known pegs are mentioned in the text. The policy employed in the previous edition of this guide, that of giving a date when the peg was last *known* to be in position, has been discontinued. This is because as an indicator of reliability it could not take into account the type of peg, whether it was in a drainage line, the effect of prevailing conditions on the state of the peg, etc. Esoteric debate about stainless steel pegs is irrelevant at this time. The main rule on all crags, but especially on sea-cliffs, should be **do not trust *in-situ* gear**. This includes jammed wires and slings.

Ethics

Few climbers can be unaware of the controversy surrounding the use of drilled pegs and bolts in West Penwith in the past. Pegs have been used in the area for many years, but were to an extent justified in the 'old days' by the absence of other protection techniques. That excuse no longer has any validity. The placing of bolts underwent a revival, although a generally unpopular one, in the 80s. At a BMC South Western and Southern Area

Committee meeting in 1993 attended by about sixty local and locally active climbers, it was agreed by an overwhelming majority that bolts and other modern fixed gear had no place on the sea-cliffs of West Penwith. The majority of the bolts in the area have been removed.

In addition to bolt use, chipping and hold-creation have taken place on a number of climbs in West Penwith. Such action is condemned by all climbers.

Amenities

West Penwith is well supplied with a wide choice of accommodation although it is sparse in the Bosigran area. There are a number of first class campsites throughout the district, but 'wild' camping is prohibited. Trevaylor campsite between Botallack and St Just is worthy of special note as they sell chalk and some other climbing gear. The newly refurbished Count House bunkhouse at Bosigran is owned by The Climbers' Club but can be booked by members of other clubs. Youth Hostels are another choice. St Just YHA (Letcha Vean, St Just, Penzance. Tel. 01736 788437) is situated in the beautiful Cot Valley. Penzance YHA is at Castle Horneck, Alverton, Penzance (Tel. 01736 363666). There is also a backpackers' lodge at the Old Chapel, Zennor.

Public transport is variable at present in an area which has long stretches of sparsely populated coastline. Apart from Land's End and Sennen, few of the main climbing areas are well-served by regular public transport. The local bus company is First Western National, which has an office in Penzance (Tel. 01209 719988). Rail travel into the area is now in the hands of three separate operators (Great Western, Wales and West, and Virgin Trains). For national rail enquiries telephone 0345 484950. Perhaps a better bet would be the BMC's car share noticeboard at http://www.thebmc.co.uk/. St Just has a post office, banks, and a chemist. There is a small supermarket open from 8 a.m. to 11 p.m. seven days a week. Cape Cornwall Golf Club has a small indoor swimming pool which is open to visitors. Penzance and St Ives have the usual social amenities although neither is well situated for the cliffs. There are Tourist Information Centres in Penzance (Tel. 01736 362207 or 352341) and St Ives (Tel. 01736 796297). There is a casualty department at **West Cornwall Hospital** (Tel. 01736 874000) in Penzance. This is located at the top of Penalverne Drive, just up the road from the Police Station.

The Lizard peninsula tends to have a quieter, more relaxed feel to it than Penwith. The main town is Helston, with Falmouth being not too far away. Helston is famous for its 'Furry Dance' which takes place on 'Flora Day', on or about May 8th every year. The town is also well known for the Blue Anchor pub, one of the oldest inns in the country still brewing its own beer, which is known as 'Spingo' and is definitely not to be under-estimated. The peninsula is home to Europe's largest helicopter base, RNAS Culdrose. Further south, at Goonhilly Downs, ancient monuments stand side by side with the latest in communication technology. The Lizard also suffers from a sparse public transport system, although Lizard town itself is reasonably well served. There are several good campsites on the peninsula and, again, 'wild' camping is prohibited. Coverack YHA is situated close to the last mainland cliff in this guide at Park Behan, School Hill, Coverack (tel. 01326 280687). There is a Tourist Information Centre in Helston (Tel. 01326 565431). The nearest casualty department is at the **Royal Cornwall Hospital**, Treliske, Truro (Tel. 01872 250000).

Unfortunately car theft is a problem at many of the more isolated parking places, particularly on the north coast. The normal precautions concerning leaving valuables in cars should be taken.

Sea-Level Traverses and Deep-Water Solos

In the 1950 guide, A W Andrews detailed a number of his 'coasteering' expeditions. The West Penwith coastline, and particularly the section from Great Zawn to beyond Trevowhan Head, offers abundant opportunities for this never fashionable but very adventurous sport, which consists of finding the lowest possible passage above the sea, mostly by advanced scrambling, climbing the odd pitch of up to Severe or more, and swimming where necessary. In perfect conditions much fun can be had on the more friendly stretches in trainers and trunks; or one can take things more seriously with all the necessary for advanced Tyroleans.

Since these little-frequented spots are at the mercy of everything that the Atlantic can hurl at them, it is unlikely that Andrews's 50-year-old descriptions, based probably in many cases on experiences of half a century earlier, will bear much resemblance to current reality. In any case, the lines have never been as popular or organized as their limestone counterparts at Torbay and Swanage. It seems better, therefore, to allow enthusiasts to rediscover the delights on offer for themselves.

Such expeditions are not to be undertaken lightly, especially where swimming, voluntary or involuntary, is likely to be involved; an apparently calm blue sea can mask a heaving swell or vicious current. Nevertheless, thorough research, especially of tides, conditions, and exit and escape routes, can reopen a whole old world of genuine adventure and discovery.

The opportunity for deep-water soloing is limited in West Cornwall, and few new routes have been claimed in this style. Unlike the limestone cliffs of Dorset and Devon, few of the cliffs in West Cornwall fall straight into deep water, and the influence of the Atlantic on the waves, swell, and current mean that days are few when conditions are right. Gurnard's Head is a serious venue for strong swimmers only. More amenable are Porthcurno Bay and the Logan Rock area.

Bouldering

Carn Brea (OS Ref 685 407), a local landmark above Redruth and Camborne, provides excellent bouldering.

The Wave at Basset's Cove (OS Ref 637 442) is a futuristic – so futuristic that the only problems completed avoid the main challenges – sweep of overhanging rock above perfect landings. Take the B3301 coast road from Hayle towards Portreath. After Gwithian the road rises and runs parallel to the cliffs. Stop in the second car-park on the left. From the cliff edge, descend an indistinct steep path and then downclimb to a secluded beach, where The Wave is found.

Godrevy Point is the best bouldering spot in West Cornwall, and is described on its own in the main text.

St Ives Station. The retaining wall below the station is the best man-made traversing wall in the area.

Clodgy Point (OS Ref 507 414) lies north-west of St Ives and offers a wide variety of good quality greenstone bouldering above a shingle beach.

The Bosworlas Boulders (OS Ref 379 306) are approached from the hamlet of Kelynack, which is on the St Just to Sennen road. Follow a minor road inland from Kelynack for a kilometre, whereupon the boulders are visible on the left. Parking is available by a public footpath sign.

The Pednvounder Beach area gives excellent granite bouldering and some good traverses.

Cribba Head: the east-facing overhanging wall which is passed when approaching the top of the headland from Penberth.

Gilingvase Beach, Falmouth. The 2-kilometre-long sea-wall is made of granite blocks and is between 3 and 6 metres high. Traverse territory.

Other bouldering spots are Zennor Hill (OS Ref 463 384) and Rosewall Hill (OS Ref 493 393).

Guidebooks

Details of the availability and prices of a wide range of guidebooks, including Climbers' Club guides, can be found on the Cordee website at www.cordee.co.uk.

Historical

Before the Flood

The cliffs of West Penwith were first climbed by desperate men.

Centuries ago shipwrecked sailors attempted epic escapes from rocky cove or deep zawn – if the sea spared them. They left no record of length, grade, or esoteric name. They sought the line of least resistance and in most cases never found it.

Later generations of Cornish men and women foraged the cliff sides for a living. Birds' eggs were collected for food, and fishing-stations were established on promontories and rock ledges amidst the stink of birdlime, seaweed, and salt spray. In King Lear, Shakespeare wrote of the samphire gatherers whose 'dreadful trade' sent them down cliffs to harvest the plant. The Cornish cliffs are still dense with samphire.

Such work went on for centuries, during which time the cliffs were treated as heathen wasteland if they failed to yield profit. Nobody loved them; they sank ships, killed people, and were convenient for throwing rubbish over.

Commercial exploitation of West Penwith's cliffs intensified during the 18th century as copper and tin miners worked the rich mineral seams, or lodes. Miners explored with remarkable zeal. There is hardly a stretch of Penwith's north coast where the 'old men' have not left some trace of their enterprise. Lodes were worked in from cliff-faces while drainage tunnels (adits) were sliced out from the swamped galleries into lonely zawns and coves. Miners 'climbed' after a fashion and there is one fascinating record of a miner who 'back-and-footed' up a thirty-metre chimney to escape from rising flood water.

Climbing as a gloriously pointless exercise came to West Penwith with the Victorians and then only as a home-brewed extension to Alpinism. The noted Alpinist and literary critic Sir Leslie Stephens climbed, 'gangling and prehensile', a chimney at Gurnard's Head in 1858, seven years before Whymper conquered The Matterhorn. Stephens's antics were probably justified as geological or botanical explorations rather than as gratuitous 'climbs', but the seed of climbing as a sport was sown by such scholarly 'field work'. There were climbing precedents of another sort. In the early part of the 19th century, local guides made a living from taking visitors to the famous Logan Rock at Treen and even into the awesome Tol Pedn cavern at the eastern end of Chair Ladder. Victorian adventurers scrambled about the cliffs of Cornwall, including those of West Penwith. Dr Tom Longstaff explored the atmospheric Culm Coast of North Cornwall as early as 1887, although he was uneasy about climbing above the sea, an experience that he felt was the antithesis of mountain-top freedom. 'The surf confines us with elemental restraint; thus far and no further,' quoth the good doctor, unknowingly launching a tradition of elegant *bon mots*.

The Edwardian/Andrews Era 1902-1912

One significant event firmly within the Victorian era was the purchase of the handsome house of Eagle's Nest above Zennor by John Westlake in 1873. Westlake's nephew, Arthur Westlake Andrews, son of a Wiltshire rector, spent many childhood holidays at Eagle's Nest. Young Arthur, a born athlete, may have clambered on the substantial rocks that lay close to Eagle's Nest; rocks with names such as The Snuffbox that in later years became 'bouldering' test-pieces for visiting climbers.

Arthur Westlake Andrews was born at Hastings in 1868 and enjoyed a Victorian middle-class life of the robust variety. His mother was a prodigious writer of historical biographies and novels and from her, no doubt, Andrews acquired subtle literary skills, which, enhanced by a classical education, later produced some fine poetry and the extremely well written 1950 climbing guide to West Penwith. At Oxford, Andrews had rooms below the leading Alpinist, Revd W A B Coolidge, with whom he became friends. Coolidge introduced Andrews to the finest mountaineering library in the country, but climbing was low on Andrews's agenda at first. The versatile Arthur was an exceptional tennis player, was picked for the university team, and represented Oxford in cross-country running and the high jump; *then* he went climbing.

Visits to North Wales in 1890 were preceded by an Alpine season and followed in 1891 by the first ascent of Norway's East Ringstind and by Alpine and Norwegian visits over the next 10 years. By 1902, Andrews had begun his lifelong involvement with West Penwith rock-climbing. With his formidable younger sister Marion Elizabeth, 'Elsie', he climbed and scrambled at Wicca Pillar below the family home. *Bosigran Ridge*, except for its first pitch, became their first multi-pitch 'course' in West Penwith. It was Atlantic Alpine enough. Andrews described the great feature as a 'remarkable serrated ridge of granite, ending in a wild and isolated combe'. Isolation was certainly the norm. There was little exploitation of the Bosigran coast at that time, least of all recreational. Andrews and his companions were climbing in a 'lost world', the textures and colours of which would be subtly different to those of today. Climbs were also done on Porthmoina Island in 1902 and the first pitch of *Bosigran Ridge* was added by J B 'Bretland' Farmer and Andrews in 1905. The pair climbed the top pitches of *Ledge Climb* in the same year, the first recorded route on Bosigran Main Face. Their climbing style was vividly described by Geoffrey Winthrop Young when he wrote, 'Andrews rubber-roamed, goat-like, up ribs while Bretland Farmer followed or preceded him with the sinuous slither and something of the look of a seal at the zoo...' These men could alliterate like sibilant snakes.

All this was still good Alpine 'training'. The following year, Andrews and Farmer made an 'outstanding expedition' by traversing The Meije in the Alps. Andrews wrote a lengthy account of West Penwith climbing for the Climbers' Club Journal of 1905, in which Wicca Pillar received detailed description unmatched by modern reviews. A reluctance to admit that climbing was gratuitous fun still prevailed. The article leaned heavily on geology with entertaining photographs of 'geological features'. Here and there, climbers peered round corners trying to look scholarly, although Andrews's jolly nature keeps breaking through. On one occasion he found a climber asleep on top of the Pillar and took a photograph of him; after which, 'I woke him up and we went home to tea and Cornish cream...' On the house of course; Andrews was most certainly not into the tourist trade.

The 1905 article featured a telling photograph of Bosigran Main Face with a crowning ribbon of whitewash staining the upper part of the Seaward Cliff. The whitewash mark was to give the lighthouse keepers at Pendeen two miles to the west some indication of visibility. When they could no longer see the paint mark the keepers fired up the fog-horn. In spite of Man's benign neglect, the cliffs were still being used for brutally practical purposes. The article was also a pointer to the area's climbing potential, although Andrews and his family and friends had it to themselves for many years to come.

The Victorian-Edwardian spirit of full-blooded adventure prevailed; and it led Arthur and Elsie to embark on the wildly eccentric plan of traversing the entire coastline of Britain between high and low water marks. West Penwith was the obvious place to start and brother and sister were soon crabbing their way along the tide-line through spectacular rock scenery. Elsie brooked no male timorousness when it came to serious water sports. She took the rope between her teeth and swam across channels to fix a Tyrolean for Arthur to bumble across carrying the gear. One advantage of such mammoth traversing was the discovery of acres of virgin rock. In his 1905 article, Andrews stated, 'I think I may claim with confidence that there is on the Cornish cliffs an almost unexplored region of the greatest interest.' Some say there still is...

The fruits of the Andrewses' sea-level explorations were harvested throughout the rest of the pre-war period, with climbs being recorded at the newly discovered Boswednack, Pedn Kei, Porthmeor Cove, Rosemergy Ridge, and Brandys Zawn. In 1912, Winthrop Young visited West Penwith and climbed the shapely little ridge at Carn Lês Boel with George Leigh Mallory, while Professor J E Littlewood climbed at Chair Ladder on several occasions pre-1915. He probably made several ascents, including *Western Chimneys*, although he left no record. Noel Odell climbed at Wicca, Bosigran, and points between with the Andrewses in 1912. Odell and Andrews were members of the Pen-y-Pass group, which included Mallory. The infamous occultist and self-styled 'Great Beast', Aleister Crowley, was certainly associated with the group, though whether Crowley would have joined any organization that would have him as a member is another matter. Crowley was on the loose in West Penwith for some time but there is no record of him climbing. He was probably too busy dancing naked around megaliths.

The Silent Decade 1912-22

For the next ten years, the First World War impinged on every aspect of life in Britain and reduced the opportunities for climbing trips, especially to such remote outposts as Cornwall. A visit was made to Penwith in 1915 by Arthur Thomson, who tried a full frontal ascent of Porthmoina Island. Thomson had less purple prose to spare, in keeping with the grim times, when he said, 'A crack was the obvious way to the summit but the position of the leader was sensational, the holds small, and the result of a fall too awful to contemplate. We returned the way we came...'

Bosigran's Count House had a vague association during the war years with the novelist D H Lawrence, who came to Cornwall soon after eloping with his German lover Frieda von Richthofen. The couple stayed for a time near Zennor at a cottage below Eagle's Nest and there Lawrence wrote parts of *Women In Love*. Lawrence did not climb, something that must be a great disappointment to the sport's hagiographers. He was, however, a frequent visitor to the Count House, which was owned by Andrews's uncle and was occupied at the time by a young musician, Cecil Gray. In climbing terms, Lawrence was the right man for dark chimneys and fecund zawns. He craved action and had immense moral courage; but he was frail despite being always ready to throw himself into the muscular work of the Zennor farms with a sometimes embarrassing enthusiasm. A revered matriarch of the Zennor farming community later said of him with lofty disdain, 'I knew Lawrence and I did not like him'. Full stop to anyone's reputation.

The Inter-War Years 1922-1940

Post-1918, Andrews explored Carn Lês Boel Pinnacle and recorded a number of pitches and traverses, while Odell climbed at Cape Cornwall, where the rock is solid only in small doses. Odell visited Chair Ladder at the same time but left no record of his exploits. In 1922, Andrews bought Tregerthen, the large but less striking house just below Eagle's Nest. The latter was by then owned by Mark Arnold-Foster. A delightful comment from Virginia Woolf's 'Diary' for 30 March 1921 states: 'Visited Arnold-Foster's at Eagle's Nest... Endless varieties of nice elderly men to be seen there, come for the climbing...', a comment which in one way neatly defines an entire generation. There was continuity also. Virginia Woolf was Leslie Stephens's daughter.

Tregerthen saw many of the nice but not so elderly as well. In 1922, Mallory, just two years before his disappearance on Everest, made the natural lower connection to *Ledge Climb* on Bosigran. Being a very nice man indeed, he was accompanied by Elsie Andrews and the Misses S and W Cox.

The following year, Sir T K Rose, Bertrand Jerram, and Maurice Guinness climbed *1923 Route*, a pleasant chimney above the vast zawn of the Horse's Back below Zennor Head. Jerram, often in the company of Captain Donald Romanis, made prolific explorations throughout Cornwall. Romanis kept meticulous diaries but seldom publicized what had been done. The pair were active from the 1890s to 1940 and Romanis's diaries, which survive, but which are unavailable, represent a lost era of climbing activity that might demand the rewriting of history one day. Climbs like *1923 Route* represented the developing style of individual 'direct' lines, although Andrews maintained the great tradition of traversing.

In 1923, Andrews traversed into Great Zawn via *Green Cormorant Ledge*, a significant event in the history of Cornish climbing. Ethics were based on first principles in those days. Andrews described the manœuvre thus: 'From a large platform a cleft must be crossed to a ledge. This is the crux of the climb and involves a very delicate finger-traverse (probably Hard Severe). A hitch or rope ring is advisable. A second might hold a rope over a small notch at the cliff end of the cleft. From the end of this ledge nearest to the Great Zawn the second must use the rope as the wall is not climbable and there is a slight swing to the left. There is a hitch but it is hard to find and a piton may be necessary.'

The reference to the piton was retrospective because Andrews did not use pitons until much later, but the creative rope-work was vintage. Andrews also built a 'pyramid of stones' to help him escape from the other side of the Zawn. It was still a striking adventure and he must surely have lingered in that great green place where his climber's eye noted the potential of the West Face.

It was not until the 30s that West Penwith's other great traditional cliff, Chair Ladder, gained 'official' status. Andrews had been there, certainly, but he was primarily a north coast man, probably for the mundane reason that transport from Zennor to the south coast was time-consuming and quite complex in those days. In the early 30s, Littlewood returned to this strikingly handsome and pure 'sea cliff'. With unknown companions he climbed *Cleft Route*, the upper part of *Pendulum Chimney*, *East Chimney*, and *Great Slab Route*. These were notable ascents that are perhaps more classically defined as sea-cliff climbs than Andrews's more complex and creative projects on the north coast.

In 1938, The Climbers' Club leased the Count House from Andrews's uncle, thereby taking West Penwith climbing firmly into the public domain. In August that year Colin Kirkus paid his first visit to West Penwith and climbed *Black Slab* at Bosigran and *Original Route* at Chair Ladder. During his stay, Kirkus made a bold solo attempt at the line of *Nameless* on Bosigran and is reputed to have got as far as the start of the final pitch before retreating.

Barrie Page (c.1957)   Photo: M Banks   Jim Simpson (1990)   Photo: J Atherton

Members of the CCAW (1950s). Zeke Deacon is on the extreme left and Mike Banks is second from right, front row.   Photo: Banks col.

Rawdon Goodier (1951)   Photo: J Hampton

Mike 'Mac' McDermott (1966) Photo:K Wilson

Mike Banks (1960s)   Photo: Banks col.

Joe Barry   Photo: John Barry col.

The last recorded route before business was suspended as the world again went to war was the delightful *Terrier's Tooth* at Chair Ladder, climbed by John Mallory and party. The route had its variation starts, including the testing left-hand first pitch added later in 1940 by J E Q Barford, the whole climb being known variously as *Wolf Buttress Climb*, *The Pinnacle*, and finally *Terrier's Tooth*.

The Early Forties – Commando Climbing

The first three years of the War saw only sporadic visits to the Count House and no records of any new routes in West Penwith. Menlove Edwards came in June 1943 and spent a lonely visit exploring traverse lines at Carnelloe and climbing pitches on Porthmoina Island and Bosigran's Western Ridge. The 75-year-old Andrews dryly described Edwards's rope work on his Porthmoina Island route, *Eastern Slant*, as 'Welsh tactics – lassoing'. From 1940-45, the most significant activity on the West Cornwall cliffs was the cliff-assault training of commandos. Geoffrey Rees-Jones, a Captain with 5 Commando stationed in Falmouth, began training his troops at Black Head and Kynance Cove on the Lizard peninsula and in West Penwith. The Everest climber Noel Odell, who was briefly seconded to the unit, partnered Rees-Jones on an 'extensive reconnaissance' of much of the Cornish coastline. Later the Commando Mountain and Snow Warfare Training Centre was moved from Scotland to St Ives in preparation for D-Day, and cliff assault training began in earnest. With the unit was Rees-Jones's chief instructor, Captain Joe Barry.

Sennen was also found to be ideal for cliff-assault training, although climbing technique as such was subsumed for hard 'grappling' in every sense; heavy metal from top to toe, the commandos were laden with tin hats, full gear, rifle, and nailed boots, their rope work being more Tarzan than tied-on. Only sea-hammered granite could survive such onslaught. A taste of things to come was Joe Barry's ascents of *Demo Route* (solo) and *Vertical Crack* in 1943, although the full significance of the commando influence was to make itself felt later with the emergence of some of the finest and hardest natural climbers from the ranks of instructors.

The commando influence contributed also to the general climbing culture of Penwith through notable figures like Jim Smith, an instructor with the Cliff Assault Wing. Like many commandos, Smith settled locally. He served as custodian of the Count House for many years and encouraged numerous locals into climbing with his generous enthusiasm.

Post-War Prizes

After 1945, the Commando Cliff Assault Wing was based at St Ives for post-war training and many of its instructors emerged as brilliant pioneering climbers in their own right. In 1947, Barry opened the commando account with the tough and characteristic *Genge's Groove*

Flannel Avenue (HS), Chair Ladder
Climber: Helen Board   Photo: David Wilkinson

Delilah (E2), Sennen
Climber: Nick Hancock   Photo: Andy Grieve

Fun Curve Factory (E5), Carn Vellan
Climber: Ken Palmer   Photo: Nick Hancock

Right Angle (HS), Gurnard's Head:
Tim Noble with a wave breaking
10 metres above his head
Photo: Andy Russell

at Sennen, which can still repel invaders. On Chair Ladder's dazzling granite, CCAW members established great classics like *Flannel Avenue* and *Red Wall*. The most significant advance in West Penwith climbing came from Jim Cortlandt-Simpson, who closed the half-century with major contributions to Bosigran and Chair Ladder.

On Bosigran Main Face, Simpson, partnered by R G Higgins and Admiral Keith Lawder, climbed *Zig Zag*, a major advance for Cornish climbing though still not matching Welsh standards of the time. *Zig Zag* had a rare cachet about it, however, being an imaginative attack on a daunting section of what was still a fairly unexplored cliff. Simpson's aim was 'to make an encroachment on the overhanging central area.' His achievement in terms of contemporary equipment and standards is exhilarating in its testament to climbing's purest principles. 'I scrambled to the top of the great pile of blocks, put a sling over the topmost spike and had a go at the steep wall behind. It was getting late in the day and, by the time I had clawed my way up to the niche, the light was beginning to fail and I was getting worried. The rising traverse to the left with its beautiful inverted holds beckoned me on and by that time the idea of reversing the moves down the wall seemed a very unattractive alternative. So I went on hopefully, although dismayed by the lack of running belays available then, and managed to make it to the top.'

Simpson maintained the standard at Chair Ladder, where he climbed the now classic line of *South Face Direct* with Eric Stones. He described the ascent as a tough challenge; it still is. A year later, Simpson put his mark on centre-stage Bosigran by climbing *Doorway*, again partnered by Hutchinson. It is fair to point out that in the fairly protectionless circumstances of the times, seconds were often just as bold as their leaders, especially on such complex climbs as *Doorway* where lack of protection meant that they often had to follow rising traverses, or make horizontal moves, with some vicious pendulums being the price of a fall. The first attempt at *Doorway* has been vividly described by Simpson, who retreated from just before the final traverse under the roof because of the shaky nature of the rock and the not unrelated fact that he had climbed the awkward and, at that time, grass-choked crack without runners. Simpson later climbed down on a top rope courtesy of Admiral Keith Lawder and fell off when he stepped on a quartz nodule that snapped. He managed to remove some other tottery quartz before returning to lead the climb in its entirety.

A marvellous postscript 40 years on: Jim Simpson repeated *Doorway* many times, and on one such occasion in the late 80s, when he was in his seventies, Jim and his companion arrived at the start of the climb to find the first pitch already occupied by one team while two young climbers waited their turn. The waiting climbers had no idea who Jim was. With refreshing courtesy they asked Jim if he would like to go ahead of them. *Doorway*'s first ascensionist declined with equal courtesy. 'It's all right,' said Jim; 'I can wait. I've climbed it before.'

The Fertile Fifties

The first climbing guide to West Penwith was published in 1950. The guide was written by Arthur Andrews and Ted Pyatt and is still the fine mix of climbing information and entertainment, enhanced by well-informed essays on the flora, fauna, and geology of West Penwith, as it was then. Pyatt described his research for the book in the company of the 80-year-old Andrews as being distinctly hair-raising: 'We went out in a boat from Porthgwarra with a boatman aged 75 to photograph (Chair Ladder) from the sea. We were terrified when Andrews stood up in the bows, rocking the boat as he peered into the viewfinder of his ancient camera, but there were no accidents and we got some good pictures.' Not only were the pictures and content good, but the book coincided with an end to post-war petrol rationing and a general resurgence of leisure activity. Wales and the northern crags drew most action but the Andrews/Pyatt Guide attracted many climbers to West Penwith.

The Marines had established the delightful *Land's End Long Climb* in 1946, beginning the development of that area's remarkable and challenging cliffs. Pordenack Point got its first climb of significance in 1951 with *Muscle Chimney* by M J Ridges and J F Lilly, and, the same year, the pair climbed *Diocese* at Chair Ladder, although a prior claim rests with R Handley and E Phillips. The definitive line was said to have been top-roped solo by the remarkable Trevor Peck in the late 40s using a friction 'shunt'-style device. In March 1952, Carn Barra won attention from Alan Imrie and Rawdon Goodier, a pointer to the latter's future significance as one of the great band of Marine climbers who dominated one part of the Penwith climbing scene throughout the 50s. Another Marine climber made his mark in 1955 when Mike Banks climbed *Zig Zag* at Sennen.

In May 1953, an important day's work at Bosigran in typically wild Atlantic weather produced *Nameless*, climbed brilliantly by Dennis Kemp and Nea Morin. The route was something of a 'consolation' after Kemp, Morin, Norman Albon, and Menlove Edwards backed off from attempting the sea-level Window Ridge below Monolith Slab in a full gale. Being a genuine sea-dog, Edwards was probably a touch miffed; he went off soloing and again missed out on involvement with the kind of significant West Penwith route that his genius deserved. He had already climbed the biting *Doorway Direct Start*, however; fame enough. On Chair Ladder, one of the greatest of all the Marine climbers, John 'Zeke' Deacon added *The Mitre*, the top pitch of which gives one of the most grippingly exposed situations in West Penwith climbing.

Cornwall saw one of its mythical summers in 1955: sunrise to brilliant sunset, seas of aquamarine, dry golden rock, mild breezes, and a Mediterranean ambience overall. It was the 50th anniversary of *Ledge Climb* at Bosigran and the dawn of modern development, albeit with a metallic hue. Hamish Nicol made a significantly bold entry at Bosigran with *Beaker*

Peter Biven

Photo: N Biven col.

Route at Whitsun. Goodier made further inroads to Carn Barra, while Deacon definitely put his name to things with *Zeke's Route* at Pordenack.

In July, the Biven brothers and Trevor Peck came, saw, and set about conquering West Penwith.

The Biven Years

Peter and Barrie Biven and Trevor Peck are part of that hierarchy of innovative and pioneering climbers that includes A W Andrews, Zeke Deacon, Rawdon Goodier, Frank Cannings, Pat Littlejohn, and Rowland and Mark Edwards, each of whom defined style as much as content in the development of climbing in West Penwith.

Leicester-born and grit-trained, Peter Biven especially was an ambitious and creative climber, tellingly described by Jim Perrin as being 'assertive, intelligent, cultured, and involved'. Add to this Barrie Biven's deeply felt summation of his brother's climbing style as a mirror of the man: 'His joy was not so much in the finished product of his pioneering but the act of creation. His keen eye for a route and the tension of the climb as he sought to match his mental photograph of the route were at the core of his passion for climbing. He gave the rock another dimension; he made it pliable and supple in his hands.'

The Bivens were inspired by their first visit to Cornwall. Its remoteness in the 50s meant little in the face of the enthusiasm that took Peter Biven and his closest companions on 'fast drives to the sea strapped in some wreck of a car being blitzed by Beethoven and Brahms'. The Bivens met the successful businessman and climber Trevor Peck through thumbing a lift to Stanage in the latter's white Rolls Royce. (An apocryphal story but true in essence.) A remarkable aspect was that Peck gave each of the Bivens the initial 'lift' from the same Leicester traffic lights, but on separate occasions and unknown to each other. It was the beginning of a rare friendship for all three.

Some time later, after much tough work on the gritstone edges, they brought their welded finger-strength and athleticism to Cornish granite and began what was to become an historic development of Bosigran Main Face. Their activities were well matched by Rawdon Goodier and John Deacon. Over a period of six weeks in late summer 1955, the Biven team's activities, with those of Goodier and Deacon, represent a major stage in the development of Bosigran. *Hopeless Slab* on the seaward face, the first to go, was followed by Barrie Biven's now classic *Doorpost*. A day later, Peter Biven struck through the heart of Bosigran with the creation of another great Penwith route, *Suicide Wall*.

Like all the Bosigran first ascents of the period it was an on-sight lead. Peter Biven made short work of the traverse pitch, wearing plimsolls and gardening as he went. Barrie Biven describes the commitment that inspired

Iain Peters, Keith Lawder, and Dennis Bateman (1961)   Photo: Bateman col.

Barrie Biven   Photo: N Biven col.

Trevor Peck (1950s)   Photo: N Biven col.

them: 'Pete confidently trusted that at the end of the traverse there would be a stance and a way up. All those leads of ours were blind... One had to believe that, should a stance be unavailable, a reverse of the traverse was possible.' On that first attempt, Peter Biven did indeed reverse *Suicide Wall* from the materialized stance because he had no pitons with which to belay.

The same week, Rawdon Goodier 'arrived back to Cornish sunshine after Chamonix rain'. Inspired by the description of the Biven routes in the Count House logbook, Goodier and Deacon made the second ascent of *Suicide Wall*, and then set out on a girdle traverse of the Main Face to produce *String of Pearls* over two scorching days. A week later, the Bivens produced *Little Brown Jug*. Peter Biven was with the RAF at the time, stationed in Northumbria. *LBJ* was the conclusion of a 1200-mile round trip on Barrie Biven's old motorcycle, which included a wild dash down unlit roads with a bicycle lamp for a headlight. Two weeks later, Goodier bounced back with *Autumn Flakes* and finished off the season in the company of Deacon on the black-browed *Raven Wall*.

The Climbers' Club held its 1956 Whitsun Meet at Bosigran. It was the opening of another important year. Biven rang in the new with *Anvil Chorus*, Verdi being the musical mentor this time. Ten years later, *Anvil Chorus*'s third pitch had earned a reputation for seriousness and had 'given rise to a controversy over the overall standard of the climb'; (to this day the route is still considered 'serious' and views differ over its grade). *Ochre Slab Route I* was climbed, while Peter Biven and Peck joined forces with Deacon to work out the girdle of *Diamond Tiara*. Amity prevailed amongst leading climbers: 'We got on extremely well with the Marines,' said Biven; 'there was no rancour, no acrimony, no bitching – just pleasant climbing with good friends'.

Another visitor during the Whit weekend was Cliff Fishwick, who was to become a close friend of the Bivens and Peck. Fishwick shared in many first ascents as well as making his own fine contributions like *Helluva Slab* at Porthgwarra. Fishwick recalled his companions with great affection: 'Barrie was the most powerful climber, the strong-arm man. Peter moved magically and Trevor had no weight, seeming to stick to everything, a phenomenon repeated later in Pat Littlejohn.' The respect and affection were mutual, with Fishwick providing a stable and supportive presence for the much younger Bivens both on and off the rock. Fishwick was an artist of great stature and he enhanced successive Penwith guidebooks with accomplished cliff diagrams and drawings.

The Bite of the Piton

In August 1956 the Bivens and Peck returned and made history by free-climbing Andrews's *Green Cormorant Ledge* into Great Zawn and exiting via *Garden Walk*. Their eyes must have gleamed at the vision of the West Face. But in Peter Biven's own words: 'There were hundreds of thousands of

John 'Zeke' Deacon (1950s)   Photo: M Banks

Frank Cannings (1967)   Photo: K Wilson

Pat Littlejohn (1990s)   Photo: I Smith

Toni Carver (1990)   Photo: C Sanger

seabirds in the old days. Great Zawn was full of them and Chair Ladder stank. Trev and I preferred Bosi as no seabird had ever been known to nest there. The Marines were made of sterner stuff and didn't mind ploughing through the slime.' This last was in respect of the more wide-ranging achievements of Deacon and co. on the south coast throughout the late 50s, including *Bishop's Rib* at Chair Ladder. Meanwhile, Biven and Peck concentrated their attention on the great overhangs of Bosigran Main Face to produce the fierce aid lines of *The Ghost* and *The Phantom* that nevertheless included some hard free-climbing. They also slipped back into Great Zawn to peg *Great Zawn Chimney*.

The following year, Deacon and Mike Banks leapfrogged the Biven team to challenge Great Zawn by making the long-considered link between *Green Cormorant Ledge* and the Western Ridge with the impressive *Green Cormorant Face*. By midsummer, Peter Biven and Peck were heads down on *The West Face* amidst a blizzard of screaming seabirds. Ten hours of whack and dangle and the mangling of Biven's thumb with a hammer saw the symbolic, heavy-metal conquest of the zawn. A month later, West Penwith met the Northern Lights through a visit by the Rock and Ice Club. Don Whillans later dismissed Cornwall as being the kind of place to go climbing when you retired – a classic put-down. Brown left his mark all the same, adding to Penwith's stature with the first pitches of *Bow Wall*, the great compelling line that takes centre stage on Bosigran before veering out across the 'rounded haunches of the overhang'. Meanwhile, only slightly off-stage, Deacon and Derek Holroyd ranged across the southern cliffs making highly valued contributions like *World's End*, at Land's End, the remote *Excalibur* at Carn Boel, and the fine *Martell Slab* on Tater-du's isolated greenstone.

At Bosigran calm descended as the decade ran out. It had been a golden time for all those involved. They were a talented few who had Penwith virtually to themselves. A contributing factor to the 'Renaissance' mood was the generational and social mix. The Bivens were in their teens when they first came to Penwith. Peck and Fishwick were much older; Andrews was in his late eighties but was a frequent spectator of activities at Bosigran, including the first ascents of *Ghost* and *Phantom*, 'an impish grin betraying his pleasure'. The Marine connection was already strongly established through Deacon, Goodier, and others, and was further emphasized through Wilfred Noyce and the redoubtable Banks and by Barrie Biven's own membership of the Marine's Cliff Assault Wing. Close climbing friends of the Bivens included the author Al Alvarez, who matched literary stature with a boisterous toughness and a taste for fast cars and fast lunges for distant holds. The Bosigran Count House was the focus. Peck lived his own carefully regulated life outside the Count House in his famous 'Alpine Wagon', a 50s version of a motor trailer with iced Ribena always on tap and sliding oak drawers full of fruit and climbing gear. The others survived on 'Spaghetti Bosigrano' in the wonderfully evocative atmosphere of the Count House – rats, ghost, and all. Out on the cliffs the sun did shine a great deal and the clear accurate light of the Atlantic on opal seas must have fairly seduced those up-country lads with its hint of the Mediterranean in cold old Blighty. They kept coming back for more, aware only in later years perhaps of the magnificent legacy they had created.

Whitsun 1958 produced the attractive *Variety Show* on the sunny seaward flank of Great Zawn, climbed by Peck, Barrie Biven, and Fishwick; while John Smoker added *Armchair* on Raven Wall Cliff. But the closing years of the 50s finally belong to John Deacon, Vivian Stevenson, and Mike 'Mac' McDermott, tough, adventurous climbers who continued to develop the testing cliffs of Land's End with serious and committing climbs like *The Parasite* and *Death Rattle Gulch*. *Longships Wall* also fell to Deacon, while he and Stevenson, the latter leading, climbed the strenuous *Excelsior* at Chair Ladder.

The first great surge of modern development now eased off into the 60s. Moods changed, leading players moved on, the rocks remained.

The Slow Sixties

West Penwith has never had a large pool of local climbers. Distance from cities, no student population, and the healthy indifference of the native Cornish to such crazed pastimes as rock-climbing have meant erratic and idiosyncratic climbing development. In 1960, for example, Zeke Deacon moved away and the Bivens, though living in the South West, were active in other areas as well as Cornwall. The main focus of front-line climbing was in the north of England and, unless committed to the long journey down the interminable peninsula to Land's End, few saw West Penwith as other than a fine holiday venue.

During the early 60s, however, local clubs were founded in mid Cornwall. The Truro School Rock Climbing Club was set up by pupils in a remarkable example of juvenile anarchism. The club produced highly talented and individual climbers like W A (Toni) Carver, who came from St Ives. Carver was a natural pioneer. His early activities in company with Peter Stanier were at mid Cornwall's Cheesewring Quarry and, although the Truro club held many meets at the Count House, they assumed that West Penwith 'belonged to someone else and that everything we could climb must have been done'. Before long, Carver was to make up for such innocence.

Development in Penwith continued, however, and the pace built steadily through the decade towards the first stirrings of the free-climbing revolution. The early 60s saw a number of good new lines on all the main cliffs, including *Venusberg* at Bosigran and *The Bishop's Chain* girdle at Chair Ladder. Peter Biven and Viv Stevenson were working independently on new guides for the north and south coasts respectively, a job guaranteed to take the edge off free-ranging exploration, despite occasional diversions. Stevenson added good lines at Fox Promontory, a true ocean venue, and explored more remote south coast cliffs like Pendower Coves. A significant Penwith debut was made in 1964 by Frank Cannings, who pegged the black crack of *Kafoozalem*, increasing the stature and challenge of Bosigran's Raven Wall area.

McDermott also maintained the vigorous tradition of the Marines but in partnership now with local climbers like Dennis Bateman, who was to make his own quietly prolific mark on West Penwith over the next twenty years. *Golva* at Sennen and *Birthday Route* at Carn Barra were McDermott contributions.

At Bosigran, Peter Biven and Peck returned to the fray with *Beowulf*, a stylish route of historical and ethical significance because of the use of several bolts. Although the pair's reaction to exposure and lack of protection led to the placing of the bolts in the first place, Biven himself was uneasy about their use for protection or aid. 'Tired by the effort of drilling and harried by bad weather, the party used the last two bolts for aid on the first ascent,' Biven wrote later with a fine degree of pained objectivity but with admirable candour. Soon after, Phil Gordon led the pitch free.

McDermott forced the hard line of *Grendel* accompanied by a very young Iain Peters, who was following in the family tradition of his grandfather, Admiral Keith Lawder. In August 1966, Peters struck out for himself into deep country at Gurnard's Head to produce *Right Angle*. This was a remarkable piece of exploration on West Penwith's greenstone cliffs, which had been neglected since Andrews's adventurous days. Equally impressive was Frank Cannings's *Boldfinger* on Bosigran's Seaward Cliff, while on the south coast Hugh Banner opened up the striking but hidden heart of Bosistow with a clutch of testing middle-grade routes.

Free Expression

In line with the political climate of the decade, 1968 sparked some revolutionary action. In April, Bosigran produced the elegant *Visions of Johanna* from Mark Springett, who used to climb strapped onto the 60s equivalent of a personal stereo until it dropped off near the top of *Doorpost*. Bob Dylan was on the tape of course and flew past a startled Cannings wailing, 'And your gravity fails and negativity don't pull you throughhhhhh…' The day after *Visions of Johanna*, Cannings struck out west into Rosemergy Zawn, reflecting a restless spirit that was to inspire the development of West Penwith climbing into the 70s. On the same day, the wildly talented Martin Jones set about the savage line of *Vulcan* on the Bosigran overhangs. A Marine helicopter pilot, Jones added to flying time on his first attempt and was fielded by Mark Vallance. Jones was back the next week with Toni Carver holding the ropes. 'Martin went for the crux with a peg between his teeth and stabbed it in like a dagger,' said Carver, who was so impressed by Jones's ultimate success on the line that he understandably failed to follow. Soon after, Jones took up other pastimes like surfing and hang-gliding because climbing had 'lost its excitement'.

Springett and Steve Young pegged the wonderful *Xanadu* on Great Zawn's east-facing wall, reopening the door on the Zawn after almost ten years, although it wasn't until December that M J Guilluard and R M Wilson aided *The Dream*. The year closed significantly with the first recorded Penwith route by Pat Littlejohn, who soloed from sea-level the tricky little *South East Face Direct* at Chair Ladder, a fitting Penwith debut. It was as if he had slipped quietly ashore to take over.

Local climbers led by Don Brown made their mark in 1969 with exploration of the remote and delightful St Loy cliff on Penwith's south coast. Carver also got into his stride with a vengeance, climbing the tough *Tuco the Terrible* at the dark-faced Robin's Rocks on the north coast. This was the first extreme outing on greenstone, matched within days by Littlejohn and Steve Jones with their fine *Behemoth* and *Shark* at Gurnard's Head.

The decade ended with a flourish in Great Zawn, where over a period of a few weeks during 1969 Cannings and the 17-year-old Littlejohn instigated a major advance in standards and approach. In August, the key event came when Littlejohn went into Great Zawn with Jones and free-climbed *Great Zawn Chimney*, a shaky old aid route. 'I don't think it was that loose, apart from the odd bit of friable granite', Littlejohn said later with typically cool appraisal. He and Jones also climbed Great Zawn's *Girdle Traverse*. Within two weeks Littlejohn was back in Great Zawn with Cannings. This was a formidable combination. Cannings was a seminal influence on Littlejohn's development. They had already joined forces on major routes in the South West like *Dreadnought* on the Old Redoubt at Berry Head. Arnis Strapcans ably summed up the combination when he said: 'Frank had considerable influence on Pat's climbing. His bold lead of the 'space-walking' *Dreadnought* was very much in the mood of the ascents that Pat was to devote himself to later on.' The impetus for the pair's Great Zawn developments came from Cannings. It was the perfect catalyst for Littlejohn's natural talent and ambition. Over the space of a September weekend they alternated leads on freeing *Green Cormorant Face* and free-climbed *Zarathustra* and *Omen*, with Littlejohn tackling the crux pitch of the former and Cannings the latter. Cannings rounded things off by leading the exquisite *Desolation Row*. New era dawning…

Seventies Spirit

The 60s closed on the heels of the Biven and McDermott biblical North Coast Guide, which, as 'Cornwall Vol. I', came out two years after Stevenson's Vol. II: an eccentric logic appreciated only by guidebook writers. With genuine logic for the times, Biven had famously predicted that the 'large unclimbed walls beyond Bosigran Ridge will soon feel the bite of the piton'. He was quite right, since the piton continued to bite for some time. Biven added, 'new techniques will be evolved', and the oft-repeated claim that he had not foreseen the free-climbing revolution is specious. Biven was mentor to Cannings, Littlejohn, and the remarkable Keith Darbyshire, and it showed. Littlejohn paid tribute to Biven's inspiration when he said, 'Pete's climbing code certainly influenced the way in which many more difficult climbs in the South West were tackled'.

The same code was reflected in Cannings's approach to the challenge of aid elimination. In 1970, he wrote an impressionistic piece on the free-climbing imperative in which he said: 'Every minute hold, piece of lichen, and discolouration in the rock has its impression firmly stamped upon my mind... I try every hold and every combination of hold.' The intellectual transformation, from the assessment of mechanical placements on steep or overhanging rock to the ideal of attempting every move by free and natural technical means, had taken place.

The free climbing spirit had also been expressed by Hugh Banner, who had free-climbed Springett's *The Scabbard* at Carn Boel in 1967. Cannings's and Littejohn's Great Zawn routes of 1969 marked the major breakthrough, while the new approach reached its apogee in May of 1970 with Cannings's free lead of key sections of the awesome *Liberator*. Points of aid were used on other sections of the route but it was a statement of intent all the same and the opener to a remarkable decade. It was effectively Cannings's curtain call in West Penwith. A demanding business career took up more of his time, although he did return to Great Zawn in 1974 for a famous piece of *déjà vu*.

Throughout the early 70s, development of new and remote cliffs rested with locals. In the summer of 1970, Carver homed in on the awesome Carn Vellan and climbed the nicely eccentric line of *My Mule Don't Like You Laffin*, while Phil Gordon made his emphatic mark at St Loy with *Chlorophyll Cluster*. Littlejohn and Carver joined forces the following year to produce *The Spire* at Chair Ladder, a serious, but brilliant line, while Deacon returned to old haunts after eleven years to contribute the fine little line of *Cormorant's Bill* at Land's End with Fishwick. On the last day of the year, Littlejohn and Darbyshire took their remarkable combined talents onto the great sheet of killas slate at Kenidjack and climbed *The Shield*.

A number of visiting climbers added a handful of routes in 1972. Paul de Mengel climbed *Ra* at Carn Barra, aided *Gillian* at Sennen, and rounded things off with a flourish with the savage aid route *The Lid* at Carn Vellan. Littlejohn and Darbyshire stayed 'deep zawn' at the stupendous Zawn Duel, climbing *The Adversary*, still one of Cornwall's great adventures. Ed Grindley climbed the fine *Black Power* at Land's End, Ian Duckworth produced *Axis* and *Dialectic* at Carn Barra, while Deacon and Fishwick kept on going with the first recorded routes at Pendeen. Les Williams and Dennis Bateman began extensive development of the charming granite outcrops at Trewavas Head on the Mount's Bay coast where Romanis and Jerram had first exploited the possibilities. The main event of the following year was the free-climbing of *The Ghost* and *The Phantom* by Ed Drummond and Tom Proctor. Drummond raised the wind by seeking to rename both routes, a move that earned measured but overwhelming opposition. The original names stayed in place, not least as a fitting tribute to the late Trevor Peck.

During 1973, Carver discovered three pleasant climbs at Zennor's upper cliff, while Rowland Edwards paid an early visit to West Penwith and made a bee-line for Great Zawn to produce *Candy Man*. A quick glance round must have really started him thinking. Locally, apart from Carver's free-ranging activity, there was a small but strong nucleus of climbers led by Mike White, a Mancunian exile. Their new-route activity was low key, although White free-climbed *Delilah* at Sennen and produced some fine pitches at Carn Guthenbras on Chair Ladder's western flank. More importantly, in the early 70s, White with Roger Gook produced an interim guide to Chair Ladder that treated the cliff to a thorough revision and established a logical division of the complex buttresses. A comprehensive guide to the south coast by Bob Moulton and Terry Thompson appeared in 1975. It had great clarity, and the dramatic cover picture of Frank Cannings on *The Mitre* remains hard to beat.

Mid Seventies Peak

By 1974, Littlejohn was firmly established as a dominant force in British rock-climbing; certainly he was without peer on the more remote and 'loose-living' sea cliffs of the South West. *Il Duce* at Tintagel and *Darkinbad the Brightdayler* at Pentire had already fallen to Littlejohn. *America* followed in 1973, while further afield he climbed routes such as *Pagan* on South Stack, Gogarth. The same commitment produced *Finesse* and *The Baldest* at West Penwith's St Loy in 1974, while his intricate *Saxon* at Kenidjack proved that the pioneering spirit could produce reasonably graded routes of quality.

Great Zawn was the scene of a stylish and historic piece of climbing with the ascent of the smooth 'vertical' slab flanking *Dream* by American ace Henry Barber, seconded by Frank Cannings. *Déjà Vu* was the result. The line had been spotted by Cannings, who felt it was not for him as a lead. 'Here was a line that I'd seen and I couldn't do. And here I had the chance to throw one of the world's top rock climbers at it.' The pair first went to view the line from the sea: literally – by swimming round into the mouth of Great Zawn to discuss the possibilities. The route was climbed the following day, but only after Barber jibbed and gibbered at making the infamous leap across The Crevasse for a good half hour. Once across, the remarkable 'Hots' resumed civilized activity and made a fine and faultless on-sight lead of the extremely bold and sparsely protected *Déjà Vu*. During his visit to Penwith, Barber also attempted a solo of *Bow Wall*, retreating after half an hour from half-way across the crux moves, an achievement guaranteed to bring sweat to the palms of ordinary mortals even now. Ron Fawcett did the *Bow Wall* solo a few years later, but Hot Henry led the way.

Later in 1974 Littlejohn and Darbyshire continued the serious work of deep exploration with Darbyshire's fine *The Aggressor* at Whirl Pool Buttress. The high profile event of the period was the American Broadcasting Corporation's

Wide World of Sport extravaganza featuring Barber plus a cast of thousands. Leading players included genuine 'character actors' Al Harris, Al Rouse, and Pete Livesey. The entire event is now shrouded in the mists of myth and other substances but was certainly unmatched by any other visitation to Penwith's reclusive cliffs other than those of a Force 10 gale. Livesey's ABC visit and starring part with Barber on *The Dream* – 'never before had (Hots) climbed with one so lacking in ethics and money as me...' – inspired him to put up some key routes on Cornish granite, while making his emphatic mark on North Cornwall's Pentire Head on the way.

The heatwave summer of 76 brought northern carpetbaggers back in force. Tom Proctor and Geoff Birtles rode into the Land's End sunset and snatched the remarkable *Yankee Doodle*, a stunning crack climb that appeared overnight at word of their coming. Having remained as a major Land's End attraction for many years, the mighty *Doodle* certainly *disappeared* overnight when the great gales of 1990 demolished the entire buttress, leaving the left-hand edge of the famous jamming crack in ghostly silhouette. Livesey with Al Evans and Jill Lawrence established the serious *Thick Wall Special* at Bosigran and the technically advanced *Red Tower* and *The Steeple* at Chair Ladder.

Midsummer of 1976 saw the shocking and tragic death of Peter Biven following a fall from Giant's Cave Buttress in the Avon Gorge, a devastating loss to family, friends, and the British climbing community. Biven was 40; his mature potential was immense after years of great and inspirational climbing. His legacy resides in his own intense climbing principles still maintained by protégés like Pat Littlejohn. His true memorial is woven across Bosigran's great cliffs.

The mid 70s were a bleak enough time for South-West climbing personalities. The year before Peter Biven's death, Keith Darbyshire had been killed while exploring Nare Head on Cornwall's south coast. Darbyshire and Littlejohn had developed a strong partnership, inspired not least by Biven. For Littlejohn, the double loss of such close companions must have had a profound effect. For some time after Darbyshire's death Cornwall saw little action from Littlejohn, but by 1976 he had resumed his lonely and inspiring journey by climbing the highly individual *Roraima* in the vast spray-curtained amphitheatre of Great Moor Zawn, one of Penwith's most spectacular 'lost worlds'. Littlejohn was accompanied on many of his routes by seconds such as Dave Garner, Steve Jones, and Chris King, first-class climbers in their own right, whose involvement deserves high tribute. Carver also struck out into Andrews's wilderness coast in the summer of 76 with testing climbs like *The Good, the Bad, and the Gruesome* at Trevowhan Zawn, named to commemorate a meeting with Frank Cannings, Bob Moulton, and Ken Wilson, though not necessarily in that order.

The intensity of climbing development elsewhere in the country touched West Penwith in the closing years of the decade. Ron Fawcett contributed *New Medium* to Bosigran's Main Face, while the same motivation that produced

1978's Gogarth bonanza brought Jim Moran to West Penwith to climb the tough *Saddle Tramp* and *Pump It Up* at Bosigran. But Littlejohn advanced the overall standard with *The Leer* and *Evil Eye* on Bosigran's Raven Wall Cliff. He also climbed *Black Sapper* at Robin's Rocks, *Cain* at Pordenack Point, and the pioneering *Burning Gold* on the great golden wall opposite Carn Lês Boel's Bosistow Island that was later named Paradise Wall.

The wall had seen early aid attempts that had left a legacy of scrap, including a rash of bolts on the stance at the end of pitch one. Although Littlejohn climbed clean and free he was later to have the presence of the old bolts thrown at him during the later bolt controversies. Littlejohn's 1978 contribution was his last in Penwith for a decade. The stars in their courses swung, Pembroke swam into the light, habits and tastes changed, and Penwith ran out of fashion in spite of Ed Hart's spartan but excellent Bosigran guide of 1978. In the absence of the mob, Rowland Edwards staked his claim as the inheritor of a peninsula that had seen gold struck but that had plenty of nuggets left after thirty years.

The Edwards Era Part I

Edwards came to live at Sennen in West Penwith in 1978. With his wife, Esther, he set up a private rock-climbing school that developed into a successful business. Edwards had an empire of rock to play with. In the late 70s, he started on the big cliffs of the north coast with a flourish, combining adventurousness with great technical skill and experience. Gurnard's Head yielded the major line of *Mastodon* after cleaning and inspection. Edwards's second on his early ascents was Sam Salmon, a local climber and surfer. Although not leading at extreme standards, Salmon played an important role in West Penwith climbing during the 80s by keeping alive the easy-going sociability for which the area was noted.

For the closing years of the 70s and into the 80s, Edwards had West Penwith virtually to himself, although the talented Devon climber Pete O'Sullivan climbed a number of routes including *The Intruder* at Robin's Rocks. During the next decade O'Sullivan made a major contribution to climbing in West Cornwall with his pioneering work on The Lizard and West Penwith, and also with his guidebook work. Edwards added good middle-grade zawn routes at Zennor with Salmon, but soon his eldest son Mark began seconding on fine routes like *Rock Dancer* at Kenidjack and the stylish *Illustrated Man* at Carn Barra to close the 70s with a taste of what was to come.

Lizard Life

The Lizard Peninsula, Cornwall's 'heel' to the 'toe' of West Penwith, had always been out on a limb in climbing terms. There was little climbing on The Lizard before the 80s, although adventurers in plenty had explored the area's dark cliffs. An early record of a remarkable piece of accidental rock-climbing is reported in the book, *A Week at The Lizard*, by the Revd

Mark Edwards and Rowland Edwards (1980s)   Photo: I Smith

Pete O'Sullivan (1990)   Photo: D Hillebrandt

Tony Penning (1990)   Photo: Penning col.

Charles Alexander Johns, published in 1848. The Revd Johns was an accomplished naturalist and his forays on The Lizard reflected the area's importance to botanists. On an August day in 1831 he was cut off by the tide while exploring Asparagus Island near Kynance Cove. He escaped by climbing the landward cliff. His description of the feat has the palm-sweating immediacy of all good climbing writing, right down to some exquisite asides. While hanging by his fingers, his feet, 'dangling... on every side in search of a resting place', the Reverend remarks that; 'a spontaneous agitation of all the nerves in my body commenced'. We know the feeling.

Apart from such eccentric epics, there seem to be no detailed records of climbing on The Lizard until 1979, when Pete O'Sullivan and Iain Peters, two of the West Country's finest, paid their first visit to the area. This was not golden granite country. The Lizard's mix of rock types, mica and hornblende schists and serpentine, suggested potentially loose cliffs. O'Sullivan and Peters were the right men to find out just how loose; they were inspired pioneers of many fine climbs on the Culm coast of North Devon and Cornwall, the ploughed fields of British rock. On their first visit to The Lizard the pair paused briefly at a local gift shop for a quick scan of an OS map of the area, the kind of forward planning that wins wars. Decisions made, they headed unerringly for the worst imaginable piece of rock on the whole coast, Pigeon Ogo. The vast cliff here is a triumph of appearance over substance. The 'loathsome' Pigeon Ogo, is how Peters later described it; 'all overhanging walls, oozing green slime'. Nothing daunted they abseiled in. 'Pulling the ropes down after us was a profound mistake,' wrote O'Sullivan with masterly understatement. 'It forced us into climbing the line of least horror to escape'.

At one point in the pair's upward slither through what was seriously extreme country, Peters tossed a handful of coins into the sea. 'This was in hopes of placating the spirits of the crag,' according to O'Sullivan, 'It was about fifty quid short.' They called the route *Loose Change*, and left Pigeon Ogo for good, but not The Lizard as a whole. During the years that followed, O'Sullivan and Peters persevered in exploring The Lizard between bouts of pioneering work in Devon and elsewhere in Cornwall. In 1983 they eventually struck good rock at the splendid Vellan Head where, accompanied by Peters, Colin Robins, and Yorkshireman Renny Croft (to add some seasoning to the Devon Cream), O'Sullivan climbed *True North*, the classic of the crag. Peters later contributed the bold and intricate *The Fix*. The pair developed Coastguard Cliff, where O'Sullivan's *Aboriginal Sin* on Tower Buttress and *The Big Heat* on Hollywood Walls, rank as classics. A number of excellent middle grade routes were also climbed on the Hollywood Walls. Lizard life had begun with a flourish.

Eighties Enterprise
Back in West Penwith, Rowland and Mark Edwards went into the 80s as a team unmatched for dedication and determination. Professionally involved

with climbing, they were on the rock virtually every day of their lives and within shouting distance of vast potential. In 1980 they produced numerous climbs on a range of cliffs, although in the early part of the year it was Edwards senior climbing with other partners who produced such fine lines as *American Dream* at Zawn Kellys, *Stone Boom* at Pordenack, and the splendid *Astral Stroll* through the great sea-sucked overhangs of Carn Gloose. By the spring of the year, father and son had started their intensive development of the productive Carn Barra with *Grande Plage* and *Sunny Corner Lane*. Back on the less than sunny greenstone, the pair diverted themselves on *Ziggurat* at Carn Vellan and by September had launched their series of 'immaculates' with *Immaculate Crack* and *Immaculate Groove* at Carn Boel.

In the summer of 1981, Devon climber Chris Nicholson turned up in West Penwith for a few happy-go-lucky summer weeks, teaming up with Sam Salmon to develop some neat little climbs at Pedn Kei and Windy Zawn on the north coast. One high point of the year was Australian Kim Carrigan's free ascent of *Vulcan*, a major effort that gave Penwith its first emphatic technical advance of the 80s. And at Chair Ladder, Jon de Montjoye free-climbed *Caliban* to add further to the technical lists on granite.

However, the Edwardses more than matched all this with their major Land's End achievement of *Atlantic Ocean Wall*, launching out on the back wall of Longships Zawn on a much-eyed line. Committing, strenuous, technical, and wildly exposed, the line is one of the milestones of West Penwith climbing. But it had its critics, as will be seen below. The Edwardses' development of Paradise Wall at Carn Lês Boel produced astounding lines such as *Interspace*, *Cool Diamonds*, and *Hot Line*, which, with Littlejohn's pioneering line of *Burning Gold*, turned the wall into a major venue for hard climbing in magnificent surroundings.

Light But Local Relief

During the early 80s, Sam Salmon continued on his merry way, contributing pleasant lower-grade routes at Kenidjack with others at Carn Barra and Tater-du. He even found his way to the small but delightful granite rocks of the Isles of Scilly, where he climbed a number of routes at Peninnis Head on St Mary's. There was a long tradition of climbing on the Scillies, where the Cornish climber-canoeist Dave Bassett, pioneer of the classic *Aviation* on Hay Tor, had established seven adventurous routes.

Salmon was involved with development of the attractive Levan's Wall area on Penwith's sunny south coast. Martin Doyle and John Hooper had been there first and climbed the excellent *Bermuda Wall*, but had left the further potential for a later date. The talented young climber Andrew Trevorrow, accompanied by newcomer to the Penwith scene, Des Hannigan, and an assorted gang of locals added more, including Trevorrow's excellent Sennen-like gems, *Devil's Meridian* and *Midnight Express*.

Salmon also added some routes to Trewavas, while a marvellously independent development was started at Basher's Harbour by Mike Freeman, who climbed a number of routes in the best traditions of principled anonymity. Basher's became something of a medic's medium. Freeman was an anaesthetist and drafted in locally based houseman Pete Sykes to climb some harder lines, while GP David Hillebrandt contributed the attractive slab climb of *Footloose*.

On the north coast, the estimable Dennis Bateman had looked closely beyond the industrial wasteland of the Levant mining cliffs and eyed up the potential of the dark shattered walls below the sentinel mine shafts. With Les Williams and Paul Murray – the three fielding a near double century of years between them – Bateman climbed a number of lower-grade routes at Trewellard. Of these, *Skylight* has become something of a classic V Diff. Bateman then called in Andrew Trevorrow to climb the stylish *Shambhala*.

Local climbers such as Bateman, Salmon, and Hannigan, between them pioneered scores of routes throughout the peninsula, either as leaders, or as seconds to notable climbers such as Mac McDermot and Hugh Banner, Rowland Edwards, and Pete O'Sullivan and Mike Raine respectively. Bateman and Hannigan developed the Trewellard and Pendeen areas without lavishing stars or hyperbole on what were minor yet adventurous venues, while over the years accomplished local climbers like Justin Ford, Steve Elliott, Luke Pavey, and John Hooper got on quietly with their climbing and contributed several fine routes on a range of cliffs.

The Edwards Era Part II

Having already worked on a supplement to North Cornwall and West Penwith with Bob Moulton, Pete O'Sullivan produced an excellent guide in 1984, bringing the traditional north and south coast areas between the same covers for the first time since 1950. By then Rowland and Mark Edwards were well advanced in developing a vast number of routes, especially on the southern crags. Sennen was a forcing ground of strenuous test-pieces such as the roof-crack of *Super Jam*. Technically, the Edwardses made even greater advances, with their routes at Land's End and Carn Barra in the mid 80s. These included *Edge of Time* and *The Last Dance* as well as Mark Edwards's trio of desperates, *Lost Souls, Virgin on a Crisis*, and *The Dawning*, all at Land's End, and his contributions of *Footless Madness, Dog Town*, and *Carmen* at Carn Barra, initially given grades of 6c in the E5/6 range.

All this was something entirely new for West Penwith. Outside interest from their climbing peers was slow but inevitable and was well deserved, given that the Edwardses' portfolio of routes recorded high technical achievements to match developments elsewhere in Britain. In 1986 the most significant achievement was Mark Edwards's *Tears of a Clown* at Sennen's Black Zawn, Penwith's first E7. The Edwardses were active in developing new crags, often in unlikely venues. Folly Cove between Carn Barra and Fox Promontory yielded a series of routes, while Moon Buttress at Pendower Cove produced the crack climb of *Isis*, originally reported as being 6b but settling down at 6a.

More Life on The Lizard

On The Lizard Pete O'Sullivan continued to search out promising venues. In 1986 he climbed *Amnesty* on the West Face of Pen Olver, to the east of Lizard Point. The route was a fund-raising effort for Live Aid 2. That same year O'Sullivan and Ken Hosie discovered Bass Point. From the coast path the cliff is hard to see in its entirety and, on the day, it was being hammered by huge waves that made close appraisal impossible; but O'Sullivan could tell there was great potential. He returned with Steve Bell two weeks later. Legend has it that the pair divided the spoils from the cliff path with O'Sullivan taking understandable precedence by booking the obvious face climb that was to become the impressive *Dawn*. Bell was the first to clamber down to the base of the cliff, where he discovered a seductive crackline that had been out of sight from above. This became *The Cull*, one of the great classics of The Lizard. With the exquisite courtesy for which he is renowned, O'Sullivan graciously conceded the line to Bell (or words to that effect). *Dawn* was a fitting conclusion to O'Sullivan's Lizard exploration, a development that had a colourful and genuine West Country spirit to it.

Fringe Elements

During the mid-1980s in West Penwith there was some minor action outside the fast lane of the Edwardses' development. On the north coast, Graham Hobbs and Des Hannigan rediscovered the potential of the Pendeen cliffs. With other locals they developed a number of pleasant middle-grade routes such as the wiltingly exposed *Hot Lettuce*. At the same time – galvanised perhaps by the activities of such upstart, yet ageing, newcomers such as Hannigan – Toni Carver emerged from quietude and hard sea-canoeing and, with Peter 'Piggy' Johnstone and Roger Mitchell, developed the independent little cliff of Boswednack that Andrews had explored at the beginning of the century. Carver's *Ways to Be Wicked* was a characteristically tough proposition. London 'Cornishman' Paul Rogers was emerging as a bold and talented climber and had contributed a number of idiosyncratic routes at Bosigran and on Carn Barra's Central Wall. Rogers also climbed some lines on the hanging grey face on the east side of Bosigran Ridge but with his notoriously relaxed attitude did not record details.

On the south coast, a sprinkling of routes was added to Levan's Wall. Sam Salmon climbed some interesting lines on the east-facing wall of Cribba Head including the tough *Geologist's Route*. A sad loss to the local scene came in 1985 with the tragic death from an illness at the age of 20 of the talented Andrew Trevorrow, a born climber who had boldness, integrity, and impeccable style and had just started to put up new routes like the tough, yet elegant *Devil's Meridian* at Levan's Wall.

The Edwards Era Part III: The Bolt Debate

Winter climbing in Spain, where the Edwardses had seasonally expanded their business, saw Mark Edwards's ability and ambition advance even further. By 1988 he was back in Cornwall developing a number of projects. These resulted in his *Kingdom of the Deep* in the Atlantic Ocean Wall area and the very bold *Baptism of Fire* at Sennen. Climbers from outside Cornwall had been drawn to West Penwith during the 80s attracted, not least, by the cornucopia of new routes established by the Edwardses, who had turned cliffs like Carn Barra into major venues and attracted climbers to a range of exciting and challenging climbs.

At this point, it is necessary to step aside from the history of achievement and deal with an issue that has caused much controversy and bitterness in many areas of the UK, and probably in none more than West Penwith: that of deliberately modifying the rock in order to create protection where no natural opportunity exists or, even more seriously, to manufacture or improve holds.

Until the early 70s, bolts had been used on artificial climbs quite freely on certain big walls around the world, but only very sparingly in Britain, where there were few crags on which the needs and the rewards justified the effort involved in drilling (almost invariably on lead and by hand). During the 70s, aid climbing dropped out of fashion, but the rise in free-climbing standards and the increase in the numbers of climbers wanting to make first ascents on crags with a dwindling potential for new routes led to some seeing the occasional bolt as the answer to bringing into play the blank areas of rock that were otherwise unprotectable.

In 1963, far from West Penwith, the first bolt on Cloggy was placed by the reigning champion, Pete Crew, and three years later others were placed by Rowland Edwards. That same year, Cornwall saw the placing of bolts on *Beowulf* by those deified pioneers, Pete Biven and Trevor Peck, although this was later acknowledged as a mistake by Biven himself. In the 70s, Edwards gained experience of placing bolts on a number of first ascents of impressive artificial climbs on North Wales Limestone. It was inevitable that the water in West Penwith would be tested: although the vast majority of British climbers would have regarded the placing of protection bolts on natural sea cliffs as unacceptable, Ron Fawcett's bolts on *The Cad* on Anglesey's North Stack in 1978 had not been universally condemned.

In January 1981, Rowland and Mark Edwards climbed *Immaculate Arête* at Pordenack Point with a mild steel peg for protection, but subsequently replaced it with a stainless steel bolt. Later the same year, *Atlantic Ocean Wall* featured a variety of placements including long stainless steel tubes in soft kaolinized granite and a number of pegs; several of these, too, were then replaced by bolts. The substitution of an unsightly motley of degradable metal by durable, secure, and neat bolts proved a seductive proposition, and although critical voices were raised (and some of the bolts were chopped), most people probably assumed that these would be isolated instances and remained non-committal.

Over the next few years, an occasional belay bolt appeared as, for example, in 1986 on *Isis*, here at the top of the first pitch below an indifferent crumbly upper pitch. The provision of abseil or lower-off 'stations' on single-pitch limestone routes was becoming fashionable, and abseiling from the *Isis* bolt became the norm.

Later in 1986, Rowland Edwards developed the dark forbidding wall left of *Immaculate Crack* at Carn Boel, where he placed one protection bolt on the first pitch of *Total Eclipse* and two others on a belay ledge. Visible scars following the ascent were attributed by some to vigorous cleaning. Allegations of chipping were also made by those who felt that the line between cleaning of loose rock and deliberate hold improvement had been crossed. Climbers from outside Cornwall expressed strong disapproval of this bolting and heavy cleaning, establishing from the start that the 'Cornish controversy' was not simply a provincial spat between local climbers.

By 1987 Mark Edwards was recording technical grades at levels as high as any in Britain. In Sennen's Black Zawn area he climbed *29 Palms*, an E6 6c with four pegs, which he then replaced with drilled pegs. At Chair Ladder he moved into overdrive with three testing pieces on Wolf Buttress, including the 7a *Rats in a Rage*, on which he placed a drilled peg as well as a 'small bolt'. The reaction, by climbers locally and nationally, was again one of anger that the granite of a much-loved 'traditional' cliff had been drilled. In 1988, Edwards climbed *Red Rose* on the sensational granite wall just round the corner from *Demo Route* at Sennen. The route was graded E8 7c (one of the highest ratings in the world at the time) and sported three bolts. There was more strong criticism, but the claimed grade certainly launched a provocative challenge to top climbers elsewhere, and several leading activists repeated some of the Edwardses' harder routes. Opinions were mixed, ranging from generous praise for the pair's pioneering spirit, to serious concern about the resulting climbs.

In 1989 the simmering pot of controversy finally boiled over. It did so with sensation. Leading rock stars Andy Pollitt and Chris Hamper went to West Penwith with a number of Mark Edwards's hardest routes, including *Red Rose*, in their sights. The pair discovered that *Red Rose* had been, in their words, 'obscenely' chipped. Hamper stated in an article in *High* magazine, 'A line of holds had been chipped up one of the best looking lines I had ever seen. No, not chipped, drilled with an electric drill, then cleaned with a chisel. Some were blatant holes, others made by chipping around crystals to make them stand out like little blunt horns, the damage is extensive and irreparable.'

When they confronted Mark Edwards about the matter, he stated that many of his routes had been chipped after his ascents by local climbers out to discredit him. Rowland Edwards supported his son's claim, but no evidence was offered to back up such serious allegations against what was a small and identifiable group of no more than a dozen local climbers active in the area. This allegation, more than any other incident, had the effect of stifling debate about topics which were of profound importance for the future of climbing in the area.

The Edwardses' *Red Rose* allegations were followed by a deluge of comment, opinion, and contradiction. It was reported that one leading climber found evidence of hold creation on *Red Rose* before the first ascent. Another climber said that the route bore no signs of chipping after Edwards climbed it. Whatever the truth is in this sorry affair, what a shame that that which is blameless, that which inspires us, that which gives us so much enjoyment – the rock – has been the main casualty!

In December 1990 the BMC South West and Southern Area Committee held a meeting at the Count House that was attended by over sixty climbers. After thorough debate an overwhelming majority agreed that drilled placements had no place on Cornish granite. Only three voted against the motion. Some confusion resulted from the careless wording of the resolution – since it was the activities on the granite cliffs between Sennen and Chair Ladder that had triggered the controversy, there was thus a failure to ensure that *all* the West Penwith sea-cliffs were embraced. Furthermore, this was two years before the BMC had formulated a national policy on bolting, which itself gave its Area Committees responsibility for interpreting it locally. The resolution, therefore, had no authority beyond an, albeit emphatic, statement of local opinion. By their own account, the Edwardses interpreted the motion as implying that it was acceptable to bolt on the Killas cliffs. Thus the matter was far from settled.

In 1991, Rowland Edwards entered into discussions with the Land's End Management about installing bolt and chain abseil points on routes at the famous headland 'which have been identified as environmentally sensitive'. The scheme was justified on the grounds that bolts would be placed only to protect the environment or for safety reasons. When the company realized that no official climbing body, such as the BMC or the Land's End Climbing Club, had been consulted, the plan was dropped. Meanwhile, Mark Edwards began development of sport climbs on the killas/greenstone of Carn Vellan.

In the spring of 1993, Rowland Edwards put proposals to the BMC's Access and Conservation Officer that bolt abseil points should be installed at a number of locations in order to curtail the erosion of cliff-tops and descents. A further large-scale debate was held, now with formal BMC authority. This time the outcome was unchallengeable – there was to be no bolting on any Cornish sea-cliff. Very soon after, most of the 50 or so bolts at Carn Vellan were chopped. A BMC meeting in Penzance in 1995 saw the decisive defeat of yet another motion in favour of rebolting Carn Vellan, and a five-year moratorium was placed on further bolt debate.

Major technical achievements of the late 80s came inevitably from Mark Edwards with a range of daunting routes. At Sennen his lead of *Amazonia* was topped by his remarkable solo of *Hell Hath No Fear*. He also produced *Diamond Life* at Land's End and *Off the Mark* at the engaging north coast cliff of Robin's Rocks. All of these were hard E7s. In a remarkable eleven years, Rowland and Mark Edwards had added hundreds of new routes to West Penwith, many of which are of great stature. But part of the legacy meant that the rock had been drilled at Gurnard's Head, Carn Vellan, Sennen, Land's End, Pordenack, Carn Boel, Carn Lês Boel, Pendower Coves, Folly Cove, Porth Loe, and Chair Ladder.

Renaissance

By the late 80s there was a veering back to the far South West by old hands like Littlejohn, whose *The Absolution* at Bosigran proved that a traditional cliff could still render up inspirational lines to the truly inspired. Littlejohn added to The Lizard's increasing stature with *Beauty and the Beast* at Vellan Head and *Lazarus* at Bass Point. Littlejohn's reappearance in Cornwall also produced *Prophecy* and *Fated* on the headwall of Great Zawn in 1988. The same year brought the strong Gloucestershire team of Tony Penning and Peter Cresswell into action to add *Free Spirit* and *Dead Lucky* to the headwall. Pete Saunders returned with Andy Grieve in 1988 to the challenging Whirl Pool Buttress where they added *The Evil Empire* alongside *The Aggressor*. The north coast was back in fashion.

Penning acquired a taste for West Penwith and paid regular visits throughout 1989. With Peter Cresswell and Roger Lanchbury he turned his sights on the stupendous Zawn Duel, where he and Cresswell forced the tough line of *Pete's Party Piece* on the spectacular headwall. Penning and co. were soon joined by David Hope, who added new lines to Brandys Zawn and to Kittiwake Zawn at Gurnard's Head.

On the south coast, local climbers Steve Young and Roger Mitchell developed the charming Tregiffian area of slabs to the west of the dark-browed Tater-du. Young was a West Penwith veteran with a number of first ascents to his credit over the years. He and Mitchell added steadily to the Tregiffian area, turning it into an ideal spot for easy-going, lower-grade climbing in the sunny south. Basher's Harbour had a visit from Littlejohn and Irish climber Eddie Cooper, who between them added three hard lines, with *Catch a Falling Star* being the best of them.

Sporadic development had continued at the attractive Cribba Head to the east of Logan Rock where McDermott and Bateman had established two tough little climbs in 1965. Martin Boysen and Al Hubbard had added two further pitches in 1981, while Andy Grieve and Nick Hancock, two of the

West Country's most accomplished climbers, contributed the outstanding lines *Pass the Pigs* and *Lovely, Lovely, Lovely* in the late 80s, to give this accessible venue some excellent short pitches on perfect rock. A major addition to Cribba, and of great significance to Penwith as a whole was Nick Dixon's stunning arête climb of 1989, *Pre-Marital Tension*. The pitch was technically 6c and poorly protected. Meanwhile, in Great Zawn, Stevie Haston and Celia Bull climbed the savage overhanging groove previously aided by *Captivator* to give *Opium*, a big route through classic country.

During the winter of 89/90 West Penwith suffered a minor apocalypse as the worst storms for decades thudded into the south and west coasts and began major dismantling of a number of cliffs. Chair Ladder underwent some harsh ocean surgery, while the most spectacular piece of natural chipping ever seen removed the entire *Yankee Doodle* buttress at Land's End. It seemed an ironic, and dramatic, reminder that the weather and the sea were the real masters of the cliffs. That old pioneer of West Penwith, Arthur Andrews, had had the first and last word when he wrote years before:
Granite is not for Man's convenience,
To chip a block into a human form.
And for its shaping there is but one tool,
The alchemy of water etching it,
And water born of water fretting it…

Into the Nineties

The first year of the new decade saw two separate strands of development on Penwith's north and south coasts. Penning, Hope, and friends carried on with verve and vigour at Pedn Kei with a range of routes throughout the grades including the excellent *Linda's Choice*. Penning added hard test-pieces in awesome surroundings with *The Party's Over* at Zawn Duel and *Ride a Cock Horse* at Horseman's Zawn. On the south coast, during 1990, the delightful cliff at St Loy drew the attention of O'Sullivan, whose long association with West Penwith was rekindled after years of high profile development in Devon. St Loy already had Littlejohn's seminal *The Baldest* on the central sweep of bare and beautiful slab. The indefatigable Edwardses executed a scissors movement from the right to give *The Barber* in 1983, while Carver and Ford added a lower flanker in 1987 with *The Barbary Coast*. O'Sullivan took the challenge head on and climbed the bold, direct line of *The Damned*. With Martin Dunning, Nick Crowhurst and Hannigan, O'Sullivan added a clutch of shorter routes on St Loy's eastern outcrops, of which *Monochrome Men* has become a deserved classic. Later that year, with Hannigan in tow, O' Sullivan climbed the striking line of *Earthly Powers* on the north coast's Whirl Pool Buttress, while before winter closed in O'Sullivan and Dunning struck out west into the wilderness country of Trevowhan where Andrews, Littlejohn, and Carver had gone before.

Iain Peters (1993)   Photo: D Hillebrandt

Des Hannigan (2000)   Photo: Hannigan col.

Mike Raine (1995)   Photo: S Ohly

Shane Ohly (1996)   Photo: Ohly col.

Environmental Concerns

Coincident with the Land's End affair and the 1993 debate, the National Trust launched a national review of the impact of outdoor activities on all Trust properties. The result of this review in West Cornwall was the setting up of the West Cornwall Access and Conservation Liaison Group made up of representatives of the BMC, The National Trust, English Nature, and the Land's End Climbing Club. From this group there emerged thoughtful and experienced environmentalists such as local climber Steve Elliott, who planned and carried out practical environmental improvements such as the repair of the eroded Pinnacle Gully descent at Chair Ladder. The Group also published *The Green Guide*, a booklet offering advice to climbers on environmental care of climbing venues in West Penwith and The Lizard.

Fresh Perspectives

In 1991, the very experienced Yorkshire climber Mike Raine moved to West Cornwall to take up a teaching post. Raine repeated some of Mark Edwards's test-pieces and climbed new adventure routes. Raine also integrated with the local climbing community and became an influential and often inspirational figure within it. Coincident with Raine's arrival in Cornwall the teenage Shane Ohly burst onto the local scene with a raw exuberance that in any field usually led to ambitious Cornish youngsters leaving the county for a wider arena. But Ohly stayed close to his roots for several years. His natural talent for climbing was apparent from the start and his boundless enthusiasm lit up the Cornish scene. Also new on the scene in the early 90s was an exhaustive two-volume guide, the result of a major reappraisal of the area by Des Hannigan.

The early 90s in Penwith saw new climbs in plenty. At the same time as he was producing bolted routes, Mark Edwards was achieving the highest standards on traditionally-protected climbs, such as the E7 *Howling at the Moon* on Paradise Wall, a cliff that the Edwardses had made emphatically their own. Other achievements included the 1992 routes *Eye of the Crystal* at Carn Barra and the E8 *Frogs in a Frenzy* at Levan's Wall. Enthusiasm and ambition led Ohly to attempt repeats of Mark Edwards's harder climbs and his first effort of note was a bolt-free ascent of the 1989 *Art of the Slate* at Gurnard's Head. Ohly made repeat ascents of others of Edwards's hardest climbs such as *Hell Hath No Fear* and *Virgin on a Crisis* and began establishing his own highly-graded virtuoso pieces in Penwith, often in company with Gavin Slade. This new generation of Cornish climbers was soon to be joined by other young locals, such as Barnaby and Tobi Carver, Toni Carver's sons, who were soon climbing new routes in the family tradition, and instigating typically adventurous developments such as that at Black Head. Amongst Ohly's strong contributions were *Manslaughter* at Coffin Cove, and *14 Lives, 13 Souls* at Union Star Cove. Ohly also teamed up with Raine to add the major routes of *Leviathan* and *Babylon and Back* at Gurnard's Head, where Ohly also added two inspired lines, *Fuji Frenzy* and *Voodoo Child*. At the same time, Noel Craine and Crispin Waddy wandered quietly in to establish the powerful *Magog*, adding to the cliff's portfolio of outstanding climbs.

In the early 90s, Raine repeated *The Adversary* in Zawn Duel. First climbed in 1972, the route had only received two or three ascents in the intervening twenty years, yet ranked as one of Penwith's finest adventures. Spurred on by the experience, he made his most impressive contribution to Cornish climbing by developing the awesome black walls of Freedom Zawn near Botallack. Freedom Zawn was a surprisingly neglected area, an entirely undeveloped cliff, until Pete O'Sullivan breached the lower wall of the 50-metre West Face in 1992 with two good pitches up to a midway ledge. In 1994, Raine, seconded by Hannigan, put up nine routes in the zawn, all of which were climbed on sight through extreme and often loose territory. Of these *The Hood* and *The Piano* have potential classic qualities. Freedom Zawn was a quiet but emphatic reaffirmation of Penwith's status as an adventure climbing area, where the rock, rather than the climber, dominated proceedings.

Edwards Unabated

From the mid 90s Rowland and Mark Edwards spent more and more time in Spain. They returned to Cornwall for a few months each summer to run domestic courses and during these periods continued to put up hard new routes. Mark Edwards, especially, established a number of pitches at the highest technical grades; these included *Placa del Edwards* and *The Paragon Returns* at Sennen, and the E8 6c *Question Mark* at Cribba Head, where Edwards placed bolt anchors to facilitate top-rope practice. *Question Mark* has seen only one repeat to date, by the outstanding Devon climber Ken Palmer.

As the century, and millennium, drew to a close, the emphasis of new climbing in Penwith was on short, but extremely intense granite lines and on high grades. Shane Ohly climbed several E6 to E8 test-pieces in the Logan Rock area, and added *Aero Dynamics* at Chair Ladder and *Audacity* at Carn Barra. He climbed short hard pitches on the sea walls below Bosigran Main Face, including *Spiderman's Nightmare*, while Mark Edwards pitched in at his old stamping ground of Land's End with another eponymous E8, *The Edwards Edge*. At Bosigran, Littlejohn rounded off his epic 20th century contribution to Cornish climbing with *Morgawr*, a line through the overhangs directly above the Coal Face. A fine contribution came at Vessacks West on Penwith's south coast where Devon climber Brian Wilkinson, seconded by Margaret Grapes, developed a new area of cliff by climbing a number of routes including the excellent *Madonna of the Waves*.

The Lizard continued to attract first ascensionists. Raine contributed the strenuous *Total Body Wag* at Diamond Head and *International* at Pen Olver, where Ohly and Leo Houlding also climbed the hard line of *Gweek*. Martin Crocker, having survived a horrifying accident on his *Three Score Years and Ten, Amen* in Bosigran's Great Zawn in 1993, climbed, invincibly (no other word for it), the intense *Obseam*, E7 6c, at Vellan Head. By way of contrast,

Pen Olver offered up a selection of worthwhile routes in the lower grades to the Hope family and friends

Back in West Penwith, Cribba Head's portfolio of exacting routes was enhanced by *Mary*, a solo by visiting Lakeland activist Dave Birkett, while Mark Edwards climbed the E8 6c *Son of Satan* at Porthgwarra. Edwards raised the stakes as the millennium drew to a close. In 1998 came his *The Human Skewer*, an E9 6c in the dark depths of Zawn Rinny on Chair Ladder's flanking walls. Even more notable was the 45-degree overhanging E10 7a *Rewind* at Carn Vellan, an ascent of his earlier bolted route *Blue Sky Lightning*, this time with traditional gear. Edwards reported that both these routes had suspect rock as well as poor protection, a 30-metre groundfall being a possibility on *Rewind*.

Countdown to a New Millennium

At the end of the 20th century West Cornwall has survived as a magnificent adventure-climbing venue. The majority of those who climb in Penwith and on The Lizard come from outside the area and are drawn by the exhilarating promise of adventurous sea-cliffs where the rock remains in charge and where the future is not robbed of its promises and its challenges. The future may confound every shade of opinion, of course, and probably will. There is still potential for good new routes in the area in spite of the intense development of the past two decades. Future developments may include bouldering on the scores of granite and greenstone facets and isolated monoliths that crowd the peripheries of cliffs and the shorelines of isolated coves. It will be 'wilderness bouldering' indeed, and the queues will be short. Some may believe that Dorset-style, deep-water soloing has a future in West Cornwall, but vicious tides and killer swell may have the last words on that. They don't surf much in Dorset.

Through all the messiness and conflict that characterized certain aspects of Cornish climbing in the final decades of the 20th century, the reality of the area's one hundred years of climbing shines through triumphantly. This is due to the achievements of numerous activists at all levels, and to the pleasure that the Cornish cliffs have given to thousands of ordinary climbers, the sport's true constituency. It seems entirely fitting that one of the first new routes of the 21st century was a typically Cornish E2, *Evening Star*, at the delightfully 'hidden' venue of Progo Arch by the local climbers John Hooper and Bob Banaster.

On this note, this record closes at the beginning of a new millennium with a celebration of the sea-cliff wilderness of Cornwall. It seems fitting, therefore, to end this historical overview with the cool serenity of Nea Morin's words about Bosigran in the misty summer dusk, as fine a eulogy to the Cornish cliffs as you could wish for: 'There was something about it quite different from anything I had previously experienced... There was an indefinable atmosphere of melancholy, tenderness and peace.'

Godrevy Point

(Devonian fine-grained slate) OS Ref 580 432

Outlook: West.
Tidal: Access is for approximately two hours either side of low tide.
Coastguard Identity: Godrevy Point.

Godrevy is a favourite bouldering spot for local climbers. The problems are short and sharp, on solid sea-washed slate. It is best visited when low tide is in the afternoon or evening, even better if it is sunny. Godrevy is always sheltered from the wind and dries quickly after rain. It is best to avoid Godrevy on humid days, as the rock stays damp.

Approach: Take the A30(T) to the large roundabout on the north-east side of Hayle. Follow signs for the B3301 to Helston and Hayle. Almost immediately, at a double mini roundabout, turn right to follow the B3301 to Gwithian and Upton Towans. Pass through the hamlet of Gwithian after a mile, cross a narrow river bridge a quarter of a mile later, and then turn left into Godrevy.

Godrevy is owned by The National Trust, and a parking fee is charged, but it is free after 5 p.m. Park near the headland and follow the coastal footpath until a gate, wooden steps, and a handrail lead down to a sandy beach. The best bouldering area lies on the line between Gwithian Beach and Godrevy lighthouse.

A distinctive 8-metre overhanging wall and some shorter rock walls close by give at least 20 problems; some are bold but all are fun!

Another particularly good area lies 100 metres to the north, just short of a large sandstone boulder lying on top of the slate. There are two good gullies with overhanging west and slabby east faces. Many problems are found here, all less than 6 metres high and on perfectly solid slate. A foot mat and chalk are the only gear required. Problems exist from beginners' climbs up to intricate sequences of 6b and 6c.

West Penwith

Wicca Pillar (Granite)   OS Ref 464 400

Outlook: West.
Non-tidal but can be dangerous in heavy seas.
Coastguard Identity: Wicca Pool.

Wicca Cliff is the only granite intrusion on a ten-kilometre coastal stretch of dark greenstone and killas. It has a number of short enjoyable routes and traverses.

Approach to Wicca Pillar is along the coast path, north-east from Zennor Head or south-west from Treveal Cove, the latter being gained by the right-of-way from the B3306 at OS Ref 473 394. The approach from Zennor Village via Zennor Head is a good 3 kilometres while the Treveal approach is about 2 kilometres from the road. Wicca Pillar is about 20 metres high and is easily identified at the base of Wicca Cliff. The Pillar's offshore twin pinnacle of Trilley or Fox Rock lies to the south-west. A sketchy path (sometimes overgrown by late summer) leads down steep, bracken-covered slopes to Wicca Pillar. On the west side of the Pillar and separated from it by the cleft of Wicca Chimney is a smaller rock mass, the top of which forms a flat platform 10 metres below the top of the main mass. This is separated from the landward cliff by another flat-topped ridge running almost parallel to the cliff.

Descent. The gap between the flat-topped ridge and the cliff is filled with boulders. It is possible to reach the top of the ridge by easy scrambling. On its far side descend a prominent slab to a ledge about 6 metres above the sea. A number of routes start from here. Alternatively, there is a more interesting, harder approach, though this can be done only below half tide: climb down into the gap between the cliff and the flat-topped ridge by way of a 15-metre chimney. From the top of a boulder, climb a crack to the top of the ridge. Descend the seaward side of the ridge by another crack to a square recess; in the left corner of this is a rift that is descended to sea-level at the foot of Wicca Chimney.

Wicca Chimney   20 metres   Very Difficult   (1902)
Climb the chimney awkwardly to a platform. From here there are two options: take a shallow rake out to big ledges on the north face and then climb to the top; or make a short traverse right to a small ledge on the landward face and then climb straight up to the top.

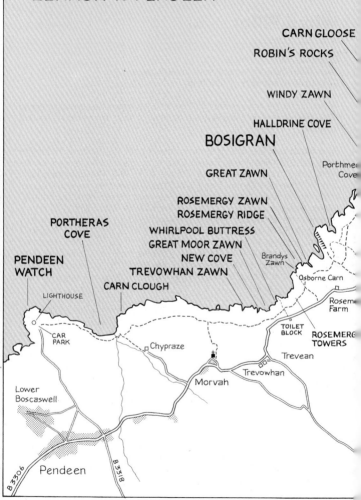

NORTH COAST
ZENNOR TO PENDEEN

CARN GLOOSE

ROBIN'S ROCKS

WINDY ZAWN

HALLDRINE COVE

BOSIGRAN

GREAT ZAWN

Porthmeor
Cove

ROSEMERGY ZAWN
ROSEMERGY RIDGE

PORTHERAS
COVE

WHIRLPOOL BUTTRESS

GREAT MOOR ZAWN

NEW COVE

Brandys
Zawn

PENDEEN
WATCH

TREVOWHAN ZAWN

Osborne Carn

CARN CLOUGH

Roseme
Farm

LIGHTHOUSE

TOILET
BLOCK

ROSEMERG
TOWERS

CAR
PARK

Chypraze

Trevean

Trevowhan

Morvah

Lower
Boscaswell

Pendeen

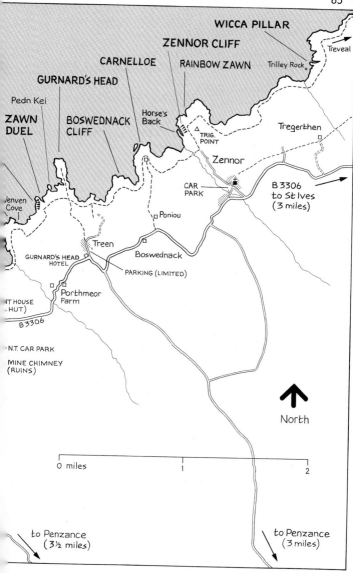

The four climbs on the landward face start from the ledge reached by the descent. They are short and obvious.

The Corner   15 metres   Very Difficult   (1902)
A pleasant climb on good holds starting at the left-hand end of the ledge.

The Cracks   12 metres   Severe   (1902)
The thin cracks in the centre of the face. The right-hand crack is the harder.

The Sloping Ledge Climb   14 metres   Difficult   (1902)
A few metres above the right-hand end of the ledge, another ledge sloping up to the left is climbed using good handholds.

Edge Climb   15 metres   Severe   (1912)
Climb the right edge of the landward face on small holds.

The east face of the Pillar rises above the platform, which slopes down to sea-level. Features on this face are a shallow recess with a crack in each corner, and two obvious horizontal cracks, which divide the Pillar into thirds. The seaward face has a number of ledges and platforms as well as a rib, which drops down to the sea. This rib can be traversed from the seaward face to the foot of the east face near sea-level, where the following climb starts.

The Rib Climb   8 metres   Difficult   (1902)
Follow the rib from sea-level to the platform that extends across the top of the seaward face.

The Sea Spray Climb   17 metres   Very Difficult   (1902)
Start a metre or so from the upper end of the east face ledge and climb straight up to the recess at the foot of the left-hand crack. Traverse right and climb the right-hand crack to the top. Following the left-hand crack to the top makes a harder, more direct route.

Diagonal Route   20 metres   Very Difficult   (1938)
Start as for *The Sea Spray Climb* and move up for 2 metres and then traverse right to a sloping ledge. Move across to a higher ledge and gain *The Rib Climb*'s platform by an awkward pull-up.

Wicca Pillar Traverse   18 metres   Severe   (1.4.52)
Start at the right edge of the landward face and climb for 3 metres before traversing rightwards onto the east face. Follow a diagonal crack, and finish with a layback and an interesting move onto a small ledge at the extreme seaward end.

Wicca Basket   20 metres   Severe   (11.10.63)
A high-level traverse from left to right around three sides of the Pillar with a stroll across the seaward face. The hardest moves are on the east face.

There are two climbs on the slabby landward cliff that runs parallel to the flat-topped ridge.

Bonnie   20 metres   Very Difficult   (16.10.69)
Start from the boulder-filled gap below a fine crack. Climb past a bulge to a large ledge. Traverse right for 2 metres and then climb diagonally leftwards to a horizontal band. Go up and then move right to a grassy ledge and belay.

Clyde   25 metres   Very Difficult   (16.10.69)
Start from sea-level below the slabs and climb a distinctive wide crack for about 6 metres to break left onto the top of a flake. Continue to a large ledge and then trend rightwards to the cliff-top by a series of delicate and exposed moves.

Zennor Cliff (Greenstone/Killas)   OS Ref 447 392

'The walls above the Horse's Back Zawn are killas and not safe for climbing.'
                                    (Andrews and Pyatt. CC Guide 1950.)

Outlook: West.
Non-tidal generally, but the routes on the lower cliff can be affected by swell.
Coastguard Identity: Pendour Cove (near Zennor Head).

The Zennor cliffs are 100 metres high in places, jet black in their lower sections and bearded with green and gold lichen above mid height. Some of the rock needs to be treated with care but it is generally honest with positive holds and ample protection. The Lower Cliff has a powerful atmosphere. The routes here are exposed and call for both commitment and nerve.

Approach. There is a car-park at Zennor village. The cliffs are reached on foot by following the private lane (right-of-way) that leads between the competing attractions of church and pub and then turns sharply left behind the pub. After 800 metres the lane ends by the gate of a private house. Continue along a narrow path and join the coast path heading in the direction of St Ives to reach a cluster of rocks with a memorial plaque set into one of them. The main climbing area is on the western side of the headland and includes the easily accessible Upper Cliff, the remote Lower Cliff, and the ridge of the Horse's Back. There are two climbs in the isolated Rainbow Zawn, which lies to the north-east of the main area.

Rainbow Zawn

Approach. From the plaque, continue along the coast path to the north-east for 100 metres until a prominent granite pillar can be seen on the seaward slopes below. The zawn lies directly below this pillar. Rainbow Zawn is a charming hellhole with two worthwhile routes. Green and purple algae covering the boulders in the zawn bed gave rise to the name.

Descent is by the eastern rim of the zawn via grassy slopes before scrambling leads back and into the zawn's mouth to gain a scooped platform 10 metres above high water mark.

Strongbow   37 metres   E2 5b   (1.8.81)
A lonely lead. From the ledge, gain the east face by some hard moves; then follow the lines of weakness leading steeply rightwards across the face to a muddy gully. Final belays are available in the gully, but a fixed rope from rocks above can be useful.

Blackthorn   20 metres   Hard Very Severe 5a   (1.8.81)
The start can be reached for three hours either side of low water. Climb down greasy rock from the *Strongbow* ledge into the zawn bed. Climb the fractured cracklines opposite.

Zennor Cliff

There are three main sections. **Descent** to each is described starting from the memorial plaque at the top of the western headland.

Upper Cliff

An accessible cliff with middle-grade routes of strong character. There is some dense lichen on parts of the routes.

Descent. From the memorial plaque, follow the path down the left side (facing out) of the headland rocks for 50 metres to a grassy platform that separates the Upper Cliff from the 60-metre drop into the zawn below. The Upper Cliff is split by a distinctive chimney: *1923 Route*.

The Rumbles   17 metres   Severe   (1.11.81)
Start below the steep crack in the flanking wall, 5 metres up from the far left arête of the cliff.
1 11m. 4b. Climb the corners past a bulge and make an awkward move onto the slab on the left. Climb the slab and belay on the right below a small overhang.
2 6m. 4a. Climb up to a ledge and step onto the right wall above the overhang to finish via a loose block.
Variation
The Bumbles (Very Severe 5a 5.82) takes the steep crack direct with a hard move onto the ledge.

Cross Town Traffic   35 metres   Hard Severe 4b   (14.11.81)
A rising traverse of the main face. Start just right of the left edge of the face.
1 15m. 4a. Climb gently to the natural traverse-line and follow it to a flake and then up to a ledge. Move right to belay in the chimney of *1923 Route* above the prominent chockstone.
2 20m. 4b. Traverse right for 3 metres and move up and rightwards past a large hollow flake to a good ledge. Finish easily rightwards to a grassy bay.

Greensleeves   27 metres   Severe 4a
From blocks 3 metres left of the deep chimney of *1923 Route*, climb a rightward-slanting crack to a ramp. Continue direct, keeping right of a perched block and move left through a 'needle's eye'.

1923 Route   25 metres   Very Difficult   (1923)
Climb the prominent chimney.

★★**Rosebud in June**   27 metres   Hard Very Severe 5a   (3.6.73)
Pick of the cliff. Take the shattered crack just right of *1923 Route* for 5 metres; then make a thin, poorly-protected move right and up into a niche. Climb direct for a metre or two and then traverse left to the base of a lichenous crack that looks daunting but sports holds like gold.

Blind Furry   27 metres   E2 5b   (12.5.96)
A confusingly-named eliminate between *Rosebud in June* and *The Royal Forester*. Start at the thin crack right of the start of *Rosebud in June*. Climb the crack until it slants left, and then move up and right (with runners behind a flake/block on the right). Step left and climb directly up the wall in the line of a very faint crack to a letterbox slot in a break. Mantel onto the ledge above and finish up a thin slanting crack.

★**The Royal Forester**   27 metres   Very Severe 4c   (29.4.73)
An entertaining pitch. Climb the distinctive V-groove in the centre of the face right of *Rosebud in June* and then take the small overhang at 6 metres on its right (a rich source of abandoned runners). Follow the shattered crack with care; then step left and climb past a hollow flake to a ledge on the right. Step back left and climb the crack.

Blind Fury   27 metres   E1 5b   (4.4.80)
Start just left of the deep niche on the right-hand side of the face. Climb to a hollow flake below the small black roof; then move neatly left for 3 metres before making strenuous moves through the break above to a foot-ledge on the right. Finish direct via a slab and overhang.
Variation E1 5c (5.9.97). Instead of moving left at the roof, climb it direct and finish as normal.

Choking Back the Cheers   20 metres   E1 5b ††   (31.12.90)
A pleasant pitch which started just right of *Blind Fury*. It climbed the shallow corner just left of the deep niche to a large flake before continuing in a direct line up the slab above. It is not known how the loss of the flake has affected the climb.

Sheep Crook, Black Dog   24 metres   Very Severe 4c   (13.5.73)
Climb the deep niche on the right of the crag by its right side; then make strenuous moves through the break. Follow the snaky crack up the slab and climb a final small overhang.

Lower Cliff (Seaward End)

There are several rewarding routes here, with the long and adventurous *Climb to the Sun* being the main attraction.

Descent. From the seaward side of the memorial plaque rocks, follow a vague path towards the sea, keeping in a direct line with the square-cut top of an offshore pinnacle, until the edge of the cliff is reached. A 30-metre abseil down a V-groove from good anchors gains a large platform that is awash at high tide and in heavy seas. The open wall above the platform gives three climbs.

Cry Tough   30 metres   Hard Very Severe 5a   (18.4.84)
Climb the pocketed crackline near the left edge of the wall to a small ledge and then follow the diagonal crack left of the edge.

Digital Wall   33 metres   E1 5b   (5.8.79)
A line up the centre of the wall, starting left of a big step. Creative route finding. Climb direct to a ledge and then the short crack above, before moving right to a rightward-slanting crack, which is climbed until it fades. Trend left to a faint groove that leads to a ledge and a short final wall.

Proctoscope   30 metres   Very Severe 4b   (24.5.79)
The obvious corner at the right end of the wall. Hop onto the big step and take the corner gently on friable holds.

The next five routes take exciting lines into the narrow sea-washed chasm formed by the Horse's Back and the main face. The traverse along the base of the main face is above the tide-line but can be hit by heavy seas. The routes share the same start from narrow ledges at the right-hand end of the big platform.

Angelus   45 metres   Hard Very Severe   (12.8.79)
1 37m. 5a. From the starting-ledges, traverse easily right for 12 metres to the base of a chimney (belay possible). Climb the chimney (often damp) past overlaps, and continue up a steep corner before moving right to ledges.
2 8m. Climb the yellow-stained rock above.

Sail Race 45 metres Very Severe (14.8.79)
1 18m. From the starting ledges, traverse easily rightwards past the chimney of *Angelus* to the obvious descent groove of *Climb to the Sun*.
2 15m. 4b. Take the wall left of the faultline to good bird-nesting ledges.
3 12m. Climb the broken rock above.

The original approach to the start of the next two climbs was by abseil, but better is to follow pitch 1 of *Climb to the Sun*.

Glockspud 77 metres Severe (20.7.79)
1 40m. 4a. *Climb to the Sun* pitch 1.
2 24m. 4a. From the left end of the ledge, climb up for about 5 metres, and then traverse up and left to good ledges.
3 13m. Move right from the belay ledge and go straight up on good rock, passing the band of overhangs at its left end.

Avoided Issue 95 metres Severe (25.5.79)
A wandering traverse-line through interesting scenery at a reasonable standard.
1 40m. 4a. *Climb to the Sun* pitch 1.
2 10m. *Climb to the Sun* pitch 2.
3 30m. Step down from the belay and follow a rising traverse-line leftwards across easy ledges to the left end of the prominent overhangs. Belay in a corner with a big spike on the left.
4 15m. Go straight up from the spike for 6 metres to finish up steep grass.

★Climb to the Sun 100 metres Hard Very Severe (23.7.79)
A rewarding jaunt with a serious feel to it. Less noisome outside the nesting season.
1 40m. 4a. From the starting ledges, traverse rightwards for 18 metres to the obvious descent groove (belay advised). Move down and continue for 12 metres until an awkward move is made onto a comfortable ledge. Belay at the far end below a corner-crack. An overhead runner at the left end of the ledge can protect the second.
2 10m. Climb the corner-crack above the belay to a good ledge on the right.
3 40m. 4c. Vegetated. From the belay, move right along a narrow ledge for 5 metres; then break onto the upper wall and climb direct past a pocket, keeping clear of some loose flakes on the left. Belay on the grassy ledge at the top of the wall.
4 10m. 4a. A jungle finish. Climb the right side of the vegetated tower to a ledge; then step left and up. Otherwise, walk off to the right and go up past the Upper Cliff.

Lower Cliff (Landward End)
Descent: From the memorial plaque, follow the path down the left-hand side (facing out) of the headland rocks and then bear left along a path

through leg-stripping blackthorn and gorse. Where the path skirts the head of the zawn there is a convenient abseil block once used by Don Whillans; feel free. Abseil down steep grass into the zawn bed. The start of *Zennorphobia* is reached by a direct abseil from the terrace at the base of the Upper Cliff.

Paper Moon   52 metres   Very Severe   (5.8.79)
Start at the slab and corner on the right edge of the second buttress to seaward from the back of the zawn.
1 12m. Climb the slab and corner to a small ledge below a pillar.
2 40m. Climb onto the pillar; then go up and left for 6 metres over poor ground and onto the lichen-covered wall above. Continue up the wall over two grassy ledges (belay possible on upper one) before moving right to the edge of the wall and finishing direct.

The Eyass   72 metres   E1 5b ††   (12.7.79)
Impressive, but handle with care, especially now a rockfall has been reported. The climb is centred on the clean-cut roof on the left of the first buttress to seaward from the back of the zawn and directly under the Upper Cliff. Start at some piled blocks below the roof.
1 37m. 5b. Climb leftwards up the mustard-coloured break and then up a shattered crack. Move right beneath the roof and across the steep slab to make an airy swing around the right end of the roof onto the lichen-smothered upper wall. Belay 3 metres higher at the base of a striking crackline.
2 35m. 4b. Go left to the edge of the wall and then follow cracks direct.

★Zennorphobia   48 metres   Hard Very Severe   (26.3.89)
An exciting and exposed route with a challenging abseil entry. The line takes the hanging gangway to the right of *The Eyass* overhang to gain the impressive vertical crackline running up the face. The gangway is reached by abseil from blocks at the right-hand end (facing in) of the Upper Cliff. Belay at a small niche above the block at the right-hand end of the gangway (peg belay).
1 14m. 4c. Step down onto the gangway and make a delicate move left on undercuts across a gap. Traverse the gangway, taking care with footholds, until it is possible to step up onto a wall of dark rock, where a move left gains a rocking block at the base of the vertical crack.
2 34m. 4b. Climb the crack, following its left side, to an area of cracked white slabs below an overlap (belay possible). Step left below the overlap and pull over on small but good holds; then follow the wide, slanting crack in the headwall to finish.

The Horse's Back
Approach down the western side of the ridge at low tide.

Now of historic interest, this remarkable feature was explored by Andrews, while two chimney climbs (Very Difficult) on the seaward nose were recorded by Kirkus and Fallows in 1938. A third route, **When I Was on Horseback** (30 metres Very Difficult 13.5.73), serves as an exit route from the zawn up the east face of The Horse's Back on shaky rock. It takes a short wall at the low-water mark to gain a break before going up and left to finish up a crack.

Carnelloe (Greenstone)

OS Ref 442 390

Outlook: North-west.
Tidal and affected by swell and rough seas.
Coastguard Identity: Carnelloe.

Carnelloe is a small headland of tumbled greenstone which is too broken to give defined climbing. However, it provides some low-grade climbs and adventurous scrambling along the marvellously complex eastern shore of Porthglaze Cove.

Approach by public right-of-way from Poniou on the coast road (B3306) a mile from both Gurnard's Head and Zennor. Follow the broad track (non-vehicular) that leads from the roadside for one kilometre until past an isolated single-storey house on the crown of the headland (the old Count House of Carnelloe Mine). Beyond the house at the point of the headland are some fine rock columns overlooking an undercut, sea-washed zawn. The striking Carnelloe Island lies just offshore beyond a deep narrow channel. The Island has been reached in the past by swimming.

Descend the obvious chimney of **Disgruntled Chimney** (15 metres Difficult in descent 2.6.52) to just above high-water mark and about 10 metres from the back of Carnelloe Zawn.

More So   20 metres   Difficult   (2.6.52)
Start just above high-water mark beneath a prominent bulge near the base of *Disgruntled Chimney* and go up rightwards to a broad ledge below a slab. Finish up the slab.

Carnelloe Zawn has been traversed high up at Severe, going right to left, but precise details of the line are unrecorded.

Pinnacle Slab Route   50 metres   Very Difficult   (4.88)
1 20m. From Carnelloe Zawn, climb the obvious slab to the right, leaving the 'pinnacle' to the left, to a belay overlooking the zawn.
2 30m. Continue over rocky steps to the top.

Torrey Canyon Slab   30 metres   Difficult   (16.4.67)
Start at the base of a slab on a broad platform at the high-water mark
opposite the extreme southern end of the Island.
1 20m. Climb the slab to a small niche.
2 10m. Move up and slightly left; then finish direct.

Boswednack Cliff (Greenstone/Killas)   OS Ref 438 386

Outlook: West.
Tidal and affected by swell and rough seas.
Coastguard Identity: Boswednack Cliff.

Boswednack is a delightfully secluded headland with a mix of intriguing
climbs. It has a rare pedigree, A W Andrews having recorded the ascent of
two chimneys here in 1907. The rock is basically sound but with some
superficial looseness.

Approach. As for Carnelloe to join the coast path below the isolated house
on the headland. Follow the coast path westwards for about a kilometre
around the rim of Porthglaze Cove until abreast of the walled corner of a
field on the left of the path. To the right of the path a slight fisherman's
track leads to seaward across a featureless vegetated slope. The start of the path
can be difficult to identify in mid summer. The path leads to bird-limed rocks
at the top of Boswednack Cliff. An alternative approach can be made from
Gurnard's Head by walking east along the coast path for two kilometres
until abreast of the walled corner that marks the beginning of the seaward
path to the top of the cliff.

Andrews Zawn
This is the small zawn on the northern side of the Boswednack headland. It is
reached by descending the seaward point of the headland and then bearing
right (facing out) just above the sea near a **deep unprotected mine
shaft**. The large block that forms the back of the zawn has chimneys on
both sides. These are Andrews's 1907 climbs. The south east wall of the
zawn has four very obvious lines.

Shiny Shiny   15 metres   Hard Severe   4b   (6.86)
Take the face of the small buttress.

Shiny Boots of Leather   15 metres   Very Severe   4c   (6.86)
Climb the direct line up the steep wall just right of the buttress.

Whiplash Girl-child   20 metres   Very Severe 5a   (6.86)
Climb the crack and groove-line that splits the wall towards the back of the zawn.

In the Dark   20 metres   E2 5c   (6.86)
The bulging wall to the right of the previous route.

Zawn Dredd.
Zawn Dredd, the narrow zawn at the northern end of the main cliff, can be approached from either side at low to mid tide.

Judge Dredd   20 metres   Hard Very Severe 5a   (18.6.95)
The obvious undercut crackline at the back of the zawn gives some fine sustained climbing. Follow the crack until 5 metres from the top, where a diagonal exit left avoids a looser finish.

Main Cliff
Descent. A scramble down left, facing out, 70 metres south-west of the mine shaft leads to a platform at mid height. On the left there is a large sea-cave. A further descent to the right and around a corner leads to the Justice Face. The cliff is broken and ragged at its right-hand end (facing in). It is divided centrally by a leftward-leaning corner-ramp which gives the line of *No Justice*. On the extreme left of the face where it turns to seaward there are two grooves.

The Chief Justice   20 metres   Very Severe 4c   (29.6.86)
The left-hand groove, gained awkwardly via a protruding block.

★**Justice on the Runs**   20 metres   Hard Very Severe 5a   (15.6.86)
Clever, sustained climbing. The right-hand groove is gained by thin moves up a steep slab and a cheeky move out right. Climb leftwards until interesting moves right gain the upper groove.

Right of the previous routes is a slender overhanging prow with a groove on its right bounded by a prominent nose.

☆☆**Pull the Wires from the Wall**   20 metres   E4 5c †   (22.3.98)
An improbable and sparsely-protected excursion up the prow. Start up the groove to the right of the prow. Climb for 5 metres until a handrail leads wildly out left, where a hard move up gains a good rest and runners on the left side of the prow. Move back onto the face using a prominent flat jug, and climb to a thin flake on the right arête. Pull up the arête to a diagonal crack and finish over the capping roof via a jammed flake.

★**Blind Justice**   20 metres   Hard Very Severe 5b   (8.6.86)
Start below the groove of *Pull the Wires...* and make hard moves into it; continue awkwardly to easier ground.

Wicked Lady   20 metres   Very Severe 5a †   (13.7.86)
The crack and groove right of the prominent nose are climbed strenuously and an awkward exit is made onto the ramp above. Climb the ramp to the top.

Taki Justice   20 metres   Hard Very Severe 5a   (22.6.86)
Start below a short face at a diagonal right-to-left crackline. Climb the face via the crackline to a strange crux move, which gains a ledge. Easier climbing follows.

Rough Justice   20 metres   Hard Very Severe 5b †   (29.12.89)
Start right of *Wicked Lady* below a niche. Climb to the base of the niche and then move left to a crack. Go up left to gain the top of a nose. Move up and back to the right to finish.

Last Minute Reprieve   20 metres   E1 5b   (29.12.89)
Climb to the niche of *Rough Justice* and follow a crack up and rightwards to a ledge on the arête. Finish easily up the ramp on the right.

The next feature to the right is an obvious corner-ramp.

No Justice   20 metres   Very Difficult   (8.6.86)
One metre left of the corner, a shallow groove leads to a large ledge at 5 metres. From the ledge, climb the narrow ramp to the top. An easier alternative is to climb the corner direct.

To the right of the corner-ramp, a broad crack runs down the face to widen into an inverted V with a prominent stepped overhang on its right at 8 metres.

★**Lone Justice**   20 metres   E1 5b   (8.6.86)
Steep, sustained, and technically pleasing. Start at the left-hand base of the faultline and climb to where the fault narrows. Break out left; then move up and back into the crack, which is climbed until it is convenient to step out right onto the face, and finish direct.

★★**Ways to Be Wicked**   20 metres   E3 5c   (29.6.86)
Interesting climbing. Start below the prominent overhangs. Climb to the second overhang and arrange protection. Step back down to the first overhang, where a long reach finds a flat jug on the arête. Swing out and move up to the thin crack, which provides sustained climbing to the top.

Ordinary Justice   20 metres   Severe   (27.6.86)
The prominent jagged-edged fault to the right.

Groovy Justice   20 metres   Severe 4a   (29.6.86)
Worthwhile. The crack and fault just right of previous route.

Jus'dis Slab   15 metres   Hard Severe 4b   (27.6.86)
The slab at the right-hand end of the cliff. Start in the left corner and climb
the slab diagonally rightwards until steeper moves gain the right-hand side
of the face.

Gurnard's Head Area (Greenstone/Killas)

---

*'The crag is elegant in its geometry. Two sheets of coal-black rock meet at 90
degrees.'*
(Chris Jackson: Extreme Rock)

Outlook: West.
Non-tidal on headland climbs but affected by swell and rough sea.
Mainly tidal on Right Angle Cliff but bases of routes on the far right-hand
wall are accessible for two hours on either side of low water (neap-tides are
less generous). The entire cliff is extremely susceptible to heavy swells and
rough seas. The *Right Angle* in particular having been the scene of several
desperate accidents. Kittiwake Zawn is **tidal** at the seaward edge and is
similarly affected by big swells and rough seas.
Coastguard Identity: Gurnard's Head.

Gurnard's Head is a significant and spectacular climbing area with great
exposure and commitment. The Head is a dramatic feature. It was the site of
an Iron Age cliff-castle and still has the remains of ancient hut circles on its
eastern slopes. The impressive cliffs that fringe the western neck of the
headland as natural defences provide some of the best climbing in Penwith,
with the reasonably-graded *Right Angle* offering an exciting challenge for
competent teams. The rock is generally very sound and clean. There are
three areas of climbing – The Gurnard's Head, Right Angle Cliff, and
Kittiwake Zawn.

Approach by following the lane that leads seawards from the main B3306
at the Gurnard's Head Hotel to a row of old coastguard houses. From these,
a right-of-way leads over a stile and is followed for nearly a kilometre
through fields until the neck of the headland is reached.

The Gurnard's Head   OS Ref 432 388
There are several short, steep climbs and problem pitches on the broken
walls that ring the true seaward end of Gurnard's Head. Two longer routes
are recorded. To reach these follow the path from the neck of the headland
along its eastern flank until below a steep depression that rises above the
remains of concrete steps.

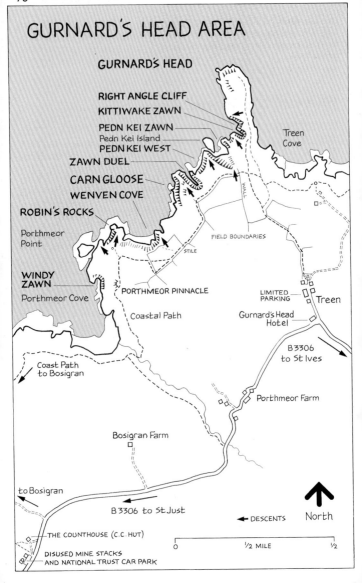

GURNARD'S HEAD AREA

GURNARD'S HEAD

RIGHT ANGLE CLIFF
KITTIWAKE ZAWN
PEDN KEI ZAWN
Pedn Kei Island
PEDN KEI WEST
ZAWN DUEL
CARN GLOOSE
WENVEN COVE
ROBIN'S ROCKS
Porthmeor Point
WINDY ZAWN
Porthmeor Cove

Treen Cove

WALL

FIELD BOUNDARIES

STILE

PORTHMEOR PINNACLE

LIMITED PARKING

Treen

Gurnard's Head Hotel

Coastal Path

B 3306 to St Ives

Coast Path to Bosigran

Porthmeor Farm

Bosigran Farm

to Bosigran

B 3306 to St Just

← DESCENTS

North

THE COUNTHOUSE (C.C. HUT)

DISUSED MINE STACKS AND NATIONAL TRUST CAR PARK

0   ½ MILE   ½

Green Stuff Chimney   30 metres   Very Difficult   (4.4.52)
From the concrete steps, scramble for about 30 metres rightwards (facing in) to the centre of a broad platform.
1 15m. Climb to a block on a ledge; then move to the right and up a gully onto a ledge below an overhang.
2 15m. Traverse left for 3 metres; then finish up a vegetated gully.

Lookout   20 metres   Very Difficult   (2.6.52)
Start directly below the huge central block of the headland to the right of the previous route and about 10 metres above sea-level. Climb the block directly to the top.

Right Angle Cliff   OS Ref 432 386

For Right Angle Cliff, take a higher line from the path that runs out to the Head and follow a path on the higher western edge of the headland until above a spectacular 50-metre vertical corner that is flanked by large cliffs. This corner gives the key line of *Right Angle*. Most routes are concentrated on the magnificent back wall of the corner with the striking line of *Leviathan* taking the central challenge. The steep corner opposite *Right Angle* is *Shark*.

Environmental Issues. Gurnard's Head is an SSSI and is owned by the National Trust. The slopes leading to the start of *Right Angle* support important crevice communities. Please descend on bare rock, where possible, and avoid treading on plants. Sea Aster, Sea Beet and Cliff Spurrey are vulnerable here.

Descent. For *Right Angle* and all the routes left of *Mastodon*, continue along the cliff edge to the right (facing out) of the *Right Angle* corner and go down easy-angled slabs until an obvious steep-sided niche about 12 metres above the sea is reached. From here, an inviting traverse-line runs out rightwards across the middle of the face. A common alternative approach to the routes starting from the cave ledge is by abseil down *Right Angle's* final corner.

★★**Right Angle**   75 metres   Hard Severe   (26.8.66)
[Photo p.32b.] An outstanding climb; technically reasonable, but requiring some commitment from both leader and second owing to its exposure and inescapability.
1 15m. Traverse rightwards onto the face to reach a good belay ledge.
2 20m. 4a. Continue for 10 metres to a descending crack and move down this to a ledge just below the main corner.
3 40m. 4b. Climb the slab into the corner and continue with pleasure to the top.
Variations
1a 30m. Very Severe. The stance below the final corner can be reached by a lower traverse. Start about 6 metres below the niche at the start of pitch 1. Not recommended in heavy seas. Not recommended at all in fact.

80

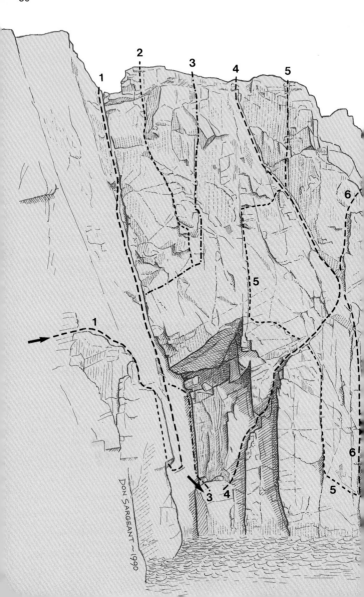

Don Sargeant ~ 1990

GURNARD'S HEAD AREA ~ RIGHT ANGLE CLIFF

1	Right Angle	HS
2	The Kraken	HVS
3	Pure Juice	E1
4	Behemoth	E2
5	Mastodon	E3
6	Black Magic	E2
7	Shark	E1
8	Tropospheric Scatter	E4
9	Probe	S

ABSEIL DESCENT

KITTIWAKE ZAWN

2a 20m. Very Severe 4b. The most commonly climbed variation avoids the descent on pitch 2, either through choice or because of heavy seas. Continue along the traverse-line by fingery moves beneath an overlap to a small and exposed stance in the corner.

The following two routes are poor variations on the magnificent theme of *Right Angle* as they are loose in places.

Surf Wall   68 metres   Severe   (2.6.68)
1 20m. *Right Angle* pitch 1.
2 30m. Continue for 10 metres and then take a diagonal rising line rightwards on big holds until a small stance in a shallow corner is reached.
3 18m. Turn the overhang above on the left, and finish direct on poor rock.

Rota Guta   50 metres   Severe   (2.6.68)
1 15m. *Right Angle* pitch 1.
2 35m. From the far end of the ledge, gain a steep arête and climb it to a shaky flake. Move right and climb the wall direct.

☆☆**Over the Ocean**   100 metres   E4 6a †   (1.6.97)
An excellent and sustained solo traverse from left to right of the whole cliff, needing calm seas and a lowish tide. Mostly above deep water. Approach as for *Right Angle* but descend to just above the high-tide line. Traverse right across faceted walls via sustained and interesting climbing to a respite at the move to *Right Angle* below the main corner. Stride the gap and enter the groove below *Behemoth*. Cross the steep-sided wall and turn the arête of *Leviathan* with considerable difficulty, above some exposed rocks. Continue along the main wall to the platform below the corner of *Shark*. Finish easily rightwards, and then scramble up the ridge.

The following routes can be reached by abseiling down the *Right Angle* corner or by following the first two pitches of that route.

The Kraken   40 metres   Hard Very Severe   (28.7.77)
Start at the end of *Right Angle* pitch 2, below the final corner.
1 20m. 5a. Climb *Right Angle* until above a chockstone; then traverse out onto the right wall below an overhang. Skirt the overhang on its right to better holds and step left to belay.
2 20m. 4c. Climb the obvious crack on the left and then follow a groove to the top.
Variation
The start of the second pitch can be reached by climbing a short distance above the chockstone and traversing rightwards on a higher line. This variation is called **Nemesis** (20.9.78).

Parabola   60 metres   E2   (17.2.80)
An exposed girdle. Start at the end of *Right Angle* pitch 2, below the main corner.

1 20m. 4a. Climb up to the corner of *Right Angle* and belay 3 metres higher.

2 15m. 5b. Traverse across the right wall, passing a square-topped pinnacle, to a shallow groove. Climb this with difficulty; then go right and back left to belay on a good ledge.

3 15m. 5c. Descend to a nose and climb around it. Climb a thin crack and make hard moves right to gain the top of a block.

4 10m. 5b. Climb a crack to a small ledge and then traverse right around the arête. Easier climbing to finish.

The following two routes start from a hanging belay midway up the last pitch of *Right Angle*, level with the roof of the sea-cave. An abseil approach is best.

Fuji Frenzy 37 metres E6 6b † (17.7.96)

A bold pitch throughout with some looseness in the middle section. The stunning arête directly opposite the finish of *Right Angle* provides the crux and the best climbing on the route. From the belay, step right and climb through the small overhang protected by a single *Micromate 1*. Continue boldly up the loose wall above, finishing up the obvious arête.

☆**Voodoo Child** 46 metres E6 6b † (6.7.96)

Committing and atmospheric climbing up the centre of the back wall. Belay as for *Fuji Frenzy*. Step right and airily traverse the lip of the sea-cave to an obvious foothold with a thin crack above; follow this for 8 metres until the crack peters out and good holds are reached. Move slightly right and climb directly up the wall split by a thin seam. Finish via the short groove and small roof.

The following routes start from the impressive cave-ledge at the left-hand base of the back wall. It is reached, with interest, from the ledge at the end of *Right Angle* pitch 2. Dampness and greasiness are the norm here, and the ledge is affected by rough seas and swell.

Pure Juice 55 metres E1 (30.8.78)

1 18m. 4a. From the cave-ledge, climb the chimney to the roof, traverse left, and then go up the crack to belay after 3 metres.

2 17m. 5b. Traverse across the right wall, passing a square-topped pinnacle, to a shallow groove. Climb this with difficulty; then go right and back left to belay on a good ledge.

3 20m. 4c. Follow the steep groove above to the top.

★★★**Behemoth** 48 metres E2 (30.8.69)

The next great challenge to follow on from *Right Angle*. Adventurous, stylish, and committing, it seeks out a central line up the formidable back wall of the zawn. Start from the cave-ledge. Best tackled in the evening to avoid 'verglas' on the first pitch.

1 25m. 5c. Climb the two greasy overhanging corners to small airy ledges leading around the arête to an optional hanging belay shared with

Mastodon and *Leviathan*. Follow the line of least resistance up and rightwards and belay at a flat-topped spike below a smooth shallow groove leading back left.
2 23m. 5b. Climb the leftward-leading groove and the larger groove above (stiff) to a pedestal (optional belay). Continue to the top.

Magog   46 metres   E5 †   (1994)
Start from the cave ledge.
1 35m. 6b. Bridge up the central corner at the back of the ledge in the sea-cave and onto the slab. Continue up and use a small ledge to move right onto the hanging wall. Traverse rightwards across the wall immediately below the roof (small wires) until good holds permit a pull onto the arête. Strenuously climb the chimney above to join the base of the crack on *Mastodon* and continue to the belay. (If rope drag is a problem it is possible to move left midway up the crack to join the *Pure Juice* belay.)
2 11m. 5c. *Mastodon* pitch 3.

★★**Leviathan**   45 metres   E4   (12.4.94)
The striking arête of the cave provides a harder alternative to *Mastodon*. Start from the right-hand side of the cave ledge.
1 15m. 6a. Swing right across the steep wall to two good holds and continue into the corner, before teetering along a ledge and pulling onto the arête with considerable difficulty. Continue boldly up the arête in a superb position to the hanging belay shared with *Mastodon* and *Behemoth*.
2 30m. 6a. Climb up rightwards from the belay to gain a large undercut flake. Follow the flake up to the left and then step back right onto a steep wall below a crackline which runs down from the left-hand side of a pedestal. Climb the wall and crack to the pedestal before finishing up the groove of *Behemoth*.

Descent to *Mastodon* and the routes on the far side of the huge back wall of Right Angle Cliff by breaking off to the west before the neck of the headland. Scramble down steep grass slopes to seaward until above the 15-metre corner of *Probe*, opposite the *Right Angle* wall. Abseil down this corner, at low tide and when there is no swell, and traverse to the tidal ledges at the base of the inner corner of *Shark*. An alternative is to abseil down *Shark* itself, so that the abseil rope is to hand for shifting the belay higher in a hurry; this can be useful!

★★★**Mastodon**   53 metres   E3   (3.9.78)
The third great development; uncompromising, strenuous, and exhilarating, this splendid line takes the wall head on. Protection is slight in places. Start at the base of the clean-cut corner of *Shark*. Pitches 1 and 2 are often combined.
1 20m. 5b. The first part is usually wet and greasy and can be awkward. Climb up left into a triangular scoop, then left again into another triangular scoop at the foot of a long crack. Climb this and traverse left to

the line of *Behemoth* and a thin hanging belay. (Step up from the belay to find a good wire placement.)

2 23m. 5c. Move left onto an awkward ledge at the base of a crack and climb this (peg above). Move right on fingerholds and then go back left into the crack again. From the top of the crack, traverse right onto a pedestal belay on *Behemoth*.

3 10m. 5c. Finish up the short, arm-pumping crack behind the belay.

★★Black Magic   34 metres   E2 5b   (2.10.78)
A fine sustained pitch. Start as for *Mastodon* and follow that route via the left-leading scoops. The first part is often wet and greasy. In between the first and second scoop, climb to a smaller scoop. Continue direct for a few metres and then move left to a flat-topped spike. (Optional belay.) Climb to the traverse of *Behemoth*, and take the shallow groove to an obvious crack, which is followed to finish.

★Shark   24 metres   E1 5b   (29.8.69)
The soaring clean-cut corner on the right of the central wall. Climb the corner to the overhangs; then take the obvious line on the right wall to finish.

The Silence of a Lamb   30 metres   E6 6b   (1991)
An impressive looking, bold and sustained line up the right arête of *Shark's* corner. Technical and unprotected at the base, but higher the climbing eases and there is marginal protection.

★★Tropospheric Scatter   29 metres   E4 5c   (2.10.78)
Start at the base of the steep wall right of the *Shark* corner. Climb the overhanging crack to a small roof. Move right and go straight up to the right of the next roof. Pass this on the right by a long reach/lunge to gain a small ledge (badly corroded peg). Traverse left and climb a thin crack to the top.

Art of the Slate   27 metres   E5 6a   (1989/20.4.94)
Start 3 metres right of *Tropospheric Scatter*. Best climbed on a calm high tide on account of the poor protection. Climb straight up the steep wall. The low crux consists of a series of long reaches protected by small hard-to-place wires. The climbing eases as height is gained although the rock becomes increasingly loose.

☆☆Babylon and Back   57 metres   E3 †   (15.4.94)
This girdle traverse is the ideal choice here when the base of the cliff is affected by swell. Start on a large ledge just down from the top of *Probe*.

1 15m. 5c. Climb diagonally left, across *Art of the Slate,* past the badly corroded peg on *Tropospheric Scatter*, to a large hold on the arête. Move left onto the overhanging wall and a diagonal crack, drop down onto a large, flat hold and gravitate leftwards to a hanging stance on *Shark*.

2 9m. 5a. Traverse left to the hanging stance of *Behemoth*.

3 18m. 5c. Climb *Mastodon* but instead of moving right above the peg go straight up until it is possible to traverse left below a nose. Climb up to the ledge stance on *Pure Juice*.
4 15m. 5c. Climb the orange groove between *The Kraken* and *Pure Juice*: surprisingly good.

Probe   15 metres   Severe
The abseil descent line. Best reached by abseil although the traditional approach was by descending grassy slopes to sea-level and then traversing in. Climb diagonally left up a slab and continue up the corner.

Kittiwake Zawn   OS Ref 432 385
This is the deep and narrow zawn immediately west of Right Angle Cliff. It is tidal on its seaward edge. The long-established routes here have had few ascents and their nature may have changed.

Environmental Issues: Kittiwake Zawn is owned by the National Trust and is an SSSI. Breeding Fulmars, Herring Gulls and Shags can be found here. The surrounding area is a British Trust for Ornithology registered site of local importance. Friable descent slopes support important maritime species and there are very good crevice communities. Sea Aster, Samphire, and Sea Spleenwort are vulnerable. Although not formally restricted, this area sometimes has a large number of birds and may be best avoided during the nesting season.

Approach by breaking off to the west before the neck of the headland to reach the rim of the zawn's east wall. Scramble with care along the top of the steep and broken slopes to seaward as far as possible; then continue left, again with care, down rock and grass steps to the sea-level mouth of the zawn before traversing in (low tide required). An abseil descent is also possible. The zawn-bed can also be reached down the grassy western edge, then over ledges to the lowest entry, where a short wall can be descended by down-climbing or abseil (low tide required). Just left (facing in) of the descent line on the eastern side of the zawn there is an obvious crack leading to a square-cut corner. This is *Free Fall Gull*.

Free Fall Gull   12 metres   Severe 4a   (28.5.89)
Climb the crack and the square-cut corner.

Darkling Thrush   15 metres   Very Difficult †   (28.5.89)
About 6 metres right of *Free Fall Gull* is an irregular groove, which is climbed to broken ledges.

African Grey   15 metres   Severe 4a †   (28.5.89)
Start at a deep pool. Climb the leftwards-slanting crack in the slab above to finish awkwardly up a short corner.

Dad's Back   15 metres   Very Severe   4c †   (28.5.89)
A fine intricate pitch. Start 6 metres right of *African Grey* below an obvious
groove bounded on its left by a steep pillar. Climb the groove to a small
overhang; then step right onto a slab and climb up to a good ledge.
Continue up the reddish wall, bearing left to finish up a short V-groove.

Quadruple X   30 metres   Severe   (6.4.83)
Just past the first big boulder in the zawn-bed is an obvious
leftward-slanting thin crack. Start at the base of the crack and make a
rising traverse leftwards into a large groove. Follow the groove, which
narrows to a crack, and then exit onto a vegetated stance. Scramble to
finish.

Kittiwake   37 metres   Severe   (4.74)
Start at the foot of the leftward-slanting crack and climb to good ledges.
Take the wider crack on the left and finish up the grassy groove.

Jonathan Livingstone Seagull   32 metres   Hard Very Severe   5a † (4.74)
Start 6 metres left of the brown hanging corner at the back of the zawn,
below a thin crack. Bridge up a groove and then climb the thin crack to a
ledge. Take the finger-crack above to a vegetated groove on the right and
follow this to the top.

Herring Gull   45 metres   Very Severe †   (4.74)
Start 3 metres left of the brown hanging corner, by a shallow groove with
cracks in the right-hand wall.
1 20m. Climb the wall to a small ledge on the left at 5 metres. Continue
up the groove to a poor stance on grass (peg belay used on first ascent).
2 25m. Bear right onto a slab; then move up to a niche before stepping
right into a vegetated gully, which leads to the top.

Black-backed Gull   35 metres   Very Severe †   (4.74)
Start outside the mouth of the zawn on its south-east wall at the foot of a
small buttress.
1 15m. Climb the slab sloping up to the right. At its top, go left to a good
ledge and peg belay.
2 20m. Step right from the belay and climb to the top of a gangway; then
move left onto a slab and finish up the gully above.

Kitty's Wake   15 metres   Hard Severe   4b   (29.5.89)
Take the obvious crack/chimney on the south-east wall, passing left of the
prominent chockstone with care. Climb a short groove to its end and belay
3 metres higher.

Pedn Kei Area (Greenstone/Killas)

Outlook: North-west.
Tidal in Pedn Kei Zawn, but accessible for two hours either side of low water.
Non-tidal for most climbs on Pedn Kei West, though the whole area can be affected by swell and rough seas.
Coastguard Identity: Treen Cliff (near Gurnard's Head).

Pedn Kei Zawn   OS Ref 431 385

Approach as for Gurnard's Head (page 77) but turn west at the coast path above the neck of the headland. Walk west for 50 metres until a low wall is crossed. Continue for 150 metres before striking down steep grassy slopes with care. The final section is very steep but manageable and leads to ledges. Scramble down ledges at the north end (right-hand side facing out), although this is affected by the tide. This is Pedn Kei West. From here, traverse left to reach the zawn. Accessible for two to three hours either side of low-water spring-tides.

The zawn is reminiscent of North Cornwall's Lower Sharpnose Point – without the fins. The west wall of the zawn is large but is often wet, while the rock is unpleasantly loose. The east wall is also big but is more vegetated. The zawn is a high-pitched echo-chamber for nesting birds throughout the early part of the season. The obvious and striking feature of Pedn Kei Island has some short routes, while some pitches have been picked over and re-assembled on the seaward end of the zawn's west wall. Three interesting routes make the best use of the east wall.

Song of the Sea   60 metres   Very Severe †   (7.71)
Low tide required. Start at sea-level below a slab in the middle of the east wall.
1 10m. 4a. Climb the slab to gain a groove below an ancient peg.
2 30m. 4a. Traverse left across wrinkled, quartz-streaked rock. Continue for another 10 metres until below a thin, vertical line of quartz. Climb leftwards up a series of steps to gain a ledge.
3 20m. 4c. From the left end of the ledge, climb a leftward-slanting crack.

☆**Games Children Play**   35 metres   E2 5c †   (12.8.90)
Good climbing. Start below an obvious corner situated 15 metres above sea-level rocks. Climb past a peg trending left to a corner-ramp and follow it to below the main corner. Climb the corner to its top, and then finish direct.

Blue Lagoon   35 metres   Hard Severe   (8.4.90)
This takes the crackline just to the right of the centre of the wall. It is best approached by abseiling to a V-shaped stance about 10 metres above sea-level. Abseil stakes may be in place.

Pedn Kei Island

The south-facing wall is steep and compact with generally sound rock. Four slanting cracklines give the basis of some good short climbs on positive holds (unless they snap off), and with sound protection.

Phroggy Phobia   15 metres   Very Severe 4c †   (13.7.90)
Open, steep, and enjoyable climbing, based on the left-hand crack. Start at the cave roof below the left-hand crack. Swing out left onto the wall to reach a ledge below a slim groove. Climb this to reach a good ledge, where the crack is rejoined. Continue up the crack to finish.

☆**Beef Cheater**   15 metres   Hard Very Severe 5a †   (8.7.90)
The crack to the right starts from the left-hand side of a square-cut overhang. Climb the wall to the right of the overhang and traverse left along the lip to reach the crack. Continue up the crack to finish.
Direct Start 5a/b (13.7.90). Climb out of the left-hand side of the cave to join the crack.

☆**C Cow**   15 metres   Hard Very Severe 5a †   (8.7.90)
The next crack right. Sustained and very enjoyable. Climb the crack.

☆**Bully for You**   20 metres   E2 5c †   (8.7.90)
The right-hand crack, and the most impressive. Climb the crack, passing the overhang with difficulty. Continue up the crack enjoying holds of doubtful security but in a fine position and with excellent protection.

Mad Cow Maggie   25 metres   Severe   (26.5.90)
On the left-hand side of the narrow landward face of the island is a fine-looking crack that promises much but gives nothing. Climb the crack to a ledge at 20 metres. Scramble carefully past a tottering block to finish on top of the island.

Pedn Kei West   OS Ref 432 384

Approach as for Gurnard's Head (page 77) but turn west at the coast path above the neck of the headland. Walk west for 50 metres until a low wall is crossed. Continue for 150 metres and then strike down the steep grassy slopes with care if wet – or dry. The final section is very steep but manageable and leads to comfortable ledges above the cliff. The climbs are reached by scrambling down ledges at the north end (right-hand side facing out) although this approach is affected by the tide. An abseil approach can be made down the slabby *Oliver*.

Pedn Kei West is a small but interesting cliff with a clutch of powerful and highly enjoyable routes. The left end of the cliff (facing in) has two obvious open-book corners. These are *Fagin* and *Bill Sykes*. The first routes lie on the left-hand end, where the crag starts to take on a steeper and less broken aspect. At the left end of the main cliff is a compact black wall. On the extreme left of the black wall is a leftward-slanting easy-angled groove.

Gut Bug   15 metres   Very Difficult   (9.9.89)
Climb the easy-angled groove until a good crack on the right wall (not visible from the start) can be climbed.

Bust a Gut   15 metres   Very Difficult   (28.4.90)
Climb the easy-angled groove for 5 metres until a step right onto a ledge can be made. Make a steep pull up onto another ledge and finish up the groove above.

Salmonella Summer   15 metres   Severe   (9.9.89)
Hopefully, a final purgative. Start at the foot of the easy-angled groove but climb direct via a thin crack to finish up parallel cracks in the headwall.

☆**Smear Today, Here Tomorrow**   15 metres   E3 6b †   (10.6.90)
A smearing test-piece up the thin crackline in the centre of the black slabby wall. Climb easily to a ledge at the foot of the crack; then climb this to reach a good slot before moving left to finish up the parallel cracks of *Salmonella Summer*.

Look on the White Side   20 metres   Hard Severe 4b   (28.4.90)
From the bottom of the easy-angled groove, step up to a ledge on the right and traverse right to the arête. Make several steep pulls to reach the arête, which is followed, awkwardly at first, then more easily to finish.

To the right of the arête is the first of the two open-book corners.

The Artful Dodger   20 metres   E2 5b   (25.7.81)
Good climbing directly up the middle of the slab to the left of the left-hand open-book corner. Slight protection with a tricky move at the top.

★**Fagin**   20 metres   Hard Very Severe 5a   (25.7.81)
Climb the left-hand open-book corner. Good strenuous climbing.

Costa Geriatrica   25 metres   E1 5b   (26.5.90)
The arête between the two corners. Climb steeply into an easy groove below the arête. Step left onto the arête and make a steep pull up the wall via a quartz patch. Continue up the arête to an overhang, turn it on the right, and gain a faint groove. Finish easily up the arête.

Oliver   20 metres   Severe   (25.7.81)
Start on the arête. Move immediately right to climb the slabby wall via a crackline, midway between *Costa Geriatrica* and *Bill Sykes*.
The Direct Start is **Gruel** (Hard Very Severe 5b 14.5.95).

Nancy 20 metres E2 6a (14.5.95)
Boulder out the wall to good holds and then climb the thin crack just left of *Bill Sykes*.

★Bill Sykes 20 metres E1 5b (25.7.81)
Climb the right-hand open-book corner and finish up the slab on the left. Strenuous and with technical bridging.

★Fools Rush In 35 metres E3 (10.6.90)
An entertaining traverse from left to right, starting from the arrival-ledges above the finish of *Bill Sykes*.
1 15m. 5c. Climb down *Bill Sykes* for a couple of metres; then traverse rightwards across the hanging wall in a sensational position past three pegs into a friendlier corner (*Linda's Choice*). Continue traversing across a black slab to a foot-ledge. Belay on a peg and small wires.
2 20m. 5b. Traverse around the nose on the right on good holds and then climb diagonally right to beneath big overhangs. Climb through the overhangs by a line of weakness on the right. Belays well back.

To the right of *Bill Sykes* are two big hanging corners with a hanging groove between them.

Polymyele 30 metres E3 5c (15.9.96)
Start just left of the easy rock steps of *Linda's Choice*. Climb directly up to ledges and move left around the arête past a peg. Trend rightwards up the slab with difficulty past a peg to the top.

★★Linda's Choice 30 metres E2 5b (29.4.90)
The choice of the cliff. The left-hand corner gives a fine, satisfying climb. Start beneath the right-hand hanging corner, by some easy rock steps. Climb easily leftwards to reach an obvious quartz vein rising to the left. Go up the vein to a peg, crossing *Polymyele*. Continue traversing left to reach the bottom of the left-hand corner. Pull into the corner and climb to the overhang before finishing by the left arête in a good position. Belay to a rock outcrop 15 metres up the grassy slope.

★Flying Finish 30 metres E3 5c (9.4.90)
The hanging groove between the two corners gives good strenuous climbing. Start at the foot of the right-hand corner and climb easily to the base of the groove. Make a hard move into the groove (peg runner), and climb to its top. Step left and move up past a peg; then step back right before pulling over the bulge. Finish more easily and belay well back as for *Linda's Choice*.

When Hope Has Gone 30 metres Hard Very Severe 5a (29.4.90)
The right-hand corner. Climb easily to the foot of the corner and take the initial groove before stepping left at its top. Follow the slab more easily to finish and belay well back.

★Tea Towel and Lightning   30 metres   E3 5c   (14.5.95)
Interesting climbing up the rightward-trending stepped groove; *RPs* useful.
Start just right of the corner. Scramble up easy rock and enter the groove
by a good flake on its right. Follow the groove until forced rightwards over
the capping roof.

To the right of the previous routes there is a 2-metre step that drops down to
a continuation of the wave-cut platform.

☆Sanctuary   30 metres   E2 6a †   (10.5.87)
A distinctive clean-cut groove slices the face above the ledge. Climb the
groove to the base of an overhanging corner. Step right and climb another
groove for a few feet; then move left onto the arête and trend left to reach
the top. Belay well back on blocks in the steep grass.

★The Moon Is Down   30 metres   E3 5c   (12.8.90)
A good pitch taking the obvious corner right of *Sanctuary*. Climb the
corner, past three poor pegs, to its top. Continue directly over the bulge
above before finishing out left at the top. Belay well back.

To the right of the corner of *The Moon Is Down* is a buttress. There are two
routes up its front face, both taking cracklines.

★Dead Cert   30 metres   E2 5b   (9.6.90)
Nice climbing up the steep left side of the buttress. Climb the initial thin
cracks to a sloping ledge on the left. Move left and then follow good holds
just left of the thin cracks to reach a slabby section below a short hanging
groove. Climb the hanging groove to easy ground, which is followed to
the top with belays well back.

Goodbye Mickey Chick   30 metres   E2 5c   (9.6.90)
Excellent climbing for the first 10 metres and easy thereafter. Three metres
right of *Dead Cert* is another crack/groove-line. Gain the crack from the left
via a bulging, overhung start. Follow the crack, passing a small niche at 5
metres, until it is possible to step onto a small slab. Move right into a groove
and follow this to easy ground, which is climbed to the top. Belays well back.

To the right is a steep, wet, and repulsive zawn. Beyond is the final buttress
before the entrance to Zawn Duel is reached. There are three climbs. On the
left-hand side of the front face of the buttress is a steep broken crackline with
a jammed chockstone at its top.

A Message from the Falselands   10 metres   Very Severe   4c   (13.7.90)
Climb the crack with increasing difficulty, the final move passing the
chockstone being the most entertaining.

Three metres right, by the base of a large pulpit of rock, is a thin crack
splitting a short steep wall.

How Terrapins Tango   10 metres   Very Severe 4c   (13.7.90)
Absorbing climbing with not much protection. Climb the thin crack to
reach a good ledge; then continue up the crackline past another ledge
before making a final steep pull to the top.

How Turtles Tapdance   10 metres   Difficult   (9.9.89)
Directly behind the pulpit block is an obvious V-groove. Climb the groove
until it closes and then move left across slabby rock to an easy finish. The
climb can be used as an easy way down for this end of the cliff.

Zawn Duel and Carn Gloose Area
(Greenstone/Killas) OS Ref 429 383

Outlook: Zawn Duel – North. Carn Gloose – West.
Tidal in Zawn Duel for *The Adversary* and *Aggressor*. Tidal for routes on
seaward face of Carn Gloose Headland. **Non-tidal** for routes on West
Face of Carn Gloose, although these can be affected by swell and rough sea
on the approach pitches.
Coastguard Identity: Zawn Duel/Carn Gloose – Gurnard's Head.
Environmental Issues: The area is an SSSI. The upper cliff of Carn
Gloose in particular is a complex biological area. The right-hand section of
the upper cliff has important lichen cover. Sea Aster, Bluebell, mosses, and
liverworts are all vulnerable too. Tread carefully, do not intrude on bluebell
patches, and steer clear of lichen.

This dramatic area continues the powerful theme of Gurnard's Head. Zawn
Duel truly deserves the superlative 'awesome', while the West Face of Carn
Gloose is equally impressive though more open to the light.

Zawn Duel
*'There's never a right time to climb The Adversary, and now's as good a
wrong time as any.'*   (Nick Hancock to Steve Hill, 1996)

'Maybe we can swim out of here...'   (Des Hannigan, 1994)

Approach can be made from the Porthmeor Valley as for Robin's Rocks
(page 101). This is longer than the Gurnard's Head approach but gives a
full frontal view of the magnificent amphitheatre of Carn Gloose West Face.
The quicker approach is from Treen hamlet as for Gurnard's Head (see
page 77) to reach the coast path. Go west along the coast path for 200
metres to the rocky summit of Carn Gloose where the coast path crosses a
low wall before it turns abruptly inland. From the summit of Carn Gloose, a
broad rocky ridge drops due north to seaward. A prominent notch splits the

ridge just below the summit rocks. Zawn Duel – the Devil's Zawn – lies a short distance to the right (facing out) of Carn Gloose summit. The zawn begins innocuously a few metres down from the coast path as a narrow grassy depression which deepens and then plunges suddenly between massive black cliffs which enclose one of the most formidable and atmospheric venues on the entire Cornish coast. Two powerful routes, *The Adversary* and *Aggressor*, take similar lines up the towering west wall, while there are shorter but equally dramatic pitches on the beetling headwall.

Descent. The shared start for the routes on the headwall is gained by abseil. For the start of *The Adversary* and *Aggressor* a long abseil to the tidal bed of Zawn Duel is made down the west wall. Joined ropes are advised although the descent can be split. It is best to view the treat in store from the sharp eastern rim before entering the zawn. This also gives an excellent view of routes on the headwall and gives guidance for the best positions for fixing abseil ropes. Zawn Duel is wet and sea-damp in the winter, and can be wet in places even in summer. *In-situ* pegs should be treated with caution.

The following three routes are on the savage headwall of the zawn, where the rock is more likely to be dry than on the side walls. All three routes start 45 metres up the headwall from a gripping stance on a small ledge on the wall's right-hand side. The ledge contains an angular-shaped block. The stance is reached by abseil, fixed at blocks high up on the grass slopes above the zawn.

☆☆**Pete's Party Piece**   25 metres   E5 6b †   (2.7.89)
Powerful and sustained, with great commitment. From the stance, traverse left past a peg to another two pegs. Make a difficult move to gain a thin vertical crack (peg) and climb it to the overlap. Continue up the crack to a scoop where awkward moves enable good holds to be reached. Climb more easily to the final crack and follow it to finish.

★**The Party's Over**   25 metres   E5 6a   (29.4.90)
High-quality climbing but very strenuous. From the stance, climb the groove directly above to a peg at its top. Step across left to a peg at the foot of an impending crack (taken by the next route). Traverse left past two pegs to a short crack. Climb the crack and the bulge above (peg) to a ledge. Finish up the crack above.

☆**Night over Day over Night**   25 metres   E4 5c †   (10.9.89)
A strenuous pitch taking the groove and crackline from the stance. Climb the groove to a peg at its top. Step across left to a peg at the foot of an impending crack. Climb the crack strenuously but with good wire placements, before moving left to easy ground. Climb the easy corner above.

The Adversary and *Aggressor* require dry conditions. In winter and early spring the west wall of Zawn Duel is permanently wet. The routes are committing and potentially serious undertakings. The original abseil for *The Adversary* was made down the east wall but this is not advised. The best approach is by abseil down the west wall, 10 metres left of the obvious grassy ledges, where a distinctive shallow gully splits the upper part of the wall for 20 metres to end at a narrow ledge. This is the belay at the top of pitch 1 of both climbs. From the top of the wall, abseil down to the right (facing in) of the gully to the ledges at its base. A further partly free abseil of 35 metres gains a sloping, half-tide ledge at the foot of the wall. (Joined ropes give a continuous abseil.) The abseil rope may be needed for a belay on the narrow ledge.

★★The Adversary   65 metres   E4   (29.8.72)

An impressive achievement for its day and still of powerful character as the definitive 'zawn experience'. The climb follows a sinuous groove system in the west wall to beneath the shallow gully. It then breaks left and takes a vague open scoop in the upper walls. Start at the left end of the sloping ledge at the foot of the abseil.

1 40m. 6a. Gain the groove and follow it until the holds peter out at a bulge. Move left with difficulty into the steep groove and climb to a small ledge. Climb the quartzy wall on the right to a crystal-filled hole. Follow the groove once more to gain the ledges at the foot of the shallow gully.

2 25m. 5b. Traverse left beneath an overhang on large holds to reach vertical cracks above it. Climb direct until beneath another overhang, step left across an open groove, and climb a broken scoop to the final wall. Climb to the top via a rightward-slanting groove with a sharp-edged finger crack. Belay well back on an outcrop.

Aggressor   65 metres   E2 †   (2.8.85)

There is some doubt as to the grade, but you probably won't be able to find the route anyway. This climb *may* cover similar ground to *The Adversary*; the description is retained should some brave soul wish to enter the depths of the zawn to sort it out for the next guidebook. Start at the left end of the sloping ledge.

1 35m. 5b. Climb down left and then cross into the groove on the left. Follow this, moving slightly leftwards at the top, to gain the belay at the foot of the shallow gully.

2 20m. 5a. Climb left onto the narrow buttress and move left into a steep groove. Climb the groove moving left to a ledge in the far corner.

3 10m. 5a. Climb the corner and wall to finish.

Carn Gloose

'Astral Stroll at Carn Gloose – Cornwall's answer to A Dream of White Horses...'   (Ken Wilson: Extreme Rock 1988)

The following routes are at the seaward end of Carn Gloose headland. *Lower Deck* lies further into Zawn Duel and has the bonus of giving a fine low-level view of the zawn.

Descent is by way of the broad ridge that drops seaward over the 'notch' from the summit rocks of Carn Gloose Headland or, more comfortably, down the grassy slopes flanking the ridge on its right (facing out). A small detached pinnacle is reached near the lower end of the ridge. Seaward of the pinnacle, across two small boulders in a dip, is a rocky platform covered in orange lichen. This is The Quarterdeck. The early routes are engagingly nautical in name, the first explorer being an Admiral. For *Lower Deck*, go down right from the two small boulders in the dip until a line of large platforms leading into Zawn Duel is reached. From the top of the first big platform, climb down a crack for 10 metres (Very Difficult), or abseil, to a niche near sea-level at the base of a steep black wall.

Lower Deck   40 metres   Very Severe   (29.4.67)
1 20m. 4c. Climb the wall in the corner to a platform.
2 20m. Continue up the corner and then go easily over broken blocks to the top.

For the next route go down right from the two small boulders in the dip and scramble easily to seawards down sloping ledges that lead to the base of a black 25-metre wall.

☆**Black Gold**   25 metres   E3 5b †   (25.6.89)
Good, solid climbing, but with scant protection. Start at the middle of the base of the wall below the left end of a sloping ledge at 3 metres. Climb to the ledge and a rightward-slanting crack, where good wires can be placed. Step left and climb direct to the top.

At low tide it is possible to traverse to the front face of the ridge, although the next two routes can be gained by abseil from the good finishing ledge at the top of *Black Gold*.

Snap Dragon   25 metres   E3 5c †   (25.6.89)
An enjoyable pitch climbing the wall on the left of the seaward face and right of an obvious groove. Start below an overhang. Climb onto a ledge at 3 metres and then climb easily to the overhang (cam placements). Move left under the overhang into the centre of the wall and climb directly past a peg to the top. At high tide it is possible to abseil to and start from the ledge at 3 metres, provided there is no swell.

Catalyst   20 metres   Hard Very Severe   5a †   (2.7.89)
The obvious crack to the right of *Snap Dragon*.

The following routes are reached from The Quarterdeck by climbing down awkward slabs and corners at the west side of the ridge at Difficult standard; or by abseiling to gain the sea-level platform below The Quarterdeck.

Port   30 metres   Very Difficult   (23.4.67)
Start on the left of the platform below a corner topped by a small overhang. Climb the corner to the overhang and then move left to a slab; continue up another corner and an easy slab.

Soloing at Zennor Head
Climber: Shane Ohly   Photo: Shane Ohly col.

Starboard   30 metres   Very Difficult   (23.4.67)
Start at the crack-system 5 metres right of *Port*. Follow the faultline to a
perched block about half-way up the crack. From the block, either climb
into a corner, or move right and mantelshelf, before continuing up the
crack to The Quarterdeck.

Mazurka   50 metres   Very Severe   (5.6.71)
Start from the right-hand side of the platform.
1 10m. Climb diagonally rightwards to a stance around the corner.
2 20m. 4c. Traverse 5 metres right to a corner. Gain a small ledge on
the right and follow the line right to a larger ledge.
3 20m. Scramble to the top.

Carn Gloose – West Face

If the Gurnard's Head approach has been used, the full glory of a view of the
West Face is missed. In some ways this is an advantage since the descent to
the climbs and the entry pitch onto the face give a dramatic revelation of
what's in store. Of the four routes crossing the huge undercut face, *Astral
Stroll* offers a remarkable challenge at an amenable grade, although
commitment is required.

Descent is by the broad ridge to seaward of the summit of Carn Gloose as
for The Quarterdeck climbs. The last 10 metres to just above sea-level is at
Difficult standard and is best abseiled if the sea is rough or the rock is wet.

★High Frontier   50 metres   Hard Very Severe   (26.1.80)
1 15m. 4b. Climb around onto the west face and cross a series of short
grooves rising rightwards to reach a slab. Traverse this into a corner and then
out onto another less steep slab. Belay at the far end below a leftward-leaning
groove. (If the sea is too high, a start can be made a little higher up the groove
at the base of the ridge – 4c. Cross the right wall and make a difficult move onto
a ledge on the seaward side of the ridge. Cross this and go around the arête to
a steep slab from where a descent is made to the belay.)

2 25m. 5a. Climb the slab until an awkward move right can be made
onto a small ledge at a corner. Climb the corner to a larger ledge.
3 10m. Climb the left-hand groove above and then scramble to the top.

Babylon Five   42 metres   E3 ††   (1991)
Originally graded VS, this climb appears to have suffered a rockfall at the
start of pitch 2, and should therefore be approached with caution. The
new grade is merely an estimate.
1 15m. 4b. *High Frontier* pitch 1.
2 12m. 5c. Climb diagonally up and right, very steeply, to an undercut
slab. Continue right more easily to a well-positioned belay in a
leftward-slanting corner.
3 15m. 4c. Climb the slab to the top.

★★★**Astral Stroll**   70 metres   E1   (31.3.80)

An outstanding climb combining intricate route-finding and epic positions.

1 15m. 4b. *High Frontier* pitch 1.

2 15m. 5b. At the obvious impasse make an awkward descent to a slab below large overhangs. Traverse right, either low if the swell permits, or higher with slightly more difficulty, to a belay below the rightward-trending roof-crack.

3 20m. 5b. Climb up to the roof and follow a strenuous line diagonally rightwards until just before a black wall. Cross this and make some impressive moves across short grooves to gain a semi-detached foot-ledge below an obvious overhang with an open corner above.

4 20m. 5a. Climb the overhang, and then follow the corner and the slab on its right with little protection to the top.

★**Space Race**   40 metres   E3 5c   (8.6.80)

Astral Stroll with a variation final pitch. From the belay at the end of pitch 3 of *Astral Stroll*, move right and descend slightly to the start of a steep wall on the right. Climb to the roof and traverse right across the steep wall beneath a small overhang with a roof-crack. Step down to a large block and move right to a broken, lichenous ramp. Follow this and then finish up a steep wall and an arête.

The next three routes lie on the right-hand wall of Carn Gloose – West Face.

Descent. From the summit of Carn Gloose, cross the low wall breached by the coast path and go directly down easy grass slopes between rock outcrops before working back to the right (facing out) until below the 'notch' in the headland. A steep grassy ridge then leads down to the top of a rocky ramp, The Gangplank, which runs down to the base of the huge undercut north-facing wall – an ideal position for photographing the West Face routes. *Hornpipe Corner* is the soaring corner crack on the more amenable right side of the face near the base of The Gangplank.

Dangerous Visions   60 metres   E6 6a 1 pt aid   (24.4.80)

A startling and dramatic line up the impressive north-facing wall of Carn Gloose. The rock can be damp in places and the climb presents a formidable challenge in its now peg-free state. The aid point is for leaving the ground, either by lassoing a spike, or by combined tactics. Start near the bottom of The Gangplank below a groove hooded by overhangs.

1 35m. 6a. Get into the groove, one way or another, and climb to its top. Traverse left with difficulty to a good hold below the roof. Continue up to the roof and make a long move over it to a good hold on the right. Pass two more good holds and then make a hard traverse left to cross a narrow slab to a corner (possible belay). Climb the steep wall on the left and make another stretch to holds that lead rightwards to a small ledge below a steep corner.

2 25m. 5b. Climb the corner; then traverse rightwards to the foot of another steep corner. Climb this, then the wall above. Exit on the left to a large grassy ledge.

The Loose Goose 35 metres Hard Very Severe 5a †   (1982)
This takes a parallel line to *Hornpipe Corner*, the soaring corner crack near the bottom of The Gangplank. Start 3 metres to the left of *Hornpipe Corner*. Climb awkwardly rightwards; then continue up the wall, more or less directly, with some exposed moves around an overhang (crux) to a loose finish.

Hornpipe Corner 30 metres Very Severe 4c   (29.4.67)
Some looseness. Follow the corner crack to a sloping ledge on the left (optional belay). Continue up the crack, handling the rock carefully, towards overhanging earth and rubble at its top. Break out left to reach a thread belay on the right-hand side of the final block.

From a position slightly higher up The Gangplank from *Hornpipe Corner*, a descent can be made to a lower ledge. From here, a traverse-line leads rightwards towards a narrow zawn.

Gangway Zawn
The Gangway 45 metres Severe   (29.4.67)
1 30m. Traverse rightwards directly above the sea until below a small overhang lying below the top of The Gangplank ramp.
2 15m. 4a. Take the overhang to finish.

The next four routes are approached at low tide during calm seas by an awkward traverse in from the seaward mouth of the zawn. Descend The Gangplank, turn left (facing out), and traverse the south-facing wall of the zawn to a point where a jump can be made onto a rib of rock below the left side of the face. Alternatively, abseil in. All the climbs give good climbing on generally excellent rock.

★Walking Wounded 30 metres E3 5c   (6.5.96)
1 15m. 5b. Climb the middle of the steep wall on the left side of the face, above the trough, to a small belay on the right below a break in the overhang above.
2 15m. 5c. Pull through the overhang with some difficulty and continue steeply to the top.

Seriously Damaged Folk 20 metres Very Severe   (6.5.96)
Climb the first groove in the wall a few metres right of *Walking Wounded*.

★Drowning by Numbers 20 metres E3 5c   (2.6.97)
Climbs the overhanging right arête of the first groove by strenuous and poorly-protected moves on perfect rock, with a deep landing in the event of failure. Start at the foot of a ramp that leads down from the right almost to the arête. Trend up leftwards on small holds towards the arête and pull up into an awkward groove and the first good protection. Follow this through steeper terrain to an easier finish.

Special Needs   20 metres   Very Severe 4c   (6.5.96)
This route climbs the right-hand groove in the zawn, just before it becomes
wet and green due to seepage.

Wenven Cove (Greenstone)   OS Ref 428 380

Outlook: North.
Non-tidal but the base of the cliff is wave-swept in heavy seas.
Coastguard Identity: Wenven Cove.
Environmental Issues: The area is an SSSI. Although Wenven Cove is not
formally restricted, a protected bird breeds in the vicinity, so please avoid the
area from March to June inclusive.

Approach: This small cliff lies between Carn Gloose and Robin's Rocks and
can be reached along the coast path, south-west from Gurnard's Head. There
is a wooden stile on the level section of the coast path, south-west of
Carn Gloose headland. Thirty metres further on, a faint track leads seawards
to a narrow grassy ridge. The cliff is below and to the left. From the ridge,
scrambling leads to a gully on the seaward end of the cliff.

Descent is by abseil or by climbing down to narrow ledges just above the sea.

The lower half of the cliff and its left edge (facing in) are easy angled. The
central part of the cliff has a steep headwall with a prominent perched block.
At the left end of the face there is a distinctive groove.

Barnacle Bill   25 metres   Very Difficult   (28.3.82)
Start 5 metres left of the distinctive groove. Climb to a broad ledge by a
groove and mantelshelf; then take the wall above by a quartz vein.

Happy Returns   25 metres   Very Difficult   (28.3.82)
Climb leftwards from the base of the distinctive groove to a platform (belay
possible). Continue up a shallow corner.

Sea Pink   25 metres   Very Difficult   (28.3.82)
Climb the slab left of the distinctive groove; then go over a diagonal overlap
and finish up a groove. Alternatively move left to a ledge and finish direct.

Mein Kampf   25 metres   Severe 4a   (28.3.82)
Take the distinctive groove direct and finish up a steep wall.

At the extreme right end of the face there is a blocky arête.

Stone Fall   30 metres   Severe 4a   (28.3.82)
Climb the arête. Belay possible midway.

Robin's Rocks (Greenstone)

OS Ref 426 380

Outlook: North-west.
Tidal. Accessible 3 hours either side of low water. Wave-washed by swell and heavy seas.
Coastguard Identity: Robin's Rocks.

Robin's Rocks is Gothic greenstone; a hard-faced cliff with great atmosphere and a clutch of powerful routes.

Approach. From the coast path, either south-west from Gurnard's Head or north from Porthmeor Cove. (The cove is reached by following the right-of-way from the B3306 down the south side of the valley below Porthmeor Farm.) Robin's Rocks lies on the headland between Porthmeor Cove and the great incut bay of Carn Gloose. Where the coast path curves around the shoulder of the headland, strike down a miners' path towards the top of the cliff, passing a deep trench and some spoil-heaps. For *Sensible Shoes* and *The Intruder*, which both start from the top of the cliff, go right (facing out) and cross the impressive chasm. *Sensible Shoes*, which makes ingenious use of otherwise redundant rock, starts above a bottomless groove in a right-angled corner of the seaward cliff.

★★★**Sensible Shoes**   40 metres   Very Severe 4c   (25.9.78)
Descend the bottomless groove for 5 metres. (Subtle back-rope cover can protect a second with a runner fixed in the slab to the right (facing in) of the start of the descent. Two ropes required for this.) Cross the slab on the right and climb over onto a second slab. Continue to the flanking arête and climb it.
Variation Start (Very Severe 4c 1988). When the tide is low a very good start can be made from the tidal platform. Climb the shallow groove just to the right of the bottomless groove to the roof and move left and up to rejoin the parent route.

The following routes (apart from *The Intruder*) start from the sea-level platform, which is reached from above by scrambling down the left-hand side (facing out) of the cliff and crossing greasy rocks above a narrow channel.

Black Cleft   24 metres   Very Severe 4c   (1991)
Start on the sea-level platform, to the right of *Sensible Shoes Variation Start*, at a groove leading up to the overhang. Climb the groove and skirt around the roof to gain the wall of the cleft. Continue up this in a fairly direct line to the top.

★**The Intruder**   58 metres   E1   (7.79)
A left-to-right girdle of the main face. Start 5 metres up from the jammed boulder in the chasm.

1 30m. 5a. Descend to the light-coloured break and follow it to below roofs in the middle of the face. Step right and descend to a crack for a hanging belay.
2 15m. 5b. Move directly up to the slab; then traverse right and step down below good handholds. Climb up and right to a ledge (on *Tuco the Terrible*); then go right and down slightly to a corner stance.
3 13m. 5b. Move up to an obvious hold and swing around into a groove. Step right into a second groove before taking a foot-ledge to an easy finish.

Porthmeor Chimney   30 metres   Severe   (1908)
Victorian values. The chasm is climbed in the traditional manner.

★★**Black Sapper**   34 metres   E4 5c   (18.5.78)
Modern values. An unrelenting line up the main face. Start 10 metres right of the chasm. Climb for 6 metres and then move left to the start of a left-slanting break. Climb the break and move up into blind cracks above the left end of the roof. Continue direct for 6 metres; then trend right before climbing straight up the impending wall past a small roof.

☆☆☆**Off the Mark**   36 metres   E7 6c †   (1989)
Post-modern values. A major route giving very steep and strenuous climbing which takes the roof and leaning wall right of *Black Sapper*. Start just right of the light-coloured vein. Follow a line of weakness up and right to a ledge below the roof. Move up to the roof and surmount it at a short crack. Continue up the witheringly steep wall in a direct line to the top. Abseil inspection recommended.

★**The Silver Arrow**   33 metres   E5 6b †   (1991)
A steep and exciting route which climbs the overhanging rock right of the faultline of *Tuco the Terrible*, but starts below the overhanging wall, a metre or two left of that route. Climb the wall past 2 pegs to reach *Tuco the Terrible*. Move right to gain a bottomless groove (peg) and climb this to reach the roof (peg). Move left slightly and surmount the roof (peg) to gain easier angled rock and the top.

★★**Tuco the Terrible**   37 metres   E2   (24.8.69.)
Sixties values and the first greenstone extreme in West Penwith. Tough and exhilarating.
1 18m. 5a. Start at the right-hand side of the main face. Climb the obvious overhanging corner and make an awkward move onto a slab on the left. Continue up and left to a small ledge below a chimney.
2 19m. 5b. Take the overhanging V-chimney above and then move left into its continuation. Make some hard moves past a sloping foothold to easier ground.

★**Black Napkin**   30 metres   E2 5c   (11.6.88)
A fine pitch. Climb *Tuco the Terrible* for 5 metres until bold moves rightwards lead into the right-hand of two grooves. At the top of the groove, take the roof above and finish direct.

The shorter wall right of the last route gives two worthwhile pitches.

Monsoon   20 metres   E3 6b †   (1992)
Climb the left-hand of the two obvious cracklines to finish up a thin crack.

★Robin Hood   20 metres   E1 5c   (1991)
A good strenuous line taking the right-hand of the two cracklines.

One hundred and fifty metres to the west of the last route is a dark zawn with west- and east-facing walls. The base is sea-washed at high tide and is reached by descending a Moderate chimney on the east side of the zawn.

Timpson's Arête   20 metres   Hard Severe   (8.8.98)
This route takes the obvious crack on the dark west side of the zawn, finishing up the arête to the right of the crack.

Windy Zawn (Granite and Killas)   OS Ref 425 377

Outlook: West.
Non-tidal but affected by swell and rough seas.
Coastguard Identity: Porthmeor Cove near Gurnard's Head.

Windy Zawn lies on the eastern shore of Porthmeor Cove. It is a geological feature of great note formed millions of years ago when a huge bubble of molten granite punched its way through the overlying sedimentary rock. It finally popped, leaving a roofless cavern of granite surrounded by darker killas. Sea breezes whisper in and out, and the routes here are a delight, be they ever so short.

Approach via Porthmeor Cove. The cove is reached by following the right-of-way from the B3306 at OS Ref 432 370 down the south side of the valley below Porthmeor Farm. From the cove, follow the coast path north for 400 metres until the path bends sharply right and uphill just before a lichen-covered tower of killas, the Porthmeor Pinnacle. (The central crack in the tower gives a 15-metre Severe.) From the coast path, follow a vague path for a few metres to seaward until the ragged rim of the zawn is reached. Walk around the rim of the zawn to the right (facing out); then go down its right edge to comfortable ledges.

Descent. A short abseil can be made into the zawn from just below the ledges. The 25-metre granite face of the zawn is fringed at either end by killas slate and crowned with layers of killas. There is some minor looseness at the exits from each climb because of this.

The Mansfield Mob   18 metres   Severe 4a   (7.8.81)
The black, broken crack towards the left end of the face.

Gritstone Delinquent   20 metres   E3 5c   (7.8.81)
Be warned, the first ascensionist is reported as being 3 metres tall. Where
the granite begins, there is a slab in a recess. Climb this for 5 metres until
hard moves are made across the left wall onto a high ledge. Finish
leftwards.

☆**Thoroughbred**   22 metres   E3 6a †   (4.83)
On the wall right of the recess, take the rightward-slanting groove; then
climb left to a thin crack and follow the groove above.

★★**The Guilty Snowflake**   20 metres   E1 5b   (7.8.81)
Great name, great little route. Climb the sustained finger-crack on the left
side of the smooth central slab. Step left at its top and follow the corner
above.

Koala   20 metres   Very Severe 4c   (28.8.81)
Right of the central slab, there is a large ledge at one-third height. Gain
this from the left; then make a bold Australian move up and left to a good
hold and easier ground.

Aristocracy   20 metres   Hard Very Severe 5a   (1984)
Climb the recessed corner right of *Koala* on slightly shaky rock.

Kangaroo   20 metres   E2 5b   (28.8.81)
Just before the killas impinges on the right of the granite face, there is a
prominent nose of rock. Climb cracks to the base of the nose; then swing
right into the corner and climb this until even bolder moves can be made
leftwards to easier ground.

Breeze   20 metres   Very Severe 4c   (6.83)
Where the mixed rock begins, climb to a ledge and then make a difficult
move into a shallow groove, which is followed to the top.

Greenstone Junction   20 metres   Hard Severe 4b   (6.83)
Climb the corner at the right-hand end of the face.

Halldrine Cove (Granite)

OS Ref 418 372

Outlook: West.
Non-tidal but affected by heavy seas and swell.
Coastguard Identity: Halldrine Cove.
Enviromental Issues: Vulnerable plant life includes Bluebell and Heath Spotted Orchid. Tread carefully and avoid bluebell patches.

This is a friendly little cliff in spite of its relatively exposed position above a deep water inlet. The cliff is dominated by a handsome tower above an incut recess. There are several pleasant lower-grade climbs with optional variations.

Approach from the coast road 30 metres north of the Count House by following the wide track that merges into a path leading down to the right-hand shoulder of Bosigran Headland. Where the path meets the main coast path, bear right and continue downhill. Halldrine Cove lies down to the left and a subsidiary path leads down left from the coast path until the obvious rocky summit of the aforementioned tower is reached. Go down left onto a broad rocky ledge. The first routes are reached by traversing leftwards (facing in) along ledges and slabs to a comfortable niche below an incut recess with a black slab running up its centre. The traverse is not difficult but novices should be protected along its length.

Limpet Slab   30 metres   Very Difficult   (28.7.56)
Climb the black slab and the airy arête on the left of the recess, moving back right at the top.

Inverted V-Groove   30 metres   Difficult   (1955)
Climb the central groove in the recess.

Shrimpet   30 metres   Very Difficult   (10.4.86)
Follow the line of grooves and cracks right of the recess. Steep in the upper section.

Barnaclet   33 metres   Very Difficult   (10.4.86)
A go-as-you-please line through the mild overhangs 6 metres right of the central groove.

Geological Groove   30 metres   Difficult   (1955)
Start at a black-coated slab down and left of the broad rocky arrival ledge. Climb the slab to a groove that leads to a small overhang, which is passed by a move out to the left.

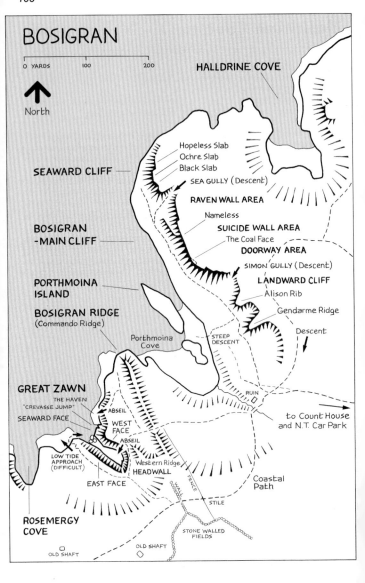

BOSIGRAN

0 YARDS 100 200

↑ North

HALLDRINE COVE

SEAWARD CLIFF

Hopeless Slab
Ochre Slab
Black Slab
SEA GULLY (Descent)

RAVEN WALL AREA

Nameless

SUICIDE WALL AREA

The Coal Face

DOORWAY AREA

SIMON GULLY (Descent)

BOSIGRAN
-MAIN CLIFF

LANDWARD CLIFF

Alison Rib

PORTHMOINA
ISLAND

Gendarme Ridge

Descent

BOSIGRAN RIDGE
(Commando Ridge)

Porthmoina
Cove

STEEP
DESCENT

RUIN

to Count House
and N.T. Car Park

GREAT ZAWN

THE HAVEN
"CREVASSE JUMP"

SEAWARD FACE

ABSEIL

WEST
FACE

ABSEIL

LOW TIDE
APPROACH
(DIFFICULT)

Western Ridge
HEADWALL

EAST FACE

FENCE

WALL

STILE

Coastal
Path

ROSEMERGY
COVE

OLD SHAFT

OLD SHAFT

STONE WALLED
FIELDS

Bosigran (Granite)

OS Ref 416 368

'There was a driving mist, through which we had glimpses of pale ghosts that might have been rocks and as it lifted in a gust of wind, towers of granite raised their heads and part of a jagged crest showed up and then vanished as the curtain fell.'

(A W Andrews recalling his first visit to Bosigran in 1902)

'Most of the great natural lines on Bosigran have now been climbed...'

(Peter Biven. 1968)

Outlook: West.

Non-tidal except for several routes on the Seaward Cliff and above the broad sea-level ledge.

Coastguard Identity: Bosigran Main Face.

Environmental Issues: The Bosigran area is an SSSI owned by the National Trust and is home to a number of species of birds, which are best avoided in the nesting season. The area supports patches of Bluebell, Heath Spotted Orchid, and dwarf Oak, which climbers should try to avoid. (The dwarf Oak grows above the path that leads across the top of Simon Gully.)

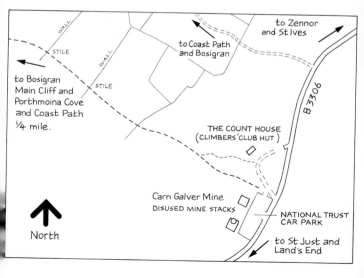

Bosigran is the focus of climbing in West Penwith. Much of its appeal as a 'sea-cliff' lies in false pretence, however, since the main cliff is pitched 45 metres above the tide-line. It is generous, accessible, and it keeps your feet dry. The 100 plus routes on Bosigran cover most grades. Quality climbing on clean, honest granite is the rule, while protection and convenient belaying are generous. Above all the great thrust of Bosigran Head breaks through a coastal 'weather window', the clear break between different sets of weather conditions at sea and on land. The cliff is often bathed in sunshine while the rest of the world is shrouded in Andrews's curtain of Cornish mist. Bosigran is now a climbers' playground, yet in Andrews's day it was a remote wilderness clothed with lichen, bramble, and ivy. Until the 40s, peregrine falcons nested in the *Suicide Wall* area and in 1955 *Raven Wall* had its raven's nest, while foxes and badgers colonized the caves and clefts below *Thin Wall Special*.

Approach to Bosigran is from the National Trust car-park by the two old mine-stack ruins on the B3306. From here, a rocky track leads down to the coast path above Porthmoina Cove and near the ruins of a former grist-mill and tin-stamps. High on the left is the dragon's back of Bosigran, also known as Commando, Ridge. Below lies Porthmoina Island, while Bosigran Main Face just shows to seaward on the right. Follow a rocky path across the right-hand slope (do not drop down too far or else steep grassy slopes are encountered) and scramble over blocks at the base of an obvious ridge. This is **Gendarme Ridge**, which gives a route of 55 metres (Difficult). Beyond here, the path leads unerringly along the base of the most famous climbing cliff in Cornwall.

Cliff Layout: Bosigran is a complex cliff. For descriptive purposes, the cliff has been divided into five sections over its 300-metre length. These are, working from left to right and facing in: Seaward Cliff, the Main Face (which comprises Raven Wall Area, Suicide Wall Area, and Doorway Area), and finally Landward Cliff.

Seaward Cliff is the independent stretch of cliff low down on the far left of Bosigran, featuring the Ochre Slab climbs and flanked high on its right side by the conspicuous break of Sea Gully.
Raven Wall Area runs from Sea Gully to *Autumn Flakes*, which starts just above the distinctive step-down on the path that runs along the base of the cliff. **Care should be taken on this step** as it is highly polished and there is considerable exposure; the path below is quite narrow and there is a big drop.
Suicide Wall Area runs from *Autumn Flakes* to The Coal Face. A key feature which is easily spotted from the approach path, The Coal Face is a polished black slab running up through the heart of the cliff to some imposing overhangs.
Doorway Area runs from The Coal Face to Simon Gully, which is the long rambling gully that divides the more continuous part of the cliff from its broken right-hand end.
Landward Cliff runs from Simon Gully to *Alison Rib*, which lies on the first substantial buttress reached after *Gendarme Ridge*.

The alternative approach to Seaward Cliff and Raven Wall Area is to follow the coast path steeply rightwards from its junction with the initial approach path near the ruins of the old grist-mill and tin-stamps. At the top of the slope go left onto the headland of Bosigran Castle and continue along the rim of the cliff and descend to a rocky outcrop. Sea Gully lies below and to the left. Descend the slabby gully with care. From the base of Sea Gully, Raven Wall Area lies immediately left (facing out) while Seaward Cliff is reached by following an eroded track downhill to meet the main path along the base of the cliff, which is then followed to the right.

Seaward Cliff

Bright, clean rock; archetypal golden granite on the splendid Ochre Slab with the sea for close company. Seaward Cliff is reached from the main approach to Bosigran by following the path along the base of the cliff to the independent section of cliff at the seaward end of the headland. The main feature is the distinctive black slab running up to overhangs. This is Black Slab. On its left is the impressive sweep of Ochre Slab. There are excellent routes on the area of cliff below Ochre Slab. These are accessible for three hours either side of low tide but should be avoided at all states of the tide when there is a swell running. They are reached by traversing the ledge system that leads leftwards (facing in) from the base of Black Slab as far as the terminal platform directly below Ochre Slab. From here descend with care to reach seaweed-covered ledges at sea-level. The smooth jet-black slab on the left is *Hopeless Slab*.

Hope   45 metres   Very Difficult
A line up the left of *Hopeless Slab*.
1 17m. From the left end of the ledges, take the black groove on the left to a large platform.
2 28m. Climb over ledges and break through the wall above, continuing up the black faultline.

The Edge of Hope   50 metres   Very Severe 4c   (30.1.98)
Start at dead low tide in calm conditions.
1 15m. 4c. Climb a barnacle-encrusted corner to a narrow groove just right of the arête. Climb the groove to a large ledge.
2 35m. Continue easily up the slabs to reach the grassy slopes above.

★**Hopeless Slab**   45 metres   Hard Very Severe   (6.8.55)
Care is needed with gear placement on the first pitch. There is plenty about in the form of micro wires but you will have to be alert.
1 18m. 4c. Start below the right-hand corner of the slab and 'barnacle' up the wall for 3 metres before moving slightly left. Go straight up on diminishing holds to a large scoop, and follow a chain of footholds out left to a belay ledge.
2 9m. 4b. Move back right onto the slab and layback around the overhang above.

BOSIGRAN ~ SEAWARD CLIFF

1	Hopeless Slab	HVS
2	Simla	VD
3	Promontory Traverse	S
4	Shallow Chimney	D
5	Ochre Slab Route II	S
6	Ochre Slab One Point Five	EI
7	Ochre Slab Route I	VS
8	Black Slab	D
9	Red Slab	S
10	Golliwog's Cakewalk	HS
11	Belle	VS
12	Ding	VS
13	Dong	S
14	Sunny Corner	M

RAVEN WALL AREA

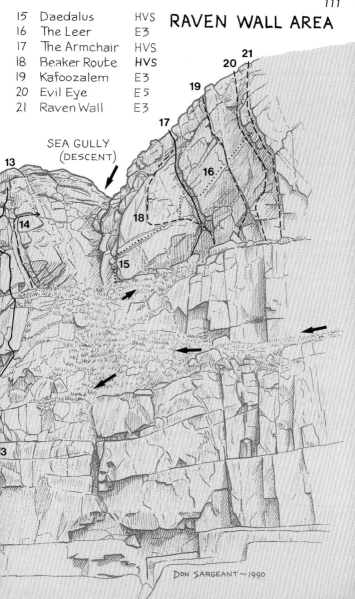

DON SARGEANT ~ 1990

3 18m. Move slightly right, then climb the beaded rib, and continue easily to finish.
Variation
1a 14m. 4b (30.1.98). Climb a broad groove 3 metres left of the normal start to reach the slab, and follow the line of holds up to the left to the belay ledge.

★**The Pessimist** 45 metres   E2   (22.8.90)
An optimistic pitch up the centre of the slab. Start on the ledge at 4 metres and belay in the right-hand corner.
1 27m. 5c. Walk left until below the middle of the slab then climb direct up a thin line of weakness to a small overlap below a shallow groove. Move up into the groove, step left to a thin crack, and follow it boldly to a narrow ledge. Take the layback crack above to the ledge of *Promontory Traverse*.
2 18m. Scramble up slabs to finish.

★**Geronimo** 45 metres   E1   (13.4.68)
A fine route taking the distinctive corner and overhang on the right edge of *Hopeless Slab*. Strenuous, but technically reasonable; thoughtful rope work required.Upgraded following the loss of a useful hold at the crux.
1 27m. 5c. Climb over a ledge and continue thinly up the corner before traversing left beneath the roof. Follow the obvious groove to a large ledge.
2 18m. Finish up the easy slabs on the right.
Variation
1a 27m. E2 5b † (25.8.90). An exposed and strenuous pitch which enhances the strong theme of the parent route. Follow *Geronimo* to the roof; then traverse right on big holds in an airy position to pull into an overhung niche. Step right and layback up the fine edge to the ledge of *Promontory Traverse*.

★**Boldfinger** 45 metres   E3   (22.9.66)
Serious with scant protection: the rib on the right of *Hopeless Slab*.
1 22m. 5c. Climb a crack and a black slab to a sloping ledge on the right. Continue up the pocketed slab to beneath the overhang, where good protection can be placed. Surmount the overhang on the left and gain a small ledge with difficulty. Either climb the groove directly above on improving holds, or move right and up to a good hold. Continue to a stance in a bay.
2 23m. 4a. Climb the crack behind the bay and take the large overhang on its left. Finish up the lichenous slabs.

★★**Silas Marner** 48 metres   E2   (23.8.90)
An intricate line in a good position. Start 3 metres left of the black seam of *Strike* at a short greasy corner.
1 24m. 5b. Climb the corner to a ledge; move up and then step right to gain the top of the black seam. Climb over the notched overhang; then

traverse left and swing around onto a sloping ledge to follow the hanging groove above to the ledge of *Promontory Traverse*.
2 24m. 5a. Climb direct to the roof; move right and pull onto the slab with difficulty. Continue more easily to the top.

Strike 45 metres E2 (18.9.66)
Takes a black seam up open rock right of *Boldfinger*.
1 25m. 5b. Follow the seam to a notched overhang, which is passed with difficulty on the right. Break back left above the overhang and follow the seam to a smaller overhang. Climb this direct to a broad platform.
2 20m. Climb the continuation of the seam to grassy slopes.

Seaspray 47 metres E1 (17.3.83)
Start at an overhung niche 5 metres right of *Strike*, at low tide.
1 35m. 5a. Climb left out of the niche to a chockstone and then move right to an arête. Climb a slab rightwards and then a cracked flake to a ledge.
2 12m. 5c. Climb overhanging cracks 3 metres right of a gully and bear right to finish.

Simla 42 metres Very Difficult (2.8.50)
From the base of *Black Slab*, scramble down to a lower platform. Go 12 metres to seaward to a projecting nose of rock above the seaweed-covered platform.
1 27m. Climb the rib on the right and then trend up and left before continuing direct to a platform stance.
2 15m. Climb diagonally to the left of the lichen-covered overhang above the stance, and follow a vague faultline until a grassy ramp is reached.

The following routes all start from the platform at the end of the ledge system which leads leftwards from the base of *Black Slab*.

Promontory Traverse 30 metres Severe (6.8.55)
1 12m. 4a. From the platform, traverse left around a rib and into a recess. Climb steeply left onto a broad ledge (exposed).
2 18m. Traverse left to reach a broken, lichenous slab.

Shallow Chimney 36 metres Difficult (1909)
The turf-filled chimney left of Ochre Slab. An Andrews original.
1 30m. Follow the chimney to the left end of the ledge beneath the capping overhangs of Ochre Slab.
2 6m. Climb the easy gully above.

★Ochre Slab Route II 36 metres Severe
Exhilarating. Start from the platform, at the base of a short triangular slab.
1 24m. 4a. Climb easily to a short headwall below Ochre Slab proper and then swing up left over huge flakes. Continue up a vein for 2 or 3

metres; then traverse right with stylish exposure to break through the lip of the upper slab, and continue to belay on the ledge below the big overhang.
2 12m. 4a. Climb the wall left of the overhang.

Ochre One Point Five   40 metres   E1   (23.5.64/12.84)
1 24m. 4c. Start from the platform and take the short headwall direct before continuing up the main line of the slab to the ledge below the big overhang.
2 16m. 5b. Climb the lichenous left edge of the overhang.

★★Ochre Slab Route I   40 metres   Very Severe   (3.56)
Devious but delightful.
1 27m. 4c. From the platform, climb rightwards up the short triangular slab to its right-hand edge to reach the headwall. Make blind and balancy moves right into a black seam, which is followed to a stance at the top of *Black Slab*.
2 13m. 5a. Tackle the inverted V-overhang above *Black Slab*. If tall, bridge; if small, back-and-foot facing left, to make a precarious but surprisingly smooth move to good holds and a final upward swing on big jugs and thin air.

★★Black Slab   33 metres   Difficult   (3.8.38)
The obvious black, pock-marked slab on the right of Ochre Slab. A beginner's delight with huge holds and huge exposure. Start 6 metres below and to the left of the base of the slab.
1 22m. Climb up a steep wall on good holds to a pinnacle just below the left-hand corner of the slab. Climb the crack behind the pinnacle to its top and gain the slab proper to follow its left edge to below the roof. Belays can be found on the slab using thin flakes and threads but these should be backed up by placements in the cracks above.
2 11m. Walk off left along the narrow top of Ochre Slab (with thoughtful protection for beginners) and follow the easy gully at the end of the ledge system.

Marking Time   18 metres   E6 6b †   (1994)
From the belay of *Black Slab*, climb directly through the roof. A range of cams would be useful.

Red Slab   30 metres   Severe   (13.6.54)
The top pitch is awkward and often wet.
1 21m. Climb cracks in the reddish slab just right of *Black Slab* to belay under the inverted V-overhang in the roof.
2 9m. 4a. Step right onto the wall and gain the V-groove by a steep move. Old fashioned back-and-footing or bridging gets you out.
Variation
1a 30m. Hard Severe 4b. Climb the initial cracks of pitch 1 and continue direct up a knobbly black vein in the wall above.

Rapture 53 metres Very Severe (31.5.97)
Start at the base of *Red Slab*.
1 33m. 4c. Climb the obvious left-to-right leaning crack on the right to
reach the vein of *Schorl Slant*. Step up and right to traverse the crack
rightwards between the recess of *Ding* and the crack on pitch 2 of *Belle*.
Continue traversing right under the line of overlaps and turn them on the
right. Climb to the belay of *Dong* below a V-groove.
2 20m. 4a. Climb the V-groove and arête just right of *Dong*.

Gollywog's Cakewalk 40 metres Hard Severe (4.9.62)
The steep red wall right of *Black Slab* has two black spots at 12 metres.
1 20m. 4b. Climb the right side of the wall to where it steepens; then
move right to a black vein, which is followed to a recess.
2 20m. Follow the black vein past a second recess.
Variations
1a 20m. 4c. Climb the wall to where it steepens; then move up and left
to a large flake. Climb diagonally rightwards above the two black spots
and rejoin the parent route at the recess on pitch 2.
1b Schorl Slant 15m. Very Difficult (25.6.50). Take the black vein that
slices diagonally leftwards across the face to reach the first recess on the
parent route.

Belle 48 metres Very Severe (20.5.64)
Disjointed but appealing. Damp for a while after rain. Start just left of the
base of the black vein (*Schorl Slant*), below three small stepped overhangs.
1 12m. 4b. Climb direct, with a bold swing up and right to clear the third
overhang, to a sloping stance.
2 16m. 4c. Move up and right on good holds before stepping left to the
base of a rightward-slanting crack, which is followed with minimum pause
before moving left and up to a grassy bay.
3 14m. 4c. Skip up the broken corner at the back of the bay and climb
the wall above on mini-flakes to a stance below a short grey wall.
4 6m. 5a. 'Boulder' up the wall via a hard move.

★★Ding 49 metres Very Severe (14.4.57)
A fine breezy climb with a testing first pitch. Start at the base of the
distinctive black vein (*Schorl Slant*).
1 26m. 4c. Climb the centre of the wide but shallow recess to a small
overhang, which is passed by moving right (awkward) and climbing to a
scoop. Surmount the next bulge and follow the crack above to a belay
ledge below a prominent spike.
2 23m. 4b. Climb to the spike; then move left to climb a scoop, and
continue direct over the larger of two overhangs.
Variation
Dung 26 metres Hard Severe 4b (11.3.72)
Start a metre right of the base of *Schorl Slant*. Climb the steep short wall to
a small orange-coloured slab below a W-shaped overhang, which is
climbed direct. Follow thin cracks and finish up *Ding*.

★Dong   48 metres   Severe   (14.4.57)
A pleasantly eccentric line with some tricky moves. Start below a jagged crack at the right-hand end of a usually damp ledge where it meets the path from the main cliff.
1 10m. 4a. Climb the crack to a belay.
2 18m. 4a. Move right and climb around a nose of rock. Traverse left and up to climb a steep wall; then move right to belay at the foot of an open V-groove.
3 20m. 4b. Climb the groove and hop onto a prominent spike. From the spike, gain a small sloping ledge by an awkward mantelshelf (given some point by the spike between your legs). Move right and finish up a narrow slab.

Sunny Corner   17 metres   Moderate   (26.2.54)
Of interest as the only recorded Moderate on Bosigran. Best used as an exit from one of the finest sun-bathing spots on the cliff. Take the groove and shallow chimney rising from the grassy platform 50 metres left of the base of Sea Gully.

Anniversary Problem   15 metres   Hard Very Severe 5b   (29.11.97)
An extended boulder problem. Climb the centre of the short wall right of *Sunny Corner*. Move right and back left at the top and continue direct up the easy slabs above.

Bosigran Main Cliff
Raven Wall Area
This area of cliff lies at the left-hand end of the Bosigran Main Face. It rises from a broad grassy terrace that runs rightwards from the base of Sea Gully to a huge pile of blocks leaning against the cliff. Raven Wall Area can be gained by branching right and upwards where the path along the base of the main cliff drops down towards Seaward Cliff. An alternative approach is down Sea Gully from the top of the cliff. There is a concentration of steep, hard routes on this section of cliff. Although shorter than those on the main face, such routes as *Raven Wall*, *Kafoozalem*, and *Evil Eye* are noted for their sustained technical difficulty and high quality. There is an even greater sense of 'inland' climbing here although the vast expanse of sea to the west gives satisfying exposure. The cliff is split centrally by the obvious break of *The Armchair*, while the thin black vein of *Kafoozalem* running up the smooth, diamond-shaped wall on its right is a classic feature. *Raven Wall* is the impending corner at the right-hand end of the cliff. The cliff is often damp in the morning but tends to dry out later in the day.

Fallout   30 metres   Severe   (22.5.61)
Takes a line up the left edge of the cliff overlooking Sea Gully.
1 15m. 4a. Start from wet ground at the right-hand base of Sea Gully. Climb a short slab and make a difficult bridging move up and right onto a sloping ledge. Continue up a groove to a ledge.
2 15m. Step left and follow the black vein to finish.

Sinistra   28 metres   Very Severe   (7.55)
Stiff for the grade but with friendly protection. Start below the jagged black vein to the right of Sea Gully.
1 18m. 4c. Climb the crack and slab to a short corner at 12 metres. Hand-jams and high kicks gain the edge of the upper slab and the grassy terrace above.
2 10m. 4a. Scramble rightwards to a steep black corner, which is climbed on chunky jugs.

Artificer   24 metres   Hard Very Severe 5b   (27.8.69)
Reasonable, but unprotected on the easier upper slab. Start below the jagged black vein right of Sea Gully. Gain the top of a flake on the right at 6 metres. Swift layback moves lead to the upper slab, which is climbed delicately to the grassy terrace. Finish up the groove just left of the black juggy corner on the far right of the terrace.
Variation Start
Artifact E5 6b (1984). Climb direct to the flake at 6 metres.

Daedalus   45 metres   Hard Very Severe   (5.7.69)
Cunning. A snaky line up the wall right of *Artificer*. Start below the jagged black vein right of Sea Gully.
1 15m. 5a. Climb to the flake on the right at 6 metres, as for *Artificer*. Move right along the obvious parallel bands to a grassy stance just left of the central break of *The Armchair*.
2 18m. 5a. Move left to a foothold, and then up and right to a sloping ledge, before climbing towards the central break. Move left to gain the top of an incut flake and flop into 'The Armchair'.
3 12m. 5a. Take the right arête above.

The Leer   48 metres   E3   (16.6.78)
Getting serious. A stylish, rising traverse of the cliff from the left base to the top of *Raven Wall*. Start below the jagged black vein to the right of Sea Gully.
1 24m. 5b. Climb to the flake on the right at 6 metres. Move right along the obvious parallel bands to some small ledges. Climb a thin crack for 5 metres, and traverse right, rising slightly, to a recess in the break of *The Armchair*.
2 24m. 6a. Swing around the corner and traverse right for 10 metres; then move up into a short groove. Follow the rising traverse-line into the corner of *Raven Wall* and finish direct.

Lurch   30 metres   E2 6a   (4.76)
The most 'bouldered-off' start of any route in Cornwall. Start 5 metres right of the previous routes below a black vein. Follow the vein and make a hard move up right to a ledge (belay possible above here). Follow the vein to the grassy terrace and finish up the black juggy corner on the right.

BOSIGRAN ～ MAIN CLIFF

RAVEN WALL AREA

15	Daedalus	HVS
16	The Leer	E3
17	The Armchair	HVS
18	Beaker Route	HVS
19	Kafoozalem	E3
20	Evil Eye	E5
21	Raven Wall	E3
22	Patience	E2
23	Dominator	E2
24	Zig Zag	VS
25	Zig Zag Variations	
26	Western Hero	E2

SUICIDE WALL AREA

27	Autumn Flakes	HS
28	Broadstairs	E2
29	Paragon	HVS
30	Paradise	E1
31	Nameless	VS
32	Beowulf	E2
33	The Phantom	E3
34	Suicide Wall	E1
35	The Absolution	E6
36	The Ghost	E3
37	Vulcan	E5
38	New Medium	E4

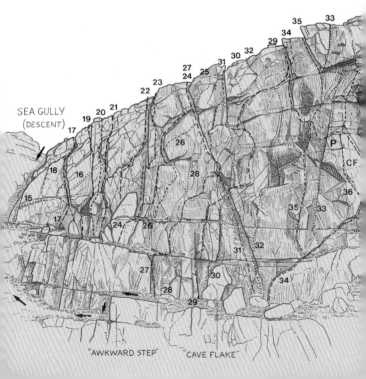

SEA GULLY (DESCENT)

"AWKWARD STEP"   "CAVE FLAKE"

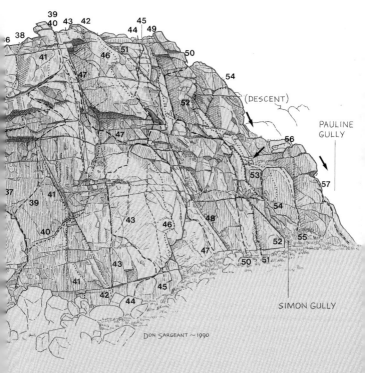

DON SARGEANT ~ 1990

P : PEDESTAL
CF: COAL FACE

★**The Armchair**   35 metres   Hard Very Severe   (3.8.58)
Fine, sustained climbing; occasionally damp. Start below the obvious
central break to the left of a positive layback crack. The first few moves are
top end of the grade and on polished rock.
1 15m. 5a. Step off a boulder onto a steep black slab and make thin
moves up to the 'neck of the beaker' in the obvious central break.
Continue steeply but on good holds into a niche; then move left and go up
into *The Armchair* (thread belay in the wall).
2 20m. 5a. Climb the crack above and finish up the black juggy corner.

★**Beaker Route**   45 metres   Hard Very Severe   (5.55)
Intricate and challenging; occasionally damp in places. Start beneath the
'neck of the beaker', the obvious central break.
1 15m. 5a. Take the layback crack on the right to the headwall. Traverse
delicately left before breaking through the 'neck' and move left to grassy
ledges.
2 20m. 4c. Traverse left over clean rock and climb delicately up the slab
to the grassy terrace.
3 10m. 4a. Finish up the black juggy corner on the far right.

★★★**Kafoozalem**   36 metres   E3 6a   (28.6.64/27.6.77)
[Photo p.96b.] A magnificent route taking the distinctive black crack that
splits the smooth diamond-shaped wall right of the central break. Start 5
metres right of the break. Climb a corner on sharp slots. Move up and right,
and then gain the black crack by difficult moves from the right. Continue up
the crack until forced left into a scoop. Continue direct for 3 metres up a
groove to a ledge; then finish up the layback crack in the wall on the left.

★★★**Evil Eye**   36 metres   E5 6b   (16.6.78)
A sustained and splendid pitch. It takes the shallow groove to the left of
Raven Wall, the distinctive impending corner above the right-hand end of
the grassy terrace. Start behind a detached triangular pinnacle and gain
the big triangular ledge at 5 metres. Climb the overhanging corner from
the back of the ledge to gain the groove. Continue direct before moving
up and left to the foot of a slab. Climb to a bulge, and take the wall above
to a rounded ledge, before breaking left to finish.

★★**Raven Wall**   36 metres   E3 5c   (19.9.55/1977)
Bosigran's hard classic; steep and solid climbing up the impending corner
above the right-hand end of the grassy terrace. Start 6 metres right of the
detached triangular pinnacle. Climb cracks in the wall, taking the
overhang at 6 metres on its left to reach a big ledge below the corner.
Bridge up the corner to a bulge; then make hard moves up and right to
the cracks beside a pinnacle. Step left and climb the continuation groove.

★★**Grendel**   39 metres   E2 5c   (30.6.66/5.71)
The black hanging corner and slab to the right of *Raven Wall*: an
intriguing pitch. Start 6 metres right of the detached triangular pinnacle

and climb easily to a ledge. Take the overhang above via the crack on its right to another ledge. Arrange gear and move up and left onto the steep slab. Make sustained moves up to and through the black break on the right to a sloping ledge (awkward belay possible). Step left and follow the black vein to the top.

★★Pump It Up 39 metres E3 6a   (17.6.78)

A hard pitch. Start from some small, slabby boulders at the right-hand end of the grassy terrace and just left of the chimney formed between the huge pile of blocks and the cliff. Climb the crack above the boulders for 3 metres and move left to a ramp. Follow the ramp and then move up to a break. Gain the wall above by strenuous moves over a downward-pointing flake. Climb a shallow crack leading right, move left, and finish via a flake.

★★Saddle Tramp 39 metres E4 6b   (16.6.78)

Another tough pitch. Start as for *Pump It Up* and climb the crack above the slabby boulders to a steep diagonal crack, which is followed for a few metres to a weakness in the wall above. Climb through this and up a large flake. Move right to finish up the wall above.

★★Patience 40 metres E2 5c   (15.6.57/8.70)

Excellent, strenuous climbing tackling the slim black groove directly above the top of the huge pile of blocks. Start just left of the chimney formed between the blocks and the cliff. Climb the wall, moving slightly right to a small overhang. Traverse left for 6 metres to a block and move up to gain a steep diagonal crack beneath overhangs. Follow the crack rightwards to enter the black groove strenuously. Finish up the groove.

★★Dominator 36 metres E2 5c   (1983)

Steep climbing just to the right of *Patience*. Start from the niche at the top of the pile of blocks by scrambling up the chimney formed between the blocks and the cliff. The slim black groove of *Patience* hangs above. Climb the overhanging corner to the base of the groove. Move around the arête on the right and up to the roof. Pull up and left to a sloping ledge and then climb the steep and exposed wall to finish.

★★Zig Zag 46 metres Very Severe   (9.48)

One of the first big lines on Bosigran, *Zig Zag* threads its way through a daunting area of cliff and is a delight. Start at the prominent spike below the jumble of blocks at the right-hand end of the terrace.
1 10m. Climb the front of the blocks to belay at their top.
2 12m. 4c. Some testing moves. Go rightwards over a flat-topped block and climb a ragged black vein, moving steeply left and up to gain a smooth sloping ledge on the right.
3 24m. 4c. If done in one pitch careful rope work is required. Move up leftwards beneath the overhung wall and step around delicately before climbing direct to the base of a deep rightward-rising trough (cramped

belay possible). Follow the trough to make a puzzling move across a slab and into an easy break (the top of *Autumn Flakes*), which is climbed direct to finish.

Variations

2a 12m. 4c. From the top of the jumbled blocks, take the corner above and climb up to a spike handhold. Move up and then traverse right to the sloping ledge. A harder variation is to continue direct up the crackline groove above the top of the spike to belay at the base of the trough.

Variation Finish 12m. 4c (4.85). From the base of the easy break at the top of the trough, climb the grassy crack leading up and rightwards; then finish direct.

Western Hero 43 metres E2 5c   (20.6.78)
A harder zag on *Zig Zag*. Start at the prominent spike at the right-hand end of the terrace and climb the jumble of blocks for 5 metres to a ledge. Move out right to the base of a steep ramp, which is followed to a large overlap. Traverse left to the sloping ledge on *Zig Zag* (optional belay). Climb up and left for 2 metres; then step up and right to the steep hand-traverse-line and follow it to easier ground.

Lower Raven Wall

Lower Raven Wall is the short tier either side of the step-down in the path beneath the base of the Main Face. This section of cliff has been walked past many, many more times than it has been climbed upon; time will tell whether the pitches here will be climbed more often now their descriptions are in one place.

Raven Wall Optional Start 12 metres Very Severe 5a
Start well to the left (facing in) of the step-down in the main path, beneath a distinctive jutting block. Climb cracks in the wall below and right of the block, move left into a scoop, and finish direct.

Zig Zag Optional Start A 12 metres Very Severe 4c
Climb the black corner that lies 15 metres left of the step-down in the path.

Zig Zag Optional Start B 12 metres Very Severe 4b
Just right of the black corner is a steep crack, which is climbed on excellent holds.

Dominator Optional Start 22 metres E1   (20.5.90/10.6.90)
1 12m. 5b. Just left of the step-down in the main path is a gravestone slab leaning against a black-faced corner. Step up from the top of the slab and follow twin cracks to finish on the grassy terrace by an overhanging boulder.
2 10m. 5a. From the top of the prominent spike at the base of a huge pile of blocks, step up onto the sharp-edged block above and make a thin

move up left to gain a lichen-covered slab. Climb cracks in the slab to belay in the niche at the top of the jumbled blocks below the groove of *Patience*.

Western Hero Optional Start   9 metres   E2 5c   (1990)
From the left-hand end of the grassy tongue above the step-down in the path, climb the thin crack which runs up the smooth wall to finish just right of the overhanging boulder.

Suicide Wall Area

This is the the central section of Bosigran Main Face. It is bounded on its left by *Autumn Flakes* and on its right by the distinctive Coal Face, the polished black slab that sits beneath the great central overhangs and is strikingly visible from the approach path to the cliff. To reach the start of *Autumn Flakes* and the other routes on this section, follow the main path to where it drops down through boulders and rocky steps below the base of the Coal Face. Continue for about 50 metres to where the path again drops down a distinctive rock step. Just before the step-down, an obvious flake (the Cave Flake) leans against the base of the cliff. To its right, a prominent reddish-coloured rake begins its left-leaning track up the cliff. This is the rake of *Nameless*.

Parody   55 metres   E1   (30.7.94)
1 12m. 4b. Start just above the rock step in the terrace path and to the left of a slanting crack (*Autumn Flakes*). Gain a scoop and move left; then climb direct to a grassy ledge. Continue up the short wall above to a large flake.
2 25m. 5b. Climb the flake and then traverse left into a groove. Follow good cracks to reach the big overhang right of *Zig Zag*. Traverse right into another groove and pull out right over the overhang to reach the ramp of *Autumn Flakes*. Go up to the belay below the final pitch of *Nameless*.
3 18m. 5c. *Paradise* pitch 3.

★★Autumn Flakes   53 metres   Hard Severe   (3.9.55)
A classic outing that is quite testing for its grade. Careful route-finding is important. There have been **serious accidents** on *Autumn Flakes* which may have been caused by confusion over the crux traverse of pitch 3. Start to the right of the step-down in the path at a slanting crack.
1 6m. 4a. Climb the crack to belay beside a large flake that leans against the cliff.
2 20m. 4a. Climb up the flake and the short wall above before trending up and rightwards via cracks and ledges to a chunky red and black vein that rises up the cliff. Belay on a small ledge. It is important not to go too high on this line, otherwise the belay below the final pitches of *Nameless* is reached with little chance of retreating.
3 27m. 4b. Climb up for a metre or so until level with a scooped bay, across to the left from which an obvious rising faultline leads up and left.

Gain the bay by delicate moves left and follow the rising faultline until an
easy break leads directly to the top. Careful rope work essential throughout.
Variation Start 6m. Very Difficult. Climb the small overhang right of pitch 1.

Broadstairs 52 metres E2   (12.7.59/5.71)
Strenuous but intriguing. Start just above the rock step in the terrace path
and to the right of a slanting crack (*Autumn Flakes*).
1 12m. 5a. Gain a small ledge up on the right and continue over a
grassy ledge to climb the short wall above.
2 24m. 5b. Climb thin cracks in a reddish wall to move right beneath the
distinctive roof. Make hard moves over the roof and reach an obvious rake
rising leftwards (final pitch of *Autumn Flakes*). Continue up the slab above
the rake to reach an exposed bay and belay beneath a final crack and
corner (final pitch of *Nameless*).
3 16m. 4c. Follow the crack past a triangular ledge.

Lil' Devil 50 metres E2 †   (22.11.98/14.3.99)
A direct eliminate with some good moves.
1 30m. 5b. Climb the narrow black ramp of *Paragon* to the good ledge.
Climb the slab just left of the corner, move left, and take a short crack to
meet *Autumn Flakes* at a ledge. Climb boldly up the orange wall above,
keeping left of *Autumn Flakes*. Belay on a flat quartz ledge.
2 20m. 5a. Follow the crack in the shallow corner above until it ends at a
ledge. Move left and climb a thin, widening crack to the top.

★★Paragon 60 metres Hard Very Severe   (24.5.56)
Nicely named. An excellent, if wandering line: exposed, technical, and
fairly tough for the grade. Start 3 metres left of the Cave Flake.
1 18m. 5a. Climb a narrow black ramp to a good ledge. Make hard
moves out right and then up left into a groove. Continue up a black corner
to belay on the broken rake on the right.
2 20m. 4c. An airy pitch. Traverse right for 8 metres until below a black
crystal-filled hole 6 metres above. Move up to it and disappear through
the overhang on a surprising jug. An exposed traverse left along flakes
leads to an awkward move up into an open bay with a hanging crack at
its right-hand end. Belay at the left end of the bay below thin cracks, as for
Nameless.
3 10m. 5a. Move back right and climb the hanging crack to a large
open niche.
4 12m. 5a. Top end of the technical grade. Take the corner at the back
of the niche by a wide bridging move, using the juggy flake on the right
wall and a high jam.

Paradise 60 metres E1   (3.4.67/12.78)
Pleasant rather than heavenly, with a strenuous and exposed top pitch.
Start just left of the Cave Flake.
1 18m. 4b. Climb the wall on thin slots and continue up the black
corners to belay on the red rake.

2 24m. 4c. Move right for 3 metres and climb a black, pock-marked slab rising leftwards. Step left at the top of the slab and climb steeply into a large open bay. Belay at the left end of the bay below thin cracks, as for *Nameless*.
3 18m. 5c. Right of the cracks is a shallow groove below an overhang. Climb the groove, take the thin lip of the overhang on the right, and continue up cracks and grooves.

★Nameless   57 metres   Very Severe   (2.5.53)

Pleasant climbing on a line of least resistance. The polished top pitch can be treacherously difficult when wet. Start at the base of the reddish-coloured rake that rises up the face from just right of the Cave Flake.
1 27m. Follow the rake to where the cliff steepens.
2 12m. 4b. Climb right, then left and up, into a large open bay. Belay at the left-hand end of the bay beneath thin cracks.
3 18m. 4c. Follow the cracks past a small ledge. Resident, head-banging gulls from a long line of defenders are an added hazard during the nesting season. Continue up the steep corner.

★★★Beowulf   61 metres   E2   (3.6.66)

A good, stylish climb. Granite at its finest. Start right of the Cave Flake at the base of the reddish-coloured rake of *Nameless*.
1 27m. 4c. Follow the rake for 6 metres and climb the thin black crack into a big bay. Move up and make an awkward and strenuous traverse right to belay on top of a large flake/block.
2 18m. 5c. Traverse left along the lip of the overhang and onto a small ledge. Use a hidden layback hold in the groove to swing left onto a small foothold. Climb the groove with increasing difficulty to gain a ledge on the right (*Suicide Wall* stance). Take the shallow groove from the left end of the ledge (hard) and reach a large bay.
3 16m. 5c. From the extreme left end of the bay, move left using small undercuts to gain a slab, and follow flakes to an exit to the left of a small overhang.

★★The Absolution   54 metres   E6   (14.4.87)

A bold, independent line that slices through the traverse of *Suicide Wall* and finishes up a highly technical crux groove. Start 6 metres right of the Cave Flake where a short corner leads to a rake that slants up to the right.
1 24m. 5c. Gain the rake and climb it for 5 metres; then move left up a smooth ramp to grooves and bulges that lead to a huge flake/block at the right end of a bay (the *Beowulf* stance).
2 30m. 6c. Follow the line of flakes directly up the wall to the traverse-line of *Suicide Wall*. Step up to a horizontal crack; then go right and through a bulge. Move to the left edge of the slab and boldly climb to a rounded ledge beneath a black groove. Climb the overhanging groove slanting up to the left, with increasing difficulty, to a flat shelf. Swing left and finish easily.
Direct Finish 5c (5.87). Climb the arête above the final groove.

★The Phantom   59 metres   E3   (28.8.56/19.4.73)
Direct and demanding, forcing the main overhang at its left end. Start 6
metres right of the Cave Flake where a short corner leads to a rake that
slants up to the right. The rake can also be gained by short but
entertaining variations on the wall to the right.
1 27m. 4c. Gain the rake and climb it for 8 metres; then bear up left to a
V-groove, which is climbed to a ledge. Climb the crack on the right to the
distinctive Pedestal.
2 17m. 5c. Climb direct and break through a small overhang by a bold
mantelshelf. Continue to the roof on diminishing holds and traverse left to
a large belay ledge. Alternatively, climb the steep slab rightwards to the
main overhang and finger-traverse left to the ledge; both are serious
pitches. Nut and *Friend* belays advised at the stance (*in-situ* pegs in decline).
3 15m. 6a. Swing back down right, pull strenuously through the
overhang, and follow the crack above.

★★★Suicide Wall   64 metres   E1   (8.8.55)
Rightly famous for its splendidly exposed central traverse pitch, at the very
heart of Bosigran. Start as for *Phantom*, 6 metres right of the Cave Flake
where a short corner leads to a rake that slants up to the right.
1 24m. Climb the rake easily bearing right to the base of the Coal Face.
An alternative approach can be made from the right by scrambling up the
deep ragged break that curves up leftwards from above where the path
rises through a narrow jumble of rocks (the *Bow Wall* approach).
2 14m. 4b. Move back left and climb the crack that runs diagonally
leftwards up the Coal Face. Step across left and down onto The Pedestal.
3 8m. 5a. Top end of the technical grade. Move left and then up a
difficult groove before traversing left using good flake holds. Thoughtful
moves lead up to a cam-eating, horizontal crack. Keep going left until a
hidden hold allows a neat step-up onto a rounded belay ledge. (Make the
move too soon and you end up on your belly rather than the belay, with
an undignified shuffle to follow.) *In-situ* peg belays should be firmly backed
up with wires and a foot-level cam.
4 8m. 5c. Climb the crack above the ledge to a large bay. (Combined
tactics reduce the moves to 5a.)
5 10m. 4b. Climb the right wall to a juggy flake and swing around right
into a hanging pod. Pop out onto an easy slab above.
Variation 5b. Take the wide crack directly into the pod. Cuddly off-width.

Doorway Area
This is the complex area of cliff which lies between The Coal Face and Simon
Gully, the obvious break where Bosigran Main Face ends. It is breached in its
middle section by the distinctive recess and capping overhang of *Doorway*.
The first six routes are gained by scrambling up a deep ragged break that
curves up leftwards to the base of the Coal Face. The break starts from just
above the point where the path along the base of the cliff drops down
through a narrow jumble of rocky steps.

★★★The Ghost 53 metres E3 (26.8 56/20.4.73)

Breaches the main overhangs with exhilarating exposure: space walking.
1 20m. 4c. Descend slightly leftwards to a short, vegetated break slanting up left. Climb the left edge of the Coal Face to the distinctive Pedestal stance of *Suicide Wall*.
2 24m. 5b. Move back right and climb to the overhang. Step left and climb over a bulge with difficulty to a resting place beneath the roofs. Traverse right along the lip of the lower overhang to a break, which is climbed on large holds to a stance 5 metres up to the right.
3 9m. Finish easily direct.

☆☆Morgawr 50 metres E6 † (5.6.96)

Cornwall's very own sea monster, sighted many times last century. This route climbs the obvious vein that crosses the main overhang directly above the Coal Face. Outrageous moves and positions. Start as for *The Ghost*.
1 18m. 5b. Climb straight up the middle of the Coal Face; then move left to a stance on the Pedestal.
2 32m. 6b/c. Move right and follow *Ghost* to the main overhang. Attack the vein direct and gain a poor knee-bar half-way across the roof, where it is possible to get a hand free to place a runner. Battle on to layback holds around the lip and make a final gripping rockover to stand in balance. The vein above gives a pleasant ramble to the top.

★Vulcan 57 metres E5 (14.4.68/30.7.81)

Fierce and testing.
1 14m. 5a. Climb the wall right of the Coal Face to an obvious traverse-line, before moving left to gain an overhanging niche and belay.
2 18m. 6b. Climb to a higher traverse-line leading rightwards and follow it past a nose to a deep horizontal crack. Continue rightwards until below a thin crack which was previously climbed with aid; now free but ferocious. At the top of the crack, traverse right to a restricted stance above the lip of the overhang (*Bow Wall* stance).
3 25m. 5b. *Bow Wall* pitch 2.

New Medium 55 metres E4 (8.78)

Ghost-busting, with a tough section through the roofs.
1 15m. 5a. Climb the wall right of the Coal Face to an obvious traverse-line, before moving left to gain an overhanging niche and belay.
2 40m. 6a. Move left to a crack and skirt the roof on its left-hand side by a hard move to gain a slab on *The Ghost*. Follow the traverse-line to the right for a metre or two before climbing two overlaps to gain a flake/groove with difficulty. Finish up the groove.

★The Marksman 59 metres E7 (1994)

[Photo p.128a.] This exciting and exposed route climbs through the roof above the sentry-box of *Bow Wall*.
1 14m. 5b. Climb the wall just left of *Bow Wall* to reach the sentry-box.
2 20m. 6c. Two pegs. Follow the thin line of weakness above and

surmount the roof to belay at the bottom of the wide crack.
3 25m. 5a. Climb the wall left of the crack to the top.

★★Bow Wall   51 metres   E2   (7.57/1958)
Joe Brown – his mark. A marvellous, intimidating, but amenable climb.
1 14m. 4c. Bear diagonally right up the impressive wall. Reach a spike,
move up, and traverse left into a small sentry-box stance.
2 12m. 5b. Climb diagonally right, and then more strenuously up the
crack above onto a distinctive 'pancake'. Arrange good gear; then step up
right onto a smooth, steep slab and edge right again before climbing
through the lip above to a small stance.
3 25m. 5b. Traverse left along the lip of the overhang in mid-air to a
bay. Follow the diagonal fault leading up and right and finish up a slab.

★★Doorpost   56 metres   Hard Severe   (7.8.55)
The great classic line on Bosigran. Elegant and exhilarating with
magnificent situations.
1 18m. 4a. Scramble up the deep ragged break for about 6 metres to
where a thin flake juts out. A distinctive traverse-line curves out to the right.
Follow the traverse-line using underclings until a few awkward moves lead
up and back left to a stance.
2 12m. 4b. Climb the twin cracks above, first by the left and then the
right to a large ledge.
3 26m. 4a. From the left side of the ledge, climb a thin crack which spills
out onto big chunky holds leading pleasantly to the cliff-top.
Variation Start 5m. Hard Very Severe 5b. Climb the thin crack just left of
the first pitch of *Shaft* to the ledge.

Shaft   61 metres   E3   (1983)
A highly strung eliminate through *Bow Wall* country.
1 24m. 5b. About 3 metres right of the deep ragged break that leads up
to the Coal Face is a left-curving flake. Make a hard move onto a ledge at
5 metres. Climb the groove above, cross the traverse-line of *Doorpost*, and
continue up a broken vein to the sentry-box belay of *Bow Wall* below the
headwall.
2 12m. 6b. Follow the steep crack above (as for *Bow Wall*); then break
through the roof and the one above to gain a slab and a restricted stance.
3 25m. 5a. Climb the roof into a groove and thin crack and finish via a
hollow.

Permanent Waves   61 metres   E4   (26.9.86)
A sketchy line based on the thin black crack on the right of the *Bow Wall*
face. Start 3 metres right of the ragged break leading to the start of *Bow
Wall* etc. below a curving flake.
1 18m. 5b. About 3 metres right of the deep ragged break that leads up
to the Coal Face is a left-curving flake. Make a hard move onto a ledge at
5 metres. Climb the groove above to the traverse-line of *Doorpost*, which
is followed to its first stance.

The Marksman (E7), Bosigran
Climbers: Sven Scholz and Heike Arnold   Photos: Egbert Dozekal

The Dream (E3), The Great Zawn
Climber: unknown   Photo: David Hope

2 43m. 5c. Step left onto the wall and climb up to where a thin black crack rises up the face above. Climb the crack and arête with minimal protection, and finish direct.

★★Thin Wall Special   61 metres   E1   (26.5.56)
Two good, strong pitches. The first puts you centre-stage of Bosigran on a busy day and is an excellent piece of climbing. Start 6 metres right of the deep ragged break that leads up to the Coal Face. A distinctive black seam rises leftwards up the face.
1 23m. 5b. Climb the black seam by a couple of thoughtful moves to a niche and continue up the rounded crack (crux) to a good belay. From the niche, a bolder alternative (**The Chicken Run** E2) takes the scoop on the right. This is a very fine piece of climbing but has a serious feel to it.
2 12m. Climb up to the large belay ledge below the big corner.
3 26m. 5a. Climb the corner crack to the roof, which is taken on its right by wild but engaging moves.
Variation
The Boysen Variant   49 metres   E1   (5.6.60)
2a 18m. 4a. Follow the line of holds up across the slab on the right to a good ledge in the midst of jumbled blocks. This is the stance below pitch 3 of *Little Brown Jug*.
3a 31m. 5b. Climb the steep slanting crack above to a foot ledge at the base of a small black ramp (peg). Traverse left to a groove below an overhang. Reach the lip of the overhang with difficulty and pull up onto a ledge. Traverse left to reach a stance under the roof at the top of pitch 3. Take the roof on its right.

Toad Wall Special   61 metres   E3   (30.12.82/2.1.83)
Hard but well protected. Start 8 metres right of The Coal Face, below a thin ragged crack (just right of *Thin Wall Special*).
1 36m. 5c. Climb the crack; then move right to gain a shallow rightward-leaning groove. Climb this until forced onto the right wall, which is climbed on tinies to a horizontal break. Move back left, then up to a large belay ledge.
2 12m. Climb the corner of *Doorway* for 6 metres and move right to a small stance.
3 13m. 6a. Take the thin zigzag crack diagonally leftwards finishing as for the last few moves of *Thin Wall Special* at the end of the roof.
Variation
2a 6m. 5b. Climb the roof right of *Doorway*'s corner pitch to the small stance.

About 25 metres right of the Coal Face there is a rise in the path beside a distinctive sentry-box. Right again is a smooth black slab rising leftwards in a V-groove. Bearings should be taken from these features for the following routes.

BOSIGRAN ~
DOORWAY AREA / LANDWARD CLIFF

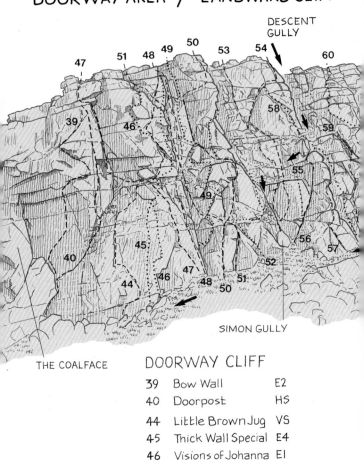

DESCENT GULLY

THE COALFACE

SIMON GULLY

DOORWAY CLIFF

39	Bow Wall	E2
40	Doorpost	HS
44	Little Brown Jug	VS
45	Thick Wall Special	E4
46	Visions of Johanna	E1
47	Doorway	S
48	Clob	VD
49	Venusberg	VS

ALISON RIB
65

GENDARME RIDGE

PAULINE GULLY

D.J.S. ~ 1991

LANDWARD CLIFF

53	Mark	HS
54	T-Tour	HVS
55	Fungus Face	E3
56	Trapeze	HVS
57	Big Top	VD
58	Simple Simon	HS
59	Pauline	HS
60	Picnic	VS
61	Oread	VD
62	Oread By-pass	VD
63	In-Between	VD
64	Kate	VD
65	Alison Rib	D

50	Anvil Chorus	VS
51	Ledge Climb	VD
52	Andrew	VD

★★★**Little Brown Jug**   64 metres   Very Severe   (21.8.55)
A marvellous and absorbing line; quite stiff for its grade and with an
elegant crux pitch. Start 5 metres left of the sentry-box at the left end of a
tapering grassy ledge.
1 22m. 4b. From the right end of the ledge, follow a line of flakes rising
leftwards to reach a shallow groove leading direct to a good belay.
2 18m. 4a. Follow the line of holds up across the slab on the right to a
good ledge in the midst of jumbled blocks.
3 24m. 5a. Climb the steep slanting crack above to a foot-ledge at the
base of a small black ramp (peg). A rounded black bulge on the left is
gained by a difficult step, followed by delicate moves up and right to gain
a good flake. Continue up and right into a trough and get tough with the
steep crack directly above to finish.
Variation Start 8m. Hard Very Severe 5a. From the left end of the starting
ledge, take the small overhang by its right side to join the rest of the pitch.

Feast of Fear   36 metres   E6 6b   (26.8.85)
Bold and bare. Start 5 metres left of the sentry-box, just right of the start of
Little Brown Jug. Climb the wall to a ledge with a good thread on the left.
Move back right and manufacture a way up to a small ledge from where
thin moves lead to a handhold on the left and a direct finish. (Walk off
right or finish via *Little Brown Jug*'s top pitch.)

★**Thick Wall Special**   55 metres   E4   (4.76)
A challenging and intense first pitch.
1 30m. 5c. Start 3 metres left of the sentry-box and climb the wall to a
small overlap at 9 metres (poor gear). Make difficult but logical moves up
left and continue more easily to belay amidst a jumble of blocks (belay of
Little Brown Jug).
2 25m. 4c. Pull onto the flying arête on the right and follow it until level
with a deep trough slanting up leftwards (*Ledge Climb*). Either climb the
arête and crack above, or step left up the trough and climb to a horizontal
crack. Move back right and finish direct.

★**Visions of Johanna**   54 metres   E1   (13.4.68)
Stylish and satisfying but with crucial first moves. Start below the broken
edge of the wall just left of the sentry-box.
1 20m. 5b. Move up for 3 metres and make harder moves up to a small
overhang on nervy gear, before moving right and up to climb the wall
above to a good stance.
2 10m. Continue easily to a ledge amidst a jumble of blocks (belay of
Little Brown Jug).
3 24m. 4c. Climb the steep slanting crack above to a foot ledge at the
base of a small black ramp. A rounded black bulge on the left is gained
by a difficult step (as for *Little Brown Jug*). Move left for a metre or so; then
climb a bulge and a neat slab to make surprisingly reasonable moves up
a cramped V-chimney.

Variation
2a 24m. 5b (4.11.86). Move a metre left and climb a faint crack and a roof to join the main route.

★★Doorway 59 metres Severe (1949)

A delightful line focusing on one of the great natural features of Bosigran. The final pitch can be serious when wet. Start about 3 metres left of the long black slab in the V-groove.
1 20m. 4a. Climb a thin ramp to a ledge. Climb through a steep break and continue pleasantly to a ledge.
2 12m. Walk left to belay in a sloping recess beneath the large corner.
3 27m. 4a. Climb the corner to below the roof. Traverse left and finish easily direct. Careful rope-work required.
Variation
1a 20m. Hard Very Severe 5a (5.53). This is a tough little number at the top end of the grade. Start in the sentry-box. Climb to the roof and make hard moves out and right, and then move up to the ledge on the parent pitch. Climb through the steep break and continue to the belay.

Clob 49 metres Very Difficult (5.1.65)

Start at the foot of the long black slab in the V-groove.
1 26m. Climb the black slab and groove to a ledge and then go direct over turf ledges to a good stance – with seat – to the right of a jutting blade of rock and a steep chimney (*Ledge Climb* pitch 2).
2 23m. Climb the wide ragged crack above the left end of the stance. Trend left at 8 metres to join the last few metres of the *Ledge Climb* chimney and so to a good ledge. Climb a short black-veined wall on the right to finish up an easy-angled chimney.

★Venusberg 55 metres Very Severe (30.4.61)

Nicely technical and varied. Small wires need to be carefully placed for protection. Start at the V-groove as for *Clob*.
1 10m. 4a. Climb the black slab; then take a steep crack out on the right to an awkward mantelshelf onto a ledge. Often wet, but still surmountable. Belay at a large pinnacle in a bay.
2 15m. 4b. Chimney up behind the pinnacle and traverse left into a corner. Climb the corner by some neat moves to a good ledge. A harder and more interesting alternative is to go directly left from the belay spike and climb the corner in its entirety.
3 20m. 4c. Walk left with care along a narrow grass ledge and scramble up to the top of a spike below a steep wall (belay recommended). The wall has twin cracks on its right-hand side and a black vein on its left. Traverse left to a small ledge and climb the black vein. Step left at its top and climb a short wall to a ledge, before stepping awkwardly back right around a nose of rock to a niche.
4 10m. 4b. Follow the corner above to a roof; then make a tricky move out left and climb the black vein above.

★★Anvil Chorus   58 metres   Very Severe   (19.5.56)
Great name, great climb; but the scene of several unfortunate accidents
on the splendid crack of pitch 3, which can shrug you off without a second
thought. There are ample protection possibilities, so use them. Start a
metre or so right of the black-sided V-groove of *Clob*, below a neat little
face.
1 18m. 4b. Climb the crack in the face passing a small ledge at 6 metres
to continue up the crack to a larger ledge
2 15m. 4b. Move up easily to a small roof on the right at 6 metres and
pass it boldly on the right. (Dozens of visiting V Diff leaders have climbed
this under the impression that it was pitch 2 of *Andrew*, an experience that
either ruined their holiday or rapidly advanced their standard.) Continue
up to a large belay ledge. From here, it is best to walk left along the
narrow grass ledge and scramble up carefully to a belay at the top of a
pinnacle below a smooth recessed wall.
3 17m. 4c. A cracker in every sense. Bold if laybacked, steady if
jammed. Occasionally wet at the top. Climb the twin cracks on the right of
the smooth wall. From the top of the crack (belay possible) move right
along the narrow ledge and make an interesting mantelshelf move up to a
belay. A flexible cam placed in the bottom of the crack will help to reduce
the chance of the runners higher up being lifted out in the event of a fall.
4 8m. 4c. Hard. Step up left to reach a horizontal crack and climb the
thin crack above.
Variation
4a 9m. Hard Very Severe 5a. Step up to the horizontal crack and follow
it left into a corner. Move left into a steep wide crack which leads to the
top.

Jolly Green Giant   21 metres   E2 6a   (8.78)
A fierce line up the lichenous buttress right of pitch 3 of *Anvil Chorus*; high
in the grade for the low in height. Start from the top of the pinnacle at the
base of the twin cracks of *Anvil Chorus* pitch 3. Move up right past an old
peg and into a niche. Climb to a small roof and take a thin crack on the
left to the traverse-line of *Anvil Chorus* pitch 3. Climb cracks to the final
roof and finish to its left.

★Ledge Climb   52 metres   Very Difficult   (1905/1922)
Classic climbing with some challenging moves. Start just left of a narrow
grey slab that slants up to the left (the start of *Andrew*), at a deep, ragged
crackline with a chockstone at 6 metres. Pitch 3 is at the top of its grade.
1 9m. Climb the crack (quite tricky) to a good ledge.
2 20m. Make a rising traverse leftwards over broken ground and then
climb a short slab and blocks to a good stance.
3 14m. Slither under the jutting blade of rock on the right, and move
around to a chimney, which is climbed to a stance.
4 9m. 'The Ledge'. This is the delightfully exposed trough rising leftwards.
A less nervy escape can be made up the short black-veined wall above the
stance and then up the easy chimney. But you wouldn't, would you?

Andrew   58 metres   Very Difficult   (13.9.58)
A good-natured and enjoyable climb, although escapable between
pitches. The top two pitches are quite challenging for the grade. Start at a
narrow grey slab at the right-hand edge of the main face and just left of a
narrow gully (Simon Gully).
1 15m. Climb the slab and some chunky flakes above to reach the left
end of a ledge that slopes gently down towards a grassy gully on the right.
2 15m. Ignore the continuation groove that leads up to a small roof
directly above. Instead, step a metre or so right and make a tricky move
up right onto the short inset wall above the grassy gully by using hidden
incut holds in its left corner. Move right and climb to a large platform.
3 12m. There is a ragged crack above and left of the stance. This is
reached from the right, and is climbed to easier blocks leading to the steep
flanking wall of the upper buttress. An easy alternative is to move around
to the right from the stance and then to scramble up blocks.
4 16m. Climb the steep, black flanking wall of the buttress to reach
excellent jugs for a pull over onto a ledge, and continue easily up to the
right. Alternatively, climb the grubby corner to the right of the wall.

The Wasteland   10 metres   Hard Very Severe 5b   (8.57)
The bottomless groove in the wall above the left end of the ledge at the top
of *Andrew* pitch 1. So called because it connects 'nothing with nothing'; an
entertaining problem all the same.

At the top of Simon Gully and just right of *Andrew*'s final pitch are three short
pitches above a slab with a black patch on its left side. All three pitches are
tricky but diverting. **The Rib Climb** (10 metres Severe 1922) climbs the rib
to the right of pitch 4 of *Andrew*. **Como Crack** (10 metres Severe 30.9.48)
takes the overhanging cracks just right of *The Rib Climb* and above the left
side of the slab. **Sloping Slab** (10 metres Severe 1922) climbs the crack on
the right side of the slab before traversing left and up an open groove.

Below Bosigran Main Face steep slopes and rocky tiers drop to sea-level.
There are some short lines on the cleaner walls towards the seaward end of
this lower section of Bosigran. A large ledge at sea-level can be reached by
traversing in from the bottom of *Black Slab* and overcoming a few obstacles
such as gaping zawns, etc. A descent down the steep grass and rock slopes
below *Nameless* can also be made, but with care.

The Giant Steps   95 metres   Very Difficult ††   (9.5.57)
Start from sea-level between the island and the Bosigran face where a line of
big ledges rise up to the left. A large flake has fallen from the higher platform
of this route. Walk along the sea-level ledge to a break, and climb rightwards
to a large platform. On the wall behind is a prominent black corner and a
bulge with a good finger-crack running diagonally up to the left. Either of
these lines can be followed to another large platform. Walk along the platform
for about 35 metres to a short arête (12 metres left of a large corner). Climb
the arête and follow various cracks over ledges to reach the terrace path.

Sea Wall Exits
Three short pitches start from a broad ledge near sea-level below the
Autumn Flakes area. The ledge ends on its left above a small zawn. The
pitches follow three obvious faultlines.
A 17m. Very Severe 4b. This pitch takes the chimney on the other side of
the small zawn, turning the overhang on the right by a delicate traverse to
a ledge. Continue up thin cracks to a belay. Easy climbing gains the
terrace path.
B 14m. Very Severe 4c. Directly above the small zawn is a crack that
overhangs at its base.Climb this with difficulty at first to a large platform.
Finish up the black crack above.
C 12m. Very Severe 4c. Climb the obvious open corner at the landward
end of the ledge. Frictional.

Some hard additions have been made on the short wall above the broad
ledge. An abseil from the Cave Flake deposits one close to a leftward-facing
corner. Five metres right of the corner, **Emergency Exit** (10 metres E4 6a
12.96) climbs flakes up the central line of the wall and the slab above. Fifty
metres further right is a wall covered in undercuts. The left side of the wall is
taken by **Racy Stacy** (10 metres E5 6a 12.96). Climb a large undercut flake
to a thin crack and the slab above, move right, and finish up a rounded flake
to reach a flat ledge. The direct line over the bulges between *Racy Stacy* and
...*Seven Seconds* is the escapable **Tragic Kingdom** (10 metres E7 6c
3.97). **The Return of the Seven Seconds** (10 metres E5 6a 12.96) is the
route of the wall, despite having no protection. It climbs rightwards to finish
up the central groove. **Spiderman's Nightmare** (10 metres E8 6c †
12.96) takes the two central overlaps, while 3 metres to the right is **Virtual
Insanity** (10 metres E5 6b 12.96): climb the wall and escape rightwards
onto the arête.

Girdle Traverses
There are two girdles of Bosigran Main Face, both of which are good long
outings offering absorbing route-finding at a reasonable but still quite
testing standard. *Diamond Tiara* is a high-level girdle and is the easier
option. *String of Pearls* is a challenging girdle across the heart of the Main
Face.

★**Diamond Tiara**   205 metres   Hard Very Severe   (21.5.56)
The route follows a line that keeps about 6 to 10 metres below the top of
the cliff. It is easily escapable at a number of points although the first
section is committing. Start at the base of Sea Gully below the jagged
black crack of *Sinistra*.
1 18m. 4c. *Sinistra* pitch 1: climb the crack and slab to a short corner at
12 metres. Hand-jams and high steps gain the edge of the upper slab and
the grassy terrace above. Belay below the black corner on the right.
2 37m. 5b. Sustained and at the top end of the adjectival grade. Step
down and right to follow the traverse-line across the top of the *Kafoozalem*

wall. Use undercuts to descend to a small overhang, step down, and move across the corner of *Raven Wall* to the small pinnacle on the right rib. Climb diagonally rightwards to belay under an overhang about 6 metres from the top of the cliff.

3 18m. Continue rightwards and then drop down an easy break to a small ledge at the top of a groove slanting down to the left (*Zig Zag*).

4 18m. 4a. Descend the rake that drops down to the right (*Autumn Flakes*) to a small bay. Move up and right to belay at the foot of twin cracks (final pitch of *Nameless*). An alternative is to climb the grassy cracks leading up rightwards from the stance before moving right to descend the *Nameless* cracks for 6 metres to the stance (4c).

5 10m. 5a. Climb the short distinctive crack on the right to a comfortable ledge (pitch 3 of *Paragon*).

6 18m. 5a. Climb the cleft on the right (*Suicide Wall*) and move up the slab to the final short corner near the cliff-top (break for lunch?). Step down to the right and swing around a rib to a spike belay just left of the final crack of *The Phantom*.

7 30m. 4c. Continue traversing rightwards to a spike. Follow the easiest line past another spike to belay under the roof at the top of the impressive corner of *Doorway*.

8 30m. 5a. Follow the obvious crack in the right wall to move around the rib. Continue up and rightwards to a trough below the steep final crack of *Little Brown Jug*.

9 18m. 4c. Descend the trough. Traverse rightwards, moving across the top of the twin cracks of *Anvil Chorus* to make the tricky mantelshelf at the end of the traverse.

10 8m. 4c. *Anvil Chorus* pitch 4: step up left to reach a horizontal crack and climb the thin crack above.

★★String of Pearls   179 metres   E1   (13.8.55)
A fine girdle tracing an inquisitive line from left to right across the face. There are some testing moves on the first pitches. Start at the foot of *Beaker Route* in the middle of the Raven Wall Face.

1 21m. 5b. Climb the crack to its top and hand-traverse to the right. Clear the bulge and continue rightwards to the ledge below the steep corner of *Raven Wall*.

2 21m. 5b. Traverse easily to reach a steep diagonal crack running up to the right. Follow this crack until it is possible to step across a slab (below the hanging groove of *Patience*) into a diagonal crack in the opposite wall. Climb this crack to a belay niche at the base of a deep rising groove on the right (*Zig Zag*).

3 26m. 4b. Climb the groove to a ledge at its top; then descend the rake leading down to the right (*Autumn Flakes*) to a small bay.

4 27m. 4c. Continue traversing and move down slightly to good holds just above a narrow, black, pock-marked slab (*Paradise*). Descend this; traverse right past the rib of *Paragon*, and then down onto a large sloping triangular ledge (*Beowulf*). Climb up a corner and hand-traverse rightwards to some blocks. Climb a corner to The Pedestal on *Suicide Wall*.

5 28m. 4c. Step around the rib onto the Coal Face and climb up to its top right-hand end. Traverse 3 metres right and descend an overhung niche to a ledge; then traverse a further 3 metres into a sentry-box stance on *Bow Wall*.

6 16m. 4c. Continue rightwards into the twin cracks of *Doorpost*. Descend these for 3 metres to the recess belay of *Doorpost*.

7 18m. 4a. (*Little Brown Jug* pitch 2.) Follow the line of holds up across the slab on the right to a good ledge in the midst of jumbled blocks.

8 22m. 5a. (*Little Brown Jug* pitch 3.) Climb the steep slanting crack above to a foot-ledge at the base of a small black ramp. A rounded black bulge on the left is gained by a difficult step followed by delicate moves up and right to gain a good flake. Continue up and right into a trough and climb the steep crack directly above to finish.

Landward Cliff

This is the broken but interesting area of cliff first reached when approaching Bosigran directly from the car-park on the coast road via the base of *Gendarme Ridge*. Its main feature is *Alison Rib*, an obvious crested ridge which is flanked on its right by a black, pock-marked slab. The deep gully left of the *Alison Rib* area is Pauline Gully, which gives a useful descent route from the top of the cliff. Left of Pauline Gully is a series of small buttresses including the distinctive Big Top Buttress, which is flanked on its left by the narrow cleft of Simon Gully.

Mark   35 metres   Hard Severe   (18.5.59)
Start on a grassy ledge on the right, 5 metres up Simon Gully, below a small lichenous buttress.

1 9m. 4b. Climb cracks on the left edge of the buttress before moving rightwards up a break to a large ledge.

2 12m. Continue up the vegetated slabs above to the left side of the upper buttress, where a steep dark slab runs up to the right.

3 14m. 4a. Climb steeply left using a big flake hold. Step left and continue via ledges and gorse bushes to the top.

T-Tour   35 metres   Hard Very Severe   (9.7.82)
Two short steep pitches split by easy rock. Start just right of *Mark*.

1 8m. 5b. Climb the flake and thin cracks in the centre of the small lichenous buttress to a large ledge.

2 12m. Continue up the vegetated slabs above to the left side of the upper buttress, where a steep dark slab runs up to the right.

3 15m. 5a. Make hard moves up the slab moving right and up. Scramble off leftwards.

Big Top Buttress is the distinctive buttress crowned by a huge block that dominates the lower half of the Landward Cliff to the right of Simon Gully.

Fungus Face 18 metres E3 6b (1986)
Start at an isolated block at the left side of Big Top Buttress below a grassy groove leading up to a steep crack (*Trapeze*). Make the choice between runners and holds before climbing the groove for 5 metres and following the minimal crack in the left wall.

Trapeze 27 metres Hard Very Severe 5a (7.4.64)
Short but fierce, though worthwhile. Start at the isolated block at the left side of Big Top Buttress. Climb the grassy groove and the steep strenuous corner above, exiting left.
Variation
The Peck Variant 28m. 5a. Top end. A wicked hand-traverse rightwards from the top of the steep corner.

★**Big Top** 28 metres Very Difficult (31.5.58)
A pleasant little route. Climb the crack directly below the summit block of 'The Big Top', and a shorter crack on the right to below the overhang. Move up and right onto a narrow slab leading to a ledge and finish via the break on the left.

Flat Top 28 metres Hard Severe 4b (21.1.79)
Start below the right flank of 'The Big Top'. Climb to a grassy ledge and take the short wall above. Step right and pull onto the black, cracked slab on the right. Continue to an overhung niche, which is exited via a ledge on the left.

Simple Simon 58 metres Hard Severe (28.5.56)
Several pitches stitched together make an interesting ramble with the top pitches being particularly worthwhile. Start 10 metres right of 'The Big Top'.
1 10m. 4b. Climb a slab to a broad ledge and block belays.
2 12m. Take the left-slanting groove to pass a triangular roof on its left and continue up the wide crack above. Scramble up to the attractive upper buttress, on which a generous faultline curves up to the left.
3 18m. 4b. Climb the faultline to its top and step up to large ledges.
4 18m. 4b. On the right of the upper wall is a steep black crack. Stagger up it to easy slabs. (There is an easier escape to the right.)
Variations
2a 13m. 4b (22.6.96). Climb straight up the wall to beneath the right-hand end of the triangular overhang. Go straight up the corner on good holds to a ledge, and climb the wide crack and slab above.
3a The Pieman 15m. Very Severe 4c (10.12.86). Start a metre or so left of the start of pitch 3. Make a hard move up the thin crackline and continue direct crossing the deep fault to reach the upper ledges. Finish up pitch 4 of *Simple Simon*.

Above Big Top Buttress, and easily seen from the descent route, is a wall with a bow-shaped left arête (between the third pitches of *T-Tour* and *Simple Simon*. **Poison Ivy** (20 metres E3 6a † 29.11.97) takes the cracked arête. **Fungus** (20 metres E6 6b † 1995) climbs up just to the right of the arête.

Crazy Man Michael   23 metres   Very Severe   4c   (1978)
A line up the right-hand flanking arête of *Simple Simon's* upper buttress.
Start up and right of the start of *Simple Simon* pitch 3. Make steep moves
up the arête via cracks and bulges gained awkwardly from the right. Finish
up the steep black crack of *Simple Simon's* top pitch.

Pauline   38 metres   Hard Severe   (19.5.59)
A wandering line up the buttresses that make up the left side of Pauline
Gully. Start at the left-hand base of the gully.
1 8m. Climb a crack to the right of a large boulder to block belays on a
ledge.
2 12m. 4b. Climb to a steep crack and make strenuous moves to its top.
Scramble to the right-flanking wall of the upper buttress.
3 18m. 4a. Gain a ledge below an overhanging wall. Make steep moves
up the wall and step right into a pleasant crack leading up to the right to
finish.

Sampan   30 metres   Very Difficult   (30.5.58)
Start 10 metres up Pauline Gully below a left-leading ramp.
1 12m. Climb up to the base of the ramp and follow it to a slab that
leads up right to a grassy ledge.
2 18m. Walk left along a path for 10 metres until below the left flank of a
small buttress. From a triangular block, climb up and through breaks to
the top.

Picnic   34 metres   Very Severe   (30.5.58)
Two unconnected but entertaining picnics. Start 10 metres up Pauline Gully
below a yellowish corner on its right wall.
1 15m. 4b. Climb the wall and follow the shallow corner to a grassy
ledge. The corner is sometimes wet near the top.
2 19m. 5a. Walk left along a path for 10 metres until below a small
buttress with a distinctive left-leaning crack running up its left side. Climb
the crack – technically interesting initial moves – and continue via a deeper
crack before stepping left to finish.
Variation
2a 18m. Very Severe 5a. Climb the wall direct, just right of pitch 2. Poor
protection. Move left and join the upper part of pitch 2.

Oread   53 metres   Very Difficult   (5.8.55)
A bold first pitch, which can be tricky if wet. Start to the right of the base of
Pauline Gully and just left of a prominent groove (*In-Between*).
1 30m. Climb a rib, making a short traverse to the left and back again to
avoid an overhang. Make a delicate mantelshelf onto a ledge. Move left
and climb the wall on small but good holds.
2 9m. Continue easily over grass and boulders until below the recessed
corner groove in the left side of the upper tower of *Alison Rib*.
3 14m. Climb over a block and finish up the groove on reassuring holds.

Oread Bypass   59 metres   Very Difficult   (5.8.55)
Start below the centre of the buttress to the right of Pauline Gully.
1 33m. Climb an arête to a ledge at 10 metres. Traverse left over two
overlaps to reach an orange-coloured streak. Move up to the right on
sloping holds.
2 12m. Go left for 4 metres to a ledge and climb an exposed inverted-V
corner to the terrace below the recessed corner groove in the left side of
the upper tower of *Alison Rib*.
3 14m. Climb over a block and finish up the groove on reassuring holds.

In-Between   34 metres   Very Difficult   (12.10.63)
A pleasant pitch. Start below the V-groove and small overhang on the left
of *Alison Rib*.
1 18m. Climb the groove, and take the overhang on the left to a ledge
by an interesting move. Step up, again with interest, to the ledge above.
2 16m. Continue direct or by trending right to gain the top of *Alison Rib*.

Kate   30 metres   Very Difficult   (9.3.63)
Short-lived but enjoyable. Start 3 metres left of the base of *Alison Rib*.
1 15m. Climb the edge of a slab to the headwall and follow the steep
crack above on excellent holds to a stance.
2 15m. Continue to the crest of *Alison Rib* and follow it to the top.

★★Alison Rib   49 metres   Difficult   (1923)
A 20s classic. Start at the base of the black slab that flanks the rib on its right.
1 31m. Climb the slab for 6 metres; then trend left to the crest of the rib
and follow it to a large platform. (This pitch can be split midway, which is
advised if seconded by a beginner.)
2 18m. Climb a crack in the left wall of the upper buttress and continue
up and left via cracks.

Fafnir   36 metres   Difficult   (30.4.61)
Often wet. On the right of *Alison Rib* is a large pinnacle. Start at its base.
1 18m. Climb the front of the pinnacle to gain a V-groove, and climb a
small overhang by its right side. Follow cracks above to a ledge.
2 18m. Continue up slabs.

Fasolt   36 metres   Very Difficult   (30.4.61)
Start 10 metres right of *Alison Rib* at a left-leaning ramp.
1 12m. Climb the ramp and make steeper moves to gain a rounded ledge.
2 12m. Take the scooped slab by pleasant moves until below an
overhanging block.
3 12m. Follow the rib above to finish.

Between *Fasolt* and *Gendarme Ridge* (page 108) are a number of short
walls and cracklines which give entertaining bouldering pitches. These can
be linked with short disjointed pitches above to give escapable routes for
beginners.

Porthmoina Island (Bosigran Pinnacle)

(Granite) OS Ref 416 368

Outlook: East and west facing.
Tidal. Not accessible for two hours either side of high water. Affected by heavy swell.
Coastguard Identity: Porthmoina Cove.
Enviromental Issues and Approach Advice: Recently the National Trust identified areas within its properties nationally that merit freedom from human intrusion in order to benefit conservation. Porthmoina Island, below Bosigran Main Face, was proposed as a sanctuary site within an otherwise popular and heavily-used leisure area. It is a breeding and roosting site to which many seabirds have moved from Bosigran Main Face due to that cliff's popularity with climbers. The Island has important maritime plant habitats, good crevice communities and vulnerable marine environments between high and low water marks. There are recorded climbs on the island going back 60 years. The BMC supports the National Trust's proposal of Porthmoina Island being a voluntary sanctuary area. **All visitors to the Bosigran area, whether climbers or not, are asked to respect this measure.** Because of the above, the following climbs are not described.

Pinnacle Traverse (1912), **Lower East Face Traverse** (1902), **Lower West Face Traverse** (1907), **Middle East Face Traverse**, **Western Slant** (both 1910), **Higher East Face Traverse, Guillemot Ledge, Central Climb** (all 22.9.38), **Eastern Slant** (6.43), **The Spider's Climb** (16.4.54), **Hake Slab** (10.9.56), **Crackers** (1.1.60), and **Canary Legs** (9.81) ranged in difficulty from Difficult to Hard Severe.

Bosigran Ridge Area (Granite)   OS Ref 415 367

Outlook: Mainly west. Bosigran Ridge runs north-west to south-east.
Tidal at base of first pitch of the Ridge and on the seaward climbs on its lower west face. Swell also affects these areas.
Coastguard Identity: Bosigran Ridge.
Enviromental Issues: SSSI. The area is home to a number of species of birds, which are best avoided in the nesting season. Avoid damage to dense lichen cover or to the patches of vulnerable plants, which include Bluebell and Heath Spotted Orchid. This is an area of immense natural beauty and care should be exercised at all times.

Bosigran Ridge is the great 'dragon's back' of pinnacled granite that rises in sweeping steps from sea-level on the west of Porthmoina Cove. Bosigran Main

Face and the Ridge complement each other perfectly, the latter offering the longest rock climb in Penwith with nearly 200 metres of delightful climbing in stunning positions at only Very Difficult standard. *Bosigran Ridge* should not be missed, although it is not necessarily a novice's expedition unless done with competent companions. The run-outs are long and involve true ridge traverses with substantial drops on either side. On the sun-trap western side of the lower ridge are a number of short hard pitches of quality. From the top of *Bosigran Ridge*, a smaller, less positive feature, the Western Ridge, drops down to the rim of the magnificent Great Zawn. Between the two ridges is a grassy 'hanging valley'.

A number of routes have been climbed on the steep grey face on the lower east side of *Bosigran Ridge*. All require abseil approach and hanging belays. No details are available.

Approach from the direction of the Count House by following the path towards Porthmoina Cove to the junction with the coast path. Go left here and cross the Porthmoina Stream by a rock bridge, and then leave the main coast path to cross an area of damp ground to a well-worn path along the grassy rim of Porthmoina Cove. This leads to the boulder-strewn base of the coxcombed upper ridge beneath a memorial plaque to the Marine Commandos, whose Cliff Assault Wing trained here.

There are two routes running up either side of the memorial plaque face.

Secretary's Pitch   18 metres   Very Difficult   (31.8.46)
Climbs the narrow lichenous slab crowned by a bulbous pinnacle on the left of the face. Start from some jagged boulders below the line of the slab. Climb left for a few feet; then move right to a ledge and climb the slab.

Plaque Pitch   15 metres   Hard Very Severe 5a   (14.6.63)
A tough little nut. Start at the right side of the face below an overhung corner. Hop onto a ledge and take the black jagged crack to a blunt spike; then follow the lichenous slab running up leftwards.

Descent. To reach the base of *Bosigran Ridge*, several crossings of the Ridge from east to west are possible. Below mid height, however, the east side of the ridge is precipitous. The best approaches are through breaks on either side of the memorial plaque face. The upper break leads down foot-ledges to the base of the headwall of the hanging valley. The lower break, lying behind the big pinnacle block, 6 metres right of the memorial plaque face, leads to similar foot-ledges but is a steeper and less reassuring crossing. A well-worn path is then followed down towards the sea, closely in line with the west side of the Ridge, until a steeper rocky section above easy-angled rippled slabs is reached. Descend the steep rocky section easily but with consideration for novices. A final judgement on sea conditions for the traverse around the base of the Ridge should be made here, since tide and swell can be vicious and unexpected. The top of the lower pitches of *Bosigran Ridge* can still be reached from well above the sea, in one piece – and dry.

★★Bosigran Ridge   198 metres   Very Difficult   (1902)

If sea conditions permit, a start can be made by traversing easily around the base of the nose onto the more dramatic east side of the Ridge with impressive views across to Porthmoina Island and Bosigran Main Face.

1 26m. Gain a sloping platform directly above the deep zawn on the east side of the nose. From the platform's upper end, either move out left onto the wall and climb up to a ledge or climb the corner above to the same ledge. Continue up the steep face on lustful holds to a platform. (This pitch looks quite spectacular from Bosigran Main Face.)

2 23m. From the platform, scramble over boulders to the foot of a chimney, which is climbed in traditional fashion to a stance below a handsome, beaked boulder.

3 18m. Move up to the beak and traverse left between two towers; then descend a short corner to a gap. Climb a crack and slab to the base of a large isolated pinnacle crowned with a triangular block.

4 15m. Traverse the left side of the pinnacle for about 5 metres to a groove, which is climbed to a stance by the triangular block.

5 33m. Move down the left side of the knife-edged flake to a break in the ridge and scramble up boulders and grass to a platform.

6 20m. Cross a small gap and continue to a large platform with a huge triangular block (thread belay at its base).

7 33m. Traverse the right side of the block and move down to an isolated pinnacle and a stance on its top.

8 30m. The Ridge continues over easy blocks to an avoidable feature, The Armchair. This calls for an awkward mantelshelf from a foot-sized spike onto a sloping ledge. It is of a much harder standard (4b) than the rest of the climb, but is protectable by an overhead runner and is in keeping with the line, which finishes by an easy scramble to the summit rocks.

Several excellent short climbs take the walls and corners that rise from the easy-angled slabs at the base of the western side of Bosigran Ridge. The seaward pitches are tidal and subject to swell, while in very big seas the whole area is no place for fully qualified survivors. The main feature is an attractive diamond-shaped slabby wall seamed with cracks that lies about 15 metres up from the seaward end of the Ridge. *Gallipoli* takes a loping, zigzag line up this wall. The climbs are described from the seaward end of the Ridge.

Dolphinarium   15 metres   E1 5b   (4.6.93)

Climb the thin crack in the seaward nose of Bosigran Ridge. A difficult pull up to and over the overhang leads to an easy finish up the arête on the left.

Kiss my Wrasse   19 metres   E2 5c   (4.6.93)

A great little pitch up the arête right of *Dolphinarium*. Gain the arête with difficulty from the left and follow it via the obvious jug to a ledge. Finish up the flake crack in the arête.

☆☆**The Girl Can Wait**   12 metres   E4 6a †   (5.7.98)
An excellent if bold little pitch up the left arête of the *Anzac Day* wall. Move up to a break and climb the right side of the arête with difficulty to a jug on the arête. Finish up the easier but now unprotected arête.

Layback and Think of England   12 metres   E1 6a   (19.6.88)
Start near the left end of a broad, coffin-shaped tidal ledge that lies at the base of the Ridge. Difficult moves lead to a niche. Step left and climb a short wall via a crack.

Cure by Choice   30 metres   Hard Very Severe 5b   (1986)
Start in the middle of the coffin-shaped tidal ledge at a short steep wall below a rightward-slanting ramp that leads to a roof. Climb the wall (crux) and follow the ramp rightwards to the small roof, which is surmounted to reach the top.

★**Anzac Day**   30 metres   E1 5b   (4.85)
Climb the ragged crack in the arête just down from the base of the approach slabs to a niche at the top of the ramp. Climb the overhang above and finish direct. Stiff for its grade.

Slippery People   18 metres   E3 6a   (9.5.87)
Climb the steep, dog-leg corner at the base of the approach slabs, moving left across the roof to finish.

★★**Imphal**   18 metres   E2 5c   (4.86)
An interesting technical pitch taking the steep, stained corner above a neat little quartzy basin in the deck. Sustained but with good gear.

★★**Kohima**   20 metres   E3 6a   (4.86)
Climb the leftward-rising crack running up the base of the diamond-shaped wall of *Gallipoli* towards the upper niche of *Imphal*. Climb directly up the wall to the upper break, and finish up fluted cracks. Hard and bold moves at the start.

★★**Gallipoli**   23 metres   E1 5c   (4.85)
Impeccable climbing on an intricate line. Start below the right-hand side of the diamond-shaped wall, below a small black-coated overhang at 6 metres. Climb a crack to fix runners near the overhang. Step down and make a difficult move leftwards to a small foothold on the wall. Climb thin cracks to a break; then move up and left along a diagonal crackline to finish up fluted cracks at the apex of the diamond.

Mandalay   20 metres   Hard Very Severe 5a   (6.86)
To the right of *Gallipoli* is an irregular-sided overhang. Climb a thin crack to its left end and pass the overhang strenuously. Continue up the blunt arête on the left.

To the right of the *Gallipoli* area, the cliff becomes more broken and indeterminate. Various ways of reaching the top of Pitch 2 of *Bosigran Ridge* at the prominent beaked pinnacle can be taken up the walls, slabs, and cracks at a Very Difficult standard; harder variations are possible.

The Great Zawn (Granite)   OS Ref 415 366

'One of the most secluded and unknown sanctuaries of the cliffs...'
(A W Andrews. 1950)

Outlook: Mainly west-facing.
Non-tidal but wave-washed in the *The Variety Show* to *West Face* section.
Coastguard Identity: Great Zawn near Bosigran.
Enviromental Issues: SSSI. The area is home to a number of species of birds, which are best avoided in the nesting season. Avoid damage to dense lichen cover and to areas of dense plant life. Vulnerable plants include Bluebell and Heath Spotted Orchid. This is an area of immense natural beauty and care should be exercised at all times.

Great Zawn truly deserves its greatness. Hallowed by tradition and developed by generations of great climbers into a major venue, the zawn is first and foremost an exquisite natural place. There is a striking contrast between the zawn's golden seaward cliff and its green and shaded heart. Flanked by towering granite walls, Great Zawn holds a collection of major routes. The fierce nature of some of these is mellowed by the zawn's delightfully persuasive atmosphere and its visual beauty.

The Zawn has four distinct faces. The Seaward Face, with *The Variety Show* and *Green Cormorant Face*, lies at the mouth of the zawn on its north side. This face merges into the formidable West Face with its cluster of splendid routes, which include *The Dream* and *Liberator*. The West Face then turns inland to the slabby wall of *Desolation Row*. Beyond here lies the independent Headwall, which acquired some hard lines in the late 1980s. From the Headwall, a broken vegetated amphitheatre encloses the back of the zawn until it merges into the East Face, which, though holding few routes, makes up for it with the excellent *Xanadu*.

Approach. Seaward Face: for *Side Show* to *Déjà Vu*; also for *The Dream*, as a way of avoiding its often slimy corner start from inside the zawn-bed. Approach as for the west side of *Bosigran Ridge* until the slabby ledges near sea-level are reached. Go left from here (facing out) to a gently sloping rock terrace above the impressive mouth of Great Zawn. An abseil of 15 metres gains a broad platform originally dubbed The Haven. (Nicely mis-named: pure Hell in heavy seas at high tide. Be warned.)

Approach. For the West Face, Headwall, and East Face there are two possibilities:

1 Take the approach for *Bosigran Ridge* and, after crossing the ridge at the Commando memorial plaque, follow a sketchy path going directly across the 'cwm' at the same level to reach a grassy niche on the rim of Great Zawn. Go through a rock notch on the left (facing out) and drop down to a grassy terrace. A few metres further on, the terrace narrows above a steep, vegetated break. Just above the break, there is an excellent abseil spike, which can be backed up with gear. This area is like a garden from May onwards and can be a sun-trap. It lies directly above The Headwall on the left and *Desolation Row* wall on the right and gives an excellent view of the East Face and *Xanadu*. A 40-metre abseil from the spike reaches the steep grassy slopes of the upper Zawn.

2 Alternatively, follow the coast path from the small bridge above the ruined mine buildings above Porthmoina Cove. Do not take the path that leads along the top of Porthmoina Cove to the clearly visible *Bosigran Ridge*, but stay with the coast path, which climbs steeply uphill and then levels off and crosses a wooden stile. The summit rocks of *Bosigran Ridge* are passed on the right. Continue through a low boulder wall. A few metres further on, a distinct but sometimes overgrown path leads seawards down a grassy depression. (The path can be obscured by high bracken in late summer.) Follow the path until the edge of Great Zawn is reached. Entry can be made from left or right (facing out):

Right entry The most convenient and open entry. From the top edge of the zawn continue along its right edge and down the stepped grassy terrace to reach the abseil spike mentioned in **1** above.

Left entry Follow the path leading down the broad ridge on the left side of the zawn until steeper ground is reached. Descend a short grubby chimney and continue to large terraces just above the sea. From the terraces, a Severe descent or a short abseil gains the massive jammed boulders in the zawn-bed. This approach gives impressive views of The West Face but is lengthy. Heavy swell makes it dangerous.

A short pleasant route lies directly above the abseil spike. It gives some of the flavour of Great Zawn without the commitment.

Ivory Tower   30 metres   Very Severe   (6.86)
1 12m. 4b. Climb the slabby wall a metre or so right of the abseil pinnacle and move left to a perched block below the upper arête. Move up the steep little crack on the right to a ledge.
2 18m. 4a. Walk around the corner to the right and climb the flaky crackline past a protruding block to finish up the wall above.

GREAT ZAWN ~

SEAWARD FACE

1	Side Show	HVS
2	Exit Route	HS
3	Smiley Culture	E3
4	The Variety Show	HVS
5	Great Zawn Chimney	E2
6	Zarathustra	E2
7	Green Cormorant Face	E2
7a	Green Cormorant Variations	
8	Deja Vu	E4

WEST FACE

9	The Dream	E3
10	Canute	E4

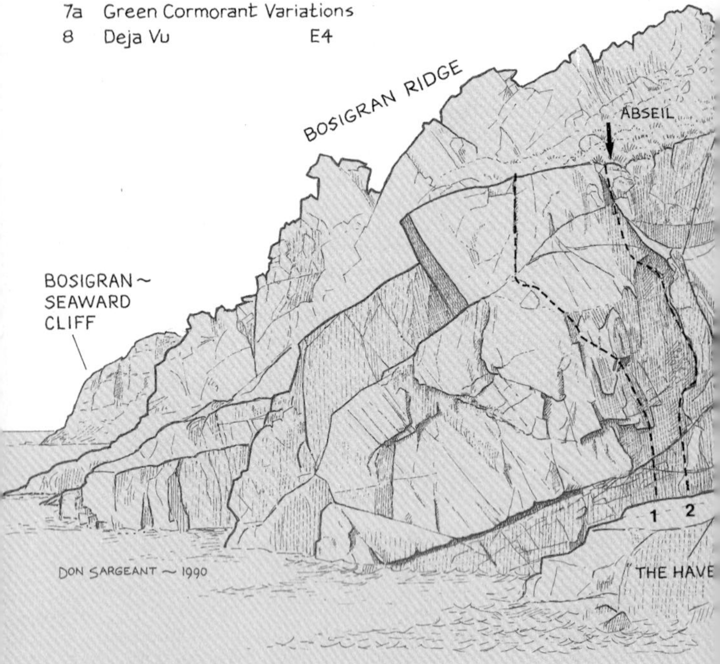

BOSIGRAN RIDGE

ABSEIL

BOSIGRAN ~
SEAWARD
CLIFF

DON SARGEANT ~ 1990

1 2

THE HAVE

N.B. Great Zawn is so deep and narrow that it is not possible to see the whole of Seaward / West Face from one viewpoint. The mouth of the zawn has been "widened" slightly in this drawing.

GREAT ZAWN

THE CREVASSE

The Seaward Face
The first few climbs start from The Haven.

Side Show   20 metres   Hard Very Severe 5a   (11.4.71)
Start below the vague thin crackline running up the short wall to the left of the abseil descent. Climb directly to the crack and then continue until it is possible to move left to a flake. Climb the smooth wall above to the platform.

Exit Route   20 metres   Hard Severe 4a
The broken corner in the general line of the abseil. Follow the corner past quartzy holds to a short steep section. Step right and climb a shallow groove; then move left and up to finish. Some looseness, which is being abseiled into submission.

Smiley Culture   27 metres   E3 5b †   (28.8.86)
Bold and serious. The smooth wall right of *Exit Route* is broken by the curving crack of *The Variety Show*. Climb over ledges and up an overhanging groove that leads to the curving crack. Continue up the crack (all so far as for *The Variety Show*); then move left onto the black-streaked wall and climb it direct with little protection.

★★**The Variety Show**   46 metres   Hard Very Severe   (25.5.58/23.5.70)
An excellent first pitch, only slightly let down by its continuation. Start below the curving crack in the wall right of *Exit Route*.
1 26m. 5a. Climb over ledges and up an overhanging groove to follow the tasty crackline to a horizontal break at 23 metres. Either continue directly up a steep crack, or move right and up to a small stance on slabby rock.
2 20m. 4c. Go straight up the slabby rock and climb the overhung corner on generous holds to follow the groove above.

★**Three Score Years and Ten, Amen**   35 metres   E6 6b   (3.5.93)
The almost fatally attractive arête to the right of *The Variety Show*. A protracted runout from a mediocre *RP*-cluster at half height will require a focused effort. Start at the bottom of a crack which runs up to the roof. Climb the crack, move left, and surmount the roof by a line of weakness. Move up for a metre or so, climb diagonally right to the arête, and follow this with difficulty and a rising fear count to the horizontal break. Resist the temptation to repeat the first ascensionist's descent and climb up left to belay. Continue up *The Variety Show* to escape.

Great Zawn Chimney   40 metres   E2   (30.8.56/8.69)
This takes the impressive tapering fault at the back of the platform. Slight protection and some shaky rock. Start at the left-hand side of the fault.
1 20m. 5a. Climb the left-hand side of the fault to a poor resting place at 15 metres. Follow a steep crack to exit from the chimney on the right to a stance on the slabby rock above.
2 20m. Climb the left-hand chimney above and exit through the needle's eye at the top to block belays.

★Zarathustra   46 metres   E2   (12.9.69)

Fine sustained climbing although the start can be damp. It takes the arête right of *Great Zawn Chimney*. Start at the right-hand corner of the fault of *Great Zawn Chimney*.

1 26m. 5b. Climb the corner for 5 metres to step right into a cramped corner. Traverse delicately right along a narrow slab to the arête and swing up and around onto the exposed edge of the *Green Cormorant Face*. Climb on good holds to a large flake; then step up left and follow a thin crack and shallow groove for 5 metres, from where a small incut flake up on the left can be reached. Move up and leftwards to belay as for *Great Zawn Chimney*.

2 20m. Take the right-hand chimney.

The following routes start from the famous Green Cormorant Ledge, which is reached from The Haven by a bold leap across a cleft, The Crevasse. The starting ledge can also be reached by a traverse with cunning use of back ropes. The leap to the ledge can be loosely protected by belaying but do not sell yourself short of loose rope when leaping. Above the starting ledge lies the crack-system of *Green Cormorant Face*, while up to the right is the black-streaked slabby wall of *Déjà Vu*.

★★Green Cormorant Face   45 metres   E2   (21.4.57/12.9.69)

A splendid classic for which committment is required. Jump across The Crevasse to the starting belays.

1 20m. 5a. From the right-hand end of the ledge, move upwards and slightly right to pass the overhang at its narrowest point. Climb to a large flake and move up to a horizontal crack. Then, either move right and up to a stance, or move left and up at the same standard.

2 25m. 5c. Follow the old peg crack that starts from the middle of the wall above the belay ledge to reach the black diagonal crack, which leads up to the left. Alternatively, pull onto the sloping ledge at the base of the black groove on the left, from which steep moves gain the black diagonal crack. This is at the top end of the grade. Follow the groove more easily to finish.

Variations

2a The Barber Variant E3 6a (5.74). Layback straight up the groove above the sloping ledge.

2b The Littlejohn Variant E2 5c (4.85). From the sloping ledge, move left and climb the left arête of the groove. Probably the easiest option of all.

★★★Déjà Vu   50 metres   E4 6a   (5.74)

Stylish main pitch with sparse, nervy protection. '... *suddenly one cannot retreat and it's fifteen thin feet to the micro-jugs...*' according to Pete Livesey. The climb takes the distinctive black slab in the centre of the wall above and to the right of the Green Cormorant Ledge. Leap to the ledge and belay at its far end.

1 20m. 5b. Move up and right to a groove (on *The Dream*). Climb left around the blunt arête and continue diagonally left to a short open-book corner, which leads to the belay ledge at the top of pitch one of *Green Cormorant Face*.

2 30m. 6a. Traverse right into the centre of the steep black slab, and climb directly and delicately to reach a slim ramp-line (on *The Dream*) that runs up leftwards. Follow this over the deep slanting crack in the small overhang above; then move right along the line of a horizontal crack to take the weakness in the wall above to a small stance (possible belay). Finish up slabs and blocks.

Green Cormorant Ledge
                    10 metres   Hard Very Severe 5b (1923/20.5.56)
This is the classic leap from The Haven to the Ledge, followed by the traverse into Great Zawn. Having gained the ledge, continue rightwards. Descend a greasy black corner (*The Dream* in reverse); then traverse rightwards on smooth and often wet rock to the huge boulders at the mouth of the zawn. The original traverse continued up a black slab and corner crack on the opposite side of the zawn.

The West Face
The West Face is the focus of Great Zawn climbing, with a roll call of long-established, outstanding routes like *The Dream*, which threads its elegant way up the powerful seaward arête, and its dark companion, *Liberator*, shadowing the inner wall. *The West Face* itself takes the central groove and crack-system, while a final change of mood comes with the right-hand section of the face where the attractive line of *Desolation Row* relaxes the steepness but not the sheer quality.

★★★**The Dream**   64 metres   E3   (12.68/26-27.4.72/6.76)
[Photos: rear cover and p.128b.] A truly 'great' route: strenuous, technical, and exhilarating. Start from the huge boulders at the mouth of the zawn.
1 12m. 5a. Traverse leftwards from the boulders and climb the greasy black corner to a ledge. (This ledge can be reached from The Haven approach, involving the leap to Green Cormorant Ledge and a traverse into the black groove.)
2 24m. 6a. Follow the groove above the belay, moving right under a small roof into a groove capped by overhangs. Climb this groove and then make hard moves rightwards and up to a horizontal break below a metre-wide roof. Clear the roof by a long-reaching swing up and left onto a slim steep ramp, and follow it delicately for 5 metres. Thin cracks are then climbed to a large horizontal break. Traverse right to the arête and move thinly around onto a small sloping stance shared with *Liberator* and *The Girdle Traverse*.
3 28m. 5c. Bold and strenuous laybacking leads to a shallow groove. From here, climb a crack in the lichenous wall to a large ledge beneath a V-shaped overhang (belay possible). Bear diagonally left to avoid the overhang and finish easily up a break.

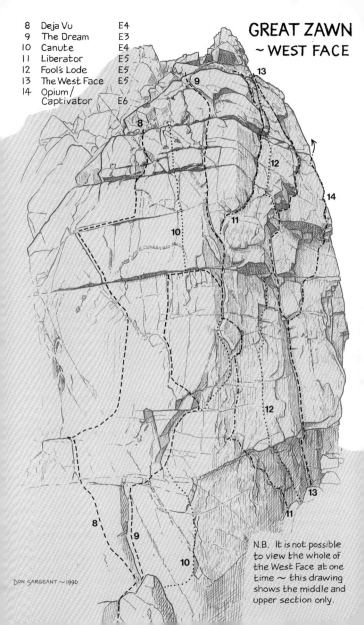

GREAT ZAWN
~ WEST FACE

N.B. It is not possible to view the whole of the West Face at one time ~ this drawing shows the middle and upper section only.

DON SARGEANT ~ 1990

Canute   65 metres   E4   (26.8.82)
An eliminate line based on the arête, and depending for much of its length
on *The Dream* and *Liberator*, but with some hard independent sections.
Start as for *The Dream* from the huge boulder wedged across the foot of
the zawn.
1 12m. 5a. Traverse leftwards and climb the greasy black corner to a
small ledge in the groove just right of the ledge on pitch 1 of *The Dream*.
2 26m. 5c. Step right onto the arête proper and climb up to some deep
holds; then follow a thin crack on the left side of the arête to join *The
Dream* 5 metres below the overhang on pitch 1. Climb to the overhang
and step right to join *Liberator*, which is followed until it is possible to
ascend leftwards under an overlap beneath the sloping stance of *Liberator*
(hard) to regain the arête. Move right to the *Liberator/The Dream* stance.
3 27m. 6a. Move left around the arête, reversing *The Dream*, and
continue left to the foot of a very thin crack starting in the overhang 3
metres left of the arête. Make hard moves up the crack to a horizontal
break, and continue up easier cracks to broken ground.

★★★**Liberator**   66 metres   E5   (24-25.5.70/4.76)
A technical and strenuous masterpiece, following the right side of the
seaward arête. Start at a black-and-white-streaked, ragged crack that runs
up to the long overhang in the wall. The distinctive layback crack of *The
West Face* is 10 metres to the right.
1 36m. 6a. Make hard moves up the crack and pull up to a large
foothold on the left. Traverse left with difficulty and cross a groove; then
move up to clear the roof onto the wall above. Climb diagonally left to
gain a small ledge close to the arête (used on early ascents as an
uncomfortable stance). Step right to an undercut hold and climb past
another undercut hold until beneath a small triangular overhang. Move
right for a metre; then go up and finger-traverse back left to belay on the
small sloping stance shared with *The Dream*.
2 30m. 5c. Take the overhung layback cracks above into the smooth
groove. Traverse right below the overhang to a large incut foothold and
follow the thin slanting crack to the horizontal fault below a sharp groove
(restricted belay possible). Climb the groove and crack above, moving left
at the top to avoid a grassy exit.

★★★**The Dream – Liberator Connection**   67 metres   E3
This is a logical – and magnificent – combination taking the first two
pitches of *The Dream* and the second of *Liberator*.

★**Fool's Lode**   60 metres   E5   (6.77)
A hard and serious eliminate line sketched up the wall between *Liberator*
and *The West Face*. Start below and left of the distinctive layback crack of
The West Face.
1 30m. 6a. Climb diagonally left until under the roof. Move left to a point
just before the roof ends. Pull over the roof and follow the excellent crack
in the middle of the wall above, moving right at the top to a good

foothold. Climb straight over the roof above; then move right into the smooth groove of *The West Face* to belay.

2 30m. 6a. Traverse left around the lip of the roof at the top of the groove to gain a small ledge on *Liberator* pitch 2. Step back right and follow a thin crack, trending right at the horizontal break, to reach a lichenous rib that leads up to the left-hand side of a prominent roof. Layback around the rib and continue straight up the wall to block belays.

★★★The West Face   55 metres   E5   (12.6.57/1975)

Pure power on an unrelenting line that takes the groove system in the centre of The West Face wall. Start directly below the overhang that leads to the striking layback crack at the foot of the grooves.

1 21m. 5c. Climb the black wall and swing up into the start of the crack. Climb the crack until it is possible to break out right beneath a blunt-nosed overhang and move up to a small square stance beneath a large overhang.

2 24m. 6b. Traverse left and climb the smooth-sided groove above until it begins to overhang. Break rightwards through the crack into a restricted corner on the right. Move right under a roof and climb up into a second corner. Follow the crack rightwards to a good belay.

3 10m. Climb easily up the crack to the top.

★★Opium/Captivator   55 metres   E6   (6.70/8.89)

A late 80s inspiration, freeing the aid line of *Captivator*.

1 21m. 5c. The West Face pitch 1.

2 24m. 6c. Climb the groove above and traverse right to a ledge (serious). Continue direct to a horizontal break and climb over the roof on the left. Climb the gritstone-style 'pod' above by a technical thrutch to a good stance shared with *The West Face*.

3 10m. Climb the easy crack above.

Variation

3a 15m. 4b. Step up to the right and follow the diagonal fault up rightwards to grass slopes.

★The Girdle Traverse   70 metres   E2   (26.8.69)

Fine positions on a high line across The West Face with a short, well-protected crux. Start from jammed boulders below a groove with a gently-angled black left wall 15 metres up from the start of *The West Face*.

1 30m. 5c. Move up the slabby black wall and gain a line of handholds on a section of wrinkled rock which leads to *The West Face*. Cross the groove and continue, using undercuts, until forced down where they end. Traverse left at the same level until a difficult finger-traverse enables the stance of *Liberator* to be gained.

2 17m. 5b. Move left around the arête until it is possible to climb down to the ramp of *The Dream*. Follow this to reach a deep slanting crack, and continue left below this to a good ledge above the hard section of *Green Cormorant Face*.

3 23m. 4a. Step down to the left and make a gently rising traverse to an overhung corner. Pull over this to block belays. Scramble to finish.

GREAT ZAWN ~ WEST FACE
(UPPER SECTION)

Access from the Bosigran Ridge path
can be made via the gap below
the prominent spiked-pillar
on "Western Ridge".

18

X
ABSEIL SPIKE

19

17

steep grassy terrace.
(Exit from West
Face routes.)

16

14   15

ABSEIL
CORNER

GREAT ZAWN ~ HEADWALL

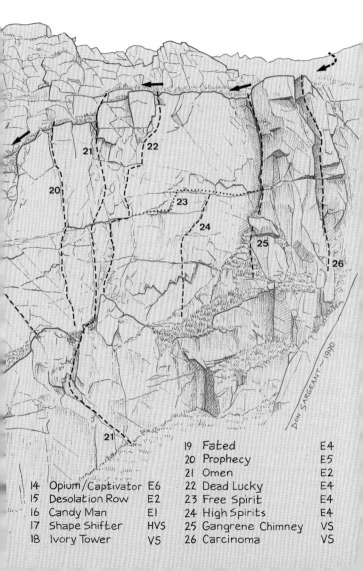

DON SARGEANT ~ 1990

				19	Fated	E4
				20	Prophecy	E5
				21	Omen	E2
14	Opium/Captivator	E6		22	Dead Lucky	E4
15	Desolation Row	E2		23	Free Spirit	E4
16	Candy Man	E1		24	High Spirits	E4
17	Shape Shifter	HVS		25	Gangrene Chimney	VS
18	Ivory Tower	VS		26	Carcinoma	VS

Something in the Air   43 metres   E3 5c   (5.86)
Start as for *The Girdle Traverse* from jammed boulders below the groove,
15 metres up from the start of *The West Face*. Climb the groove direct to
clear the overhang and break right onto the small arête on the right
(*Desolation Row*). Climb up the arête and onto the slabby wall above; then
make a thin and bold traverse left to reach the groove/diagonal crackline
of *Opium/Captivator*. Finish up this.

★★Desolation Row   36 metres   E2 5b   (14.9.69)
A fine subtle pitch of sustained delicacy following the thin cracks to the
right of the arête between the main wall of the West Face and its
easier-angled right-hand section. Conventional protection is sparse but
camming gear has made things less worrisome. Start at a shallow groove
5 metres above and to the right of the jammed boulders that mark the
start of *The Girdle Traverse*. Gain the groove from the right and climb to a
small overhang at its top. Step left and climb the rib to reach the
right-hand end of a large overhang (poor peg). Move up and right to
follow a thin crack-system to good footholds. Continue direct past a
sloping foothold to the final difficult section, which leads boldly to the
grassy terrace left of the abseil spike.

☆Hurricane   35 metres   E4 6a †   (1.9.90)
Sustained and intricate with a serious lower section, this pitch takes a line
between *Desolation Row* and *Candy Man*. Follow *Desolation Row* to the
small overhang but continue direct to a peg. Difficult moves lead to a
good hold. Traverse right to below a thin crack. Several hard moves lead
to a good ledge, from where a runner can be placed in *Candy Man*. Move
up diagonally left from the ledge to gain a shallow left-to-right groove and
follow it to the grassy slopes above.

★Candy Man   34 metres   E1 5c   (6.73)
Less stylish than *Desolation Row* but a good pitch nevertheless, it takes the
line of vague cracks up the centre of the slabby wall. The lower part can
often be greasy. Start beneath the centre of the wall, where an indistinct
crackline leads over two ledges. After hard moves at 10 metres, continue
pleasantly in a more or less direct line to the grassy terrace.

Ocean Rain   34 metres   E2 5b   (1985)
A good honest pitch taking the crack to the right of *Candy Man*.

Shape Shifter   36 metres   Hard Very Severe 5a   (23.6.77)
This climbs the cracks just left of the abseil descent. Start at a large sloping
ledge at the foot of the abseil corner. Climb the groove to the overhang;
then step left to gain thin cracks and follow these to a niche on the right.
Move up right to a sloping ledge, step left, and climb the crack until it is
possible to move right to gain the final slab. Climb this to a grassy exit to
the terrace.

★Scalpel 55 metres Hard Very Severe (30.5.70)
An exciting traverse across the *Desolation Row* wall and the upper section of *The West Face*. It is quite challenging for the grade. Start at the foot of the abseil entry.
1 28m. 5a. Follow the thin horizontal crack that leads from a sloping grassy ledge to a small ledge at the junction with *Desolation Row*.
Continue traversing more delicately and with slight protection around a blunt arête to the large stance on *The West Face*.
2 15m. 4b. Traverse left along exposed horizontal cracks; then swing up to a ledge on the arête and a good stance below an overhang.
3 12m. Climb diagonally left to avoid the overhang, and then go up an easy break to the top.

The Headwall

This is the steep headwall to the right of the abseil entry. It can be damp but catches more sun than the other faces. *Omen* takes the thin crackline above a prominent sharp-pointed spike about half-way up the centre of the face. To approach the routes it is possible to either abseil in from the spike above *Shape Shifter* and then climb the first pitch of *Omen* or abseil straight to the ledge at the end of that pitch.

★Fated 20 metres E4 6b (4.4.88)
A compelling, poorly-protected line taking the prominent leftward-slanting black dyke that runs up the left side of the headwall. Start at the right-hand end of a sloping grassy ledge 5 metres left of the spike. Follow the dyke to a big hold at 12 metres (peg). Move back and up left (or left and up in dry conditions) and continue steeply up the dyke on better holds to finish.

★★Prophecy 20 metres E5 6a (4.4.88)
A sustained line of grooves and cracks to the left of *Omen*. Start below and 3 metres left of the prominent spike. Climb to a peg in the first break and continue steeply and boldly to better holds and a resting place at the half-way break. Climb the line of shallow cracks above until it is possible to exit left to a sloping ledge. Finish up the grassy and lichenous groove above.

★Omen 36 metres E2 (14.9.69)
Strenuous classy climbing on the top pitch. Start directly below the prominent spike by a leftward-curving ramp-line.
1 15m. 4b. Follow the ramp to its end and climb a slabby groove to ledges. Walk to the spike on the right.
2 21m. 5b. Step left from the top of the spike and follow the steep broken crack to a horizontal break. A difficult move is followed by strenuous moves on better holds, leading to a chockstone in a shallow chimney. Climb over this to finish.

★Dead Lucky   27 metres   E4 6b   (26.5.88)
Dramatic wall climbing to the right of *Omen*. Climb the groove above the
spike past two pegs to a horizontal crack that runs across the wall. Move
right (peg), and then climb steeply until a long reach gains a good hold
just below the next break. Climb the crack on the right and the V-groove
above to finish.

★Free Spirit   55 metres   E4   (25.5.88)
A committing and wildly strenuous line traversing the wall right of *Omen*
into the grubby cleft of *Gangrene Chimney*.
1 40m. 6a. Climb the groove on the right past two pegs to the horizontal
traverse-line. Continue rightwards past two pegs to a third where a move
up gains the start of an upper faultline (peg). Continue traversing
rightwards past a peg near the end of the faultline to make committing
moves into the chimney (thread belay).
2 15m. 4a. Finish up the chimney.

★High Spirits   30 metres   E4 6a   (4.6.90)
Start about 10 metres to the right of the pointed spike, at a short crack.
Climb the crack and move left to two poor pegs. Continue steeply past
another peg to the break of *Free Spirit* and traverse right along the break
into *Gangrene Chimney* to belay. Finish up the chimney.

Seamantics   24 metres   E6 6c †   (24.3.92)
The thin black seam that slices across the headwall left of *Gangrene
Chimney*. Start 3 metres down and left of the base of the chimney, at a
thread belay. From a short line of finger-pockets, make a long reach for
the break (peg on *High Spirits*). Move left and reach over the bulge to the
base of the seam (peg). Follow the seam (crucial blind pre-placed *RP3*)
past three pegs (third one minimal) to an exit groove on the left.

There are two short climbs at the back of the zawn. **Gangrene Chimney**
(18 metres Very Severe 4a 19.4.57) is the green-walled chimney that
borders the headwall. Exit left at the top to belay well back. **Carcinoma** (18
metres Very Severe 4c 6.70) takes the chimney on the other side of the
buttress right of *Gangrene Chimney*.

The East Face
Starved of sunlight, often damp, and with a broken and vegetated left
section, the East Face is literally overshadowed by the zawn's other walls. At
its seaward end, however, is the striking line of *Xanadu*. Just the view of The
West Face from the 'domed' base of *Xanadu* makes the zawn worth visiting.

Garden Walk   47 metres   Very Severe + A1   (20.8.56)
A generally wet route with much vegetation although the line has some
style. Start at the centre of the left-hand section of the face beneath a huge
flake, the grassy top of which lies below a black-streaked slab.

Fun Curve Factory (E5), Carn Vellan
Climber: Ken Palmer   Photos: Nick Hancock

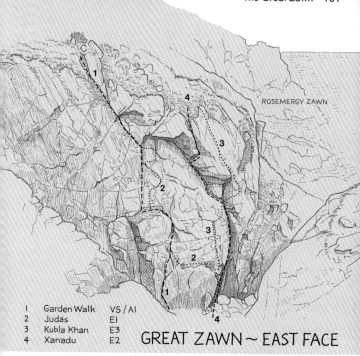

1 Garden Walk   VS / A1
2 Judas   E1
3 Kubla Khan   E3
4 Xanadu   E2

ROSEMERGY ZAWN

GREAT ZAWN ~ EAST FACE

1 24m. Peg up vertical cracks until free climbing on large holds leads to the wide crack on the right side of the flake. Continue to belays on top of the flake.

2 23m. 4b. Climb directly on aid for 6 metres; then free climb a corner to exit right to a grassy finish and block belays.

☆**Clueless**   52 metres   E2 †   (8.8.98)
A devious start leads to a line between *Judas* and *Xanadu*. Start right of *Garden Walk*, below the right-hand side of the large flake taken by *Judas*.
1 40m. 5b. Climb up for 2 metres, step rightwards to a ledge, and move up to the right to join *Judas* on its ramp. Take the short groove on the left as for *Judas* before moving right onto another ledge. Climb straight up past three undercut flakes, until delicate climbing leads up right to a stance shared with *Xanadu* just below the overhang.
2 12m. 5a. *Xanadu* pitch 3.

★Judas   73 metres   E1   (30.3.70)

This takes a line up the centre of the slabs left of the obvious corner of *Xanadu*. Start at the base of the initial groove of *Xanadu*.

1 15m. 5a. Climb the groove for 6 metres and then follow the ramp on the left to a short groove. Climb this to a stance.

2 15m. 4c. Move leftwards and slightly upwards along the ledge system. At the left end, move up for 3 metres to belays on the grass-topped flake.

3 28m. 5b. From the left end of the ledge, move up to an undercut flake; then traverse right to a short corner. Move back left, following the higher line on undercuts. Climb over a bulge to good flakes and follow a black seam in the slab to the big overhang. Traverse left to a small stance beneath the roof.

4 15m. 4b. Step up left into a corner and follow this to exit right onto steep grass.

★★Kubla Khan   60 metres   E3   (11.8.84)

High in the grade. Start at the base of the initial groove of *Xanadu*, below the leftward-slanting ramp on its left.

1 30m. 6a. Climb the ramp to the first horizontal break. Move rightwards to a narrow groove and climb it to a flat hold. Move back leftwards to another horizontal break and climb the crack on the right to gain the slab above. Traverse rightwards to a stance shared with *Xanadu* just below the overhang.

2 30m. 5b. Move onto the right arête and climb up. Traverse left onto a narrow slab above the overhung niche. Follow this leftwards to the foot of a crack which leads up the larger slab to the top. Belay well back.

★★★Xanadu   60 metres   E2   (5.68/4.70)

[Photo p.160a.] Exhilarating and full of character; a Great Zawn classic, lacking only regular sunlight. It takes the long stylish groove at the seaward end of the face before bearing left beneath the line of overhangs to break through them via an overhanging crack. The initial groove is often greasy, especially early in the day. Start below the leftward-curving groove.

1 30m. 5b. Climb the groove, which is at the top end of the grade in its mid section. (The pitch can be varied by moving out on the right wall.) A large flake is reached at 20 metres. Continue on improving holds to a cramped stance in the niche below the overhang.

2 18m. 5b. Move left to a blunt spike. Make hard moves up and left, and traverse on to the foot of a black seam in the slab below the main overhang. Continue left to a small stance beneath the roof.

3 12m. 5a. Step back right and pull across the overhanging wall of a groove and into a wide crack, which is climbed past a chockstone to a grassy finish.

Piledriver   88 metres   Very Severe (1 pt aid)   (29.12.69)

A right-to-left girdle of the East Face. Start from the grassy slopes right of the face.

1 12m. Traverse easily left along ledges to a good stance at the edge of the face just down and to the right of the large sharp flake on *Xanadu*.

2 21m. 4c. Climb up to the flake and hand-traverse it to reach the *Xanadu* groove. Use the rope to descend 3 metres down the groove until it is possible to traverse left to the long narrow ledge that divides the slab.
3 10m. 4a. Climb the wide crack on the left to belay on top of the grassy ledge.
4 45m. Traverse left into a gully and climb the grassy rib on the left to the top. Not much fun.

Heart Attack Machine   54 metres   Hard Very Severe (2 pts aid) (6.70)
The most seaward route on the East Face. Start from the boulders at the base of the zawn.
1 30m. 4a. Follow the curving black corner to a belay 5 metres right of the sharp flake on pitch 1 of *Xanadu*.
2 24m. 5a. Climb the short crack and bear leftwards to an overhanging groove. Use two pegs to gain a grassy ledge, and continue up a short corner to belay well back.

Horseman's Zawn

Immediately west of the grassy rib on the western edge of Great Zawn is a small zawn with a steep back wall. Two excellent routes take striking lines up the wall. Approach as for Great Zawn Left Hand Approach, to move left (facing out) from half-way down the steep grassy rib. The base of the wall is best reached by abseil from substantial blocks above the steep grass that crowns the wall. The abseil ropes are also useful for the finish up the steep grass. Joined ropes are advised for the abseil. The first route starts just left of the centre of the wall, at a corner.

☆☆**Ride a Cock Horse**   33 metres   E5 6b †   (3.6.90)
Climb the corner for 5 metres and then move right to a ledge. Climb the short crack on the right to another ledge. Step up onto the big flake and move left to a groove (peg). Make difficult moves to gain the groove, which is climbed with difficulty past a peg until a good hold is reached above the top of the groove. Climb the wall above to a horizontal break and traverse right along this to the final crack of *The Fifth Horseman*, which is followed to a ledge. Belay using the abseil rope if available, or a *Friend 4* and large nuts. Finish up the steep grass with care or by using the abseil rope.

☆☆**The Fifth Horseman**   33 metres   E5 6a †   (29.8.88)
An excellent and sustained piece of climbing. Start 5 metres right of the start of *Ride a Cock Horse* and climb a thin crack direct to the big flake on that route. From the flake, climb a thin crack (jammed wire) with difficulty to an overhang (peg). Pull over the overhang to a good ledge. Climb the wall directly above(peg) to a crack, which is climbed to a ledge on the left. Belay using the abseil rope if available, or a *Friend 4* and large nuts. Finish up the steep grass with care or by using the abseil rope.

Rosemergy Cove (Granite)   OS Ref 414 366

Outlook: North-east.
Tidal. Accessible for about 3 hours either side of low water. Affected by heavy swell.
Coastguard Identity: Rosemergy Cove.
Enviromental Issues: SSSI. A very sensitive area for both plant life and sea-birds; see notes for Rosemergy Ridge area (page 166).

This is the dark-cornered zawn that lies about 150 metres west of the mouth of Great Zawn and beyond Horseman's Zawn. It is reached at low tide by following the Great Zawn Left Hand approach to sea-level ledges from where a traverse is made via a slab (Very Difficult), to some other ledges. These lead to the east-facing zawn wall which, although often damp, sports some fine climbs. The long groove on the left-hand side of the face is followed by *Dylan*. The base of the wall can also be reached by abseil at low tide and in quiet sea conditions.

The first two routes can be climbed at high tide, but with quiet seas, from a low ledge which can be reached by abseil. They both start at a thin crack just left of a long groove on the left-hand side of the face. The groove itself is taken by *Dylan*.

★Ordinary People   30 metres   E4 6a   (30.5.89)
An excellent face and crack climb up the steep white upper wall of Rosemergy Cove. Climb the thin crack to a small overhang and pull directly over this to a ledge (peg above). Move left to a small ramp and follow it to the right. Continue diagonally right to below a peg at the foot of the headwall. Climb past the peg to the break. Step left and continue up (passing a peg) in a fine position to the top.

★★Lunar Sea   33 metres   E3 5c   (7.5.89)
Fine atmospheric climbing up the walls to the left of the *Dylan* groove. Climb the thin crack to a small overhang and pull directly over this to a ledge (peg above). Move left and up to climb diagonally leftwards across the wall to a poor peg. Continue direct via cracks and finish up a grassy slope.

★Dylan   30 metres   Hard Very Severe 5a   (13.9.69/7.5.89)
An interesting pitch. It finishes on steep grass and may merit an abseil entry, so that the abseil rope can be used for security on the exit. The climb follows the long groove on the left-hand side of the face. Start at the base of the groove. Climb the right-hand crack to a ledge. Follow the groove to a bulge and continue with increasing difficulty to the capping overhang. Move up right to a small ledge. Follow the slab above and finish with care up a grassy ramp.

★Sea Sharp 33 metres E2 5b   (7.5.89)
A pleasant but poorly-protected climb taking the groove to the right of
Dylan. Climb the first 9 metres of *Dylan*; then traverse right to the groove,
which is climbed to its top.

Palm Beach 33 metres E3 5b/c   (1993)
This takes the fine open arête between *Sea Sharp* and *Run for Your Wife*.
Climb *Zebedee* until just below the overhang of *Run for Your Wife*. Follow a
line of good pockets out left to a blunt flake and then step left to the arête.
Climb for 2 metres to a peg in a ledge on the left. Continue up the arête to
finish up an easier-angled ramp.

Zebedee 34 metres Hard Severe   (14.4.68)
There is a Z-shaped overhang half-way up the face to the right of the
groove of *Dylan*. Beneath the overhang is a jamming crack.
1 17m. 4b. Climb the crack over a small lip to a restricted stance.
2 17m. Follow a slab up to the right; then traverse right until a step down
leads to a groove, which is climbed to the top.

★Run for Your Wife 35 metres E3   (28.8.88)
A stylish second pitch taking the Z-shaped overhang on the left.
1 17m. 4b. *Zebedee* pitch 1.
2 18m. 5c. Climb to the overhang to place protection, and step back
down to a flat spike. Climb across the wall to the left and move up to gain
the slab above the overhang. Climb the slab and groove above to finish.

Sea Thief 30 metres E4 5c   (28.8.88)
Strenuous climbing up the overhanging crack to the right of *Zebedee*.
Climb cracks easily to the overhanging crack and move up this (peg) to the
slab above. Climb the slab and finish up the thin crack in the headwall.

Florence 30 metres Very Difficult   (14.4.68)
The corner crack to the right of the face. Climb the corner keeping to the
slabs on its right to finish right of the tower up a short wall and crack.

Dougal 30 metres Very Difficult   (2.9.68)
Start just right of *Florence*. Climb a crack to gain a smooth, light-coloured
niche on the right. Climb left out of the niche and bear diagonally right to
the broken arête, which is followed to belays.

Black Rabbit 30 metres Severe 4a   (29.5.89)
A line up the thin black crack at the extreme right-hand end of the slab of
Dougal. Start from a sloping ledge at sea-level and climb the crack to the
ridge, which is followed to its top.

Rosemergy Ridge Area (Granite) OS Ref 413 366

Outlook: North-west.
Tidal at the base of Window Ridge and Brandys Zawn Wall. Non-tidal at
Monolith Slab.
Coastguard Identity: Brandys.
Enviromental Issues: The Rosemary Ridge to Trevowhan Cliff area is an
SSSI and apart from Trevowhan Cliff is owned by the National Trust. The
area is very rich in numerous species of south-western flowering plants,
lichens, mosses and liverworts. There are important wet flushes, mires, reed
beds and other fragile habitats here. Vulnerable plant life include Bluebell,
Heath Spotted Orchid, Royal Fern, Sea Spleenwort, Marsh Cinquefoil, Bog
Asphodel and Cotton Grass. This is also a major sea-bird breeding-area,
and protected birds breed in the Great Moor Zawn/Trevowhan Head area.
This is a remote and particularly beautiful piece of coastline of great
environmental value. There is a long tradition of climbing here with some
excellent routes that are not intrusive provided the climber isn't either. Large
numbers of birds nest here and it is best avoided in the nesting season.

Approach from Porthmoina Cove, Bosigran, by following the coast path
west for about one third of a mile, until a walled mine shaft is reached. From
here, a track leads seawards to the top of a rocky carn (Osborne Carn). A
fisherman's path leads down grassy slopes on the right side of the Carn
(facing out). Rosemergy Ridge is on the right and at its base is the obvious
Monolith Slab (more wall than slab). Directly below the slab is Brandys
Zawn, flanked on its right by Window Ridge and on its left by Brandys Zawn
Wall below the distinctive Brandys Zawn Pinnacle.

Monolith Slab
First explored in 1906, the front of the slab finally yielded some fine pitches
in 1956.

Rosemergy Ridge (Ordinary Route)   59 metres   Very Difficult (1906)
1 20m. Climb the chimney on the left side of Monolith Slab and belay
where the slab meets the ridge.
2 39m. Follow the ridge to a gap. Descend this and climb the wall and
crack opposite. Scrambling follows.
An alternative first pitch takes the wide chimney on the right of the slab
(Difficult).

Peswar   18 metres   Hard Very Severe 5a   (27.5.56)
Top end of the grade. Start below the centre of the slab, just left of a
jagged crackline. Climb up for 3 metres; then traverse delicately left to a
crack near the left edge of the slab, and climb the crack to a niche and on
to the top of the slab.

★When the Music Stops 18 metres E2 5b (11.9.88)
A fine, strenuous line starting as for *Peswar* and continuing directly up the centre of the slab and through the small overhang at mid height. Slight protection.

Try 20 metres Very Severe 4c (27.5.56)
Climb the left-hand of two jagged cracks on the right side of the slab to a niche on the left and continue up the lichenous crack.

Deu 20 metres Very Severe 4c (27.5.56)
Climb the right-hand crack to the niche and continue up the lichenous crack.

Onen 18 metres Very Severe 4c (27.5.56)
Climb the thin crack on the right flank of the Monolith to a ledge that leads around into the backing chimney at 6 metres. Step up to the left and make a thin move up the crack to reach up and left to a good hold. Continue past a large hollow flake and move right and up a slab.

Window Ridge Zawn

This is the dark, sea-stained, corner zawn, to the east of Window Ridge. Approach by following a faint track eastwards from Monolith Slab for 100 metres before dropping down left to an easy-angled black slab that leads down to the zawn. The facing wall has an obvious 'window' feature, and some resident shags. At its base is the Moon Pool, a rounded pool isolated at low tide. The back wall of the zawn is steep and 'hot-coloured'. The climbs here have a rare character.

Shadow Line 27 metres E1 5a (24.9.87)
A traverse-line from the top of the slab across the back wall with sparse protection. From ledges, climb easily up and left before moving right up the ramp-line and across the wall. Just before the back corner, move up a left-slanting groove.

Moon Pool Wall 21 metres E1 5b (22.9.87)
Get your arms out for this one. Climb the overhanging crack in the middle of the back wall to a ledge and then follow the left-slanting crack, using flake holds on the wall.

★Louder than Bombs 30 metres E1 5b (14.7.87)
The striking line up the back corner of the zawn.

The dark brooding wall of Window Ridge was explored as early as 1922.

Sue 24 metres Hard Very Severe 5a † (22.9.87)
Low-tide start. Climb the awkward corner from the left end of the Moon Pool; then trend rightwards to the higher corner and up to the lime-slime ledge. Continue direct to the crest of the ridge.

Recess Climb   27 metres   Hard Very Severe 5a   (18.9.45)
Take the right-hand crackline near the seaward edge of the wall to the
lime-slime ledge, before traversing left and through the Window.
Variation
Recess Direct (25 metres Hard Very Severe 5a 1948) continues direct from
the ledge to the crest of the ridge.

Lower Monolith Ridge   40 metres   Hard Severe   (13.4.57)
The ridge from sea-level to the grass below Monolith Slab, reached by
scrambling down Window Ridge.
1 18m. Follow the line of the ridge to a belay.
2 6m. Climb a corner and a short slab on the left.
3 9m. Continue up a cracked wall.
4 7m. 4b. Finish up some rounded blocks. Provoking.

Brandys Zawn

This is the broad-mouthed zawn below and west of Monolith Slab. It is
flanked on the east by Window Ridge and by an attractive western wall
below the prominent 5-metre-high Brandys Zawn Pinnacle.

Descent is by the ridge below Brandys Zawn Pinnacle to a platform above
the 18-metre-high wall that faces Window Ridge. Abseil down the wall to
ledges. Several of the climbs on the landward sections of the zawn are
crowned by steep grass. Abseil down the route, and use the abseil rope to
exit up the steep grass where described below. The zawn is accessible for
three hours either side of low water and is wave-washed in heavy swell.

Stamp of Office   43 metres   E1 †   (12.11.89)
Varied though broken climbing starting up a black open-book corner in
the back wall of the zawn. Abseil approach can be made from the base of
Monolith Slab.
1 14m. 4b. Climb the corner taking care with some suspect rock.
2 29m. 5b. Climb a groove immediately behind the belay, and then step
right at 3 metres to go into an easy-angled groove. Continue diagonally
rightwards across a ledge to a wide crack above a small triangular niche.
Climb the crack to the next ledge and cross this to a fine steep crack in the
headwall. Climb this crack with difficulty; at its top, swing left and up into a
short chimney. Pull up left onto a small slab, and then pull over onto a
final small slab leading to a grassy finish.

★Seal of Approval   23 metres   E2 5c   (31.5.89)
An atmospheric line up the obvious groove in the back wall of the zawn.
Approach can be made by abseil from a huge block lying 30 metres west
of Monolith Slab. Abseil on joined ropes to a ledge at the foot of a corner.
Climb a crack just right of the corner; then step right to climb the overhang
on big holds to the foot of a groove. Climb the groove to its top and a
ledge on the left before finishing up steep grass using the abseil rope.

Jammy Dodger   15 metres   E2 5b   (4.9.93)
At the left-hand end of the back wall, below a crack left of *The Masochism Tango*, is a prominent open-book corner, which is a jamming and laybacking test-piece.

The Masochism Tango   21 metres   Hard Severe 4b   (6.6.89)
Finishes up Grade IV grass. Start at the left side of the north-facing wall of the zawn that is bounded on its right by a wide grassy gully running up from half height. Climb a short crack to reach a good ledge. Traverse out left to the arête and follow the short crack just right of the arête to reach the top and the grass exit.

Half Man Half Brandy Snap   15 metres   Hard Severe 4b   (25.6.89)
A pleasant pitch starting 3 metres right of *Masochism Tango*. Climb a steep wall and cracks to a ledge at 6 metres. Continue up the cracked wall above to step right at the top and finish up steep grass.

Devastating the Lilies   24 metres   Severe   (4.9.93)
Just to the right of the previous route is a prominent schorl crack. Climb this for 10 metres to an obvious traverse-line. Sally forth rightwards across ledges to finish up blocks at the top of *Brandys Zawn Chimney*.

Comfortably Dumb   27 metres   E1 5a/b   (6.6.89)
Start at a black crack slanting up to the left directly below the wide grassy gully. Climb the crack to the good ledge at half height (belay possible). Climb the deep crack rising from the right-hand end of the ledge. Tricky.

Clutching at Straws   22 metres   E2   (9.8.87)
1 11m. 5b. Start at a steep crack, left of a corner in the middle of the wall. Climb the crack and bear left to a good ledge and spike belay.
2 11m. 5a. Climb cracks and flakes from the left end of the ledge into a final groove and an 'exciting' exit up steep grass.

Brandys Zawn Chimney   18 metres   Hard Severe 4b   (1912)
Climb the distinctive black groove that flanks the right-hand side of the seaward wall.

A Gift of Wings   23 metres   E1 5b   (4.9.93)
Start at a leaning groove. Purposefully climb the groove to stand on the large flake to the right. Climb the face above to finish up the thin crack in the headwall.

Schnapps   27 metres   Hard Severe 4b   (28.5.89)
Climb the arête immediately right of the leaning groove and swing around into a slabby groove. Go up the groove to its top and move left across the black groove to reach parallel cracks, which are followed to finish up steep grass.

★**Opening Thrust**   18 metres   E1 5b   (14.6.87)
The left-hand of two cracklines.

★**Swing Out Sister**   18 metres   E3 5c   (9.8.87)
Strong technical moves up the right-hand crack.

Cereal Killer   18 metres   E3 5c   (4.9.93)
Ten metres right of the cracklines is a sentry-box leading to a
leftward-slanting crack. Climb up to the crack (peg) and make a difficult
move diagonally left to reach the easy-angled groove above. Finish up
this.

Osborne Carn

The slabby, west-facing wall of Osborne Carn can be climbed almost
anywhere at easy grades. There are a number of climbs on sea-level cliffs
below the Carn. Approach as for Rosemergy Ridge and Brandys Zawn to
reach sea-level to the west of these areas. The following routes climb slabs
on the far side of an obvious cave. Finishing belays are difficult to find due to
the loose nature of the ground so a **preplaced abseil rope** is a wise
precaution.

Blood Smear   25 metres   Very Difficult   (1992)
Start up the left-hand crack before moving left along a ledge and up to an
overhanging nose. Climb through the gap and finish up a corner.

Notch It   25 metres   Severe 4a   (1992)
Climb the crack above the square-cut recess. Move right and up to a
ledge; then delicately climb the slab above.

Flaky Toes   25 metres   Severe 4a   (1992)
Climb the crack on the right-hand wall of the recess via a flake. Continue
to a ledge and then finish up bulbous flakes.

Waterfall Slab   25 metres   Difficult   (1992)
This climb lies in a zawn with a waterfall some 200 metres west of the
main area and follows a line up the left-hand side of the slab.

Rosemergy Towers (Granite)   OS Ref 413 362

Outlook: West.
Non-tidal.
Coastguard Identity: Long Carn.
Enviromental Issues: SSSI. See the Rosemergy Ridge Area (page 166).

The Towers are easily accessible granite outcrops with entertaining little climbs only metres from the coast path. Ideal evening work as an alternative to the pub. Or as a prelude to the pub.

Approach from the small car-park with the square toilet-block on the coast road half-way between Bosigran Count House and Morvah at OS Ref 412 360 (beware car thieves). Bear left across the road from the car-park and take the path by the National Trust sign to a junction with the coast path. Turn right and go over the first rocky ridge. Rosemergy Towers with the distinctive *Hard Times* slab are visible 300 metres ahead and just below the coast path. Continue along the coast path until abreast of the towers; then strike left and follow a path down through deep heather and gorse until below the outcrop. The Towers are made up of typically fractured granite blocks. A huge slab of rock has broken away from the main face and now forms an impressive open-ended cave.

There is one recorded route on the stepped ridge 100 metres left (facing in) of the cave outcrop.

Goat's Ridge   36 metres   Very Difficult   (6.4.67)
1 9m. From the lowest point of the ridge, climb a steep V-corner and cracks to a ledge.
2 9m. Step left and climb a short wall to the top of the first tier. Follow the blocky arête to the foot of the second tier.
3 18m. Follow the arête; traverse left at half height.

The following routes are on the cave buttress.

Crabber's Nip   30 metres   Hard Very Severe   (20.7.83)
Below and to the left of the cave is a small buttress with an overhang at half height. Start at the lowest point below a short crack.
1 10m. 4a. Climb the crack and the slab above and then take the overhang by a move right. Bounce and scratch your way across the big heather ledge to a recess at the foot of the upper face.
2 20m. 5b. Steep and strenuous. Climb onto a ledge on the left and take the cracks in the steep wall above to another ledge. Make bold layback moves up the steep ramp above. The upper ledge can be gained by easier moves up the steep corner on the right of the recess.

Finger Winch   30 metres   Very Severe   (11.7.83)
Two interesting pitches. Start just outside the left-hand entrance to the cave.
1 10m. 5a. Climb the ragged crack in the wall and continue up the
rounded rock above to a belay ledge.
2 20m. 4c. Traverse left onto the steep wall and climb to a ledge (belay
possible). Climb the series of flake cracks above.

East Tower Arête   20 metres   Difficult   (6.4.67)
Climb the arête above and right of the belay ledge at the top of pitch 1 of
Finger Winch.

Funnel Chimney   36 metres   Very Difficult
1 18m. Udge and grudge up the inside of the cave close to its right-hand
end and squeeze (quickly) through a small skylight. A genuine 'Fat Man's
Agony'. Continue on the right to a smooth ledge and belay.
2 18m. Climb the right-hand arête of the face above.

The Soundings   18 metres   E2 5c   (24.6.95)
Start at the bottom left-hand edge of the *Hard Times* slab. Follow a
diagonal traverse rightwards to gain the slab proper. Delicate moves lead
to a blind finger-crack and the good protection on *Hard Times*. Continue
right and make a hard move to gain the prominent knob and then the top.

The Lucky Sea   15 metres   E2 5c   (5.92)
Start just left of *Hard Times*. Climb a shallow flake followed by a line of
weakness to a large ledge. Step right onto the upper wall, move up, and
escape leftwards to a rounded finish (crux). Very good climbing.

★Hard Times   15 metres   E1 5c   (11.12.83)
A bold micro-gem taking a direct line up the outside face of the slab
forming the cave/cleft. Climb cracks in the right side of the slab to where it
steepens at a break. Move up and left onto a foot-ledge and then
crimp-the-quartz up the rounded rock above.

NC Madness   11 metres   Very Severe 4c   (5.92)
Climb the right arête of the slab via an obvious low knob and then make a
long reach to get established on the arête itself. Finish up it.

Devious Do   12 metres   Hard Very Severe 5b   (5.92)
Start right of the slab below a wall with an obvious overhang above a slab.
Climb the short wall, slab, and overhang by its right side.

Nipper's Crab   15 metres   Severe   (14.8.84)
Start just right of the vegetated V-groove outside the right-hand end of the
cave. Climb a thin groove and make a neat move right before continuing
easily up the slab above into the right-hand gully. Finish up the right edge
of the wall above, passing a small overhang.

Flash Back   15 metres   Severe 4a   (23.6.83)
Start at the V-groove 6 metres right of the cave. Climb the groove and step right onto a slab. Climb this and the steep crackline above.

Sam's Greasy Thumbprint   15 metres   Severe 4a   (12.9.83)
Start at a depression just right of *Flash Back*. Climb the thin crack onto the slab and finish up the rounded cracks above.

Go Shorty   12 metres   E2 5c   (5.92)
Climb the wall right of the depression to a ledge and make a series of bold and very long reaches to gain the top.

Bolder Problem   11 metres   Hard Very Severe 5a   (6.3.83)
At the right-hand end of the face is a clean crack leading to a heathery ledge. Climb the crack onto the ledge and then make bold moves up the short groove on the right.

Whirl Pool Buttress (Granite)   OS Ref 410 362

Outlook: North-east and north-west.
Tidal. All routes are affected by heavy swell and rough sea. Whirl Pool Buttress rises from tidal sand, the depth of which can vary substantially from year to year. *Light in August* and several other routes on the seaward face of the buttress were first climbed when the sand build-up was high and when they could be gained comfortably from uncovered sand at low water of a spring-tide. At present there is sand in the bottom of the zawn but this can change dramatically after winter storms so be prepared to improvise. Abseil descent to hanging belays will be required if the sand is absent.
Coastguard Identity: Whirl Pool.
Environmental Issues: An SSSI which is a very sensitive area for both flora and fauna: see notes on Rosemergy Ridge area (page 166).

Approach from the small car-park with the square granite toilet-block on the coast road half-way between Bosigran Count House and Morvah at OS Ref 412 360. There is a history of car thefts from this car-park so take precautions. From the car-park, cross the road diagonally left until a National Trust plaque is located. Take the path leading seawards behind the plaque until it divides just before joining the main coast path. Take the short left-hand branch, cross the coast path, and follow a well-used fisherman's path down steep slopes towards the sea. On the right (facing out) is the rocky crest of Long Carn Ridge. Down to the left is the rocky top of Whirl Pool Buttress. For *Earthly Powers* and *Light in August* continue down the fisherman's track where it winds its way close to Long Carn Ridge. Below and left of the lower section of Long Carn Ridge is a rocky cove whose dark north-east-facing wall runs back into a high and narrow cave. *Earthly Powers* traces an exhilarating line up the main wall, while *Light in August* climbs the shallow corner which runs up the wall's seaward edge. If there is no sand in the zawn *Earthly Powers* can be started by scrambling down Long Carn Ridge to seaward and then by working back into the cove and crossing seaweed-covered rocks to tidal ledges below the left edge of the main face. Accessible two hours either side of low water but less so during neap-tides. The wall is crowned with steep grass and a **preplaced abseil rope** is advised to take the sting out of this, unless one is looking for the authentic North Coast experience of terror, incontinence, etc.

★★★Earthly Powers   60 metres   E2   (9.8.90)
A splendid climb that strikes its way up the impressive black wall left of *Light in August*. Start from the sand if this is possible or from the lower end of the seaweed-covered slabs at the left-hand side of the wall.
1 25m. 5c. Climb the shallow groove that trends up slightly leftwards to a flake/groove at 10 metres. Enter the groove; then make a wild move rightwards to gain a delectable jug. Swing around onto the main wall and move to the right down the obvious break for 6 metres before climbing direct to a ledge system. Continue to a sloping belay ledge.
2 35m. 5a. Move left from the end of the belay ledge to reach a diagonal crack leading up left. Follow the crack to where it fades; then move right and climb to a good hold. Continue with care over some perched blocks and finish either up steep grass, also with care, or pull up on the abseil rope.

★Caravaggio   65 metres   E3   (3.8.96)
A technical route which climbs an obvious right-to-left line of weakness. Start 5 metres right of *Earthly Powers*, below the line of weakness and a rounded foot-ledge at 2 metres (invariably wet).
1 30m. 6a. Climb with great difficulty to the obvious ledges at 10 metres. Move up left into the groove, step out left onto the short hanging wall, and gain the large flake. Brisk laybacking gains the left-hand end of the obvious ledge system.
2 35m. 5a. *Earthly Powers* pitch 2.

Chiaroscuro   34 metres   E1   (28.8.90)
Start as for *Light in August*.
1 22m. 5b. Climb for about 4 metres until a thin line of foot-ledges lead out left (often greasy). Follow the foot-ledges to a narrow ledge where friction improves. Avoid a shallow groove on the left (*Caravaggio*) and instead climb direct to an overlap. Make a long move over this to a good flake and continue to the sloping belay ledge on *Earthly Powers*. Climb the cracks above the ledge, and belay using the abseil rope.
2 12m. 5a. Climb the obvious vertical crack above the belay; then move right and use the abseil rope to scramble up the grass to the top.

★Light in August   30 metres   Hard Very Severe   (16.8.74)
A fine, well-protected climb. Start below the corner if sand build-up allows;
otherwise abseil from above and take hanging belays.
1 23m. 5a. Follow the crack to reach a pointed flake. Take the crack on
the right to a block belay.
2 7m. Climb the mixed rib above and scramble to a belay.

The next routes are on the north-west-facing wall of Whirl Pool Buttress
around to the right of *Light in August*. Approach is best by abseil from blocks
from the top of the buttress at low tide to reach the sandy floor of the zawn.
Some of the routes can be started from hanging belays. On the left side of
the face is a smooth gangway running up to the right into a chimney.

Fingers   36 metres   Hard Very Severe †   (11.6.83)
Start 2 metres left of the base of the smooth gangway.
1 18m. 5b. Climb a slippery left-facing corner and then a short
overhanging crack in the right wall. Continue up a ramp to a ledge.
2 18m. 5a. Climb a groove to an overhang, step left, and finish up
ledges.

Corkscrew   37 metres   Hard Very Severe 5a   (4.7.76)
Better and more difficult than it looks. Start below the smooth gangway.
Follow the gangway to the chimney and move up this using the groove on
the left. Above, good holds lead to a steep finish directly up a crack.
Continue over several ledges to a belay.

★★The Evil Empire   39 metres   E3 6a   (12.6.88)
A fine route with sparse protection in its lower half. The starting-belay is on
an abseil rope 3 metres above the zawn floor in a damp open groove in
the middle of the face. Climb the difficult groove; then move up and left to
a series of finger-ledges leading to the large roof (skyhooks used for
protection). A rightward descending traverse allows sloping ledges to be
gained. Move up via huge jugs and bear left to vertical cracks to finish at
an overhanging block.

Two Tribes   37 metres   E4 6a †   (26.6.88)
A powerful line taking the crack 5 metres right of the previous route. Start
from a hanging belay at 2 metres. Climb left of the crack to a peg and
swing down right to gain cracks, which are followed to a bulge. Take the
bulge on its right and move up to a ledge. Step left; then climb direct to
finish at the overhanging block.

★Ship of Fools   34 metres   E2 5b   (11.6.88)
The deep crack 3 metres right of *Two Tribes*. Belay at the base of the crack
at low tide, from where a greasy start leads to fine climbing.

★★The Aggressor   40 metres   E2   (16.8.74)
A fierce, bold route, taking the obvious crackline formed by a distinctive
flake at the right-hand end of the face. Camming gear has improved
protection possibilities. Start at dead low tide.
1 12m. 5a. Climb the chimney to a stance and belays.
2 15m. 5b. Move up to the hanging flake and layback around it to enter
the crack above. Strenuous jamming leads to a sloping ledge. Climb a
crack in the wall behind to a larger ledge on top of the flake.
3 13m. 5a. Move right and up to the top of a pile of blocks. Step up, and
then traverse left for 3 metres using a line of undercuts. Climb directly up a
rib to the top and scramble to belays.
Direct Start: 12m. 5a. Climb direct to the stance of pitch 1.

Great Moor Zawn (Granite)   OS Ref 409 361

Outlook: North-north-west.
Tidal on approach.
Coastguard Identity: Trevean Cliff.
Enviromental Issues: An SSSI which is very sensitive on account of bird
life and plants. See notes on Rosemergy Ridge area (page 166) for further
details.

Great Moor Zawn is a remote and spectacular place, hemmed in by a vast
curtain-wall of rock over 60 metres high. For most of the year it is damp and
dripping. There are two waterfalls into the zawn. One spouts dramatically
from the rim of the cliff in a free fall and is blown to and fro by the wind. The
other floods more quietly down the right-hand side of the zawn. Between the
two is a striking mass of orange and red granite, bearded with sedge and
grass. *Roraima* takes an imaginative and exotic line up this wall. Its only
ascent to date was in the drought year of 1976 and dry conditions are
advised.

Approach as for Whirl Pool Buttress, but go left (facing out) before the top
of the buttress is reached and descend a marshy slope to reach some wet,
slabby rock that drops down to sea-level. Descend with care until just above
a rounded tidal pool at sea-level. Traverse left to reach the mouth of a
narrow rock-channel, which runs back into the vast amphitheatre of the
zawn between its east wall and a bulging rocky fin that lies in the centre of
the zawn bed. At low tide, a boulder at the mouth of the channel is
uncovered and the central fin can be reached and traversed into the zawn.
Alternatively, an abseil can be made down the inner part of the east face
before it rises in height; either way, wet feet are likely. *Roraima* starts roughly
in the middle of the wall, below some leftward-rising diagonal faults by a
projecting cloven foot.

Roraima 75 metres E4 † (6.7.76)
A remarkable route with sparse protection and friable rock on the first pitch. A serious commitment for the truly adventurous.
1 45m. 5b. Climb for 6 metres; then go diagonally right, following a line of shallow grooves and sloping ledges to a good crack at 15 metres. Gain the steeply sloping ledge on the right and then go up a face crack until just below an overhang, where a difficult traverse leftwards is made to a rounded spike. Climb straight up the steep wall above for 6 metres; then step right to good holds leading to a large sedge-covered stance (spike and nut belays).
2 30m. 5b/c. Step up from the left end of the ledge and climb diagonally left to a rib. Move up to a turfy ledge on the left, step right into a shallow groove, and climb this. Take the short corner above and continue rightwards until it is possible to break left to finish. Belays well back.

Trevowhan Cliff (Granite) OS Ref 407 361

Outlook: North to north-west.
Tidal in New Cove, Trevowhan Zawn, Trevowhan Head, and Rabman Zawn. All these venues are seriously affected by swell and rough sea.
Coastguard Identity: Trevowhan Cliff.
Enviromental Issues: An SSSI which is very sensitive: see the notes regarding birds and plants given for Rosemergy Ridge Area (page 166) for further details.

This is a beautiful and remarkable area of cliff with an honourable tradition of adventurous climbing that began with Arthur and Elsie Andrews in the first years of the century. The cliffs are north-facing and often crowned with steep grass. They remain damp from seepage and sea-spray late into the year and are more amenable in summer and early autumn. All the sea-level cliffs pose challenging problems of approach. Extra ropes are advised for abseils and optional belays on grass finishes. The area is genuine 'wilderness' and encourages respect. It offers an environment strikingly different from that of the more traditional and accessible cliffs of Penwith.

Approach can be made as for Whirl Pool Buttress from the toilet-block car-park on the B3306 (beware of car thieves). On reaching the coast path, go west for approximately 400 metres to reach a boggy area that is laid with paving stones. From here, a square-cut rocky ridge can be seen on the cliff slopes ahead; this is Carn Fran-kas. Follow the coast path down rocky steps to a small stream that is crossed just before the path rises steeply to a wooden stile. The stream drains into New Cove and is often choked with vegetation. The same point can be reached from the coast road near Trevean Farm and Trevowhan Hamlet at a corner (OS Ref 408 356) a few metres north of the junction of the coast road with the road inland to Penzance. A rather boggy and overgrown right-of-way crosses the New Cove stream to follow its left bank to the junction with the coast path as above. From the coast path, the approach to New Cove, Trevowhan Zawn, and Trevowhan Head is made by following a faint path that leads down the left bank of the stream to seaward past some small patches of granite rubble. After a few metres the path rises steeply left and leads to thickly vegetated slopes where it becomes more distinct. Follow the path down the steepening slopes towards a flat-topped rocky promontory that juts out into the sea. West of the promontory is Trevowhan Head. East of the promontory is the small but impressive Trevowhan Zawn with the much larger New Cove lying further east again. The last two are separated by a grassy spur that extends onto a rocky lower ridge. For New Cove and Trevowhan Zawn, veer off to the right down this grassy spur.

New Cove
Descent. The zawn is tidal but the base of the climbs can be reached at low water, preferably on a spring-tide. Descend the ridge to sea-level, and then traverse back into New Cove (Difficult). An abseil entry is possible from the lower rim of the cove's east-facing wall.

Zawn Alley Rumble   52 metres   Very Severe †   (18.7.76)
This climb takes the crack system on the right-hand side of the east-facing wall to the left of a huge flake crack. Start beneath the crack system.
1 31m. 4c. Climb the wall and then a wide crack to a grassy stance. Thread and nut belays.
2 21m. 4c. Bear diagonally left up the wall above to the top.

The Bandsman   60 metres   Hard Severe 4b †   (7.76)
Start below the east-facing wall at the base of a conspicuous band of blackish rock (schorl) that runs diagonally left to right up the cliff. Follow the band until it rounds the end of the spur between New Cove and Trevowhan Zawn, and then follow a break to the top.

Trevowhan Zawn
Descent. The bed of the zawn is tidal but can be reached for three hours either side of low water when there is no swell. Climb down the west-facing wall (Difficult) or abseil from the rim.

The Good, the Bad, and the Gruesome   46 metres   E1 † (17.7.76)
Impressive name for an impressive climb that follows the splendid black corner between the zawn headwall and the protruding pinnacle buttress on its right. It finishes up a steep and very loose arête which is a cruel betrayal of the striking first pitch. The climb is a serious undertaking because of this and because of the lack of an adequate belay at the end of pitch 1. Barely adequate peg belays were used on the first ascent.

1 23m. 4c. Climb the corner to the top of the buttress. Very poor peg and nut belays.
2 23m. Climb the steep and very loose arête to the top and a block belay.

Trevowhan Head

The cliff lies just west of the rocky promontory. It is reached by following the path down to the promontory, and then by descending a short greasy gully (abseil descent recommended) that leads to a sea-washed platform which can be very slippery. The first feature is a steep brutal crack chopped off at the base. This is *Blackguard*.

Blackguard   15 metres   E1 5b †   (9.9.90)
Climb the steep crack strenuously.

Roughneck   17 metres   Hard Very Severe 5b †   (21.8.90)
This takes the groove capped by an overhang to the right of *Blackguard*. Harder than it looks. Climb the groove to the roof, and then squirm up into a cleft in a roughneck sort of way and finish direct.

Dilettante   24 metres   E2 5b †   (21.8.90)
The corner right of *Roughneck* is climbed steeply to a ledge at half height. From here, technical bridging leads up to where it is possible to break out left in an exposed position to finish.

I Am a Cormorant's Toilet   40 metres   Severe 4b   (30.7.98)
From ledges at the extreme right-hand end of the cliff, traverse rightwards into the zawn until a tricky, often wet, crack is reached. Make some bold moves up this and follow the slabs above avoiding the eponymous cormorant and exit onto grass. Belay at a bluff of rock. It is advisable to remain roped up to overcome the fearsome grass cornice above.

For Carn Fran-kas, Rabman Zawn, and Rabbit Carn, continue along the coast path from the New Cove stream. Cross the wooden stile and continue for about 150 metres to a square-cut stone stile just before some ruined mine buildings. A wire fence runs directly to seaward from the stile. On the right of the fence (facing out) stands one wall of a ruined building.

Caution: Do not enter ground on the right of the fence, where there are open mine shafts.

Follow the left side of the fence to seaward down parallel tracks for 80 metres until level with a small detached section of wall on the left that is crowned with earth and gorse. Cross the wire fence on the right and follow an indistinct path for a few metres onto a bare area of cliff slope. Continue across the brow of the slope (with Bosigran directly ahead in the distance) following small exposed boulders until the point where the slope drops away more steeply. Look for a single-slab wall that runs horizontally across the slope just below. Rabbit Carn is the rocky ridge lying well down to the left. Rabman Zawn lies directly below. Carn Fran-kas is the square-cut ridge, the top of which can be seen a short distance down to the right.

Carn Fran-kas

The buttress is reached by following the slab wall to the right to where it ends at a small, ivy-crowned ridge. Go down the left side of the ridge; then bear right to the narrow front face of the buttress.

Hidden Cornwall   24 metres   Hard Very Severe 5a   (5.85)
Luckily for the climbing world this is not a very accessible cliff. Some loose rock. Start at a detached lichenous block below a steep crackline leading to a small black niche. Climb to the niche and finish up the blocky lichenous ridge.

Rabman Zawn

Approach as for Carn Fran-kas but bear left from the base of the ivy-clad ridge to follow the zawn's eastern rim through deep heather; then go down between some rocky bluffs to a more level area studded with boulders. The climbs lie to seaward on the steep black walls directly below here. The base of the cliff may be sea-washed in swell and rough sea.

Descent is by abseil. Two separate ropes are required with a third rope advised for safeguarding the final steep grass exits of *Raiders…* and *Stella Maris*. From a position looking out to sea, the abseil rope should run down to the right of a distinctive, projecting slab on the cliff-top. (The preplaced safety-rope for *Raiders…* and *Stella Maris* should be lowered down to the left of the projecting slab.) An initial 35-metre abseil leads to a ledge beside a flat-topped flake-pinnacle. The second rope is anchored here for a further abseil to the sloping platform at the base of the wall. The cliff is dominated by a smooth black wall capped with overhangs. *Stella Maris* takes an impressive line up this wall. Right of this (facing in) is a black corner leading to a large ledge at 18 metres.

Stella Artois   27 metres   Very Severe 4b †   (20.8.90)
On the left (facing in) of the arrival platform is a step-up to a smaller platform. Start from the right-hand end of this. Climb the wall above direct on good though occasionally fragile holds to the flake-pinnacle. Climb a wide crack to the top of the pinnacle and pull over on large blocks to belay on the abseil rope.

✩✩✩**Stella Maris**   26 metres   E3 5c †   (20.8.90)
A sustained and powerful route. Start below the black wall at a short corner. Climb a series of short but difficult walls to reach a crack. Technical climbing on finger-jams leads to a ledge. Move right in a very exposed

position and then up to a roof-crack, which is followed spectacularly to the top. (Large cams are useful.) The preplaced rope is advised for belaying to avoid the frighteningly succinct request 'Make sure you take that runner out, I need it for the belay'.

Raiders of the Lost Zawn   27 metres   E1 5b †   (20.8.90)
Climb the black corner on the right of the black wall to reach the large ledge. Strenuous. Move right and climb a mix of grass, rock, and earth to the top of the ridge. The preplaced rope is advised for belaying.

Rabbit Carn
For Rabbit Carn, follow the slab wall to the left and go down the narrow vegetated slopes above the west wall of Rabman Zawn to reach a boulder-terrace below the broken east face of the Carn.

Sheerwater   33 metres   Very Severe 4c   (1978)
A pleasant climb. Take the steep crack on the left of the Carn's east face to a broad ledge (belay possible). Climb the good crack above (quite hard) to another ledge. Continue up the lichenous slab above, bearing left to finish up a short chimney.

Rabbit Gully   20 metres   Difficult   (1978)
The obvious gully right of the previous route.

Hlao-Roo   20 metres   Severe 4a   (1978)
Climb the crack and groove system to the right of *Rabbit Gully*.

Minions Mens Institute   20 metres   Very Difficult   (1978)
This takes a direct line up the arête between the east face and the seaward face of the buttress.

Bonny Black Hare   23 metres   Hard Severe 4b   (1978)
Start at the right-hand side of the seaward face. Climb a crackline to the black band that snakes across the face at mid height. Follow the band leftwards to the arête and make an interesting move left and up, bearing right to finish.

Carn Clough (Granite)   OS Ref 390 358

Outlook: West.
Tidal on lower cliff.
Coastguard Identity: Carn Clough.
Enviromental Issues: An SSSI which is a very sensitive area due to birds and plant life; see notes on Rosemergy Ridge Area (page 166).

Carn Clough is the last granite outpost before the black killas cliffs of Penwith's mining coast. There are some delightful pitches here, although lines are indistinct except for a few short routes on the higher cliff. Carn Clough overlooks the handsome Portheras Beach, where sun, sea, and sand outshine the climbing. Unfortunately, the beach is marred by pieces of dangerous wreckage from a vessel called the *Alacrity*, whose sharp-edged remains are periodically uncovered at low tide. Care should be taken if swimming off the middle of the beach.

Approach from the B3306 at an unmarked turn-off just west of Morvah at OS Ref 398 353. There is a convenient parking-field at Lower Chypraze Farm (small payment appreciated). From the car-park, follow the wide track that winds down towards the beach. Carn Clough is on the eastern side of the beach and is reached by following an indistinct path directly along the cliff edge from where the main track swings sharply down to the left above the beach at a wreck warning sign. There are two areas: Ridge and Lower Cliff, and Clough Buttress. The latter is the first obvious rocky feature reached along the approach path and is independent of the rest of the cliff. For The Ridge and Lower Cliff, continue beyond the rocky top of Clough Buttress and descend a path to seaward to a square-cut, perched block in a grassy bay facing Pendeen Watch. On the left side of the grassy bay (facing out), a narrow right-angled 'squeeze' leads through a jumble of rocks to The Lawn, a delightful grassy terrace. The top pitches of several climbs take the walls above The Lawn. For the start of the following routes, scramble down a wide break in the cliff directly below the grassy bay. From sea-level ledges at the base of the descent break, The Ridge lies to the left (facing in).

Ridge And Lower Cliff
Various scrambles and bouldering pitches are possible to the left of the ridge.

Ridge Direct   35 metres   Difficult
The crest of the ridge is followed, with optional variations, from a triangular platform below a rusting iron spike.

To the right of the base of the descent break there are sea-level ledges. The next routes start from a narrow, barnacle-covered ledge at low tide.

Free Rein   30 metres   Very Difficult   (26.5.61)
1 24m. From the ledge, climb leftwards up the slab and continue up a series of blocks to the left edge of The Lawn.
2 6m. Climb a black knobbly vein in a steep crack to an awkward finish.

Brown Slab   45 metres   Severe   (26.5.61)
A pleasant route. Start from the ledges, as for the previous route.
1 30m. 4a. Move diagonally rightwards up a short wall and make an awkward mantelshelf onto a brown-streaked slab. Continue up the slab and over a bulge to The Lawn.

2 15m. 4b. Climb the short cracked wall to the left of the small overhang in the face above to a platform. Make some delicate moves to the right and continue up the knuckly face to finish.
Variation
2b 5b. Take the small overhang direct.

Blinkers Slab   40 metres   Very Difficult   (22.5.61)
Start from a higher ledge to the right of the previous starts.
1 25m. Climb directly up the slab to The Lawn.
2 15m. Climb the wall above, starting in the break to the right of the small overhang. After 5 metres, move onto the knuckly face and finish direct.

Clough Buttress

This is the small, slabby-sided buttress just below the approach path, and easily reached from the path down its left-hand side (facing out). The main feature of the buttress is a deep recess at 5 metres, with a steep chimney crack running up to its left and an overhang with a groove above on its right. There are two pleasant pitches centred on the recess and two harder pitches on the right side of the buttress.

Popse   20 metres   Severe   (16.6.61)
Start 6 metres left of the recess.
1 6m. Climb a black vein in a groove; then traverse right into the recess.
2 15m. Climb the steep chimney crack. Hollow rock.

Nutse   20 metres   Hard Very Severe   5b   (26.5.61)
This takes the overhang to the right of the recess. Start below the recess and climb the shallow groove to make tough, strenuous moves through the overhang into the groove above, which is climbed to the top by difficult moves.

Ragtag   20 metres   E1   5c
A testing little problem. Make hard moves up the steep black crack on the right of the buttress to the overhang; there is an easier alternative crack to its left. Move right to the lip of the overhang and step up delicately to finish up easier rock.

Bobtail   18 metres   Hard Very Severe   5b
The small overhang leads around to the right flank of the buttress. Start below its right edge and climb the black stained wall. Using the spike on the right, make a hard move up and left. Continue up and right and finish easily.

The slab on the right of this route, which starts from a grassy ledge at 5 metres, gives a pleasant climb of Very Difficult.

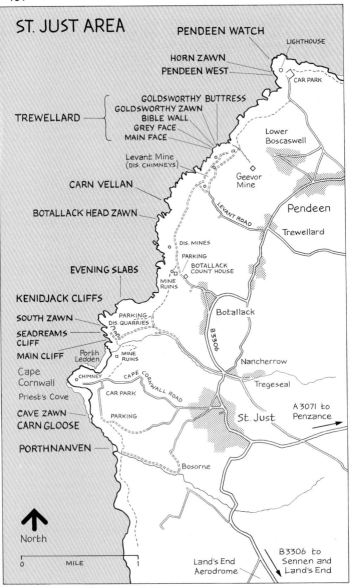

ST. JUST AREA

PENDEEN WATCH

LIGHTHOUSE

HORN ZAWN
PENDEEN WEST

CAR PARK

GOLDSWORTHY BUTTRESS
GOLDSWORTHY ZAWN
BIBLE WALL
GREY FACE
MAIN FACE

TREWELLARD

Lower
Boscaswell

Levant Mine
(DIS. CHIMNEYS)

Geevor
Mine

CARN VELLAN

Pendeen

LEVANT ROAD

BOTALLACK HEAD ZAWN

Trewellard

DIS. MINES

PARKING

EVENING SLABS

BOTALLACK
COUNT HOUSE

MINE
RUINS

KENIDJACK CLIFFS

Botallack

SOUTH ZAWN

PARKING
DIS. QUARRIES

B 3306

SEADREAMS
CLIFF

MAIN CLIFF

Porth
Ledden

MINE
RUINS

Nancherrow

Cape
Cornwall

CHIMNEY

CAPE CORNWALL ROAD

Tregeseal

Priest's Cove

CAR PARK

A 3071 to
Penzance

CAVE ZAWN
CARN GLOOSE

PARKING

St. Just

PORTHNANVEN

Bosorne

North

0   MILE   1

Land's End
Aerodrome

B3306 to
Sennen and
Land's End

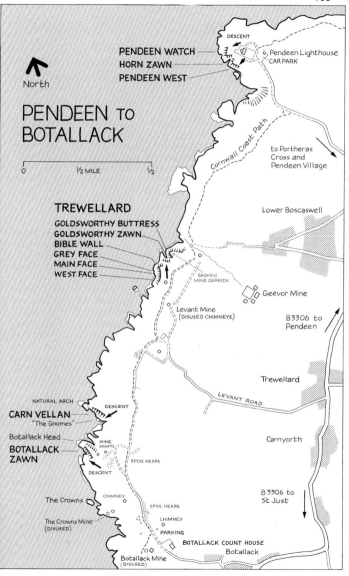

North

PENDEEN TO BOTALLACK

0   ½ MILE   ½

PENDEEN WATCH
HORN ZAWN
PENDEEN WEST

DESCENT

Pendeen Lighthouse
CAR PARK

Cornwall Coast Path

to Portheras
Cross and
Pendeen Village

Lower Boscaswell

TREWELLARD

GOLDSWORTHY BUTTRESS
GOLDSWORTHY ZAWN
BIBLE WALL
GREY FACE
MAIN FACE
WEST FACE

BROKEN MINE DERRICK

Geevor Mine

B3306 to
Pendeen

Levant Mine
(DISUSED CHIMNEYS)

Trewellard

LEVANT ROAD

NATURAL ARCH

DESCENT

CARN VELLAN
"The Gnomes"

Botallack Head

BOTALLACK
ZAWN

DESCENT

MINE
SHAFTS

SPOIL HEAPS

Carnyorth

The Crowns

CHIMNEY

B3306 to
St Just

The Crowns Mine
(DISUSED)

SPOIL HEAPS

CHIMNEY

PARKING

BOTALLACK COUNT HOUSE
Botallack

Botallack Mine
(DISUSED)

Pendeen Cliffs (Killas)   OS Ref 378 360

Outlook: Mainly west.
Tidal sections in all areas although many routes are above the tide level. All areas are affected by swell and rough sea.
Coastguard Identity: Pendeen Watch.

The Pendeen Cliffs lie below and to the west of Pendeen Lighthouse, which is reached from the B3306 at Portheras Cross. There is adequate car-parking at the road end above the lighthouse. The cliffs are clean and unvegetated and offer fine, short routes at most grades on generally good rock. Pendeen is a good afternoon or evening venue, with the benefit of some of the shortest approaches in the area. There are three separate sections of cliff called Pendeen Watch, Horn Zawn, and Rip Tide Wall.

Pendeen Watch
Approach. From the car-park, walk down the approach drive to the lighthouse and go through a small gate on the right, just before the entrance to the lighthouse compound. Go down stone steps onto grassy slopes. Follow a path down left, to a small block wall above a deep zawn. A sewage outlet from the lighthouse discharges from the other side of the wall and spoils the atmosphere of the routes in the zawn, although this may be less of a problem now the lighthouse is automated. Routes on the seaward faces are unaffected. Skirt the rim of the zawn on its right-hand side to a recessed ledge where rucksacks can be left. From here, an abseil or a descent at Very Difficult standard over a stepped pulpit block can be made to a vast rock platform sloping down to the sea. The climbs are concentrated on the left-hand, seaward, wall and the face of the pulpit block leading around into the zawn wall on the right (facing in). The seaward wall is tidal but can be approached by an abseil from its rim. The pulpit block wall is non-tidal.

Below the seaward wall is a huge boulder with a smaller boulder wedged beneath its right-hand side.

First Slip   15 metres   Very Difficult   (12.5.86)
Start from the left end of the huge boulder, and climb a weakness in the face on the left.

Second Slip   15 metres   Severe 4a   (12.5.86)
Climb the vertical crack from the huge boulder.

Square Leg   17 metres   Severe 4a   (12.5.86)
Step up from the left side of the huge boulder, and follow the jagged edge leading rightwards.

Gymslip   20 metres   Very Severe 5a   (16.5.86)
Climb the wall direct from the top of the smaller boulder. Thin for the first 6 metres.

Seventeen Schoolgirls   24 metres   Very Severe 5a   (16.5.86)
Climb a groove from the right-hand base of the smaller boulder; then continue direct up the wall past a ledge, to finish by thin moves up the short wall to the right of the lower rim of the cliff.

★Pork Ordinaire   34 metres   Hard Very Severe 5a   (12.6.86)
A fine little route up the right-slanting crackline beneath the huge overhang. Traverse left beneath the overhang to a ledge and finish up a crack.

Gardener's Wall   30 metres   E1 5b   (18.7.87)
Start just right of the preceding route and climb to a spike at 6 metres. Continue direct to the left edge of the roof, and finish as for the preceding route.

The cliff now turns rightwards across a smooth impending wall before making another sharp turn onto the pulpit block face.

★★Hot Lettuce   30 metres   E2 5b   (20.8.86)
This route takes the left edge of the pulpit block wall. Climb easily leftwards from the centre of the base of the wall to a good ledge on the arête. Move up the narrow slab, and then make airy moves rightwards beneath the roof and onto the wall. Finish up the left edge.

☆☆Prime Remover   30 metres   E5 6b †   (18.7.87)
Climb direct up the left arête to the ledge on the arête of *Hot Lettuce*. Pull over the left side of the roof on the right and continue direct to join *Hot Lettuce* (peg runner used on first ascent: no longer *in situ*).

☆☆Writings on the Wall   30 metres   E5 6b †   (18.7.87)
Climb the centre of the wall to the roof, pull over this (peg runner), and join the upper part of *Slot Machine*.

Slot Machine   30 metres   E1 5c   (25.4.86)
A strenuous and amusing route. Take the corner-crack between the wall and the pulpit block to gain the latter through the slot by a hard move. Traverse left from the edge of the pulpit block and climb the weakness in the centre of the upper wall more easily and pleasantly.

Wave Dancer   20 metres   Severe   (5.8.79)
Gain the top of the pulpit block, and climb the wall above to a ledge; then follow cracks from its left edge and finish over a small roof.

Sea Music 20 metres Very Difficult (5.8.79)
Gain the top of the pulpit block, climb the broken arête on the right on good holds, and then finish up a white wall.

Foam Follower 20 metres Hard Very Severe 5a (5.8.79)
A recent rockfall has left this route a serious undertaking with poor protection. From below the right side of the pulpit block, traverse rightwards for 5 metres and climb the clean-cut groove direct.

★Sick Dreams 30 metres E2 5b (17.7.87)
The obvious right-facing corner-crack in the wall running back into the zawn. Bold and friable at the finish. Approach by a rightward traverse from below the pulpit block or by abseil. Climb the lower wall to ledges at the foot of the steep corner-crack, which is climbed to the top.

The back wall of the zawn offers some obvious challenges to the less fastidious climber.

The following routes take lines on the right-hand wall of the outfall zawn (facing in). The sewage discharge is intermittent, and does not affect the routes directly. The routes are approached by following the left-hand rim (facing out) of the zawn from the blockwork wall above the sewage outlet, and then by scrambling down onto the comfortable platform above the zawn's narrow, tidal channel.

The first few routes are slightly loose in places.

Hypocrite Arête 25 metres E3 5c † (17.7.87)
Climb the arête on the far left side of the wall to the top. (From a small ledge on the arête, it is possible to traverse left to finish up a groove.)

Fair Play 25 metres E1 5b † (17.7.87)
Climb the groove just right of the preceding route to a roof and follow the rightward-slanting crack above.

A route has been claimed to the left of *Impendeen Wall* at VS, but two generations of guidebook writers have been unable to locate it.

Impendeen Wall 26 metres Very Severe 4c (30.8.72)
Take the prominent groove to the left of the stepped corner. A fine line which is slightly loose in its upper part.

Stoneflasher 24 metres Severe 4a (5.8.79)
Climb the stepped corner passing two large terraces on the right.

Yellow Slab   24 metres   Severe 4a   (30.8.72)
This route lies at the sunnier mouth of the zawn. Climb an overhanging
corner below an orange slab, which is climbed pleasantly up and to the
left. Traverse right around an arête to finish up an easy slab.

Horn Zawn

This is the black cliff directly below the great twin funnels of the foghorn and the
west wall of the lighthouse, and was originally used as a Trinity House rubbish
tip. However, Horn Zawn has a charm of its own and some pleasant routes.

Approach from the car-park by walking along the west wall of the
lighthouse compound for about 100 metres and then dropping down to the
left over broken ground until above the southern rim of the zawn. The north
wall has a distinctive long overhang at mid height. There is an impressive
rock island to the west beyond a narrow tidal channel. Abseil down the south
wall to a platform above the sea. The seaward side of the north wall is tidal.
The floor of the zawn can be hit by big swells or rough sea.

Brothel in Brighton   24 metres   Hard Very Severe 5a   (3.9.89)
Start below the centre of the long overhang. Climb a short right-slanting
crack with difficulty, continue up leftwards on good holds to the left edge of
the overhang, and finish up the steep corner-crack.

Pink Foaming Transvestights   55 metres   Hard Severe †   (3.9.89)
A girdle starting from the zawn and traversing the north wall to finish
across and up the seaward wall opposite the rock island. Start below the
north wall, from the boulders beneath the right edge of the big overhang.
1 37m. Traverse up and leftwards beneath the overhang and continue
around onto the seaward face to a smooth scoop in the wall opposite the
rock island. This pitch can be split where it turns onto the seaward face.
2 18m. From the scoop, traverse left, and then make steep exposed
moves up the wall to finish direct.

★Painted Lady   30 metres   Hard Very Severe 5b   (20.10.89)
The steep crackline just right of the big overhang. A very pleasant pitch.

Houghmagandie   45 metres   Very Severe †   (18.9.89)
An adventurous route which gains the groove in the back right-hand wall
of the zawn by a long traverse from the right. Start below the right-hand
end of the wall at a jagged crack running up to the obvious traverse-line.
1 15m. 4b. Climb the jagged crackline and then traverse left past a
protruding block: awkward. Belay below a break.
2 15m. 4c. Climb up through the break to a groove (taking care with the
rock). Break out left to easier ground and move up to a belay ledge.
3 15m. 4b. Continue up the groove to exit carefully over a jammed
block. Belay to the large block above. There is a cunning thread-through
wire placement at the back of the block.

Rip Tide Wall

This small section of cliff faces west and has some pleasant routes.

Approach from the car-park by walking along the west wall of the lighthouse compound for about 50 metres before dropping down left over grassy slopes to some broken ledges. The cliff is to the right of the ledges (facing out). It is gained by following a ramp, directly below the ledges, to seawards, to where a short abseil or a greasy scramble leads to a comfortable ledge between the base of the cliff and the rocky pinnacle further seaward. The ledge is just tidal and is sheltered from swell and rough sea by the rocky reef lying beyond it. Caution is advised, however, since unexpected swells can swamp the ledge without warning. The attractive corner-crack on the right (facing in) is *Rip Tide*. All the routes start from the ledge.

The first three routes take similar lines up the left-hand side of the wall. Inspection from the seaward boulder is advised to confirm that the correct line is being taken.

Very Ordinary Route   30 metres   Severe   (26.4.87)
Traverse leftwards from the ledge for 15 metres and climb a narrow crackline to a large ledge. Finish up the quartzy wall above.

The Outlaw   27 metres   Severe 4a   (9.5.86)
Traverse leftwards from the ledge for 12 metres and climb a narrow crack.

Deep Six   24 metres   Severe 4a   (30.4.86)
Traverse leftwards from the ledge for 9 metres and climb direct over a slight bulge to ledges.

Seamstress   34 metres   Hard Severe 4a   (11.5.86)
From the ledge, edge leftwards, and move up over light-coloured rock to a deep, rightward-leading crack, which is followed to a niche. Step left and climb the wall direct.

Slanderous Accusations   30 metres   Hard Very Severe 5a   (20.9.86)
Climb directly up the wall from the middle of the ledge over a small overlap (poor protection) to a niche (shared with *Seamstress*). Continue to a second niche and up the rattly chimney above.

★**Malicious Gossip**   24 metres   E1 5a   (20.10.89)
Climb directly up the wall between *Slanderous Accusations* and the corner-crack of *Rip Tide*. Poor protection.

★**Rip Tide**   24 metres   Very Severe 4c   (30.4.86)
The layback crack starting at the right-hand end of the ledge.

Hang-Over Cure   16 metres   Hard Very Severe 5a †   (8.11.98)
Strenuous and rather contrived. Climb the thin crack in the steep wall just
right of *Rip Tide* until the crack ends. Step into *Rip Tide* and follow it for 3
metres; then move back right to the top of the arête.

Radiator   16 metres   Hard Very Severe 5a †   (11.10.98)
The arête five metres right of *Rip Tide* is poorly protected.

Flower Girl   24 metres   Hard Severe 4b   (26.5.86)
The deep chimney to the right of the ledge, climbed via moves on its left wall.

The crackline at the base of the approach ramp is **New Belt and Braces**
(10 metres Severe 4a 7.5.86)

Trewellard (Killas)   OS Ref 370 349

Outlook: North-west.
Non-tidal. The majority of routes at Trewellard start above high-water
mark, although heavy swell and rough sea seriously affect the start of all
routes on Goldsworthy Zawn, Bible Wall, Grey Face, and Main Face.
Coastguard Identity: Trewellard Zawn.

The Trewellard cliffs consist of killas slate and pillow-lavas with numerous
other intrusions. There are no outstanding climbs but they offer a quiet and
picturesque venue. The cliffs fringe an area of industrial chaos that is also a
treasure-house of mining archeology. The rock is generally sound but loose
in a few places.

Approach from Trewellard village by following Levant Road, the narrow
road that leads to the coast from opposite the Trewellard Inn car-park. After
three-quarters of a mile, the road reaches the Levant Beam Engine House
(National Trust). Park here, just before a barrier across the track, which is
locked outside the Engine House opening hours.

Follow the track downhill and around to the right for 300 metres, past two
mine stacks on the right, before bearing left to a mine-stack at the edge of
the cliffs. About 30 metres below and to the right (facing out) is a large,
comfortable platform (The Sundeck). This lies above the left end of the Main
Face and is convenient for leaving 'sacks. The Sundeck is easily reached by
going to the right (facing out) and scrambling down rocky steps.

From The Sundeck, a narrow gully with a jammed block at its top drops to
the base of Main Face, which can be reached either by abseiling or by
climbing down the gully at Difficult standard. The broken walls directly below

the cliff-top mine-stack, and to the left (facing out) of The Sundeck are Brown Face and Black Cliff.

For Goldsworthy Buttress and Goldsworthy Zawn, walk north-east from the cliff-side mine-stack for about 200 metres until above the concrete platform of a capped mine shaft down on the left. Goldsworthy Zawn lies directly below the capped mine shaft while Goldsworthy Buttress is the orange-tinted buttress lying to its right (facing out). From Goldsworthy Buttress, a short, fiercely overhanging wall, the Bible Wall, lies 200 metres to the south west. Grey Face leads on from Bible Wall to join Main Face, which in turn leads around to West Face below The Sundeck.

Goldsworthy Buttress
Approach from the capped mine shaft by scrambling straight down to the cliff edge (this is Goldsworthy Zawn) and then scramble down to the right, via broken rock and an easy-angled slab to a flat broad ledge 15 metres above the sea.

Double Take   67   Severe   (13.7.84)
A slightly artificial line, but pleasant.
1 27m. 4a. From the broad ledge, traverse left, taking the lower of two ledges, which leads around the edge of the buttress. Scramble with care across greasy ledges to the foot of a 10-metre corner. Climb the corner to ledges.
2 40m. 4a. Above and to the right is another 10-metre corner; climb this to a big ledge and continue easily to the top of the buttress.

Sea Fever   40 metres   Difficult   (1.12.83)
1 18m. From the broad ledge, step left onto the wall and continue via a niche to a big ledge and huge block.
2 22m. Climb a steep slab and wall; then move across to the upper tower and take the break on the left.

★**Bright Morning**   38 metres   Very Difficult   (1.12.83)
1 18m. From the broad ledge, climb leftwards and follow the slanting break back right to a niche. Continue to the big ledge and huge block.
2 20m. Scramble rightwards over blocks and climb the thin crack on the right of the tower.

☆**The Return of the Lemming**   29 metres   Very Severe †   (29.4.2000)
1 13m. 4c. From the broad ledge, climb the centre of the face between Bright Morning and Isosceles to a large ledge under an overhang.
2 6m. 4c. Climb straight over the overhang to the apex of the face.
3 10m. 4c. Climb the tower above to finish on its right-hand arête.

Zero Gravity (E3), Carn Vellan
Climber: Andy Grieve   Photo: Dave Turnbull

Biggles Flies Undone (HVS), Aire Point.
Climber: Andy Grieve Photo: Ken Palmer

★Isosceles   24 metres   Very Severe   4b   (27.5.84)
Fine climbing with poor protection. Start from the broad ledge and climb diagonally rightwards on small pockets to the right-hand edge of the large platform.

Goldsworthy Zawn

This is the deep and narrow zawn below Goldsworthy Buttress. The pitches on the main wall give excellent climbing. The zawn is occasionally damp but dries well after midday.

★Chain Link   75 metres   Hard Very Severe   (11.4.87)
An interesting left-to-right girdle of the zawn face with increasing exposure. Take care to protect the second on pitch 2.
1 18m. 4b. From the broad ledge below Goldsworthy Buttress, scramble down a short chimney to seaward to reach a ledge, flanked on its right (facing in) by a black slab. Take a rising line across the slab to a small ledge on its right edge. Continue across the right-angled corner to belay on a sloping ledge where the wall turns into the zawn.
2 27m. 4c. Move right strenuously for 6 metres on good holds before making a harder move around onto the main wall. Continue for another 18 metres to a belay niche.
3 30m. Easy but exposed climbing along the pock-marked upper wall leads to a final chimney above a narrow cave at the back of the zawn.

There are three short pitches on the smaller face near the seaward end of the zawn, gained by abseiling down a wall from the broad ledge at the base of Goldsworthy Buttress. Move down and right to a ledge beneath the face. The pitches are: **Sweet Metal** (4.7.85) – the left-hand overhang; **Claymore** (17.5.85) the right-hand overhang; and **Thin Tin** (4.8.85) – the corner at the right-hand end of the face. All three are strenuous, Hard Very Severe 5a.

The following routes all start from the ledge below the main wall of the zawn. Abseil down the centre of the wall from good belays. The wall is split near the left end of the ledge by a deep crackline. This is *Cold Iron*, named after a wedge of rusty metal jammed in a crack at its base, a relic of early mining activity. Direct starts can be made from the zawn-bed at very low tide.

Cluny   37 metres   Hard Severe   (17.7.85)
1 30m. 4b. From the base of *Cold Iron*, traverse left to the left edge of the face and climb direct to a niche.
2 7m. Climb the steep wall on the right.

Parrot Face   27 metres   E1 5b   (24.6.87)
Take a direct line up the main face a metre or so from its left edge.

★What Red Parrot?   24 metres   E3 5c   (4.7.85)
The boldest line on the wall, with poor protection. From the foot of *Cold Iron*, climb diagonally left to the centre of the face. Finish direct via a break to easier rock.

★Eric Goes to the Seaside   24 metres   E1 5b   (11.7.85)
Fine, sustained climbing on a direct line up the wall a metre or so left of *Cold Iron*.

Cold Iron   24 metres   Hard Severe   4b   (25.7.84)
A pleasant climb up the obvious deep crackline. Difficulties ease after the first few metres.

Steely Dan   24 metres   E1 5b   (17.7.85)
There are two slanting grooves right of *Cold Iron*. Climb the first of these to the break and continue up the easier rock above.

The Confluence   24 metres   E1 5b   (11.7.85)
The right-hand groove.

D.B. I Presume?   24 metres   Hard Severe   4b   (4.7.85)
Climb the wall towards the right-hand end of the ledge via a large pocket; then trend up and right to a groove.

Targe   24 metres   Hard Very Severe   4c   (24.7.85)
Step off the right-hand end of the ledge and climb to a small overhang at 10 metres (poor protection). Move right below the overhang and climb the arête and crack.

Had It Chimney   30 metres   Very Difficult   (24.7.85)
The deep chimney at the far back of the zawn is climbed by traversing from the end of the ledge. This is usually wet or greasy. A variation finish is possible by traversing rightwards from the chimney onto the back wall to its right-hand end and then climbing left of the gully.

A number of routes have been claimed between all the original lines. These have little independence.

Bible Wall

This is the black, overhanging wall 200 metres west of Goldsworthy Zawn. The base is above high tide level, but may be sea-washed at any tide. It is north-facing and sunless. Access is by climbing or abseiling down the left-hand side of the wall (facing in), or by a low tide approach from the Main Face.

Geriatrics   15 metres   Severe   (6.7.85)
The crack and ledges on the extreme left of the wall.

Fringe Benefit   12 metres   E1 5b   (4.7.85)
The direct hanging crack at the left end of the wall proper offers fierce jamming.

Grey Face

There are two sections to this face. The first leads on directly from Bible Wall at a slightly easier angle. The second section is a further continuation leading at a right-angle inwards to a junction with Main Face. It is best to approach these walls at low tide from The Sundeck down the access gully at the right-hand end of Main Face, before crossing a greasy tidal channel to higher ledges below the walls. Alternatively, an abseil entry can be made down *Rainmaker*.

Philosan Crack   12 metres   E3 5c   (25.6.87)
Take the steep crackline just around the corner right of Bible Wall.

The centre of the seaward wall is recessed. The top of the recess has been affected by rockfall, and is loose.

Ancient's Way   18 metres   Very Severe   (8.3.84)
Climb the back of the recess, then finish carefully up its left side.

Niwl   23 metres   Very Severe 4c   (16.6.88)
A rising traverse of the wall from right to left (poor protection). Start below the recess and climb a slab to a yellow-coloured overhang; then move left and traverse to an obvious slim grey ramp. Make a precarious exit from the ramp.

Levant Jug Route   18 metres   Hard Very Severe 4c   (4.8.85)
To the right of the recess, climb an awkward wide crack to a ledge. Finish steeply up shattered rock.

Wayfarer   20 metres   E3 5b †   (25.6.87)
This route takes the wall between *Levant Jug Route* and the broad, yellow-stained arête that leads around to the right-hand face. Start below the left edge of the arête. Climb to a shattered orange-coloured overhang and climb it direct.

★Rainmaker   20 metres   Hard Very Severe 5a   (30.6.85)
A sharp little problem with good protection. Climb the shallow groove on the right of the broad arête to a cracked overhang. Move out right and climb a steep, ragged groove.

Variations on *Rainmaker* have been climbed at the same standard, but have little independence.

★Skylight   27 metres   Very Difficult   (7.12.83)
A good route in fine positions. From the ledge beneath the left end of the
face, climb the grey wall, trending rightwards into a steep corner. Go up a
slab to a recess (belay possible). Exposed moves through the skylight to the
right lead to a finishing groove.

The Crab   27 metres   Difficult   (13.2.84)
Start as for *Skylight*. Climb the grey wall to a recess; then move right for
10 metres to easier ground to finish up the brown wall on the left.

★Bateman's Boots   36 metres   Hard Very Severe   (7.5.84)
Full of character, like the boots.
1 20m. 4b. From the ledge below the left end of the face, traverse
rightwards along a crackline above the zawn; then take the greasy
chimney above to a belay niche.
2 16m. 5a. Follow the broken crackline up and left to make a hard,
exposed move through the overhang and into a V-groove.

Twilight Zone   37 metres   E3 5c †   (26.6.87)
A line up the deep recess between Grey Face and Main Face. Traverse
leftwards above the tidal pool from greasy ledges on the right. Climb to the
crack on the right wall of the recess and follow it to an undercling crack. Step
left across the void into a hanging groove and follow it to easier ground.

Pussy Foot   33 metres   E3 †   (26.6.87)
Start as for *Twilight Zone*.
1 15m. 5b. Climb to the crack on the right wall; then move rightwards
across the wall and up to the ledge which extends rightwards.
2 18m. 5c. Climb the arête on the left. Poor protection.

Main Face
An impressively steep face, with several attractive routes, gained from The
Sundeck by abseil from a jammed boulder, or by descent at Difficult
standard down the deep gully below the boulder.

Debutante   18 metres   Hard Very Severe 5a   (23.4.84)
Short but strenuous and exposed. Climb the steep crack from the left end
of the ledge beneath the face.

★Shambhala   27 metres   Hard Very Severe 5a   (24.2.84)
A stylish and pleasant route which takes the shallow crackline left of the
centre of the face.

Sundog   27 metres   E1 5b   (24.4.85)
Short-lived difficulties, but tough. Start below the middle of the face and
take a direct line over the bulging mid section on small fingerholds to
steep but easier ground.

John Knox   37 metres   Hard Very Severe   (16.3.84)
An interesting line.
1 27m. 5a. Start at the right-hand end of the face and climb diagonally
leftwards to reach the top of a small pinnacle beneath a bulging crackline.
Climb the crackline and traverse right at its top to a cave belay.
2 10m. 5a. Climb strenuously out of the cave via the hanging crack
above.

Space below My Heels   32 metres   Severe   (7.12.83)
Pleasant and airy.
1 12m. Start at the right-hand end of the face. Climb to the left; then
trend right to a steep scoop and a cave belay.
2 20m. 4a. Traverse steeply left for a metre and continue direct to a
platform. Climb the corner on the left to the top.

Initial Crack   37 metres   Very Difficult   (23.11.83)
Climb the crack flanking the right-hand end of the face to a jammed
block. Continue up the chimney and go over the chockstone to finish.

Moxibustion   34 metres   Severe   (23.11.83)
From the right-hand end of the face, step right and climb black rock (often
greasy) to easier ground. Continue to a steep slab and either take this
direct (poor protection), or climb the corner on the right of the slab to a
ledge.

West Face

This is the small face below and to the left (facing out) of The Sundeck,
running inland from Main Face. Approach by easy scrambling down its
left-hand side (facing out) from The Sundeck.

Solo   18 metres   Severe 4a   (27.5.84)
A direct line at the left end of the face, via a thin crack in the smooth upper
wall.

Microcosm   21 metres   Difficult   (13.2.84)
An easier pitch just right of *Solo*. Start at the foot of *Welsh Wizard*, and
climb diagonally leftwards.

Welsh Wizard   18 metres   Difficult   (23.11.83)
The main break in the wall, with two small caves.

Trio   18 metres   Difficult   (23.11.83)
Climb the wall to the right of *Welsh Wizard* via cracks and grooves.

Route Four   16 metres   Very Difficult   (1984)
Start at the right-hand end of the face. Step up and left onto the face, and
finish up a very shallow groove. Poor protection.

The area of cliff running west from The Sundeck is set back into the land and lies well above the sea. It has been quarried in the past and is all that remains of what may once have been a substantial cliff face. There are a number of short pleasant climbs, although care should be taken because of minor looseness. There are two main features separated by a broken, mineral-streaked gully.

Brown Buttress
This is the buttress to the left of the gully. The broad right-facing corner gives the line of *Sunset Walls*.

Brown Jack   37 metres   Very Difficult   (1.12.83)
From The Sundeck, scramble down a short gully to a break in the wall on the left.
1 21m. Climb the wall to a corner and follow this to a belay.
2 16m. Cross to a short final wall; then climb the finishing tower.

Sunset Walls   37 metres   Difficult   (1.12.83)
Start as for *Brown Jack*.
1 21m. Climb up the break onto the wall on the left; then move steeply into a corner, which leads up a wall to a recess.
2 16m. Take the left-hand corner of the recess to finish on the tower.

Russet Wall   34 metres   Moderate   (7.12.83)
1 12m. Follow *Sunset Walls* for 10 metres. Move right to a platform.
2 22m. Climb a black-streaked wall via a flake; then go up a scoop and walls to finish up the right side of the tower.

Black Cliff
This is the area of dark, broken rock lying to the right of the gully. The most obvious feature is the deep V-groove of *Grey Groove*, towards the left side.

Rainbow   18 metres   Severe 4a   (20.6.85)
Start just right of the broken area of rock on the left of the cliff, and below a wall with fine bands of orange and black rock. This is just left of the deep V-groove. Climb a steep wall and move right to climb a second wall.

Grey Groove   20 metres   Very Difficult   (2.2.84)
Climb the deep groove to a ledge on the left, at its top, and finish up a crack.

Slanting Crack   18 metres   Severe 4a   (14.4.84)
Climb the slanting crack to the right of *Grey Groove*; then step right and finish directly up the wall.

Andrew   18 metres   Severe 4a   (24.2.84)
Start 5 metres right of the deep V-groove, below a left-facing corner. Climb
over a series of bulges to the final steep corner.

Three other routes have been climbed on the rock to the right. These are
Black Shadow (Severe 4a 24.2.84), **Shades** (Severe 4a 20.6.85), and
Grey Shadow (Difficult 24.2.84). The lines are rather indefinite.

Carn Vellan (Killas)   OS Ref 364 343

Outlook: South-west.
Tidal except for the right-hand side, although heavy seas affect the base of
all routes.
Coastguard Identity: Carn Vellan.
Environmental Issues: This SSSI has rich maritime heath and grassland,
good crevice communities, and fragile approach slopes. Sea Beet, Sea Aster,
Golden Samphire, Dyer's Greenweed, and Sea Spurrey are vulnerable
here, so please keep to the approach described and tread on rock wherever
possible. This is an important geological and mineralogical area and the
nearby mine tips are the world type locality for rare minerals.

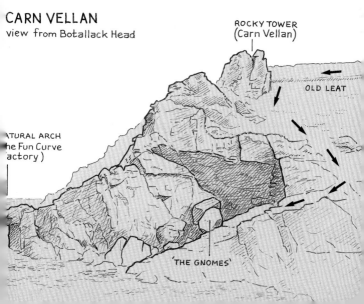

CARN VELLAN
view from Botallack Head

ROCKY TOWER
(Carn Vellan)

OLD LEAT

NATURAL ARCH
(The Fun Curve
Factory)

'THE GNOMES'

Carn Vellan is a fine crag of great character, with a good selection of routes. It can become a suntrap on a sunny afternoon, although in winter the combination of sea-spray and seepage means it is best avoided. The cliff's main feature is a massive overhang on the right-hand side, and slightly less steep rock to the left. Beneath the left side of the massive overhang are some huge wedged boulders, known as The Gnomes.

Approach along a wide track leading northwards from the village of Botallack, keeping left of Manor Farm, to reach ample parking just past the Count House (National Trust). From here, continue along the wide track passing some houses. Half a kilometre beyond the houses the rocky tower of Carn Vellan can be seen down to seaward. Follow the track to where it dips down into a shallow valley, and follow the right side of the stream bed downhill. Pick up a path which follows the line of an old water course along the grassy shoulder to the tower, which is split where the water course was blasted through the rock. The base of Carn Vellan is easily gained by going leftwards (facing out) down the slopes below the tower to the cliff edge, and working back seawards to reach big ledges beneath the cliff.

Routes on the seaward cliff, in the area of *The Fun Curve Factory* can be approached by going through the gap in the tower and descending a well-marked path in a broad gully to the huge black platform that runs to seaward beyond a remarkable rock bridge. Just before the flat top of the rock bridge go left (facing out) down ledges to seaweed-covered rocks at the base of the cliff. This approach should be made at low tide and in quiet seas only.

At low tide and calm seas, the entire base of the crag can be traversed by boulder-hopping.

★★★The Fun Curve Factory 20 metres E5 6a (1991)
[Photos pp.32a and 160b.] Steep, well-protected climbing on good rock. Climb the rib to the right of the arch; then traverse left above it in a fine position via a sentry-box.

Sooty 18 metres Severe 4a † (1990)
The chimney to the right of the arch.

Joy Riders 18 metres E3 5c † (1991)
Start right of the chimney. Climb the wall to a short groove and bulge, and continue direct.

Insurance Drain 18 metres E3 5c † (1992)
Climb the wall right of *Joy Riders*.

Kurtzer 33 metres Very Severe 4c (30.7.81)
This route lies at the far left end (facing in) of the main part of the crag. Start from barnacle-covered ledges just left of the left arête of the main face and

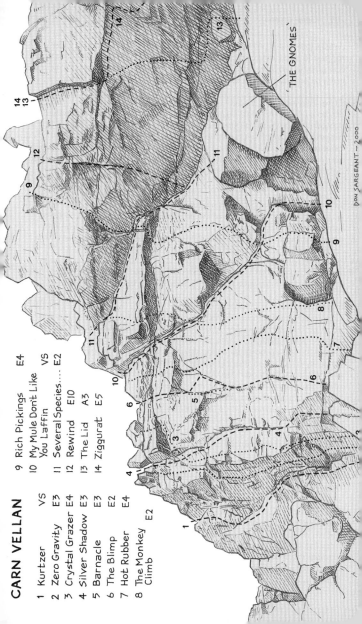

CARN VELLAN

1 Kurtzer   VS
2 Zero Gravity   E3
3 Crystal Grazer   E4
4 Silver Shadow   E3
5 Barnacle   E3
6 The Blimp   E2
7 Hot Rubber   E4
8 The Monkey   E2
  Climb

9 Rich Pickings   E4
10 My Mule Don't Like
   You Laffin   VS
11 Several Species..... E2
12 Rewind   E10
13 The Lid   A3
14 Ziggurat   E5

'THE GNOMES'

DON SARGEANT ~ 2000

directly below the projecting flake at the top of the cliff. Climb a wide ragged fault running up to the left to the base of a steep corner. This point can also be reached direct from below. Move up the steep corner and then traverse out right in an exposed position to finish up a short corner.

★★**Zero Gravity**   33 metres   E3 6a   (24.8.80)
[Photo p.192a.] A tough, sustained route on good rock with reasonable protection. Start from barnacle-covered ledges directly below the projecting flake at the top of the cliff. Climb a short steep wall to the overhang on the left. Go over this onto the wall above, and climb straight up on large but well-spaced holds to a small groove on the left; climb this before traversing right below an overhang to easier-angled rock and the final cracks.

☆☆☆**Crystal Grazer**   33 metres   E4 6a †   (1991)
A route centred on the arête at the left end of the cliff. Two peg runners were used on the first ascent, but are no longer *in situ*. Start below the projecting flake at the top of the cliff, and just left of a short corner containing a wide crack. Climb the arête, pulling through the first overhang, and go slightly right at the next major overhang. Continue up a short slab to gain an easy crack, joining *Silver Shadow*, but leave this route by a spectacular traverse up and right beneath the final overhang.

★★**Silver Shadow**   36 metres   E3 5c   (11.4.80)
Committing and strenuous, this fine pitch follows a natural line up the left edge of the main face. Start at a short corner opposite the slabby face of a huge seaward boulder. Climb the corner for 3 metres to a small ledge. Follow the faint groove up and to the right with difficulty to another small ledge by a strange cluster of nodules. Traverse directly left on small holds until it is possible to gain the obvious crack with small stepped overhangs at its top. Follow the crack and then move left onto the rib, which is climbed to a good crack. Continue up it, over an awkward bulge; then trend left on enormous holds towards the projecting flake. Reach the top by a good crack on its right side.

Barnacle   33 metres   E3 5c †   (1991)
A variation on *The Blimp*. Start at a roofed corner just left of that route. Climb the corner with difficulty, exiting right to easier rock. Climb up to the niche of *The Blimp*, and go up an arête to a crack. Climb rightwards through the bulge to join *The Blimp* again to finish.

★**The Blimp**   33 metres   E2 5b   (9.10.71)
Sustained climbing on an intricate line, tackling the main face about 15 metres left of The Gnomes and close to the start of *Silver Shadow*. Start from the pointed end of a large seaward boulder below an orange-streaked wall. Step off the top of the boulder and climb up to a horizontal break. Bear up and left past a good hold to a higher horizontal break. Climb the wall above to gain a niche below the overhanging upper

wall. (Possible belay.) Step right and climb the wide, rightward-slanting crack for 5 metres. Traverse left across the base of a smooth wall to a short vertical crack and move up and left to good holds. Finish direct.

☆☆**Hot Rubber** 33 metres E4 5c †   (1992)
Start about 5 metres left of a crack that widens into a cave at 5 metres. Climb steeply up and right beneath small stepped roofs to easier rock. Climb the right side of a smooth wall, crossing the right-slanting crack of *The Blimp,* and finish direct through a bulge.

Shades of Last Summer 35 metres Hard Very Severe 5a (7.6.70)
The original direct line up the right-hand side of the wall leads to an airy finish just left of *My Mule*… Sparse protection. Start from a large boulder 6 metres right of *The Blimp* and just left of the crack that widens into a cave at 5 metres. Climb the wall left of the cave through a band of light-coloured rock and continue up to a scoop with a shallow corner on the right. Climb the corner until a short hand-traverse leads out leftwards onto the wall. Turn the bulge and continue boldly straight to the top.

☆☆**The Monkey Climb** 45 metres E2 †   (1981/1992)
Start from a 2-metre-wide boulder, just left of the chimney-crack.
1 15m. 4b. Climb the left-hand groove awkwardly to a stance on the faultline of *My Mule*…
2 40m. 5c. Step up and right onto the blunt arête, and climb to the roof. Pull leftwards through this and climb the slab above to the horizontal break of *Several Species*… before moving left to finish via a grassy niche.

☆☆☆**Grand Illusion** 46 metres E4 †   (1993)
A long and varied route through the smaller overhangs to the left of the great overhang. It has not been possible to locate the first (6b) or fourth and fifth (5c) pitches.
1 20m. 4a. *My Mule*… pitch 1.
2 13m. 5b. Climb the orange-flecked wall to a diamond-shaped roof. Move into a hanging groove above and right, and exit left beneath another small roof. Pull over the next roof, and belay on the right, in the break of *Several Species*…
3 13m. 6a. Climb through the bulge on the left, to the left of the bulging crack of *Life's Moments*, to easier gound. Belay on the left, then escape leftwards.

☆☆**Rich Pickings** 41 metres E4 †   (1993)
A fine climb through some impressive overhangs. A peg runner was used on the last pitch (not in place). Start from a 2-metre-wide boulder, just left of the chimney-crack.
1 6m. 5a. Step off the boulder into a curving crack and follow this to a niche on *My Mule*…
2 20m. 5c. Step up then right onto the blunt arête, and continue to the overhang. Pull through rightwards to a niche on *Several Species* …

3 15m. 6b. Follow the wall beneath the right-slanting overhang to its end, and then climb direct to easier ground.

☆**Life's Moments**   62 metres   E4 †   (1993)
Another impressive but elusive route. A fourth and fifth pitch have been climbed at 5c, but it has not been possible to locate them.
1 6m. 4b. *The Monkey Climb* pitch 1.
2 40m. 5c. *The Monkey Climb* pitch 2, but step right at the horizontal fault to belay.
3 16m. 6b. Climb the bulging crack to easier ground. Belay on the left, and then escape leftwards.

★**My Mule Don't Like You Laffin**   58 metres   Very Severe   (6.6.70)
An interesting and adventurous route which follows a natural line up the diagonal fault in the main wall and finishes up walls above. The top two pitches are escapable but the second pitch is quite serious due to loose rock. Start in the shadow of The Gnomes below and right of the base of the fault at a steep break.
1 20m. 4a. Climb the break, often wet but negotiable, and climb easily up the fault to a midway belay.
2 16m. 4c. Follow the fault over big plate holds before moving left in an exposed position to exit up a crack.
3 12m. 4a. Climb the short wall above by a bold move, bearing right towards the top. Scramble over easy ground to a stance beneath a second wall.
4 10m. 4c. Climb the wall, passing the overhang on the right, to finish up the short, steep groove above.

★**Several Species...**   23 metres   E2   (9.10.71/1990)
Another adventurous route taking a strong line to the left of the great overhang. Start from the top of The Gnomes.
1 18m. 5b. Step down across a gap and climb a slab to a small open corner. Make strenuous moves to gain the niche above the overhang. Move up and left to a good ledge.
2 5m. Traverse left to exit through a grassy niche on the skyline.

☆☆☆**Rewind**   40 metres   E10 7a †   (1999)
A truly astonishing route taking the left-hand side of the huge overhang on a fairly obvious left-to-right line. The line was originally climbed as a sport route. The bolts were then chopped, and later it was reclimbed with traditional leader-placed protection. According to the first ascensionist 'Technical climbing in extremely powerful positions requiring a degree of mental control to overcome the seriousness of the climb. Serious ground-fall impact from a great height guaranteed if you fall off.' There is some gear available, but it is hard to place and may be unreliable due to poor rock. Start from The Gnomes and head towards a finishing crack/groove.

Two other routes tackled the great overhang: a right-hand start to *Rewind* called **Nuts Are Not the Only Fruit** (40 metres F8b † 1991); and **Monster Munch** (45 metres F8b+ † 1993). Their bolts have been chopped.

An aid route **The Lid** (42 metres A3 16.8.72) takes the most continuous crackline through the overhang, right of centre. The line is gained by a traverse from the right, and finishes at the second belay of *Ziggurat*.

★★★Ziggurat   53 metres   E5   (24.6.80)
A strenuous and sensational route, gaining and following a horizontal faultline to gain the hanging left-facing corner. The line can be wet. The assorted *in-situ* gear should be treated with caution. It may be advisable to reinforce the belay at the end of pitch 2 in advance, or be prepared to continue up the final pitch. Start to the right of *The Lid*, below a steep broken wall capped by an overhang at 6 metres.
1 16m. 5b. Climb the wall for a metre or so, and then traverse left. Harder moves up and left across the corner lead to a short wall below a roof. Move left again to a small ledge.
2 24m. 6b. Climb rightwards across the white-streaked slab to a short groove and move up to good holds at its top. Move strenuously left to get into the faultline (peg runner). A technical and strenuous hand-traverse leads left along the faultline to a stance.
3 13m. 6a. Move left and reach out over the roof to good holds. Difficult moves lead into a groove with good jams. Climb this to belays well back from the top.

From the belay at the end of the second pitch of *Ziggurat*, **1025** (18 metres F7c † 1992) took the roof and wall above. Its bolts have been chopped.

☆☆☆Bridge of Sies   24 metres   E7 6b †   (1991)
A very serious route up the blind open corner at the right end of the huge roof. It was originally climbed with several poor peg runners; these were removed and two bolt runners placed, which have now been removed. The grade is an estimate based on its present state. Start as for *Ziggurat*, but pull over the first overhang direct onto the white-streaked slab. Continue up the corner-line with difficulty, passing a bulge.

☆☆Wild at Heart   24 metres   E6 6b †   (1991)
The crackline in the wall right of the corner, gained by climbing diagonally left across a rather loose wall, is harder than it looks.

Other lines have been climbed on this wall, but they are loose and cannot be recommended.

To the right of Carn Vellan (facing in), a narrow, crumbling zawn cuts into the land. There are three short routes near its mouth. They are reached by going down to sea-level ledges at the base of Carn Vellan and then continuing left (facing out) at low to mid tide. The first feature is a steep wall with diagonal cracklines. Right of this is a groove.

Ordinary Route   18 metres   Very Difficult   (1986)
Climb the groove direct.

The Fugitive   27 metres   Very Severe 4b   (1986)
Right of the preceding route is a ramp. Climb the ramp to an overhang. Finish left and up a groove.

Midnight Trundler   27 metres   Very Severe 4b   (1986)
Start 10 metres right of *The Fugitive*. Climb a corner, slab, and pillar, and finish left.

Botallack Head Zawn (Killas)   OS Ref 363 338

Outlook: South-west.
Tidal. Accessible for three hours either side of low water in calm seas.
Coastguard Identity: Botallack Head.
Environmental Issues: An SSSI with vulnerable plants as at Carn Vellan (page 199).

Botallack Head Zawn is delightfully atmospheric, black, and brooding; ideal during heat-waves. There is some impressive climbing in the lower grades, with *The Dungeon* a challenging but technically reasonable adventure. The seaward face of the main wall catches the afternoon sun but some dampness is inevitable deeper into the zawn. The rock is smooth, with many sloping holds, and becomes slippery when wet.

Approach along a wide track leading northwards from the village of Botallack, keeping left of Manor Farm, to reach ample parking just past the Count House (National Trust). From here, continue along the wide track passing some houses. About 500 metres beyond the houses, the rocky tower of Carn Vellan can be seen down to seaward. Carn Vellan forms the northern arm of a craggy bay and Botallack Head its southern arm. From the track, strike down towards the southern side of the bay across mining spoil-heaps to reach a mine shaft blocked with a metal grille, with a sturdy retaining wall, on the edge of a dripping zawn. The knuckly pinnacles of Botallack Head are to the left of this zawn. Botallack Head Zawn lies on the southern side of the Head. (There are views northwards across the bay to Carn Vellan with its seaward rock bridge). Cross over the broken ridge to grassy slopes and rock ledges where 'sacks can be left. The zawn slices deeply into the slopes below and is approached by going down left (facing out), to skirt the left-hand edge of the zawn to a series of huge rocky steps dropping to seaward. A short abseil or a scramble to seaward at low tide gains the zawn bed. All the climbs are on the big south-west-facing wall.

Low tide and calm seas are needed to enter the zawn by scrambling, although the incoming tide rarely reaches the back of the zawn.

Ninevah   45 metres   Hard Severe   (28.9.68)
Follows a line up the left end of the wall where it falls away to seaward.
1 18m. 4a. Climb a slanting crack close to the mouth of the zawn until it is possible to gain a small ledge on the right below a short steep corner.
2 27m. 4b. Climb the corner and the slab above to exit via a shallow V-groove to a grassy ledge.

Visiting Hours   70 metres   Severe †   (25.5.97)
Start near the mouth of the zawn. The climb is a rising traverse along the prominent strata.
1 20m. Climb a shallow rightward-facing corner to an overhang and then traverse rightwards to a belay niche.
2 25m. Traverse rightwards to the belay niche on *The Dungeon*.
3 25m. (The rock requires care near the end of this pitch.) Continue the traverse until above the jammed boulders at the back of the zawn. From here, climb up to a belay.

Strangeways   40 metres   Hard Severe   4b   (5.92)
Climb the obvious groove at the mouth of the zawn to an overhang. Pass the overhang and continue somewhat boldly to the top.

★Jailer   37 metres   Very Severe   4c   (6.6.80)
Nice climbing with poor protection up a line of cracks on the central section of the face. Start just left of the slightly recessed central section of the face below a shallow leftward-slanting crackline. Climb this with difficulty, traverse right to a crackline splitting the central wall, and follow it to a grassy bay.

The Scrubs   40 metres   Hard Very Severe   4c   (5.92)
Start between two scoops. A poorly-protected first section. Climb up to a horizontal crack, make a tense move up left, and continue slightly left of vertical to finish up the last 5 metres of *Jailer*.

★The Dungeon   50 metres   Hard Severe   (29.12.71)
A splendid adventure, especially if the route is approached by scrambling at low tide, when a real feeling of commitment can be experienced as the tide cuts off retreat. This challenging line is more reasonable than its truly Gothic surroundings suggest. It takes the deep, slanting crackline running up the wall near the back of the zawn.
1 30m. 4b. Climb the wall below and right of the bottom of the crack (often wet) and surmount an overhang to a break. Climb to a stance in the uppermost of three niches.

2 20m. Either continue reasonably up the crack to ledges and move right to climb a short wall to the top, or step right from the belay niche and follow the thinner crack to the top (4a).

The slabby walls and small buttresses above the zawn offer several short pitches and scrambles. Three little routes climb the slabby area of rock above the grassy slopes directly above the zawn.

Close Encounter   25 metres   Severe 4a   (1978)
Very vegetated. Start at the left end of the wall. Climb a small open-book corner until a steep move left gains a leftward-slanting crack, which is followed to the top.

Big Ears   25 metres   Severe 4a   (23.6.78)
Equally vegetated. This is the wide crack between *Close Encounter* and the obvious chimney to the right.

Noddy Esquire   25 metres   Severe 4a   (28.9.68)
Pleasant climbing on rough rock. Pull steeply onto the middle of the brown slab and finish up a green V-groove.

On the approach to the zawn after crossing the upper part of the ridge, a series of short buttresses are passed. The first substantial buttress gives three short routes. The buttress is split by an obvious break with an overhang to its right. The wall left of the break gives **Jam** (12 metres Severe 4a 8.7.90). The central break gives **Sand** (12 metres Very Difficult 8.7.90), while the overhang is taken direct and strenuously to give **Wich** (12 metres Very Severe 4c 8.7.90).

Freedom Zawn (Greenstone/Killas)   OS Ref 362 336

Outlook: South and West
Tides. Partially tidal at the base of the South Face which is awash for only about two hours either side of high water. Even then, routes can be reached by easy traversing if the sea is calm. Most of the lines on the West Face are unaffected by tide. Swell may affect the starts of all the South Face routes and of *The Hood* and *Grand Piano* on the West Face.
Coastguard Identity: The Crowns, Botallack.

A powerful venue with intricate and sometimes strenuous climbing on very steep rock. The routes were climbed on sight and were unprepared. Consequently there may be some remaining looseness, especially on the upper sections.

After prolonged rain, seepage on the West Face affects the routes from *Grand Piano* rightwards and it may take a day or two of sunshine for this area to dry out. The South Face and the line of *The Hood* dry very quickly. The South Face catches the sun from midday onwards and the West Face is at its best from mid-afternoon through to evening.

Approach from the north end of Botallack village. Follow the rough track around left keeping left of Manor Farm to reach a parking area just beyond the old Count House building (National Trust). Several paths lead down through old mine buildings to the cliff edge from where a broad track is followed down to the distinctive Crowns Mine engine houses. Continue past the upper mine building and follow a narrow path that leads ahead below broken cliffs to reach a flat area. The seaward edge of this flat area is directly above a covered-over mine shaft and should be avoided. Freedom Zawn lies down to the right and is reached down an earthy and grassy rake, and then down a rock ramp. The zawn comprises two very steep faces of mixed metamorphic rock lying at right-angles to each other. The faces are separated by a corner-chimney that becomes a chossy break in its upper reaches.

The South Face is about 30 metres high and is the more amenable with several fine steep routes. The West Face is 45 metres in height. It is very steep and intimidating and has some good lines. The starts of the West Face routes are given some character by the deep rock trench that separates the face from the starting ramp. Protection is generally good. There may be some loose rock on the upper sections of both faces.

South Face
Easily accessible from low to mid tide. At high tide, with a calm sea, routes from *El Cuco* rightwards can be reached by hopping across a gap to gain the chimney at the right end of the face, and climbing it easily for 5 metres. Easy ledges can then be descended to the start of the chosen route.

Wham   37 metres   Hard Severe   (4.6.95)
Start on a tidal ledge on the left-hand side of the South Face. Climb the chimney/groove to a rock platform and continue up easier slabs on the right.

El Cuco   34 metres   E2   (15.5.94)
The main feature of the climb is a short, hanging corner near the left end of the South Face. Start at low tide, on the largest boulder beneath the centre of the face.
1 18m. 6a. Climb to a small ledge, from where it is possible to traverse left, between roofs, into a groove below the hanging corner. Climb the groove and make a hard move into the corner, which is followed to a ledge on the left.
2 16m. 5a. Make wild moves over the roof above the ledge on large holds. Climb easily to the top.

★★Nelson   30 metres   E1 5b   (12.5.94)
Steep climbing on good holds. Start at low tide at the base of the middle of
the South Face and below the thin rightwards-trending crack that splits the
steep wall above. Climb easily to a good ledge below the crack. From the
left end of the ledge, follow good holds in the steep wall to the horizontal
break. Pull through the roof above on fine holds onto a slab. Climb the
slab; then exit leftwards over a bulge. Finish easily up the arête.

★The Flow Country   30 metres   E2 5c   (12.5.94)
Steep and exhilarating. Start just right of *Nelson* and climb to the good
ledge. Climb the wall just left of the slanting crack until it is possible to
move right and up on good pockets to below an overhung niche.
Engaging moves gain the fine pocketed wall above. Steep but easier
climbing leads to a small ledge below an impending flake crack. Swing
left on brittle holds and follow the flake boldly to the top.

The Unqualified   34 metres   E4 6a †   (4.6.95)
Climbs the centre of the wall directly to finish as for *Cappucino*. Start in the
centre of the wall and scramble up to the sloping ledge below an obvious
slanting crack and leftward-facing corner. Between these two features is a
thinner crack (often wet) running up a steep wall to an overhang. Climb
the crack and continue straight through the widest point of the overhang.
Climb the headwall to finish as for *Cappucino*.

★Cappucino   34 metres   E1 5b   (7.5.94)
Mostly straightforward, but with a hard finish. Climb the right edge of the
South Face. (Possible stance at 5 metres, if the zawn bed is awash.) Climb
diagonally left across the quartzy section to reach a ledge. Trend right up a
groove and then climb easily left to reach the right-hand end of the
narrowest part of the capping roof. Move up and left using holds over the
roof to reach a good incut, pull around the lip, and finish steeply.

A Very Severe leading from the start of *Cappucino* along a leftward-rising
line to finish up *Nelson* has been climbed.

West Face
The lower part of the west face is split by a number of left-facing corners.

★★★The Hood   40 metres   E4   6a   (22.5.94)
An outstanding pitch that increases in steepness and intensity to a final
strenuous crux. Start on the rock ramp, 3 metres left of the leftmost corner.
Make a very hard pull across the gap onto the pocketed wall, and follow a
thin crack to the horizontal break. Move up for 3 metres through quartz
streaks, step right, and climb steeply to reach a good side-pull. Continue
direct to reach horizontal breaks, and then move right and up into a niche
(resting place). Pull out of the top of the niche on good holds and gain a
small incut at the base of a quartz-filled crack. Step left and pull up

strenuously into a quartz band. Move diagonally right to reach the break at the top of the cliff. Belay at the outcrop 6 metres up the grass slope. Big hexes and cams are useful for the belay.

★★Grand Piano   43 metres   E3   (8.5.94)
A challenging climb. Start below the leftmost corner.
1 15m. 5b. A stiff pull across the gap onto the wall leads to excellent climbing up the black corner to a good ledge.
2 28m. 5c. Climb the shallow groove immediately above and to the left of the stance to an area of brown rock. Swing right to gain the impressive but nerve-wracking flake. Layback steeply up the flake on good holds to a tenuous mantelshelf. Make another mantelshelf move, and teeter rightwards to a good hold in a hidden crack just below the grass. Make a tricky step left to reach good holds on a rib, which allows an exit onto the grass.

Play It Again Sam   35 metres   E2   (1994)
Start 2 metres right of the leftmost corner (between *Grand Piano* and *The Piano*).
1 15m. 5c. Pull across the gap and climb steeply to better pockets. Bear right to what looks like a blunt spike in a quartzy pocket, and continue up and left to the ledge.
2 20m. 5c. *Nkosi Sikelele* pitch 2.

★★The Piano   43 metres   E2   (4.5.94)
Intricate climbing. Start below the second corner.
1 18m. 5c. Step down into the gap and make a very hard move to good holds. Continue more easily up the corner and move delicately left to gain a fine stance.
2 25m. 5c. Climb the steep ramp above by a continually absorbing series of moves.
Variation Start
1a 20m. 5c. The corner to the right of pitch 1 is technically harder overall but has a less testing start. Descend into the gap and then make strenuous layback moves to reach easier ground level with where you started. Good technical climbing then leads to a ledge. Belays can be taken here, or an awkward step left gains the stance at the top of pitch 1.

The next two climbs are split by a broad terrace. The upper pitches have some friable rock which requires careful handling.

★★Nkosi Sikelele   35 metres   E4   (7.5.94)
Two powerful and technical pitches. Start below the steep pocketed wall behind the large boulder and just left of the rightmost corner.
1 15m. 6a. Climb the fine wall on diminishing pockets to a hard finish onto a broad ledge.
2 20m. 5c. The headwall has a striking diagonal crack which provides the line, but not the holds. Good climbing up a short groove gains a pedestal below the diagonal crack. Make bold and strenuous moves up the steep line of the crack on good holds.

Buthelezi   36 metres   E3   (12.5.94)
Intense, a little devious, and rarely straightforward. Start below the rightmost (often wet) corner at the right-hand side of the crag.
1 18m. 4c. Climb the corner, and follow the fine crackline in the wall on good pocket holds to a large sloping ledge. Go down the ledge for about 5 metres and belay below the right-hand of two shallow grooves.
2 18m. 5c. Climb the right-hand groove past a spike, by wide, technical bridging, to a good ledge. Step left and climb carefully past a sandy flake on good pockets, before swinging left on a small hold to enormous jugs on the overhanging wall. A swift pull leads to the top.

Crowns Mine Cliff (Killas)   OS Ref 362 336

Outlook: Mostly west.
Tidal on the seaward face but with a few non-tidal routes.
Coastguard Identity: The Crowns, Botallack.

Approach as for Freedom Zawn (page 209), but after passing the higher of the two buildings, descend polished rocks to a flat grassy platform between the buildings. Continue carefully down the disintegrating slope between the buildings, past wooden and metal debris, and scramble around to the right (facing out) to reach the front of the buttress. The climbs are pleasant, on good rock, and with generally good protection.

Lardy Boys   20 metres   Severe †   (26.5.97)
Start near the left-hand side of the seaward face and climb up to the shoulder at half height. From this large platform, climb an easy crack to the top.

Unhalfbricking It   20 metres   Very Severe 4c †   (26.5.97)
Start in the middle of the face and climb straight up to the top.

Norman Conquest   20 metres   Very Severe 4c †   (26.5.97)
Start near the right-hand side of the seaward face at a rightward-slanting crack. Climb the crack past an awkward bulge at 5 metres. When the crack ends, step left and follow the right-hand side of the face to the top.

Dismembered Members   20 metres   Severe †   (26.5.97)
Start 5 metres right of the last route, at the yellow recess on the right-hand side of the seaward face. Follow the wide cracks to a slab on the right below an overhang. Avoid this at its left-hand end and finish easily.

On the south face of the buttress is a slab with an overhang at 5 metres.

King Shark   20 metres   Severe   †   (26.5.97)
Start just left of the overhang. Climb the crack up and rightwards to the top.

Slab and Tickle   20 metres   Hard Very Severe 5a †   (26.5.97)
The protection is rather sparse. Climb to the overhang and cross it at the slight corner on the right. Climb the middle of the slab to its top, and continue up the slanting corner to finish at a gap in the skyline.

Above the grassy platform are two walls at right-angles. The left wall has a diamond-shaped recess at half height, and the right wall is pink and slabby on its left, becoming black and steeper further right. This is a useful place to climb, well above the sea and sheltered from the worst of the wind. However, the area is very busy with tourists in the season. The restored engine-houses are legally protected.

Crown Green   16 metres   Hard Very Severe 5b †   (31.1.99)
This route takes the centre of the left wall. Climb steeply to enter the recess, and leave it for a ledge on the left. Step right into the continuation groove to finish.

Local Wall   18 metres   Very Severe 4c †   (1990s)
Start up the easy groove on the left side of the right wall to gain a hand-traverse leading rightwards to a final wide crack.

Evening Slabs (Killas)   OS Ref 356 328

Outlook: North-west.
Non-tidal but spray-washed in heavy seas.
Coastguard Identity: Wheal Edward Zawn.

The Slabs are part of a small area of attractive killas slate cliffs on an otherwise brooding coastline of rattling zawns.

Approach along a wide track leading northwards from the village of Botallack, keeping left of Manor Farm, to reach ample parking just past the Count House (National Trust). Join the coast path just below here and walk south for a kilometre to a gate across the path. (The same point can be reached from the Kenidjack cliffs by following the coast path north for a similar distance.) About 300 metres ahead, on the right of the path, is an old shooting butt banked up with grass on its landward side. Make for this and follow an indistinct path down the slope trending leftwards. This leads to an easy-angled grassy spur almost at sea-level. On the right of the spur is a grassy hollow containing a 2-metre-long tilted block, where gear can be left.

To reach the slabs, continue down the spur and then go sharply right down black rocks to cross a narrow rock bridge above an impressive gully. Cross short ragged slabs and piled blocks to reach a sweep of slabs that is skirted by a short entry wall and crowned by a gruesome headwall. As the name suggests the climbs here are at their best later in the day.

Just past the rock bridge there is one short, slightly loose route that takes the right-hand side of the first ragged slab. This is **Hack** (18 metres Very Difficult 22.6.88). Belay on the tilted block using a spare rope.

There are three enjoyable routes on the main slab. All share the same finish, which is often wet but still manageable.

Notbad   36 metres   Very Severe   (22.6.88)
1 18m. 4c. Start below the left end of the slabs where the entry wall falls away to the ragged flanking wall. Climb a steep jagged crack onto a sloping ledge and continue through the break onto the slabs proper. Belay 5 metres above.
2 18m. Continue in a direct line to the grassy exit.

Notrilleachan   43 metres   Hard Severe   (22.6.88)
1 15m. 4b. From directly below the middle of the slabs, make an awkward move up the stepped wall to a ledge and continue up a short crackline to a belay in the middle of the slabs.
2 28m. Continue direct; then traverse left across mixed ground to the common exit up grass.

Notidwal   50 metres   Very Difficult   (15.6.88)
Start at the right-hand end of the slab (facing in), below a square-cut niche.
1 20m. Gain the niche, either direct, or from the right by an awkward step, and continue on a rising traverse leftwards to a belay ledge in the middle of the slabs.
2 30m. Continue in the same line, rising towards the top left-hand edge of the slabs where an exit is made up grass to a block belay.

Kenidjack Cliffs (Killas)   OS Ref 354 326

Outlook: Main Face – South. Seadreams Cliff – South-east.
Non Tidal on Main Face and South Zawn. **Tidal** on Seadreams Cliff and Grooved Face.
Coastguard Identity: Kenidjack Castle.

The Kenidjack cliffs lie to the north-east of Cape Cornwall and at the northern, seaward, end of a deep valley outside the town of St Just. The whole area was intensively mined, particularly during the latter part of the 19th century, and the valley and its environs retain a wealth of industrial remains.

The cliffs offer an excellent venue for the middle-grade climber as they face south, the Main Cliff is unaffected by the tide, and the central part (including *Saxon*) dries quickly. The Main Cliff offers slabby climbing, often with well-spaced protection.

Approach. Start from the crossroads at Nancherrow (OS Ref 370 319) on the B3306 between Botallack and St Just, at the bottom of a steep valley. Follow the road towards the sea, and then a track in the same direction. Where this forks, keep right, uphill, to a parking possibility 50 metres after the fork. Walk, bearing left along an increasingly rough track, through a metal gate to some boulders blocking the track. Continue for a short distance to some distinctive quarries.

South Zawn
This is the wide zawn immediately north of the quarries. Follow the path northwards from the quarry around the grassy rim of South Zawn. The climbs here are contained on the big area of slab on the zawn's grassy north wall, high above the sea. The slab is not as steep as it first appears, but there is some loose rock.

Descent to the base of the slab is best done by abseil from an outcrop set well back from the top (two ropes needed, one to go around the outcrop), although it is possible to descend very steep grass towards the back of the zawn on its northern side.

D I Blues   40 metres   Hard Very Severe 4c   (3.5.80)
Fine slab climbing with scant protection. Start in the centre of the slab, and move diagonally left after 10 metres to the corner of the large overhang. Move left and up across the lip of the overhang; then go straight up to the top.

Scouse Slab   37 metres   Very Severe 4b   (3.5.80)
A contrived line up the slab, starting in the centre and wandering up the rock between the centre and the big corner on the right of the slab.

Drag Artist   37 metres   Very Severe 4b   (5.10.80)
Climb the big, left-facing corner on the right of the slab.

CARN KENIDJACK ~
MAIN CLIFF

1	Gneiss Gnome	HS
2	In The Gallery	HVS
3	Rock Dancer	E1
4	Saxon	HVS
4a	Saxon Direct	HVS
5	Super Direct	E2
6	The Shield	E1
7	Thane	E1
8	Sunny Cellophane	E2
9	Stormbringer	E3

DON SARGEANT ~ 1991

Seadreams Cliff

This pleasant little cliff lies on the southern side of the grassy spur bounding the south side of South Zawn and just below the last quarry at the end of the track, where the path proper begins. The base of the cliff is tidal and wave-washed in westerly swells but is accessible for three hours either side of low water.

Descent is from the quarry by walking to seaward down the grassy spur directly below the start of the path, with the deep inlet of South Zawn on the right. The cliff is reached by contouring left (facing out) from the base of the grassy spur where the grass gives out on rock ledges, stepping across the top of an impressive corner (*Seadreams*), and scrambling down sloping ledges to sea-level.

For routes from *Great Central* rightwards, final belays are scant and the best anchors are at a solid block on the grassy slopes about 20 metres above the *Seadreams* corner. This can be reached with 50-metre ropes. If several routes are to be climbed, it may be more convenient to rig a spare rope from the block down to the cliff-top.

Seaspray   23 metres   Very Difficult   (1982)
A traverse of the cliff from left to right starting from a stepped ledge high on its left edge. The ledge is reached from above by easy scrambling. Traverse slabby rock on good holds, and finish up the crack of *Great Central*, which runs up the left edge of the *Seadreams* wall.

Seahorse   30 metres   Hard Severe 4b   (1982)
A longer and harder left-to-right girdle starting from 8 metres up a short corner on the extreme left of the cliff. Skirt the lip of the left-hand overhangs to cross the wall before finishing up *Seadreams*.

Crazy Horse   18 metres   E2 5c †   (4.96)
Start 5 metres left of *Maneater* at a groove and arête. Move up into the smooth groove with difficulty (high runner in the corner just left). Reach up and move right at the overhang to a welcome good hold but poor runners. Continue directly up the easy slab above to belay well back.

Apocalypse   20 metres   E2 5c †   (4.96)
Start 2 metres left of the corner of *Maneater*. Make steep moves on good holds to a large sidehold under the big overhang (small wire placement to the right). Make a very long reach around the overhang, and continue easily up the slabby pillar above. Belay 5 metres back on the right.

Maneater   23 metres   E1 5b   (1983)
Start just left of the small bay flanking the left edge of *Seadreams* wall. Climb a short crack leading up to an overhang and move out right to finish straight up the rough slab above.

Pink Knight   24 metres   Hard Very Severe 5b   (8.87)
Climb a groove and a crack above from the small bay flanking the left edge of the *Seadreams* wall.

Great Central   23 metres   Severe 4a   (18.4.81)
Climb the obvious crack that snakes up the left side of the *Seadreams* wall.

Salmon Splitter   23 metres   Very Severe 4c   (1982)
A direct line up the middle of the wall just left of *Seadreams* corner. Poor protection in the lower half.

★**Seadreams**   23 metres   Hard Severe 4b   (18.4.81)
Climb the corner on delightful holds.

The Castle   17 metres   Hard Very Severe 5a   (1982)
Climb the blocky arête right of *Seadreams*. Strenuous and bold.

★**Sieging the Castle**   17 metres   E4 6a   (1982)
Fierce climbing up the thin, fingery crackline in the impending wall right of *The Castle*, joining that route to finish.

Foamflower   14 metres   Hard Very Severe 5a   (1982)
The crackline up the corner, a metre or so right of *Sieging the Castle*, is often wet.

Fifty Year Storm   8 metres   Hard Very Severe 5c †   (9.8.97)
Climbs the arête left of *The Roof Is Leaking* on its seaward side. Climb the lower arête to a break and make difficult moves up and right to finish more easily.

The Roof Is Leaking   6 metres   E2 6a   (8.87)
A short problem over the normally wet roof at the right-hand end of the cliff. Crucial holds over the roof are generally dry.

Black Beauty   37 metres   E1 5b   (24.4.87)
Start from ledges well into the deep black zawn right of the *Seadreams* area. Climb a left-to-right crackline that leads to beneath a hanging groove. Move into the groove and then climb rightwards onto the big flake on the right-hand wall and continue direct. The rock is poor near the top.

Grooved Face and Main Cliff

Descent to this area is by the grassy slopes that lie directly below the quarries at the end of the track. Half-way between the two large quarries is a much smaller quarry, with a small boulder on the seaward side of the track. Looking down the slope just to the right (facing out) from this small boulder, two rock outcrops can be seen about 30 metres below. The descent path runs down between the outcrops, trending first right then left, to a steep grassy ridge which has become well-marked by foot-traffic. The last 5 metres of the descent is on easy but steep rock to a quartzy platform.

Grooved Face lies to the left (facing in) of the descent line and is accessible for about three hours either side of low water provided there is no swell.

Submariner   68 metres   Hard Very Severe 5c †   (5.96)
Start at low spring-tide, from boulders at the start of an obvious leftward-leading traverse which leads around onto the seaward end of the buttress. A sunny afternoon helps dry out the crux.
1 18m. 4b. Step onto the traverse-line and follow it with scant protection until a crack is reached. Place good nuts, before descending the crack to a large ledge.
2 5m. 5c. Climb the overhanging wall to the obvious ledge above, via a crack and some slippery moves. Good nut belay.
3 45m. Take the black slab behind the belay to a groove, left of a block. Continue up to a ridge, and then easily up a steep slope. Belay on a dubious block or stakes (removed).

Little Plum   33 metres   Very Severe   (12.11.72)
Worthwhile, although the finish is dirty. Start near sea-level about 30 metres left of the foot of the descent, below a large detached block with a deep crack curving up its right-hand side.
1 6m. Climb the face of the block or the right-hand crack to a good ledge.
2 27m. 4b. Step left into the start of the groove between the left wall and a triangular pinnacle. Climb the groove to the apex of the pinnacle before continuing up and left to a chimney behind a flake. Climb the chimney to grass slopes and belay well back.

Nothinmega   27 metres   Very Severe 4b   (1982)
Climb the right-hand crack of the *Little Plum* block, and then the groove that runs up the right side of the triangular pinnacle, to finish up *Little Plum*.

Sesquipedalian   27 metres   Very Severe 4b   (1982)
The wide blocky groove right of *Nothinmega*.

Beyond here, Grooved Face becomes broken and loose and loses height.

Main Cliff is unaffected by the tide although swell can be dangerous. From the base of the descent line, walk right (facing in) along a broad ramp to the boulder strewn base of the cliff. Main Cliff is a handsome sweep of black slate, dense and compact in places, but with characteristic bubbly rock and quartz intrusions. Its central area is taken by *Saxon*, which traces a line from the right-hand base of the wall starting along the obvious ramp. On the right of this section is a big corner which is taken by the challenging line of *Thane*. Right of these the cliff becomes impressively complex and, though sometimes wet in places, holds a number of good routes. The first route takes the dark corner at the left-hand side of Main Cliff.

Gneiss Gnome   27 metres   Hard Severe 4b   (31.12.71)
A good introduction to the cliff. Start from the approach ramp and climb a quartzy wall (slightly loose) to enter the corner. Follow it to a belay in a niche alongside the descent path.

Sword at Sunset   45 metres   Hard Very Severe   (10.10.80)
A sustained left-to-right rising diagonal, which links some good climbing. Start just right of *Gneiss Gnome* at the base of a groove with a diamond-shaped overhang at 5 metres.
1 27m. 5a. Climb the groove for about 3 metres and then make steep moves up and right on slightly friable rock. Continue in a diagonal line to cross *Saxon*. Go up steeply for 3 metres and move across to the groove of *The Shield*, which is climbed to a belay.
2 18m. 5a. Step up and follow a thin diagonal crack to the corner of *Thane*, which is followed to the top.

★In the Gallery   37 metres   Hard Very Severe 5a   (20.4.79)
Start to the right of *Gneiss Gnome*, below a thin crack where the approach ramp levels off. Climb the crack and wall through a horizontal band of quartz at 3 metres to a flake on a long ledge at 15 metres. From the top of the flake, follow a faint crackline until it runs out at an easy-angled slab above and left of the prominent horizontal crackline running across the upper wall. Climb the slab near its right edge.

★★Rock Dancer   46 metres   E1 5b   (17.4.79)
Challenging and direct. Start from a long flat boulder below the mid-point of the ramp-line that runs across the wall about 8 metres up. Make a strenuous pull up and gain the ramp-line. Continue for 12 metres before moving left and up into the obvious sloping 'slot' ledge. Traverse left until it is possible to climb directly to the top of the cliff past a horizontal break.
Variation Start
The Wooden Box E2 5c (5.85). Start 3 metres to the left. Pull leftwards through the bulge into a shallow groove. Step right and climb direct to the ramp-line. Continue up *Rock Dancer*.

★★★Saxon   50 metres   Hard Very Severe   (31.3.74)
One of West Penwith's great routes: exposed and exhilarating. Careful rope-work is needed. Start at the right-hand base of the central wall, just left of a huge boulder leaning against the cliff.
1 43m. 4c. Gain the easy ramp by a gymnastic move and follow it left for 10 metres to where it peters out (belay possible). (The ramp can be gained less strenuously by back-and-footing between the huge boulder and the cliff or by traversing from the top of the huge boulder.) Move up left for a metre, and climb direct to a shallow niche with good runners. Move up; then follow a line of scooped footholds rising leftwards towards

the edge of the wall before stepping up to gain the horizontal break. Traverse right along the break to a stance on top of the block where the wall recesses.
2 7m. 4c. Make an interesting move up and left onto the wall above and finish diagonally leftwards.
Direct Start 5a. Climb directly up the wall to reach the left-hand end of the ramp. Poor protection. (This is to the left of both *Rock Dancer* and *its* direct start.)
Direct Finish 5a (2.4.79). Instead of traversing right to the belay, continue direct from half way along the horizontal break.

The following routes are based on the steep recessed section of the cliff bounding the *Saxon* wall on its right.

Super Direct   37 metres   E2 5b   (20.4.79)
Well-spaced protection, but low in the grade. Start from the top of the huge boulder which leans against the right-hand end of the cliff. Step off the boulder and follow a faint crackline on the left past a horizontal break. Where the crack peters out, continue to a small overhang. Move left beneath this and up, avoiding the blocky groove further left. Go back right up a smooth slab to the earthy break. Climb the wall above direct using small pockets, finishing on better holds.

Viking's Dawn   40 metres   Hard Very Severe 5a   (10.10.80)
A rising traverse of the Main Cliff from right to left following a natural line and giving good sustained climbing. Start from the top of the huge boulder. Climb direct to a horizontal fault at 5 metres and bear left up a slanting crack to beneath a quartz patch. Make some steep moves; then continue traversing left to the niche on *Saxon*. Traverse left rising slightly with feet at about the level of the parallel diagonal cracks, to reach the groove of *In the Gallery*. Finish up the groove, exiting right up a small rib.

★The Shield   35 metres   E1   (31.12.71)
A fine sustained route with sparse protection on pitch 2. Start on the huge boulder which leans against the right-hand end of the cliff.
1 20m. 4c. Climb direct to a horizontal fault at 5 metres, then bear left up a slanting crack to beneath a quartz patch. Continue direct to a line of holds leading to a corner formed by a large block. Gain the top of the block (the stance of *Saxon*).
2 15m. 5a. A bold pitch. Step up, then right. Continue rightwards, rising slightly, almost as far as the large open corner on the right, and then climb directly to the top. Block belay well back.

Facedancer   35 metres   E2 5b   (1993)
Start on top of the boulder. Climb direct, passing to the right of the prominent small overhang at mid height, to reach an earthy break. Finish directly on small pockets, as for *Super Direct*.

★★Thane   40 metres   E1 5b   (31.3.74)

Impressive and direct, taking the open corner which bounds the wall high up on its right-hand side. Start on top of the huge boulder. Climb rightwards over quartz-streaked rock passing a long narrow overhang to enter a groove system that slants up leftwards. Pleasant climbing leads to bulging rock beneath the corner. Keep right of the diagonal earthy break, and make steep moves up to and over the left side of the bulge to enter the corner, which is followed over the top.

Sunny Cellophane   45 metres   E2   (30.6.79)

The steep arête right of *Thane*. Start at the foot of a cracked slab at the junction of the main wall and the right-hand cliff.
1 12m. 4b. Climb to the leftward-sloping blocky groove of *Thane* and belay at a ledge.
2 33m. 5b. Move up, and then right into a corner. Move left and go over the roof into the corner of *Thane*. Climb delicately across the right wall (old peg), and make a difficult step onto the arête. Take this and the wall above to the top.

★Stormbringer   45 metres   E3   (30.6.79)

Good climbing on the second pitch, with well-spaced protection.
1 12m. 4b. *Sunny Cellophane* pitch 1.
2 33m. 5c. Climb up, go right into a corner, and then move right onto the arête. Make a strenuous move up to the roof, followed by some difficult moves right to enable the lip of the next roof to be used to get onto a sloping ledge. Move back left onto the steep wall which leads to the top.

Slanter   42 metres   Very Severe   (29.6.79)

This route takes the upper of two diagonal lines across the right-hand wall of the cliff. Take care with the rock.
1 12m. 4b. *Sunny Cellophane* pitch 1.
2 30m. 4b. Traverse right onto the small slab and continue up right onto the larger slab. Pull up onto steeper rock and follow this past a fin of rock to large blocks. Climb these and then go right to belay around the corner, or go straight up grooves to belays a further 15 metres up the grass slope.

Short Circuit   45 metres   E1   (8.79)

Start at the foot of a slab at the junction of the main wall and the right-hand cliff.
1 15m. 4b. Climb direct; then move onto the large, lower slab cutting diagonally right. Follow this up to the right for 10 metres to belay on a ledge.
2 30m. 5b. Move back left down the slab; then climb boldly over the roof at a slight groove. Climb directly up to join and follow *Slanter* to the top.

Diagonal   45 metres   E2   (1979)

1 15m. 4b. *Short Circuit* pitch 1.
2 30m. 5b. Climb up right for a few metres, and break back left up steeper rock to reach the exit of *Slanter*.

Carn Gloose: Cave Zawn

(Granite) OS Ref 352 314

Outlook: West.
Tidal. Accessible three hours before and after low water.
Coastguard Identity: Carn Gloose (near St Just).

This area of fine-grained granite lies south of Cape Cornwall and marks the break from the north coast killas. It offers enjoyable short climbs, the names of some of which are every bit as tasteless as their shaky finishes.

Approach: Cave Zawn can be reached at dead low tide along the rocky beach that runs south from Priest's Cove, just south of Cape Cornwall. There is a large car-park above the cove, which is reached from St Just down the narrow lane sign-posted to Cape Cornwall. The best approach to the crag, however, is from the summit of Carn Gloose, which is reached by road from St Just; take the Cape Cornwall road and turn left almost opposite the cricket club. There is convenient parking at the road end.

Carn Gloose is crowned by three distinctive rock outcrops. From the road end, walk north along the track between two granite gateposts until abreast of the northern summit. Look for the faint beginnings of a fisherman's path which leads down the right-hand side (facing out) of the northern summit to the seaward edge of Cave Zawn. Most of the climbs are on the wall running back into the zawn. The first short wall has several obvious cracklines that have been climbed at about Hard Severe. On the next, higher section of the cliff, an overhang at 12 metres is breached by a groove. This is *Cheddar*. All the routes on the north wall have loose finishes.

Cheddar 20 metres Very Severe 4c   (3.3.82)
At the top end of its grade. Climb to the overhang at 12 metres and crank through the groove on gravelly rock.

The cliff right of *Cheddar* is centrally split by a deep cleft.

Addanardon 18 metres Hard Very Severe 5b   (1984)
The first in a sequence of pleasant routes. Start 2 metres right of the central cleft. A few neatly technical moves lead up twin black ramps to an impending headwall and corner-crack to finish.

Narcissus 20 metres Hard Severe 4b   (3.3.82)
The pleasant black and broken crackline right of the previous route.

Hard On 18 metres Hard Very Severe 5a   (1984)
The wall right of *Narcissus* is climbed by a leftward-trending series of corners, and then by finishing rightwards over ledges.

Hard Up   18 metres   Very Severe 4c   (1984)
Climb a slight ramp just right of *Hard On* to a crack formed by a hanging
flake. Climb the crack and continue over a bulge to the top.

There are two routes on the grey, sunless wall that forms the south side of the
zawn. Accessible from the north wall area at low tide or by abseil from the
top of the south rim of the zawn after negotiating mixed slopes, with care,
from above.

Twinkletoes   18 metres   Very Severe 4c   (3.3.82)
Worthwhile. Climb the centre of the grey wall to a ledge at 12 metres. Step
right and up, around a steep nose, and continue to the top on weary rock
to a finish with one of the best views in Cornwall.

First Entry   18 metres   Severe 4a   (3.3.82)
The right-hand corner of the wall is climbed direct.

Porth Nanven (Granite)   OS Ref 355 306

Outlook: West.
Tidal at base of the cliff but accessible for three hours either side of low
water. Affected by swell and rough sea.
Coastguard Identity: Porth Nanven.

Pompey Wall offers delightful short pitches, some of which give good testing
moves.

Approach from the road end at Porth Nanven at the mouth of the lovely
Cot Valley (sign-posted from St Just). From the car-park, cross a small
footbridge and walk south along the coast path for about half a kilometre to
where the path turns sharply left up some rock steps. Follow a subsidiary
path leading directly ahead towards a rocky ridge. The path runs below the
mouth of a dangerous mine shaft with warning notices. From a point just
before the ridge, follow a faint path down steeply to the right over stony
ground; then move down left to a boulder-strewn ledge above Pompey Wall.
The base of the wall can be reached by easy scrambling down its left edge
(facing out) or by a series of reverse mantelshelves down its right side,
although an abseil rope is more convenient.

Pompey Wall rises to a height of 10 metres from a smooth, tidal platform.
The wall is flanked on its left (facing in) by a small stepped ridge. **Curving
Crack** (Very Difficult 1960-63) takes a line over ledges just right of the
corner between the stepped ridge and the main wall. **Doorstep** (Difficult
1960-63) is a direct line over the ledges. **Slope** (4b 1960-63) takes the

clean shallow corner to the right of *Doorstep*. The central section of the cliff features a handsome little wall with nicely spaced horizontal cracklines. **Larboard** (5c 6.84) follows the neat groove on the left of the wall after a tricky start. **Midships** (5b 6.84) takes the faint central crackline and **Starboard** (5b 6.84) climbs the right side of the wall, keeping left of the big ledge in the central chimney. The chimney gives **Bosun's Whistle** (Difficult 1960-63). Right of the chimney there is a step down in the starting ledge. Above this is the striking little line of **Tall Ships** (5b 6.84) up a narrow hooded slab. The arête right of this gives **Shellback** (5a 6.84). A 2-metre step leads up to a final ledge below a short wall with an obvious 'box' feature at two-thirds height. **Box** (Very Difficult 1960-63) goes up the curving ledges to gain the box from the right. **Fingernail** (4b 1960-63) starts up the thin crack just right of *Box*, and then trends rightwards to finish up a crack. **Exit** (Moderate 1960-63) takes a line up the right edge of the wall past a triangular recess.

Progo Arch was a fascinating feature until it succumbed to the forces of tempest and gravity during the winter of 97/98. Its priapic remains are reached by following ledges down to sea-level to the right (facing in) of Pompey Wall, giving access to a wide flat beach with bouldering opportunities on flanking outcrops. The beach is covered variously with silver sand or knee-deep, stinking seaweed. The imposing Pogo Wall lies behind the pinnacle and has two good routes, which can be reached 3 hours either side of low water.

☆☆**Evening Star**   25 metres   E2 5b †   (27.3.2000)
An attractive crackline, sustained and varied, but bold. Start on a large rounded boulder beneath a vertical crack, 2 metres from the right-hand end of the steep wall. Gain the crack and climb it to a ledge. Traverse delicately left to gain a shallow groove and hard-won protection. Make tenative moves out left from an overhung niche to gain a second niche and better runners. Climb twin cracks to a flat-topped block, which requires gentle handling, and continue via a groove to the top. Scramble left (some looseness) to multiple belays.

Archipeligo   25 metres   Severe   (19.4.98)
A pleasantly exposed route on good rock. Start at the right-hand end of Pogo Wall. Follow the narrow slab until it peters out and continue steeply to the right via a crack to a ledge. Climb diagonally leftwards across a short steep wall to another ledge. Sling and large hex belay. Traverse carefully off leftwards.

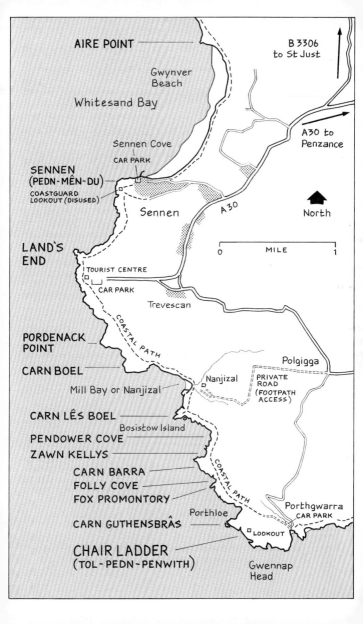

Aire Point (Granite) OS Ref 358 282

Outlook: West.
Non-tidal but can be affected in big swell.
Coastguard Identity: Aire Point.

The crag which bears the name Aire Point is an attractive granite buttress rising to a height of 20 metres from a broken platform that lies well above sea-level. Situated just beyond the northern end of Whitesand Bay, it has a decidedly fresh 'open sea' atmosphere with a marvellous outlook towards Sennen and The Longships Lighthouse.

Approach is best from Gwynver (pronounced Gwenver) Beach. There is a paying car-park above the beach, which is reached from the Penzance – Land's End road by taking a lane to seaward at OS Ref 371 270. (On the main road just south of the lane's turn off is a sharp corner by a Methodist Chapel.) After half a mile the lane branches: take the right-hand branch to a car-park at a distinctive round gate-house. From the car-park, go straight down to the beach and follow the coast path northwards to the rocky headland of Aire Point, which forms the northern limit of Whitesand Bay. The crag itself, with the obvious vertical cleft of *Aireline*, can now be seen about 300 metres to the north.

Varicose Zawn

On the north side of Aire Point's main buttress is a wide-mouthed zawn with an undercut slab forming its back wall. The slab is split centrally by a break, while a crumpled black vein runs diagonally up the slab from left to right.

Varicose   25 metres   Very Difficult (10.77)
Climb the black vein; awkward to start.

Claudication   20 metres   Very Severe 4c (21.7.85)
A pleasant pitch taking the dog-leg crack on the right side of the slab to where it fades out at some thin moves. Start by the earthy break on the right.

Stealth   20 metres   Hard Very Severe 4c (10.91)
Climb directly up the slab to the right of *Claudication*. Bold.

There is one route on the steep wall to the right of the undercut slab.

Cargo Route   18 metres   Severe 4b (30.6.88)
A black vein runs from left to right up the wall. Climb the vein (difficult to start) to the higher of two ledges, and finish up an orange arête.

Aire Point

The south-facing main wall of the buttress is centrally split by a V-shaped cleft, which is climbed by *Aireline*. To its left is a steep wall guarded by overhangs at one-third height. Left of the wall there is a recess flanked on its left by a lichen-covered tower.

An Gof   18 metres   Severe †   (29.5.97)
Start on the seaward face and climb through an obvious V-notch, to finish left of the lichen-covered tower.

The following routes are on the south face.

Night Flight   18 metres   Severe   (29.7.77)
The slab and broken crack on the left side of the face.

Dick Dastardly   18 metres   E2 5b   (1.9.85)
The overhang at two-thirds height is breached on its left by a break. Climb through this; then go left up a ramp and finish up an arête.

★★**Spitfire**   18 metres   E3 5c   (21.7.85)
A good steep pitch. Climb through the central V-shaped break in the overhang and continue directly up the wall.

Wiki Wiki Wheels   18 metres   E3 6a   (1.9.85)
Climb the right-hand break in the overhang; then go up the thin crack above and through a bubbly band of rock to reach a diagonal line leading left to finish up *Spitfire*. (Alternatively, finish direct for an extra E-grade.)

★**Aireline**   18 metres   Very Severe 4c   (29.7.77)
A tough, stylish line taking the central V-cleft.

★**Biggles Flies Undone**   18 metres   Hard Very Severe 5a   (3.9.84)
[Photo p.192b.] Start up twin cracks just left of the right-hand edge of the face; then climb the excellent flake before finishing leftwards beneath the final roof.
Variation E2 5b. Climb the final roof direct.

Landing Strip   40 metres   Severe 4b   (21.7.85)
A girdle starting from the right-hand edge of the face, following an obvious line crossing the cleft of *Aireline*, and traversing the ledge system above the central overhang on the *Spitfire* wall.

Max Crack   15 metres   E2 5b   (10.91)
Start below the right-hand end of the diagonal break. Climb the obvious hanging crack to the roof, undercut the crack and layaway around the lip. Finish with a struggle up the off-width crack. Good natural thread.

Airport   15 metres   Severe   (29.7.77)
On the broken right flank of the main face there is a wide chimney which
contains a slab with cracks on either side. Just below and to the right is a
shallow scoop, which is climbed to a ledge. Move left to finish up the
chimney.

Two short pitches make the most of the landward-facing wall to the right.
Hello Salar (10 metres Very Difficult 1.10.77) climbs strenuously to the left
end of the recessed ledge, and then moves up and right by a series of flakes
to finish up a short crack. **Biggles** (9 metres Moderate 30.7.77) takes a line
up the bubbly wall starting from a black seam.

John Wayne Memorial Crag (Granite)   OS Ref 362 278
Outlook: South-west
Tidal. This cliff can only be climbed on near low water and in calm seas.
Coastguard Identity: Aire Point

This interesting outcrop, although small, is well worth a visit. It is composed
of solid sea-washed granite and contains a number of good routes. The cliff
is best visited after midday when it is a sun-trap; it is always uncrowded and
has excellent bouldering close by.

Approach as far as the beach as for Aire Point (page 228). Turn right,
follow the coast path northwards crossing a stream after 100 metres, and
continue for another 400 metres to an orange lifebelt sited on a headland.
The cliff, which is flat topped and not easy to see, is found 150 metres further
along the coastal path, some 200 metres before Aire Point. Scramble down
boulders and continue over them to arrive at the base of the cliff.

The cliff has easy-angled black slabs at the left-hand end, then a chimney,
an overhang, and a series of corners before the impressive steep central
face is reached. A leftward-leading diagonal break marks the right-hand
end of the cliff.

The first climb is found at the left-hand end of the cliff at a black slab with
four horizontal breaks. A huge rounded boulder looms over the start of the
slab.

The Duke   8 metres   Severe 4a   (7.3.99)
Start beneath a thin crack that runs up the slab. Climb the crack to the
final break, where a difficult move gains an easier finish.

True Grit   8 metres   Very Difficult   (17.2.99)
Start at the base of the black slab just right of the thin crack. Climb the
centre of the slab by delicate moves and long reaches between the
horizontal breaks, finishing up a little flake near the top.

Rio Bravo   8 metres   Severe 4a   (20.2.99)
Start at the right edge of the slab at a very rounded arête. Climb the arête
delicately to the second break; a thin move up using rounded holds (easier
for the tall) gains a good ledge, from which an easy finish follows.

Rooster Cogburn   8 metres   Severe 4a †   (17.2.99)
Start at a black V-shaped groove. Climb the groove and the wide crack
above, using a crucial good hold high on the left. Finish easily up the wide
crack above.

The Big Trail   8 metres   Severe 4a †   (17.2.99)
Start at the right-hand edge of the black V-shaped groove. Climb the edge
of the groove before moving up and right to a tiny ledge. Make a bold
move up the bulge above using a rightward-leaning crack and gain a
wide ledge. Finish easily up broken rock.

Fort Apache   8 metres   Very Difficult †   (17.2.99)
Start just right again at a little overlap, to the left of an off-width crack.
Climb the overlap strenuously, and then traverse 3 metres right to a faint
white quartz crack. Ignore this and instead climb the thin crack above to
finish just right of a loose projecting block.

The cliff continues with a wide overhang, above which is a pair of parallel
white quartz veins trending rightwards.

The Alamo   8 metres   Very Severe 5c   (20.2.99)
Start on boulders at the lip of the overhang beneath a big quartz vein.
Climb the overhang using the vein; once over, continue up the vein more
easily to finish.

The Quiet Man   8 metres   Severe 4a †   (17.2.99)
Start just right of the overhang. Climb up towards the larger quartz vein and
pull strenuously onto it. Follow the vein more easily rightwards to the top.

Cheyenne   8 metres   Hard Very Severe 5a †   (20.2.99)
Start in the middle of the red wall. Climb the wall leftwards, using spaced
incuts, to gain the ramp. Hand-traverse rightwards up this to finish.

Blood Wagon   10 metres   Very Severe 4c   (1984)
Start at the base of the corner, which has a black wall and a prominent
undercut arête to the right. Climb the corner, using projecting wedged
blocks carefully, and finish direct.

Vigilante   8 metres   Severe 4a †   (20.2.99)
Start beneath a vertical black crackline that runs just left of a ledge at 3
metres height. Overcome a steep start up the thin black cracks to get
established on the slab; continue up the cracks to a good ledge and a
scrambling finish.

Deputy Sheriff   10 metres   Very Severe 4c   (1984)
Start in the middle of a small slab that leads to a ledge at 3 metres. Climb
the slab using flakes to gain the ledge. From the right-hand end of the
ledge, climb the arête using two horizontal breaks. Gain the layaway crack
above by a nicely technical move to finish in a good position.

The Searchers   10 metres   Very Difficult   (5.4.99)
Start to the right of the small slab at a wide leaning crack. Grunt up the
wide crack (difficult to start), moving leftwards to a ledge. Continue more
easily up the corner-crack.

Sheriff   10 metres   Very Severe 4c   (1984)
Start as for The Searchers at a wide crack that leads to a ledge at 3 metres.
Climb the crack to the ledge. From the right-hand end of the ledge, step
up and out right onto a slab, and then climb a rightward-leaning crack to
the top.

Cow Girl   10 metres   Very Difficult   (1977)
Start just right of the wide crack. Climb a thin crack, which leads to the big
leaning chimney. Climb the chimney mainly using its right edge to a steep
and exposed finish.

Now follows the most impressive part of this cliff, a fine steep wall broken
centrally by a leaning crack. Further right, beyond an overhanging wall, is a
crack and hanging corner; right again is a black-coloured slanting ramp
that leads up easily leftwards.

Hit the Deck, Here She Comes   10 metres   E2 6a   (1984)
Start 6 metres right of the base of the chimney, at a leftward-leaning crack.
Use a flake left of the crack to gain a little slab. Move up the slab to
horizontal breaks and a short thin vertical crack. Climb the crack, move
right to the leftward-leaning black cracks, and climb these with difficulty to
a sudden finish onto a ledge. Finish up the chimney of Cow Girl
immediately behind the ledge.

Reagan's Regression   10 metres   Hard Very Severe 5b   (1984)
Start 6 metres right again, where a vertical crack leads to an interesting
hanging corner. Climb the crack, move up into the corner, and continue
up it to a slab. Finish up a crack and the ramp above leading leftwards.

Stagecoach   8 metres   Very Severe 5c †   (2.96)
Start 2 metres right again, beneath a short wall criss-crossed by cracks.
Climb to the short vertical crack, move up and then use layaways on the
little arête above to gain the ramp. Climb the overhanging wall behind, by
a pink crystalline hollow, using a good hold to gain the sloping ledge
above. Finish easily up blocks.

Red River   8 metres   Very Severe 5c †   (7.3.99)
Start just right again. Climb to a small overlap and then move up with
difficulty to mantelshelf onto the ramp above. Finish as for *Stagecoach* up
the overhanging wall.

An easy ramp now follows, which is handy for ascent from or descent to the
climbs on the central wall and southern end of the cliff.

The Long Voyage Home   10 metres   Severe 4a †   (7.3.99)
Start 5 metres to the right of the ramp beyond a loose, overhanging wall,
at a black and white vein. Step onto the vein and climb steeply to a
leftward-leaning ramp, which is followed to an easy finish.

Sennen: Pedn-mên-du (Granite) OS Ref 347 263

Outlook: West.
Non-tidal apart from The Forgotten Wall, Black Zawn and Irish Lady Cove.
The whole cliff can be affected by big waves at all states of the tide; in addition
the Central Area is subject to a spectacular waterspout, from a blowhole.
Coastguard Identity: Pedn-mên-du.

Pedn-mên-du, the 'Black Headland', is West Penwith's answer to the Gritstone
Outcrops: a Roaches-by-the-sea, although Cornish partisans would give
granite the edge. Sennen's granite is certainly close to being impeccable:
steep, clean, immensely varied, and solid. The shortness of the climbs is
compensated for by their compact style: plenty of moves in short order. All
grades exist from Moderates through classic Severes to the upper E-grades.

The cliff is made up of a beautifully-structured series of walls and corners,
each facet changing in character of rock and outlook. The entire area is a
sun-trap in spring and summer, although the Black Zawn can be sea-damp
at times. With Sennen Cove and its magnificent surfing beaches nearby,
though out of sight, what more could the climber ask for?

Sennen was first developed by the Cliff Assault Wing of The Royal Marines,
which had taken over cliff assault training from the war-time Commando
Mountain Warfare Training Centre. The commandos' wartime activities
involved manic assaults with grappling irons, full combat gear, and a
hundredweight of steel on either foot. Latterly, however, the Marines produced
remarkable climbs and climbers, and for years after the war their contribution
to climbing in West Penwith was immense. Sennen was the Marines' ideal
venue and remains a favourite training crag. The presence of military
trainees and commercial climbing groups can sometimes overcrowd the
cliff, but the Marines were there first.

Sennen has had a reputation for under-grading; this may just reflect the strenuous and compact nature of the harder pitches. Most routes are amenable with the lower grades being very relaxed. Protection is generally excellent.

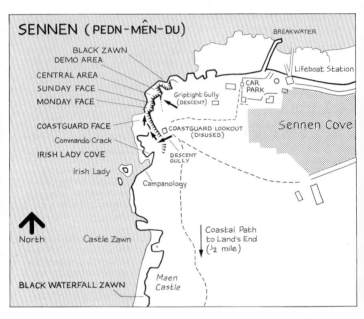

The cliffs run north to south. They rise from a series of stepped platforms situated below the old coastguard lookout on the prominent headland west of Sennen Cove. From the car-park at the western end of Sennen Cove village (a very busy car-park by mid-morning in July and August), the coast path leads up to the lookout.

Descent. There are several ways to reach the base of the cliffs, the first being the safest:
1 Climbers on their first visit should take their bearings from the coastguard lookout, which is now a National Trust information point. The easiest, though longest, approach to the base of the cliff from here is to the south. Behind the lookout, a deep gully with jammed blocks near its top falls to the south. To the right of the gully (facing out) is a rib with a split boulder perched on top.

Go down to the right of the split boulder and scramble easily down a narrow gully in line with the distinctive offshore rock of the 'Irish Lady' with its strange summit boulders. An eroded path descends, passing the steep-sided Irish Lady Cove on the left, and then leads rightwards onto a large, open area of ledges and boulders below the sun-trap walls of Coastguard Face. The rest of the cliff is reached by a pleasant scramble northwards over a series of steps and ledges beneath Monday Face and Sunday Face, culminating in a 5-metre descent, The Aisle, onto the large platform beneath the main part of the cliff.

2 A sea-level approach beneath The Forgotten Wall and into Black Zawn at the north end of Pedn-mên-du is possible along the foreshore from Sennen Cove. This can be **extremely dangerous** and should be attempted only at low water, on spring-tides, when the sea is calm.

3 A more direct access to the main part of the cliff is by climbing down *Griptight Gully* (Difficult). The top of the gully can be located by walking due north from the lookout (with the stump of the flag-pole behind you) for about 80 metres towards the farthest part of the cliff, on which there is a flat perched block. This leads to a break in the cliff-top, the top of *Griptight Gully*, with the impressive *Demo Route* wall beyond. *Griptight Gully* has a steep central section with large holds. Near its base it is easier to cross right (facing in) to avoid the undercut foot of the cliff. The gully is sometimes wet and a traverse to the right (facing in), after the first 10 metres of descent, provides an alternative. This leads to a large ledge. From its far end, huge holds lead down the lower section of *Main Face Climb* (Difficult) to the base of the cliff. **Warning:** This descent involves steep, although relatively easy down-climbing and this should be taken into account if novices are involved.

The climbs are described from left to right facing in and the divisions of the cliff are as follows: The Forgotten Wall, Black Zawn, Demo Area, Central Area, Sunday Face, Monday Face, and Coastguard Face.

The Forgotten Wall
This short, steeply overhanging wall lies at the most northerly tip of the cliff and can only be climbed at low water when the sea is very calm. Belay immediately on arrival to guard against being washed away.

The Forgotten Wall   10 metres   E5 6a †   (1994)
Start just to the left of the main face, at a little groove capped by a roof. Climb the groove and then the roof above. The right-hand arête may be climbed instead of the groove at a bolder E6 6a.

Placa del Edwards   18 metres   E7 6c/7a †   (1994)
One of the hardest lines at Sennen. Start at the left-hand end of the main face, below a small roof. Either climb the roof direct or traverse in from the left, climb powerfully up the wall past two pegs, and finish up a shallow groove.

236

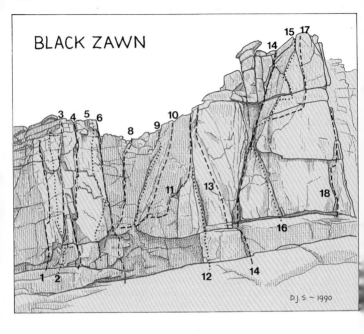

BLACK ZAWN

1	Prow	E4
2	High Street Blues	E5
3	Delilah	E2
4	Zig Zag	HVS
5	Tears of a Clown	E7

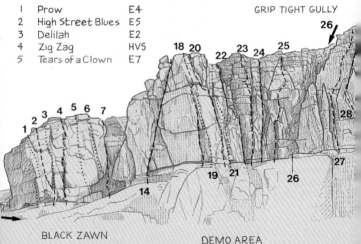

GRIP TIGHT GULLY

BLACK ZAWN   DEMO AREA

SENNEN : PEDN-MEN-DU

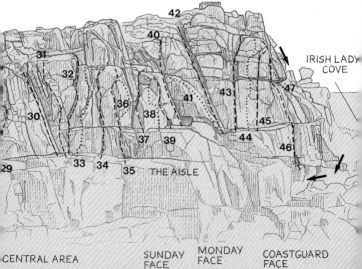

CENTRAL AREA · SUNDAY FACE · MONDAY FACE · COASTGUARD FACE · IRISH LADY COVE · THE AISLE

The Paragon Returns   18 metres   E7 6b †   (1990s)
A serious route, with scant protection. Start beneath the overhanging arête 5 metres left of the entrance to Black Zawn. Climb the arête and finish up the wall right of the top groove of *Placa del Edwards*.

Black Zawn

This steep-walled zawn at the northern end of the cliff, which can be sea-washed any time after half-tide, provides many of the harder routes at Sennen. Its left wall contains the prominent staggered crackline of *Zig Zag*, while in the shadowy back of the zawn is the distinctive black slab which gives *Slippery Slab*, with *Congo Route* on its right. To the right of this, above a stepped ledge, is an impressively steep wall broken by the deep crackline of *Genge's Groove*, and ending on its right at the blunt arête of *Samson Arête*.

★**Prow**   17 metres   E4 6a   (8.87)
Start below the left arête of the *Zig Zag* face. Climb the wall on well-spaced holds to a small ledge. Continue up the wall on the right to finish up a groove.

★★**High Street Blues**   17 metres   E5 6a   (8.87)
Start as for *Delilah*, by gaining a ledge and slim triangular niche. Step up leftwards onto the wall and follow slight cracks leftwards up the wall to a break; then follow faint cracks to another break. Move rightwards over an overlap and finish up the steep wall above. Alternatively finish straight up the wall left of the overlap.

★**Delilah**   17 metres   E2 5b   (1956/1973)
[Photo p.32a.] A tough little pitch with good moves. Start below the slim triangular niche at the base of the thin crack on the left of the face. Gain a good ledge and climb the short pillar above. From the top of this, climb the crack to a sloping recess; swing left and climb the short wall to the top.

Cool Curl (20 metres Hard Very Severe 5b 7.85) climbs *Zig Zag* to mid height and then traverses the crack that runs leftwards to join *Delilah*, which is climbed to finish.

★**Zig Zag**   18 metres   Hard Very Severe 5a   (10.7.55)
The eye-catching, staggered crackline running up left of centre of the face. Strenuous but enjoyable. Start at the foot of the crack and climb to the sentry-box. Move out and continue up the wide crack to a sloping ledge. Move right and then climb the final overhang on good holds.

29 Palms (20 metres E6 6c 11.87) was a very technical route up the wall right of *Zig Zag* over two slim overlaps. From the ledge right of *Zig Zag*, climb the wall to the first overlap. Pull over this to a second overlap and then continue up the wall to the top. (The four pegs and the four drilled pegs which replaced them are no longer in place.)

☆☆☆**Tears of a Clown**   23 metres   E7 6b †   (7.86)
Another very technical line, which takes a direct line up the wall to the right of *29 Palms*. Long reaches and strenuous moves with only small wires for protection make this a serious lead.

★**Ace of Spades**   26 metres   E4 5c   (17.8.82)
Bold with slight protection, taking the jet-black arête just left of the back left-hand corner of the zawn. Start from a slim ledge about 5 metres up *Norge Corner* and gain the arête on the left. Follow the arête on its right-hand side to the top.
Direct Start   24 metres   E5 5c   (7.9.85)
Gain the arête from directly below. Protection: nil.

Thieves Carnival   30 metres   E6 6b †   (1988)
A right-to-left traverse of the *Zig Zag* wall at mid height, starting up *Norge Corner* and finishing up *High Street Blues*.

Norge Corner   24 metres   Hard Severe 4b
A welcome easing of difficulty, though giving quite strenuous climbing up the left-hand back corner of the zawn. Start below the break at the back of the zawn and gain a ledge. Continue up and left to a ledge below the dark corner proper (belay possible). Climb the corner on good holds to the overhang, which is taken boldly using a small foothold on the left.

Skid Mark   21 metres   E4 6b †   (1994)
Follow *Slight Pause* up past its second ledge to a horizontal break. Hand-traverse leftwards into the centre of the wall and climb up boldly to good holds. Finish directly up the overhanging headwall with difficulty.

Slight Pause   24 metres   Very Severe 4c   (11.6.81)
Start below the break at the back of the zawn. Climb onto the first ledge of *Norge Corner* and follow the scoop up the right-hand corner to a ledge (belay possible). Finish up the steep crackline to the left of the corner of *Slippery Slab*.

Slippery Chute   24 metres   Very Severe 4c
This climb takes the corner left of the black slab. Start at the back of the zawn. Climb onto the ledge and follow the scoop up the right-hand corner to a ledge (belay possible). Climb the 'chute'-like corner on the left edge of the slab, past an awkward mantelshelf, and continue on small holds until it is possible to make a thoughtful move left onto a ledge.

Slab Happy   21 metres   E3 5b †   (2.87)
Start as for *Slippery Chute* and climb the unprotected area of slab between *Slippery Chute* and *Slippery Slab*.

★Slippery Slab   27 metres   Very Severe 5a   (31.7.55)
A delightful way of deciding how steep a slab should be; nicely balanced,
the line follows cracks in the centre of the distinctive black slab. Start at
the back of the zawn. Climb onto a ledge, and follow the right-hand corner
until 5 metres below the belay ledge of *Slippery Chute*. (A runner can be
placed higher up to take the edge off the next moves, which are often
greasy.) Make an awkward move across the undercut groove on the right
and go up to a good ledge. Climb the crack above to a deep, square-cut
hole. (An alternative to crossing the greasy undercut groove is to continue
up *Slippery Chute* to the awkward mantelshelf on that route, where a
rightwards traverse leads to the deep, square-cut hole.) The thin crack
above is followed, with the hardest moves at its top.

Dark Comedian   34 metres   E3 5b   (8.85)
Climb the slab between *Slippery Slab* and *Congo Route*.

Congo Route   34 metres   Very Severe   (1.8.61)
A line up the right-hand side of the black slab. Start at the back of the
zawn.
1 22m. 4c. Start as for *Slippery Slab*, but having crossed the greasy
undercut groove continue rightwards along the good ledge to belay at its
end.
2 12m. 4c. Climb up above the belay to reach a small ledge. A difficult
move up to the right gives access to a scoop leading more easily to the
top.

Trip across the Slip   37 metres   E2 5c   (4.87)
Climb to the right-hand end of the ledge as for *Congo Route*, and then
traverse leftwards across *Slippery Slab* at mid height to finish up *Slippery
Chute*.

☆☆Much Ado about Nothing   12 metres   E6 6c †   (1991)
Start beneath the dank overhang split by two cracks, below and to the right
of *Slippery Slab*. The left-hand crack across the roof is climbed
acrobatically and strenuously past a triangular slot (*Camalot 4* useful).
Above the roof, trend leftwards to gain the black slab, and finish up *Dark
Comedian*.

The following routes start from the stepped ledge 5 metres to the left of the
deep break of *Genge's Groove*, beneath an impressive leaning buttress.

Congo Crack   23 metres   E1 5b   (27.8.66)
A satisfyingly tough jamming pitch taking the corner crack 5 metres to the
left of the deep break of *Genge's Groove*. Follow the crack and the wider
one above until it is possible to swing round, awkwardly, onto an easier
section leading up to where *Congo Route* comes in from the left. Climb the
easier crack to the top.

Congo Tribute 26 metres E2 5c (1987)
A harder variation on the theme of *Congo Crack*. Climb the first section of
Congo Crack, continue over the roof, and take a leftward-rising
foot-traverse to finish up the steep section of slab right of *Slippery Slab*.

★★★**Amazonia** 21 metres E7 6c (1989)
A highly technical test-piece with poor protection. One peg, now removed.
Start 3 metres right of *Congo Crack* at a sensational groove. Climb the
groove for 5 metres and continue rightwards up a thin crack to an overlap
before finishing more directly.

☆☆☆**Rainbow Warrior** 20 metres E7 6c † (1990)
A poorly protected and highly technical alternative to *Amazonia*. Climb the
groove for 5 metres and continue leftwards up the wall via a crack and
leftward-leaning overlap to a steep finish.

★**Genge's Groove** 23 metres Hard Very Severe 5a (1947)
The overhanging corner and groove splitting the left section of the face.
Start above a V-trough in the stepped ledge. Climb the overhanging
corner until a high left handhold enables a strenuous move to be made
onto a ledge on the right. Continue up the steep groove trending
rightwards to the top.

☆☆**Let the River Live** 23 metres E6 6b † (1987)
Climb *Genge's Groove* for a few metres and then move leftwards to the
arête, following a faint crackline. Finish up *Amazonia*.

Two variations on *Genge's Groove*, **Eeny** and **Meany**, finish up cracks in
the wall left of the steep groove at the same grade (1980s).

Genge's Right Hand 24 metres Hard Very Severe 5b (9.69)
Climb to the first ledge of *Genge's Groove*, traverse delicately right for 3
metres to a crack in the arête. Climb this crack past a break and then
move right to a ledge. Step back left onto the flake above and follow
cracks on the edge above to the top.

Finale 24 metres E2 5c (1973)
A line to the right of *Genge's Groove*, finishing up *Genge's Right Hand*.
Start 3 metres right of the V-trough, below an impending crack. Climb up
and left to gain a ledge. Climb the crack to a niche, traverse delicately
right for 3 metres, and climb the crack in the arête. Climb this past a break
and move right to a ledge. Step back left onto the flake above and follow
cracks on the edge above to the top.

★★**A Swift Flight of Fancy** 23 metres E3 6a (25.4.84)
[Photo: front cover.] A brisk, exhilarating pitch. Start as for *Finale*, 3 metres
right of the V-trough, below an impending crack. Climb up and left to gain
a ledge. Climb the crack to a niche, traverse delicately right for 3 metres,

and climb the crack in the arête. At the first break hand-traverse a few metres right and make a long reach for the break. Finish up the overhanging face above via a small leaning corner and then a crack.

Red Rose (20 metres E8 7a † 6.88) was centred on the distinctive short groove high in the middle of the magnificent wall to the right of *Genge's Groove*. Its three controversial bolts have been removed. The grade was given for its former state.

Samson   22 metres   E5 6b   (8.57/7.74)
The tough crack and overlap just before the blunt arête on the right of the wall.
1 14m. 6b. Climb the crack, clear the overlap by hard moves, and continue up the crackline to a good long ledge on the right.
2 8m. 4b. Climb directly up the slab to the left of the nose to finish.
Variation
2a The Rock Hopper   8 metres   E4 6a   (1993)
For a wild, poorly-protected finish, climb the crack in the left edge of the slab above.

Demo Area
This section of the cliff introduces an easing of the harder standard of Black Zawn and includes one of Cornwall's most famous climbs, *Demo Route*. The area covers the two walls flanking the prominent corner 20 metres left of the base of *Griptight Gully*. *Demo Route* is strikingly obvious from the line of its spectacular upper pitch traversing under the hanging nose high on the left wall.

★**Samson Arête**   20 metres   E2 6a   (7.74)
This hard but attractive pitch gains the crack that slices the left arête of the *Demo Route* wall. The crack is gained by climbing up the left edge of the wall to a break and then making strenuous moves up and left into the crack. Continue to the long ledge below the hanging nose and finish to its left.

Demolition   20 metres   E6 6a   (8.85)
A speedy belayer could prove useful. Climb straight up the grooved wall just right of the arête to the horizontal break. Continue up using small flakes on the wall above, step left into a thin crack, and follow it to a large ledge. Pull over the roof, move right onto the nose, and finish steeply using cracks and flakes.

★★**Demo Route**   24 metres   Hard Severe   (1943)
[Photo p.256a.] Pure climbing pleasure. Start at a flake left of and below a V-chimney in the wall at mid height.
1 15m. 4b. Climb the flake to a shallow groove leading to the foot of the chimney, which is followed to a good ledge and belay. Gear placement requires some thought.

2 9m. 4b. Move up; then using the undercut nose for handholds, step down and left. This enables good holds to be reached for the pull over onto the slab, which leads pleasantly to the top.

Intermediate Route   20 metres   Very Difficult   (c.1940s)
Start at the small overhanging block just to the right of *Demo Route*. Climb onto the block with some difficulty; before moving right and up the edge of the slab to a good ledge. Continue easily up leftwards via a black vein to a ledge (common with *Demo Route*). Climb the steep corner above on good holds.

Andrimne   20 metres   Severe 4a   (5.7.70)
A harder variation of the climbs to either side. Start just right of the small overhanging block. Follow a rightward-trending crack before climbing direct to the top, passing a good thread runner just right of the belay ledge of *Demo Route*.

★**Corner Climb**   20 metres   Very Difficult   (c.1940s)
A pleasant climb on good holds, although tricky in places. Climb the left wall of the big corner and move left and up to a good ledge. Follow the corner above on large holds to the top.

Corner Crack   20 metres   Severe 4a   (6.52)
Climb the corner and then move right into the wider crack. The crack leads upwards until the final part of *Corner Climb* can be followed to finish.

Protein   25 metres   Very Severe 4c   (7.60)
A strenuous climb, with poor protection on the crux. Climb a short distance up the corner, move right onto the steep wall, and climb to the arête, where good protection can be placed. Traverse left for 2 metres; then make bold moves up a thin vein on small, widely spaced holds (hard) to a huge block in the corner. Finish up the awkward overhanging groove. Direct Finish
Hot Tuna   20 metres   Hard Very Severe 4c   (23.7.86)
Follow *Protein* and climb the final roof direct.

Post the Postman (20 metres Very Severe 4c 4.87) starts up *Protein* and then climbs a crack just right of the crack of *Civvy Route* to a large ledge (belay possible). Continue up the overhanging arête.

Civvy Route   25 metres   Hard Severe   (c.1940s)
Pleasantly steep. Start just right of the corner.
1 15m. 4b. Climb awkwardly up to the right onto an arête, which leads to a steep crack. Follow this to a good ledge above.
2 10m. 4b. Climb the flake on the left to reach an overhung ledge. From the right of this, make an awkward pull onto a gangway and continue leftwards across the overhanging exposed nose to the top.

Walter's Chimney   23 metres   Difficult   (c.1940s)
This climb follows the chimney left of *Griptight Gully*, past a bulge at 6 metres, to the good ledge of *Civvy Route/Letterbox*. Continue up the chimney above the ledge.

Letterbox   27 metres   Severe   (c.1940s)
A good climb, with unusual moves on the second pitch. Start below the corner 3 metres right of *Walter's Chimney*.
1 15m. 4a. Climb the corner to a ledge that runs across into the chimney. Continue straight up the steep corner until good holds lead to the slab above. Take this to a good ledge and belay.
2 12m. 4b. Gain the sloping ledge on the right, with difficulty, using a good high hold (The Letterbox). Easier ground leads to the top.

Griptight Gully   20 metres   Difficult
This can be climbed by numerous variations, but the least unpleasant and greasy way is to jump across to a ledge from a flat-topped block, and climb the left-hand side of the gully. The steeper section near the top is climbed on huge holds.

Central Area
This large section of cliff runs from *Griptight Gully* to the distinctive step, The Aisle, that leads down from the Sunday Face and Monday Face areas. It includes a large number of excellent low to middle grade climbs with the harder lines concentrated at the right-hand end on Double Overhang Buttress. Easily located features include the high, narrow, banana-shaped flake protruding between two grooves just right of *Griptight Gully*. Further right is a rounded, 8-metre-high, black slab, undercut on its right and lying below an obvious, steep chimney. The route, *Black Slab*, starts up here and then goes left below the steep chimney, which gives the upper line of *Gilliwiggle*. Further right, a recess in the cliff is flanked on its left by a distinctive, narrow black ramp rising steeply to the left. This is *Staircase*. The steep buttress to the right of the depression is Double Overhang Buttress, with *Africa Route* on its left-hand side. Most of the routes are described as one-pitch climbs although in many cases excellent belays can be taken *en route*.

Immediately right of *Griptight Gully* and above the large block used to enter the gully is a steep black wall some 10 metres high. It gives three short routes leading to a large ledge at half height. **Gully Wall Left Hand** (10 metres Severe 4a 2.8.62) starts from the top of the block and climbs the left edge of the wall on small holds. Quite a bold little climb. The poorly-protected **Centre Pitch** (Very Severe 4a 1980s) climbs the centre of the wall to the ledge. **Gully Wall Right Hand** (10 metres Very Difficult 2.8.62) gains the block from the right and continues up a groove to a niche. Move left and gain the big ledge direct.

The Flakes   25 metres   E1 5b   (1983)
Take the small bulging face just right of the large block of *Griptight Gully*.
A difficult move gains upward-pointing flakes (much harder for the short).
Continue up the wall above to the half-way ledge, and climb the upper
wall on its left side.

Banana Crack   25 metres   Hard Very Severe 5c   (1983)
Climb the thin crack right of *The Flakes* (hard to start), before moving up
and left. Continue rightwards on better holds to the half-way ledge.

Left Banana Flake   20 metres   Difficult   (1940s)
Starting 5 metres right of *Griptight Gully*, this climbs the groove on the left
side of the banana-shaped flake to the half-way ledge. Continue up the
left edge of the face above.

Orange Slice   25 metres   Very Difficult   (1983)
Climb the arête formed by the banana-shaped flake to the half-way ledge
and finish directly up the wall above.

Now follows a pair of black V-shaped grooves

Black Groove   25 metres   Very Difficult   (c.1940s)
Climb the larger left-hand groove to the half-way ledge. Finish up the face
above.

★**Banana Flake**   26 metres   Very Difficult   (c.1940s)
A pleasant climb. Start below the right-hand groove.
1 14m. Move leftwards up steps and into the right-hand groove, which is
climbed to the half-way ledge.
2 12m. Climb the centre of the steep wall at the back of the ledge,
moving right near the top to a flat ledge with a short overhanging wall
above. Climb the centre of this to the top.

Banana Split   27 metres   Hard Very Severe 5a   (28.6.85)
The steep black wall right of *Banana Flake*, finishing direct up an arête and
the bulges above.

★**The Arête**   27 metres   Very Severe 4b   (1.8.61)
This follows the arête right of the banana-shaped flake in a direct line.
Start below the arête. Climb the steep wall to a point where an easy rake
(*Main Face Climb*) crosses leftwards. Mantelshelf awkwardly onto the
sloping ledge on the right (sometimes greasy) and take the steep little
corner to a nice position astride the top of the arête (belay possible). Move
right and climb the delightfully exposed and overhanging face on large
holds. Follow the line of the arête over two short overhanging noses to the
top.

Main Face Climb   25 metres   Difficult   (c.1940s)
An attractive little climb well suited to beginners. Start below a little
overhang. Climb up rightwards and follow the encouraging line of flaky
holds diagonally left to the right-hand end of the half-way ledge (belay
possible). Follow the right-hand corner to the top.

Fruit Salad   18 metres   Very Difficult
Start as for *Main Face Climb*, below a little overhang. Climb to a good
yellow-topped spike above and on the right. Follow the leftward-facing
flake above, until it is possible to move right on good holds to a ledge.
Finish up *Black Slab* pitch 2.

Black Jack   18 metres   Severe   (2.8.62)
Start at a V-shaped pod on the right edge of a small slab. Climb the twin
cracks that rise from the pod to a ledge. Continue up the twin cracks
immediately above.

Gilliwiggle   20 metres   Severe   (24.6.63)
Climb the twin cracks just right of the start of *Black Jack* to a good ledge.
Move down to the right to a gently overhanging chimney, which is taken to
finish (awkward at the top).

Marionette   18 metres   E2 5c   (18.6.74/8.76)
Right of *Gilliwiggle* is an overhanging crack high on a smooth impending
wall. Climb to the base of this crack and climb it strenuously on jams to the
top.
Variation
No Pack Drill   18 metres   E2 5c   (1994)
Follow *Marionette* to the base of the final overhanging crack. Move right a
metre; then climb up and follow a wide crack above to the top.

★Black Slab   30 metres   Very Difficult   (1940s)
Good climbing. Start just right of a wide crack to the left of the black slab.
1 13m. Climb the slab to the overhanging chimney, which is followed a
short way before moving left to a fine ledge and belay.
2 17m. Follow the flake on the left to a niche and climb over the bulge
above into a small cave. Move right and then go left up a groove to the
top.

No Name   20 metres   Very Difficult   (c.1940s)
Top end of the grade. Start below a groove around to the right from *Black
Slab*. Climb the groove to a good ledge. Step delicately right and up a
short slab to finish up a V-groove on the right.

No Number   20 metres   Very Severe 5a   (21.7.83)
This climb is a much harder version of *No Name* with a tough finish. Climb
the steep flaky wall just to the right of the groove of *No Name* and finish
up the steep crack left of the V-groove.

★Staircase   18 metres   Difficult   (c.1940s)
A good route for beginners, but protection should be placed for seconds to avoid a big swing off the ramp. Start at the foot of the narrow black ramp that runs up to the left where the face is recessed. Climb a short corner to reach the slab, which is followed on splendid holds after an initial steep move.

Skewcrack   20 metres   Severe 4b   (22.8.83)
Start at the base of the *Staircase* ramp. Climb the steep slab until beneath overhanging cracks, which criss-cross the wall above. Move up and left into a steep groove that runs above and parallel to the *Staircase* ramp, and follow this over a small overhang to finish.

Truescrew Crack   20 metres   Very Severe 4c   (1980s)
Climb *Skewcrack* for 5 metres, move right, and climb the overhanging crack until it eases. Finish much more easily up the slab above.

Overhanging Wall   20 metres   Very Severe 4c   (12.11.62)
Hard for the grade, but well protected. Start at the base of the *Staircase* ramp and then climb the steep slab to the overhanging corner. Move up to the left and climb the criss-crossed overhanging cracks strenuously until a spike is reached. Pull over onto a small ledge and continue to the top on better holds.

Overhanging Corner   23 metres   Very Severe 4c   (9.9.55)
A fine sustained pitch though occasionally greasy. Start at the foot of the narrow black ramp of *Staircase*. Climb the steep slab to the right to reach the corner. Continue up the steep slab right of the corner to a bulge. A delicate step-up followed by a difficult mantelshelf leads to a large sloping ledge on the left. Follow the corner-chimney to the top.

☆☆**Mark Up Another One**   20 metres   E5 6a †   (1993)
Start 3 metres right of *Overhanging Corner* directly beneath a flake of rock shaped like Africa. Climb the wall direct to the double break where good protection can be placed (*Tricams*). Continue up the slab above to the Africa-shaped flake; move up to a ledge and climb just left of an arête to a steep and very bold finish.

★Africa Route   18 metres   Very Severe 5a   (10.55)
A satisfying pitch running up the left face of the buttress to the right of the recess. The first few moves to gain excellent holds on the lower wall can be problematic. Start at the left edge of the wall, where it falls away leftwards. Use a small black knob up on the left to step up, swing right to reach a good jug, and climb to the ledge above. Traverse left and go up the slab to a flake below a groove. Gain a sloping ledge on the right; then move left under the thin V-shaped nose and finish, with difficulty, up the cracks above. A technical gem of a climb.

SENNEN: PEDN-MÊN-DU
SUNDAY FACE, MONDAY FACE, COASTGUARD FACE

1	Double Overhang	VS	
2	Dexter	VS	
3	Dextrose	HVS	
4	Windows of Perfection	E5	
5	Sinner's Route	D	
6	Windows of Perception	E5	
7	Messenger from the Furnace	E5	
8	The Quaker	E1	
9	Church Window	VD	
10	Catholic Girls	HVS	
11	Altar Route	VS	

12	Tombstone	E1	
13	Senior's Route	D	
14	Junior's Route	D	
15	Pots Arête	HVS	
16	Monday Face	VS	
17	Slim	VS	
18	Vertical Crack	HS	
19	Gillian	E3	
20	Golva	E2	

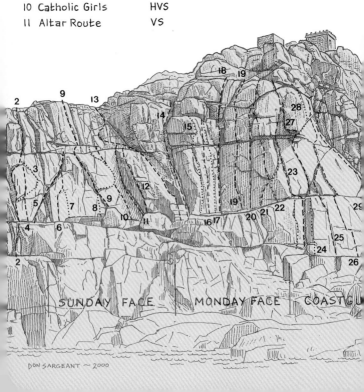

DON SARGEANT ~ 2000

IRISH LADY COVE

30 31

FACE

White Man's Burden   20   Very Severe   5a   (6.76)
Start below the middle of the lower wall and gain the ledge using fingery
holds. Move slightly right and take the overhanging scoop on airy moves
to gain a pinnacle (belay possible). Move left and climb the short,
overhanging corner to the top.

★**Double Overhang**   18 metres   Very Severe   4c   (c.1940s)
A steep solid climb on classic holds. Start at a steep red quartz vein near
the right edge of the *Africa Route* wall. Climb the vein to a ledge, move
left, and take a gently overhanging groove on good holds to a pinnacle
(belay possible). Move left and climb the short, overhanging corner to the
top.

Devo   18 metres   Very Severe   4c †   (6.84)
Start just right of a steep red vein. Climb the overhanging grooved arête
just right of *Double Overhang* to gain a pinnacle. Move left and finish up a
short overhanging corner as for *Double Overhang*.
Variation Finish
Devotee   18 metres   E1 5b †   (1993)
A harder finish to *Devo*. Follow the groove of *Devo* to the final pinnacle
block of *Double Overhang*. Move up onto the flake on the right and make
a hard step up onto the final slab.

★**Dexter**   17 metres   Very Severe   4c   (1954)
A varied climb, which is quite bold for the grade. Start a few metres right
of the red vein of *Double Overhang* beside a short black slab. Climb the
blunt arête to enter a groove at mid height by an awkward move. Follow
the groove up to the right of the pinnacle block of *Double Overhang* and
then step left onto the pinnacle (belay possible). From the top of the
pinnacle, make a bold move out right, and hand-traverse along the top of
the large flake until a mantelshelf can be made onto it. From here, make
an interesting step onto a black knob (harder for shorter climbers) and
climb the groove above to the top.

Dextrose   17 metres   Hard Very Severe   5a   (12.11.62)
Some tough moves. Follow *Dexter* into its groove. Follow the groove for a
few metres; then traverse right along a distinctive horizontal band and
make a long reach onto a sloping foot-ledge at the base of a vertical
scoop on the right side of the huge flake. Climb up the scoop to a big
black chicken-head on the right and hand-traverse left along the flake until
a mantelshelf can be made onto it. From here, follow *Dexter* again by
stepping onto a black knob and climbing the groove above to the top.

☆**Windows of Perfection**   14 metres   E5 6b †   (1989)
A difficult eliminate version of *Dextrose*, that attacks the wall centrally. Start
at the steep wall directly above The Aisle, two metres right of *Dexter*'s
groove. Climb directly up the flake, past a black chicken head, to finish up
Dexter.

Near the foot of *Main Face Climb* is a deep fault in the platform, which is the top of a narrow chimney that leads up from a sea-level cave. This is **Waterspout Chimney** (8 metres Hard Severe 4b), an eccentric little route which can be done only at low tide in quiet sea conditions. The waterspout that forces its way up the chimney in heavy seas can be sudden and is always spectacular. A whole new grading-system would be needed for a high-tide, high-sea ascent! The base of the chimney is reached by descending an easier chimney on the right (facing out) to sea-level ledges, and then traversing left to the mouth of the cave. The chimney is strenuous and usually wet and greasy (don't get stuck). There are a number of short pitches along this lower tidal wall.

Sunday Face

This small section of cliff runs from the top of The Aisle to the higher corner ledge of Monday Face. It has a fierce concentration of hard, short climbs with a welcome break or two in the general intensity. The central feature of the lower wall is the deep-set niche of *Church Window*. On the left of the wall immediately above The Aisle is the rightward slanting break of *Sinner's Route*. To the right of *Church Window* is the often damp but attractive corner of *Altar Route*, flanked on its right by an overhanging black wall.

Sinner's Route   14 metres   Difficult   (c.1940s)
Start at the foot of the slanting break above The Aisle. Take either the right or the left entry; then follow the groove on good holds to a large ledge, and scramble to finish.

The low traverse from *Sinner's Route* to *Overmarked* gives a sustained boulder-problem: **White Wedding** (20 metres 6c 26.7.2000). The crux is near the start.

Stairway to Heaven   15 metres   E1 5a   (4.87)
From 3 metres up *Sinner's Route*, move right around the arête onto a foot-ledge at the base of a steep slab. Traverse right to a corner and climb it to a ledge. Poorly protected.

The next few climbs are concentrated in a very small area of rock and all are successful solutions to the attractively smooth wall to the right of *Sinner's Route*. The climbs are very close together and blinkers may be necessary to avoid adjacent climbs!

Windows of Perception   15 metres   E5 6a   (4.88)
Start below the arête just right of *Sinner's Route*. Climb the right side of the arête, move onto the slab on the right, and finish direct. Alternatively, when level with the slab, traverse right and climb its centre.

Black Widow   18 metres   E3 6b   (5.87)
Climb the wall right of the arête using two side-pulls to gain a small hold.
Move up and right into the corner-groove above and then move back left,
when possible, into the centre of the slab via a mantelshelf. Climb the slab
to the top.

☆☆**Messenger from the Furnace**   15 metres   E5 6c/7a †   (1992)
The most direct way up the wall; fiercely technical and protectionless.
Climb the faint sketchy cracks in the wall, move up and left to the lip of the
wall, and get established on the slab above. Finish with relief up the centre
of the slab.

Exodus   18 metres   E3 6b   (17.6.84)
Start 2 metres left of the crack of *Angels Highway*. Climb the faint
rightward-leaning cracks to a blunt flake (on *Angel's Highway*) and move
directly up via a thin layback to gain better holds on a flake above. Move
up and finish boldly up the corner/groove above.

Angel's Highway   23 metres   E2 6a   (23.10.69/7.78)
Start below the hairline crack in the narrow-faced arête on the left of the
Church Window recess. Climb the crack, using a blunt flake. Move right to
the larger crack and then to the *Church Window* recess. Climb left around
the square arête onto a steep slab and take the centre of the slab left of
the corner to finish.

Communion Crack   15 metres   Hard Very Severe 5c   (1972)
Climb the wider crack below the right edge of the narrow-faced arête to
the *Church Window* recess. Finish up the corner above as for *Church
Window*.

The Quaker   18 metres   E1 5c   (8.77)
Start in the middle of the short wall beneath a slabby recess, at a thin
crack leading up to a slab. Climb the crack with difficulty to a blunt flake
and move up to gain the slab above. Move up rightwards, traverse further
right beneath an overlap using undercuts, and follow the curving crack of
the flake leftwards to the top.

Church Window   23 metres   Very Difficult   (c.1940s)
Start from a large boulder below and slightly right of the deep-set central
slabby recess.
1 14m. 4a. From the boulder, mantelshelf onto the ledge above and step
left into the crack, which leads to the slabby recess. Traverse left across the
small slab to gain a low pinnacle below the overhanging corner. Climb the
corner to a large ledge below a slabby wall.
2 9m. 4a. Climb the slab, using the scooped crack on its right and small
black knobs on the face.

Variations
1a Hard Severe 4c. Instead of the mantelshelf move, climb the vertical crack direct to the window. Break out onto the right-hand face by a flake forming a crack. Steep, thin moves lead to twin cracks, which are followed to the large ledge.
2a Hard Very Severe 5a. Climb the centre of the slab. Unprotected.

Catholic Girls   15 metres   Hard Very Severe 5c   (30.7.85)
Climb the wall directly to the traverse of *The Quaker*, move up to gain the curving flake, and finish just to the left of the chimney of *Altar Route*.

Altar Route   23 metres   Very Severe 4c   (c.1940s)
A pleasant little climb which becomes particularly treacherous when wet. Climb the right-hand corner on small holds to reach a rounded crack, which leads neatly to the large ledge. The last part of the corner is nearly always greasy. Take the overhanging chimney at the back right-hand side of the ledge, past a loose chockstone, to the top.
Variation 15 metres Hard Severe 4c. At about 10 metres, a flake crack (on *The Quaker*) starts on the left and once gained, is climbed more easily to a large ledge.

Tombstone   23 metres   E1 5b   (15.2.81)
This takes the overhanging wall with a V-pod in it, right of *Altar Route*. A very strenuous climb that is not easy to protect.
1 15m. 5b. Climb the corner of *Altar Route* for 3 metres to a small ledge; then move right into the pod and climb this to its top. Move out on the right and continue straight up on good, well-spaced holds. A very pumpy pitch so don't hang around!
2 8m. 4a. Climb the wall just left of the steep chimney.
Direct Start E3 5c (2.88). Climb the leaning black wall direct to reach the pod.

The bold **Catacombs** (15 metres E6 6b † 7.98) is a tight eliminate, only half being new climbing. Start just right of *Tombstone Direct Start*. Climb the overhanging wall, between *Tombstone* and the right edge, and finish up the easy slab of *Overmarked*.

Monday Face
This small area of cliff lies to the right of Sunday Face. It has some delightful routes on perfect granite and is unaffected by the sea except in ferocious storms. It can be a sun-trap in the afternoon and evening. The central feature is the handsome line of *Vertical Crack* flanked on its right by the striking wall of *Gillian* and *Golva*. Left of *Vertical Crack* is the narrow wall of *Slim* ending at a steep rounded arête. Left of this, two gangways slant up to the left.

Overmarked   20 metres   Hard Severe 4a   (1983)
This starts at a little overhang just right of the leaning face of *Tombstone*.
Climb out of the left-hand side of the cave, trend left up slabs, and finish
on the right-hand end of the ledge above.

Senior's Route   20 metres   Difficult   (c.1940s)
Climb the wider (left-hand) gangway to the large ledge above Monday
Face (belay possible). Finish up the corner on the right.

Junior's Route   20 metres   Difficult
The right-hand black-patched gangway leads direct to the top.

International Groove   18 metres   E3 5c †   (1994)
Climb the slab and the left-leaning groove and crack just right of *Junior's
Route*. At a bulge, make difficult moves up and slightly right to a break.
Finish over the bulges above, moving slightly leftwards at the top.

Pots Arête   18 metres   Hard Very Severe   (28.10.83)
Start at the steep, lichen-covered rounded arête with a low pinnacle at its
base.
1 10m. 5a. Climb the low pinnacle. From its top, move up and left to
make a hard move over a bulge before continuing up the grooved arête
above.
2 8m. 4c. Move up to a crack and follow it to a ledge via a prominent
black knob. Move left and finish easily to a ledge.

Monday Face   20 metres   Very Severe 4b   (c.1940s)
This takes the left edge of the lichen-covered face left of *Vertical Crack*.
Protection is not generous. Start at the steep rounded arête. Climb the low
pinnacle before moving right onto the face, which is climbed direct using
pinch-grips to a ledge. Finish direct.

Slim   20 metres   Very Severe 5a   (12.11.62)
A nice little finger-cracker starting just left of the corner of *Vertical Crack*.
Climb the thin crack to a good ledge and continue up the wall just left of
the right-hand chimney over bulges.

★★**Vertical Crack**   20 metres   Hard Severe 4c   (1943)
A well-protected route. Climb the corner-crack, with judicious bridging into
Slim at the start. From a ledge at 12 metres, follow the right-hand side of
the chimney above.

Squeeze Me   23 metres   E3 6a   (2.88)
Start just right of *Vertical Crack*, beneath a bottomless crack. Climb the
wall boldly to gain the crack and slight protection. Continue up the crack
in a direct line to a break. Move up and slightly right before finishing
rightwards over a bulge and twin cracks.

★★★Gillian 32 metres E3 5c (8.7.72/8.77)
[Photo p.256b.] A delightfully elegant line up the golden wall right of *Vertical Crack*. Start about 3 metres right of *Vertical Crack*. Follow the thin crackline slanting up left, before climbing steeply to gain a large pocket. Move up and right to a small break; then go over a bulge. Climb past a horizontal break to another break; move right over a bulge and take the twin cracks to the top.
Direct Start E4 5c. Take the wall below the large pocket direct.

ExSqueeze Me 20 metres E5 6b (1994)
From the start of *Gillian*, climb directly up, cross the overlap, and continue straight up to join *Gillian* again at the first big break.

★★Golva 35 metres E2 5c (16.4.64/8.76)
Excellent thuggy climbing up the steep crackline that splits the wall. Climb the crack, passing a small overlap, to the second of two breaks. Move up rightwards to a crack below the roof. Follow it to a chicken head and use this to move up into a shallow groove leading to the top.

Pinch the Egyptian 27 metres E6 6c (1992)
Start at a narrow slanting flake crack just right of *Golva*. Climb the flake crack to a narrow roof. Cross the roof just left of a crack in the wall above and continue up the wall on small crystal pulls and long reaches to a break. Finish more easily up *Golva*.

★Tango in the Night 30 metres E3 6b (8.87)
A right-to-left ascending traverse of the *Gillian* wall. Climb the rightward-slanting flake crack right of *Golva* to the narrow roof, and then traverse left into *Golva*. Continue left, following the downward-pointing flake overlap to the large pocket on *Gillian*. Climb the pocketed wall on the left to a break and continue up the bubbly crack above. Move back right and pull over the bulge to finish up the crack of *Gillian*.

Smeagol 30 metres Hard Very Severe (19.10.73)
Tense but good moves on the first pitch. Start where the ledge narrows on the right of the wall, below a leftward-curving crack.
1 12m. 5a. Climb the crack to the narrow roof and then move right to a foot-ledge. Make an awkward move up and continue direct to belay below an overhanging crack.
2 18m. Make a long traverse back left to finish up the shallow groove of *Golva*.

Coastguard Face

From below the corner-ledge of Monday Face, a series of broad steps runs rightwards to the large open area of ledges and boulders below the southern end of the cliff. This is the area that is reached down the easy gully running south from the coastguard lookout. The Coastguard Face is the clean stepped face that rises above here, terminating in an impressive bulging overhang with a deeply grooved crack on its under-face. The overhang is tackled by two climbs, *Super Jam* and *Flair for the Theatrical*. On the left, lower edge of Coastguard Face is a steep chimney rising from a square corner. This is Genge's Crack, the first pitch of *Dolphin Cracks*. At the base of the 10-metre lower wall of Coastguard Face, there is a wide ledge from where most of the routes start. Coastguard Face is flanked on its right by the long rambling gully of *Hayloft*, beyond which the cliff falls away into a broken area of walls and pinnacles that gives good scrambling and bouldering.

Just below the right-hand end of the Monday Face ledge is a large flake-spike that juts from a crack. **The Cut Price Comedy Climb** (10 metres Hard Very Severe 4c 8.85) starts here. Step off the spike and move rightwards to the central scoop. Climb this to the top. Unprotected and with a nasty landing. **Stunted Arête** (8 metres Hard Very Severe 5a 8.85) takes the crack with the black 'cloven hoof' just right of the previous pitch and just left of the first pitch of *Dolphin Cracks*.

★**Dolphin Cracks**   25 metres   Hard Very Severe   (1947/9.9.55)
Impressive and bold climbing on the first pitch. On the left, lower edge of Coastguard Face is a steep chimney rising from a square corner.
1 10m. 5a. Genge's Crack. Climb the steep corner crack and make a difficult exit on to the ledge above.
2 15m. 4c. Move left into a crack running up the wall and climb this to a small overhang. Pull over into a groove and follow it to the top.
Variation
2a Top Banana E5 6a (2.11.97). Climb the slab 2 metres right of the crack via flakes and a chicken-head mantel.

★★**Hell Hath No Fear**   15 metres   E7 6c   (1988)
Climb the right arête of Genge's Crack, starting from the block beneath. Climb the arête on its left side: a bold, protectionless lead with no room for failure.

Baptism of Fire   15 metres   E5 6b   (2.4.88)
The same arête climbed on the right. Make bold moves up the arête to a break and poor runners. Move up right via a tricky mantelshelf, which leads to a faint crack and horizontal break. Finish straight up the right edge of the arête.

★**Terrace Cracks**   40 metres   Hard Very Severe   (7.76)
Steep and sustained on pitch 1. Start at the extreme left end of the comfortable ledge at the base of the first 10-metre wall of Coastguard Face, below a tasty crackline.
1 20m. 5a. Climb the thin crack, moving left at its top into another crack to reach a ledge (belay possible). Climb the leftward-slanting flake on the right to gain a scoop below another slab.

Demo Route (HS), Sennen
Climber: unknown   Photo: David Simmonite

Gillian (E3), Sennen
Climber: Mark Edwards Photo: David Simmonite

2 20m. 4c. Climb the slab, moving right to the deep-set top of *Hayloft Gully*, and then take the overhanging black corner on the left, climbing it by its left wall.

Slanting Crack 10 metres Hard Very Severe 5a (7.76)
[Photo p.288a.] The same breed as *Terrace Cracks*, taking the steeply slanting crack that starts half-way up the lower wall. Climb the wall to the right of the start of the slanting crack to a good hold at the horizontal break. Move left and then up to the crack and follow it to a ledge above. (Alternatively, continue straight up from the good hold at E1 5a.)

Arang Atang 23 metres Hard Very Severe 5a (4.84)
A mid-height leftwards traverse of the lower wall starting up the steep crack at the right end of the ledge and finishing up the first pitch of *Terrace Cracks*.

★★Super Jam 20 metres E5 6b (4.84)
Skin-stripping and power-packed, taking the roof at its left end. Start near the end of the ledge above the first pitches of the previous routes, below a flared crack. Climb the crack to the roof. Swing left to the roof-crack, and traverse left until the crack widens. Continue up the crack, which eventually narrows into a corner that leads to the top.

★★A Flair for the Theatrical 20 metres E4 6a (8.84)
A spectacular climb. Start, as for *Super Jam*, near the end of the ledge, below a flared crack. Climb the crack and slab above to the roof. Climb the roof using a creative hold on the lip and finish direct.

☆Rib and Flake 10 metres E3 6b † (1990s)
To the left of the second pitch of *Hayloft* is a short wall with a flake near its top. Start from the first belay of *Hayloft*. Step left and climb a rib before moving left to gain the flake and easy ground above.

★Hayloft 42 metres Very Severe (c.1940s)
Enjoyable climbing although each pitch is escapable. Start on the ledge below the main break in the lower wall.
1 10m. Climb the break in the wall and the V-groove above to a ledge.
2 10m. 4c. Bold. Climb the slab on the left of a big block in the gully to a black knob (good nut placement), and use it to make a delicate step up to a ledge.
3 12m. 4a. Across the gully is a steep dark groove that after an awkward start leads to a short corner below a large ledge on the right.
4 10m. 4c. The Hayloft. Traverse left along a ledge to a corner, and then make a hard move up into the undercut recess on the right. Squirm up the short chimney to the top.
Variation
1a Hayloft Cracks Hard Very Severe 5a (1984). Climb the wall 2 metres to the right using a flake and crack.

Donna   40 metres   Hard Severe   (17.2.67/8.7.67)
A contrived but pleasant climb. Start below the corner at the right-hand
end of the ledge below the lower wall.
1 15m. 4b. Climb the steep corner-crack to a broad ledge and walk left
to belay below a short crack slanting up right.
2 25m. 4b. Climb the short crack to a ledge. Climb the small slab
above, just left of the gully, to a short impending wall. Move left with
difficulty to a prominent knob above the wall, and follow a slanting ledge
to the left to finish up a short wall.

At least two variations on *Donna* have been recorded: **Gargoyle** (8.7.67)
and **Gargoyle's Ear** (4.7.70). They follow similar lines and converge on
the prominent 'gargoyle' knob on *Donna's* final pitch.

On Your Marks   30 metres   Hard Very Severe †   (1985)
Start on a ledge at the base of the initial corner of *Donna*.
1 10m. 5a. Climb cracks in the right-hand wall to a sloping ledge and
belay.
2 20m. 5a. Climb the flake crack above the belay until moves leftwards
can be made towards a conspicuous overhang. Climb this via a crack on
the right and then continue in a direct line to finish.

Hayloft Gully   40 metres   Difficult   (c.1940s)
Start below the easy-angled corner with a small pinnacle at its foot, to the
right of Coastguard Face. Follow the gully above until it becomes steeper
at the top. Climb a flake on the right and then a short step to gain the top.

There are a number of short pitches on the walls below and to the south of the
open area of ledges and boulders below Coastguard Face. On the seaward
end of the ledges is a square-cut black corner. A steep crack on its left,
seaward-facing, wall gives **Plucky** (10 metres Hard Very Severe 5b 8.85).

The Green Beret   160 metres   E1   (4.59)
This left-to-right girdle of Sennen has a fine pedigree. It has two
contrasting sections, the first one being relatively light-hearted, the second
being quite technical in places. The whole route is escapable from many
positions but some of the more technical sections are serious. Start at the
top of *Demo Route*.
1 to 5 60m. Descend the top pitch of *Demo Route* and cross the face
easily via *Civvy Route*, the *Banana Flake* routes, *Black Slab*, and *No Name*
to a stance at the top of *Staircase*. Belays are liberal.
6 17m. 5a. Traverse along the ledge crossing *Overhanging Wall* until above
the bulge of *Overhanging Corner*. Descend the bulge and immediately
traverse across *Africa Route* to the pinnacle belay of *Double Overhang*.
7 10m. 5a. Hand-traverse along the flake of *Dexter* and continue down
the hand-traverse of *Dextrose* to a belay part way up *Sinner's Route*.
8 10m. 5b. Move down a touch before crossing the slab and making
hard moves around the nose into the recess of *Church Window*.

9 18m. 5a. Traverse rightwards into the corner of *Altar Route*. Climb to a niche and then traverse across the overhanging black wall of *Tombstone* to a stance on the gangway of *Senior's Route*.

10 10m. Traverse easily to the stance half-way up *Vertical Crack*.

11 25m. 5a. A belly-traverse leads to below the final groove of *Dolphin Cracks*. Continue with difficulty just below the overhang to a stance in the gully below The Hayloft.

12 10m. 4c. The corner to the left of the break of The Hayloft is climbed to the top.

The Irish Lady Cove

Descent. Irish Lady Cove is reached by following Descent 1 on page 234 until the gully opens out. Immediately below is a steep, loose gully opening into the Irish Lady Cove itself. The walls of the gully give a number of climbs and there are more climbs on the left-flanking wall of the cove. The bed of the gully is reached by scrambling down leftwards (facing out) from the descent path on decomposing rock and over massive jammed boulders to the narrow mouth of the gully, where there are magnificent views to the Irish Lady and the Longships Lighthouse.

On the right (facing towards the Irish Lady) is a steep wall with a flake crack on its right edge rising steeply to curve over to the left at two-thirds height. This is *Commando Crack*. To its right is a steep chimney, *Commando Corner*. At the back of the gully above the jammed boulders, is a long lean buttress with a huge flaky pillar leaning against it (non-tidal). The charmingly named *Grot* goes up the left side of the buttress. Opposite the *Commando Crack* wall are the twin leaning chimneys of *Irish Lady Chimneys*. The cliff then turns sharply to the left (facing out) across the *Chi Squared* wall. The other routes lie beyond here on the far wall of the cove.

At the seaward end of the wall is a short crack: Very Severe.

Knight Move   25 metres   E2 5a   (7.86)
Start at a crack just right of the short crack. Climb the crack, move into the next crack on the right, and follow this trending leftwards towards the top.

The Big Blade   20 metres   E3 5c   (7.9.85)
Start 3 metres right of *Knight Move*, where a shallow crack starts 2 metres up the face. Climb to the shallow crack and follow it until moves leftwards gain thin cracks, which are followed to finish.

Six Blade Knife   18 metres   E2 5b   (5.84)
Start just left of a flake and chimney at a crack. Climb the crack for 8 metres, trend leftwards, and continue up to a finish just right of *Big Blade*. Direct Start 16m. E2 5c (1985). Start 3 metres right of *Big Blade*. Climb the second crack right of *Big Blade* to join the parent climb by moving rightwards at 10 metres.

Commando Crack   15 metres   Very Severe 5a   (1950)
A strenuous and gritty climb. Start at the right edge of the wall, at the base
of the deep chimney crack. Climb the steep flake crack just left of the
chimney, and move leftwards near the top to finish at blocks.

Stone The Crows   15 metres   E4 6a   (1986)
An impressive line. Climb the arête and overhang just right of the deep
chimney crack.

Commando Corner   17 metres   Very Severe 4c   (1950-66)
Gritty. Start at the base of the arête. Climb diagonally right to the foot of
the steep corner, which narrows to a chimney leading to the top.

Ostrobogulous   20 metres   Very Difficult   (21.2.68)
Climb the centre of the tapering slab that lies at right angles to the
Commando Crack wall. Pass a ledge at 10 metres and finish up the loose
arête on the right.

The long lean buttress with the huge flaky pillar leaning against it at the back
of the gully, above the jammed boulders, gives two climbs.

Grot   35 metres   Very Severe   (8.4.72)
What's in a name? Quite pleasant all the same. Start at the left edge of
the buttress.
1 25m. 4c. Climb direct on friable rock to the foot of a groove on the left
edge. Continue up the groove on improving rock and break out right at
the top of the groove onto a ledge. Climb the arête above until a good
ledge and belay is reached.
2 10m. 4c. Move right, climb the short chimney with difficulty, and
scramble to finish.

Tartarus   20 metres   Severe 4a   (21.2.68)
Climb the chimney between *Grot* and the huge flaky leaning pillar.

Geordie Boy   35 metres   Hard Severe   (7.8.91)
Start 3 metres right of the chimney of *Tartarus*, at a black slab.
1 23m. 4b. Climb the thin crack in the slab before trending rightwards
past a black knob to a small ledge.
2 12m. Climb the two small slabs above to finish.

The next routes lie on the barrel-shaped buttress on the lower left wall of the
zawn opposite the *Commando Crack* wall.

Dublin Wall   20 metres   Very Severe 5a   (1975)
Start just right of a big square-faced block at the base of the buttress.
Climb a vague crack on the right of the buttress; then move left and climb
direct to the top.

Irish Lady Chimneys 18 metres Very Difficult (1940s)
Start below the leaning chimneys and take either one to a large ledge.
Climb the corner on the left, taking care with the rock.

The following routes lie on the short compact wall around to the left (facing
out) from *Irish Lady Chimneys*. The wall faces directly on to the Irish Lady Rock.

Brain Drain 15 metres E3 5c (4.7.87)
Climb the left arête of the wall.

Sky Train 15 metres E2 5b (6.84)
Start 2 metres right of the arête, at two thin cracks. Follow the thin cracks to
the first break. Move left and follow more cracks to a final
orange-coloured bulge. Climb the bulge via a crack and flake to finish.

Chi Squared 15 metres Hard Very Severe 5a (18.2.68)
Start below the centre of the wall at an open groove and crack. The rock is
quite poor. Climb the crack to a ledge at 4 metres. Continue up an
awkward crack to another ledge and then a loose finish.

Flexitoys 15 metres E3 6a (6.84)
Start in the middle of the wall 3 metres to the right again. Climb the wall,
and at the third horizontal break move slightly leftwards before finishing
straight upwards.

Plastic Edge 15 metres E2 5b (6.84)
Start just right of the arête. Climb up and left to gain the arête and then
climb it direct.

Right again, there is a deep recess crowned with spectacular hanging
boulders. Beyond this the cliff runs below more hanging boulders embedded
in earth and then turns sharply rightwards across a steep wall streaked and
stained with water-marks.

Speleology 22 metres Hard Very Severe (1 pt aid) (16.7.72)
This sustained climb takes the right-to-left slanting chimney on the left side
of the steep wall, and then traverses right to clear a hanging block at the
top of the wall on its right side. Pegs required. Start in the corner on the
left, and scramble 10 metres to a large ledge to the right of a loose break.
1 12m. 5a. Climb the chimney and use a peg (not *in situ*) to exit from it.
Continue on some shaky rock to a niche.
2 10m. 4c. Traverse right along the exposed, horizontal ledge for 6
metres and climb up to the right of the hanging block.

Stout Crack 23 metres E4 6a (1991)
Often wet. Start just right of the slanting chimney, at a left-leaning fault.
Climb the crack (peg) until the ledge on pitch 2 of *Speleology* is reached.
Finish to the right of a hanging block.

The North Wall   30 metres   Very Severe   (9.7.72)
This follows the easiest line to the right of the blank reddish-coloured, overhanging wall in the middle of the face. Start below and left of the obvious leftward-slanting overhangs that fringe the right side of the wall.
1 10m. 4a. Climb on flakes for a few metres to a ledge and then go up to another ledge immediately above and on the left. Step up to the right and traverse for about 3 metres along a streaky ledge below the narrow impending wall.
2 10m. 5a. Climb onto a slimy ledge below an overhanging crack; then make a hard move up to the right and continue awkwardly around the corner. Traverse a metre or so to the right and then climb to the foot of the black-streaked wall.
3 10m. 4c. Climb up the centre of the wall by a small slab and take the overhang direct on good holds; above this the angle eases.

★Campanology   23 metres   Severe 4a   (8.7.72)
Start 2 metres right of *The North Wall* and gain a staircase of small ledges leading diagonally rightwards to a vertical corner crack. Climb this for 2 metres; then step right onto a sloping greenish ledge and climb to another ledge on the right. Move up, and turn the bulging wall above by moving left onto a ledge. Climb easily up the corner and belay on the right.

☆Dead Ringer   23 metres   Hard Very Severe 5b †   (16.6.88)
Start just right of *Campanology* below the central crackline of the wall. Climb the crack for 6 metres and then move left onto a ledge. Continue up the crack above to a ledge and corner and finish up the corner.

☆☆Coconut Cove   20 metres   E5 6b †   (7.87)
Climb the left-leaning crack in the wall right of *Dead Ringer* for a few moves before crossing the bulge above with difficulty. Continue up the wall to a horizontal break. Finish more easily using a crack up to the left.

Teleology   20 metres   Severe 4a   (7.8.69)
Climb the ramp to a chimney behind the left edge of the trapezium-shaped block and continue steeply up this. Finish up the steep wall above.

Soft Touch   15 metres   E2 5b †   (4.7.87)
The arête right of *Teleology*, starting up a slanting crack from the chimney and finishing up the wall above.

Face Lift   15 metres   E3 5c †   (4.7.87)
The face 3 metres right of the arête of *Soft Touch*, finishing up the crack on the right.

Feeding the Mouse   17 metres   Very Difficult   (27.7.89)
Follow the slanting chimney right of *Face Lift* to finish up the corner above.

On the next steep wall there are three more climbs.

Dark Lady 23 metres E1 5a † (4.8.86)
Start at the foot of a left-slanting white vein. Climb the white vein leftwards
for 15 metres and finish up the steep wall above.

Retail Therapy 15 metres Very Severe 5a † (3.10.89)
Start as for *Dark Lady* at the foot of a left-slanting white vein. Climb the
vein for a few metres and then move up to a good flake below a
prominent vertical crack. Finish strenuously up the crack.

Christine 20 metres Severe 4a † (1987)
Climb the wall, starting a couple of metres right of *Dark Lady*.

Right of *Christine* is a small tower; the front face gives **Final Line** (8 metres
E1 5b † 4.7.87).

Mayon Castle Cliff
Approach. Mayon Castle Cliff is the first headland south of Sennen, and is
best approached from there. It can be identified by a small stone wall, which
is part of the castle ruins.

Environmental Issues. Take care on the approach, as the area is very
environmentally sensitive. The headland is owned by The National Trust.

The routes are on the impressive overhanging wall below the seaward face
of the cliff. The cliff catches the afternoon sun and is non-tidal provided the
sea is calm. The rock is of variable quality, but is mostly reasonable. The
routes have strong lines and are bold.

Rourke's Rift 13 metres E1 5b † (1990s)
Start below the short lower tier on the left side of the cliff. Climb the central
crackline up the smooth wall to finish up a short groove.

The next two routes and variant start beneath a recess in the tall central
wall.

Sugar and Dust 33 metres E6 6a † (1990s)
Bold, powerful climbing on an obvious line up crumbly rock. Climb up
over easy ground, turn the roof on the right, and break left above it. Follow
cracks and flakes to the top.

☆☆☆**Mean Crack** 33 metres E6 6b † (1990s)
The obvious rightward-slanting crackline of the tall central wall. Gritty rock.
Climb easy ground and then the recess to the roof. Move out right and
follow a powerful but punishing crack, to finish direct using flakes.
Direct Start 33 metres E7 6b † (1990s). Powerful and thin technical

climbing. Start up easy ground as for *Mean Crack*. Boldly climb the left-slanting faultline before rejoining *Mean Crack*.

☆☆☆**Copacabana**   25 metres   E5 6b †   (1990s)
A strong line with excellent rock and reasonable protection up the steep right-hand wall. From a sloping ledge, climb the obvious crackline. Pull up rightwards at the overlap and continue up another crack. Exit to the right of the capping roof/nose.

Black Waterfall Cove   OS Ref 347 258

This small cove lies about 800 metres south of the old coastguard lookout at Pedn-mên-du. It is best reached from Sennen by walking along the coast path towards Land's End as far as the impressive remains of Maen Castle, a pre- 300 BC Iron Age cliff castle. A small stream runs down the depression to the south of the Castle promontory. Follow the stream down to the edge of the cliff where it drops as a waterfall into the rocky cove below. There are two routes on the slabby right-hand wall (facing out) of the cove. The bed of the cove is best reached by walking south along the cliff edge for about 80 metres to where a break leads down crumbly rock to sea-level. Traverse north along the rocky foreshore at or near low tide to reach the base of the climbs.

There has been a small rockfall from the mid point of the slabby wall, and the rock throughout should be treated with care. The wall is split on its left side by a deep, earthy crack. Left of the crack is a slabby pillar taken by **Electric Blue** (30 metres Hard Severe 4a † 1984) and to the right is the slab of **Wind Hanging** (30 metres Very Severe 4c † 1984).

Land's End Area (Granite)   OS Ref 342 250

'The Land's End terminates in a poynt or peak of great rocks which runs a good way into the sea. I clambr'd over them as farre as safety permitted me...'   (The Journeys of Celia Fiennes, 1698.)

Climbing at Land's End is long established. However, the headland is privately owned and is one of the country's major tourist attractions. The current owner of Land's End has honoured the custom of previous owners in allowing climbers access to the cliffs without charging a parking fee. You may be asked to provide evidence that you are a climber; a quick flash of the rope is usually adequate proof. It is worth pointing out that if you don't want to be just another attraction in the Land's End Experience you had better climb elsewhere! As this book goes to press the owner has asked that climbers sign in on arrival.

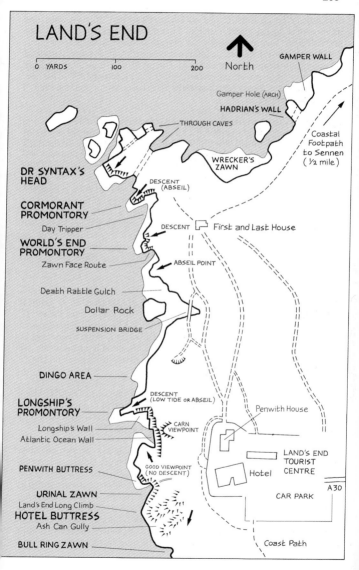

Outlook: West on most climbs on Dr Syntax's Head and the walls and promontories to the south. Gamper Hole Area and Hadrian's Wall face north-west and west respectively, while Wrecker's Zawn Cliff faces north-east.

Tidal in most areas. Accessible for about three hours either side of low water in most areas except where mentioned. The whole area is seriously affected by swell and rough sea except on the few climbs that start well above the sea. There have been deaths from drowning here: be aware of both the state of the tide and the swell.

Coastguard Identity: Land's End.

Environmental Issues: The area is a breeding site for Kittiwake and Razorbill as well as Fulmar, Shag, and Herring Gull,. Dense nesting areas are best avoided during the nesting season. The slopes above the cliffs are very fragile in places, and heathland and crevice communities are vulnerable, so tread carefully. See also the specific advice for Trevescan Cliff.

Land's End is a remarkable phenomenon, and not least as a climbing venue. The complex series of jutting cliffs and promontories that confront the Atlantic head on at this 'Seat of Storms' offer a splendid selection of challenging climbs, always in impressive surroundings, though quite often on rock that is not of prime quality. The exits from a good number of the routes prove to be particularly challenging. If in doubt, a fixed rope is a good idea, always assuming you can identify the finish of your chosen route from above.

The 'real world' of the adjoining Land's End Experience is incidental to the climbing. In areas like Cormorant Promontory climbing as a genuine spectator sport has been well established for far longer than indoor TV spectaculars. Top out with style and you can bask in the genuine applause of the multitude picnicking on the natural galleries of Dr Syntax's Head. Despite this, some areas of Land's End are remarkably secluded once below the cliff edge, while the advantages of the greatly improved facilities of the Land's End Complex itself can be a bonus, après-climb.

Approach to Land's End is obvious, just keep driving west! On a first visit it is best to identify the layout of the main climbing areas. Although the cliffs are continuous, there are individual and complex sections, each served by separate descents (see map on page 265).

Cliff Layout: First locate Penwith House. This is the smaller detached building to the right (facing out) of the large State House Hotel and is on the seaward side of the complex. The route from the car-park to Penwith House is via the entrance archway, or by detouring less conspicuously around to its right. Walk directly to seaward from in front of Penwith House. Go down a granite step to cross a gravelled area; then go down rocky steps to reach a pile of boulders on top of a seaward promontory. The boulder pile (or carn) is directly above *Atlantic Ocean Wall* and the Longships Promontory area. It is an ideal viewpoint from which to identify the main climbing areas as listed below.

To the north (right facing out) from the viewpoint, the farthest feature visible is the impressive promontory of Dr Syntax's Head. This is the most westerly projecting point and is the site of the official 'Land's End'.

East of Dr Syntax's Head, and out of sight from the viewpoint, is Trevescan Cliff, incorporating Gary Cooper Wall, Gamper Hole, Hadrian's Wall, and Wrecker's Zawn.

South (back towards the viewpoint) from Dr Syntax's Head, the next visible feature is the elegant Cormorant Promontory, identified by the curving corner of *The Cormorant's Bill* capped by its helmet-shaped overhang.

South of Cormorant Promontory is a large zawn sporting routes like *Black Power* and *Day Tripper* but hidden from view by the orange-coloured top of World's End Promontory, where routes like *World's End* and *Zawn Face Route* are located.

South of *World's End* is Abseil Point Area flecked with large bunches of greenery on its upper walls. To the right of this and just out of sight is a steep friable wall taken by *Death Rattle Gulch*. The next obvious feature is Dollar Rock, the decaying island that lies at the entrance to the gulf spanned by the 'Land's End Experience' swing-bridge.

South of the swing-bridge, the cliffs fall off in height to Longships Promontory and Longships Zawn, which lie directly below the viewpoint. The black, schorl-coated top of Longships Wall lies down to the right.

To the south (left) of the viewpoint lies the stepped profile of Hotel Buttress, up which *Land's End Long Climb* threads its way. Beyond here but out of sight is Bull Ring Zawn with climbs such as *Aberdeen Angus* and *Crystal Fingers*. Beyond Bull Ring Zawn there is a stretch of unstable cliff. The next climbs are on Armed Knight Buttress, which lies at the far end of the southern run of Land's End cliffs and opposite the rock island of The Armed Knight.

For Trevescan Cliff, Dr Syntax's Head, Cormorant Promontory, and World's End Area, follow the wide tourist track north from the State House to reach the isolated building called The First and Last House, which stands on the inland neck of Dr Syntax's Head.

Trevescan Cliff

This is the north-facing section of Land's End. It lies east of Dr Syntax's Head and is approached from The First and Last House.

Environmental Issues: There are important sections of heathland, wet flushes, and mires in this area which are susceptible to damage from trampling. Spring Squill is abundant, but Bog Asphodel, Cottongrass, Royal Fern, and Sea Spleenwort are vulnerable. The foreshore is an important marine biological site. Although the area is not formally restricted, Kittiwake, Shag, Herring Gull, and Fulmar breed here, so climbers are asked to avoid the area in the nesting season.

Gary Cooper Wall

Gary Cooper Wall lies just to the east of the projecting buttress of Gamper Wall (see below). The area is north-facing and has not proved popular. The rock is generally solid, but a number of routes have unstable finishes. The routes in the centre of the bay are tidal, those towards the extremities less so.

Approach from The First and Last House by following the coast path north-east towards Sennen for about 150 metres to a point above the distinctive arch of Hadrian's Wall. Continue in the same direction to the projecting pillar of Gamper Wall, then another 40 metres to a second projecting ridge, down which an awkward scrambling descent is possible.

To the right of the descent (facing the cliff) is a south-west-facing flat wall with a prominent straight crack bounding its right side.

Route One   10 metres   Very Severe 4c †   (1994)
Easy ledges give access to the crack, which is steep and short.

Candy   10 metres   Hard Severe 4b †   (1994)
Starting from the foot of the steep crack of *Route One*, follow the thinner crack just to the right.

The next four routes climb the grooved wall just to the right of *Candy*, starting from tidal ledges in the base of the zawn.

Espron Negro   18 metres   E3 6a   (1988)
Start on the left side of the bay and climb a groove to ledges. Continue in a direct line passing the left edge of a projecting overhang to finish up a shallow groove.

Pump It   18 metres   E2 6a †   (1994)
Start two metres right of the groove of *Espron Negro*. Climb the wall via a thin crack to a ledge at the base of a groove. Climb this until it is possible to move out left; then continue up the narrow buttress until forced left into the final groove of *Espron Negro*.

Yet Again   18 metres   Very Severe 4c †   (1994)
Follow *Pump It* to the ledge at the foot of the groove. Climb the wall on the right until it is possible to step back left and finish up the continuation of the groove.
Variation Finish
And Another   18 metres   Very Severe 4c †   (1994)
This short variation takes the right-hand upper groove on poor rock.

The back of the bay is a smooth decaying wall bounded on its right-hand side by a striking thin crackline with a wider crackline right again.

★Fast Lane   18 metres   E4 6a   (1988)
The thin crack proves to be the best route in the zawn, giving good hard crack climbing which is well protected throughout.

OK Corral   18 metres   Hard Very Severe 5a †   (1994)
The wide crack is followed to a bulge and the continuation crack leads to a ledge. Finish up the wider corner crack taking care with the exit.

To the right is the projecting buttress that is Gamper Wall. There are four routes on the left-hand side of this feature.

☆High Noon   16 metres   E1 5b †   (1994)
Climb into a recess in the open corner and pull leftwards onto the wall. Climb this trending right and then left to a position below stepped roofs and a hanging fang. Pull around the right-hand side of this to a steep finish. It is also possible to climb the left-hand side of the fang at E2 5c or to escape right into the next climb at HVS 5b.

Tumble Weed   16 metres   Very Severe 5a †   (1994)
Start as for the previous climb but pull right into the open corner and climb it to an evil deep slot. Chimney this and finish up the steep groove and crack above.

Pony Express   16 metres   Very Severe 5a †   (1994)
A right-hand variant to the previous climb avoids the slot by pulling onto the right wall and then climbing this steeply to enter the upper groove of *Tumble Weed*.

True Grit   18 metres   E2 5b †   (1994)
The slanting off-width in the wall to the right gives an ungainly struggle to the security of a good ledge. Escape out right to finish.

Gamper Hole Area
Gamper Hole lies on the north side of the distinctive archway of Hadrian's Wall, which is clearly visible looking north-east from The First and Last House. The area tends to be gloomy and damp, though it dries out late in the day. The rock is generally solid, but a number of routes finish through earth and decaying rock bands, so care is required.

Approach from The First and Last House by following the coast path north-east towards Sennen for about 150 metres to a point above the distinctive arch of Hadrian's Wall. Descend the spine of the arch over loose ledges stained with yellow lichen and bird lime. Near sea-level, drop down to the right (facing out) into the dark mouth of Gamper Hole, passing below an obvious pinnacle and then onto the boulder-strewn floor of the zawn. The crack-seamed Gamper Wall lies on the left. Right of the wall is a depression flanked on its right by the arête of *Looking over the Edge*. An abseil descent down the buttress of Gamper Wall is also possible, but check the state of the tide first.

The next climb is on the seaward face of the Gamper Wall buttress taking an obvious line up its front face.

★Bulging Arête   18 metres   Hard Severe 4b   (25.7.59)
Start at lowish tide at the base of a short chimney formed by a block. Climb the chimney and then follow the deepening crack to a ledge. Continue up the steeper crack and finish up a short wall.

The following climbs are on the west side of Gamper Wall buttress.

Mind Bubble   18 metres   Hard Very Severe 5b †   (30.7.88)
Start between the left arête and a wide crack that slants to the right. Climb the wall to the second of two breaks; then traverse rightwards to reach a developing crack, which leads to a ledge. Finish up the wall on the left.

Sunset Crack   18 metres   Hard Very Severe 5a †   (6.6.88)
Climb the wide crack in the centre of the wall, initially slanting to the right and then following it to the top of the buttress.

Fading into Black   18 metres   E2 5c †   (30.7.88)
Start below the blunt arête in the centre of the wall. Climb the arête to reach flakes close to the *Sunset Crack* and then follow the right-hand crack to the top.

Double Take   18 metres   Very Severe 5a †   (22.7.88)
Start in the corner on the right side of Gamper Wall. Climb to a recess and then go up to the roof. Move up and traverse left using a good crack to where it is possible to step up to reach a slanting, downward-pointing flake. Step left and follow *Fading into Black* to the top.

The Long Reach   18 metres   E4 6b †   (1988)
Follow *Double Take* to the roof, but where that route traverses left, step right and climb to a sinuous crackline. Follow this until it veers right close to the corner, step back left, and climb the centre of the wall to poorer rock and the top.

Looking over the Edge   40 metres   E1 5b †   (25.8.88)
The earthy finishing section should be treated with caution. Start at the foot of the obvious arête on the right of the deep corner with the block and cave at its back. Climb the arête directly to an area of convoluted rock and continue over this to a short corner capped by a small roof. Climb onwards to another corner leading to a small ledge on the right. Steep broken cracks lead to the top and a thread belay in the grassy area above.

Children of Laughter (42 metres E4 6b † 9.8.88) started behind the pinnacle in the middle of the zawn. It climbed ledges, the arête, a small roof, and a wall to a ledge (possible stance). A wall then led to an earthy finish. The hangers were removed from the two bolt runners by the first ascensionists, who gave it the above grade first.

Hadrian's Wall

Approach from The First and Last House by following the coast path north-east towards Sennen for about 150 metres to a point above the distinctive arch of Hadrian's Wall. The climbs are on the smooth west face of the archway and can be reached by scrambling down the north-east arête of the buttress and following ledges around to below the west-facing wall.

★Hadrian's Wall   15 metres   Hard Very Severe 5a   (18.7.59)
Start from the ledge below the left edge of the wall. Gain a ledge on the left before traversing diagonally right to a horizontal fault (peg). Make a difficult mantelshelf to reach a horizontal break and then continue on small holds to the top.

☆SPQR   15 metres   E3 6a †   (19.8.82)
Start below the right edge of the wall. Climb a steep crack on the left to a hanging recess on the left-hand side of the roof; then continue up the thin crack in the upper wall.

Hadrian's Nose   15 metres   E1 5b   (21.6.82)
Climb the steep wall and the crack that splits the hanging nose, and then finish up the crack above.

Across the tidal inlet to the right are three more climbs on rock that is unsound in places, especially towards the cliff top. They can be approached from Hadrian's Wall or Wrecker's Zawn (see below) at low tide. The first two routes start on blocks across the inlet from the west-facing Hadrian's Wall.

Cassio   30 metres   E2 5c †   (1982)
Follow a continuous thin crack up the left-hand side of the buttress, and continue up its crest to a direct finish that requires care.

Brutus   30 metres   Hard Very Severe 5b †   (1982)
Climb a short corner on the right side of the buttress to gain a large left-facing flake, which is followed to easier terrain.

To the right is an unclimbed angular corner and then a large slab.

Caesar's Groove   30 metres   E2 5c †   (1982)
Follow a crack that slants rightwards to end at the slab. Continue up the slab, before pulling rightwards through an overlap and an overhang to finish up the obvious steep corner.

Wrecker's Zawn

This is the large zawn lying to the east of Dr Syntax's Head. There are two recorded routes on its impressive north-east-facing wall. The wall is prone to seepage, does not get much sunlight, and has its share of poor rock. Dry conditions and a visit after midday are advised.

Approach from The First and Last House by walking to seaward down the grass slopes from the western end of the wooden fence that cordons off the inland rim of the zawn. Continue parallel to the rim of the north-east-facing wall and then scramble down with care to sea-level boulders. Traverse back into the zawn over boulders to the base of the big wall.

The climbs here finish on steep grass and a **preplaced belay rope** is advised as the block belays are a considerable distance up the slope.

☆☆**Infinite Design**   60 metres   E4 †   (6.5.88)
A technical and strenuous climb taking the obvious steep wall with a rightward-slanting crack just right of the leftmost bottomless corner of the wall. Start below the pillar just right of the corner.
1 42m. 6a. Climb the pillar to gain a ledge on the right. Go over the small roof into the corner; then continue up to the roof. Swing right onto the steep wall and then move up into the crack, which is followed to its top. Move right and up to a shallow corner (peg). Climb the corner (peg) to its top and then move left to reach a belay ledge.
2 18m. 5a. Climb the steep slabs and walls to the boulder below the grassy top, which should be negotiated with care.

☆☆**A Winking Crack**   60 metres   E4 †   (9.7.88)
Another impressive line taking the obvious crack above the black overhang to the right of the central groove. Start 8 metres right of *Infinite Design*, below a big black roof.
1 42m. 6a. Climb direct to the left edge of the roof. Pull leftwards over the roof and then climb a groove to its top. Swing right to follow a faint crack in the arête to another roof. Make strenuous moves over this and then move right to a crack. Follow the crack to its top and belay on an orange-tinted slab.
2 18m. 5a. Climb the slab and wall above to broken blocks on the left. Pull over the blocks and ascend the grassy slope with care.

Dr Syntax's Head

This is the true westerly point of 'Land's End'. It juts out into the Atlantic, open-faced to the north, west, and south and has taken a pounding because of it. Substantial rockfalls have radically changed the structure of the West Face and a number of routes have been destroyed or changed. The surviving rock is generally sound, and there are some worthwhile climbs here.

Approach from The First and Last House by walking diagonally to the right down an obvious twisting path, which leads through boulders and out onto the distinctive promontory of Dr Syntax's Head. The top of the Head is generously supplied with abseil anchor blocks. Large rock islands lie directly opposite the North-West Face. A narrow through-cave pierces the northern extension of Dr Syntax's Head and leads from the extreme northern side of the Head to the three main faces. However, these are best approached as described below.

Descent for the North-West, West, and South Faces: It is possible to abseil down each of the three faces from the crest of the Head, but the most amenable abseil is down the South Face, which faces Cormorant Promontory. There is a big anchor block in a gap near the seaward edge of Dr Syntax's Head above the West Face. About 5 metres below and to the south of the anchor block is a big ledge above the South Face. From this ledge, the abseil gives access to good ledges, where an easy traverse can be made around left (facing in) to non-tidal ledges below the start of the climbs on the West face. A further slippery traverse at sea-level can be made around the left arête of the West Face to reach non-tidal ledges below the North-West Face. This last section is possible only at low water and in calm seas.

Alternatively, abseils can be made directly down the West Face from the same anchor block mentioned above, and down the North-West face from the anchor blocks above its rim. The ledges at the foot of all the walls can be reached at most states of the tide but they can be dangerously affected by rough sea and swell at any state of the tide.

North-West Face
The first climbs are in the black-walled bay on the northern side of the Head.

April Fool   22 metres   E2 5b †   (1.4.88)
Climb the extreme left-hand crack on the left wall of the bay; then move left under a diagonal overlap, where the crack fades, to gain the left arête. Make bold moves up the arête to the top.

Exit Visa   22 metres   Hard Severe 4b †   (10.84)
Climb the deep groove just to the right and then traverse left at the top to finish.

Copy Cat   22 metres   Very Severe 4c †   (10.84)
Climb the obvious crack on the narrow face just around to the right of the previous route to a blocky exit.

Perfect Prescription   22 metres   E3 6a   (10.84)
The centre of the face left of the narrow through-cave. Climb the thin crack that splits the overhang and continue up the groove above.

CORMORANT PROMONTORY

Don Sargeant ~ 1991

DR. SYNTAX'S HEAD

CORMORANT
PROMONTORY

LANDS END ~ NORTH

DR. SYNTAX'S HEAD

1	Born Free	HVS
2	Second Chance	E1
3	Time Out	E3
4	Land's End Micro Climb	HVS
6	Blitzkrieg	E1
7	New Waves	HVS
8	Edge of Time	E4

CORMORANT PROMONTORY

9	Hors d'Oeuvre	VS
10	A Sudden Splash	E3
11	Cormorant Slab	S
12	Cormorant's Ben	E2
13	The Cormorant's Bill	HVS
14	Lost Souls	E5
15	The Last Dance	E4
16	Johnstone's Route	S
17	Split Minds	E1
18	Backlash	E1
19	Witch Hunt	E2
20	Black Power	E2
21	Oliver Twist	HVS
22	Tide Race	VS
23	Day Tripper	E4

WORLD'S END PROMONTORY

24	Edge Control II	E5
25	Virgin on a Crisis	E6
26	The Prodigal's Return	HVS
27	Strongbody	HVS
28	Procyon	VS
29	The Dawning	E5
30	World's End	HVS
31	Sunset Wall	E3

ABSEIL POINT AREA

32	Voices	E3
33	Echoes	E3
34	The Parasite	E2
35	Initiation	E2
36	The Maiden	HVS
37	Deception	HS
38	Piton Route	HVS
39	Land's End Short Climb	E1
40	Death Rattle Gulch	E2

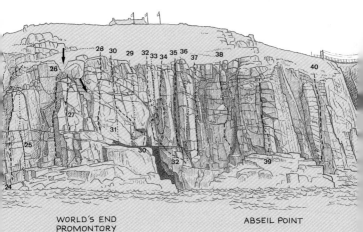

WORLD'S END PROMONTORY

ABSEIL POINT

Soloer's Paradise   48 metres   Severe 4b †   (1983)
Start at the entrance to the through-cave. Traverse right at sea-level on good rock to reach the arête, which is climbed direct on big flake holds. A more direct start is also possible at 4a.

West Face
This face has suffered major rockfalls, which have erased established climbs. Some have survived but with structural changes.

Born Free   22 metres   Hard Very Severe 5a †   (6.11.83)
Start 3 metres right of the left arête of the face. Climb the wall on good holds and then continue direct on smaller holds to where it is possible to step onto the arête. Climb a crack and a square-cut corner to finish.

Easy Way Out   22 metres   Very Difficult   (1987)
As the name suggests, a useful escape route. Climb the shallow groove right of the arête to a ledge and then follow the easy upper section of the previous climb.

☆☆**New Release**   22 metres   E2 5c †   (1990)
Follow the deeper (capped) groove on the right to its closure, before pulling left and back right to enter the continuation crack leading to the top.

★**Second Chance**   30 metres   E1 5a   (19.5.86)
A worthwhile pitch up the thin crack in the centre of the face which has been exposed by rockfalls. Finish up the deeper continuation crack.

Recycled   22 metres   Very Severe 5a   (1987)
Start under the centre of the face but trend right to enter the big left-facing groove, which is followed to ledges on the right.

☆☆**Time Out**   25 metres   E3 5c †   (4.10.83)
Start below the wall to the right of the big left-facing groove of *Recycled*. Climb the steep wall to a fault; then step left to climb a thin crack to a ledge. Continue up the steep wall and arête (right of the deep groove) past horizontal breaks to reach a vertical crack. Climb the crack and the shallow groove to the top.

Land's End Micro Climb   22 metres   Hard Very Severe 4c   (5.10.83)
Climb the right arête of the West Face for 6 metres, and then move around to the right and onto the South Face to climb the steep crack which splits the upper wall.

Right of here the south face deteriorates into poorer rock for about 18 metres to where a chossy break rises from a sea-level cave. On the other side of this break is the wedge-shaped Entrance Wall. The wall flanks the impressive Great Cave, which pierces the neck of Dr Syntax's Head.

Entrance Wall

Descent is by abseil down the south face of Dr Syntax's Head as described above. From here, traverse in towards the Great Cave at Very Difficult standard. It may be possible to reach Entrance Wall from the foot of Cormorant Promontory by boulder-hopping across the mouth of the Great Cave, although very low tide and calm seas would be required.

Blitzkrieg 42 metres E1 5b †   (13.3.85)
From stepped, sloping ledges, climb the chimney/crack up the left-hand side of Entrance Wall to reach a thinner exit crack.

New Waves 45 metres Hard Very Severe 5b   (13.3.85)
Follow the chimney/crack of *Blitzkrieg* for 12 metres; then move rightwards along a horizontal break for two metres and climb the flaky wall before trending up and left to finish.

★★**Edge of Time** 45 metres E4   (16.4.85)
A powerful and serious route keeping close company with the mouth of the Great Cave. It is probably best done in one huge pitch to avoid belay difficulties. Start at an obvious rightward-slanting crack to the left of the cave entrance.
1 15m. 5c. Climb the crack to a ledge which leads into a roofed recess.
2 30m. 6b. Step left to the arête and then climb the steep wall to the roof (peg). Move left around the arête and into a shallow groove. Continue direct; then trend left to a narrow ledge. Continue to a square recess, and climb it to a flat ledge before moving right to finish.

> **Heritage of Follies** (45 metres E5 5c 6b 1988) is a variation going directly over the roofs. It originally used two bolt runners, and the grade reflects this.

☆☆**Mark in Time** E5 6a †   (1990s)
Climb the obvious crackline in the overhanging wall opposite *Edge of Time*.

Cormorant Promontory & World's End Promontory

The climbs in this area are best reached by a descent of *World's End Approach*. This is a 10-metre chimney of Difficult standard that gives direct access to the World's End area. The approach can appear quite intimidating and is slightly loose. Most parties abseil rather than down-climb, and an abseil rope left in place can also be reassuring in this tidal area from which there are few easy escapes.

Approach: To locate *World's End Approach*, start from The First and Last House. Follow a rocky path down right for several metres to where it forms a T-junction with a path running across the slope. Go directly across this path and descend grassy slopes to seaward, keeping to the left of some small pinnacles and boulders, to reach flat ledges at the cliff edge. Cormorant Promontory is dramatically visible down to the right.

Descent. Below the flat ledges there is a vegetated break that can be down-climbed, with great care, to a ledge above steeper rock. *World's End Approach* (Difficult) is the continuation chimney with a chockstone at its head. It can be descended to the platform at the base of World's End Wall. Alternatively, an abseil can be made from good anchors.

To reach Cormorant Promontory from the base of World's End Wall, descend to the boulder beach, which is accessible for about three hours either side of low water but which can be affected by swell and rough sea. During the high-water period of spring-tides an alternative and convenient abseil can be made from the summit blocks down *Cormorant Slab* on the seaward face of the Promontory.

The first climbs lie close to the Great Cave, around to the left from *Cormorant Slab*.

The Crypts of Lieberkuhn   25 metres   E1 5b   (16.7.89)
From a platform to the right of the Great Cave, traverse around to the left to a small ledge just above sea-level. Climb leftwards towards overhanging rock. Traverse right; then move up into a wide crack, which is followed to the top.

The next two climbs tackle the left wall of the deep recess to the right of the Great Cave, and have common climbing for their last 10 metres.

Irish Whiskey   25 metres   Hard Very Severe 5a †   (1990)
The wall and shallow groove on the left-hand side of the recess.

Hors-d'œuvre   25 metres   Very Severe   (25.7.59)
1 15m. 4c. Climb the pillar on the right for a short distance; then make a long step across onto the left side of the arch. Move up on small holds to a good ledge at the foot of a pillar on the right.
2 10m. 4b. Climb the pillar to the summit block; then scramble to finish.

The steep wall to the right of the deep recess has three taxing offerings to the left of the incised groove of *Lindy*.

☆**Magnet Fever**   28 metres   E6 6b †   (1990)
The steep smooth wall immediately to the right of the step-up that leads into the dark recess is split by a variety of sinuous cracklines and climbed with great difficulty to reach easier-angled terrain.

☆☆**Synchromatic**   28 metres   E4 6a †   (1990)
To the right a wider left-slanting crack is climbed (two pegs, although one may be missing) to join the easier-angled upper section of the previous route.

☆☆**Technotronic**   28 metres   E4 6b †   (1990)
The steep corner to the left of the start of *Lindy* is followed until the
rounded and flaky left arête can be gained. Follow this (peg) until an
easier groove leads to a huge block. Finish up the easier corner above.

Lindy   30 metres   E3 5b   (20.3.73)
A direct line up the obvious corner/groove on the left flank of Cormorant
Promontory. Protection is poor in the groove and the rock is friable in
places. Start around to the left of *Cormorant Slab* below a short chimney,
which is climbed to a ledge. Climb the groove for 10 metres to where the
crack becomes more amenable at a chockstone runner and a resting
position. Continue in the same line to the top.

☆**A Sudden Splash**   30 metres   E3 5c †   (15.7.88)
Start below the thin crack on the extreme left edge of *Cormorant Slab*.
Climb to the crack and follow it to a block. Continue up the arête to the
top of the pinnacle.

★**Cormorant Slab**   25 metres   Severe 4a   (1957)
A pleasant climb in classic Land's End surroundings. Start below a short
left-facing stepped corner on the left section of the slab. Climb the corner
to a crack and follow this to a ledge (belay possible). Move right into a
crack and then follow better holds to the top of the slab, from where a
scramble leads along the top of the promontory and back to the fleshpots.

Cormorant's Ben   25 metres   E2 5b   (10.4.81)
A direct line up thin cracks 2 metres to the right of *Cormorant Slab*. Climb
the deep first crack to its thinner continuation and then climb the
orange-coloured, lichenous wall on some shaky flakes to a small ledge
below another thin crack. Climb the crack and step left to finish as for
Cormorant Slab.
Direct Finish E2 5b (1981). From the top of the first crack, traverse up
and slightly rightwards across a steep slab, and go straight up to gain the
finish of *Cormorant Slab*.

★**Lost Souls**   30 metres   E5 6b   (8.3.85)
A bold route. Climb up as for *The Cormorant's Bill*, but after a short
distance move left onto the arête (peg – not *in situ*). Climb the arête by a
series of tenuous moves to gain an awkward foothold; a micro-wire can
be pre-placed around to the right, although this may not be necessary
now a stainless steel peg has appeared near the top. Use a vein of rock
high up to reach easier ground.

★★**The Cormorant's Bill**   28 metres   Hard Very Severe 5b   (29.8.71)
A stylish and strenuous pitch that follows the steep leaning corner around
the arête to the right of *Cormorant Slab*. Start at the right-hand end of the
platform below the slab. Climb past a ledge and then mantelshelf onto a
small sloping ledge below the main groove. Follow the groove on small

holds to the capping overhang and then use a good hold on the left wall to aid the pull over. Continue on good holds to the top.

★★The Last Dance   28 metres   E4 6b   (1985)
From the ledge at the base of *The Cormorant's Bill*, move right and climb boldly up the steep slab to the break. Continue in the same line to a shallow groove and climb this to an exposed exit onto the right arête. Step left, pull through the overlap and finish up the slab and arête above. Two pegs.

★Last Dancer   40 metres   E5   (12.4.85)
A technical climb up the right-hand side of the arête to the right of *The Cormorant's Bill*, finishing as for the previous climb. Start at the base of the wall below a crack that fails to reach the ground and just left of a wide crack (*Split Minds*). Four pegs.
1 10m. 6c. Climb the steep pock-marked wall to a peg and continue up the widening crack above to a belay on a large ledge.
2 30m. 6b. Climb the wall on the left and then swing around the arête onto the wall. Continue traversing; then move up into the shallow groove of *The Last Dance*. Climb the steep slab above to a horizontal fault. Surmount the overlap above the fault onto another steep slab. Climb up to another faultline; then move rightwards to the arête, which is climbed to its top.

☆☆☆The Edwards Edge   38 metres   E8 †   (9.97)
1 10m. 6c. *Last Dancer* pitch 1.
2 28m. 6c. *Friends* required for horizontal breaks. Step up left onto the arête and arrange a poor cam in a horizontal break. Climb the overhanging wall with increasing difficulty and move left onto the arête proper. Follow the arête before moving right at the second break. Climb the wall to make committing run-out moves past two edges. Move left to regain the arête and continue past a peg on *Last Dancer* to the top.

Split Minds   30 metres   E1 5b   (16.7.81)
Start below the distinctive wide crack just right of *Last Dancer*. Climb the wide crack to a ledge and possible stance. Climb the wall on the left to a crack; follow the crack to a good ledge on the right. Step left across the wall and then climb steep cracks (large cams) to the top.

★Johnstone's Route   28 metres   Severe   (1957)
A fine route with considerable exposure and atmosphere. Start below a large triangular niche (the stance on the previous two routes) about 6 metres right of the front face of Cormorant Promontory.
1 14m. 4a. Climb red and black rock, bearing right slightly at first, and then work left over ledges to take a stance in the corner.
2 14m. 4a. Follow the right-hand corner for a short distance to where a narrow ledge leads left to the final crack. Climb the crack, which is awkward to start and crumbly to finish.

The next two routes are best avoided as they are not particularly pleasant and their upper sections are home to considerable volumes of exotic herbage.

Backlash 34 metres E1 (28.8.72)

Start below the wide, rightward-leaning crack just right of *Johnstone's Route*.

1 16m. 5b. Climb the wide crack to a point just past a small overhang in the back of the crack and before a section of poor rock. Move left around the rib on a small foothold and then climb to the foot of the vertical crack that splits the upper part of the wall. Traverse left into the corner of *Johnstone's Route* to belay.

2 18m. 5a. High in the grade. Return to the crack and follow it to the top; the hardest moves are below half height.

Witch Hunt 40 metres E2 5c (8.77)

Start a metre or so right of *Backlash* at a thin crack that splits a blunt rib. Climb to small ledges and then follow a thin crack diagonally left to the chimney of *Backlash*. Climb the shallow chimney and a difficult section up cracks above to where a good horizontal crack cuts right across the buttress, 8 metres from the top. Step left and make a hard move up a blind crack to reach a flake crack on the right. From here, another move gains the top.

★Edge of Light 32 metres E3 5b (1994)

Start as for *Witch Hunt*, but climb the increasingly sharp arête on its left-hand side to the top.

★Black Power 32 metres E2 5b (27.8.72)

A stylish and direct line up the buttress to the right of the previous routes. Protection is poor in the V-groove. Start as for the previous two climbs. Climb a short corner/groove to gain a small ledge on the rib; then traverse rightwards until below a small white niche. Climb to the niche and then continue up the steep crack above until this eases and a ledge on the right is reached. Step into the V-groove on the left and climb it to a point where the left rib can be used. Move up the rib; then step back into the groove, which is followed to a finish up cracks.

Oliver Twist 32 metres Hard Very Severe (19.7.59)

There is loose rock on the first pitch. Start below the steep narrowing chimney that is the next main feature of the wall.

1 18m. 5a. Climb the chimney, which becomes harder as height is gained, until forced out left into a steep groove. Follow the groove to a good ledge.

2 14m. 4c. Climb the corner above and then make a long step left to a ledge. Gain another ledge further left by a mantelshelf. Make a hard move onto the sloping ledge above; then continue straight to the top.

Beyond the deep chimney of *Oliver Twist* is a narrow buttress that runs rightwards into a groove and thence into a chossy corner. Right of the corner is an impressive buttress undercut at its left-hand side. The front face of the narrow buttress is climbed by:

★Dancing on Crystals   42 metres   E5 6b   (1994)
Climb to a ledge on the prow of the buttress and then move left and up to a notch that splits the overhang. Follow the sustained thin cracks above (many small wires) to a stance at the junction with the next route. Finish up this or, more pleasantly, lower off a pre-placed rope.

Tide Race   40 metres   Very Severe   (1959)
A pleasant if somewhat gritty climb in impressive surroundings for the grade. Start below an open groove to the right of the arête of the previous climb.
1 20m. 4b. Climb to a ledge at the foot of the steep groove and then traverse left to the foot of a second groove. Climb the second groove passing some loose flakes to reach a good ledge on the right. The first groove has also been climbed at the same grade.
2 20m. 4a. Climb the short and rather grotty crack above; work left and then right through bulges to finish. Alternatively, lower off a pre-placed rope to avoid the unstable, vegetated top section.

★★Day Tripper   38 metres   E4   (4.4.81)
A powerful and technical route of quality, although still with some crunchy rock in places. It follows thin cracks in the broad arête of the undercut buttress. Start below the obvious roofs at the base of the buttress.
1 32m. 6a. Climb the initial wall strenuously to the first roof and move around into an overhanging V-groove. Go up the V-groove to reach holds high up on the left and pull over onto the wall above. Climb to the next roof, and then rightwards to a finger-crack. Continue to a horizontal break; then make difficult moves up to a small triangular ledge. Move left with difficulty into a another finger-crack, which is followed to a good ledge.
2 6m. 4c. Climb into the wide crack on the left and follow it to the top, taking care with the rock, or lower-off a pre-placed rope.

★★A Bridge Too Far   45 metres   E5 6b   (1994)
Around the rib to the right of the start of *Day Tripper* is a severely overhanging groove; this is the line! The optional hanging stance offers a way of reducing rope-drag. Bridge and contort your way up the leaning groove (two pegs) until it is possible to pull around onto the vertical face. Either take a hanging stance here (on a single large *Rock*) or continue up the cracks that trend diagonally leftwards to join the upper section of *Day Tripper* and climb this to its good belay ledge. Finish as for *Day Tripper*.

Flash Control (25 metres E3 6a 1990) followed the leaning open groove at the back of the bay, past six pegs, some in drilled placements, to a twin-peg belay. The pegs have been removed. An upper pitch is available at a very unstable E2 5b.

The cliff now juts forward as a buttress split by a wide horizontal break at half height and bounded by a deep crack on its left side.

Currying Favour   30 metres   Hard Very Severe 5a   (1990)
The open groove on the left-hand side of the buttress leads into a deeper corner-crack, which is followed as it curves over to the right to a stance on top of the buttress. Large nuts required.

★★★**Edge Control II**   30 metres   E5 6b   (25.11.88)
The left edge of the seaward-facing wall. Start just left of a short corner and below a thin crack. Climb the crack and the wall above to reach a horizontal fault (peg). Move left to the arête; then go straight up cracks to the small roof above the wide horizontal fault. Pull over the roof (peg) and climb the arête to a series of small sloping ledges. Climb the edge to the top and a belay block. Escape via ledges behind the block. The route has been climbed without the pegs at E6.

★★**Virgin on a Crisis**   30 metres   E6 6c   (4.85)
A bold, direct line up the middle of the wall, starting right of a short corner. Climb the striking crack with the boldest climbing at the top. The climb has two pegs (one of which is stacked), but has been repeated without them at the same grade.

Svetio Polacek's Route   30 metres †   (1986)
The loose corner to the right has been climbed just once, as an on-sight solo. No grade was offered for the outing.

Beyond Cormorant Promontory, a dark, jutting buttress marks the left extremity of World's End Promontory.

The Prodigal's Return   28 metres   Hard Very Severe 5a   (16.8.71)
A line near the left edge of the dark buttress starts on the sea-level platform, below a V-groove. Climb the V-groove to a large ledge and then move right and take the steep wall above by cracks to reach the bottom of a flake. Climb the flake to finish.

Black Wednesday   28 metres   E5 6b   (1991)
The thin crack in the centre of the wall just to the right was climbed with a peg on the first ascent. The first ascensionist subsequently replaced it by a bolt.

The following routes are on the seaward face of the World's End Wall.

Strongbody   15 metres   Hard Very Severe 5a   (1.71)
Start from the highest ledge below the crack in the seaward face, immediately left of the *World's End Approach* descent chimney. Climb the crack to a niche below an overhang, which is climbed strenuously. Continue to a belay.

Just to the right is the chockstone-blocked chimney of **World's End Approach** (Difficult), which makes a useful descent route, although great care is needed here and an abseil may be preferred. The following climbs lie on the wall above the ledge right of *World's End Approach* and can be reached at any state of the tide.

Procyon   22 metres   Very Severe 4c   (22.2.72)
Start just right of *World's End Approach*, below an obvious right-facing layback crack, and climb this to make an awkward move onto a ledge. Follow the short crack above to another ledge; then move right onto a wall and finish up this.

Sunset Wall   28 metres   E3 5c   (9.3.85)
Boldly climb the thin cracks in the wall directly below the final bubbly faultline of *World's End* and finish up this. Poor protection is provided by small *RPs*.

★★**The Dawning**   25 metres   E5 6b   (17.3.84)
Hard, serious, and sustained climbing. Small wires required. Start at the arête to the left of the big sickle-shaped overhang. Climb the overhanging groove in the arête to beneath the overhang. Traverse left for a metre; then climb a thin vertical crack just to the right. Continue up a short corner to where a delicate move right brings better holds leading to the top.

The very thin and technical **It's a Square World** (22 metres E4 6c 25.8.87) was climbed with a bolt for protection, hence the grade. It took the initial groove of *The Dawning* to the *World's End* break, and went out right across the smooth wall past the bolt to a jug on the arête. The arête was climbed to finish up *Zawn Face Route*.

★★**World's End**   25 metres   E1 5a   (1957)
A tough, rewarding pitch, very much at the top end of the grade. Start under the big overhang. Climb the steep wall; then traverse left to clear the overhang. Follow the diagonal fault leftwards and then continue up the bubbly faultline to the top.

The Outside Man   25 metres   E1 5b †   (15.7.84)
Start as for *Zawn Face Route Variation Start*; then cross *Zawn Face Route* and take a direct line over roofs and up walls to the top, keeping just left of *The Time Lord*.

★★**Zawn Face Route**   26 metres   Hard Very Severe   (1957)
A memorable approach to a unique little trip into the steep zawn on the right of World's End Promontory. Start under the big overhang.
1 18m. 4c. Slither rightwards under the overhang and carefully gain a standing position in an open groove. Climb the groove (often damp) to easier-angled rock on the left. Traverse left more easily under an overlap and then climb to a large ledge on the left.

2 8m. 4a. Climb the crack above the left end of the ledge.
Variation Start 6 metres Very Severe 4c (1971). The non-slither start for climbers who suffer from claustrophobia. Pull up under the seaward face overhang, using a flake 3 metres to the right of *World's End*. Traverse right; then pull up around the overhang to move up and join the parent route.

The Time Lord   30 metres   Hard Very Severe 5a   (4.77)
Follow *Zawn Face Route* along the stomach-traverse to reach the open groove. Climb the groove for a couple of moves; then swing right to follow an obvious line of flakes to the top.

Abseil Point Area (Deception Zawn)
Descent: Abseil from a boulder-strewn ledge above the seaward-facing buttress to the south of *Zawn Face Route*. The abseil ledge is reached by veering left from the northern end of the swing-bridge to reach a cluster of small rocks above the cliff edge. The abseil ledge lies directly below these. The easiest climbing escape from this section of cliff is by the Hard Severe climb *Deception*, which has loose rock. The sensible alternative is to leave the abseil rope in place with the option to jumar out.

Going left (facing in) around a small headland from the arrival platform leads to the south side of the zawn of *Zawn Face Route*. The steep groove at the back of the zawn (and above a narrow ramp) is taken by *The Parasite*, and the wall to its left by *Voices* and *Echoes*. *Initiation* takes the deeper groove to the right of *The Parasite*. All these routes and *The Maiden* start from a triangular ledge on the edge of the zawn, at the foot of a groove. There are some excellent climbs here but unstable rock in the upper section of the cliff demands care.

Echoes   30 metres   E3 5c   (4.85)
A left-hand variation on *Voices*. Follow *Voices* to the overhang just before the chimney and then move left to a steep crack. Follow this to an overhang, climb leftwards through it, and finish directly up the wall above. One peg runner.

★**Voices**   30 metres   E3 5b   (8.77)
A fine route in a good position, which has unfortunately been affected by rockfall. Start on the triangular ledge. Climb leftwards along the narrow ramp to below the corner of *The Parasite*. Pull left onto the back wall and climb a steep crack until a short distance below the overhang. Move right and climb a shallow chimney for 3 metres; then step left above the overhang to a good small foothold. Climb directly up the face to a line of handholds; from their left-hand end move up and climb the cracked face on the right to finish.

★The Parasite   28 metres   E2 5b   (1.8.59/8.77)
An impressive and significant effort for its day and a route that still retains
a serious air. Start from the triangular ledge. Traverse left along the narrow
ramp and then move up into the steep corner. Climb to the small
overhang and make hard moves to clear it. Continue up the corner on
poor holds until a hard move enables a bird-limed ledge on the left to be
reached. Continue up the corner to the top.

Edge Control   28 metres   E3 5b †   (12.5.85)
Climb the left-hand arête of the groove of *Initiation* to finish up a steep
crack.

★Initiation   28 metres   E2 5b   (3.59/6.10.79)
Fine but serious climbing up the black-sided groove in the back of the
zawn. Start on the triangular ledge and climb into the deep groove using
well-spaced holds on the right wall. Make some difficult moves at half
height and then continue up the groove to where a step right is made.
Climb a crack to the top.

Nineteen Eighty-Four   28 metres   E2 5c †   (12.5.85)
Start as for *Initiation* but follow the crack system in the right wall of that
route's steep groove to finish up an arête and short corner.

The Maiden   28 metres   Hard Very Severe 4c   (30.5.71)
Start on the triangular ledge. Climb steeply to reach the right-hand of two
grooves (*Nineteen Eighty-Four* takes the left-hand one). Continue up the
groove to a sloping ledge and then follow the groove and cracks above to
an overhang. Make steep moves over this to gain a ledge and then
continue up wide cracks to the top.

Deception   28 metres   Hard Severe 4a   (3.59)
A line up the main corner to the right of *Initiation*. Care should be taken
with the rock. Start about 6 metres right of *Initiation*, on a sloping ledge
below a right-angled corner. Climb the corner to a ledge on the edge of
the pillar. Move up and then traverse right to a chimney, which leads to the
top of the pillar. Climb the corner above for a couple of moves; then
traverse out right below a nose to finish.

Silent Shadow   28 metres   E5 6b †   (1995)
The thin and disappearing crack in the right wall of the large corner is
climbed with difficulty to where it fades. Move up and right to enter a short
corner and follow easier cracks to the top. Three peg runners.

Piton Route   28 metres   Hard Very Severe 5b   (26.7.59/1994)
There is a large triangular-shaped recess 6 metres right of the corner of
Deception. Start by scrambling up into the recess. From the left edge of the
recess, make tricky moves up and left to gain the start of a groove in the
reddish-coloured arête. Follow the groove to a corner, which leads to a

large sloping ledge on the left. From the ledge, climb a steep little corner to a detached flake. Climb the flake's left edge and then continue direct to finish.
Variation
Sabre Cut   25 metres   Hard Very Severe 5b   (1995)
Take the left wall of the recess, thereby avoiding the tricky moves up the arête.

To the right of the triangular recess is a buttress with a shallow hanging corner just left of its left-hand arête. The starts of the next two routes may have been affected by rockfall and their grades are therefore suspect.

This Year's Model   25 metres   Very Severe 4c   (1995)
From ledges, climb into the corner and follow it to its end. Move right to gain the cliff top.

Old Generations   25 metres   Hard Very Severe 5a   (1995)
Follow the previous climb into the corner. Step right and climb the crack in its right wall until it is possible to escape rightwards up a ramp.

Motivation   25 metres   E2 5b   (9.87)
Start below the left arête of the buttress. Climb the steep wall to a loose flake on the arête, step right, and continue direct up the crack above to where a move onto the right wall can be made. Climb the wall and a crack to finish.

Hidden Secret   25 metres   E2 6a   (1995)
The front face of the buttress is climbed starting over a bulge with a tough rock-over move forming the crux. Continue up the face and though the overhang via a hanging crack. Small wires useful.

Land's End Short Climb   22 metres   E1 5b   (2.10.76)
A strenuous pitch up the chimney/groove in the wall just left of the abseil descent. Start just left of the arête at the left-hand end of the seaward face. Move up and then left into a groove, and climb to a ledge. Continue strenuously up the chimney/groove on poor rock to a large ledge. Finish easily.
Variation
Down the Line   25 metres   E2 5b   (12.5.85)
Climb a crack in the rounded arête until it is possible to move left below a roof to join the parent route.

Bring On the Nubiles   25 metres   E1 5b †   (5.5.80)
The leftmost climb on the seaward-facing buttress. From the foot of the corner beneath the roof, follow a crack up leftwards to meet the arête and the roof. Gain the ledge above; then move right and climb the arête.

Come to My Aid   25 metres   E5 6a †   (9.87)
Start below thin cracks in the wall around to the right of *Land's End Short Climb*. Climb the shallow groove in the wall until it steepens; then continue up the crack (hard) to a point just short of the top. Move left and up to finish. Some loose rock.

Rockin'   18 metres   E1 5b †   (1978)
Start just left of the abseil arrival point. Mantelshelf onto an obvious ledge. Move left to a thin crack, which is followed to finish direct.

The Gannet   18 metres   Hard Very Severe 4c †   (6.10.76)
The crack immediately right of the line of the abseil has poor rock. Climb easily to the foot of the crack; then climb steeply for 5 metres. Trend left to an obvious detached block, which is unstable. Climb over the block with care and move up to an overhang. Climb left to finish up easy ground.

The next climbs lie on the face some 30 metres south of the abseil arrival point and opposite Dollar Rock. Approach by traversing south from the arrival point past a large corner to the foot of a narrow pillar. *Death Rattle Gulch* takes the chimney right of the pillar; *The Quartz Band* lies further around to the south in the next zawn.

Death Rattle Gulch   30 metres   E2 5a   (26.7.59)
The name and grade say it all; loose rock is still likely, especially near the top, where a pre-placed rope may be useful. Start at the foot of the pillar and climb diagonally right up the steep slab to the foot of the chimney. Climb the chimney, using the shallow crack on the face, to a ledge on top of the pillar. Scrambling leads to the top.

Loose Girth   28 metres   Very Severe †   (31.7.59)
Start at the foot of a rib about 10 metres right of the chimney of *Death Rattle Gulch*.
1 20m. 4c. Climb the rib on good but doubtful holds for about 10 metres to where a diagonal traverse rightwards leads around the arête to a stance.
2 8m. 4b. Climb the arête, bearing right to the top.

The Quartz Band   40 metres   Very Severe 4a   (1969)
A line up a rib of quartz in the zawn wall behind Dollar Rock. Technically easy, but the rock is in an advanced state of decay and leads to crumbling earth at the top. Start, if you really must, about 30 metres right of *Loose Girth*. Climb the quartz rib to the foot of a clean corner on its left. Move right and then continue up to a terrace at the top of the quartz pillar. Traverse 5 metres left to a shallow chimney, which is followed to exit left on steep earth.

Slanting Crack (HVS), Sennen
Climber: Mark Edwards   Photo: David Simmonite

Bouldering at Peninnis Head, The Isles of Scilly. Climber: Sean Howden. Photo: Andy Grieve

Dingo Area

These climbs lie on the northerly buttress of the small zawn south of Dollar Rock. The top of the cliff is reached from the State House by descending easy slopes to a point about 40 metres north of the viewpoint carn above Longships Promontory. The base of the cliff is reached by descending *Dingo* (10 metres Difficult) at the lowest point of the cliff-top. The top of *Dingo* is located just north of a small, rounded bouldery ridge that rises from the grassy slopes above the cliff edge. Descend a faultline through a series of steps to the starting-platform. A few metres right of *Dingo* is the prominent *Longships Chimney* and right of that is the oblique crack of *Longships Crack* on the zawn wall opposite Longships Promontory.

Fair Dinkum   16 metres   Very Difficult   (1959)
Start just above sea-level, below and to the left of *Dingo*, at the foot of a steep corner-crack. Climb the corner-crack and continue up to a platform on the left. Climb the groove in the centre of the wall above to a finish on flakes.

Dingo   10 metres   Difficult   (1959)
Climb steps in the faultline to the top.

Longships Chimney   15 metres   Very Difficult   (1959)
Climb the prominent chimney right of *Dingo*; it is often damp.

Whacko   15 metres   Very Difficult   (23.6.63)
Climb the black vein just right of *Longships Chimney* to a ledge at 5 metres; then continue up two corners to the top.

Blue   15 metres   Hard Severe 4b   (23.6.63)
A steep little climb. Start 2 metres right of the black vein of *Whacko*, by a narrow quartz vein. Climb the vein on widely-spaced holds to a niche. Move right and climb the steep wall to a flake. A difficult mantelshelf onto the flake gains a short finishing crack.

Longships Crack   18 metres   Very Severe 4c   (1959)
Start below the oblique crack which runs up rightwards to the right of *Blue*. Climb this awkwardly to a niche below the overhang; then move up to where a difficult pull over onto the ledge above can be made. Continue easily to the top.

Longships Zawn

Longships Zawn is the square-cut zawn lying directly below the viewpoint carn in front of Penwith House. It is flanked on its north side by Longships Promontory and by the distinctive black-faced Longships Wall, while its impressive back wall is breached by *Atlantic Ocean Wall*.

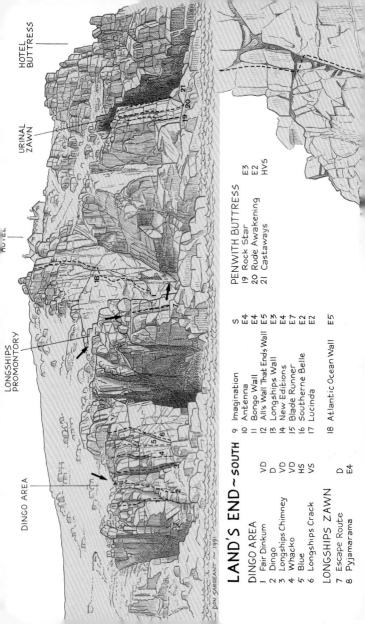

LAND'S END ~ SOUTH

DON SARGEANT ~ 1991

DINGO AREA
1 Fair Dinkum	VD
2 Dingo	D
3 Longships Chimney	VD
4 Whacko	VD
5 Blue	HS
6 Longships Crack	VS

LONGSHIPS ZAWN
7 Escape Route	D
8 Pyjamarama	E4

9 Imagination	S
10 Antenna	E4
11 Bongo Wall	E4
12 All's Wall That Ends Wall	E5
13 Longships Wall	E3
14 New Editions	E4
15 Blade Runner	E7
16 Southerne Belle	E2
17 Lucinda	E2
18 Atlantic Ocean Wall	E5

PENWITH BUTTRESS
19 Rock Star	E3
20 Rude Awakening	E2
21 Castaways	HVS

HOTEL BUTTRESS

URINAL ZAWN

LONGSHIPS PROMONTORY

HOTEL

DINGO AREA

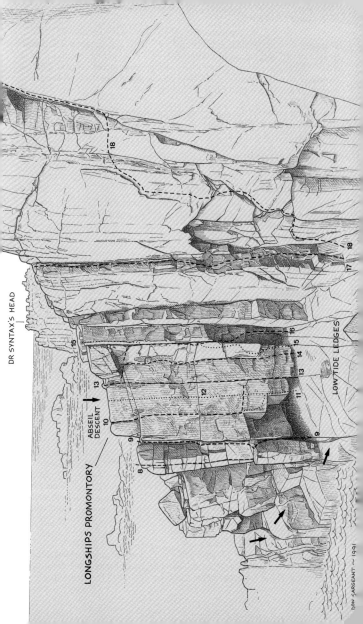

DR SYNTAX'S HEAD

LONGSHIPS PROMONTORY

ABSEIL DESCENT

LOW TIDE LEDGES

DON SARGEANT ~ 1991

Descent is by scrambling down Longships Promontory to reach a flat ledge at its seaward end, about 12 metres above the sea. A short, steep groove in the southern side of the promontory is then descended. This is **Escape Route** (10 metres Difficult 1959). Alternatively, abseil directly down Longships Wall, first ensuring that nobody is climbing on it!

The easiest exit from the zawn is via *Escape Route*. This becomes cut off by the flooding tide quite early on in the cycle, so leaving a rope in place down Longships Wall is advised.

To reach the first climb, traverse left (facing in) along a ledge to the north side of the promontory.

Rory   18 metres   Very Difficult   (1959)
Start at the end of the ledge. Move left until a mantelshelf leads to a wide crack, which is climbed on good but sometimes greasy holds to a small platform. Continue up the steep wall to another wide crack, which is followed to the top.

The next climbs are all within the zawn proper and are reached by a short traverse around to the right (facing in).

★★★**Pyjamarama**   20 metres   E4 6b   (10.3.86)
Climb the overhanging crack on the left-hand side of Longships Wall to a ledge (as for *Imagination*). Traverse left and climb the thin crackline in the front of the square prow.

Imagination   22 metres   Severe 4a   (1959)
Climb the overhanging crack on the left-hand side of Longships Wall to a ledge. Climb the corner past another ledge, taking care with friable rock.

The steep schorl-covered wall to the right is home to a series of hard and closely-packed pitches.

Bongo Wall   25 metres   E4 6a   (1978)
The clean-cut hanging rib that forms the left edge of the wall provides a tough direct start to *Antenna*. It may leave short climbers well and truly grounded.

☆☆**All's Wall that Ends Wall**   25 metres   E5 6c †   (6.5.88)
An eliminate graded for an ascent without side-runners. Start below the hanging rib of the lower overhang and climb the rib (as for *Bongo Wall*) to reach a thin crack. Continue boldly up the centre of the wall. Small wires are useful.

★★**Antenna**   28 metres   E4 5c   (6.77)
A fine, sustained route. Climb the thin crackline to the right of the stepped overhangs (*Longships Wall*) for 8 metres and then traverse left to the tip of the higher of the two overhangs. Continue in a direct line to the top.

★★Longships Wall   25 metres   E3 5c   (1959/8.73/6.77)
  Good, honest, and well-protected face climbing. Start beneath the thin
  crackline just right of the stepped overhangs. Climb the crack direct, which
  is sustained with the hardest moves half-way.

★★New Editions   25 metres   E4 6b   (20.3.86)
  A fine pitch. Start just right of *Longships Wall* below a hanging blade of
  rock. Climb into a groove to the left of the blade. Follow the groove past a
  small ledge at 18 metres. Continue to the capping overhang, move right,
  and pull through it to finish. One peg.

☆☆Blade Runner   25 metres   E7 6b †   (23.11.88)
  Climbed with runners in *New Editions* and *Southerne Belle*. Start below the
  hanging blade of rock. Climb to the roof; move left and then back right to
  gain the blade. Climb the left side of the blade (peg) to where it is possible
  to move into the crack on the right. Climb the crack and then follow the
  corner until it bulges. Move onto the arête and follow it (peg) to the top.

Southerne Belle   25 metres   E2 5c   (1978)
  Start in the corner on the right-hand side of *Longships Wall*. Climb the
  corner to a hanging hand-jam crack and follow this to a pull out left to a
  horizontal break. Follow the corner above to where the rock deteriorates,
  and then break out left below the overhang to finish at the top of
  Longships Wall.

Glory   25 metres   E5 6a   (1990)
  The right wall of *Southerne Belle* is climbed with difficulty to enter the
  hanging groove above. This is followed on indifferent rock.

The jagged arête on the right was the left-hand side of the classic jamming
crack **Yankee Doodle** (4.76). *Yankee Doodle*, along with several other
climbs, disappeared during the great storms of the winter of 1989/90
leaving many a tick-list well tuckered. The other deceased were the arête of
A Perfect Lady (26.3.86) and the off-width crack of **Buffalo Gorge**
(4.76). Two routes replace the three.

Counting Pixies   28 metres   E6 6b †   (21.3.99)
  Start beneath the upper arête. Climb the wall to a ledge before climbing
  the upper arête. Bold climbing, hard-to-place protection, and some loose
  rock all add to the experience.

Well That's Just Dandy   28 metres   E3 5b †   (1990)
  A bold line which also has its share of looseness. Climb the corner-crack
  behind the arête.

Lucinda   42 metres   E2 5a ††   (1981)
  This surviving route takes the prominent groove to the right of the ghostly
  imprint of Yankee Doodle Buttress. It had friable rock from the start and

may have become more unstable. Care advised. Start from the large platform that remained after the rockfall. Either traverse right or, more easily, descend a couple of moves and gain the prominent groove. Climb this, moving left onto the rib below bulges, and then back right above them. Finish direct up the narrower groove above.

The stupendous back wall of Longships Zawn sports a number of hard routes including the classic *Atlantic Ocean Wall*, a line of great note and notoriety involving dramatic and intense climbing in highly exposed positions.

A serious left-to-right traverse of the Atlantic Ocean Wall, **Hands across the Ocean** (90 metres E6 6a, 6a † 1989), started from the top of *Lucinda* and followed the obvious line across the wall in two pitches, before finishing up the top pitch of *Atlantic Ocean Wall*.

The following two routes climb the 'blank' wall left of *Atlantic Ocean Wall*.

Kingdom of the Deep   65 metres   E7 6b †   (10.88/1989)
From the hanging belay of *Titanic*, climb leftwards into a scoop. Follow the scoop, move left, and climb a thin crack to its top. The route has been climbed without clipping the original bolts, but not since they were removed.

Titanic   60 metres   E8   (2.86/28.10.94)
Start at the left-hand base of the main wall just right of *Lucinda*. The route has been climbed without clipping its drilled pegs, which are still in place if not necessarily in good condition.
1 32m. 6b. Climb a groove, traverse rightwards beneath roofs, and pull over them to a hanging belay.
2 28m. 6c. Follow an intricate line up the wall on the right (past a series of pegs).

★★★**Atlantic Ocean Wall**   70 metres   E5   (1.8.81)
The original line of the wall. A great route to have done, though the state of some of the rock detracts a touch from the actual pleasure of the climbing. Start from the enlarged platform created by the *Yankee Doodle* rockfall.
1 7m. Traverse right and then descend slightly to climb a short wall to a good ledge below the corner of *Lucinda*. Large cam belay.
2 8m. 6a. Climb the crunchy corner to the first horizontal break. Traverse right along the gritty break to reach a sloping ledge. This section is affected by seepage and is often wet.
3 25m. 6a. An intense and harrowing pitch. Climb a thin crack to a slanting break, which is followed to a steep red-coloured wall. Climb the wall to a poor resting-place and then take the narrow corner on the left to reach an undercling flake on the right. Climb rightwards to a good flake and then step to the right across some poor rock to a narrow sloping ledge. Cross the ledge to a stance at the base of the groove that bounds

the right edge of the upper wall. There are wire-clip bolts here, though good medium *Friend* placements are available a short way up the next pitch.
4 30m. 5c. Climb the groove to the roof; then move around into the continuation groove (many rotting pegs and scaffolding tube runners). Go up to the next roof. Move left and climb the wall to a small groove above a roof. Follow the groove to a crack, which is climbed to the top.

☆☆☆**Astrodome**   81 metres   E6 †   (16.4.88/7.98)
This weaves a line parallel to *Atlantic Ocean Wall* and then climbs the wall to the right of the main groove of that route. The route was originally climbed with pegs and a bolt. It has since been climbed without the bolt. The pegs may not be in place.
1 6m. *Atlantic Ocean Wall* pitch 1.
2 30m. 5c. To the right of the ledge is a steep wall split by a rightward-slanting crack. Climb the steep wall to the crack and follow it to the arête. Step around to the right and follow a groove to the second horizontal fault on the left. Climb leftwards along the fault to belay as for *Atlantic Ocean Wall*.
3 28m. 6b. Traverse rightwards using an awkward undercling to a peg. Move right onto a very steep orange section of rock (peg) and climb it (peg) to roofs on *Atlantic Ocean Wall*. Pull over these and layback steeply to an undercling resting place (as for *Atlantic Ocean Wall*). Climb left and then up the wall (peg) to a sloping ledge. Peg belays in the next break up.
4 17m. 5b. Climb the steep wall above past two pegs to the top
Variation Start
1a 48m. This variation misses out the first belay of the parent route. The pitch is usually wet and low tide is required. Start from the very bottom of the zawn, below the deep chimney. Climb up into the chimney and into the corner on its left. Follow the corner to the roof (peg). Move left and up onto the steep orange wall (peg) to join pitch 2 of the parent route.

The Great Green Wave   30 metres   E7 6c †   (1991)
A hard and dangerous outing, with friable rock and one poor peg, up the black streak on the right-hand side of the *Atlantic Ocean Wall*. It is approached by scrambling carefully down the buttress that bounds the right side of the wall.

A narrow buttress protrudes from the southern end of Longships Zawn and is home to three 30-metre climbs that are all share a common top pitch. From left to right, these are **Western Approaches** (Very Severe 4c), which climbs the dog-legged crack in the left-hand wall, finishing up the arête. **Rap City in Blue** (Very Difficult) climbs the jagged groove in the front face past a large block, and finishes up the black slab above. **Farewell to Friends** (Very Severe 4c) starts as for the previous climb but swings around the corner to climb the crack. All were first climbed in 1995.

Penwith Buttress

Although non-tidal, this small attractive buttress lies about 60 metres south of Longships Zawn. It is affected by swell and heavy sea. It is the seaward northern face of the odious Urinal Zawn but the climbs are not affected by any discharge.

Descent. The buttress can be approached via the Longships Promontory descent about three to four hours either side of low water. Alternatively, an abseil entry can be made from good anchors at the top of the buttress (though you might well get pizzled by the drizzle). The top of the buttress is reached by descending the grass slopes lying to the left (facing out) of the rocky summit of *Atlantic Ocean Wall*.

Rock Star   28 metres   E3 5c   (1.4.84)
Start behind a huge perched boulder. Climb the left-hand side of the face via a shallow groove, a slab, and a wall, finishing over a small overhang.

Rude Awakening   28 metres   E2 5c   (1.4.84)
Climb a thin crack in the centre of the face to reach a triangular niche. Continue up the wider crack above.

Castaways   28 metres   Hard Very Severe 5a   (26.3.84)
Climb the right arête of the face using a thin crack to reach a ledge; then continue up a groove past a small overhang to the top.

Urinal Zawn

This is the deeply recessed cave/zawn to the right of Penwith Buttress, and is named after an ancient sewage pipe outlet. For those who really must, the zawn is gained from the base of Penwith Buttress or by scrambling around at low tide from the base of Hotel Buttress. There are two routes.

Chiotte   28 metres   Severe 4a   (4.4.52)
Great name for a gruesome route. Start just around the arête to the right of *Castaways*. Climb the black-veined recessed corner with strange organ-pipe fluting in its upper half. Now please wash your hands.

Giant's Staircase   28 metres   Hard Severe 4b   (1.8.55)
Climb the back corner of the zawn to finish via an overhanging 'pile'.

Hotel Buttress Area

This is **non-tidal** for routes on upper sections of the buttress and is also **non-tidal** for the start of *Land's End Long Climb*, although very big swell and rough sea may affect the lower pitches of this route. Care required. The area is **tidal** at the start of *The Vein* and *Capillary Cracks*. These routes are accessible for about three hours either side of low water and again they are affected by swell and rough seas.

The summit blocks of Hotel Buttress lie directly in front of the State House. To reach the foot of the buttress, follow an eroded path down the left side (facing out) of the buttress until the piled blocks of *Land's End Long Climb* can be seen. For *Land's End Long Climb* and *Pinnacle Route*, continue easily down to the right to big ledges at the seaward base of Hotel Buttress.

★★Land's End Long Climb   73 metres   Very Difficult   (1946)
Mountaineering meets the Atlantic. A good classic outing, with short pitches, easy variations, and sections where progress is made by leaps and bounds. Start just left of centre of the lower buttress, about 10 metres above sea-level.
1 16m. Climb over rock steps and then through a narrow gap to reach the foot of a wide crack. Climb the crack to a recessed platform with a steep corner-crack at its back.
2 10m. The Elbow Crack. This is at the top end of the grade. Climb the corner-crack on rounded holds to a good ledge. The crack can be avoided by traversing around to the left to climb an easy chimney.
3 10m. Climb the slab behind the belay block and then jump (or stride) across the cleft to a ledge below a short wall.
4 7m. Climb the wall to a ledge, from where a steep crack is climbed to reach the foot of a large detached pillar.
5 10m. Walk around the pillar; then chimney up the cleft until a step across onto the inner face can be made. From the top of the face, a tricky little move up and to the right gains a big ledge.
6 5m. Traverse right delicately around a small buttress to reach the top of Ash Can Gully. Alternatively, a bold jump across the Gully onto the lower ledge on the opposite side can be made. Go on… you can do it.
7 8m. Climb easily right and then go up a short corner to a good ledge at the foot of the lichenous face.
8 7m. The Green Face; another pitch high in its grade. Climb the centre of the steep and exposed face to the top.

Pinnacle Route   76 metres   Hard Very Severe   (2.9.85)
The variations to *Land's End Long Climb* can be combined to give a harder route.
1a 16m. 4b. Start 3 metres right of the start of pitch 1. Climb walls and ledges, and move left to belay below The Elbow Crack.
2a 16m. 4c. Make a rising traverse across the right wall of the recess and step around the arête to climb flakes on the right to reach the top of the pinnacle.
3 to 6 32m. As for the regular route.
7a 12m. From the stance in Ash Can Gully, an easier finish can be made up the chimney in the corner to the left of The Green Face.

Part-way down the path and to its right is an area of small stepped buttresses. The small buttress up on the right (facing in) has an engaging little problem: **The Tier** (10 metres Hard Severe 4b) climbs easily into the first sentry-box and then moves left onto the steep wall. Gain the upper recess by difficult moves and then climb the short corner above to the top.

The more substantial buttress below and left of *The Tier* (facing in) has a large detached flake/block leaning against its left-hand side.

Hotel Chambermaid   25 metres   E1   (1984)
Start below the crack that rises above the right-hand, sloping edge of the detached flake.
1 10m. 5b. Climb the crack to a big ledge.
2 15m. 4b. Climb a crack behind the pinnacle at the back of the ledge; then boulder-hop onto the wall above. Follow the left-slanting crack in the final wall.

The Bearded Clam   25 metres   E1   (1984)
Start at the right edge of the buttress.
1 10m. 5b. Climb the clean crack past a horizontal break to the big ledge. Take the right-hand crack above that trends away to the left.
2 15m. 4b. Climb the blunt arête some way back to reach a grassy ledge, and then finish up the obvious chimney and wall on the right.

The Hairy Lobster   22 metres   E4 6a   (15.10.88)
Start around to the right of *The Bearded Clam*, below the lichenous flanking wall of the buttress. Climb the face via a shallow crack to gain a horizontal break. Move up to a faint crack and then gain the big ledge. Continue direct to the cleaner line of *The Bearded Clam* and finish up this.

The next climbs lie on the broken buttress below and to the south of Hotel Buttress. Go down the approach path as for Hotel Buttress. Keep descending to the left (facing out) to reach the sea-level base of a broken buttress that rises above a small rock trench. *The Vein* starts up the obvious line in the steep block to the left (facing in) of the main buttress.

This area is tidal and affected by swell and rough sea. It gained notoriety when four schoolboys were swept from sea-level rocks and drowned in 1986. The tragic victims had found their way down the Hotel Buttress path. There was a heavy sea running but to the uninformed it was deceptive. This should be a lesson to all of us who court the sea.

The Vein   30 metres   Very Difficult
Start from the sea-washed platform to the right of Ash Can Gully and at the foot of a quartz vein that runs up a short steep wall.
1 15m. The thin vein is climbed awkwardly to a large ledge. Follow the red vein on the right to the foot of a steep little corner.
2 15m. Climb the corner to a ledge and then continue over a block and up the rib behind to the top.

Capillary Cracks   41 metres   Very Severe   (9.7.67)
Start 6 metres to the right of the previous route, on a long flat ledge at the foot of a vertical crack. There is some friable rock.
1 16m. 4c. Climb the crack to a ledge; then follow the right-angled corner on the right. A red quartz vein runs up the corner.

2 25m. Continue up a chimney in the same line to a big block. Climb strenuously over this, finishing on top of a tower.

Bull Ring Zawn (Crystal Walls)
Tidal. Accessible for about four hours either side of low water. Affected by swell and heavy seas.

The Bull Ring area has a number of amenable routes on good granite with harder test-pieces on its back wall. There can be stubborn dampness in the shadier recesses after rain.

Approach via the Hotel Buttress descent path to reach *The Vein*. From here, traverse to the right (facing in) for about 15 metres and then descend slightly to move around into an attractive shallow zawn with a narrow left-hand wall seamed with cracks. *Aberdeen Angus* and *Iron Hand* go up this wall, which ends at an arête on the right. The cliff then falls back into a recess above a sea-stained brown ledge. The face above the ledge is split by a deep chimney, to the right of which lie hard routes like *Crystal Fingers* and *Diamond Life*. An alternative approach to the Bull Ring can be made by descending the broken chossy slopes to the south of the zawn and then traversing back left.

Spare Rib   43 metres   Very Severe   (21.4.84)
Start at a narrow groove at the outer edge of the left-flanking wall of the zawn.
1 25m. 4c. Climb the groove, and then the crack to a large ledge. Continue up a short wall to belays on the left.
2 18m. 5a. Climb to the arête and follow it on small holds, or use cracks just to the right, to the top. This upper pitch is overgrown and is best left to blossom.

Matador   30 metres   Hard Very Severe 5a   (21.4.84)
Climb the open corner-crack to the right of the previous route and finish up the right-facing groove above.

Silly Old Moo   30 metres   Hard Very Severe 5a   (1984)
Start up the straight crack of *Aberdeen Angus* and then transfer into the thinner crack to the left. Follow this to an easier finish up a blocky arête.

★Aberdeen Angus   25 metres   E2 5c   (8.77)
A worthwhile crack climb. Start below the left-hand of two continuous cracks in the main wall. Climb the wide black crack to where it narrows and then continue up the thinner crack to gain a ledge. Finish up the crack directly above.

★Iron Hand   30 metres   E2 5c   (21.4.84)
Another cracking crackline. Climb the thin crack right of *Aberdeen Angus* to reach a ledge. Finish up the crack left of the arête.

☆☆**Desert Hawk**   28 metres   E6 6b †   (1985)
The right-hand arête of the wall is climbed past an overlap to a protruding nose.
Pull rightwards over this and continue to ledges. Finish up the arête behind.

The next two routes lie around to the right of the arête.

Birds of Prey   25 metres   E2 5c   (7.84)
Climb a groove just right of the arête to a position below the roof; then
move left around the arête to climb a finger-crack on the left to ledges.
Follow the crack on the left to the top.

★**Cactus Crack**   25 metres   E1 5b   (2.6.84)
Climb the groove in the arête as for the previous climb; then surmount the
roof to finish up a crack in the right wall.

The following routes lie on the back wall of the zawn to the right of the deep
dark chimney.

☆☆☆**Diamond Life**   30 metres   E7 6c †   (1988).
A bold route with one peg. Start below the left edge of an overlap at 10
metres and climb a shallow groove to the overlap. Pull around the left
edge of this and the next two overlaps, step back right under the fourth,
and finish up the centre of the wall above.

★★**Crystal Fingers**   30 metres   E3 6b   (29.6.84)
A highly technical but well-protected pitch provided the *in-situ* pegs are
sound. Start on the brown ledge below a wide crack on the right side of
the wall. Climb the wide crack and then a thinner one on the left leading
to the roof. Traverse left along the fault past two pegs to a thin vertical
crack. Climb the crack and then a groove to finish.

Gemstone   28 metres   E5 6a   (1995)
The obvious direct finish to *Crystal Fingers* gives a hard pitch.

Dynosaurus   28 metres   E3 6c   (1995)
The black-stained wall just to the right is climbed passing many horizontal
breaks. A long reach and a rack of cams may both prove essential.

Quartz Crystal   18 metres   Hard Very Severe 5a   (29.6.84)
Climb the groove in the right-hand side of the wall to finish across a crack
at the top.

In the next large zawn south of Bull Ring Zawn there is one route. The bed of
the zawn can be reached at low tide by descending the broken rib between
the zawn and Bull Ring Zawn.

The High Traverse   28 metres   Very Difficult †
This crosses the steep north wall of the zawn in an exposed position. Start
below the north wall at the base of a pinnacle. Either climb a corner-crack

on the left to gain a block on the pinnacle, or climb the steep corner formed by the pinnacle. From the block, traverse to the right along a wide ledge and then climb a crack to the top.

Variation Above the block is a lichenous slab with a crack on its right that is climbed direct (Difficult).

Knight's Buttress

Tidal: accessible for about three hours either side of low water.

The following routes are on the headland facing the impressive rocky island of The Armed Knight. The headland marks the southern end of the main run of Land's End cliffs where they turn sharply eastwards. It is reached by going down sweeping slopes to the south of the State House to the lowest point of the cliffs, where a stream runs down to a boulder-beach. An old concrete-block pumping-house stands by the stream, while there is a holding-tank and outlet at a lower level. Scramble down rocks to the left (facing out) of the stream and then go left to the headland.

The steep wall to the left of the arête (facing in) is composed of friable rock. There is one route on the right edge of this wall.

The Jouster 22 metres   Very Severe 4c †   (22.11.85)
Climb the corner-crack just left of the arête, passing ledges at half height.

Armed Knight Crack 22 metres   Hard Very Severe 5a †   (22.11.85)
Climb the steep crack 3 metres right of the arête.

Call to Arms 22 metres   E3 5c †   (22.11.85)
Climb a fin of rock in the bay just right of *Armed Knight Crack* to a downward-pointing flake. Finish up cracks above.

The Mace 22 metres   Hard Severe 4b †   (22.11.85)
Climb the groove and wall right of *Call to Arms*.

The Brave Warrior 22 metres   E1 5b †   (22.11.85)
Start on the right side of the bay. Climb the wall to a small groove and finish up slabs above.

Jester's Blues 22 metres   E3 5c †   (22.11.85)
Climb the crackline on the left of the next bay south.

The Armed Knight and the distinctive arched island of Enys Dodnan to the south have been explored, traversed, and topped-out on by a number of parties. Enys Dodnan has been incorporated in a massive ramble involving abseils, Tyroleans, swims, jumars, and a cast of thousands. It should be noted, however, that both venues are key nesting-sites for large numbers of birds and they do not enjoy being disturbed.

First Ascents

This list is as comprehensive as possible. Due regard should be paid to early pioneers – and some contemporary ones – who made ascents with a healthy distaste for posterity and left no record.

A number of route duplications have been noted. Some involve routes climbed and recorded many years ago, omitted from previous guidebooks and then subsequently climbed and claimed with good intent. Where possible the subsequent ascent is mentioned. It is hoped that first ascent vanity does not produce too much quibbling. In some cases, the authors have had to make judgements on routes which have questionable independence over existing ones. Again the initial line has taken precedence.

The policy of retaining the original name of an aid route that has been totally free-climbed is generally followed, unless the new name is in common use. In either case, both names are given in this list.

AL and VL in brackets indicate alternate and varied leads respectively. The number of any points of aid known to have been used on a first ascent is given in brackets after the name of the climb; the word Aid indicates that the climb was originally climbed as an aid route or with an aid section.

No details for:	**Greensleeves, Probe, Hope, Ochre Slab II, Raven Wall Optional Start, Zig Zag Optional Starts A & B, Sea Wall Exits A B & C, Funnel Chimney, Ridge Direct, Ragtag, Bobtail, Slippery Chute, Fruit Salad, Junior's Route, The Tier, The Vein, The High Traverse**
1858	*Sir Leslie Stephens climbed a chimney on Gurnard's Head. No details yet.*
Pre-1900	*General scrambling and exploration carried out by a number of 'mountaineers' with A W Andrews at the forefront. D G Romanis and Sir Bertrand Jerram were probably active in West Penwith during the 1890s.*
1902	**Bosigran Ridge** A W Andrews, Miss E Andrews *Pitch 1 was added in 1905 by J B Farmer, A W Andrews. Atlantic Alpinism.*
1902	**Wicca Chimney, The Corner, The Cracks, The Sloping Ledge Climb, The Rib Climb** (Wicca Pillar), **The Sea Spray Climb** A W Andrews, Miss E Andrews
1902	**Lower East Face Traverse, Ordinary Traverse** A W Andrews
1905	**Ledge Climb** A W Andrews, J B Farmer *They traversed in at half height. Pitch 1 was added in 1922 by G H L Mallory, Miss E Andrews, Miss S Cox, Miss W Cox.*
1906	**Rosemergy Ridge** A W Andrews, Miss E Andrews
1907	**Lower West Face Traverse** A W Andrews, Miss E Andrews
1908	**Porthmeor Chimney** A W Andrews
1909	**Shallow Chimney** A W Andrews, O K Williamson

1910	**Middle East Face Traverse, Western Slant** A W Andrews
1912	**Edge Climb** A J Clark
1912	**Brandys Zawn Chimney** A W Andrews
1912	**Pinnacle Traverse** G W Young, G H L Mallory
1921	**Carnelloe low level traverses** A W Andrews
1922	**Sloping Slab, The Rib Climb** (Bosigran) A W Andrews, Miss E Andrews
1922	**West Face Slab** A W Andrews

This route at the foot of Bosigran Ridge was destroyed by rockfall.

1923	**1923 Route** T K Rose, C B Jerram, M Guinness
1923	**Alison Rib** D G Romanis
1923	**Green Cormorant Ledge** A W Andrews

Using knots, hitches, lasso, and stone pyramids. Climbed free by P H Biven, H T H Peck, B M Biven on 20 May 1956.

| 1938 Aug 3 | **Black Slab** (Bosigran) C F Kirkus, P S Fallows |

A pitch for posterity.

1938 Sept 22	**Higher East Face Traverse, Central Climb, Guillemot Ledge** F R Dodd, J B (the only recorded details)
1938	**Diagonal Route** C F Kirkus, P S Fallows
1938	**Horse's Back Chimney** C F Kirkus, P S Fallows
1938	**Angle Climb** F R Dodd, J B

Destroyed by rockfall.

| 1943 June | **Western Ridge Direct** J M Edwards |

The lower section had been climbed by A W Andrews in 1922. The climb was in the vicinity of Ivory Tower but cannot now be identified with certainty.

1943 June	**Eastern Slant** J M Edwards
1943	**Demo Route, Vertical Crack** J F Barry (the first, solo)
1945 Sept 18	**Recess Climb** (Window Ridge) C A Fenner, A J Nicholson, J W Mitchell, W G Standring

Recess Direct was climbed by members of the CCAW in 1948.

1946 Aug 31	**Secretary's Pitch** F H Keenlyside, W Allen, T G Osborne
1946	**Land's End Long Climb** Royal Marines
1947	**Genge's Groove** J Barry

A hard man's pitch for its day. Still is, some say. Eeny and Meany variations climbed by R Edwards, M Edwards in the 1980s.

| 1947 | **Dolphin Cracks** T Genge |

First pitch only. Pitch 2 added by J Deacon, R Goodier on 9 September 1955. Top Banana variation climbed by S Ohly on 2 November 1997.

| 1948 Sept 30 | **Como Crack** H Longley-Cook, Mrs N E Morin |
| 1948 Sept | **Zig Zag** (Bosigran) J Cortlandt-Simpson, R G Higgins, K M Lawder |

The first multi-pitch route of significance on Bosigran. Optional Finish P R Littlejohn, M Burgoyne April 1985.

| 1948 | **Loco Route** H Longley-Cook, N Morin |

This route at the foot of Bosigran Ridge was destroyed by rockfall.

| 1949 | **Doorway** J Cortlandt-Simpson, W J Hutchinson |

The Direct Start was added by J M Edwards, N E Morin, N Albion in May 1953. Another significant achievement by Jim Simpson through territory still 'well-grassed'. Creaky rock on the final traverse caused a judicious retreat initially.

1940s	**Hayloft Gully, Hayloft, Monday Face, Senior's Route, Altar Route, Church Window, Double Overhang, Griptight Gully, Irish Lady Chimneys, No Name, Main Face Climb, Banana Flake, Letterbox, Walter's Chimney, Civvy Route, Corner Climb, Intermediate Route, Sinner's Route, Staircase, Black Groove, Left Banana Flake, Black Slab** (Sennen) *All these excellent routes were climbed by members of the CCAW whose anonymity says quite a bit about the urge to name-claim on new routes. Such routes still get climbed. Pure legacy.*
1950 Aug 2	**Simla** K M Lawder, P B Lawder
1950	**Commando Crack** M E B Banks, J Eliot
1950	***Cornwall* by Arthur Andrews and Ted Pyatt** *The first guidebook to the climbing in West Penwith also described the walks on the coast and the moors.*
1952 April 1	**Wicca Pillar Traverse** A J Imrie, R Goodier
1952 April 4	**Green Stuff Chimney** A J Imrie, R Goodier
1952 April 4	**Chiotte** H Tantem, D Kemp *Classical scatology if not classic climbing.*
1952 June 2	**Lookout** P A Warland, J M Warland, A E Simpson
1952 June 2	**Disgruntled Chimney, More So** A E Simpson, P A Warland, J M Warland
1952 June	**Corner Crack** R Handley, E H Phillip
1953 May 2	**Nameless** D Kemp, N E Morin *A further key breach in defences first scouted by Kirkus.*
1954 Feb 26	**Sunny Corner** (Bosigran) K M Lawder, W A Hutchinson
1954 April16	**The Spider's Climb** J A E Hassell, R Bruce
1954 June 13	**Red Slab** K M Lawder, J Andrew *Variation climbed by D Hannigan, G Hobbs in June 1988.*
1954	**Dexter** J W Kinnaird
1955 May	**Beaker Route** H Nichol, R Brooke *A first imaginative sortie on this delightful area of cliff.*
1955 July 10	**Zig Zag** (Sennen) M E B Banks
1955 July 31	**Slippery Slab** P H Biven, H T H Peck, W B Bacon *Sennen starts to shape up.*
1955 July	**Sinistra** D Holdroyd, A Blackshaw, A Day
1955 Aug 1	**Giant's Staircase** P H Biven, B M Biven
1955 Aug 5	**Oread** P Jaynes, E Byne (AL)
1955 Aug 5	**Oread Bypass** E Byne, C W Ashbury
1955 Aug 6	**Hopeless Slab** P H Biven, H T H Peck, W B Bacon, B M Biven *Variation climbed on 30 January 1998 by B Carver (solo).*
1955 Aug 6	**Promontory Traverse** P H Biven, H T H Peck
1955 Aug 7	**Doorpost** B M Biven, H T H Peck, P H Biven *National classic. The Direct Start, added by G Mason, O Hill, M Pollard, T Andrews on 24 October 1965, has been incorporated into Shaft and Permanent Waves.*
1955 Aug 8	**Suicide Wall** (2 pts aid) P H Biven, H T H Peck, B M Biven. *Reaching the heart of Bosigran.*
1955 Aug 13	**String of Pearls** R Goodier, J Deacon (AL) *Originally climbed from right to left. Either way, a significant piece of climbing by the military wing.*
1955 Aug 21	**Little Brown Jug** P H Biven, B M Biven (AL)
1955 Sept 3	**Autumn Flakes** R Goodier, P Henry
1955 Sept 9	**Overhanging Corner** J Deacon, R Goodier
1955 Sept 19	**Raven Wall** (Aid) J Deacon, R Goodier *'We were repulsed on the first ascent. We finally succeeded with the aid of a certain amount of pitonage of a rather dubious nature on*

the second pitch where we had to overcome some vicious bulges.'
Originally climbed with a short aid traverse out onto the left wall
to escape the groove, and subsequently climbed by exiting right
from the groove with a peg for aid. Direct Finish: P R Littlejohn in
1977. Eight classics in six weeks. Who were these guys?

| 1955 Oct | **Africa Route** R Flemming |
| 1955 | **Inverted V-Groove, Geological Groove** Cliff Assault Wing |

| **1955** | ***Climbing in Cornwall*** (New Climbs supplement) **by Rawdon Goodier, Peter Biven, Barrie Biven, et al.** |

1956 March	**Ochre Slab Route I** H T H Peck, P H Biven
1956 May 19	**Anvil Chorus** P H Biven, H T H Peck, B M Biven
1956 May 21	**Diamond Tiara** P H Biven, J Deacon, H T H Peck.

Originally climbed from right to left and begun by reversing the
traverse of Anvil Chorus. The original line included a short aid
traverse between Paragon and Nameless.

| 1956 May 24 | **Paragon** P H Biven, H T H Peck |
| 1956 May 26 | **Thin Wall Special** (1 pt aid) P H Biven, H T H Peck |

The Boysen Variant 5 June 1960.

| 1956 May 27 | **Onen, Deu, Try, Peswar** P H Biven, H T H Peck |

The Monolith Slab Climbs. Top-roped by J Cortlandt-Simpson in
1939.

| 1956 May 28 | **Simple Simon** P H Biven, H T H Peck |

Top pitches only, as a climb called Simon. The lower pitches were
climbed later as a separate climb called Simple. Variation second
pitch climbed on 22 June 1996 by M Bransby, T Owen. The
Pieman variation climbed on 10 December 1986 by M Crayton,
D Hannigan.

| 1956 July 28 | **Limpet Slab** M Hardy, R G Pettigrew |
| 1956 Aug 20 | **Garden Walk** (Aid) P H Biven, H T H Peck (AL) |

The first multi-pitch route in Great Zawn. Of no great merit but
certainly of great significance.

| 1956 Aug 26 | **The Ghost** (Aid) P H Biven, H T H Peck |

Climbed free by E Drummond, T Proctor on 20 April 1973.

| 1956 Aug 28 | **The Phantom** (Aid) P H Biven, H T H Peck (AL) |

Climbed free by E Drummond and T Proctor on 19 April 1973. A
proposal by Drummond to re-name Ghost and Phantom was
rejected. It was felt by many that to do so would set a precedent
for 're-writing' history.

| 1956 Aug 30 | **Great Zawn Chimney** (Aid) H T H Peck, P H Biven |

Climbed free by P R Littlejohn, S B Jones in August 1969.

| 1956 Sept 10 | **Hake Slab** M Harby, J A Taylor, N Kershaw, V Grey |
| 1956 | **Delilah** (Aid) J Deacon, D M Holroyd |

FFA by M White in 1973.

| 1957 April 13 | **Lower Monolith Ridge** J Deacon, M E B Banks |
| 1957 April 14 | **Ding** J Deacon, B Grey, M E B Banks |

Dung variation: D E Hope, D Atkin on 11 March 1972.

1957 April 14	**Dong** M E B Banks, B Grey, J Deacon
1957 April 19	**Gangrene Chimney** J Deacon, M E B Banks
1957 April 21	**Green Cormorant Face** (Aid) J Deacon, M E B Banks

A committing move forward – or 'leap' rather. Climbed with one
point of aid by F E R Cannings P R Littlejohn (AL) on 12 September
1969. Pitch 2A: H Barber, F E R Cannings in May 1974. Pitch 2B:
P R Littlejohn, M Burgoyne in April 1985.

1957 May 9	**The Giant Steps** (Bosigran) P H Biven, H T H Peck

1957 May 9   **The Giant Steps** (Bosigran)   P H Biven, H T H Peck

1957 June 12   **The West Face** (Bosigran) (Aid)   P H Biven, H T H Peck (AL)
Great Zawn accepts the 'bite of the piton'. Climbed with one point of aid by P Livesey, J Lawrence in 1975.

1957 June 15   **Patience** (Aid)   H T H Peck, B M Biven
Climbed free by P R Littlejohn, C R Wand-Tetley in August 1970.

1957 July   **Bow Wall** (Bosigran)   J Brown *Pitches 1 and 2 only. An unerring eye for a good line even while at the seaside. The upper pitches: B M Biven, H T H Peck with some aid in 1958.*

1957 Aug   **The Wasteland**   H Banner

1957 Aug   **Samson** (Aid)   B G N Page, M B McDermott
Climbed free by R Edwards, I Pomfret in July 1974. The Rock Hopper variation climbed in 1993 by M Edwards, T Rourke.

1957   **Cormorant Slab**   D M Holroyd, A Blackshaw, J Deacon

1957   **Johnstone's Route**   J Deacon, D M Holroyd

1957   **World's End**   J Deacon, D M Holroyd, A G Day
Hard climb, hard lads.

1957   **Zawn Face Route (Land's End)**   D M Holroyd, J Deacon
Pity the poor struggler. The variation start: I F Duckworth, P Gordon, G Morgan in January 1971.

1958 May 25   **The Variety Show** (Aid)   H T H Peck, B M Biven, C Fishwick (AL)
Climbed free by P R Littlejohn, F E R Cannings on 23 May 1970.

1958 May 30   **Picnic**   B M Biven, H T H Peck, C Fishwick

1958 May 30   **Sampan**   H T H Peck, B M Biven, C Fishwick

1958 May 31   **The Big Top**   C Fishwick, H T H Peck

1958 Aug 3   **The Armchair**   J V Smoker
One that the main-men missed.

1958 Aug 28   **Four Pips Crack** (Aid)   R Goodier, M E B Banks
This route at the base of Bosigran Ridge was destroyed by rockfall.

1958 Sept 13   **Andrew** (Bosigran)   P H Biven, H T H Peck, J Andrew

1959 March   **Deception**   M B McDermott, J Deacon

1959 March   **Initiation** (Land's End)   M B McDermott, J Deacon (AL)
Reclimbed after rockfall by R Edwards, M Edwards on 6 October 1979.

1959 April   **The Green Beret**   J H Deacon, M B McDermott (AL)

1959 May 18   **Mark**   P H Biven, B M Biven, H T H Peck, C Fishwick

1959 May 19   **Pauline**   P H Biven, B M Biven, H T H Peck

1959 July 12   **Broadstairs (Aid)**   J Deacon, S R Jarvis (AL)
Climbed free by P R Littlejohn, S M P Jones F E R Cannings in May 1971.

1959 July 18   **Hadrian's Wall**   J Deacon, V N Stevenson

1959 July 19   **Oliver Twist**   J Deacon, V N Stevenson

1959 July 25   **Bulging Arête**   J Deacon, V N Stevenson

1959 July 25   **Hors-d'œuvre**   J Deacon, V N Stevenson (AL)

1959 July 26   **Death Rattle Gulch**   J Deacon, V N Stevenson
'It was as desperate as its name implies' according to early comments regarding the first ascent. Same goes, ever since.

1959 July 26   **Piton Route** (1 pt aid)   J Deacon, V N Stevenson (AL)
FFA R Edwards (solo) 1994. Sabre Cut variation climbed by R Edwards, T Dennell in 1995.

1959 July 31   **Loose Girth**   J Deacon, V N Stevenson

1959 Aug 1   **The Parasite** (3 pts aid)   J Deacon, V N Stevenson
Free-climbed by P R Littlejohn, D Roberts in August 1977.

1959	**Dingo** (Land's End), **Fair Dinkum, Longships Chimney, Escape Route, Rory, Imagination** M B McDermott, J Deacon
1959	**Longships Crack, Tide Race** J Deacon, M B McDermott
1959	**Longships Wall** (Aid) J Deacon, M B McDermott
	Climbed with 1 pt of aid by E Grindley, P Long, C Heap in August 1973. Free-climbed by P R Littlejohn, I M Peters in June 1977.
1960 Jan 1	**Crackers** J Foster, I Stewart (AL)
1960 July	**Protein** W H Morrow
	The Hot Tuna variation was climbed by M Edwards, D James on 23 July 1986.
1960-63	**Exit, Fingernail, Box, Bosun's Whistle, Slope, Doorstep, Curving Crack** E Kelly and Portsmouth College students
1961 April 30	**Fasolt, Fafnir** P H Biven, C Fishwick (AL)
1961 April 30	**Venusberg** P H Biven, C Fishwick
1961 May 22	**Fallout** H T H Peck, P H Biven, C Fishwick
1961 May 22	**Blinkers Slab** C Fishwick, R H Williams
1961 May 26	**Free Rein, Brown Slab** H T H Peck, C Fishwick
1961 May 26	**Nutse** H T H Peck, C Fishwick
1961 June 16	**Popse** B M Biven, H T H Peck, P H Biven
1961 Aug 1	**The Arête** V N Stevenson, P Stevenson
1961 Aug 1	**Congo Route** (2 pts aid) M B McDermott, G Berbonne
1962 Aug 2	**Black Jack** V N Stevenson
1962 Aug 2	**Gully Wall Left Hand/Right Hand** V N Stevenson
1962 Sept 4	**Gollywog's Cakewalk** D Basset, G Barber
	The Schorl Slant variation had already been climbed as a separate route by J F Adams, P Smart on 25 June 1950.
1962 Nov 12	**Overhanging Wall, Dextrose** V N Stevenson, G B Wilson
1962 Nov 12	**Slim** B Wake, G B Wilson
1963 March 9	**Kate** C Fishwick, R Mavin
1963 June 14	**Plaque Pitch** M McDermott, J P Kendall
1963 June 23	**Blue** (Land's End) V N Stevenson, J M G Sheridan
1963 June 23	**Whacko** V N Stevenson, J M G Sheridan, P Stevenson
1963 June 24	**Gilliwiggle** J Paterson, V N Stevenson
1963 Oct 11	**Wicca Basket** P H Biven, C Fishwick, R Woodman
1963 Oct 12	**In-Between** P H Biven, R Woodman, C Fishwick
1964 April 7	**Trapeze** H T H Peck, P H Biven
1964 April 16	**Golva** (Aid) M B McDermott, S R C Bemrose
	Free climbed by R Edwards, M Edwards in August 1976.
1964 May 20	**Belle** P H Biven, C Fishwick, H T H Peck
1964 May 23	**Ochre One Point Five** H T H Peck, C Fishwick, P H Biven
	A top pitch was added by R Edwards, M Edwards in December 1984 and the whole climb re-named Ochre Slab Direct.
1964 June 28	**Kafoozalem** (Aid) F E R Cannings, P Badcock
	The Whore of Jerusalem – a jewel all the same. Climbed free by J Moran, D Banks on 27 June 1977.
1965 Jan 5	**Clob** C Fishwick, R Woodman
1950-66	**Commando Crack** Unknown
1966 June 3	**Beowulf (3 pts aid)** P H Biven, H T H Peck
	Bolt bagged. Climbed free by P Gordon shortly afterwards.
1966 June 30	**Grendel** (Aid) M B McDermott, H T H Peck
	Climbed free by P R Littlejohn, F E R Cannings in May 1971.
1966 June	**Congo Direct** R N Bond, W Doherty
	An artificial route up the buttress right of Slippery Slab.

1966 Aug 26	**Right Angle** I Peters, J Bember
	How to leave your mark from an early age. A famous route made more famous by being left out of Classic Rock; an omission which Ken Wilson admitted was one of the few errors of judgement he's ever made.
1966 Aug 27	**Congo Crack** H I Banner, J Gosling
1966 Sept 18	**Strike** F E R Cannings, J D Davis
1966 Sept 22	**Boldfinger** F E R Cannings, J D Davis
1966	***Cornwall Volume 2 by Vivian Stevenson***
1967 Feb 17	**Donna** M Springett, S Moore, R Hodgson
	Climbed by an artificial start, which is now Terrace Cracks. The start as described: J R Lees, G Moffat on 8 July 1967 as part of a climb called Gargoyle, which then took a line similar to Donna.
1967 April 3	**Paradise** P H Biven, H T H Peck
	Originally the line went to the top belay of Nameless and finished just right of that climb. The finish described was climbed with a point of aid by P Rigg, D Carr, M Ryan on 4 October 1973. Climbed free by P R Littlejohn, H Clarke December 1978.
1967 April 6	**Goat's Ridge, East Tower Arête** T A J Goodfellow, W A Carver
1967 April 16	**Torrey Canyon Slab** D W Bateman, M McDermott
1967 April 23	**Port, Starboard** M B McDermott, D W Bateman (VL)
1967 April 29	**Hornpipe Corner, The Gangway, Lower Deck** M B McDermott, R Payne
1967 July 8	**Gargoyle** J R Lees, G Moffat
1967 July 9	**Capillary Cracks** J R Lees, G Moffat
1968 Feb 18	**Chi Squared** R Coates, S Young
1968 Feb 21	**Ostrobogulous** S Young, R Coates
1968 Feb 21	**Tartarus** R Hodgson, S Young
1968 April 13	**Geronimo** F E R Cannings, P H Biven
	Direct Finish added by P O'Sullivan, P Bingham on 25 August 1990.
1968 April 13	**Visions of Johanna** M Springett, F E R Cannings, P H Biven
	Pitch 1 only; the top pitch had been climbed by J Taylor, P Badcock on 10 March 1968.
	The crux was 'bouldered' by Springett, who was then thrown gear with which he gratefully retreated. In the words of the song, he sat there stranded doing his best to deny it, while 'muttering small talk at the wall' before roping up and climbing the full pitch. Variation climbed solo by M Edwards on 4 November 1986.
1968 April 14	**Florence, Zebedee** F E R Cannings, A R Thompson
1968 April 14	**Vulcan** (Aid) M Jones, M Vallance
	Jones took an impressive fall on his first attempt at the crux pitch, and the party retreated. Jones returned on April 20th and climbed the top pitch with W A Carver holding the ropes. Free-climbed by K Carrigan and A Lowe on 30 July 1981.
1968 May	**Xanadu** (Aid) M Springett, S Young
	Originally broke out to the right at the top of the main groove. Climbed free with left-hand finish added by P R Littlejohn, I F Duckworth in April 1970.
1968 June 2	**Surf Wall, Rota Guta** I Peters, P Mould
1968 Sept 2	**Dougal** F E R Cannings, P Murphy, J Fowler
1968 Sept 28	**Noddy Esq, Nineveh** W A Carver, J Burley, P Stanier

1968 Dec **The Dream** (Aid)   M Gulliard, R Wilson
Climbed with 3 pts of aid by P R Littlejohn, I F Duckworth on 26/27 April 1972. The last aid point was eliminated by P Livesey in June 1976 to make the dream a reality.

1968   ·   ***Cornwall Volume 1 by Peter Biven and Mike McDermott***

1969 July 5 **Daedalus**   P R Littlejohn, P H Biven
The top pitch was added by P R Littlejohn, S B Jones on 27 July 1969.

1969 Aug 7 **Teleology**   P B Checkland

1969 Aug 24 **Tuco the Terrible**   W A Carver, M Hands
The first greenstone extreme. A local strike a week before Littlejohn got his in with Shark and Behemoth.

1969 Aug 26 **The Girdle Traverse** (Great Zawn) (3 pts aid)   P R Littlejohn, S B Jones
The freeing of Great Zawn Chimney together with the creation of the girdle was of major import at a key point of climbing development.

1969 Aug 27 **Artificer**   P R Littlejohn, S B Jones
Artifact variation climbed in 1984 by N Dixon.

1969 Aug 29 **Shark**   P R Littlejohn, S B Jones

1969 Aug 30 **Behemoth** (2 pts aid)   P R Littlejohn, S B Jones (VL)
Setting the mark on Gurnard's Head.

1969 Sept 12 **Zarathustra**   P R Littlejohn, F E R Cannings (AL)

1969 Sept 13 **Dylan** (2 pts aid)   F E R Cannings
Climbed free by T. Penning, P Cresswell, R Lanchbury, P Lanchbury on 7 May 1989.

1969 Sept 14 **Desolation Row**   F E R Cannings, P R Littlejohn

1969 Sept 14 **Omen**   F E R Cannings, P R Littlejohn (AL)
The culmination of a remarkable series of free ascents in Great Zawn over a memorable weekend.

1969 Sept **Genge's Right Hand**   D Musgrove, A Wild, D Gray

1969 Oct 16 **Bonnie, Clyde**   S R Young, N S Barnes, R D Hodgson

1969 Oct 23 **Angel's Highway**   S R Young, N S Barnes
Originally called Goonshow. Climbed free by R Edwards, M Edwards in July 1978.

1969 Dec 29 **Piledriver** (1 pt aid)   M J Guillard, P Bittner

1969 **The Quartz Band**   R J Isherwood, J M Kosterlitz

1970 March 30 **Judas**   F E R Cannings, D Steel, I F Duckworth

1970 May 24/25 **Liberator** (7 pts aid)   F E R Cannings, P R Littlejohn (AL)
The right name for a route which regardless of points of aid and two-day effort was justly seen as 'liberating' Great Zawn from artificial climbing. Recorded by a spool-full of leading photographers. Climbed completely free by R Fawcett, P Livesey in April 1976 with some variations in line.

1970 May 30 **Scalpel**   F E R Cannings, P H Biven

1970 June 6 **My Mule Don't Like You Laffin**   W A Carver, M James
Possessed by the spirit of adventure and Clint Eastwood; a fine piece of exploration.

1970 June 7 **Shades of Last Summer**   W A Carver, M James

1970 June **Carcinoma**   P H Biven, I F Howell

1970 June **Heart Attack Machine** (2 pts aid), **Captivator** (Aid)   P H Biven, I F Howell (AL)
Captivator was climbed free with variations to give Opium in August 1989 by S Haston and Ms C Bull.

1970 July 4	**Gargoyle's Ear** L W P Garland
	Eclipsed by Donna's eventually finding a home.
1970 July 5	**Andrimne** S R Young, K D A Peterson
1970 July 8	**Tramps Overcoat** R D Kift, J Dunstone, D Titt
	Sennen's first bolt. Eaten by sea-slugs. The route is no more.
1971 Jan	**Strongbody** P Gordon, I F Duckworth, G Morgan
1971 April 11	**Side Show** F E R Cannings, P Leaver
1971 May 30	**The Maiden** P R Littlejohn, F E R Cannings
1971 June 5	**Mazurka** H I Banner, D W Bateman
1971 July	**Song of the Sea** H I Banner, D W Bateman
	Lay unsung for many years.
1971 Aug 16	**The Prodigal's Return** J Deacon, A Alvarez, C Fishwick
	The line as described: E Grindley, G Higginson on 1 April 1972.
1971 Aug 29	**The Cormorant's Bill** J Deacon, C Fishwick
1971 Oct 9	**The Blimp** A McFarlane, P de Mengel
1971 Oct 9	**Several Species...** (1 pt aid) P de Mengel, A McFarlane
	The full name given to this climb was Several Species of Small
	Furry Animals Gathered Together in a Cave Grooving Together
	with a Pict. Pinkly florid in anyone's language. Climbed without aid
	point by P Craggs 1990.
1971 Dec 29	**The Dungeon** P R Littlejohn, K Darbyshire
	The variation was added by K Darbyshire, H Clarke on
	12 November 1972.
1971 Dec 31	**The Shield, Gneiss Gnome** P R Littlejohn, K Darbyshire (AL)
	Deep discovery on the killas slate.
1972 Feb 22	**Procyon** I F Duckworth, A McFarlane (AL)
1972 April 8	**Grot** D Carter, M C Gibbs
1972 July 8	**Campanology** T D Thompson, P de Mengel
1972 July 8	**Gillian** (Aid) A Mahony, P de Mengel
	Free climbed by R Edwards, M Edwards in August 1977. Direct
	Start climbed solo by M Edwards in August 1985.
1972 July 9	**The North Wall** T D Thompson, A Mahony (AL)
1972 July 16	**Speleology** (1 pt aid) T D Thompson, P de Mengel
1972 Aug 16	**The Lid** (Aid) P de Mengel, A Mahony
	Still in chains.
1972 Aug 27	**Black Power** E Grindley, G Higginson, I Roper
1972 Aug 28	**Backlash** E Grindley, I Roper, G Higginson (AL)
1972 Aug 29	**The Adversary** P R Littlejohn, K Darbyshire
	Setting the mark for modern but essentially 'classic adventure'
	climbing in Penwith.
1972 Aug 30	**Impendeen Wall, Yellow Slab** J Deacon, C Fishwick
1972 Nov 12	**Little Plum** K Darbyshire, P H Biven
1972	**Communion Crack** R Edwards, I Pomfret
1973 March 20	**Lindy** E Grindley, G Higginson
1973 April 29	**The Royal Forester** W A Carver, P Turner
1973 May 13	**Sheep Crook Black Dog, When I Was on Horseback**
	W A Carver, P Turner
1973 June 3	**Rosebud in June** W A Carver, R Nadin
1973 June	**Candy Man** R Edwards, I Pomfret
	Edwards puts his name down for future considerations.
1973 Oct 19	**Smeagol** T F Walker, M Tighe
1973	**Finale** (1 pt aid) M Tighe, B Newton

1973   ***Great Zawn* by Frank Cannings and Pat Littlejohn**

1973   ***Chair Ladder: an Interim Guide* by Roger Gook and Mike White**

1973   ***Climbing in Cornwall* by Toni Carver, Peter Stanier, and Pat Littlejohn**

1974 March 31   **Saxon**   P R Littlejohn, S B Jones
Direct Finish by R Edwards, S Salmon on 2 April 1979.

1974 March 31   **Thane**   P R Littlejohn, S B Jones

1974 April   **Herring Gull, Black-backed Gull, Kittiwake** (Gurnard's Head), **Jonathan Livingston Seagull**   J P Stranger, J L Hart (AL)

1974 May   **Déjà Vu**   H Barber, F E R Cannings
A pure, on-sight ascent of great boldness and style.

1974 June 18   **Marionette** (Aid)   D T Roscoe, R C Firth, B M Spark, T M Clarke
Climbed free by R Edwards in August 1976. No Pack Drill variation climbed in 1994 by T Dennell, S Rourke, M Edwards.

1974 July   **Samson Arête**   R Edwards, I Pomfret

1974 Aug 16   **The Aggressor** (Whirl Pool Buttress)   K Darbyshire, P R Littlejohn (AL)
Another fine piece of exploratory work.

1974 Aug 16   **Light in August**   P R Littlejohn, K Darbyshire

1975   **Dublin Wall**   R Burns, D Cook, J Cheesmond

1975   ***Chair Ladder and the South Coast* by Bob Moulton and Terry Thompson**

1976 April   **Lurch** (Bosigran)   P Livesey (solo)
Livesey's evening amble before getting down to the next day's work.

1976 April   **Thick Wall Special**   P Livesey, A Evans, J Lawrence

1976 April   **Buffalo Gorge, Yankee Doodle**   T Proctor, G Birtles
RIP.

1976 June   **White Man's Burden**   D T Roscoe, P Temple

1976 July 4   **Corkscrew**   P R Littlejohn, D Garner

1976 July 6   **Roraima**   P R Littlejohn, D Garner
Into inner space with damp patches. A climb for all seasons.

1976 July 17   **The Good, the Bad, and the Gruesome**   W A Carver, G Arthur

1976 July 18   **Zawn Alley Rumble**   W A Carver, G Arthur

1976 July   **The Bandsman**   W A Carver, G Arthur
Carver pushes out into deep coast.

1976 July   **Slanting Crack** (Sennen), **Terrace Cracks**   R Edwards, M Edwards
Terrace Cracks pitch 1 originally climbed with aid by M Springett, S Moore, R Hodgson on 17 February 1967 as part of Donna.

1976 Oct 2   **Land's End Short Climb**   J Barry, D V Nicholls
Down the Line variation by R Edwards, M Edwards on 12 May 1985.

1976 Oct 6   **The Gannet**   D V Nicholls, J Barry

1977 April   **The Time Lord**   P Rigg, K Marsden, N Metcalf

1977 June 23   **Shape Shifter**   D E Hope, A W Mills

1977 June   **Fool's Lode**   P Livesey, J Lawrence

1977 June   **Antenna**   P R Littlejohn, I Peters

1977 July 28   **The Kraken**   J L Hart, J Loxham (AL)

1977 July 29   **Aireline, Airport, Night Flight**   B R E Wilkinson, J Wilkinson

1977 July 30   **Biggles**   B R E Wilkinson (solo)

1977 Aug   **The Quaker**   R Edwards and party

1977 Aug	**Aberdeen Angus** R Abbas, T Mawer	
1977 Aug	**Witch Hunt, Voices** P R Littlejohn, D Roberts	
1977 Oct 1	**Hello Salar** S Salmon, R Hall	
1977 Oct	**Varicose** S Salmon, J Pearce	
1977	**Cow Girl** S Salmon (solo)	
1978 May 18	**Black Sapper** P R Littlejohn, C King	
1978 June 16	**The Leer, Evil Eye** P R Littlejohn, C King	

Notable advance in standards on Bosigran.

1978 June 16	**Saddle Tramp** J Moran
1978 June 17	**Pump It Up** (1 pt aid) J Moran, N Donnelly
1978 June 20	**Western Hero** J Moran, N Donnelly, S Massey
1978 June 23	**Big Ears** W A Carver, D Brown
1978 Aug 30	**Pure Juice** R Edwards, S Salmon
1978 Aug	**New Medium, Jolly Green Giant** R Fawcett, M Rhodes, S Foster
1978 Sept 3	**Mastodon** R Edwards, S Salmon

The bright dawn of the Edwards Era.

1978 Sept 20	**Nemesis** R Edwards, S Salmon
1978 Sept 25	**Sensible Shoes** P O'Sullivan, Ms C Woodhead

An ingenius use of the available rock. Variation Start climbed in 1988 by M Edwards, C Johns.

1978 Oct 2	**Black Magic, Tropospheric Scatter** R Edwards, S Salmon
1978	**Close Encounter** (Botallack Head Zawn) C P Gibson, L Vrbora
1978	**Crazy Man Michael** C Lowther
1978	**Sheerwater, Rabbit Gully** (Rabbit Carn), **Hlao Roo, Minions Mens Institute** W A Carver, P Turner
1978	**Bonny Black Hare** W A Carver, R Nadin
1978	**Rockin'** R Fawcett, S Foster, M Rhodes
1978	**Southerne Belle** S Foster, M Rhodes, R Fawcett
1978	**Bongo Wall** R Fawcett

1978	***Bosigran and the North Coast by Ed Hart***

1979 Jan 21	**Flat Top** S Salmon, N Hampson
1979 April 17	**Rock Dancer** R Edwards, M Edwards

Edwards moves onto Kenidjack and begins substantial development. The Wooden Box variation climbed in May 1985 by P Williams, S Bird.

1979 April 20	**In the Gallery, Super Direct** R Edwards, M Edwards
1979 May 24	**Proctoscope** D Hillebrandt, P Roberts

Claimed unwittingly as Charley Farley five days later by R Astley, A Davies.

1979 May 25	**Avoided Issue** D Hillebrandt, M Freeman, P Roberts
1979 June 29	**Slanter** R Edwards, M Edwards
1979 June 30	**Stormbringer, Sunny Cellophane** R Edwards, S Salmon
1979 July 12	**The Eyass** R Edwards, S Salmon
1979 July 20	**Glockspud** D Hillebrandt, P Roberts
1979 July 23	**Climb to the Sun** R Edwards, S Salmon
1979 July	**The Intruder** P O'Sullivan, S Bell (AL)
1979 Aug 5	**Digital Wall** R Edwards, S Salmon, A Gallagher
1979 Aug 5	**Paper Moon** R Edwards, A Gallagher, B R E Wilkinson
1979 Aug 5	**Sea Music, Wave Dancer, Stoneflasher, Foam Follower** D E Hope, S Hope
1979 Aug 12	**Angelus** R Edwards, M Edwards

1979 Aug 14	**Sail Race** R Edwards, M Edwards
1979 Aug	**Short Circuit** P O'Sullivan, Ms C Woodhead
1979	**Diagonal** R Edwards, M Edwards
1980 Jan 26	**High Frontier** R Edwards, M Edwards
1980 Feb 17	**Parabola** R Edwards, R Perriment
1980 March 31	**Astral Stroll** R Edwards, C Bryan

An inspired discovery to launch the 80s.

| 1980 April 4 | **Blind Fury**   C Cavey, W Wilson, R Cavey |

Variation by B Carver, W A Carver on 5 September 1997.

| 1980 April 11 | **Silver Shadow**   C Nicholson, A Gallagher |
| 1980 April 24 | **Dangerous Visions** (2 pts aid)   R Edwards, M Edwards |

A rest point was eliminated by P R Littlejohn in 1996.

1980 May 3	**D I Blues** M Dunning, R Dearn, I Collins
1980 May 3	**Scouse Slab** L Jennings, K Corrish, S Pocock
1980 May 5	**Bring On the Nubiles** M Donnan, M Corbett
1980 June 6	**Jailer** J Williams, J R Mitchell
1980 June 8	**Space Race** R Edwards, P O'Sullivan, P Lloyd
1980 June 24	**Ziggurat** (2 pts aid) R Edwards, M Edwards

Constructed in stages.

1980 Aug 24	**Zero Gravity** R Edwards, M Edwards
1980 Oct 5	**Drag Artist** M Dunning, R Bennett
1980 Oct 10	**Viking's Dawn** A Churcher, J Churcher
1980 Oct 10	**Sword at Sunset** A Churcher, J Churcher

1980   ***Trewavas Head, A Climbing Guide* by Dennis Bateman and Les Williams**

| 1981 Feb 15 | **Tombstone**   M Edwards, R Edwards |

Direct Start by M Edwards (solo) February 1988.

| 1981 April 4 | **Day Tripper**   R Edwards, M Edwards (AL) |

The first of some major contributions at Land's End.

| 1981 April 10 | **Cormorant's Ben**   S Dougherty, M Nicholson |

Direct Finish: M Edwards, R Edwards, R Barker 15 May 1981.

1981 April 18	**Great Central, Seadreams** S Salmon, D Hannigan
1981 June 11	**Slight Pause** A D Newton, D T Roscoe
1981 July 16	**Split Minds** R Edwards, M Edwards (AL)
1981 July 25	**The Artful Dodger, Bill Sykes, Fagin** C Nicholson, S Salmon
1981 July 25	**Oliver** C Nicholson (solo)

Gruel variation climbed on 14 May 1995 by M Raine.

1981 July 30	**Kurtzer** N Freemantle, S Shimitzu, D Cook
1981 Aug 1	**Strongbow, Blackthorn** C Nicholson, D Hannigan, S Salmon
1981 Aug 1	**Atlantic Ocean Wall** R Edwards, M Edwards (AL)

A major line. A number of fixed placements have been used variously over a period of time. These include metal tubes, bolts, pegs, and stainless steel pegs.

| 1981 Aug 7 | **Gritstone Delinquent, The Mansfield Mob**   R Pepperday, D Canlin |
| 1981 Aug 7 | **The Guilty Snowflake**   C Nicholson, S Salmon |

Nicholson's first use of chalk inspired a great name.

1981 Aug 28	**Kangaroo, Koala** K Lindorff
1981 Sept	**Canary Legs** A Trevorrow, S Torr
1981 Nov 1	**The Rumbles** S Salmon, M Crayton (AL)

The Bumbles finish climbed by D Hannigan, A Trevorrow, May 1982.

1981 Nov 14	**Cross Town Traffic** S Salmon, M Crayton	
1981	**The Monkey Climb** (1 pt aid) P Montgomery, K Lawlor	
	FFA by M Edwards, C Edwards in 1992.	
1981	**Lucinda** E Cleasby, M Lynch, R Matheson	
1982 March 3	**First Entry, Stilton, Cheddar, Narcissus, Twinkletoes** K Lawlor, R Dixon (VL)	
1982 March 28	**Happy Returns, Sea Pink, Mein Kampf, Barnacle Bill, Stone Fall** D W Bateman, P Murray (VL)	
1982 June 21	**Hadrian's Nose** R Edwards, M Edwards	
1982 July 9	**T-Tour** A Trevorrow, S Torr	
1982 Aug 17	**Ace of Spades** M Edwards, R Edwards	
	The Direct Start was added by M Edwards on 7 September 1985.	
1982 Aug 19	**SPQR** M Edwards, R Edwards	
1982 Aug 26	**Canute** M Fowler, S Lewis	
	The taxman cometh.	
1982 Dec 30	**Toad Wall Special** S Lewis	
	Pitch 1 only. Pitches 2 and 3: S Lewis, C Mellor on 2 January 1983.	
1982	**The Loose Goose** S Lewis	
1982	**Cassio, Brutus** R Edwards, M Edwards	
1982	**Caesar's Groove** M Edwards, R Edwards	
1982	**Salmon Splitter, Seaspray,** (Kenidjack), **The Castle, Nothinmega** M Wilson, P Custry (VL)	
1982	**Seahorse** M Wilkins, G Buxton	
1982	**Sesquipedalian** M Wilson, M Ravern, P Custry, S Cheslet	
1982	**Sieging the Castle, Foamflower** (Kenidjack) T Hodgson, I Jones	
1982	***North Cornwall and West Penwith New Climbs** by Pete O'Sullivan and Bob Moulton*	
1983 March 6	**Bolder Problem** D Hannigan, M Crayton	
1983 March 17	**Seaspray** (Bosigran) J Hooper, J Francom	
1983 April 6	**Quadruple X** R Bateson, C Snell	
1983 April	**Thoroughbred** M Doyle, J Hooper	
1983 June 11	**Fingers** J Hooper, S Blanchet	
1983 June 23	**Flash Back** M Crayton, D Hannigan	
1983 June	**Breeze** A Trevorrow, W A Carver	
1983 June	**Greenstone Junction** W A Carver, A Trevorrow	
1983 July 11	**Finger Winch** D Hannigan, R Lewis, D Hillebrandt	
1983 July 20	**Crabber's Nip** D Hannigan, R Lewis	
1983 July 21	**No Number** S Salmon, D Hannigan	
	They thought their number was up in a ferocious thunderstorm during which gear and noses glowed.	
1983 Aug 22	**Skewcrack** S Salmon, P Thompson	
1983 Sept 12	**Sam's Greasy Thumbprint** S Salmon, D Hannigan	
1983 Oct 4	**Time Out** R Edwards, M Edwards	
1983 Oct 5	**Land's End Micro Climb** M Edwards, R Edwards	
1983 Oct 28	**Pots Arête** R Tewson, S Salmon, P Thompson	
1983 Nov 6	**Born Free** M Edwards, R Edwards	
1983 Nov 23	**Initial Crack, Moxibustion, Trio, Welsh Wizard** L Williams, P Murray, D W Bateman (VL)	
	First developments at Trewellard. Collective age of trio of wizards 'approaching 200'.	
1983 Dec 1	**Bright Morning, Brown Jack, Sea Fever, Sunset Walls** P Murray, D W Bateman	

1983 Dec 7	**Russet Wall, Skylight, Space below My Heels**	L Williams, D W Bateman (VL)
1983 Dec 11	**Hard Times** D Hannigan, M Crayton, E Ford	
1983	**Maneater** M Edwards, M Peplow	
1983	**Banana Crack, The Flakes, Orange Slice** M Edwards (solo)	
1983	**Dominator, Shaft** R Edwards, M Edwards	
	Shaft incorporated the direct start to Doorpost.	
1983	**Overmarked, Soloer's Paradise** M Edwards (solo)	
1984 Feb 2	**Grey Groove** A Trevorrow, D Hannigan, P Murray, D W Bateman	
1984 Feb 13	**Microcosm, The Crab** D W Bateman, P Murray	
1984 Feb 24	**Grey Shadow** P Murray, D W Bateman	
1984 Feb 24	**Black Shadow** J Twigg, P Murray	
1984 Feb 24	**Shambhala, Andrew** (Trewellard) A Trevorrow, P Murray, D W Bateman, D Hannigan	
1984 March 8	**Ancient's Way** D W Bateman, P Murray	
1984 March 16	**John Knox** D Hannigan, D W Bateman	
1984 March 17	**The Dawning** M Edwards, R Edwards	
1984 March 26	**Castaways** M Edwards, R Edwards	
1984 April 1	**Rude Awakening, Rock Star** R Edwards, M Edwards	
1984 April 14	**Slanting Crack** (Trewellard) D W Bateman, P Murray	
1984 April 18	**Cry Tough** D Armstrong, G B Smith	
1984 April 21	**Matador** M Edwards, R Edwards	
1984 April 21	**Spare Rib, Iron Hand** R Edwards, M Edwards	
1984 April 23	**Debutante** C Gilbert, M Burt, D W Bateman	
1984 April 25	**A Swift Flight of Fancy** R Edwards, M Edwards	
1984 April	**Arang Atang** M Edwards (solo)	
1984 April	**Super Jam** M Edwards, R Edwards (VL)	
1984 May 7	**Bateman's Boots** D Hannigan, D W Bateman	
1984 May 27	**Solo** A Trevorrow (solo)	
1984 May 27	**Isosceles** A Trevorrow, S Wright	
1984 May	**Six Blade Knife** M Edwards, E Stone	
1984 June 2	**Cactus Crack** M Edwards, R Edwards	
1984 June 17	**Exodus** B Knight, B Parr	
1984 June 29	**Crystal Fingers** R Edwards, M Edwards	
1984 June 29	**Quartz Crystal** M Edwards, R Edwards	
1984 June	**Devo** M Edwards (solo)	
	Devotee variation climbed by M Edwards, T Dennell in 1993.	
1984 June	**Skytrain** R Edwards, M Edwards	
1984 June	**Flexitoys, Plastic Edge** M Edwards, R Edwards	
1984 June	**Larboard, Midships, Starboard** (Porth Nanven), **Tall Ships, Shellback** Land's End Climbing Club members	
1984 July 10	**Territorial Claim** M Edwards, R Edwards	
1984 July 13	**Double Take** L Williams, D W Bateman, D Hannigan	
1984 July 15	**The Outside Man** R Edwards, M Edwards	
1984 July 25	**Cold Iron** D Hannigan, D W Bateman	
1984 July	**Birds of Prey** R Edwards, M Edwards	
1984 Aug 11	**Kubla Khan** R Edwards, M Edwards	
1984 Aug 14	**Nipper's Crab** S Salmon, S Richards	
1984 Aug	**A Flair for the Theatrical** M Edwards, R Edwards	
1984 Sept 3	**Biggles Flies Undone** S Salmon	
1984 Oct	**Exit Visa, Copy Cat** R Edwards, M Edwards, A Wingham	
1984 Oct	**Perfect Prescription** M Edwards, R Edwards	

1984	**The Bearded Clam, Hotel Chambermaid** R Lince, M Harding
1984	**Silly Old Moo** M Edwards, C Johns
1984	**Aristocracy** D Kerr, P Whitfield
1984	**Route Four** L Williams, P Murray, D W Bateman
1984	**Hard Up, Hard On, Addanardon** R Lince, M Harding, D Ashwell
1984	**Blood Wagon** T Daniel, S Leberman, R Lince
1984	**Sheriff, Deputy Sheriff** R Lince, S Leberman, T Daniel
1984	**Cow Girl** S Leberman, T Daniel, R Lince
1984	**Hit the Deck, Here She Comes** T Daniel, R Lince
1984	**Reagan's Regression** R Lince (solo)
1984	**Electric Blue, Wind Hanging** D Armstrong, M Powell
1984	**Hayloft Cracks** M Edwards and party

1984 — ***Cornwall – West Penwith** by Pete O'Sullivan*

1985 March 8	**Lost Souls** M Edwards, R Edwards
1985 March 9	**Sunset Wall** M Edwards, R Edwards
1985 March 13	**Blitzkreig, New Waves** R Edwards, M Edwards
1985 April 12	**Last Dancer** R Edwards, M Edwards (AL)
	The second pitch had been climbed from the foot of The Cormorant's Bill by the same team on 8 March 1985.
1985 April 16	**Edge of Time** R Edwards, M Edwards
	Heritage of Follies variation: M Edwards, R Edwards 1988.
1985 April 24	**Sun Dog** D Hannigan, D W Bateman
1985 April	**Virgin on a Crisis** M Edwards, R Edwards
1985 April	**Echoes** M Edwards, R Edwards
1985 April	**Gallipoli** P O'Sullivan, D Hannigan, M Dunning
1985 April	**Anzac Day** P O'Sullivan, D Hannigan
1985 May 12	**Nineteen Eighty-Four** R Edwards, M Edwards
1985 May 12	**Edge Control** R Edwards, M Edwards
1985 May	**Hidden Cornwall** W A Carver, P O'Sullivan
1985 June 20	**Rainbow, Shades** D Hannigan, D W Bateman
1985 June 28	**Banana Split** M Edwards (solo)
1985 June 30	**Rainmaker** D Hannigan, D W Bateman, P Richardson
1985 July 4	**What Red Parrot? D.B. I Presume?** C Nicholson, D Hannigan, D W Bateman
1985 July 4	**Fringe Benefit** C Nicholson, D Hannigan, M Crayton
1985 July 6	**Geriatrics** D Roscoe, D W Bateman, B Roscoe
1985 July 11	**Eric Goes to the Seaside** C Nicholson (solo)
1985 July 11	**The Confluence** C Nicholson, I Peters
1985 July 17	**Cluny, Claymore** D Hannigan, D W Bateman
1985 July 17	**Steely Dan** D Mannix, Ms A Sheets
1985 July 21	**Claudication, Landing Strip, Spitfire** S Ferguson, M Harrison
1985 July 24	**Targe** D Hannigan, D W Bateman, S Salmon
1985 July 24	**Had It Chimney** D W Bateman
	Variation: R Edwards on 24 June 1987.
1985 July 25	**Sweet Metal** D Hannigan, D W Bateman
1985 July 30	**Catholic Girls** M Edwards, C Edwards, M McMahon
1985 July	**Cool Curl** M Edwards (solo)
1985 Aug 2	**Aggressor (Zawn Duel)** R Edwards, I Blake
1985 Aug 4	**Thin Tin** D Hannigan, P Jones
1985 Aug 4	**Levant Jug Route** P Johnstone, B le Grange

1985 Aug 26	**Feast of Fear** M Edwards, R Greaves
1985 Aug	**Stunted Arête, The Cut Price Comedy Climb, Plucky**
	M Edwards (solo)
1985 Aug	**Demolition** M Edwards, I Blake
1985 Aug	**Dark Comedian** M Hounslea
1985 Sept 1	**Dick Dastardly, Wiki Wiki Wheels** K Palmer, A Grieve
1985 Sept 2	**Pinnacle Route** M Edwards, F Keegan
	Some pitches may have been climbed before.
1985 Sept 7	**The Big Blade** M Edwards (solo)
1985 Nov 22	**Jester's Blues, The Jouster, Call to Arms** M Edwards,
	R Edwards
1985 Nov 22	**The Mace, Armed Knight Crack, The Brave Warrior**
	R Edwards, M Edwards
1985	**The Last Dance** R Edwards, M Edwards
1985	**Desert Hawk** M Edwards
1985	**Ocean Rain** G Everett, J Sonczak
1985	**On Your Marks** M Edwards and party
1986 Feb	**Titanic** M Edwards, R Edwards
	Reclimbed by the same pair without clipping the drilled pegs on
	28 October 1994.
1986 March 10	**Pyjamarama** M Edwards, R Edwards
1986 March 20	**New Editions** (Land's End) R Edwards, M Edwards
1986 March 26	**A Perfect Lady** R Edwards, M Edwards
	Destroyed by rockfall.
1986 April 10	**Shrimpet, Barnaclet** Unknown
1986 April 25	**Slot Machine** D Hannigan, G Hobbs
1986 April 30	**Rip Tide, Deep Six** D Hannigan, G Hobbs
1986 April	**Kohima** P O'Sullivan, M Grassi
1986 April	**Imphal** P O'Sullivan, C Pretty
1986 May 7	**New Belt and Braces** G Hobbs, D Hannigan
1986 May 9	**The Outlaw** G Hobbs, P Ellis
1986 May 11	**Seamstress** G Hobbs, D Hannigan, D W Bateman
1986 May 12	**First Slip** G Hobbs, D W Bateman
1986 May 12	**Second Slip, Square Leg** G Hobbs, M Crayton
1986 May 16	**Seventeen Schoolgirls, Gymslip** D Hannigan, G Hobbs
1986 May 19	**Second Chance** R Edwards, M Edwards
1986 May 26	**Flower Girl** G Hobbs, D Hannigan
1986 May	**Something in the Air** R Harrison, D Carter
1986 June 8	**Blind Justice, Lone Justice** W A Carver, P Johnstone
	News of A W Andrews's pioneering ascents at Boswednack finally
	followed up to produce a pleasing wave of development.
1986 June 8	**No Justice** R Mitchell, P Johnstone
1986 June 12	**Pork Ordinaire** P Johnstone, J Moore
1986 June 15	**Justice on the Runs** P Johnstone, W A Carver
1986 June 22	**Taki Justice** P Johnstone, W A Carver
1986 June 27	**Ordinary Justice, Jus'dis Slab** W A Carver, R Mitchell
1986 June 29	**The Chief Justice, Groovy Justice** W A Carver, R Mitchell
1986 June 29	**Ways to Be Wicked** W A Carver
	Belayed by R Mitchell who 'declined to follow'.
1986 June	**Shiny, Shiny** P Johnstone, R Mitchell, W A Carver
1986 June	**Shiny Boots of Leather** W A Carver, P Johnstone, R Mitchell
1986 June	**Whiplash Girl-child** W A Carver, P Johnstone
1986 June	**In the Dark** P Johnstone, W A Carver
1986 June	**Mandalay** P O' Sullivan, M Grassi

1986 June	**Ivory Tower**	A Churcher, J Churcher
1986 July 13	**Wicked Lady**	W A Carver, D Hannigan
1986 July	**Knight Move**	M Edwards (solo)
1986 July	**Tears of a Clown**	M Edwards

West Penwith's first recorded E7.

1986 Aug 4	**Dark Lady**	M Edwards (solo)
1986 Aug 20	**Hot Lettuce**	D Hannigan, G Hobbs
1986 Aug 28	**Smiley Culture**	P Rogers, H Simons
1986 Sept 20	**Slanderous Accusations**	P O'Sullivan, A Williams, M Godfrey
1986 Sept 26	**Permanent Waves**	P Rogers, R Fowler

This route incorporated the direct start to Doorpost.

1986	**Svetio Polacek's Route**	S Polacek (on-sight solo)
1986	**Fungus Face**	J Matthews, P Johnstone
1986	**Cure by Choice**	N Hancock
1986	**Ordinary Route**	W A Carver, P Johnstone, R Mitchell
1986	**The Fugitive**	W A Carver, P Johnstone
1986	**Midnight Trundler, In the Dark**	P Johnstone, W A Carver
1986	**Stone the Crows**	R Edwards, M Edwards
1987 Feb	**Slab Happy**	M Edwards (solo)
1987 April 11	**Chain Link**	D Hannigan, R Pryor (AL)
1987 April 14	**The Absolution**	P R Littlejohn, F Ramsey

Littlejohn's postscript with flourish to the notional 'Suicide Eliminate' attempted by Peter Biven in the Late Sixties. 'He did the groove left of Phantom as a first pitch, then tried the flakes leading up to the Suicide traverse but couldn't get protection so he eventually got a top rope from a leader on Suicide. Hopefully he would approve of the above conclusion to his efforts.'
Pat Littlejohn, Count House Log.
A direct finish was climbed by M Edwards and R Edwards in May 1987.

1987 April 24	**Black Beauty**	M Edwards (solo)
1987 April 26	**Very Ordinary Route**	S Young, R Mitchell, D W Bateman
1987 April	**Stairway to Heaven**	M Edwards (solo)
1987 April	**Post the Postman**	M Edwards (solo)
1987 April	**Trip across the Slip**	M Edwards (solo)
1987 May 9	**Slippery People**	P Saunders, A Grieve
1987 May 10	**Sanctuary**	P Saunders, N Hancock
1987 May	**Black Widow**	M Edwards (solo)
1987 June 14	**Opening Thrust**	P Saunders, N Hancock
1987 June 24	**Parrot Face**	R Edwards (solo)
1987 June 25	**Philosan Crack, Wayfarer**	R Edwards (solo)
1987 June 26	**Twilight Zone**	M Edwards (solo)
1987 June 26	**Pussy Foot**	R Edwards, M Edwards (AL)
1987 July 4	**Brain Drain, Soft Touch, Face Lift, Final Line**	M Edwards (solo)
1987 July 14	**Louder than Bombs**	N Hancock, G Butler, P Saunders
1987 July 17	**Sick Dreams, Hypocrite Arête, Fair Play**	R Edwards (solo)
1987 July 18	**Gardener's World, Prime Remover**	R Edwards, M Edwards
1987 July 18	**Writings on the Wall**	M Edwards, R Edwards
1987 July	**Coconut Cove**	M Edwards
1987 Aug 9	**Swing Out Sister, Clutching at Straws**	P Saunders, A Bonner
1987 Aug 25	**It's a Square World**	M J Crocker, M Ward

One bolt runner.

1987 Aug	**Pink Knight**	M Edwards (solo)
1987 Aug	**The Roof Is Leaking**	M Edwards (solo)
1987 Aug	**Tango in the Night**	M Edwards, I Blake
1987 Aug	**High Street Blues**	R Edwards, M Edwards
1987 Aug	**Prow**	R Edwards, M Edwards
1987 Sept 22	**Sue**	C King, J Lawrenson, H Lawrenson
1987 Sept 22	**Moon Pool Wall**	J Lawrenson, C King, H Lawrenson
1987 Sept 24	**Shadow Line**	J Lawrenson, C King, H Lawrenson
1987 Sept	**Motivation**	R Edwards, M Edwards
1987 Sept	**Come to My Aid**	M Edwards, R Edwards
1987 Nov	**29 Palms**	M Edwards, R Edwards

Four pegs were replaced by drilled pegs by the first ascensionists.
The drilled pegs have been removed.

1987	**Christine**	M Edwards, C Johns
1987	**Recycled**	R Edwards, M Edwards
1987	**Easy Way Out**	R Edwards (solo)
1987	**Let the River Live, Congo Tribute**	M Edwards
1988 Feb	**Squeeze Me**	M Edwards (solo)
1988 April 1	**April Fool**	M Edwards (solo)
1988 April 2	**Baptism of Fire**	M Edwards
1988 April 4	**Prophecy, Fated**	P R Littlejohn, E Cooper, G Taylor

Back to old haunts.

1988 April 16	**Astrodome**	R Edwards, M Edwards

Originally climbed with drilled pegs and at least one bolt. Climbed
without the fixed gear in July 1998 by M Edwards, R Edwards,
I Blake.

1988 April	**Windows of Perception**	M Edwards (solo)
1988 April	**Pinnacle Slab Route**	S R Young, J R Mitchell
1988 May 6	**Infinite Design**	R Edwards, M Edwards
1988 May 6	**All's Wall that Ends Wall**	M Edwards, R Edwards
1988 May 25	**Free Spirit**	T Penning, P Cresswell
1988 May 26	**Dead Lucky**	T Penning, P Cresswell

The North Coast begins to stir again.

1988 June 6	**Sunset Crack**	R Edwards
1988 June 11	**Ship of Fools**	N Hancock, P Saunders
1988 June 11	**Black Napkin**	P Saunders, G Butler
1988 June 12	**The Evil Empire**	P Saunders, A Grieve
1988 June 15	**Notidwal**	D Hannigan, D W Bateman
1988 June 16	**Niwl**	D T Roscoe, B M Roscoe
1988 June 16	**Dead Ringer**	M Edwards, C Johns
1988 June 19	**Layback and Think of England**	A Williams, P Twomey
1988 June 22	**Notrilleachan, Notbad, Hack**	D Hannigan, D W Bateman
1988 June 26	**Two Tribes**	P Saunders, P Twomey
1988 June 30	**Cargo Route**	N C J Stutchbury, D White, P B Checkland
1988 June	**Red Rose**	M Edwards

Climbed with three bolt runners, which led to a great deal of
controversy.

1988 July 9	**A Winking Crack**	R Edwards, H van Ham
1988 July 15	**A Sudden Splash**	R Edwards, C Edwards, H van Ham
1988 July 22	**Double Take**	R Edwards, J Andres
1988 July 30	**Mind Bubble**	R Edwards, H van Ham
1988 July 30	**Fading into Black**	R Edwards, H van Ham, N Mooney
1988 Aug 9	**Children of Laughter**	R Edwards, H van Ham, J Andres
1988 Aug 25	**Looking over the Edge**	R Edwards, J Andres

1988 Aug 28	**Sea Thief, Run for Your Wife** T Penning, R Lanchbury, P Cresswell	
1988 Aug 29	**The Fifth Horseman** T Penning, P Cresswell, R Lanchbury	
1988 Sept 11	**When the Music Stops** T Penning, P Cresswell, R Lanchbury, D E Hope	
1988 Oct 15	**The Hairy Lobster** M Edwards (solo)	
1988 Oct	**Kingdom of the Deep** M Edwards, R Edwards	

Reclimbed in 1989 without clipping the bolts by M Edwards, who then removed them.

1988 Nov 23	**Blade Runner** R Edwards

At one time there was a bolt runner on the lip of the roof. The route was originally graded E5, but has been reassessed by the first ascensionist as E7.

1988 Nov 25	**Edge Control II** R Edwards
1988	**Diamond Life, The Long Reach** M Edwards, R Edwards
1988	**Espron Negro, Fast Lane** R Edwards, J Andres-Avajas
1988	**Thieves Carnival** M Edwards, S Anson
1988	**Hell Hath No Fear** M Edwards (solo)
1988	**Heritage of Follies** M Edwards, R Edwards

1988	***North Devon and Cornwall* by Iain Peters**

1989 March 26	**Zennorphobia** T Noble, T Gifford

The top pitch claimed retrospectively as having being climbed in 1982 by R Edwards and M Edwards.

1989 May 7	**Sea Sharp** T Penning, P Cresswell, R Lanchbury, P Lanchbury
1989 May 7	**Lunar Sea** T Penning, P Cresswell, R Lanchbury
1989 May 28	**Free Fall Gull, African Grey, Dad's Back** D E Hope, J Cornwell
1989 May 28	**Darkling Thrush** J Cornwell, D E Hope
1989 May 28	**Schnapps** D E Hope, J Cornwell
1989 May 29	**Kitty's Wake, Black Rabbit** D E Hope, J Cornwell
1989 May 30	**Ordinary People** T Penning, P Cresswell
1989 May 31	**Seal of Approval** T Penning, R Lanchbury, P Cresswell
1989 June 6	**The Masochism Tango, Comfortably Dumb** D E Hope, J Cornwell, A Camm
1989 June 25	**Half Man Half Brandy Snap** A Camm, J Cornwell, D E Hope
1989 June 25	**Black Gold, Snap Dragon** T Penning, P Cresswell, R Lanchbury
1989 July 2	**Pete's Party Piece** T Penning, P Cresswell

Zawn Duel challenged again.

1989 July 2	**Catalyst** T Penning, R Lanchbury
1989 July 16	**The Crypts of Lieberkuhn** C Jones, B Simmonds
1989 July 27	**Feeding the Mouse** P B Checkland, K H Checkland, D White
1989 Sept 3	**Pink Foaming Transvestights** Ms D Hanningford, D Hillebrandt (AL)

A name entirely in keeping with natural phenomena: pink from the mine outfall, foaming from the sea, and the rest from Dr Hillebrandt's discovery of a large amount of lady's clothing at the top of the climb. Part of the moral decline which started with chalk and tights.

1989 Sept 3	**Brothel in Brighton** D Hillebrandt, D Hannigan
1989 Sept 9	**How Turtles Tapdance, Gut Bug** D E Hope
1989 Sept 9	**Salmonella Summer** D E Hope, P Lanchbury
1989 Sept 10	**Night over Day over Night** T Penning, D E Hope

1989 Sept 18	**Houghmagandie**	D Hannigan, S Wright
1989 Oct 3	**Retail Therapy**	S Salmon, M Easterbrook
1989 Oct 20	**Painted Lady**	A Hall, P O'Sullivan, D Hannigan
1989 Oct 20	**Malicious Gossip**	P O'Sullivan, D Hannigan, A Hall
1989 Nov 12	**Stamp of Office**	D E Hope, A Camm
1989 Dec 29	**Rough Justice**	K Waterhouse, S Clegg
1989 Dec 29	**Last Minute Reprieve**	M Corbett, N Waterhouse
1989	**Amazonia**	M Edwards, R Edwards
1989	**Off the Mark**	M Edwards, R Edwards
1989	**Hands across the Ocean**	M Edwards, S Anson
1989	**Art of the Slate**	M Edwards, S Anson

Five bolts were placed by the first ascent team. First bolt-free ascent by S Ohly on 20 April 1994. Years later, Edwards claimed to have made the first bolt-free ascent, solo, immediately after the first ascent.

1989	**Windows of Perfection**	M Edwards, S Anson
1980s	**Centre Pitch**	M Edwards (solo)
1980s	**Truescrew Crack**	M Edwards and party
1990 April 8	**Blue Lagoon**	R Lanchbury, T Penning
1990 April 9	**Flying Finish**	T Penning, R Lanchbury
1990 April 28	**Bust a Gut**	D E Hope
1990 April 28	**Look on the White Side**	D E Hope, P White
1990 April 29	**Linda's Choice**	T Penning, R W Lanchbury, D E Hope
1990 April 29	**The Party's Over**	T Penning, R Lanchbury, D E Hope
1990 April 29	**When Hope Has Gone**	T Penning, R Lanchbury, A Tierney
1990 May 26	**Costa Geriatrica, Mad Cow Maggie**	D E Hope, A Camm
1990 June 3	**Ride a Cock Horse**	T Penning, R Lanchbury
1990 June 4	**High Spirits**	T Penning, A Tierney, R Lanchbury
1990 June 9	**Dead Cert, Goodbye Mickey Chick**	T Penning, A Tierney
1990 June 10	**Fools Rush In, Smear Today, Here Tomorrow**	T Penning, A Tierney
1990 June 10	**Dominator Optional Start**	J Ford, D Hannigan

Pitch 1 only; pitch 2 was climbed solo by D Hannigan on 20 May 1990.

1990 July 8	**Jam, Sand, Wich**	D Hannigan, J Hobbs, G Hobbs
1990 July 8	**Beef Cheater**	D E Hope, P Lanchbury, T Penning, R Lanchbury, J O'Leary

Variation Start by D E Hope on 13 July 1990.

1990 July 8	**C Cow**	R W Lanchbury, T Penning, J O'Leary, D E Hope
1990 July 8	**Bully for You**	T Penning, R Lanchbury, D E Hope
1990 July 13	**Phroggy Phobia, How Terrapins Tango, A Message from the Falselands**	D E Hope, J Cornwell

The culmination of an impressive period of development and verbal gymnastics.

1990 Aug 9	**Earthly Powers**	P O'Sullivan, D Hannigan
1990 Aug 12	**The Moon Is Down**	T Penning, A Tierney, R Lanchbury
1990 Aug 12	**Games Children Play**	R Lanchbury, T Penning, A Tierney
1990 Aug 20	**Stella Artois**	M Dunning, P O'Sullivan, P Greenwell
1990 Aug 20	**Stella Maris**	P O'Sullivan, M Dunning, P Greenwell
1990 Aug 20	**Raiders of the Lost Zawn**	P Greenwell, M Dunning, P O'Sullivan
1990 Aug 21	**Roughneck, Dilettante**	P O'Sullivan, M Dunning
1990 Aug 22	**The Pessimist**	P O' Sullivan, B Adams
1990 Aug 23	**Silas Marner**	P O' Sullivan, B Adams

1990 Aug 28	**Chiaroscuro**	P O'Sullivan, B Adams
1990 Sept 1	**Hurricane**	P O'Sullivan, A Hall (combined leads)
1990 Sept 9	**Blackguard**	P O'Sullivan, M Dunning
1990 Dec 31	**Choking Back the Cheers**	R Tewson, S Salmon, P Thompson
1990	**Western Hero Optional Start**	J Ford
1990	**Rainbow Warrior**	M Edwards
1990	**Sooty**	M Edwards, C Johns
1990	**New Release**	R Edwards, C Edwards, I Blake
1990	**Irish Whiskey**	R Edwards, N Mooney
1990	**Magnet Fever, Glory, Well That's Just Dandy**	M Edwards, R Edwards
1990	**Synchromatic, Technotronic, Currying Favour**	R Edwards, S Jones
1990	**Flash Control**	R Edwards, S Jones, N Mooney
1991 Aug 7	**Geordie Boy**	J Judson, Ms A Judson
1991 Oct	**Stealth**	J Hooper, M Raine
1991 Oct	**Max Crack**	M Raine, J Hooper (on sight)
1991	**Black Cleft**	M Edwards, J M G Fraile

1991 **The Fun Curve Factory**   M Edwards, J M G Fraile, R Edwards
Unwittingly claimed, and splashed across the cover of High *magazine, by N Hancock, K Palmer as* Lost a Friend to the Sea *in 1997.*

1991	**The Silver Arrow**	M Edwards, R Edwards
1991	**Robin Hood**	M Edwards, C Johns
1991	**Black Wednesday**	M Edwards, R Edwards, I Blake
1991	**The Great Green Wave**	M Edwards, R Edwards

1991 **The Silence of a Lamb**   R Edwards, I Blake
An impressive line marred by the bolt hole drilled by the first ascensionist, who reported that he did not use it.

1991 **Stout Crack, Much Ado about Nothing**   M Edwards
The latter free-climbed Tramp's Overcoat (8 July 1970).

1991	**Joy Riders**	M Edwards, I Blake
1991	**Babylon Five**	T Dennell, S Pac (AL), J Adamson
1991	**Crystal Grazer**	R Edwards, J M G Fraile
1991	**Barnacle**	R Edwards, M Edwards
1991	**Bridge of Sies**	M Edwards, J M G Fraile
1991	**Wild at Heart**	M Edwards, R Edwards
1991	**Nuts Are Not the Only Fruit**	M Edwards

A sport climb: its bolts have been chopped.

1991   Bosigran and the North Coast by Des Hannigan

1992 March 24	**Seamantics**	M J Crocker
1992 May	**The Lucky Sea, NC Madness**	M Raine, J Hooper (on sight)
1992 May	**Devious Do, Go Shorty, Strangeways, The Scrubs**	P O'Sullivan, P Telford
1992	**Pinch the Egyptian**	M Edwards
1992	**Monsoon**	M Edwards, R Edwards
1992	**Blood Smear, Notch It, Flaky Toes, Waterfall Slab**	D Hall, O Henry
1992	**Insurance Drain**	M Edwards, M Barnes
1992	**Hot Rubber**	R Edwards, M Edwards
1992	**1025**	M Edwards, I Blake

A sport climb: its bolts have been chopped.

1992	**Messenger from the Furnace**	M Edwards, R Southall

1992	***Chair Ladder and the South Coast* by Des Hannigan**

1993 May 3	**Three Score Years and Ten, Amen** M J Crocker

On completing the pitch, Crocker was taken off belay instead of being lowered off. Luckily, he survived the resultant 20-metre plummet with 'only' broken wrists and some crushed vertebrae.

1993 June 4	**Dolphinarium, Kiss my Wrasse** P Harrison, N Jowett
1993 Sept 4	**Jammy Dodger** D E Hope, B Bigger, J Cornwell
1993 Sept 4	**Devastating the Lilies** B Bigger, J Corwell
1993 Sept 4	**A Gift of Wings, Cereal Killer** D E Hope, B Bigger, J Warren, J Cornwell
1993	**Palm Beach** D E Hope, P Lanchbury, R W Lanchbury
1993	**Mark Up Another One** M Edwards, T Dennell
1993	**Grand Illusion, Rich Pickings, Life's Moments** R Edwards, M Edwards
1993	**Monster Munch** M Edwards

A sport climb: its bolts have been chopped.

1993	**Facedancer** D Carroll, D Viggers
1994 April 12	**Leviathan** S Ohly, M Raine (AL, on sight)
1994 April 15	**Babylon and Back** M Raine, S Ohly (AL, on sight)
1994 May 4	**The Piano** M Raine, D Hannigan (onsight)

Pitch 2. Pitch 1 and variation start climbed by P O'Sullivan, D Hannigan, N Crowhurst, J Barber in June 1990.

1994 May 7	**Nkosi Sikelele, Cappucino** M Raine, D Hannigan (on sight)
1994 May 8	**Grand Piano** M Raine, D Hannigan (on sight)
1994 May 12	**Nelson, Buthelezi, The Flow Country** M Raine, D Hannigan (on sight)
1994 May 15	**El Cuco** M Raine, D Hannigan (on sight)
1994 May 22	**The Hood** M Raine, D Hannigan (on sight)
1994 July 30	**Parody** D E Hope, R Jervis (AL)
1994	**Magog** N Craine, C Waddy
1994	**Placa del Edwards, The Forgotten Wall, ExSqueeze Me, The Marksman, Marking Time** M Edwards

Eponymism writ large.

1994	**Skid Mark** M Edwards, J Fisher
1994	**International Groove** M Edwards, S Rourke, S Stotz
1994	**Route One, Candy** R Edwards (solo)
1994	**Pony Express, True Grit** (Land's End)**, Pump It** R Edwards
1994	**Yet Again** R Edwards, Mrs E Edwards

And Another variation by the same pair, same year.

1994	**OK Corral, High Noon, Tumble Weed** R Edwards, Mrs E Edwards
1994	**Edge of Light, A Bridge Too Far** R Edwards, C Edwards
1994	**Dancing on Crystals** R Edwards, M Edwards, S Rourke
1994	**Play It Again Sam** J Ford, S Elliottt

The original line went left from the quartzy pocket to join The Piano. The line as described climbed later by M Raine.

1995 May 14	**Nancy** S Ohly, M Raine, G Slade
1995 May 14	**Tea Towel and Lightning** M Raine, G Slade, S Ohly
1995 June 4	**Wham** M Raine

Raine runs out of worthy route names for Freedom Zawn.

1995 June 4	**The Unqualified** S Ohly, L Pavey, M Raine
1995 June 18	**Judge Dredd** W A Carver, B Carver
1995 June 24	**The Soundings** W A Carver, B Carver, T Carver
1995	**Fungus** S Ohly (solo)

1995	**Silent Shadow** R Edwards, M Edwards
1995	**Sabre Cut, This Year's Model, Old Generations, Hidden Secret** R Edwards, T Dennell
1995	**Western Approaches, Rap City in Blue, Farewell to Friends** T Dennell, P Birchell
1995	**Gemstone, Dynosaurus** M Edwards
1996 Feb	**Stagecoach** J Hooper (solo)
1996 April	**Crazy Horse** J Hooper
1996 April	**Apocalypse** J Hooper, P Oak
1996 May 6	**Walking Wounded** N Hancock, S Hill (AL)
1996 May 6	**Seriously Damaged Folk** L Earnshaw, S Hill
1996 May 6	**Special Needs** L Earnshaw, R Meek
1996 May 12	**Blind Furry** S Needham, Ms D Foster
1996 May	**Submariner** J Hooper, P Oak
1996 June 5	**Morgawr** P R Littlejohn, T Ralphs, M Charlton
1996 July 6	**Voodoo Child** S Ohly, M Lush
1996 July 17	**Fuji Frenzy** S Ohly
1996 Aug 3	**Carravagio** P O'Sullivan, P K Hosie
1996 Sept 15	**Polymyele** S Hill, R Meek
1996 Dec	**The Return of the Seven Seconds** S Ohly, G Slade
1996 Dec	**Racy Stacy, Spiderman's Nightmare, Virtual Insanity** S Ohly, Miss P Bale
1996 Dec	**Emergency Exit** S Ohly, D Henderson (both solo)
1996	*An Interim Guide for Black Head by Toni and Barnaby Carver*
1997 March	**Tragic Kingdom** S Ohly (solo)
1997 May 25	**Visiting Hours** N Coe, N Wright (AL), I Birch
1997 May 26	**Lardy Boys, Dismembered Members** S Wales, I Birch
1997 May 26	**Unhalfbricking It** N Coe, I Birch
1997 May 26	**Norman Conquest** N Wright, S Wales
1997 May 26	**King Shark** I Birch, S Wales
	*'Look, it's a great big ***king shark!'*
1997 May 26	**Slab and Tickle** N Coe, N Wright
1997 May 29	**An Gof** S Cardy, M Niklas
1997 May 31	**Rapture** B Carver, W A Carver
1997 June 1	**Over the Ocean** N Hancock (solo)
1997 June 2	**Drowning by Numbers** N Hancock, D Scott-Maxwell
1997 Aug 9	**Fifty Year Storm** A Connor, B Sutton
1997 Sept	**The Edwards Edge** M Edwards
1997 Nov 29	**Anniversary Problem** B Carver, S Ohly
	The 25th anniversary of the Land's End Climbing Club.
1997 Nov 29	**Poison Ivy** S Ohly, B Carver
1997	*Cornish Rock by Rowland Edwards and Tim Dennell*
1998 Jan 30	**The Edge of Hope** B Carver (solo)
1998 March 22	**Pull the Wires from the Wall** N Hancock
1998 April 19	**Archipeligo** R Banaster, C Banaster
1998 July 5	**The Girl Can Wait** M J Crocker, J Alcock
1998 July 30	**I Am a Cormorant's Toilet** P O'Sullivan, M Dunning, C Griffiths
1998 July	**Catacombs** M Edwards, Ms S Nuttall
1998 Aug 8	**Timpson's Arête** D Hillebrandt, B Rowe
1998 Aug 8	**Clueless** L Pavey, B Carver

1998 Oct 11	**Radiator** B.Carver, M J.Frith
1998 Nov 8	**Hang-Over Cure** B Carver, M J Frith
1998 Nov 22	**Lil' Devil** B Carver, M J Frith, L Pavey (on sight)
	Pitch 2 climbed by B Carver, L Pavey on 14 March 1999.
1999 Jan 31	**Crown Green** A March
1999 Feb 17	**True Grit** (Aire Point), **Rooster Cogburn, The Big Trail, Fort Apache, The Quiet Man** J Hooper (solo)
1999 Feb 20	**Rio Bravo, The Alamo, Cheyenne, Vigilante** J Hooper (solo)
1999 March 7	**The Duke, Red River, The Long Voyage Home** J Hooper (solo)
1999 March 21	**Counting Pixies** B Heason, S Ohly (headpointed)
1999 April 5	**The Searchers** J Hooper, P Oak
1999	**Rewind** M Edwards
	The hardest route in the West Country? Originally climbed in 1991 as a sport route, Blue Sky Lightning, by M Edwards.
1990s	**Mark in Time, The Paragon Returns** M Edwards
1990s	**Rib and Flake** J Brown
1990s	**Rourke's Rift** S Rourke, M Edwards
1990s	**Sugar and Dust** M Edwards, S Rourke
1990s	**Mean Crack** M Edwards, P Twomey
	The Direct Start climbed by M Edwards, 1990s.
1990s	**Copacabana** M Edwards, S Rourke, R Edwards, I Blake
1990s	**Local Wall** Unknown
	They said they were locals but didn't give their names.
2000 March 27	**Evening Star** J Hooper, R Banaster
	Finished in the dark.
2000 April 29	**The Return of the Lemming** N Pearson, J Yearsley
2000 July 26	**White Wedding** M Edwards (solo)

Index

New Climbs

Accident Procedure

First Aid

If spinal or head injuries are suspected, do not move the patient without skilled help, except to maintain breathing or if this is essential for further protection. Do not remove the patient's helmet.

If breathing has stopped, clear the airways and start artificial respiration. Do not stop until expert opinion has diagnosed death.

Stop bleeding by applying direct pressure.

Summon help as quickly as is compatible with safety. Do not delay.

Rescue

In the event of an accident where further assistance is required, dial 999 and ask for the Coastguard. The Coastguards are responsible for the co-ordination of all sea-cliff rescues, and will co-ordinate other services such as helicopters, lifeboats, cliff rescue teams, etc.

It is important to report the exact location and details of the accident and also to have someone meet the rescue team to guide them to the spot. Use the Coastguard Identity and Grid Reference of the cliff; these are given at the start of each section of the guide.

Nearest Phone Points

Bosigran – There is a pay-phone in the Count House, the Climbers' Club bunkhouse immediately to the north of the National Trust car-park. However, the bunkhouse is often locked.

Chair Ladder – There is a phone at the lookout at Gwennap Head, above the cliff. If the lookout is closed use the public phone box at Porthgwarra.

Logan Rock, Cribba Head – There is a 999-only phone near the Logan Rock headland.

Helicopter

In the event of a Helicopter evacuation **all** climbers on or off the cliff should take heed. A helicopter flying close to the cliff will make verbal communication very difficult and small stones will be dislodged by the rotor down-draught. All loose equipment should be secured and climbers in precarious positions should try to make themselves safe.

The people with the injured person should try to identify their location. **No** attempt should be made to throw a rope at the helicopter, but assistance should be given to the helicopter crew if requested. **Do not** touch the lowered crew member or his winch wire until the trailing wire has earthed the helicopter's static electricity.

Local Hospitals

The walking wounded can receive treatment in the casualty departments of the following hospitals:

West Cornwall Hospital, St Clare Street, Penzance.
Phone number 01736 874000.

Royal Cornwall Hospital, Treliske, Truro.
Phone number 01872 250000.

Follow-Up

After an accident, a report has to be compiled. Normally the details will be collated at the scene by the Coastguard or rescue team, who will then pass the information to the Mountain Rescue Council Statistics Officer.

If unreasonable equipment failure is suspected then the British Mountaineering Council's technical committee may wish to investigate; contact the BMC at 177-179 Burton Road, West Didsbury, Manchester, M20 2BB.

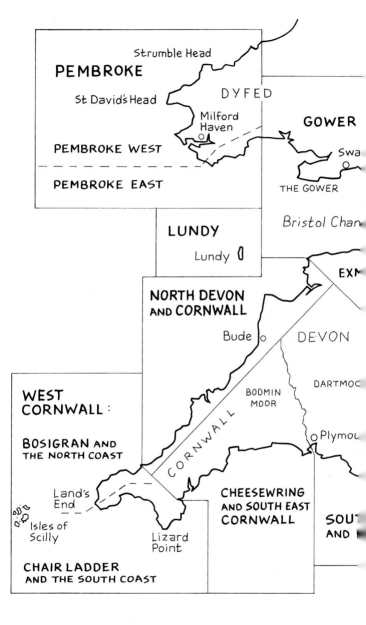

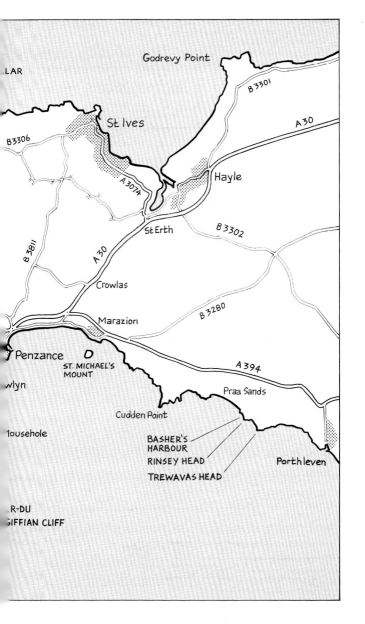

Stone Boom (E2), Pordenack Point
Climbers: Clive Davis and Jody Vallance   Photo: David Simmonite

Contents

Maps and Diagrams

Introduction

Book One contains the full introduction to climbing in West Cornwall. Printed here are the sections most relevant to the south coast of West Penwith, together with The Lizard and The Isles of Scilly.

Crag Overview – South Coast of West Cornwall

Pordenack Point   What a difference a kilometre makes. Take a stroll and leave the hordes behind. Your effort will be rewarded by a good mix of grades on mainly excellent rock. Non-tidal on the upper crags.

Carn Boel area   An interesting little headland with some worthwhile easy routes and a couple of 'Immaculate' classics.

Carn Lês Boel/Bosistow area   Well worth a visit. A rather enigmatic area where pre-war easies rub shoulders with modern desperates. Most of the more substantial routes are tidal and many require abseil approaches. The quality of the rock can be variable, especially in Bosistow Zawn. *Excalibur* is a hidden classic.

Pendower Coves   A generally friable area of granite with one or two solid bits.

Zawn Kellys   A small buttress of generally sound granite. Worth the walk for *American Dream*.

Carn Barra   Once a quiet place to get away from the Bank Holiday crowds, this crag is now much more popular, thanks to a sustained bout of E-grade activity during the early 80s. Mostly tidal, except for the excellent Central Wall.

Dutchman's Zawn   A handful of tidal extremes.

Folly Cove   Tidal climbs on sometimes friable granite.

Fox Promontory   Despite some good, mainly low to middle grade climbs, this can still be a quiet location. Watch the sea though.

Black Carn South   Now, if you want to really get away from the crowds…

Porth Loe/Pellitras area   This quiet, pleasant area is often passed by on the way to other things.

Carn Guthensbrâs   A good little crag, overshadowed by its mighty neighbour, yet with its own strong identity. Some pleasant, short pitches at all grades.

Chair Ladder   The third of West Penwith's big three requires more thought and care than the other two in terms of access, but the rewards repay the effort. Excellent multi-pitch routes of all grades, but it can get very crowded on those ledges.

Porthgwarra Buttress and Hella Point   A quieter alternative, with good routes (mostly low grades) and superb granite.

Levan's Wall/Pedn-mên-an-mere   Worth seeking out. A collection of climbs which includes a couple of treasures.

Porthcurno/Logan Rock area   This stretch of coast has it all: good beaches, isolated zawns, nude sunbathers, and a decent pub. Shoehorned in are a few half-decent rock climbs and some very good bouldering.

Cribba Head area Once a sandbagger's delight, this isolated little buttress has rather more to offer nowadays. Non-tidal and with a sheltered east face.

Penberth/Porthguarnon Quiet. Mostly easy routes in pleasant surroundings.

Coffin Cove A delightful and remote spot.

St Loy Has gained in popularity over recent years. One of the few completely non-tidal crags in the area, with some of the boldest pitches.

Tregiffian Off the beaten track, but deserves to become popular, especially with slab enthusiasts.

Tater-du The black stuff. A greenstone island in a sea of granite, with a classic VS and more besides. Don't come here in poor visibility as the nearby foghorn rattles teeth and holds alike.

Basher's Harbour/Trewavas Penwithian outliers. Trewavas, in particular, is a delightful area with a superb outlook towards the Lizard. Little treasures, much prized by locals. Mostly low to middle grades.

Predannack Head A rather complex area with mostly low to middle grade routes, though further possibilities abound.

Vellan Head The Hidden Buttress is well worth seeking out. Big multi-pitch routes of true quality in an isolated area.

Soap Rock to Kynance Cove A great deal of rock, but it tends to be of poor quality.

Lizard Point area A good selection of routes, often steep, on Britain's most southerly coast. Access is generally amenable. Tower Buttress and The Hollywood Walls are the main attractions.

Housel Bay to Bass Point Although somewhat smaller in stature, Bass Point vies with Hidden Buttress for the title of the Lizard's premier crag. *The Cull* is a must-do for those who can-do. Pen Olver provides a worthwhile selection of short routes in the Difficult to Very Severe range.

Black Head Worth a visit for its unusual rock.

The Isles of Scilly A few scattered routes and plenty of bouldering in a superb setting.

Sea Conditions

Over the years, many people, climbers among them, have died needlessly on the Cornish coast due to ignorance of, or disregard for, the dangers of rough seas. Perfect tidal conditions can mean nothing if a big swell or a heavy sea is running. Stormy weather is obvious, but in West Penwith and The Lizard swell is deceptive. Substantial swells can run into the cliffs even in windless conditions with an apparently calm sea. Swell is often present in fine weather and is caused by low-pressure areas far out in the Atlantic. The sea can look smooth offshore yet at the base of a tidal cliff it may be boiling white with a vicious rise half-way up the face. Dangerous swell can also arise suddenly with a changing tide. **If in any doubt, do not go to the foot of the cliffs.** In any case, always belay when close to the sea.

Coastguard Identity

Each cliff has a 'Coastguard Identity'. This may seem unnecessary in many cases. However, several climbing venues have acquired names known only to the climbing fraternity while some traditional names are duplicated around the coast. The list of Coastguard Identities in the guide has been agreed with HM Coastguard and Air-Sea Rescue authorities and will be used by them as a location guide. Climbers are advised to use these precise names when giving details of an emergency.

Route Descriptions and Grades

The cliffs are described in an anti-clockwise direction around the coast of the peninsula. Descent routes are described with the terms 'left' and right' relating to the climber facing out unless otherwise stated. From its base each cliff is described from left to right, facing in, without exceptions. Pegs mentioned in the text are for runners unless explicitly described as being used for aid.

West Penwith grading remains traditional without being archaic: the established adjectival system is used, that is, in order of difficulty, Moderate, Difficult, Very Difficult, Severe, Hard Severe, Very Severe, Hard Very Severe, E1, E2, etc. Numerical (technical) grades are given for pitches of 4a and above.

Climbs which are not known to have had reasonably successful on-the-lead second ascents are marked with a dagger sign: †. Some older established routes on remote cliffs may not have had ascents for a number of years and may have changed. If a route has suffered a rockfall which may have affected its grade or description and the route has not been reclimbed, it is marked with ††. Bolted and chipped routes are indented in the text.

Guidebook Disclaimer

This guide attempts to provide a definitive record of all existing climbs and is compiled from information from a variety of sources. The inclusion of any route does not imply that it remains in the condition described. Climbs can change unpredictably: rock can deteriorate and the existence and condition of *in-situ* protection can alter. All climbers must rely on their own ability and experience to gauge the difficulty and seriousness of any climb. Climbing is an inherently dangerous activity.

Neither The Climbers' Club nor the authors and editor of this guidebook accept any liability whatsoever for any injury or damage caused to climbers, third parties, or property arising from the use of it. Whilst the content of the guide is believed to be accurate, no responsibility is accepted for any error, omission, or mis-statement. Users must rely on their own judgement and are recommended to insure against injury to person and property and third party risks.

The inclusion in this guidebook of a crag or routes upon it does not mean that any member of the public has a right of access to the crag or the right to climb upon it. Before climbing on any crag in this guidebook, please read the access notes on page 17 of Book One.

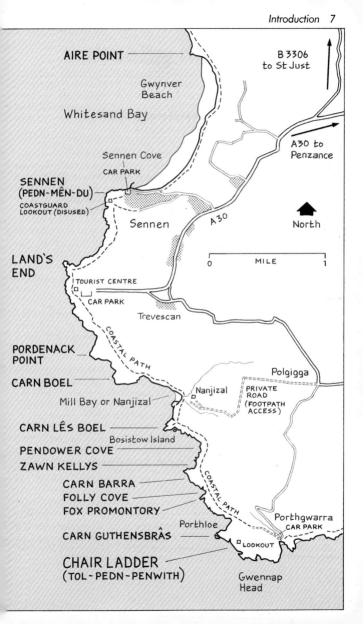

AIRE POINT

Gwynver Beach

Whitesand Bay

B 3306 to St Just

A30 to Penzance

Sennen Cove
CAR PARK

SENNEN
(PEDN-MÊN-DU)
COASTGUARD
LOOKOUT (DISUSED)

Sennen

A30

North

LAND'S END

TOURIST CENTRE
CAR PARK

Trevescan

0 — MILE — 1

PORDENACK POINT

CARN BOEL

Nanjizal

Polgigga

PRIVATE ROAD
(FOOTPATH ACCESS)

Mill Bay or Nanjizal

COASTAL PATH

CARN LÊS BOEL
Bosistow Island

PENDOWER COVE

ZAWN KELLYS

CARN BARRA

FOLLY COVE

FOX PROMONTORY

COASTAL PATH

Porthloe

Porthgwarra
CAR PARK

CARN GUTHENSBRÂS

LOOKOUT

CHAIR LADDER
(TOL-PEDN-PENWITH)

Gwennap Head

West Penwith – South

Pordenack Point Area (Granite)OS Ref 347 242

'On the summit of one of the crags a rock about five feet high is very delicately poised, and appears to be resting on a mere point; it is the most striking object of the range. Fearful as it may seem, lads of the neighbourhood do not hesitate to stand on the top of it…'
(John Thomas Blight, *A Week at the Land's End*, 1861; this edition, Alison Hodge 1989.)

Outlook: South-west.
Tidal on the Lower Cliff and Helmet Buttress and on a few climbs to the east of Helmet Buttress. These areas are accessible for about three hours either side of low water but may be seriously affected by swell and rough sea at all states of the tide. **Non-tidal** on Green Face and on a number of climbs above the main area.
Coastguard Identity: Pordenack Point.
Environmental Issues: SSSI. There are good heathland and crevice plant communities here, and English Stonecrop is vulnerable. The upper cliffs have important lichen cover. The descent path to The Squeeze is showing signs of erosion, so tread lightly.

Pordenack Point has a special atmosphere: it lies within a kilometre of Land's End yet seems a world away from the latter's overt commercialism. The Lower Cliff faces south-west and catches a great deal of sunshine, often being bone dry even in winter. There is a good mix of grades on mainly excellent rock but with occasional looseness in the cracks and chimneys.

Approach. Pordenack is the first major headland south of Land's End. From Land's End, follow the coast path to the south-east along the edge of the cliffs for a kilometre to where a path leads out onto the crest of the headland.

Sloose Zawn
There are now several climbs in this isolated zawn about 100 metres north of the crest of Pordenack Point. The left-hand side of the zawn is best reached from the summit of Pordenack Point by dropping down north-west over steepening slopes. The zawn is steep-sided, loose in places, and often wet. Please form an orderly queue to repeat these routes.

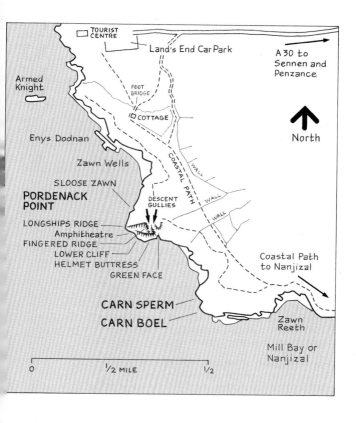

On the Loose   20 metres   Severe 4a †   (1993)
Start at low tide on the northern side of the zawn. Traverse rightwards into
the zawn and follow a long corner to the top.

Loose Feelings   25 metres   Hard Severe 4b †   (1983)
Follow the previous climb to the base of the corner. Climb the
right-slanting crack in its right wall to a short arête, and make strenuous
moves to finish.

To reach the right-hand side of the zawn from Pordenack, descend to the north-west and climb down to the south side of the zawn. Traverse in along ledges just above the sea at mid to low tide. This is dangerous in heavy seas. The routes are approached from the right. From the base of the descent route, follow narrow ledges above high tide level to a flat ledge 'at the end of all things' below a wide crack.

Through the Looking-Glass   30 metres   Very Difficult †   (1993)
1 18m. Climb the slab on the left-hand side of the buttress and then follow cracks and ledges to a larger ledge.
2 12m. Climb the wall on the left and step around the arête to reach a corner. Climb this to the top.

Smear on Sight   30 metres   E4 5c †   (1993)
1 18m. 5c. Climb the blunt arête on the right and smear up the steep slab on crystals. Continue up horizontal faults to a good ledge.
2 12m. Climb the wall left of the belay, then a crack to the top.

Step on a Cloud   30 metres   E3 5c †   (1993)
Start below the buttress a couple of metres right of the ledge at the base of the previous two climbs. Climb up ledges to a crack; follow this and a shallow groove to a roof. Traverse left onto the face around the arête before climbing slightly right to a fault and then straight up to the top.

Empty City   27 metres   E1 5b †   (1993)
In the centre of the zawn are square ledges. Start below the crack on the left-hand side of the large buttress in the centre of the zawn. Climb the crack to its top. Traverse left along a fault and climb up to a small ledge. Climb left onto a bulge and straight up a steep slab to a large ledge. An abseil descent is recommended to avoid an unstable finish.

Eye of the Owl   27 metres   Hard Very Severe 5a †   (1993)
Start as for the previous route and climb ledges just right of the arête to a small ledge and shallow corner. Climb the wall on the left up horizontal faults to a narrow ledge. Move up to the large ledge of the previous route. Abseil descent recommended to avoid an unstable finish. This line is very similar to **Star Turn** (E3 5c † 1993).

Main Area

From the arrival point at the neck of the headland, a broad grassy gully runs down to the left (facing out). The square-cut lichenous Green Face is on the upper left-hand side of this gully and *Helmet Ridge* is on its right-hand side. The gully is used for access to the Green Face climbs, *Gig in the Sky*, and a handful of routes to the east of the main climbing area.

From the seaward crest of the headland, two substantial ridges descend towards the sea. The ridge on the right is Longships Ridge; the pinnacled ridge to its left is Fingered Ridge. There are easy scrambles and some more distinctive lines on an open area of rock, The Amphitheatre, which lies well above the sea between the arms of Longships Ridge and Fingered Ridge. The main climbing area, the Lower Cliff, lies below Fingered Ridge at sea-level. East of Lower Cliff lies Helmet Buttress.

Descent for Longships Ridge, The Amphitheatre, Lower Cliff, and Helmet Buttress. All these areas are reached from the seaward crest of the headland by descending a well-worn path down the rock-studded grassy gully lying to the east of Fingered Ridge. (This gully should not be confused with the broad grassy gully leading down from the neck of the headland to the Green Face area.) Where the descent gully opens out before steepening about 30 metres above the sea, there is a flat-topped pinnacle on the right. This is The Tower, below which lies the Lower Cliff. Between the base of Fingered Ridge and The Tower is a narrow cleft, The Squeeze, which leads rightwards onto the open-faced Amphitheatre. The natural continuation of The Squeeze is a deep decomposing faultline, The Trough, which slices down the cliff to the sea-level nose of Longships Ridge and gives access to the Lower Cliff and Helmet Buttress.

Longships Ridge

The following routes are on the east face of the sea-level nose of Longships Ridge. They are reached by descending The Trough to its base. The first few routes can be reached for two hours either side of low water but are affected by swell and rough sea.

Slagroom   15 metres   Severe 4a   (16.7.84)
Start at the steep corner 3 metres from the seaward arête of Longships Ridge. Climb the corner and the cracks above.

There are two cracklines on the tiered tower. There is still some doubt which of the two was climbed as *The Harp*.

Loco Parentis   15 metres   E1 5b   (23.6.96)
Fine but short-lived. Climb the thin (left-hand) crackline on the tower and finish up a flake on the final block.

The Harp   15 metres   Very Severe 5a   (16.7.84)
The wider (right-hand) crackline.

Chopper Chimney   18 metres   Very Difficult   (10.77)
The deep chimney just left of the wide decomposing vein that rises from the base of The Trough. (This vein can be used with care as a rather loose descent line.)

PORDENACK POINT

LONGSHIPS RIDGE AND UPPER CLIFF

1	Slagroom	S
2	Loco Parentis	E1
3	Chopper Chimney	VD
4	Lesser Known Tunisians	S
5	One Inch Rock	S

23	Bubble Wall	E5
24	Ruby Nails	E3
25	Rubber Neck	E3
26	Sian	VS
27	Love Drives Me Crazy	VS
28	Depechez Vous	VS
29	Helmet Ridge Direct	VS

THE LOWER CLIFF

8	Economist's Climb	VD
9	A Pocket Full of Quartz	HVS
10	Nut Route	S
11	Swiss Route	HS
12	Zeke's Route	HS
13	King Crab Crack	VS
14	Stone Boom	E2
15	Biceps Wall	VS
16	Muscle Chimney	HS
17	Immaculate Arete	E4
18	" " direct start	E4
19	Cain	E3
20	Nothing Much	HVS
21	Friends	VS
22	Wrist Climb	VD

HELMET RIDGE

30	Gig In The Sky	E2

THE GREEN FACE

31	The Green Face	S
32	Gringo	VS
33	Mexican Pete	VS
34	Dago	VS

THE AMPHITHEATRE

LONGSHIPS RIDGE

THE TROU

LANDS END

DON SARGEANT — 1991

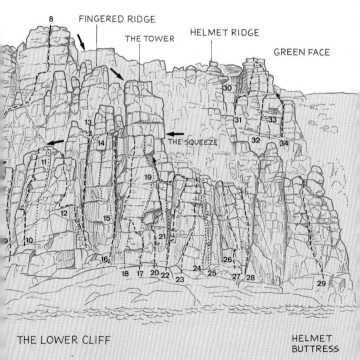

FINGERED RIDGE

THE TOWER

HELMET RIDGE

GREEN FACE

8

13

14

THE SQUEEZE

30

31   33

32   34

11

12

15

19

10

16

21

18 17 20 22

23

24

25

26

27 28

29

THE LOWER CLIFF

HELMET BUTTRESS

The Amphitheatre

The walls above the line of The Trough have been scrambled over for many years. The following routes are the most definitive and may have been climbed in the past though left unrecorded. The starts are non-tidal, although they may be affected by very heavy seas.

On the left-hand side of The Amphitheatre is an obvious sentry-box one third of the way up the cliff.

Little Trapeze   10 metres   Very Severe 5a   (1979)
Enter the sentry-box from the right and exit left at the roof. Finish up a short corner.

Little Trapeze Right-hand   10 metres   Very Difficult   (1979)
Enter the sentry-box from the right and exit right at the roof to finish up a thin crack.

To the right is a squat flat-topped pillar standing below easier terrain.

Exit Climb   12 metres   Difficult   (1979)
Climb the black crack on the left side of the pillar and continue easily.

Blood on the Rocks   14 metres   Very Severe 5a   (9.8.85)
Climb the finger-crack in the right-hand side of the pillar and continue up the easy corner on the right.

Just to the right is a taller, tapered pillar of rock.

Halfway House   14 metres   Hard Severe 4b   (1979)
Climb a thin zig zag crack and then the left-hand side of the upper tower.

Full House   16 metres   Severe 4a   (1979)
The wider central crack is followed by the right-hand side of the upper face.

The face directly above the lower part of The Trough is topped by a jutting block cut by a distinctive red vein.

Lesser Known Tunisians   18 metres   Severe 4b   (10.77)
This pitch takes a line that starts below and to the left of the jutting block. Start opposite a reddish wall seamed with cracks. The wall is gained by a cheeky step across The Trough. Continue up corners passing to the left of the jutting block to finish.
Variation Hard Severe 4c. Traverse to the right beneath the jutting block and climb the crack that splits its front face.

Big Ned 18 metres Very Difficult (1979)
High in the grade. Start as for the previous route but trend right to climb
the hanging corner on the right-hand side of the block overhang.

One Inch Rock 20 metres Severe 4a (10.9.84)
Climb the chunky red and black vein/groove that starts below and to the
right of the jutting block. Continue up a flake groove and a thin crack on
the right.

Exact details are not available for **Teetotal** (25 metres Severe 4a 1979),
which takes the rib to the right of the red and black vein.

Whisky 45 metres Very Difficult (c.1940s)
One of the first climbs recorded on Pordenack and a route that is quite
tricky for the grade. Start from a square-cut ledge 3 metres up The Trough
from the red and black vein. Climb a V-shaped groove to a ledge.
Continue up the grooves above; then take a devious line, trending
gradually rightwards towards the steep whitish wall on the skyline. Climb
the groove in the white wall on good holds to the top.

To the right the easy-angled rock can be climbed anywhere at a reasonable
standard.

The following routes lie on The Tower, the flat-topped pinnacle at the
entrance to The Squeeze and at the base of Fingered Ridge.

Mr Married Goes for a Hike 16 metres Hard Very Severe (5a 8.85)
Climb the attractive crack on the east side of The Tower.

Tower Direct 14 metres Hard Severe 4b (26.11.80)
Start just right of *Mr Married…*, below an open lichenous groove. Climb
the open groove for 4 metres to an overlap and then move right below the
overlap to finish up a wide crack.

Twist Again Like Moira Did Last Summer

14 metres Hard Very Severe 5a (16.8.85)
Start just left of a jammed boulder and climb the cracks and small roof
right of *Tower Direct*.

The Lower Cliff
This is the main climbing area on Pordenack Point. The cliff runs to the east
from below The Trough and is composed of a series of friable cracklines with
some splendid rock between them. At the left side of the face (facing in) and
directly below the top section of The Trough is a distinctive red seam running
up a steep slab; this is the first pitch of *Economist's Climb*. Right of this, the
central part of the cliff is recessed. Beyond the recessed area, a handsome
buttress of clean rock juts out. *Immaculate Arête* follows the left edge of the

buttress and *Cain* takes the striking crackline in its upper seaward face. Past the buttress the cliff falls away into the reddish break of *Wrist Climb* and beyond this are lesser rocks.

★Economist's Climb   62 metres   Very Difficult   (c.1940s)
This long and entertaining route follows the red seam running up the steep slab on the extreme left of the Lower Cliff. It crosses The Trough and finishes up the more broken face above.
1 18m. Climb the vein past a ledge on the left, move right, and continue up the vein to The Trough.
2 18m. Step across The Trough and follow the left-hand of two grooves; then climb a short red wall on the right.
3 16m. Continue easily over rounded blocks, bearing right to the foot of a steep whitish wall.
4 10m. Climb the groove in the white wall on good holds to the top. Quite tricky.

Before the next buttress are three rather friable routes.

Racing Line   18 metres   E6 6b   (2.7.95)
The steep slab has a crack which eventually fades out. Climb the crack and the slab above: crunchy and exciting.

A Pocket Full of Crystals   18 metres   E3 5b   (9.82)
The crumbly groove to the right, again on poor rock.

A Pocket Full of Quartz   18 metres   Hard Very Severe 4c (26.7.85)
Climb the initial groove of ...*Crystals* before breaking right and climbing the corner to The Trough.

Beyond here, the cliff turns around a blunt arête and begins to improve in quality. The next routes start just around to the right from a step-up ledge with a V-shaped wedge sliced out of it.

Hiroshima Mon Amour   22 metres   Hard Very Severe 5b (9.82)
Climb the blunt arête on the left utilising a thin crack which starts at half height on its left wall.

Little Cracker   20 metres   Severe 4a   (1980)
Start below a ragged crack 2 metres right of the arête. After a delicate start the route steps left and follows the nicely positioned arête throughout.

Nut Route   20 metres   Severe 4a   (c.1940s)
This also starts below the ragged crack 2 metres right of the arête. After a delicate start, follow the crack to a comfortable ledge on the arête, which is gained by an awkward move left. Climb into a niche on the right and then follow the crack direct.

Swiss Route   36 metres   Hard Severe   (1956/6.73)
Start below the thin decomposing vein to the right of *Nut Route*.
1 18m. 4a. Care is required with friable rock so this pitch is not really to
be recommended. Climb the vein to a belay in The Trough.
2 18m. 4b. Go up to the foot of the wall above the belay. Climb the
hairline crack on the left and bridge up an open groove on the left to finish.
Variation
2a Towerful 14 metres Very Severe 4c (1980). Finish up the tower on
the left.

★Vietnamerica   20 metres   E1 5b   (22.7.82)
Fine, open climbing following the thin line of cracks that twists steeply back
and forth up the wall above the right end of the starting-ledge. Gain the
crackline by a move right, and then continue past the narrow end of a big
ledge on the right (stance of *Zeke's Route*) to a short finishing-groove.

About 6 metres right of the previous routes is a clean-cut corner that drops 3
metres down to sea-level ledges below a steep buttress. The buttress is
flanked on either side by chimneys. The left-hand chimney is *King Crab
Crack*, whilst the right-hand one is *Muscle Chimney*.

★★Zeke's Route   20 metres   Hard Severe 4b   (4.7.55)
An early line of some character following the wall on the left of the deep
corner of *King Crab Crack*. Start below the corner and climb it for 12
metres. Make a long step left to a groove, which leads to a ledge. Move
up to a flake and gain a fine ledge on the left (belay possible). From the
right of the ledge, climb the steep wall and then make an awkward move
into a niche. Move left and follow the arête to the top.

King Crab Crack   20 metres   Very Severe 4c   (8.61)
This takes the prominent chimney to the right of *Zeke's Route*. The rock is
friable, particularly near the top. Climb the corner to gain the crack. Follow
this to a good stance (belay possible). Climb a steep corner to the top.

★★Stone Boom   30 metres   E2   (16.3.80)
[Photos: reverse frontispiece and p.32b.] A devious outing with two excellent
contrasting pitches involving a strenuous and airy hand-traverse and a
technical groove. Start as for *King Crab Crack*.
1 18m. 5b. Climb up to the left of *King Crab Crack* until level with a
horizontal fault running across the buttress on the right. Traverse along the
fault to the arête. Go around the arête to a ledge and then climb up and
back left to another ledge.
2 12m. 5c. Climb the open groove (small wires) above to the roof. Move
right and then finish direct.
Variations
★1a Telegraph Road 16 metres E3 6a (1983). [Photo p.32a.] Climb
the arête below the traverse of *Stone Boom* passing a small overhang
(peg) to reach the belay at the end of pitch 1 of the parent route.

2a Cable Highway E4 6b † (8.98). From the belay of the parent route, 'Climb the left side to swing around right to finish up the thin crack shared partly with *Stone Boom*'. No other details are available.

Biceps Wall   28 metres   Very Severe 5a   (9.61)
A more open variation to the rather crusty *Muscle Chimney*, which lies on the right of the *Stone Boom* buttress. Climb the initial corner of *Muscle Chimney* over good ledges to reach a small pillar at 10 metres. Move left onto the wall and climb steeply by interesting mantelshelf moves to a large ledge on the left (belay possible). Climb diagonally right to regain the chimney, and finish up this.

Muscle Chimney   25 metres   Hard Severe 4b   (1951)
Strenuous and crunchy. Follow the corner onto the small pillar at 10 metres; then continue by some tough chimneying to easier ground near the top.

★Sea Fury   25 metres   Hard Very Severe 5b   (22.8.55)
Powerful climbing up the wide, crooked crackline to the right of *Muscle Chimney*. Follow the crack to a niche below a small roof, which is climbed strenuously to a ledge. Easy climbing now leads to the top.

★★★Immaculate Arête   35 metres   E4   (10.1.81)
A stylish and striking climb on excellent rock taking the face of the blunt seaward arête right of *Sea Fury*. Start 12 metres right of the arête on a stepped ledge and directly below the right-hand end of a slim overhang.
1 30m. 6a. Step over a small trench and then climb to the overhang. Pull over this into a left-trending crack and follow this to its end. Make a long move left onto the arête to reach a good hold; then pull up to a horizontal break. Climb onto the ledges on the left and then move back onto the arête, which is followed steeply to a good ledge and belays.
2 5m. 4b. Climb the thin, steep crack right of the corner.
Direct Start 6a (24.5.87). Better and safer than the parent route. Start below the roof on the arête. Move up to the roof and go over it into a crack (peg). This crack leads to a junction with the parent route.

New Editions   30 metres   E4 6b   (1989)
The amalgamation of earlier variations to *Cain* with a more recent middle section provides an arduous and devious way up the buttress. Start just right of *Immaculate Arête*, and climb to the obvious thin crack, which is followed to join *Cain* at the end of its traverse. Climb rightwards to reverse the traverse and take the overhanging corner to a point close to the end of the bubbly crack. Continue straight up the wall and climb the prominent prow above via the roof-crack to reach a good hold over the lip. Pull up onto the right side of the prow to finish.

★★Cain   30 metres   E3 6a   (1978)
A fine, sustained and strenuous route. Its main feature is the diagonal bubbly crack that splits the upper wall of the steep buttress between *Immaculate Arête* and the reddish break of *Wrist Climb*. Start at a steep

crack in a quartz-studded wall below and to the right of the mid-height overhang. Climb the crack for 6 metres; then traverse left below a recess in the overhang to obvious holds at the overhang's left end. Move up to the next overhang and pull strenuously over into the crack. Follow this rapidly until it eases; then climb the wall on its left on good holds. Finish by the thin crack just left of the summit nose.

★Nothing Much 31 metres   Hard Very Severe 5a   (8.6.65)
Start this tough little route as for *Cain*, below and right of the mid-height overhang, at a steep crack in a quartz-studded wall.
1 25m. 5a. Climb the crack; then hand-jam left into the recess in the overhang, from where hard moves are made up and rightwards to a sloping ledge. Take the obvious groove to below the large overhang on the traverse of *Wrist Climb*. Move easily left to a stance and belay.
2 6m. Finish up the short layback crack on the right. This can be quite difficult when wet.
Variation 16m. Very Severe 4c (1.71). From the junction with *Wrist Climb*, take the overhanging wall on the right to make an interesting traverse move followed by strenuous climbing to a good ledge. Continue easily to the top.

★Friends 38 metres   Very Severe   (13.2.81/24.5.81)
A pleasant climb with good protection. Start at the conspicuous reddish-coloured chimney/break to the right of the previous routes.
1 20m. 5a. Climb the break to the roof and pull boldly around this leftwards to gain a crack. Continue up the crack to another small roof. Go over this to reach a flake, which leads to a stance in a narrow gully.
2 18m. 4c. Step up onto a large block; then climb directly up the steep wall to a ledge. Step left and continue to the top of the pinnacle.

★Wrist Climb 38 metres   Very Difficult   (22.5.55)
A worthwhile route that offers interesting and airy climbing on the exposed traverse of the second pitch. Start at the foot of the conspicuous reddish-coloured chimney/break.
1 20m. Climb the chimney to the overhang; then make a short traverse right. Continue up a groove to a stance on top of a large block on the left.
2 12m. Traverse left across the gully and step down; move left under the nose on good holds, and with considerable exposure, to reach a block belay in the corner.
3 6m. Finish up the short layback crack on the right. Quite difficult, especially when wet.

☆Bubble Wall 22 metres   E5 6b †   (15.5.87)
A tough, sustained pitch tackling the steep wall to the right of the chimney/break of *Wrist Climb*. Start 12 metres right of *Wrist Climb*, below a steep groove in the middle of the wall. Climb the groove and then gain the 'bubbly' faultline above. Follow this onto the upper wall and finish direct. The Direct Start is just to the right (E6 6c † 1987).

Pop!   22 metres   E7 6c †   (1987)
The shallow depression in the wall to the right leads to a thin seam, which
is followed to ledges. Fierce and poorly protected.

To the right are a pair of parallel cracks on the right-hand side of the buttress
and to the left of a deep chimney.

★Ruby Nails   20 metres   E3 5c   (29.2.88)
Climb the left-hand crack and then the thinner continuation crack to reach
a ledge. Finish up the easier wall above.

Rubber Neck   20 metres   E3 5c   (29.2.88)
Start below the next crack just right of *Ruby Nails*. Climb the wall just right
of the crack to a large hold; then gain the crack and follow it to a ledge.
Finish up the easier wall above.

From here, the cliff falls away into a deep chimney and then a small buttress
flanked on its right by a broken corner containing a couple of huge stacked
blocks. Right of the corner is a narrow buttress which gives the following
routes.

Siân   20 metres   Very Severe 4c   (22.10.72)
Start right of the blocks, below a thin hanging nose at 12 metres. Make a
difficult move up to a ledge on the right, climb delicately up the slabby
groove, and pass to the right of the thin nose. Above this follow the
right-hand crack to the top.

The next two climbs tackle the front of the buttress, starting up parallel
cracks.

Love Drives Me Crazy   20 metres   Very Severe 4c   (26.7.85)
Start at a lower level and climb the left-hand crack in the rounded buttress
to a break. Move left and follow the continuation cracks via a recess to the
cliff-top.

Dépêchez-Vous   20 metres   Very Severe 5a   (9.8.85)
Climb the cracks and folds in the arête on the right of the buttress to reach
easier ground.

Helmet Buttress

Beyond the *Siân* buttress, there is a broken depression flanked on its right by the
attractive Helmet Buttress, which leads up to *Helmet Ridge* and the upper slopes
of Pordenack Point. The climbs here tend to be variations on the central theme
of the steep and apparently chaotic Helmet Buttress, although they are all
enjoyable. Most of the routes are started by stepping across a deep cleft from
the large detached ledge at the base of the buttress to reach ledges and belays.

★On the Loose 22 metres Very Severe 4c (11.5.87)
The rock is better than you might think. Start below the left arête of the buttress. Climb up and left to the base of the rightward-slanting crack of *Veedy*. Continue up the arête past a square ledge to a roof. Move right to another ledge; then move up to climb the arête, finishing up a crack.

★Veedy 22 metres Very Severe 4c (1966)
Start as for the previous climb and follow the right-slanting crack to join a deeper crack (*Helmet Ridge Direct*), which leads to the top.

★Helmet Ridge Direct 20 metres Very Severe 4b (11.54)
Climb the chunky central crack with jutting blocks directly above the belay spike to a small roof. Turn the roof on the right and then move steeply back left above the roof by a long step to reach a niche. Follow the wide crack above to the top.

Saruman 20 metres Hard Severe 4b (5.3.67)
From the belay ledges, start up *Helmet Ridge Direct* until it is possible to traverse right into a small recess. Climb a short overhanging groove; then move left to a ledge. Continue over a bulge to finish more easily.

Gandalf 25 metres Severe 4a (5.3.67)
Climb the deep crack on the right into a small recess and then continue awkwardly around the rib on the left. Climb the steep groove, moving left to finish.

Helmet Ridge gives a pleasant direct climb in its upper reaches (34 metres Difficult). It can be used as an extension to the routes on Helmet Buttress or can be reached independently from the approach gully that leads down to The Squeeze.

The Green Face Area
The next cluster of climbs are reached by going down the broad grassy gully that drops down to the left (facing out) from the neck of the headland. The Green Face is on the top left-hand side of the gully (facing out). For *Gig in the Sky*, go down the grassy gully to where it opens out and then cross rightwards over grass and rock ledges to beneath the striking upper tower of *Helmet Ridge* with its remarkable perched blocks.

★Gig in the Sky 30 metres E2 (7.1.81)
A striking roof climb, well protected but ferociously strenuous. Start at the foot of a short steep wall about 15 metres below the roof.
1 8m. 5a. Climb the wall to a narrow ledge.
2 16m. 5c. Climb to a small roof; then move left and back right onto a short wall below the large roof. Climb to the crack in the roof and follow this on jams (large cams) to make strenuous moves onto the ledge above.
3 6m. Climb a crack and then scramble to the ridge.

Descent: The Green Face itself is reached by descending the broad grassy gully and then bearing left after 15 metres to reach a pleasant, seaward-facing grassy ledge with the Green Face buttress on its left (facing out). There are two lines (plus variations) on the immediate flanking wall of the buttress. Harder routes on the seaward face are reached by traversing along ledges that lead easily around to a substantial ledge below the face.

Mr Haggis   35 metres   Hard Severe 4b   (16.8.85)
A broken line above the grassy ledge. Start at the right-hand side of a wide blocky gully, directly below a bulbous overhang. Climb a crack and wall and then the left side of the overhang to finish.

To the left of *The Green Face* are two routes.

Ella-phant   15 metres   E1 5b †   (16.3.94)
Climb the left-hand side of the wall and capping overhang, where the holds are good but hard to find.

Who Ya Gonna Call   15 metres   E1 5b †   (3.94)
Climb the right-hand side of the wall and capping overhang.

Amigos   20 metres   E4 5c †   (1984)
'The bold wall on the east upper walls of The Green Face.'

★The Green Face   24 metres   Severe   (c.1940s)
A pleasant climb finishing up the exposed upper section of the seaward face. Start from the grassy ledge below the flanking wall of the buttress, at the foot of a deep chimney with a jammed block at its top.
1 10m. Climb the chimney and move right to a big ledge below a steep rippled wall. A harder variation takes the deep crack just right of the chimney.
2 14m. 4a. Traverse right from the ledge to climb a short gangway onto the pleasantly exposed seaward face. Climb this direct on widely spaced holds.
Variations
From the belay on the big ledge above pitch 1 there are three options, the first two of which reduce the overall standard to Very Difficult and Difficult respectively.
2a 16m. From the back of the ledge, traverse left and climb a corner to its top.
2b 10m. Climb the chimney behind the belay.
2c 10m. Climb the steep wall right of the chimney on sloping holds. Bold.

The following climbs start from the ledge below the seaward face.

Gringo   24 metres   Very Severe   (9.61)
A strenuous climb taking a direct line up the centre of the face. Start in the middle of the ledge, at an overhanging crack to the right of a distinctive brown streak.

1 12m. 4b. Climb the crack for a short distance; then use a good hold on the left to gain a ledge. Continue up the corner on the right to a big ledge on the right.

2 12m. 5a. Climb the steep crack just left of the edge. The first moves are quite hard and not easy to protect. Continue up the crack to the left to a junction with the top pitch of *The Green Face*.

★Mexican Pete   25 metres   Very Severe 4c   (2.74)
Gratifyingly powerful climbing. Start at a clean, brown-edged crack just right of *Gringo*. Climb the crack and then traverse left, crossing *Gringo*, to reach the base of an overhanging crack in the centre of the upper face. Climb the crack on encouraging holds to join *The Green Face* for the last couple of metres.

Bingo   25 metres   E2 5c †   (1990s)
Climb the wall and flake/crack up bulging rock to the right of the initial crack of *Mexican Pete*.

Dago   25 metres   Very Severe 5a   (1970s)
This takes a line up the right-hand flanking wall of the buttress. Start around to the right of the seaward face, below a steep crack. Climb the crack strenuously, moving left near its top to reach a large ledge. Climb the wall behind and finish up a groove.

There are a number of routes starting from sea-level directly below *The Green Face* buttress. They are best gained from the base of the big ledge below the seaward face of *The Green Face* buttress by working left (facing out) until a wide grassy gully is reached. Go down this gully to where it falls away; then move left and scramble down some unpleasant ground. Continue down left beneath a broken area of cliff to reach long narrow ledges below a steep 20-metre wall. Huge sea-washed boulders spill out from a decaying zawn to the right (facing in) of the wall. The area is tidal and may be wave-washed in heavy swell or rough seas.

Mister Fixit   24 metres   Hard Very Severe †   (12.9.87)
1 12m. 4a. Climb just left of a fault on the left side of the wall. At the top of the faultline, cross over to the right to a ledge in the bottom of a loose chimney.
2 12m. 5a. Climb the chimney for a short distance; then move left into a slanting crack that goes up to the left. Follow this to a ledge and finish up the arête above.

Water-Man   24 metres   Severe †   (12.9.87)
1 12m. 4a. *Mister Fixit* pitch 1.
2 12m. 4a. Move right onto a ledge and climb steep slabs to the top.

Sandman   24 metres   E3 5c †   (12.9.87)
Climb the wall just right of the fault to flaky ledges below a steep section. Make a hard move to reach good holds, which lead to ledges above.

Solar Explorer   25 metres   E7 6b †   (1990s)
Climb the overhanging wall right of *Sandman*, finishing up a steep flake crack.

A Job for Life   25 metres   E1 5b †   (29.5.87)
There is a pillar on the left wall of the rotting zawn. Start below the left
arête of this. Climb the ledges on the left arête until the crack in the
headwall on the right can be climbed to the top.

A Question of Time   25 metres   E2 5c †   (29.5.87)
Start on the right side of the pillar below a thin crack. Climb the crack to a
small ledge and pull over the roof into a small groove on the right. Climb
this and the wall above to a ledge, before tackling the top wall on its right
to reach a crack coming in from the left. This leads to the top.

As one walks out to Pordenack Point there is a wide grassy cirque down on
the left, before the two gullies on the left are reached. On the right side of this
cirque is a pillar.

Beelzebub's Boobs   14 metres   E1 5b †   (1994)
The overhanging brown wall on the cirque side of the pinnacle.

To the east of the Pordenack area is an impressive stretch of cliff with fluted
'terra cotta' walls terminating at the rather loose Trevilley Zawn. A route
has been manufactured here (**Fragile Earth** E5 6b † 1989) using 4 bolts
(removed), 2 pegs (removed), and a number of glued holds. The idea has
not caught on.

Carn Boel Area (Granite)   OS Ref 349 239

*'Climb up ... and sit upon its lichen-embroidered head; no king was ever
enthroned as sumptuously as you will be...'*   (A G Folliott Stokes, 1909.)

Outlook: South-west from Carn Sperm; north-west from Carn Boel.
Tidal on some climbs on Carn Sperm. All climbs on the north-west face of
Carn Boel involve an initial traverse at lowish tide and in calm conditions.
Coastguard Identity: Carn Boel.

The Carn Sperm/Carn Boel area makes up the distinctive headland lying
just over a mile to the south-east of Land's End. The area offers some
excellent climbing, from amenable lower-grade pitches to tough upper
extremes.

Approach: From Land's End, take the coast path that runs south-east from
the car-park passing Pordenack Point on the way. A kilometre beyond

Pordenack Point, leave the path above a steep grassy slope that runs down to a saddle lying between two distinctive headlands separated by a deep cavernous zawn. Carn Boel is on the left of the zawn (facing out) with Carn Sperm on the right. The deep zawn between them is known as the Lion's Den, possibly from the 'lion's head' profile of Carn Boel as seen from the east. The north-west wall of Carn Boel, which rises from Lion's Den Zawn, holds some serious and committing routes, the striking seaward crackline of *The Immaculate Crack* being a leading feature. Carn Sperm offers routes of a gentler character.

Carn Sperm
There are four climbing areas on Carn Sperm. From left to right (facing in) these are; North-West Cliff, Sea-Level Cliff, Terrace Ramp, and Terrace Wall.

North-West Cliff
There is one route on the broken North-West Cliff. It is reached by descending slopes north-west of the top of the Carn Sperm headland and then continuing down a groove to sea-level. Ten metres to the right (facing in) is a V-shaped groove with a slab above. Low tide required.

Aquastat   25 metres   Very Difficult   (5.4.79)
1 16m. Climb easily up to the V-shaped groove and follow it to the slab. Make a rising traverse left to a large platform.
2 9m. Climb a crack at the back of the platform to another platform. Move right onto the steep wall and then finish direct.

Descend for all other climbs on Carn Sperm down its north-west side via short chimney-cracks and ledges, before traversing back east to The Terrace. This is the wide level area strewn with huge blocks that lies directly beneath Terrace Cliff. (*The Immaculate Crack* and the climbs on the west wall of Carn Boel can be seen across Lion's Den Zawn from the edge of The Terrace.)

The approach described above is safer than the usual approach, a loose descent down the earthy gully from the saddle that divides Carn Sperm from Carn Boel. This descent is being steadily eroded and its lower section lies above the vertical drop into Lion's Den Zawn. A rope can be preplaced to safeguard the descent and care is required especially if at all damp. Where the gully falls away, traverse around to the right (facing out) onto The Terrace.

Sea-Level Cliff
Descent: Follow the continuation line of The Terrace around blocks to the left (facing in) to where it narrows and finally ends just above a square-cut recess with an orange-coloured left wall. The short wall that drops down from here to the wide sloping platform at the base of Sea-Level Cliff can be down-climbed at Very Difficult standard or avoided by a short abseil.

The first two climbs lie to the left of the square-cut recess.

The Immaculate Runner   25 metres   Very Severe 4c   (1985)
A neat little pitch up the left edge of the wall starting from the lower end of the platform at low tide. Climb left; then continue up a cracked wall before moving back right in an exposed position to finish back on Terrace Ramp.

Launch   18 metres   Hard Very Severe 4c   (2.4.83)
Start 12 metres left of the recess. Mantelshelf onto a ledge at head height, or gain the ledge from the left. Move rightwards along a thin overhanging crack to the base of a hanging groove, which is gained and then followed to Terrace Ramp.

The Runner   20 metres   E2 5b †   (2.4.83)
Steep climbing up the left-hand wall of the recess. Start a metre or so in from the left arête of the recess. Climb the orange-coloured wall on good but well-spaced holds before moving up and slightly left to a small foot-ledge at 10 metres. Finish up the corner above.

Immaculate Conception   22 metres   E3 6a (1 pt aid) †   (3.4.83)
Care should be taken with the rock in places. Start below the left-hand corner of the recess. Climb the right wall and swing into the corner to reach two small incuts. Move up to a cam-slot at 6 metres and then continue into the niche above. Use a wire placed out to the right for aid to move right onto improving holds. Gain the break below a small roof; then move right and pull over the lip before moving left. Either follow the groove to the top, or traverse left and mantelshelf onto a ledge.

Journey to the Stones   22 metres   E5 6a †   (4.4.88)
There is a blunt arête above a small trench on the right-hand wall of the recess. Make difficult moves up the left side of the slabby wall to the left of the arête to reach a break. Continue up the right wall of the recess above to the top.

The short wall running to the right of the easy way down has been climbed at a number of points. The overhanging corner at its right end is a strenuous 5a.

Terrace Ramp

Descent: Follow the continuation line of The Terrace as for Sea-Level Cliff, and then continue up rocky steps to reach the top of another broad ramp. This ramp slopes steeply down to the sea and is flanked by a wall on its right. There are two good climbs here. Half-way down the ramp is an obvious slab. This is the start of *Immaculate Groove*. The area can be awash at high tide and in heavy swell.

Sunburst Crack   20 metres   E5 6b   (1989)
The fiercely strenuous crack in the hanging wall left of the slab of *Immaculate Groove*.

★★Immaculate Groove 30 metres E1 (3.9.80)
[Photo p.64a.] A fine climb with an interesting first pitch that is harder than it looks. Start at the foot of the obvious slab.
1 18m. 5b. Make technical moves up the slab, using the crack on the left. The crack becomes steeper and widens higher up. Some strenuous jamming up and to the right leads to a ledge and belay.
2 12m. 4a. Traverse left to a groove and finish up this.

Terrace Cliff

This is the friendly, open-faced buttress rising directly from The Terrace. The main feature is a deep chimney/groove running up to a corner-crack at half height, the black slabby left wall of which is taken by *Bitter End*. *Longships Rib* is the obvious rib at the right edge of the buttress. *Kari* takes the diamond-shaped overhanging block high on the left edge of the main buttress.

Boulder Buttress 18 metres Severe (2.8.88)
Start below the large tower on the left side of Terrace Cliff. Climb a broken corner to a ledge; then traverse right below the roof to a good hold. Move up to a crack in the wall above and finish up this.

Blind Spring 20 metres Difficult (8.1.78)
Below the left end of the main buttress is a 5-metre broken cleft with a perched boulder at its top. Start from the grassy niche above this. Climb a short left-leaning ramp and then step up onto the lichenous slab. Climb the slab, trending from right to left, to finish up a short wall.

Wandering Worlds 38 metres Hard Severe (3.9.80)
Start 3 metres left of *Kari* at a short corner.
1 4m. Climb the corner to a ledge.
2 30m. 4b. Climb the wall and groove above to the right-hand end of the long ledge. Make a strenuous move up the steep corner on the right to another groove on the left. Climb this and the slab above to a large ledge.
3 4m. Finish up the wall above.

★Kari 40 metres Very Difficult (3.9.80)
An attractive climb, quite high in the grade. Start below a short wall about 6 metres left of the central chimney/groove of *Bitter End*.
1 4m. Climb the wall to a ledge.
2 18m. Climb the steeper wall on the left; then move right to a short groove, which is climbed to a long ledge. From the left-hand end of the ledge, make bold moves through the steep overhanging corner on good holds to follow a groove to a ledge.
3 14m. Climb the narrow slab and wall above to a ledge; awkward.
4 4m. The wall above leads to the top.

Four Directions   42 metres   Severe   (27.8.80)
A pleasant climb. Start at the foot of the chimney/groove of *Bitter End*.
1 6m. Climb the groove and then move left to a large ledge.
2 18m. 4b. Gain the groove above from the left by an awkward move to
gain a niche. Climb the back of the niche; then go left under the roof and
continue up flaky cracks in the arête to a narrow ledge.
3 14m. Take the wall and slab above to a large ledge.
4 4m. Finish up the wall.

★Bitter End   36 metres   Very Difficult   (16.5.59)
Another pleasant climb with a similar standing to *Four Directions*, taking
the black slabby wall of the central break. Start at the base of the
chimney/groove.
1 32m. Climb to the top of the chimney/groove and then follow the black
slab past an exposed narrow section to a ledge. Continue up the
vegetated groove to a wide ledge and thread belay.
2 4m. Climb the steep lichen-covered wall to the top.

Sweet and Sour   30 metres   Severe 4a   (4.74)
Start just right of the chimney/groove of *Bitter End*. Climb the wall and
short arête above to a ledge below wrinkled cracks in the upper wall.
Continue up the cracks in the steep wall for 10 metres to where easier
climbing leads to the top.

The Bitts   30 metres   Very Severe   (10.5.88)
Start below the broken wall just right of *Sweet and Sour*.
1 6m. Climb cracked grooves over small ledges to a bigger ledge below
the upper wall.
2 24m. 4c. Climb directly up the centre of the wall just right of *Sweet and
Sour*.

★Longships Ridge   30 metres   Difficult   (c.1960)
An attractive, well-positioned route up the ridge on the extreme right of
Terrace Wall. Climb a smooth, cracked slab and continue to an overhang,
which is passed on its right-hand side. Continue up the crest of the ridge
by pleasantly exposed climbing.

Carn Boel

Descent: Carn Boel's forbidding north-west wall is gained from the east
side of the headland by scrambling down ledges towards the sea. The
immediate area below the headland is ideal for bouldering, and there are
some short worthwhile pitches on the seaward face. For the lines on the
north-west wall, traverse around to the north. Climb the 6-metre chimney
formed by a large pinnacle; then traverse leftwards across a ledge onto the
face overlooking Lion's Den Zawn to a point above a steep groove. An
abseil can be made from here onto a sloping ledge for the start of *The
Immaculate Crack*. This position is unapproachable at high tide or when

there is swell or rough sea. A committing abseil descent can also be made to the chimney-crack belay at the end of the shared first pitch of the following climbs.

Total Eclipse (50 metres E5 5b,6b,5c † 30.8.86), which used several bolts, followed the first pitch of *Waiting for the Sun* and then traversed out leftwards and up to a cluster of bolts. From here, it climbed directly up the wall past thread runners. The bolts have been removed; the grade is for the climb's former state.

☆☆**Waiting for the Sun**   53 metres   E4 †   (5.8.86)
Start from a boulder in the bottom of the zawn at low tide, or from the first belay in the chimney/crack. Beware: the peg may have been removed.
1 10m. 5b. Climb the shallow leaning groove to gain a ledge to the left of *The Immaculate Crack*. Belay higher up in the chimney/crack.
2 28m. 6b. Climb the recess (peg) and then a thin crack over a roof to cracks and a ledge above.
3 15m. 5b. Continue up the wall to the left of the leaning corner.

☆☆**A Leap in the Dark**   56 metres   E4 †   (12.6.86)
Beware, the two peg runners may be missing.
1 10m. 5b. *Waiting for the Sun* pitch 1.
2 28m. 6a. Climb the chimney for a short way; then step across into the thin crack on the left. Follow this to a wider steep crack on the left. Climb the steep crack straight up to the roof. Pull over this and climb cracks leading up leftwards to a ledge on a perched block.
3 18m. 5b. Climb around the arête on the right; then continue up the wall to the top.

☆**Walking on the Light Side**   50 metres   E5 †   (24.7.87)
Beware, the three peg runners on pitch 2 may be missing.
1 10m. 5b. *Waiting for the Sun* pitch 1.
2 40m. 6b. Climb the chimney for a short way; then step across into the thin crack on the left. Follow this to a wider steep crack on the left. Climb the steep crack straight up to the roof. Pull over this onto the wall above; then move right to the bottom of a steep crack. Follow this to where it peters out, trend right, and climb the continuation crack to gain a wide fault. Finish direct.

★**The Immaculate Crack**   34 metres   E3   (3.9.80)
An excellent strenuous crack climb following the fissure up the left side of the partially detached pillar at the seaward edge of the wall. Lowish tide and quiet seas advised.
1 30m. 5c. From the sloping ledge, climb the crack. Where it ends, move left and climb the arête to ledges.
2 4m. Step across the gap on the right to finish on the large ledge.

☆**Spirit of Summer**   35 metres   E6 6c †   (1990)
The thin, and ever thinning, seam directly above the start of *The
Immaculate Crack* gives a pitch of great difficulty and considerable
boldness.

Adios Kernow   35 metres   E4 6a   (1990)
The continuous abrasive crack that splits the right-hand side of the face is
approached from the right and is climbed passing a good ledge just below
half height.

★**Blood, Sweat, and Fears**   30 metres   E1 5b   (22.6.96)
Good climbing with fine positions. Start on the sloping ledge on the right
side of the face (to the left of *The Immaculate Grovel*) and climb a short
jamming crack to a good ledge. Follow diagonal flakes all the way out to
the left arête and finish up this.

The Immaculate Grovel   27 metres   Very Severe 4b   (7.81)
An awful route which is best climbed with tongue firmly in cheek. It takes
the chimney behind *The Immaculate Crack* pinnacle, starting at the
seaward side and squirming up the outer edge of the huge flake. It is also
possible to walk up the ramp at the back of the chimney and finish by
'grovelling up the last 6 metres of the flake'.

There are two recorded routes on the seaward face.

Fiddler   34 metres   Very Severe   (1.8.86)
Start just left of the edge of the buttress where it goes into the zawn.
1 9m. 4a. Climb the sloping ramp rightwards to a ledge.
2 25m. 4c. Climb the left arête; then cross to the wall on the left.
Continue to ledges and finish up the slab.

His Nibs   30 metres   Very Severe 4b   (1.8.86)
Climb the obvious central chimney to a big jammed block.

The impressive summit block of Carn Boel is split by a wide cave/cleft. To the
right of this, the cracks in the wall have been climbed with pitons, some of
which remain, rusting *in situ*. The cracks have been free-climbed by a
number of ascensionists using a variety of methods. They are strenuous and
hard and have remained unrecorded in detail.

Carn Boel Cleft   25 metres   Very Difficult
An eccentric little climbing/caving pitch.
1 10m. Climb short walls and cracks into the cave/cleft.
2 15m. Walk into the back of the cave to where it turns sharply right.
Climb by chimneying direct to exit through a hole.

Nanjizel Bay: Zawn Pyg
OS Ref 356 235

There are two short climbs on loose rock at the eastern end of Nanjizel Bay. A stream drains onto the beach where the cliff turns to the south. A striking and obvious feature on the cliff is a narrow arch known as 'The Song of the Sea'. On the south side of the point formed by the arch, there is a corner above a small zawn. The obvious crack on the southern corner above the zawn gives **The Pyg Track** (10 metres Very Difficult † 1962). A longer route lies up the corner 4 metres to the right of *The Pyg Track*.

Pygmalion   15 metres   Very Severe †   (11.6.62)

A route that features decaying rock.

1 6m. Climb the left side of the pillar to a ledge.

2 9m. 4c. Step right from the top of the pillar and climb the steep wall on small, crunchy holds. 'Not bloody likely!' according to the 1966 guidebook.

Carn Lês Boel Area (Granite)

Outlook: Carn Lês Boel promontory – all points; Mild and Bitter Buttress, Bosistow Wall, and Paradise Wall – south; Bosistow Zawn – south-east.

Tidal around the base of Carn Lês Boel Promontory. **Tidal** at the base of the starting-slab of Mild and Bitter Buttress, but this can be gained above the tide-line; affected by heavy swell and rough sea at all states of the tide. Bosistow Wall and Paradise Wall are **non-tidal** but swell and heavy seas affect the lower sections of routes. **Tidal** in Bosistow Zawn with access possible for only about two hours either side of low water and less during neap-tides; approach is **not advised** in conditions of swell and rough seas.

Coastguard Identity: Carn Lês Boel (all sections).

Environmental Issues: SSSI. The main cliff (particularly Bosistow Island) is a breeding area for Fulmar, Herring Gull, and Shag. The adjacent caves are breeding sites for Grey Seals, which are especially vulnerable in September and October. Although not formally restricted, the area is best avoided during the nesting season for your own safety. Take care where you tread, avoiding Sea Aster and English Stonecrop in particular.

This is a complex but fascinating area of cliffs, promontories, and zawns. At its heart lies the major venue of Paradise Wall offering sea-cliff climbing at its most spectacular.

Approach: Carn Lês Boel lies about midway between Land's End and Porthgwarra. It can be approached along the coast path from either by a walk of about 2 kilometres. There is also a pedestrian right-of-way down a private lane from the B3315 at Polgigga crossroads where the side road to Porthgwarra branches off. This is the most direct route, but there is no vehicular access. The best approach is to walk westwards from Porthgwarra along the coast path to skirt the rim of the wide-mouthed Pendower Coves, which lie beyond Carn Barra.

Carn Lês Boel is the high headland at the north-west end of the coves. It is made up of several dramatic features, the most impressive being on the Pendower Coves side where Paradise Wall hides behind the massive rock pinnacle of Bosistow Island. East of here lies the hidden Bosistow Zawn. A hundred metres to the east of Bosistow Zawn is the vast Pendower Cavern, and beyond lies the long boulder beach of Pendower Coves. The main features described are obvious from the Porthgwarra approach, although Bosistow Island looks like part of the mainland at first.

The south side of Carn Lês Boel contains the magnificent area of cliff lying opposite Bosistow Island. It offers committing and in many cases fiercely technical routes, especially on Paradise Wall, where there are no routes below E2. One slight drawback is the presence of nesting sea-birds in the summer with a consequent liberal pile-up of bird-lime on and below some of the ledges. However, the open-faced Mild and Bitter Buttress, which lies on the seaward end of the headland's south flank, offers pleasant climbing at more reasonable standards.

Descent for Carn Lês Boel Promontory, Mild and Bitter Buttress, Bosistow Wall, and Paradise Wall is from the crest of the headland. From the coast path, walk out along the initially broad crest of the headland for 50 metres to reach a point just before it becomes narrow and rocky.

Carn Lês Boel Promontory
OS Ref 356 233

'A popular playground of the ancients...'
(V N Stevenson: Cornwall Volume 2, 1966.)

On the north side of Carn Lês Boel a thin, rocky promontory, varying in height from 25 to 30 metres, juts out into the sea. It is made up of two square-cut seaward blocks with three higher pinnacles leading inland to a boulder neck. There are steep walls seamed with cracks and chimneys on the north and south sides. The climbing is variable and involves optional traverses that link up with short climbs on the side-walls near the seaward end of the promontory. A girdle of the promontory is possible and a traverse of the crest gives **Pinnacle Traverse** (60 metres Difficult 1920).

The north side of the Promontory is gained by scrambling down grassy slopes and ledges to the right (facing out) of the landward neck of the Promontory. From here, ledges lead out to a short easy chimney of 6 metres separating the two square-cut blocks at the Pinnacle's seaward end. This is the easy **Northside Chimney** (1920), which is flanked on its right (facing in) by **North Wall Climb** (10 metres Severe 12.9.38).

Stone Boom (E2), Pordenack Point
Climbers: Jody Vallance and Clive Davis   Photo: David Simmonite

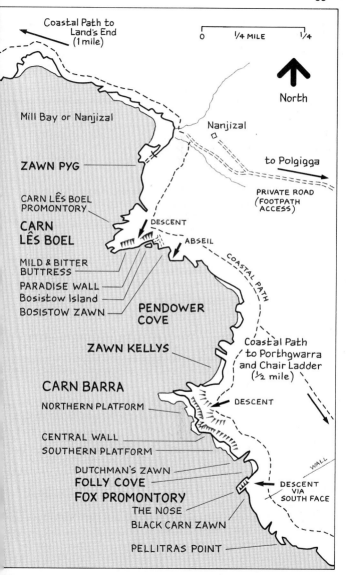

Coastal Path to
Land's End
(1 mile)

0   1/4 MILE   1/4

North

Mill Bay or Nanjizal

Nanjizal

to Polgigga

PRIVATE ROAD
(FOOTPATH
ACCESS)

ZAWN PYG

CARN LÊS BOEL
PROMONTORY

CARN
LÊS BOEL

DESCENT

ABSEIL

COASTAL PATH

MILD & BITTER
BUTTRESS

PARADISE WALL

Bosistow Island

BOSISTOW ZAWN

PENDOWER
COVE

ZAWN KELLYS

Coastal Path
to Porthgwarra
and Chair Ladder
(1/2 mile)

CARN BARRA

NORTHERN PLATFORM

DESCENT

CENTRAL WALL

SOUTHERN PLATFORM

DUTCHMAN'S ZAWN

FOLLY COVE

FOX PROMONTORY

THE NOSE

BLACK CARN ZAWN

PELLITRAS POINT

WALL

DESCENT
VIA
SOUTH FACE

On the south side of the Promontory there are several more substantial pitches. The face is best reached by **Southside Traverse** (Difficult 1920), which leads down ledges from the landward neck of the Promontory to sea-level ledges. These lead to a slab, followed by an awkward step across a rift to the foot of **Southside Chimney** (10 metres Moderate 1920).

Sunshine Slab (12 metres E1 5b 10.9.88) starts below the short overhanging wall just left of the crack between the inner seaward block and the first of the three pinnacles which crown the Promontory. It demands strenuous moves up the overhanging wall to gain a slab, which is climbed to the top.
Southside Crack (12 metres Difficult 1939) is the crack between the inner seaward block and the first of the three pinnacles. A more substantial and quite testing pitch takes the 'rib and furrow' wall right of *Southside Crack*.

The Grooves   25 metres   Very Severe 4c   (16.9.52)
Start at the base of *Southside Crack*. Climb the slab diagonally to the right below an overhang, and then continue to the top up a series of fluted grooves; the final section is quite thin.
Direct Start Climb up the main groove and to the right of the overhang (1.6.53).

Chockstone Chimney (10 metres Difficult 1920) is the chimney up the right side of the outer of the three pinnacles.

Carn Lês Boel Headland
There are two pleasant climbs on the headland proper.

Descent. Go out along the rocky crest of the headland and scramble directly down gullies and ledges to where the final gully widens. Go around to the right (facing out) and traverse down the side of the zawn opposite Carn Lês Boel Promontory to the foot of the quite well defined but broken West Ridge.

Great Western   75 metres   Very Difficult †   (22.4.92)
The climb follows the crest of the West Ridge and starts on the seaward side of the lowest of the light yellow towers.
1 15m. Climb the juggy staircase and walls to the top of the tower.
2 20m. Descend from the tower and continue horizontally to climb a low prow on the left. Scramble along the ridge for 15 metres to the foot of some slabs left of a crack.
3 12m. Climb the steepening slabs to the foot of a buttress.
4 18m. Climb the lower wall of the buttress, moving right to climb an obvious break in the wall.
5 10m. Climb down, cross a gully on the right, and climb the V-crack beyond to the summit of the final tower.

Sou'wester   50 metres   Very Difficult   (23.4.92)
This follows the broken line of the South-West Ridge, which starts opposite
the U-shaped island, where the rock steepens in a light-reddish rib.
1 10m. Climb the steep prow of the rib on jugs.
2 10m. Scramble 10 metres to steepening slabs.
3 8m. Climb the slabs to the foot of the final tower.
4 22m. Climb some blocks, which lead to a crack near the left side of the final
tower. Climb the crack, and then step right to finish up the final steep wall.

Mild and Bitter Buttress   OS Ref 357 232

Descent. Go out along the rocky crest of Carn Lês Boel and then scramble
directly down gullies and ledges to a point just above sea-level. From here,
traverse back right (facing in) to reach a platform at the edge of the lower
slabs of the buttress. All the climbs lie to the right of the platform. Bosistow
Island can be seen from this position. The base of the buttress is made up of
a smooth slab usually dotted with patches of seaweed. The climbs start from
the slab, which is gained by a short descent and then a traverse to the right
from the starting-platform. It is best to take a higher traverse-line onto the
slab at high tide or in rough conditions.

After starting up the lower sweep of clean slabs, the climbs finish with steeper
climbing up cracks and chimneys in a lichen-covered summit tower.

Xenolith   50 metres   Hard Severe   (15.7.73)
This takes a line up the left side of the buttress to finish up a short chimney
in the upper tower.
1 25m. 4a. From the starting-platform, climb the left edge of the slab to
a large ledge. Take the wall above to a flake; then move up and right to
the short crack at the top of the wall. Follow the crack to a ledge.
2 20m. 4b. Climb the awkward chimney in the corner above the belay.
Move right and climb another chimney; then pass through a notch to
belay in a grassy gully.
3 5m. Climb the cracked wall above.
Variation
1a 20m. 4a (20.6.87). Start from a square ledge well to the left of the
lower slab. Follow a stepped groove to a large ledge and spike, and then
climb a corner on the right to where it is possible to move left onto the
ledge at the foot of the chimney of pitch 2.

Mild and Bitter   50 metres   Very Severe   (15.4.57)
A pleasant climb taking a central line up the slab and then a tough
chimney pitch in the left flank of the summit tower.
1 30m. 4a. Traverse down onto the lower slab from the starting-platform
and then, from as low as possible, climb the centre of the slab to where it
becomes a short wall. Climb the wall, bearing slightly right, to reach a
large ledge and spike belay. This lies at the foot of the V formed by a line
of flakes on the left and a deeper trough on the right.

CARN LÊS BOEL ~
PARADISE WALL AREA

BOSISTOW WALL

1	Excalibur	HVS
2	The Scabbard	HVS
3	" Direct Start	HVS

PARADISE WALL

4	Modern Images	E2
5	Fantasy Crack	E3
6	Interspace	E4
7	Burning Gold	E4
8	Hot Line	E4
9	Cool Diamonds	E5

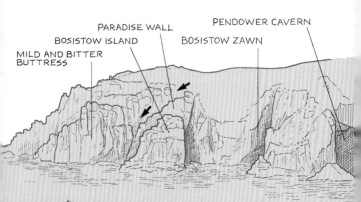

MILD AND BITTER BUTTRESS
BOSISTOW ISLAND
PARADISE WALL
BOSISTOW ZAWN
PENDOWER CAVERN

CARN LÊS BOEL ~ view across Pendower Cove from the top of Carn Barra.

PENDOWER COVE

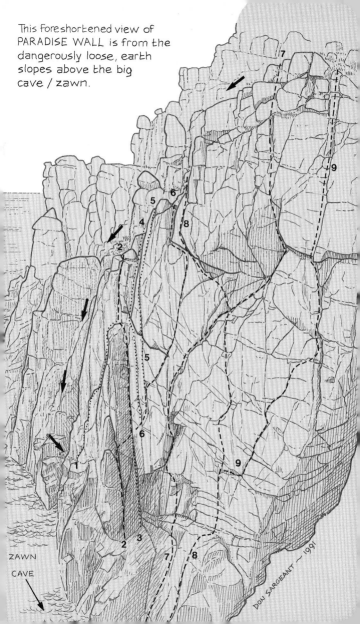

This foreshortened view of PARADISE WALL is from the dangerously loose, earth slopes above the big cave / zawn.

ZAWN
CAVE

DON SARGEANT — 1991

2 15m. 4c. Climb to the left behind the flakes; then enter the wide chimney with difficulty. Continue up the chimney, passing through a notch into a grassy gully.
3 5m. Climb the cracked wall opposite the chimney to the top.

Seal Passage   45 metres   Hard Severe   (16.4.57)
This takes a line up the right side of the buttress.
1 30m. 4a. From the starting-platform, gain the lower slab and traverse across to its far side. Climb obliquely to the right, following a rounded ledge, to reach a ledge below a rib and groove. Move left and climb the groove to the front of the V formed by the troughs. Belay as for *Mild and Bitter*.
2 15m. 4b. Climb easily to the right for 5 metres and then climb a rounded chimney running up to the left (strenuous) to the top.
Variation
2a 15m. E1 5b (15.7.73). Climb the steep crack left of the chimney; poorly protected.

The Lost Arrow   30 metres   E5 6b †   (1988)
Climb directly up the obvious jutting arête right of *Seal Passage*.

Bosistow Wall
The main feature of the wall is a huge tapering pinnacle, the left-hand and right-hand sides of which are taken by *Excalibur* and *The Scabbard* respectively.

Descent: Take the narrow grassy gully that drops steeply from just before the point where the crest of the headland becomes narrow and rocky. The gully ends abruptly at a ledge above a final 10-metre drop. Right of the ledge (facing in) is a smooth wall with blunt chicken-heads. An abseil approach can also be made down the left edge of the wall to reach the ledge at the base of the gully.

★Camelot   38 metres   E3 5c   (2.10.76)
A fine, bold climb taking the left edge of the wall. From the starting-ledge, step onto the smooth wall; climb the wall direct and then a rounded groove above. At the second break above, traverse right to the arête and then swing around to a groove. A final poorly-protected move gains a break and the top.

The Armed Knight   35 metres   E1 †   (1985)
1 15m. 4b. *Excalibur* pitch 1.
2 20m. 5b. Climb the corner past a sloping ledge (as for *Excalibur*); then move up and out left to gain a crackline rising up the face to the left. Climb this directly to finish in the descent gully.

Motivator   30 metres   E3 †   (1984)
1 15m. 4b. *Excalibur* pitch 1.
2 15m. 5c. Move up to the striking left-leaning crackline and climb it with difficulty.

★★Excalibur   35 metres   Hard Very Severe   (1957)
Excellent climbing in good positions for the grade. In the March to June period the top of the pinnacle pitch is often occupied by nesting shags. Please do not disturb them.
1 15m. 4b. From the starting-ledge, step onto the smooth wall; then traverse delicately right, leaving protection behind, to a good ledge. Continue easily up to the foot of the corner between the huge pinnacle and the face.
2 20m. 5a. Climb the corner past a sloping ledge until harder moves gain the top of the pinnacle. Climb the short wall directly above to finish.

The following routes are best approached by abseil from the top of *Excalibur* to reach a square ledge at the foot of the corner. Otherwise, the first pitch of *Excalibur* can be taken followed by an easy traverse across ledges to reach the square ledge.

★The Scabbard   30 metres   Hard Very Severe 5a (25.5.67/1.7.67)
This takes the striking corner on the right-hand side of the pinnacle. Climb the chimney formed by the smaller isolated pinnacle until it is possible to traverse into the large crack on the right. Follow the crack to an overhung niche; then escape up to the left to gain the top of the pinnacle on *Excalibur*. Finish up the short wall.
Direct Start 10m. 5a (5.8.81). Climb the grooved lower section of the corner direct to join the parent route.

Paradise Wall
'Pump City...'   (Jim Moran: Count House Log, mid 80s.)

This is the big wall to the right of the *Excalibur* pinnacle. The wall is climbed by a collection of fiercely rewarding lines, such as the seminal line of *Burning Gold*, which started exploration here, and the outstanding lines of *Interspace* and *Cool Diamonds*. The wall is usually dry and the rock is good, although there may be vestigial grittiness in places. A number of bolts were placed on Paradise Wall (c.1960s) on an early aid ascent of a line superseded by *Burning Gold*. Other bolts were placed during the 80s. Bolt removal has taken place. The certainty of the bolts' remaining available should not be assumed. Cams of all sizes are useful.

Environmental Issues. Nesting birds should be respected and the cliff is best avoided between March 1st and July 1st to avoid disturbing eggs or chicks.

Descent is best by abseil, as for *The Scabbard*. The first three routes start from a good ledge below the corner of *The Scabbard*. For *Burning Gold* and the other routes on the wall, start from a ledge just above sea-level, about 5 metres below the ledge of *The Scabbard*.

Modern Images   35 metres   E2 5c   (15.5.82)
Climb *The Scabbard Direct Start* to where the first crack out on the right wall can be gained. Follow this crack strenuously, to finish up a groove near the top.

Fantasy Crack   38 metres   E3 5c   (15.5.82)
Start as for *Modern Images*, but continue traversing to the second crack on the right. Follow this over a roof to the top.

★★Interspace   42 metres   E4 6a   (26.6.82)
Excellent sustained climbing taking a thin line of weakness across the wall right of *Fantasy Crack*. Follow that climb into the second crack; then move up until a diagonal line running rightwards up the centre of the crag can be taken to a precise horizontal crack with a thin crack above. Climb the thin crack to a niche below a triangular overhang. Move left around the overhang to gain a sloping ledge and an easier finish.

★★★Burning Gold   42 metres   E4   (21.5.78)
[Photo p.64b.] A commanding and splendid line taking the distinctive rightward-leaning weakness and then a groove through the final overhangs. Start on a ledge to the right of the black, dampish groove that forms the lower part of the line of weakness.
1 27m. 6a. Climb to a niche; then traverse left and move up to the groove. Continue up the groove to the start of the rightward-slanting weakness. Follow this strenuously to a stance beneath the overhang.
2 15m. 6a. A bold finish. Move up and right into the groove that splits the overhang. Climb strenuously to where a hard move gains easier rock above.

★★White Eagle   55 metres   E4   (18.4.82)
Another excellent route. Start as for *Burning Gold*.
1 17m. 5c. Traverse right to a crack in the arête of the slab and follow this to a good ledge.
2 38m. 6b. Climb direct and then take a horizontal break leftwards to join *Burning Gold*. Cross this; then climb up and leftwards to a layback flake in the exposed upper-middle section of the face. Climb this and then a thin and difficult crack to finish.

Grande Paradiso   47 metres   E3 †   (2.5.84)
1 17m. 5c. *White Eagle* pitch 1.
2 30m. 6a. Climb direct and then take a horizontal break leftwards to join *Burning Gold*. Continue rising leftwards to join *The Scabbard* at the top of the pinnacle. Finish up the wall above.

☆**Howling at the Moon** 52 metres E7 † (1992)
The technically hardest climb on Paradise Wall.
1 12m. 6a. *Hot Line* pitch 1.
2 40m. 6b/c. Climb to the horizontal break as for *Hot Line* and move left a few metres before tackling the centre of the wall above to gain the stance of *Burning Gold*, beneath the overhang. Move up leftwards to gain a thin, overhanging crack that leads through the large overhang, and follow the crack's continuation to finish.

★**Hot Line** 47 metres E4 (14.8.82)
Hard, sustained climbing up the wall right of *Burning Gold*. Start from a lower ledge about 10 metres down and to the right of *The Scabbard*, at the base of a slabby wall.
1 12m. 6a. Climb the centre of the wall via a shallow depression to a good ledge.
2 35m. 6b. Climb to a horizontal break above and continue up and slightly left to a line of weakness leading up to the right. Climb this to a horizontal break and then climb up and slightly left to the stance on *Burning Gold*, beneath the overhang. Traverse left into a steep groove, which is climbed to the top.

★**Cool Diamonds** 50 metres E5 (30.6.82)
A brilliant route up the right-hand side of Paradise Wall. The second pitch is sustained and strenuous.
1 10m. 6a. *Hot Line* pitch 1.
2 40m. 6b. Climb to the horizontal break, as for *Hot Line*, and traverse right to the arête. Climb cracks and slabs past an overlap, and a wide crack to beneath a roof on the right. Make hard moves over it to another roof, and pull over this to finish up a splendid crack in the headwall.

The start of the following four routes is a cave stance at the base of the menacing diagonal cleft in the right-hand corner of Paradise Wall. The stance can be approached by abseil down the cleft. The line of the cleft gives *Pendragon*.

Pendragon 40 metres Hard Very Severe (1 pt aid) † (31.5.67)
Challenging for the grade. Often wet.
1 15m. 4c. From the cave, traverse around a rib on the right and climb a groove to gain a chimney (peg for aid, not *in situ*). Climb the chimney to a possible belay where it may be best to tie onto the abseil rope if available. Alternatively, continue direct.
2 25m. 4b. Follow the chimney to the top. The last 6 metres are on poor and vegetated ground.

The Badlands 38 metres E1 † (5.7.82)
1 18m. 5a. From the cave, traverse right into a sentry-box (some loose rock). Go up this into a good crack-system and belay on a flat ledge below an overhang.

2 20m. 5b. Climb leftwards to the left edge of the overhang. Climb this using a crack and follow slabs to the foot of the headwall. Take a very thin crack to finish.

Two further routes, **No Place for Cowboys** (48 metres E1 5b † 9.7.82) and **The Last Stand** (48 metres E3 6a † 1983), made a lower traverse right from the start of *The Badlands* to a hanging bolt belay before their upward pitches. The bolts may have been removed.

Bosistow Island

The island is a spectacular feature and a major breeding site for sea-birds. It has been assaulted using various methods, including swimming and Tyrolean tactics. Cuckoo bolts and pegs have also nested here, and reported activities include easy scrambles to the summit and a partly bolted aid climb, **Bosistow Island North Face** (Hard Very Severe + A2 1983).

Bosistow Zawn   OS Ref 358 231

This is the impressive square-cut zawn east of Bosistow Island. It has a rare, guarded atmosphere yet is open-faced to the south-east. Its adventurous appeal is marred only by some shaky rock in the upper section of the cliff, more so towards the right-hand side of the main wall. The climbs are steep and serious for their grade, in line with the challenging atmosphere of the zawn.

Approach as for Carn Lês Boel. Continue past Carn Lês Boel headland for a short distance, to a point where steep slopes of shattered rock and earth lead down to the precarious ridge forming the eastern side of the zawn.

Descent to the bed of the zawn is by abseil from a large perched block on the seaward crest of the ridge. This leads to a rocky platform. A big chimney splits the upper part of the splendid wall at the back of the zawn. This is *Bosistow Chimney*. On its left, the junction of the west and back walls of the zawn gives the start of *The Cut*, well-marked by a tongue of bright green weed.

The first three climbs are reached at low tide by a 30-metre traverse into the back of the zawn from the foot of the abseil. They all start 20 metres below and just left of the foot of the chimney of *Bosistow Chimney*, at the base of an overhanging crack.

The Cut   55 metres   Very Severe   (2.7.67)
An interesting outing with climbing in some very impressive positions.
1 6m. Descend from the starting-position and traverse left to a stance and thread belay below the 'Cut'.
2 20m. 4c. Climb the 'Cut' (usually wet) and then the corner above to a good belay.
3 6m. Climb rightwards to a small stance below an overhang.

4 23m. 4c. Take the overhang at its left end; then follow the crack above. Where the angle eases, follow a ledge to the right; then climb a crack and slabs to the left of *Bosistow Chimney*.

The Crack 45 metres Hard Very Severe (24.6.67)
1 20m. 5a. Climb the overhanging crack above the starting-position and then an open cracked groove, which leads slightly left to the faultline at half height. Step right to a stance under an overhang.
2 25m. 5a. Surmount the overhang at its left end and climb the crack above on poor rock to a recess. Leave this by a leftward traverse to a good handhold. Pull over an overhang to gain some easy slabs that lead to the top.

Bosistow Chimney 45 metres Very Severe 4c (17.6.67)
A reasonably mild line technically, but still serious. Climb up a metre or two to where it is possible to move right into the break. Climb the break and the chimney above before moving onto the slabs on the left for the last 6 metres. The pitch can be split.

The Ramp 47 metres Very Severe † (18.7.67)
Below the chimney of *Bosistow Chimney* is a weakness that forms the left-hand edge of a slight tower in the lower half of the face. The right side of the tower is a shallow corner, which is taken by the second pitch. Approach from the abseil platform by traversing 20 metres around the back of the zawn to a large thread belay below and right of the shallow corner.
1 8m. Step left and climb up to a small ledge and thread belay.
2 30m. Climb the corner to the half-way break. Move left and climb a crack to a perched-flake belay at the right side of a small tower.
3 9m. Climb a groove to good holds on the right, pull up, and scramble to the top.

The next climb takes a line directly up the line of the abseil.

Easy Way Down 27 metres Very Severe 4c (3.7.67)
Climb the black overhanging groove directly above the arrival-platform for 10 metres to where easier rock leads to the abseil block.

The small buttress forming the seaward face of the eastern ridge of Bosistow Zawn provides two climbs. The foot of the buttress can be reached for two to three hours either side of low tide by scrambling down the shattered slopes to the east of the ridge and then traversing back west to reach a ledge at the foot of the buttress. Affected by swell and rough sea.

Anna's Climb 32 metres Very Severe (27.6.67)
Start from the ledge below a prominent narrow crack.
1 10m. Climb the narrow crack to a small stance.
2 22m. Step left and under the overhang to gain a groove around the corner. Follow this to the top.

Cinecs   25 metres   Very Severe 4c   (3.7.67)
Climb the wall right of the crack of *Anna's Climb*. Move left and then climb
to the overhang. Traverse right under the overhang to a groove, which
leads to a stance on the edge of the buttress.

East of Bosistow Zawn lies the vast Pendower Cavern facing the boulder-
beach of Pendower Coves. There are eight climbs on the small steep cliff on
the seaward side of the huge cavern. *Teacher's Pet* takes the impressive
staggered corner just left of the cavern.

Descent. The climbs are reached by going down the broken ground to
seaward of the Cavern and then traversing along the foot of the cliff at very
low tide. Alternatively, an abseil approach can be made down the steep
seaward wall.

Top of the Class   25 metres   Hard Very Severe 5a   (21.4.83)
Climb the left-hand of three cracks in the steep wall, and then climb
rightwards to finish up a steep wall.

Late Developer   25 metres   Hard Very Severe 5a   (21.4.83)
Climb the crack to the right of the previous route before moving rightwards
to join *Swot Crack*.

Swot Crack   25 metres   Hard Very Severe 5a †   (21.3.83)
Climb the wide crack to the right of *Late Developer* to finish up the steep
wall above.

Teacher's Pet   25 metres   E2 5b   (25.10.71)
A strenuous little route. Well protected, but not from nesting birds and their
firepower. Start at the foot of the obvious clean-cut red corner just left of
the cavern's mouth. Climb the lower corner to a stance (belay possible);
then continue steeply up the corner to the wide final crack.

Rock Citadel   45 metres   E4 6a †   (1990)
Start as for *Teacher's Pet* but climb the right edge of the corner to gain a
sloping slab. Continue up the right edge to a deep horizontal break. Move
left and climb the wall first leftwards then rightwards to a steep finish.
Three pegs.

Wolf at the Door   40 metres   E6 6b †   (1990)
Start 5 metres right of *Teacher's Pet*. Climb the wall to the right of the edge
of *Rock Citadel*, finishing just left of the overhangs near the cliff-top. Five
pegs.

The Cornishman   55 metres   E6 6b ††   (1990)
A major two-pitch route which took the wall left of the cave to a belay level
with the lip, before traversing above the cave and finishing up the
headwall. This climb has suffered a rockfall, which has destroyed the belay

point. As no subsequent ascent is known to have been made, an abseil inspection is advised before attempting this route.
Variation Start
Cerberus   25 metres   E6 6b/c ††   (1990)
Start just right again and climb the wall to join the parent route at 20 metres. The same warning applies as for the parent climb.

Pendower Coves (Granite)   OS Ref 360 230

Outlook: West-south-west and south-west.
Tidal. The foot of Pandour Buttress is accessible for about two to three hours either side of low water on a spring-tide. However, on a neap-tide the base of the buttress may still be awash even at low water. Pandour Buttress is wave-washed at all states of the tide in heavy swell and rough sea. Halfway Buttress and Moon Buttress are accessible for four to five hours either side of low water, but both are spray-washed at low tide by big seas.
Coastguard Identity: Pendower Coves.
Environmental Issues: The clifftop in this SSSI has wet flushes, mires, reed beds, and other important habitats, where Bog Asphodel, Cottongrass, Yellow Bartsia, and liverworts are vulnerable. There is sensitivity over breeding birds: Peregrines have been seen here and Cormorants occupy the zawn at the eastern end of the bay. Grey Seals breed in the caves at the western end of the bay and are especially vulnerable from September to the end of October. Although it is not formally restricted, the area is best avoided during the nesting season.

A majestic cove which features all that is best about Penwithian scenery. The unique western heath, which is crossed en *route* to the crag, is the reason for this area's designation as an SSSI. Beyond this, steep grass slopes, punctuated by mini tors, sit temporarily above the decaying granite cliffs. The giant pebble beach is a sight to behold and has provided a superb setting for photographs of exploratory routes on these cliffs. Unfortunately the cliffs here are softer than the adjacent headlands of Carn Lês Boel and Carn Barra.

Pandour Buttress   OS Ref 359 231

Approach. Pandour Buttress is difficult to locate from above. It lies a short distance east of Pendower Cavern and is reached from the coast path by identifying the rocky summits of three short ridges that drop down to seaward and have grassy gullies between them. Pandour Buttress lies directly below the middle ridge.

Descent. From the coast path, go down the right-hand (facing out) grassy gully and traverse left along grassy ledges that run across the seaward face of the middle ridge. Locate useful abseil blocks above the corner of *Demelza*.

There are one or two worthwhile routes on the buttress but the rock can be loose and mean, while the sea needs watching. The distinctive clean-cut corner of *Demelza* and a huge central nose are the main features.

One Way Ticket   38 metres   E2 5c   (11.4.82)
Le. of Pandour Buttress and across a red-veined wall is a prominent beak with a wide crack on its left. This route follows the thin cracks which run the full height of the wall just to the left. Crumbly rock.

Return Ticket   30 metres   Hard Very Severe 4c †   (1989)
Climb the narrow wall just left of the short chimney of *Dour Cracks*.

Dour Cracks   27 metres   Hard Severe   (12.8.63)
This takes the wide crack-system running up the left wall of the corner on pebble-dash granite. Start at sea-level below the obvious chimney.
1 10m. Climb the chimney to the big ledge.
2 17m. Continue up the corner for 5 metres; then move left into a gravelly groove and grovel up it until level with the top of a huge detached flake on the left. Make an awkward move onto the top of the flake and continue up friable rock to some pretty solid-feeling grass.

Demelza   30 metres   Very Severe   (16.4.76)
1 10m. *Pandour Grooves* pitch 1.
2 20m. 4c. Take the corner direct. Quite strenuous.

Pandour Grooves   30 metres   Very Severe   (12.8.63)
A pleasant and worthwhile route on the best rock available here. Start at sea-level below the big corner.
1 10m. Climb a V-groove to the large ledge.
2 10m. 4c. From the right end of the ledge, gain the small shelf on the right arête by a difficult move and then traverse across the seaward face to belay below the final crack.
3 10m. 4a. Climb the crack on good holds.
Direct Start 20 metres Severe † (1989). Follow the crack below pitch 3.

Demelza's Arête   30 metres   E2 5c †   (1989)
Start at a crack below the fine arête. Climb the crack and continue up the arête.

To the right of the arête is a deep overhung recess.

Sabre Cut   30 metres   Very Severe 4c   (1989)
Start below the recess. Climb its left-hand edge to finish just right of a triangular overhang.

Seal Chimney   30 metres   Hard Severe   (1989)
Climb the deep recess.

Stackolee   30 metres   Hard Severe   (20.8.63)
This climbs the slanting chimney on the right-hand side of the deep
overhung recess. There is some friable rock.
1 10m. Climb from sea-level to the base of the chimney.
2 20m. 4a. Follow the chimney to where an awkward move left is made
onto a ledge midway up the face. Continue left, crossing a loose vein; then
finish up the right edge of the big corner.
Variation
2a Severe 4a. Continue up the chimney instead of moving left onto the
ledge.

Kooky Crack   27 metres   Very Severe 4c   (1982)
Yet another wide crack. The next one in fact.

Blue Kazoo   27 metres   Hard Very Severe 5a   (1982)
Climb the centre of the wall right of *Kooky Crack* to an overlap and then
go over this to the top.

Time Tavern   27 metres   Very Severe 4c   (1989)
Start about 2 metres right of *Blue Kazoo*, just left of a wide crack. Climb
the right-hand side of the buttress until it is possible to move up rightwards
into a hanging flake crack. Grunt up the crack.

Before completely turning to vertical choss, Pandour Buttress provides one
last climb.

Pendower Direct   27 metres   Hard Very Severe   (1982)
Start below the last decent buttress, at a rightward-slanting crack. Climb
the crack and continue up the centre of the buttress.

Halfway Buttress
Approach is best made from Porthgwarra by walking along the coast path
to where the eastern wall of Pendower Coves turns to the west. A small
stream cuts across the coast path at this point (OS Ref 361 228), below
several granite tors.

Descend to the left of the stream valley, over grass at first then wet rocks.
Beware: retreat by the same route can be quickly cut off by the flooding tide.

When approached from the east, the western end of Pendower Coves is
dominated by a full-length corner of yellow rock. About 40 metres east of
this, a spire of better rock leans onto the back wall of the cove. Unfortunately
the good rock does not run the full height of the cliff and the first ascensionist
of the following routes placed a two-bolt lower-off point, which was soon
chopped. If, having climbed every other route in this guide, jaded locals feel
compelled to try these routes, they may find a **preplaced rope** useful for
gaining the top of the cliff.

The Edge (12 metres E3 5c) takes the left arête. **Seal Crack** (14 metres Very Severe 4b) starts up *Fatal Attractions* before moving left and following its own crackline. **Fatal Attractions** (12 metres Very Severe 4c) takes the central crack on the front face. **Right Edge** (12 metres Very Severe 4c) follows the right edge of the face. **Awksberg** (12 metres Hard Very Severe 5a) takes the right-hand retaining wall via the distinctive groove. (All routes 1991.)

Moon Buttress
OS Ref 361 230

Moon Buttress is at the far eastern end of the boulder beach of Pendower Coves. It is the small buttress of rough granite that protrudes from an otherwise decaying cliff about 100 metres left (facing in) of the base of a large decomposing gully. The buttress is split on its right side by a slanting chimney/crack. This is the line of *Rack and Ruin*. As with Halfway Buttress, a two-bolt lower-off has been placed between pitches on this buttress, and subsequently chopped. A **preplaced rope** can be used for safeguarding the loose second pitches of these climbs. Try to avoid rope damage to the vegetation near the top.

Moon Child   44 metres   E2 †   (11.8.86)

Start left of Moon Buttress below a steep groove capped by an overhang.
1 18m. 5b. Climb the crack to the roof, pull over, and continue to belays.
2 26m. 4b. Continue up the groove before stepping right to a ledge, from which the loose slabs are climbed to the top.

Time Starts Now   45 metres   E2   (24.5.86)

Start in the bay below the left wall of Moon Buttress proper.
1 20m. 5b. Climb the left-hand crack.
2 25m. 4b. Climb the slabs above. Loose.

Shadow on a Wall   45 metres   E3   (6.6.86)

Start in the bay below the left wall of the buttress.
1 20m. 6a. Climb the right-hand crack: painful.
2 25m. 4a. Climb loose slabs above.

Space Cruiser   42 metres   E3 6a   (10.4.86)

Start near the left-hand side of the front face of the buttress.
1 17m. 6a. Climb a crack and a shallow corner, and cross an overlap to easier-angled rock. Belay on nuts or the preplaced rope.
2 25m. 4a. A poor pitch up the loose slab above.

★Isis   42 metres   E4 6a   (6.2.86)

1 17m. 6a. Climb the central crack, which proves a touch friable, to an easing of the angle. Belay on nuts or the preplaced rope.
2 25m. 4a. *Space Cruiser* pitch 2.

Rack and Ruin   42 metres   E3   (5.6.87)
1 17m. 5c. Unpleasant. The chimney on the right. Break out right at the top to finish up a slanting crack.
2 25m. 4a. Climb the loose slabs above.

A line which used bolts took the right edge of the buttress. **Lunatic Owl** (55 metres E5 6b 4.5.87) climbed up a groove and left to the arête. It went over a roof (bolt runner, now removed) and up to a crack which led to a ledge and bolt belay (also removed). Loose slabs were followed to the top. The grade predates the removal of the bolts.

Zawn Kellys Area (Granite)   OS Ref 359 227

Outlook: West.
Tidal. Routes to seaward of *The Screw* are accessible up to three hours either side of low water, but those routes nearest the sea are affected very quickly on a flooding tide. The routes to the right of *The Screw* are accessible for much longer. All routes can be affected in swell and rough sea.
Coastguard Identity: Zawn Kellys.
Environmental Issues: These cliffs are situated in an SSSI, and the slopes above them have wet flushes, mires, reed beds, and other important habitats.

Approach from Porthgwarra along the coast path to a point just beyond Carn Barra where the path turns north-east along the eastern cliff-edge of Pendower Coves. Zawn Kellys lies below a marshy area of the cliff.

Frank's Zawn

Frank's Zawn lies immediately north of Zawn Kellys, the two being divided by a narrow ridge with distinctive perched blocks. Frank's Zawn is a narrow sunless breach in the cliffs and is a popular nesting-area for sea-birds. It is reached by continuing along the coast path above the edge of Zawn Kellys to cross the neck of the narrow ridge.

Descent is by the broken northern edge of the zawn. A traverse into the zawn can then be made from near sea-level. Alternatively, an abseil can be made from either the south or north rim of the zawn.

At the seaward end of the north side of the zawn is the short wall taken by **Pick It** (10 metres E1 5b † 1995). To the right is a small bay of gritty rock, the left arête of which is **Lick It** (10 metres E1 5c † 1995). **Roll It** (10 metres Severe 4b † 1995) takes a short undercut groove, **Flick It** (10 metres Moderate † 1995), a red juggy wall. To the right of the chimney at the back of the bay are two climbs: **Lil' Bitty Gritty** (10 metres Difficult † 1995) up the left-hand side of a slab and **Lil' Bitty Groove** (10 metres Moderate † 1995) up a slabby corner. **Paul's One Liners** (10 metres Very Severe 4c † 1995) is just before the right-hand arête of the bay. Climb to the roof, circumvent it to the left, and continue to the top. For **Williams Formula One** (10 metres Very Severe 4b † 1995), climb to the overhang and continue up the face to the right of the arête using a diagonal crack.

☆☆**Funeral for a Friend**   30 metres   E4 6c †   (1.8.84)
Start below a black crack just left of a through-cave on the southern side of the zawn. Climb the crack, and then continue up a steep crack in the clean wall above to finish up an equally steep groove.

☆☆☆**Farewell to Stone**   35 metres   E5 6a †   (1993)
Start on the ledge left of the arch. Climb the big groove to finish up a hanging groove on the left.

Zawn Kellys

Zawn Kellys lies on the eastern seaward edge of Pendower Coves. It is more of a cove than a zawn and has a fine open outlook. There are several good routes in spite of some shaky rock here and there.

Descent: Routes to the left of *The Arch* can be gained by scrambling down the ridge above them and traversing in. For the other routes, abseil from buttresses above the cliff.

American Dream lies on the more substantial north wall of the cove, which is split on its seaward edge by a narrow through-cave leading into Frank's Zawn.

Club Route   18 metres   Difficult   (9.9.79)
The route furthest to seaward on the north wall. Start just in from the seaward edge of the wall at sea-level. Step onto the wall, traverse right, and make a long step into a groove. Climb this and then move left onto the steep face, which is followed to the top.

Omega Man   24 metres   Hard Very Severe 5a †   (1983)
Start on a flat ledge just above sea-level to the left of the through-cave of *The Arch*. Climb to a flat-topped spike on the left wall of the arch; then climb the crack on the left.

★**The Arch**   24 metres   E1 5b ††   (18.4.80)
A fine climb on good rock… which has recently suffered a rockfall! The grade is probably unchanged. Start on the flat ledge just above sea-level, to the left of the through-cave. Climb the left wall of the arch to where a large spike once stood; then move up the arête to a narrow groove. Climb the groove to a small roof, move up to a ledge on the left, and finish direct.

A Nightmare of Nightmaidens and **Anglo-American Nightmare** (25 metres E1 5b 1993/1994) are worthless routes which cover similar ground on the crumbly slab left of *American Dream*.

Three Seals Watching   25 metres   E2 5b †   (27.7.95)
Another poor route, taking the obvious crack-system in the face just left of *American Dream*. Move right near the top to avoid vegetation-filled cracks and finish up the final slab of *Second Skin*.

★★American Dream   37 metres   E1 5b   (30.3.80)
A stylish and photogenic line with nicely sustained climbing up the face of the main buttress: the route of the crag. Start just left of a deep chimney. Gain a sloping ledge on the left and climb the seamed wall to a flat hold on the right. Climb to an overhang and pull over to reach a small ledge on the right. Continue to the next roof, which is climbed on its left to the start of a steep crack. Climb the crack to finish.

Second Skin   37 metres   E2 5b   (1983)
A counter-diagonal to *American Dream* (but better as a direct start to that route). Start at the base of the deep chimney, below a steep crack in its left wall. Climb the crack to a cave; then traverse left, crossing *American Dream*, to a small niche on the left arête. Finish up the slab.

The Screw   38 metres   E3 6a   (6.6.80)
This takes the remarkable narrow column of tormented rock on the right of the chimney. The start is fierce but protectable. Start at the base of the column. Climb the overhanging crack on the left and move right with difficulty to a good resting-place. Move back left to a fine crack. Climb the crack and another crack on its right to a hold on the arête. Follow the arête over a small roof and finish up a steep wall. Belay well back.

★★Broad Street   130 metres   E3 6a   (25.8.84)
A climb focused on the smooth upper wall right of *The Screw*. The two pegs may not be in place. The grade assumes dry conditions, but the route is usually a waterfall! Start in the corner right of the chimney. Climb a steep black slab on the left to the overlap and follow this into a groove. Climb rightwards across a steep slab to an overhung arête. Climb this and, at the first faultline, move right to a small ledge on the upper wall. Climb a thin crack in the wall. Belay well back.

The next feature is a large cave at the back of the zawn. There are three intimidating routes to the right of the cave that have failed to gain popularity. There is some shaky rock in the upper sections.

The Big Easy   46 metres   E3 †   (24.7.89)
A line taking the central grooves on the wall right of the cave. Start below the outer part of the wall.
1   30m.   5c. Climb the right-hand of two steep leftward-slanting cracks. Traverse left and pull into a shaky recess. Climb the recess and then use an

undercut to gain a good flake over the lip. Use the flake to make difficult moves onto the slab. Climb leftwards to gain a long groove, which is followed to a roof. Move out right to the foot of the final corner and a hanging belay (peg).
2 16m. 5b. Climb the corner direct.

Hare Krishna   46 metres   E3 †   (6.8.89)
An impressive line with some bold climbing. Start about 10 metres right of *The Big Easy*, in the left-hand corner of a 20-metre-high coffin-shaped recess that contains a steep, smooth slab.
1 30m. 5c. Climb the left-hand corner of the recess and move out across the slab to the left arête. Climb the arête and then a short crack. Swing back to the right onto the slab and climb it with increasing difficulty to beneath the roof, where a move back left using an undercut gains the front of the face. Make hard moves up and right into the small corner (peg). Climb leftwards across the slab to another peg and belay. Alternatively, a move down left gains the hanging-belay position below the final corner of *The Big Easy*. This is more secure.
2 16m. 5b. Climb the centre of the wall direct.

Who Knows Where the Nose Goes   43 metres   E1 5b †   (23.7.89)
This line is focused on the narrow groove capped by a triangular overhang, high up to the right of *Hare Krishna*. Start at slabby rock just to the right of some big roofs. Climb to and over a small roof. Follow the slabs up left and then move around the rounded arête into a slabby groove. Climb the groove to where it steepens and narrows. Continue direct, moving out left to finish.

Carn Barra (Granite)   OS Ref 359 225

'There are considerable climbing possibilities here as yet untouched...'
                                                    (A W Andrews, 1950.)

Outlook: South-west.
Tidal on parts of Northern Platform and Southern Platform. **Non-tidal** on Central Wall. All areas can be affected by heavy swell and rough sea.
Coastguard Identity: Carn Barra.
Environmental Issues: SSSI. Whilst there is no formal restriction, it is suggested climbers avoid the upper tiers so as to protect the splendid lichen cover. Routes have been done by several parties over the years, but they are not described for this reason.

Carn Barra is a major West Penwith venue. Most routes are under 30 metres in length but are of a high quality. They are generally steep and can be strenuous. There are climbs for all abilities, although the majority are in the middle to higher grades. The open and sunny aspect of the cliffs is a welcome bonus.

Approach from Porthgwarra car-park. Follow a narrow tarmac road uphill to open cliffland where the road curves sharply to the left at a junction of several paths. (Chair Ladder is reached by following the road around left.) For Carn Barra, take the path that leads directly ahead along the higher edge of the cliff. After about a kilometre a distinctive granite wall built from single slabs is crossed. Beyond this wall are the adjoining climbing areas of Black Carn Zawn, Fox Promontory, Folly Cove, Dutchman's Zawn, Carn Barra, and Zawn Kellys, in that sequence. Black Carn Zawn lies directly below the end of the stone wall. Fox Promontory lies about 100 metres further on, with Folly Cove biting into the land between Fox Promontory and Dutchman's Zawn, beyond which lies Carn Barra's Southern Platform.

For access to all parts of Carn Barra, continue from the stone wall for about 250 metres, passing on the way a rusty capstan, which marks the beginning of Folly Cove, and a split boulder by the edge of the path, which marks the end of the cove. About 80 metres beyond the split boulder is a wide grassy depression, with a path, vague at first, that leads down to stony ledges directly above Peel Crack Buttress. The Northern Platform lies to the right (facing out) of Peel Crack Buttress. Central Wall lies to the left, with the Southern Platform further left again. Excellent views can be had of Central Wall and the eastern end of the Northern Platform by scrambling to seaward along the bouldery crest of Peel Crack Buttress. The bottom part of this approach suffers from natural erosion and can be quite unpleasant. Alternatively, and probably more pleasantly, it is possible to make a descending traverse under the upper tiers from the slopes above Folly Cove and Dutchman's Zawn. This approach involves one or two tricky rock steps.

The Northern Platform Area
Descent. The platform can be gained from the top of Peel Crack Buttress by climbing down *Sleazy Corner* (Difficult), which is located near the seaward end of the buttress's right flank (facing out). Alternatively, a short abseil can be made down the right flank of Peel Crack Buttress.

An alternative and more convenient descent for the main routes is by abseil from a number of points along the edge of the Northern Platform cliff.

It is possible to scramble down to the far northern end of the Northern Platform. This can be reached by tracing faint paths rightwards (facing out) from the arrival point above Peel Crack Buttress. Follow the break between the rambling upper tiers and the smooth walls of the Northern Platform (crossing a 'bad step' with particular care) for about 150 metres until the scramble down broken rock is obvious. This descent is crumbly, often wet, and, towards the bottom, over seaweed-covered rock, so care is needed. A few routes lie to

CARN BARRA ~ NORTHERN PLATFORM

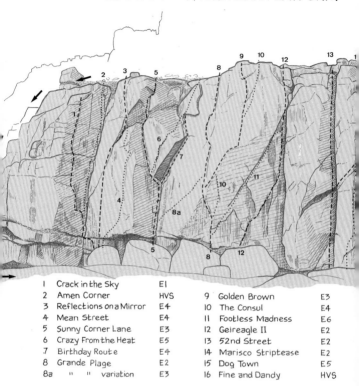

1	Crack in the Sky	E1		9	Golden Brown	E3
2	Amen Corner	HVS		10	The Consul	E4
3	Reflections on a Mirror	E4		11	Footless Madness	E6
4	Mean Street	E4		12	Geireagle II	E2
5	Sunny Corner Lane	E3		13	52nd Street	E2
6	Crazy From the Heat	E5		14	Marisco Striptease	E2
7	Birthday Route	E4		15	Dog Town	E5
8	Grande Plage	E2		16	Fine and Dandy	HVS
8a	" " variation	E3				

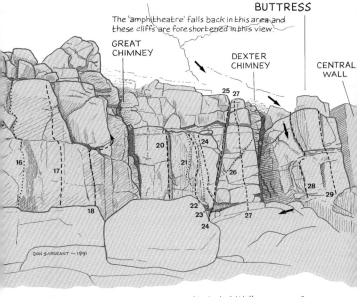

PEEL CRACK
BUTTRESS

The 'amphitheatre' falls back in this area and these cliffs are foreshortened in this view.

GREAT
CHIMNEY

DEXTER
CHIMNEY

CENTRAL
WALL

DON SARGEANT ~ 1991

17	Silent Sleeper	E2
18	Carmen	E6

SOCKET WALL AREA

20	Five Year Itch	E3
21	Sock It To Me	E1
22	Socket Arete	VS
23	Cumbelloe	HS

24	Socket Wall	S
25	Slant Crack	VS
26	Smash and Grab	E2
27	Touch of Glass	E4
28	Sleazy Corner	D
29	Peel Crack	VD

the left (facing in) of the sea-level arrival point, while the main climbing area runs off to the right as far as Peel Crack Buttress. The routes to the left of the arrival point lie on the broken walls that rise from a distinctive V-shaped boulder-channel. The middle of the wall is broken by a black greasy scoop.

Easy Touch   18 metres   E1 5b   (19.3.86)
Left of the black greasy scoop is a south-facing wall which has a steep crack. Climb the groove at the left-hand end of this wall.

Worried Warrior   15 metres   E1 5b   (25.5.85)
Climb the obvious steep crack left of the black greasy scoop.

Simplicity City   18 metres   Hard Very Severe 5a †   (19.3.86)
Climb the arête to the right of the black greasy scoop. This arête has also been claimed as **Empty Spaces** (18 metres E2 5c † 1988). The relationship between the climbs is not clear, but neither is attractive anyway.

To the right of the black greasy scoop is a rightward-leaning rake of poor rock, its upper part hidden from sea-level. A climb has been made up the rake but the **Hidden Gems** (18 metres Very Severe 4c 1988) are unlikely to attract many suitors.

Mental Breakdown   18 metres   E1 5b   (1988)
A good route. High on the crag is a distinctive triangular roof. Below this is a flake crack with a line of diagonal cracks joining it from the left. Take any route to the bottom of the diagonal cracks, follow them to the flake crack, and (surprise, surprise) pull over the triangular roof to finish.

An 'obvious hanging right corner crack' which finishes 'direct via a thin flake crack' has been climbed in the vicinity, but no other details are available (**Far North Crack** Hard Very Severe 5a † 8.98).

Hampshire Zigzag   30 metres   Difficult   (10.50)
Start from the boulder-channel at its lowest point, below a loose break that curves up to the right into a chimney.
1 20m. Follow the break to the chimney on the right, which is climbed to a stance (belay possible). Traverse right past a large block to a good platform.
2 10m. Climb the steep slab above, keeping to the right of a protruding rock, and then climb a steep groove to the top.

Hampshire Bypass   70 metres   Hard Severe   (17.7.88)
Start 30 metres up and right of the start of *Hampshire Zigzag*, below a triangular-shaped niche.
1 40m. Climb into the niche (hard to start); then go right into grooves and follow these to a ledge level with the start of *Hampshire Zigzag* pitch 2.
2 30m. 4b. Climb the steep undercut wall before moving right to finish up a groove.

The main climbing area lies to the right of the above routes. It is reached from the arrival point of the northern descent by negotiating a 3-metre drop and crossing a shallow tidal channel to a vast platform of sweeping slabby ledges dotted with huge boulders. Rising from the ledges are a series of splendid walls and corners. The northern end of the area is accessible for three hours either side of low water. Swell and rough sea can also restrict access here. The first big corner reached is *Amen Corner*, which has a massive square block at its base, cheek-by-jowl with a rounded boulder. These giants may go walkabout during very big winter storms and may end up in different positions. From *Amen Corner*, the cliff runs to the right across the impressive *Sunny Corner Lane/Powerflex* corner, the striking faces of *Grande Plage* and *Golden Brown*, and the groove-lines of *Geireagle II* and *52nd Street*. Beyond a pile of boulders the cliff loses height gradually, falling back into a more broken recessed section ending at the square-cut *Touch of Glass* wall. From here, Peel Crack Buttress juts seaward with its right flank overlooking Central Wall.

The left wall of *Amen Corner* is steep, with a striking crack in its upper left side. This is *Crack in the Sky*. Left again is a smooth wall, which is home to three hard routes on good rock. The smooth wall has four cracks in it. The left-hand crack is about hand size, slanting, and guarded by a crumbly overhang and the right-hand crack is very, very thin. Neither has been climbed yet. The middle two provide good, though comparatively short routes. Their starting-block may shift position, necessitating a traverse from the right-hand block.

Raindancer   24 metres   E3 5c †   (1992)
Start atop a large boulder in the centre of the wall. Make a tough pull up on well-cleaned pockets to a horizontal break (wire slot above). Move up again to a second horizontal break at 5 metres. Follow the crackline above, making good use of holds on the left wall. Easy ground soon leads to the cliff-top.

Hot Wire Fire   24 metres   E7 6b/c †   (1992)
Follow *Raindancer* to the second horizontal break. Swing up and right to the thin crack, which is followed with extreme difficulty and not a little boldness to ledges. Easy ground remains.

Just Another Inquisition   24 metres   E7 6b   (1992)
The right-hand arête of the smooth wall. Start on the large boulder below *Amen Corner*. Step up left and follow the lower arête precariously. The upper part of the arête is escapable to the left.

Crack in the Sky   24 metres   E1 5b   (10.5.80)
Fine climbing to a classic crack finish with a tempting slice of sky shining through it. Start from the massive block at the base of *Amen Corner*. Move up the corner for a few metres and then move out left onto a small ledge. Make hard moves up onto the small slab on the left and reach a ledge

below the steep upper wall. Climb the wall to the base of the widening crack on the left, which leads unerringly to the top.
Direct Start 6m. E1 5c (1991). Start a metre left of *Amen Corner* and climb the thin crack which leads to the route proper.

Amen Corner   20 metres   Hard Very Severe 5a   (12.8.55)
A good-looking line but with some loose rock near the top. Start from the massive block. Climb the corner until a difficult finish can be made to the left. It is possible to finish to the right but on loose rock.

★★Reflections on a Mirror   27 metres   E4 6a   (20.5.86)
Hard, technical climbing. Start from the block beneath *Amen Corner*. Climb to a peg at about 2 metres. Continue straight up past a second peg on the left to a break on the right. Finish leftwards up thin cracks.

★★Mean Street   27 metres   E4 6a   (2.3.84)
[Photo p.96a.] A testing pitch taking the staggered crackline up the wall right of *Amen Corner*. Start from the right-hand block. Climb the staggered crackline to reach a break in the arête. Move left and finish up a short wall.

★★Arc of a Diver/Psychosis   26 metres   E5 5c   (1984)
The right-hand arête of the *Mean Street* wall is a serious lead. Climb straight up the arête until it eases. From here, move left and finish up the short wall.

To the right of the arête lies a clutch of powerful routes. An obvious feature is the long narrow roof of *Birthday Route/Powerflex* slanting up to the right.

★★★Sunny Corner Lane   27 metres   E3 5c   (23.5.80)
Excellent climbing on a handsome line. Start at the base of the steep corner below the long narrow roof. Climb the corner to the base of the roof. Move left and around into the adjoining corner and climb this to a roof. Climb the steep wall into the overhanging groove above. Follow this, moving right around the roof to finish.

★Crazy from the Heat   27 metres   E5 6a   (15.6.85)
Follow *Sunny Corner Lane* up to and left around the narrow roof, before stepping back right into a slim staggered groove. Climb the groove and the slab above to finish up a thin crack in the final wall, as for *Birthday Route/Powerflex*.

★★Birthday Route/Powerflex   27 metres   E4 6a   (6.3.66/8.6.80)
A strenuous pitch that takes the rightward-slanting roof. Start as for *Sunny Corner Lane* at the base of the steep corner below the roof. Climb the corner and then the steep crack running up under the roof. The climbing gets decidedly harder until a pull over the top gains a good resting-place. Climb the thin crack in the wall above.

The next two routes follow very similar ground up the steep wall left of *Grand Plage*. It is possible that the right-hand holds on *Audacity* are the left-hand holds on *Scary Route*!

Audacity 27 metres E7 6c † (17.7.96)
From the foot of *Birthday Route/Powerflex*, follow a faint rightward-slanting crack. After 2 metres, make a balancy move to stand up in the crack. Using painfully small crimps, climb up to a thin crack (tiny cam). Pass by the corner of *Birthday Route/Powerflex* and finish up the shallow hanging corner of *Grand Plage*.

Scary Route 27 metres E6 6b † (1988)
Start on a large boulder below a faint arête (a metre left of *Grand Plage*). Pull onto the arête and climb up to the diagonal, flaky crackline of *Grand Plage Variation Start*. Now climb directly up the wall to finish up a shallow hanging corner as for *Grand Plage*.

★Grande Plage 26 metres E2 6a (23.5.80)
[Photo p.96b.] A brilliant pitch up the fine wall right of *Birthday Route/Powerflex*. Start about 10 metres right of that route, between two huge boulders at the foot of a steep wall. Climb from the right-hand boulder to a flake. Make a series of hard moves up the left-slanting crack to turn the blunt arête. Climb the continuation crack to make a move onto a small mantelshelf; then traverse left to the shallow, rightward-facing hanging corner. Follow this to exit on the right. A better finish can be made direct from the mantelshelf move. Variation Start E3 5c (10.5.84). Gain the main crack of the parent route from the foot of *Birthday Route/Powerflex* by following a faint diagonal crack.

★Golden Brown 27 metres E3 6a (1982)
Golden climbing up the wall right of *Grande Plage*. Follow *Grande Plage* for 5 metres; then move diagonally rightwards up the obvious ramp to a flake (poor protection). Step up and climb the excellent thin crack in the headwall.

The Consul 30 metres E4 6a (20.7.85)
Start as for *Grande Plage* but instead of following the crack leftwards from the flake, climb directly up broken rock (strenuous) to join *Golden Brown* before finishing a metre or so to its right.

★Footless Madness 24 metres E6 6b (6.7.85)
Muscle-busting sustained moves across the steep wall to the right of *Grande Plage*. From the start of *Grande Plage*, move up right into the thin diagonal crack and follow it across the impending wall, past a peg and a ledge, to the top.

Comedy of Errors 24 metres E6 6b † (1992)
Start at the foot of a rock step which leads to the grooves of *Geireagle II* on the right. Climb straight up to the crack of *Footless Madness*. Climb blind flakes to a resting place and then take the smooth wall straight to the top.

Geireagle II   24 metres   E2 5b   (24.5.80)
A testing pitch on rock which can be damp and greasy at times; the gear is
not all it could be either. Start 5 metres right of *Grande Plage* at the foot of
a line of grooves that are reached up two short steps. Climb the grooves
past a sloping ledge and then continue steeply to make some hard moves
to reach the foot of the overhanging headwall, which is climbed to its top.

Big Guns   24 metres   E4 6a   (1992)
The pillar between *Geireagle II* and *52nd Street*. Start on a boulder at the
foot of the grooves of *Geireagle II*, below a diamond-shaped slab. Climb
up to the right of the diamond-shaped slab and step back left onto its
crest. Reach up for a shallow, hanging, leftward-facing corner and climb it
to a sloping ledge. Finish up the right-hand side of the headwall.

52nd Street   24 metres   E2 5b   (24.5.80)
Start 5 metres right of *Geireagle II*, at the foot of a steep groove system
containing two slabby sections. Climb the groove system. Protection is not
very good.

The orange-coloured wall to the right of the groove system of *52nd Street*
has some impressive routes.

★Marisco Striptease   27 metres   E2 5b   (5.8.84)
[Photo p.128a.] An attractive line across the orange-coloured wall. Follow
the first groove of *52nd Street* before breaking out right along a diagonal
traverse-line to a ledge. Move up and right to finish up an easier groove.

★At Home/Pig City   20 metres   E5 6a   (3.87/5.87)
Climb boldly on a direct line up the right-hand side of the left-hand arête
of the orange-coloured wall. (E3 with side runners.)

★★Dog Town   20 metres   E5 6b   (3.84)
Powerful climbing up one of those irritating cracks where a choice has to
be made between fingers or runners! Start just left of the peaked boulders
at the base of the cliff. Climb the sustained crack up the orange-coloured
wall. Once the traverse of *Marisco Striptease* is reached, easier climbing
leads to the top.

Fine and Dandy   23 metres   Hard Very Severe 5b   (10.5.80)
[Photo p.128a.] The rock is not fine or dandy on this tough pitch. Start
below a ragged overlap corner. Climb the ragged corner to its top. Move
up left and then back right by a long reach to finish up easy grooves.

Scarring from a chipping episode mars the fine wall between *Fine and
Dandy* and *Silent Sleeper*. This created the unprotected **Scratchmarks**
(E6 6a † 1996), which is probably best forgotten.

About 6 metres right of the ragged overlap corner of *Fine and Dandy* is a rounded arête with a broken ledge low down. Large boulders abut the base of the cliff hereabouts.

★Silent Sleeper   20 metres   E2 5b   (27.6.85)
Start from boulders leaning against the cliff and step onto a broken ledge on the rounded arête. Move up left and climb the wall to where a horizontal crack joins a niche (peg). Swing left on the horizontal crack, using very good incuts, to where it is possible to finish direct.

Right again is a thin, brown-stained crack.

★Carmen   20 metres   E6 6b   (20.7.85)
Intense, bold, and technical. Climb the thin crack in the wall to a break, before taking the hanging flake crack on the right. Move back left onto the headwall and climb it to the top.

Vive la Difference   24 metres   Hard Severe 4b   (1984)
Climb the large groove which terminates this section of wall. Tricky at the top.

The cliff falls away to the right from this point towards the deep cleft of *Great Chimney* and an amphitheatre of shorter walls.

Credit Squeeze   20 metres   Difficult
This takes the cracked arête to the left of *Great Chimney*. It is gained by scrambling about 2 metres up onto the large ledge at the foot of a 7-metre-high column in the groove left of *Great Chimney*. Climb the crack on the left of the column to a good ledge. Follow the chimney for a few metres and then a slab on the left to some large boulders. Finish up the wall on the right, squeezing past a flake to the top.

The cleft of **Great Chimney** (20 metres Difficult 1950s) can be used in ascent or descent. Right of *Great Chimney* is a short wall with a big stepped ledge below it and a dark brown overhanging crack in its centre. The cliff then falls away to the right across the small but distinctively pock-marked *Socket Wall* area to the deep slanting break of *Slant Crack*. From here, it straightens out across the *Touch of Glass* wall to end at *Dexter's Grooves*.

★Holiday Tripper   15 metres   E2 5c   (10.8.85)
Climb the delightful orange crack and lovely pocketed wall above the left end of the big stepped ledge.

☆Five Year Itch   15 metres   E3 6b †   (25.4.87)
Climb the dark brown-stained overhanging crack in the centre of the wall. It requires dry conditions, which are rare.

NORTHERN PLATFORM

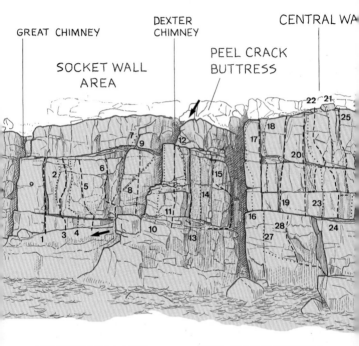

GREAT CHIMNEY

DEXTER CHIMNEY

CENTRAL WA

SOCKET WALL AREA

PEEL CRACK BUTTRESS

SOCKET WALL AREA			PEEL CRACK BUTTRESS		
1	Five Year Itch	E3	10	Spring Squill Salad	E5
2	Sock It To Me	E1	11	Peel Crack	VD
3	Socket Arete	VS	12	Edge Climb	S
4	Cumbelloe	HS	13	Razor	HVS
5	Socket Wall	S	14	The Sewing Machine Man	E5
6	The Lurch	VS			
7	Slant Crack	VS	15	The Sigh	VS
8	Smash and Grab	E2			
9	Touch of Glass	E4			

CARN BARRA ~
SOUTHERN PLATFORM

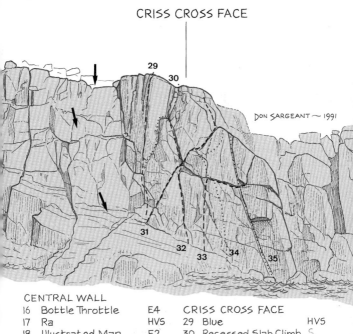

CRISS CROSS FACE

DON SARGEANT ~ 1991

CENTRAL WALL

16	Bottle Throttle	E4
17	Ra	HVS
18	Illustrated Man	E2
19	Dialectic	E1
20	Axis	VS
21	Exodus	VS
22	Fourteen Fathoms	E2
23	Relax	E2
24	Wet Barnacle	E3
25	Cruisin for a Bruisin'	E2
26	Big Bad Blues	E4
27	Twisting By The Pool	E3
28	Crystal Voyager	E3

CRISS CROSS FACE

29	Blue	HVS
30	Recessed Slab Climb	S
31	Criss	HS
32	Iron Cross	VS
33	Niche Wall	HS
34	Sea Wolf	HVS
35	Weasle	VS

Sock It to Me   15 metres   E1 5b   (10.8.85)
Climb the left arête of *Socket Wall*, moving up and left at mid height to
gain a groove slanting up to the right. Quite bold.

Socket Arête   15 metres   Very Severe 4c   (1983)
Start directly below the left arête of *Socket Wall* and climb the short wall to
a large ledge left of the arête. Follow the left side of the arête to gain a
slanting crack on its right, which is followed to the top.

★**Cumbelloe**   15 metres   Hard Severe 4b   (8.8.77)
A nicely insecure little pitch up the steep pock-marked wall just right of the
left arête of *Socket Wall*. Start below the middle of the wall and pull onto a
good hold above the overlap. Traverse left and climb the wall just right of
the crack to the top.

★**Socket Wall**   15 metres   Severe 4a   (29.6.55)
A cheeky start from below the right-hand end of the pock-marked wall,
where an undercut break runs up leftwards. Make a strenuous pull up and
left onto the face above the undercut; then climb straight up to a flake. Pull
into the groove and continue to the large platform above.

Broken Hearts   15 metres   E3 5c   (1991)
Start at the foot of *Socket Wall*. Pull stiffly up the overhanging wall to follow
a thin crack to the top.

Sundogs   15 metres   E4 6a †   (1996)
Start at the foot of *Socket Wall*. Climb the strenuous rightward-slanting
crackline to join *The Lurch* near the top.

The next major feature is the slanting line of *Slant Crack* running the full
height of the cliff.

The Lurch   15 metres   Very Severe 4c   (14.4.71)
Climb the overhanging cracks in the left retaining wall of *Slant Crack*
(often wet). A finish further left can be made.

Slant Crack   20 metres   Very Severe 4c   (5.7.55)
A tricky pitch taking the obvious slanting crack, which can be wet at times.

Smash and Grab   34 metres   E2 5c   (1.9.83)
Gain the ledge at the base of *Slanting Crack* and follow the faultline
diagonally rightwards and past a peg to the right. Finish up the arête.

Smash and Grab crosses a particularly fine wall of solid granite, which now
hosts several hard climbs. In the centre of the wall is a thin crack.

Eye of the Crystal   24 metres   E7 6c †   (1992)
Start a metre left of the thin crack. Very small holds might lead you to the faultline of *Smash and Grab*. Continue directly to a ledge by some very balancy moves. Step off left or finish as for the next route.

★★A Touch of Glass   24 metres   E4 6b   (1.9.83)
A direct and demanding pitch. Start below the centre of the wall. Climb the steep and fingery crackline past a peg in the fault of *Smash and Grab* to reach a ledge. Finish up a short wall.

☆Between the Sheets   27 metres   E5 6a †   (1991)
Start between the thin crack of *A Touch of Glass* and the right-hand arête, at a thinner crack. Follow a direct line up the thinner crack.

★Glass Arête   27 metres   E3 5c   (1.9.83)
Good moves. Climb straight up the reddish-coloured right arête.

Dexter's Groove   25 metres   Very Severe 5a   (1981)
Start in the dank recess right of *Glass Arête*. Follow the stepped grooves on the left of the recess.

Peel Crack Buttress

The cliff now turns sharply to seaward across the left flank of Peel Crack Buttress with its clean seaward face. The right flank of the buttress leads back into a deep break before the splendid Central Wall dominates the scene.

Glass of Sweet Wine   18 metres   E3   (1991)
Two disjointed pitches. Start midway between the dank recess and the arête start of *Sleazy Corner*.
1 9m. 5b. Climb disjointed cracks to the left-hand edge of a large ledge. Belay on the right below an easy corner (*Sleazy Corner*).
2 9m. 6a. Take the thin, leaning crack in the wall right of the easy corner.

Sleazy Corner   17 metres   Difficult
This is the line of the descent from the top of Peel Crack Buttress. Climb the left arête of the seaward face of the buttress to a large ledge. Follow twin cracks in the corner to the top.

Spring Squill Salad   15 metres   E5 5c   (3.87)
A short but bold little pitch. Climb the extreme left edge of the seaward face of Peel Crack Buttress.

◆Peel Crack   15 metres   Very Difficult   (2.7.55)
A little charmer, which is quite high in the grade. Start below the centre of the buttress and climb easily up to a large ledge. Climb the neat crack above.

Edge Climb   20 metres   Severe   4a   (31.3.52)
Climb to the large ledge as for *Peel Crack*. Step around the arête on the
right, and climb the strenuous chimney past an awkward bulge to the top.

★Weekend Treat   15 metres   Hard Severe   (28.8.83)
Start just around to the right of the right arête of the buttress. Climb the
steep cracked wall to the end of the large ledge; then move up and right
to finish up the arête.
Direct Start Hard Severe (1984). Climb the right end of the front face of
the buttress to the ledge.

Weekend Retreat   15 metres   Very Severe   4b   (1983)
The narrow chimney on the right flank of Peel Crack Buttress. (The upper
half is part of *Edge Climb*.)

Razor   15 metres   Hard Very Severe   5a   (1975)
Climb the obvious V-shaped corner, and then follow the crack onto the
right wall.

★★The Sewing Machine Man   15 metres   E5   6a   (1984)
Climb the bald and bold arête to the right of *Razor*.

The following four routes are reached by traversing gingerly below the
rounded arête to a ledge. The first two routes cross on a ledge at 8 metres.

★Nelson's Eye   20 metres   Hard Very Severe   5a   (21.7.87)
Take the first crack after the arête of *Sewing Machine Man*, and climb to a
good ledge. Continue up the crack on the right to a ledge; then step right
and continue up a broken crack to an awkward finish.

The Sigh   18 metres   Very Severe   5a   (11.4.71/1985)
From the far end of the ledge, climb the obvious crack leading up to a
roof; then move up and left to a small triangular ledge. Climb the
strenuous groove at the back of the ledge; then step right and climb to the
top.
Variation Finish E3 6a † (1984). From the triangular ledge, climb the
arête on the left.

In Touch   18 metres   E2   5c †   (1989)
Follow *The Sigh* to the small roof. Pull over the roof, trending rightwards to
finish up close to the right-hand edge of the wall.

Last Gasp   24 metres   E5   6a †   (1989)
Climb the overhanging cracks that run up the right side of the wall, to the
right of *The Sigh*.

Central Wall

Carn Barra's handsome Central Wall rises from the sea to a wide ledge at 10 metres. The main climbing lies on a 20-metre wall of impeccable golden granite above this ledge. The most convenient way of reaching the base of the wall is by abseil, although it can be reached from the Southern Platform by a short VS 4c or a long V Diff. The top of Central Wall is reached from the arrival point above Peel Crack Buttress by walking left (facing out) for a short distance to a comfortable ledge dotted with convenient abseil blocks. The obvious thread belays at the right-hand end of the ledge lie directly above the corner of *Axis*.

The left-hand side of the wall is terminated by a dank recess where the first route is found.

☆**The Soloist's Mist**   18 metres   E5 6a †   (1996)
Climb the right wall of the recess.

★**Bottle Throttle**   18 metres   E4 6a   (1985)
Serious and bold. Climb the wall and arête left of the corner-crack of *Ra*.

★**Ra**   18 metres   Hard Very Severe 5a   (23.7.72)
Intimidating. Good climbing up the stepped corner-crack at the left end of the wall. Large nuts or cams are advised for the upper section, which is steeper than it looks. Climb easily to the foot of the main crack, which is followed to a large ledge below the final crack. Climb the crack with increasing difficulty.

Atlantic Crossing   55 metres   Hard Very Severe   (2.1.80)
An entertaining traverse of the central wall from left to right.
1 12m. 4b. Climb *Ra* to the second ledge, below its final crack.
2 35m. 5b. Traverse right around the arête and follow the faultline below the roof to a resting-place. Continue along to a step down, and then hand-traverse to the corner. Traverse right again around the arête to a belay at a groove on the far right of the crag.
3 8m. 4a. Climb rightwards to the foot of a narrow wall split by a thin crack, which is climbed to finish.

★**Illustrated Man**   20 metres   E2 5b   (23.10.79)
An elegant and nicely structured climb. Follow *Ra* to the first break and move a few metres right to the next crack. Climb to where an awkward move gains a foot-ledge and protection potential around to the left. Clear the roof and take a steep groove to an easier finish.

The following routes climb the central part of the wall above a narrow ledge at 5 metres.

★Dialectic   18 metres   E1 5b   (30.8.72/5.80)
Fine climbing with one hard move. Start below the rounded arête at the
left-hand end of the narrow ledge, by a small flake. Use the flake to gain the
ledge; then continue up the crack in the arête above to the horizontal break.
Surmount an overhang easily and continue in the same line to the top.
Variation Starts
These are more sustained, but not as hard or as good as the parent route.
A 20m. Hard Very Severe 5a (5.79). Climb the corner left of the parent
route direct for 10 metres to the horizontal break; surmount the overhang
and continue in the same line to the top as for *Dialectic*.
B 20m. Hard Very Severe 5a (1978). Start as for the parent route and
use the flake to gain the ledge (several boulder problem starts are
available to the right). From the ledge, climb the crack two metres right of
Dialectic, joining the parent route at the overhang.

★Axis   18 metres   Very Severe 5a   (30.8.72)
An enjoyable, steady pitch up the distinctive corner that rises from the
narrow ledge. Climb a short, difficult wall to gain the ledge. The corner is
then followed steeply on delightful holds.

Exodus   27 metres   Very Severe 5a   (22.10.79)
Start as for *Axis* and gain the narrow ledge. Continue up the corner to the
prominent faultline. Move right along this for about 5 metres and then step
up into an obvious groove. Follow this and the steep crack to finish.

Variations are possible on the following pitches.

★Fourteen Fathoms   20 metres   E2 5b   (1982)
Fine, open climbing. Start as for *Axis* and gain the ledge. Climb the right
arête to the break, traverse 3 metres right, and gain a triangular niche.
Move up left onto the face; then climb straight up the thin crack to finish.

Relax   20 metres   E2 6a   (1987)
Start to the right of *Axis* below a faint arête and groove. Climb the arête to
a deep break. Follow a slight crack on the left, which trends rightwards to
the next break. Gain the triangular niche of *Fourteen Fathoms* and finish
as for that climb.

★★Wet Barnacle   20 metres   E3 5c   (1982)
Good, steep climbing. Start 4 metres right of the *Axis* corner. Three jugs
lead to the roof. Pull over on the left before climbing a flake crack to the
break. Move up left and finish as for *Fourteen Fathoms*.

★Cruisin' for a Bruisin'   20 metres   E2 5c   (6.84)
Start as for *Wet Barnacle*. Climb the steep wall and traverse right to a
roof-crack. Pull over the roof to good hand-jams; then continue up a crack
and wall to finish up a groove. The direct start is the pugnacious **Black
Eye for a Guidebook Writer** (E3 6a 8.98).

☆**Big Bad Blues** 20 metres E4 6b † (1.10.87)

Start at the extreme right end of the wall below a steep arête, just before the point where the wall goes into a shallow groove. Climb the arête to the roof using a rounded finger-pocket. Pull over the roof to a series of disjointed cracks, which lead to the break. Continue up the groove above to the top.

Kicking Steps 20 metres Hard Very Severe 4c † (22.7.87)

Start at the extreme right end of the wall. Climb the corner to a roof, step right, and climb a short groove to a ledge. Move left into a groove and climb this to finish up the thin crack of *Atlantic Crossing*.

On the sea wall below the main ledge there are two nicely eccentric routes which are approached by a further abseil from the right-hand end of the ledge, or by an approach from the extreme left end of the Southern Platform area (see approach notes below). Calm seas and dry conditions required.

☆**Twisting by the Pool** 28 metres E3 † (7.85)

From the extreme left end of the Southern Platform area, work left to a ledge below the sharp right edge of the sea wall.
1 14m. 4c. Step down and traverse left under the clean-cut overlap and across blackish rock into a corner; then go left for a few metres across the wall to a small sentry-box and hanging belay.
2 14m. 5c. Continue left (small wires) to a good vertical crack, which is climbed to the platform.

Crystal Voyager 20 metres E3 † (7.86)

1 14m. 4c. *Twisting by the Pool* pitch 1.
2 6m. 6a. Follow the crackline directly above the sentry-box to the platform.

Southern Platform

The Southern Platform of Carn Barra has a number of easier-grade climbs of character. It is best reached by traversing north-east to boulder-strewn ledges from the grass slopes above Folly Cove. Alternatively, walk left (facing out) from the arrival point above Peel Crack Buttress to pass across the top of Central Wall. Continue left across a wet and grubby break to the boulder-strewn ledges. Descend some stepped rock and down-climb a short steep section; then descend more easily to the smooth and deeply furrowed platform below the distinctive Criss Cross Face. Southwards across the bay is the handsome North Face of Fox Promontory. The Southern Platform slopes down rightwards (facing in) to sea-level and draws sweeping waves in swell and rough sea. The extreme smoothness of the rock helps in the sluicing off of moving objects – even fast ones running frantically in the other direction. Be warned! The starts of climbs near the seaward base of the platform may be awash at high tide. Criss Cross Face is characterized by wide cracks which form a huge X. *Criss* follows the branch running up from left to right.

The routes on the lower section of Central Wall can be gained from here by scrambling down at low tide to the far left end (facing in) of the Southern Platform. The starting-ledge for the main routes on Central Wall can also be reached from this approach by climbing the short smooth wall at the right-hand end (facing in) at Very Severe 4c.

The following route links the Southern Platform with Central Wall.

Samphire Wall   53 metres   Very Difficult   (15.8.68)
A wandering line, if line is the right word! This makes a long leftward traverse above the lower, northern section of the platform to finish up the right-hand side of Central Wall. Start at the left-hand end of the higher section of the platform, on a recessed ledge. This is directly above a steep corner-crack that drops down to the lower sea-washed platform.
1 15m. Climb leftwards to a tapering ledge and move left along it for a couple of metres. Climb a steep wall and short slab, moving left from this to a higher ledge. Step down from the left end of the ledge, and then traverse to a buttress with a vertical crack. Climb on poor rock to belay below a steep wall.
2 10m. Step down and left; then traverse delicately left in an exposed position to continue up a V-chimney to a large ledge.
3 10m. Step off a large rocking stone and then move over to a small buttress split by an overhanging crack. Climb the crack to a belay below a wall.
4 18m. Climb to the right of the nose above; then make some awkward moves up a corner on the right. Swing into a chimney, which is climbed to finish.

Touchwood   18 metres   Severe 4a   (23.2.82)
Start as for *Samphire Wall* and climb a square groove by the left-hand crack to a ledge. The groove is gained from a ramp on the left. Finish up a stone-filled crack at the back of the ledge.

A slabby break runs up diagonally leftwards from the left base of the Criss Cross X. Near the top of the break there is a steep crackline to the left of a recess. To the left of the slabby break is a short red-veined crack, which provides a 5b start to *Blue*. The slab left of the red-veined crack has been climbed at E4 5c: **Put the Red Card Out for the Correspondent** (20 metres 24.5.98). Alternatively, follow the red-veined crack and then step left to follow a slabby arête: **The Hog from Camborne** (20 metres E1 5b 1981).

Blue   30 metres   Hard Very Severe 5b   (1982)
Climb the steep crackline which soars proudly above the slabby break.

Recessed Slab Climb   26 metres   Severe   (31.3.52)
A pleasant pitch. Move up the slabby break; then climb, with some difficulty, into the base of the recess to follow slabs and cracks to the top.

Criss   22 metres   Hard Severe 4b   (26.5.55)
Good old-fashioned skills are called for here. Start at the foot of the crack
forming the left-to-right diagonal of the X formation. Climb the crack
strenuously to a niche; then continue diagonally right up the widening
crack to the top of the pinnacle. The short wall on the left leads to the top.

Iron Cross   25 metres   Very Severe 4c   (5.10.75)
Similar technique to that for *Criss*, following the right-to-left diagonal crack
to the niche. Continue in the same line up the flared crack to finish up
Recessed Slab Climb.

Winged Victory   25 metres   E2 5c   (1994)
Though eliminate in nature, this provides some nice climbing and an airy
finish. Start at the foot of the right-hand leg of the X, below a shallow
groove. Climb up and follow the shallow groove to a wide horizontal
break. From the break, take thin cracks in the face of a large block. From
the top of the block, step left onto the face and climb it to the top via a
shallow scoop.

★Niche Wall   25 metres   Hard Severe   (7.7.55)
[Photo p. 128b.] A pleasant little climb. Start at the foot of the steep wall
just to the right of the X formation.
1 15m. 4b. Climb the steep wall to a good ledge, where there are two
choices. The original line traverses delicately right around the arête to a
ledge at the foot of a crack. Alternatively, and better, climb the square-cut
corner and slab above to the top.
2 10m. If the original line has been taken, climb the crack in the corner to
the top.
Variation Start
Climb the cracked wall about 2 metres right of the normal start and trend
rightwards to join the parent route 2 metres below the good ledge.

★Sea Wolf   22 metres   Hard Very Severe 5a   (1983)
Start right of *Niche Wall* below the centre of the steep wall at a flaky ledge.
Climb the wall direct to the good ledge of *Niche Wall*. From the ledge,
follow a thin crack past a niche to the top. Slight protection.

★Air Tripper   22 metres   E1 5b   (1981)
A good sustained pitch if a step right into *Weasle* is avoided. Start at the
flaky ledge in the centre of the wall, as for *Sea Wolf*. Move right to a
shallow, leftward-facing, curved scoop. Climb straight up the wall to join
the variation finish of *Weasle*.

★Weasle   20 metres   Very Severe 4c   (16.4.76)
An interesting pitch, with good moves around the overhang. Low tide
required. Start at the base of a leftward-slanting groove about 6 metres
right of *Niche Wall*, at the right-hand end of the face. Climb the groove to
the overhang: a popular place to hang around, much to the chagrin of

tide-harassed seconds waiting below! Continue up a crack to a ledge (belay possible). Finish up the groove.
Variation
Touchstone 4b (26.5.82). From the ledge, step up, move awkwardly around to the left, and follow a crack in the slab above.

For about two hours either side of low water and in calm seas, a deep chimney-break can be gained from the base of the Southern Platform. This leads rightwards through a maze of rock and gives access to a small number of routes before Dutchman's Zawn is reached. At high tide, the routes described can be reached from above the extreme left end (facing out) of Criss Cross Face by descending short walls and chimneys with care.

Two climbs, **Wild Oscillations** and **Miss Selfridge** (both 1986), led up the first buttress past the deep chimney/break, but were destroyed by rockfall. What is now the first substantial wall past the chimney/break has two routes.

Rapido   10 metres   E1 5a   (1990)
Climb the blunt arête in the middle of the wall, with a move left towards the top.

Life's Moments   10 metres   E3 5c   (1990)
Climb the right-hand arête of the wall.

The next climbs lie around to the right on the broken walls overlooking the entrance to Dutchman's Zawn.

Howlin' Wolf   20 metres   E1 5b   (10.11.85)
A few metres along the flanking wall there is a square-cut recess in the cliff with a steep black backwall. The wall is climbed direct to a protruding block, from where steep moves up to the right lead to an easier break.

Sea Fox   22 metres   Hard Severe 4a   (16.2.69)
Climb the cracks in the right-hand corner of the recess to a large ledge. Continue up a corner to another ledge, and follow a steep corner to the foot of twin V-grooves. Take the left-hand groove to the top.

Pedantics   20 metres   Difficult   (16.2.69)
Start below a deep, black chimney 6 metres right of the square-cut recess. Gain the chimney and continue to a ledge. Climb the right-hand wall and a steep groove to a ledge, and then to the top.

Dutchman's Zawn (Granite) OS Ref 361 224

Outlook: South-west. Dry weather required.
Tidal. Accessible for three hours either side of low water.
Coastguard Identity: Folly Cove.

Dutchman's Zawn is a gruesome-looking place which has failed to gain any popularity and the routes described here must be treated with caution on account of damp, weak rock.

Approach as for Carn Barra from the car-park at Porthgwarra. Just beyond the twin-split boulder on the coast path the sloping rim of Folly Cove appears down to the left with the small upper buttresses and towers of Carn Barra's southern edge beyond. Dutchman's Zawn lies tucked in between Folly Cove and Carn Barra.

Descent: Cross the grass slopes above the zawn and descend broken rock towards the seaward edge of the zawn's northern side. A short abseil gains the boulder-packed bed of the narrow zawn. At high tide the routes on the South Face can be approached by abseiling to their first belays from the grassy rib that lies between the zawn and Folly Cove. It is best to view the face from the north side of the zawn in order to judge the precise abseil line.

On the right-hand side of the zawn (facing in) is the South Face. It has a fine looking but rather gritty slab high on its left side. Opposite the South Face is the steep, impending, usually damp North Face.

North Face

☆**Eat 'Em and Smile** 52 metres E6 7a † 20.5.87)
A *Friend 1* proves essential for a section near the top. Start from a large boulder next to a short groove. Gain the groove and climb leftwards to a peg. Continue straight up past more pegs to a horizontal break. Make a dynamic move for a small flake, go left on poor holds, and mantel to reach easier ground. Belay on cams and wires.

South Face

The following routes start at a shallow orange-coloured depression at the right-hand base of the face below a deep vertical crack. Subsequent ascentionists have not been impressed and these routes are best left for aficionados of damp, gritty, loose rock with poor protection.

A Walk on the Dark Side 60 metres E3 (5.5.87)
Start below the orange-coloured depression.
1 30m. 4b. Climb a short way up the depression; then traverse left along ledges to belay below a small square overhang on the far left.

2 30m. 6a. Surmount the overhang on the left and climb the crack to a small foothold. Continue up the broken groove; then traverse right onto the steep slab. Climb this past two pegs to the top.

Reflections on the Sea   61 metres   E4   (10.6.85)
This takes a series of grooves and overhangs to gain the right side of the steep slab. Start below the orange-coloured depression.
1 24m. 4b. Climb the wall just left of the orange-coloured depression; then traverse left to ledges below some overhangs.
2 37m. 5c. Climb grooves on the right of the belay and cross an overhang to the steep slab, which is followed to the top. Two pegs.

Second Time Around   52 metres   E3   (17.4.87)
A line up the right side of the buttress, to the left of the deep vertical crack. Start as for *A Walk on the Dark Side*.
1 23m. 4c. Climb the depression and then the steeper groove on the left to a narrow sloping ledge. Traverse left to belays in a corner below some roofs.
2 29m. 6a. Climb the steep broken groove to the roof above; pull over this on the left to the steep wall (peg). Climb to a horizontal fault; then move right to climb the steep wall to a peg. Continue up the wall on the right to finish up easier-angled rock. Belays are well back.

Folly Cove (Granite)   OS Ref 362 224

'I came across a deployment of falsity in the rock so massive as to be fit almost to prop up a Fascist…'
                          (J Menlove Edwards: Count House Log Book, 1953)

Outlook: South-west.
Tidal. There is an easy right-hand (facing out) approach for three hours either side of low water and in quiet seas.
Coastguard Identity: Folly Cove.

The Cove is a deeply eroded weakness between the harder outliers of Carn Barra and Fox Promontory and, while much clearance of loose material was carried out prior to first ascents, the nature of the kaolinized rock means that decay continues. Care is advised on the gritty rock found here.

Approach as for Carn Barra from the car-park at Porthgwarra. Just beyond the twin-split boulder on the coast path, the sloping rim of Folly Cove appears down to the left. The rim of the cove is grassy and has been eroded and undermined by rabbits. There is a cluster of solid pinnacles half-way along the rim of the backwall. These pinnacles lie directly above the boulder ledges and upper crack of *Solitaire*.

Descend easily a steep grassy rib on the north side of the cliff. This rib separates Folly Cove from Dutchman's Zawn. Scramble down to the left (facing out) where the grass ends; then traverse back into the cove down a sloping ramp and onto the boulder-crammed floor. The Cove has a left wall (facing in) that falls back to a wide corner depression with a big grassy ledge at half height. The cliff then runs to the right across the back of the cove through a series of ribs and bays to where its black right-hand wall turns sharply to seaward towards the outlying fin of Fox Promontory.

The first routes are on the left wall close to the foot of the approach. A thin white vein slants up across the wall from left to right.

Initiation   24 metres   Hard Very Severe 5a   (1.8.86)
Climb the steep wall and grooves on the extreme left edge of the left wall of the cove crossing the white vein on the way.

> The rounded arête right of a vertical red vein has been climbed past a peg in a horizontal break, and then past a bolt to where a short crack leads to a ledge on the arête, which is climbed to finish (**A Hollow Man** 30 metres E4 6a 26.4.87). The bolt has subsequently been removed and the grade merely reflects the climb's former status.

To the right of the previous routes, the left wall runs back into the wide depression with the big grassy ledge at half height. To the right of this is a wall with shattered pillars and boulder-strewn ledges at half height. Below and right of the pillars is an orange-coloured lower wall seamed with cracks.

Solitaire   52 metres   Hard Very Severe   (4.3.86)
Start below the middle of the lower wall.
1 26m. 5a. Climb the centre of the wall, and then trend leftwards over ledges to belay on a boulder-strewn ledge below the ochre-patched upper wall.
2 26m. 5a. Climb the central crack in the upper wall to the cluster of pinnacles on the rim of the cove.

Right of *Solitaire* is a deep vertical crack.

Sky Highway   49 metres   Hard Very Severe   (4.4.86)
Start at the foot of the buttress right of the deep central crack.
1 12m. 4b. Climb a slab to belay on a ledge.
2 37m. 5a. Climb the crack right of the belay, clearing the roof on its right to reach a wall and groove. Climb the groove to a cave; then move right to climb another groove to the top.

To the right of *Sky Highway*, the cliff declines into a recessed break of very poor rock. To the right of the break lie a series of blade arêtes.

★Technicolour Dream   40 metres   E2 5b   (12.7.86)
Start below the first arête. Climb broken rocks into the obvious groove,
which leads to a roof. Pull around into a groove on the left and follow it to
a second roof. Move left and finish steeply up the arête.

There is a belay stake on a ledge near the finish of the following four routes.

The Bush Man   55 metres   Hard Very Severe   (16.10.86)
Replace rock after use. Start about 10 metres right of *Technicolour Dream*,
at the start of a series of short grooves and walls below a thin flying arête
on the skyline.
1 25m. 4a. Climb the grooves and walls to a ledge below and left of the
flying arête.
2 30m. 4c. Climb a crack in the slab to finish up the left wall of the arête.

Right of *The Bush Man* is an ochre-coloured wall.

Hidden Glories   50 metres   E3 †   (26.4.87)
Start below the ochre-coloured wall.
1 20m. 4b. Climb the wall to the arête and gain a groove on the left.
Follow this; then step left to the belay of *The Bush Man*.
2 30m. 5c. Climb the slab on the right to reach the arête. Move right
around this; then climb it boldly to the top. Belay at its top or go up
carefully over earthy ledges and grass for a further 15 metres.

Computer Commuter   53 metres   E2 †   (2.10.86)
Start in the bay to the right of the ochre-coloured wall. The lower backwall
of the bay can be greasy. On the left wall of the bay is a steep corner-crack
with a clean wall to its left.
1 15m. 5a. Climb the corner-crack to a ledge.
2 38m. 5b. Climb the right wall; then continue up cracks in the headwall
on the left.

☆Sun Lord   53 metres   E4 †   (16.10.86)
Start below the arête right of *Computer Commuter*, between competing
greasy cracks.
1 15m. 5b. Climb the arête and the groove on the right to a ledge.
2 38m. 6a. Climb the lichen-capped pinnacle above; then follow cracks
in the right arête to another pinnacle. Climb this pinnacle to its top and
belay well back.

The Inquisition   50 metres   E2   (26.4.87)
Start as for *Sun Lord*, below the steep corner.
1 15m. 5a. Climb the steep greasy wall on the right to where it is
possible to step left into a steep crack. Follow this into a chimney and then
onto a good ledge.
2 35m. 5c. Climb the overhanging groove slanting up to the right; then
move right onto the wall to follow a crack and groove to its top. Move right
onto a ledge, and climb the wall above to the top.

Dream Machine   53 metres   E3   (2.10.86)
Start below a crack in the next buttress right of the bay.
1 10m. 4a. Climb a steep corner to a ledge.
2 43m. 6a. Climb the groove on the right and then the crack on the left
to a roof. Go over the roof and finish up a steep wall.

The right-hand wall of the cove now turns sharply to seaward.

The Music Man   49 metres   E2   (25.9.86)
The black right-hand wall has a central vertical crack.
1 34m. 5c. Climb the crack to a sloping ledge.
2 15m. Continue easily up the broken right arête.

☆**Joy Rider**   52 metres   E1 †   (1986)
1 37m. 5b. Climb the slanting crack on the right of the black wall just left
of a jutting arête to reach a sloping ledge.
2 15m. Continue easily up the broken right arête.

Folly Groove   34 metres   Very Severe 5a   (21.6.81)
Just around the arête there is a curving groove and corner. Climb the
groove to where it is possible to cross to the right to gain a slab around the
corner. Climb to the foot of a steeper corner, which is followed to the top.

Fox Promontory (Granite)   OS Ref 361 223

'…When the sea mist lays its spell upon its rocks and towers; then one seems
to be surrounded by monsters of another world, such as Dante dreamed of
and Doré tried to paint…'   (A G Folliott Stokes, 1909.)

Outlook: South, west, and north.
Tidal on The Nose and along the base of the North Face, where starts are
accessible for about three hours either side of low water, although they can
be strongly affected by swell and rough sea. **Non-tidal** on the upper
pitches of the South Face.
Coastguard Identity: Black Carn/Folly Cove.

Folliott Stokes meant every purple word. And, even for modern cynics, Fox
Promontory is still impressive; monster-backed and straining out to sea from
its tenuous boulder-bridge mooring. There is no descent into hell-fire; but
there are some excellent climbs here on steep solid rock and in fine
positions.

Approach as for Carn Barra from the car-park at Porthgwarra. About 80
metres beyond the distinctive wall of slabs that cuts across the path, the rocky

summit of the headland to which the Promontory is attached is reached. (Folly Cove lies just beyond.)

Fox Promontory is a handsome granite fin jutting westwards from the mainland. It is about 30 metres high and is separated from the mainland by a narrow steep-sided zawn and its linking boulder-bridge. The crest of the promontory is ragged but nicely horizontal, while the south and north sides are steep. The North Face is the most extensive feature and comprises a steep black wall seamed with vertical cracks. The seaward prow terminates at The Nose, which is about 25 metres high. The South Face is more broken and provides the approach to the starts of all the climbs. This face is separated from Black Wall by the narrow zawn, which can be jumped across.

Descent is via the Easy Way Down across the South Face. From the mainland, go out along the chaotic, jumbled crest of the Promontory to a small earthy platform just beyond the first high tower. There are two perched boulders on the crest to seaward. Do not go beyond these, but instead follow a break slanting down the South Face to where it steepens above a 10-metre corner with big ledges at its foot.

The corner can be descended at Difficult standard. Alternatively, go down the left rim of the corner (facing out) and make an airy step down to a flake. Shuffle left (facing in) down the flake to reach the ledges at the foot of the corner. From here, stepped ledges drop down to a final descent groove which leads to sea-level. For The North Face and The Nose, cross the sea-level rocks and then climb a short wall or a bulging corner to reach the large platform below The Nose. Traverse around to the left to reach the ledge system below the North Face.

An alternative descent can be made by traversing along the crest of the Promontory to its seaward end. From here, an abseil down the seaward part of the North Face can be made from a number of belay points.

The North Face

The North Face is a handsome expanse of black rock. It is sunless until later in the day and can often be sea-damp and greasy until the first blink of afternoon sun transforms it. A line of ledges runs along the base of the North Face decreasing in height from right to left.

At the left end of the main ledge-system is a deeply-cut corner capped by an overhang. *Folly Corner* starts up to the left of this and then continues across the yellow-lichened tower on the left. The distinctive corner 10 metres to the right of *Folly Corner* is *Cuboid Corner*. The steep crack in the centre of the face right of *Cuboid Corner* gives *Sunshine Cracks*, while right again the prominent black vein curving up to the left is climbed by *Reveille*. Right of this, and a few metres in from the seaward edge of the face, is the thin white quartz vein taken by *Curtain Raiser*. Those routes to the left of *Cuboid Corner* have the least generous tidal access.

Several variations exist to the routes on the North Face. Only the original and more obvious lines are described.

☆The Blade   18 metres   E2 5b †   (25.6.86)
Start at the extreme left end of the face, below a knife-edged arête. Climb short walls and ledges to the fine arête. Move up to a large hold that doubles as a sling runner and follow the arête proper to the top. Blinkers are required for a rather pointless variation, **The (Bogus) Blade** (18 metres E6 6b 16.7.95), which follows a thin crack to the right of the arête. From the large hold which doubles as a sling runner, step right to follow the incipient crack with great difficulty and little protection to the top.

Second Blood   18 metres   Very Severe 4b   (25.6.86)
Start just right of the knife-edged arête, below a square-cut overhang split by a crack. Climb the deeply-grooved slab to the overhang and follow the crack through it to the top.

Foxblood   27 metres   Severe 4a   (17.4.76)
A pleasant route up the left side of the prominent tower left of *Folly Corner*. Start at the foot of a distinctive red-stained groove left of the tower. Follow the groove until it steepens; then move right along a small ledge to where a strenuous move gains a larger ledge on the front of the tower (belay possible). Climb the wide crack above for 10 metres to a ledge on the right. Follow the crack to a lichen-covered slab and belays. Scrambling leads to the top.

Droplove   30 metres   Severe 4b   (5.6.86)
Climb a steep crack and shallow corner just right of *Foxblood* to a small ledge. Swing right to another ledge; then move back left onto the left face of the tower, which is climbed via steep cracks. A direct start up the front face is 4c.

Folly Corner   30 metres   Very Difficult   (27.3.51)
Start below the deeply-cut corner.
1 8m. Climb easily up the left wall of the corner to a broken ledge.
2 10m. Traverse left around the rib to a ledge. From here, easier climbing leads up the rib to the foot of a broken chimney.
3 12m. Follow the easy chimney to the top.

Vixen's Crack   37 metres   Very Difficult   (25.6.86)
Start as for *Folly Corner*.
1 8m. Climb over ledges to a steep pillar on the right of the arête.
2 23m. Climb the pillar; then step left onto the arête and follow this to the obvious crack. Climb the crack and continue up a short slab to belays.
3 6m. Finish up the pinnacle above.

FOX PROMONTORY

NORTH FACE

1	The Blade	E2
2	Second Blood	VS
3	Foxblood	S
4	Droplove	S
5	Folly Corner	VD
6	Vixen's Crack	VD
7	Tiptoe	E1
8	Pilgrims	HVS
9	Cuboid Corner	HS
10	Rough Rider	S
11	The Huntsman	VS
12	Reynard's Revenge	HS

13	Sunshine Cracks	HS
14	Dark Denizen	VS
15	Reveille	HS
16	The Curtain Raiser	VS

THE NOSE

17	Octopus	E2

20	Sports Plan	E3

21	Sinister	VS
22	The Muzzle	HVS
23	The Whisker	VS
24	Zawn Face Climb	D
25	The Outside Start	VD

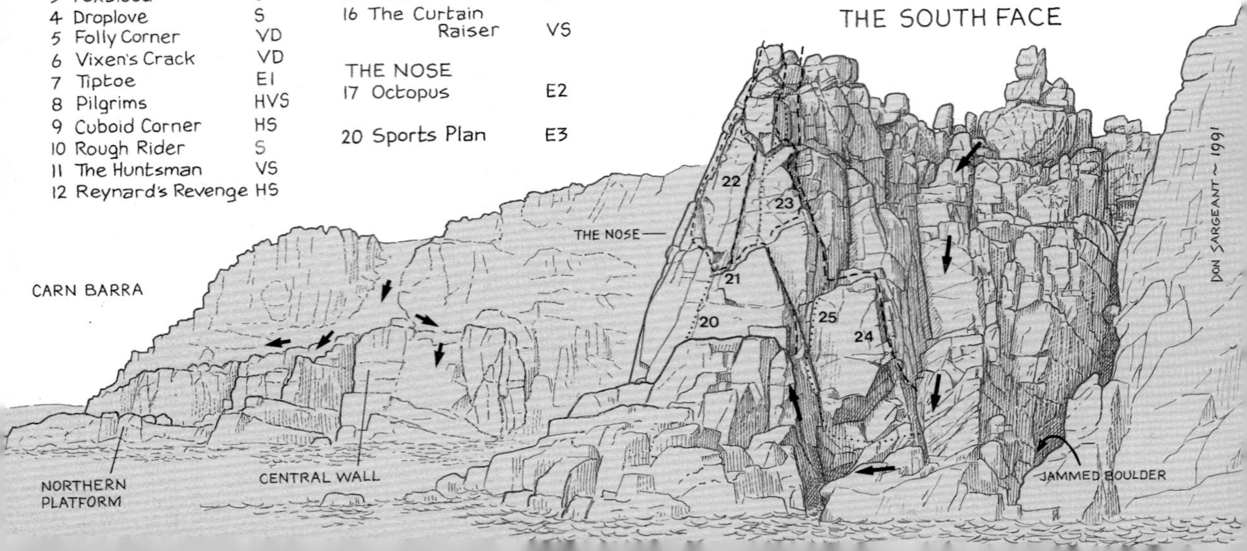

THE SOUTH FACE

CARN BARRA

NORTHERN PLATFORM

CENTRAL WALL

THE NOSE

JAMMED BOULDER

DON SARGEANT ~ 1991

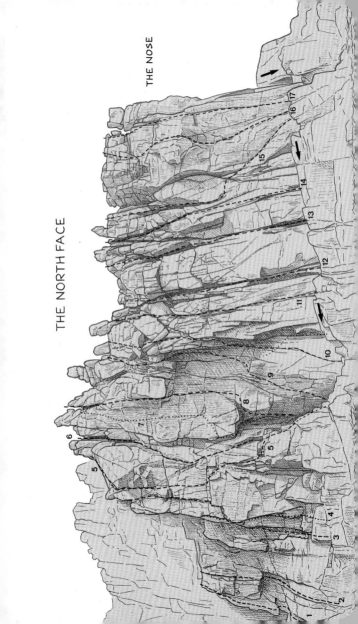

THE NORTH FACE

THE NOSE

Tiptoe   30 metres   E1 5a   (5.6.86)
Start below a triangular overhang in the centre of the face to the right of
Vixen's Crack. Climb the groove to the roof. Move left then back right onto
the steep slab on the right. Climb up right for 3 metres to follow a system
of slanting cracks and a slab to the top.

Pilgrims   30 metres   Hard Very Severe 4c   (5.6.86)
Start as for *Tiptoe*. Climb a thin flake on the right to the roof. Move right to
a small ledge and climb a steep crack to a corner on the left. Follow the
corner onto slabs, which lead to the top.

Cuboid Corner   24 metres   Hard Severe 4b   (15.8.63)
This takes a diagonal entry from left to right to climb the steep corner
about 10 metres to the right of *Folly Corner*. Start as for *Folly Corner*. Climb
the wall on the right on good holds to a comfortable ledge to the left of the
corner. Trend up rightwards to a ledge to the left of the corner. Make an
awkward move into the corner and then climb on better holds to a large
niche. Scramble up the gully to finish.
Direct Start 8m. (1.6.66). Start at the base of *Cuboid Corner*. Climb the
corner-crack, which can be greasy, for 3 metres; then move left onto the
wall to gain the first ledge of the main route.

Rough Rider   30 metres   Severe 4b   (5.6.86)
Start just left of the start of *Cuboid Corner Direct Start*. Climb the steep wall
and crack system to a sentry-box. At the roof, either traverse left onto a rib
and then go straight up to finish up slabs, or swing right onto the right
arête to follow broken cracks and slabs to the top.

★The Huntsman   24 metres   Very Severe 5a   (28.10.78)
Start about 3 metres right of the start of *Cuboid Corner Direct Start*. Climb
the twin cracks and the wall above directly to the top. Well protected.

Reynard's Revenge   24 metres   Hard Severe 4b   (1.6.66)
Climb the steep chimney right of *The Huntsman* using holds on the left
wall, before taking the overhang direct. Follow good holds to a ledge.
Move easily up the chimney, to pass a pinnacle after 5 metres. Scramble to
the top.

★Sunshine Cracks   24 metres   Hard Severe 4b   (20.5.56)
A nice direct jamming pitch taking the wide vertical crack right of
Reynard's Revenge. Dig deep and you may not have to jam. The crack, a
narrow chimney at first, is climbed to a good ledge at 3 metres. Continue
up the crack in the shallow corner above to reach a narrow sloping ledge;
then climb more easily up the short corner to a stance on the right (belay
possible). Alternatively, the left wall can be climbed rather delicately via two
ledges and a rib. The chimney above the stance is followed to the top.

Baby Bouncer   25 metres   E4 6a †   (16.7.95)
Climb the wall between *Sunshine Cracks* and *Dark Denizen* to a
leftward-facing corner. Continue more easily up the corner and the cracks
above to the top. (Side runners were used for the first section.)

Dark Denizen   27 metres   Very Severe 5a   (5.10.80)
Start below the obvious cracks 5 metres right of *Sunshine Cracks*. Follow
the cracks direct passing a tricky section at about 10 metres.

Thrutched Up   27 metres   E1 5b †   (16.7.95)
Start at the leftmost of the cracks that meet the leftward-facing curved
corner at half height. Climb the poorly-protected crack and then the
decomposing runnel in the corner. Finish up the cleft above.

★★Reveille   27 metres   Hard Severe 4b   (5.56)
Good, well-protected climbing. Start 6 metres in from the seaward edge of
the face at the foot of a black quartzy vein running up to the left. Follow
the black vein steeply but on good holds to a point below a wide rounded
crack. Traverse left across the face and then climb the left wall of a short
chimney to a block belay.

★★The Curtain Raiser   26 metres   Very Severe   (21.8.63)
An excellent open face pitch; sustained, and on small holds. Start about 3
metres in from the seaward edge of the North Face below a thin white
vein.
1 20m. 5a. Follow the vein on small holds and make a tenuous move
into a scoop at 10 metres. Continue on more generous holds to a shallow
recess; then move up right onto a slab which leads to a stance and belay.
2 6m. 4a. Climb the steep broken nose above.

Octopus   27 metres   E2 5c   (7.68)
Start just left of The Nose by a rock-pool and below a thin vertical crack.
Climb the thin crack to where it becomes rounded and most unhelpful near
the top. From here, move up and right, to finish up the obvious groove.

The Nose

The Nose is an impressive tower of granite split by a striking central crack,
which gives the testing line of *The Muzzle*. *The Whisker* takes a flanking line
from the stance at the base of the central crack around to the right of The
Nose while *Sinister* leads off to the left. The lower left section of The Nose has
been disfigured by a large rockfall which has destroyed **Aggressive Edge**
(24.7.85) and **Hallucinations** (21.6.81). In their place are:

Disappointment Arête   30 metres   E2 5b   (1994)
Start at the foot of the groove just right of the arête. Climb into the groove
and then, when possible, climb the arête with your left hand! An
unsatisfying experience.

Second Class Slab   30 metres   Hard Very Severe   4c   (1994)
A route which lives up to its name. Climb the rockfall scar, moving left at
the top.

Sports Plan   29 metres   E3   (18.4.81)
Start 3 metres right of the large V-shaped rockfall scar, below a thin
vertical crack. The first pitch is not easily protected and only succumbs to a
confident effort.
1 14m. 5c. Climb leftwards into the crack, which is followed to a good
ledge and belay.
2 15m. 5a. Step right and climb the thin crack in the edge of the wall to
the first roof. From here, it is more logical to finish leftwards up *The Muzzle*.
The original line moves right and then up onto a good ledge, from which it
climbs the right-hand crack in the green wall to the top of *The Nose*.
Direct Start 10m. E3 6a. An attractive alternative with pleasant moves
and just enough protection. Climb the line of shallow flakes to the right of
the crack which forms the substance of *Sports Plan*'s first pitch. Stepping off
the pinnacle and climbing the top part of the direct start is HVS 5b, and
was formerly recorded as the direct start to *The Muzzle*.

The next three climbs lie on the central section of The Nose and have a
common first pitch.

Sinister   26 metres   Very Severe   (5.56)
Start below a narrow slab at the right-hand side of the platform at the foot
of The Nose. The slab leads up left to a ledge below the steep central
crack of The Nose.
1 8m. Climb the steep slab to its top; then step down onto the ledge
below the steep central crack.
2 18m. 4c. A testing few moves. Traverse left from the ledge onto the
steep wall and then gain the good ledge above by a difficult mantelshelf.
Continue more easily up the groove on the right to the top.

★★The Muzzle   26 metres   Hard Very Severe   (20.5.56)
This nicely positioned and sustained pitch climbs the central crack and then
traverses left to finish up the arête.
1 8m. *Sinister* pitch 1.
2 18m. 4c. Climb the steep crack to below the overhang; then traverse
left with difficulty and on some slightly dubious rock to gain the rib, which
leads more easily to the top.

★The Whisker   26 metres   Very Severe   (21.8.63)
A good little route which climbs the right arête of The Nose.
1 8m. *Sinister* pitch 1.
2 18m. 4c. From the belay, pull up onto a gangway leading up to the
right. Move delicately around onto the slab and follow its left edge to a
large perched block. Mantelshelf onto the block and climb twin cracks on
the right to finish.

Zawn Face Climb   25 metres   Difficult   (27.3.51)
A pleasant route, although bird-limed in parts. It follows the line of the slab on the southern flank of The Nose. Start from a ledge above the final descent groove of the Easy Way Down.
1 8m. Climb steep cracks to a big platform.
2 17m. Climb the short steep corner that leads to a large slab. Climb the slab to its upper edge, where an awkward move right leads via a wide crack to the top.
Variation
The Outside Start   17 metres   Very Difficult   (16.9.62)
From the foot of the steep cracks of the normal start, move left across a scoop and then climb the bulging corner to the foot of the narrow slab taken by *Sinister* and the other routes on the front of The Nose. Climb the slab until it is possible to move right up a short crack to the large platform at the top of pitch 1.

★★The Vixen's Embrace   118 metres   Very Severe   (18.8.63)
This adventurous though contrived line girdles The Nose and North Face of the Promontory from right to left. It includes a diagonal abseil down and across *The Curtain Raiser*. Easier variations exist, but the line described is in the best sporting traditions. The fox may escape but the climber may not.
1 8m. *Zawn Face Climb* pitch 1.
2 10m. 4b. Climb a short corner to gain the left edge of a slab and descend the sloping gangway of *The Whisker* to the belay common to the routes on the central area of The Nose.
3 10m. 4c. Move left past a niche onto a steep wall and mantelshelf onto a good ledge (*Sinister* pitch 2). Continue leftwards above the crack of *Sports Plan* and then move up to a prominent spike on the arête above.
4 20m. 4a. From the spike, make a diagonal abseil of about 12 metres down the groove of *The Curtain Raiser*. At the midway point, swing left to the black vein of *Reveille* to a point just below a niche. Follow the vein; then traverse left to a short chimney leading to a belay.
5 20m. 4a. Descend to a traverse-line and move left around the arête onto a sloping ledge. Continue left and then climb down a rib to make a delicate move left onto a sloping black ledge. From the far end of the ledge, climb a crack on good holds to a comfortable niche on the left (on *Cuboid Corner*).
6 12m. 4b. Descend the corner below to a ledge on the left; then continue more easily down to a belay ledge in the centre of the black face (*Cuboid Corner* pitch 2 in reverse).
7 11m. 5a. From the left end of the ledge, make some thin moves left across a slab under the big overhang of *Folly Corner* to enter a cave on the left. These moves can be avoided by using the rope clipped into a nut placed in a thin crack above the overhang. Continue across to the large broken ledge on *Folly Corner*.
8 27m. 4a. Climb the gully above the overhang to another overhang, which is climbed direct to a good ledge. Bear left over broken ground to the top.

The South Face
The next two climbs take lines up the South Face proper.

Foot Loose   21 metres   Very Severe   (29.7.79)
Start from sea-level at the foot of the final descent groove of the Easy Way
Down and just to the left of the start of *Zawn Face Climb*.
1 15m. 4c. Climb an arête and then step right into a diagonal crack,
which is followed across the wall to a short crack. Climb the crack to a
large ledge. (At high tide, the diagonal crack can be started from the
platform above the final corner of the Easy Way Down.)
2 6m. Climb over a bulge on the right-hand side of the upper wall to
finish up a short corner.

Bloody Finger   15 metres   Hard Severe   (29.7.79)
Start from the ledge above the final descent groove of the Easy Way Down,
below a crack on the right.
1 9m. 4b. Climb the crack to a large ledge.
2 6m. 4a. Climb the centre of the overhanging wall above on
comfortable holds.

The following climbs lie on the sea-level wall of the South Face below the line
of the Easy Way Down. This wall in turn forms the left side (facing in) of the
narrow zawn which effectively separates Fox Promontory from the mainland.
The routes are approached from the sea-level base of the Easy Way Down
by traversing into the narrow zawn along ledges at low tide to a large
rounded boulder wedged between the walls. In swell and rough sea the
zawn becomes extremely lively. The obvious quartz vein running diagonally
rightwards from a point before the boulder is reached gives the line of *The
Illusion*. Just above the boulder, the wall is split by the very steep vein of
Pullover. The rock is excellent but can be damp and greasy.

The Illusion   15 metres   Very Severe 4c   (15.8.63)
Aptly named for its surprising toughness in spite of an innocent look. Start
10 metres left of the boulder, below a quartz vein. Climb the corner, using
the vein for footholds, and make a delicate move past a bulge to follow
the vein up to the right. Finish more easily up the crack above the end of
the vein.

Pullover   17 metres   Very Severe 4c   (15.8.63)
This follows the quartz vein in the steep wall on the right edge of the wall;
bold but on good holds. Start on the inner edge of the wedged boulder,
below a groove. Follow the groove to where the wall steepens and a long
reach gains good holds. Climb the overhanging wall direct to where an
escape can be made into the wide crack on the right. Continue more
easily up the crack to finish on the Easy Way Down.

★★Rejoice the Luddites 18 metres E4 6a (28.8.94)
Start below an unclimbed off-width crack 5 metres right of the jammed
boulder. Climb twin cracks directly up the overhanging wall to easier
ground and a belay below the Easy Way Down.

Lovely Cruise 36 metres Hard Severe + A1 (19.9.81)
An eccentric salute to aid climbing in its proper place. The chimney at the
back of the narrow zawn is reached from the wedged boulder by an aid
traverse along the smooth wall.
1 18m. A1. From the wedged boulder, traverse easily rightwards to
where a short section requires five tied-off blade pegs. This gains the
chimney, which is climbed to a stance at a jammed boulder.
2 18m. 4b. Climb the chimney, moving behind a huge jammed boulder
to gain a ledge on the left wall. Climb a corner on the left and finish up a
short crack.

From the top of the *Lovely Cruise* chimney, **Wavedodgers** (10 metres Hard
Very Severe 5a † 28.8.94) climbs an overhanging crack to a loose horizontal
break, crosses an overhang to a ledge, and finishes steeply.

Black Wall
On the opposite side of the narrow zawn is a steep black wall about 15
metres high which has three worthwhile climbs. It is best approached by
scrambling down the ridge to the east of the narrow zawn.

The Crack 14 metres E1 5b (24.5.98)
Climb the crack on the left side of the wall.

The Wall and Bulge 14 metres E3 5c (24.5.98)
Start just right of the crack in the centre of the wall. Make problematic
moves up to the bulge. Pull around the bulge on small but delightful
layaways.

The Arête 14 metres Severe (24.5.98)
Climb the right-hand arête.

There are many other small difficult pitches in this complex area. It is also
possible to string together some long easy routes.

Black Carn South (Granite)   OS Ref 362 223

Outlook: South-east.
Tidal. Accessible for three to four hours either side of low water, although the bases of some of the climbs are above the tide. The whole area is affected by swell and rough sea.
Coastguard Identity: Black Carn.

The coast south-east of Fox Promontory is a complex area of broken cliffs and small zawns. There is much scrambling and bouldering, with a handful of longer routes in Black Carn South Zawn.

Approach as for Fox Promontory and Carn Barra. Follow the coast path from Porthgwarra to just before the distinctive stone wall that runs out to the seaward edge of Black Carn South. The zawn lies directly below here and the climbs are on its northern side. Descend steep slopes to the right (facing out) to scramble down ledges and steps to just above the sea, where an easy traverse leads back into the zawn.

There is a narrow buttress near the back of the zawn. It is split at half height by a red quartz band. A wall to the left of the narrow buttress is split by a rightward-slanting crack.

Immaculate Off-Width   20 metres   Hard Very Severe 5a (28.2.84)
Climb to the rightward-slanting crack and then follow this awkwardly to a steep wall, which is climbed to finish.

London's Burning   20 metres   Hard Very Severe 4c   (23.5.88)
Start just right of the previous route, below the steep wall. Climb the wall to a ledge; then move right to a detached pillar. Continue up the face.

The narrow buttress has an obvious crackline running up its right-hand side:

Memento   25 metres   Very Severe 5a   (28.2.84)
Start at the base of the crack. Move left immediately and climb the rounded edge to below a ledge. Move right and then climb direct to the top.

★Shaky Fashion   25 metres   Very Severe 4c   (28.2.84)
A good, open climb. Follow the crack for 15 metres; then move left to finish up the steep hold-plastered wall.

Mina   15 metres   Hard Very Severe 5a   (28.2.84)
Start on top of a cracked boulder on the right of the previous route. Climb a steep wall to a slab; then move right and climb the rounded edge to the top.

Pellitras Point (Granite)   OS Ref 362 221

Outlook: South-west.
Just **tidal** in places. Affected by swell and rough sea.
Coastguard Identity: Pellitras Point.

Pellitras Point lies at the north-west end of the attractive and complex area of cliff lying between Black Carn South and Porth Loe Cove. Pellitras Point merges to the south-east into Porth Loe Buttress.

Approach from Porthgwarra car-park by walking up the coastguard road to where it bends sharply to the left on the open cliffland. Do not take the path that runs downhill towards an obvious low point on the coast. Instead take the main coast path leading directly ahead across heathland to a point about 100 metres before the distinctive stone wall that runs inland from the cliff edge.

The main feature of the Point is a 20-metre block rising from sea-level. It is joined to the mainland by a narrow neck.

Descent: From the coast path, scramble down the broken cliff slope and then cross the neck onto the large seaward block. Descend the right side (facing out) of the block for a few metres only and then go left along a ledge that crosses the upper part of the seaward face. This leads to an easy descent-line to the big sloping platform at the base of the block. This descent is exposed. An alternative descent can be made by climbing down a line of chimneys and grooves to the left (facing out) of the large seaward block.

There are four routes up the seaward face of the block.

The Wall   15 metres   Very Severe 4c   (7.88)
Climb the walls on the left of the obvious groove at the left side (facing in) of the block.

The Groove   15 metres   Very Severe 4c   (1983)
Climb the obvious groove and corner on the left of the block to a large ledge.

Pollyvia   15 metres   Hard Severe 4b   (19.8.63)
A testing little pitch taking the leftward-rising gangway that runs up the seaward face. Gain the gangway from the top end of the sloping platform by a difficult move; then follow the gangway up left on small holds to finish.

Phiz   15 metres   Very Difficult   (10.1.68)
Start as for *Pollyvia*. Climb grooves to the left of the right-hand edge of the seaward face; then continue over flakes to finish.

Pellitras Buttress

Behind the seaward block of Pellitras Point there is a dark zawn crammed with boulders. The landward wall of the zawn extends south-eastwards towards Porth Loe Buttress. The more open south-eastern section of the landward wall is Pellitras Buttress. It is gained via the descents for Pellitras Point.

Zero   15 metres   Difficult   (8.8.82)
The centre of Pellitras Buttress is split by a crack. Climb the crack to reach a boulder-filled chimney/gully above. This is climbed on its left side.

Second and Penultimate   15 metres   Severe 4a   (8.8.82)
Start at the foot of the open-book corner in the middle of the buttress. Climb the corner and then the chimney above.

The Greek's Knees   20 metres   Very Difficult   (14.7.82)
High in its grade. Around to the right of the previous routes is an obvious groove.
1   10m.   Climb the groove to a large ledge.
2   10m.   Climb the deep chimney above.

★Las Meninas   20 metres   Very Severe 5a   (15.8.98)
Just before the zawn that separates Pellitras Point from Porth Loe Buttress is a fine-looking layback crack at 15 metres that curves from right to left. Start below the crack. Climb the rounded arête to below a narrow overlap. Traverse left and follow a vertical crack to an overlap. Launch into the curving crack and follow it splendidly to the top.

Porth Loe Buttress (Granite)   OS Ref 363 221

Outlook: South.
Tidal at the base of the East Buttress, although the routes can be started above the tide-line in quiet sea conditions. The whole area can be affected by swell and rough sea.
Coastguard Identity: Porth Loe.

This is a charming area of golden granite with an open sunny outlook. There are some fine routes in the lower grades such as *Eileen*, while the eccentric challenge of *The Beak* is worth the effort.

Approach from Porthgwarra as for Pellitras Point to where the main coast path is joined by a secondary path coming in from the left. Go back along the secondary path for a few metres. Just before a jumble of boulders a broad grassy gully drops down to seaward.

Descent is by the grassy gully. A few metres down the gully, a branching gully descends to the left: East Gully. The continuation of the main gully is South Gully. The most convenient descent is made by continuing down the right-hand side (facing out) of South Gully, and finishing down easy grooves to reach big ledges well above the sea.

Alternatively, descend East Gully keeping to its centre over rocky steps at half height to a point about 15 metres above the sea; then scramble down right (facing out) across ledges and short walls to sea-washed ledges at the base of the slabby East Buttress.

Porth Loe Buttress is made up of a series of towers and recesses. The main feature is a lichen-covered tower capped by a large fluted overhang, the distinctive 'Beak'.

To reach the left side of the area, traverse leftwards from either descent arrival point along the base of the buttresses and recesses. Two medium-size detached boulders are passed. Beyond these, go down a sloping ledge below the attractive lower crack of *The Beak*. A short descent into a greasy niche leads on to the base of a billowing sweep of slabs taken by *Eileen*. Beyond here is a narrow boulder-choked zawn. Pellitras Buttress can be reached from here by traversing to seaward around an arête to gain the big zawn behind Pellitras Point. The seaward face of Pellitras Point can then be gained by a short, awkward traverse across a jammed boulder in the zawn channel. Dry conditions and a calm sea are required for this section.

Hay Fever 30 metres Hard Severe 4b   (1970)
This takes a line up the back of the narrow damp zawn.

★Eileen 45 metres Severe   (31.3.67)
A charming line taking the sweep of slabs to finish up an interesting chimney. The start is reached by traversing down and left from the greasy niche described above to reach a sloping ramp. Start from the top end of the ramp.
1 10m. Climb easily to a scooped ledge below a black-streaked wall; or make a harder move from the lower end of the ramp to gain the scooped ledge.
2 15m. 4a. Climb to a small ledge just right of the corner; then go up the black-streaked wall onto the slab. Climb thin cracks involving some tricky moves to reach the base of the short wall.
3 10m. 4a. Climb the corner above past a splendid thread runner to reach a ledge.
4 10m. An enjoyable continuation pitch can be made up the left edge of the large block above the platform, finishing on easier-angled rock.

Claire 45 metres Very Difficult   (2.2.69)
Start as for *Eileen*.
1 25m. Climb easily to a scooped ledge below a black-streaked wall. Move diagonally rightwards to a crack. Climb the crack for 4 metres and

then move onto a slab on the right. Go up the slab; then move left to climb a chimney.

2 10m. Climb the wall above to a grassy ledge. Step left onto a wall and continue traversing diagonally to make a high step onto a slab, which is climbed to a grassy ledge.

3 10m. Move easily up to climb a lichenous slab and then finish up a wall on the left.

★The Beak   25 metres   E1   (16.9.70)

An intriguing line. Start on the ledge to the right of the greasy niche at the base of an attractive crack.

1 10m. 5a. Climb the crack to the large half-way ledge.

2 15m. 5b. Climb the rounded groove to the overhang, which is cleared strenuously but with good protection. Finish up the lichenous rock above.

Tobacco Road   35 metres   Difficult   (27.12.72)

Start below a scooped corner around to the right of the starting-ledge of The Beak.

1 5m. Climb the corner to exit left to a large sloping ledge. Belay as for The Beak.

2 30m. Climb from the left end of the ledge to a chimney. Exit right after 5 metres and then follow a crack-system to finish.

Times Remembered   25 metres   Hard Severe   (6.5.73)

A lower pitch of 10 metres up a groove from sea-level is possible.

1 5m. Tobacco Road pitch 1.

2 10m. 4b. Quite tricky. Move up and right into the narrow undercut chimney/groove just left of the arête. Continue to a ledge.

3 10m. Move right to a break, which leads easily to the top.

Variation

1a 5m. Climb the arête right of the corner to belay below the undercut chimney/groove.

A Little S and M   25 metres   Hard Severe 4b   (25.2.82)

Start below a chimney with a detached block at its base. Climb the chimney and then a lichenous groove on the left to reach a tower (belay possible). Finish up an obvious rightward-slanting break.

Eastern Buttress

This is the sunny area of slabs and corners between South Gully and East Gully.

Just right of the base of South Gully and well above the sea is a platform below a recessed slabby wall. The wall rises to a small overhang and is flanked on its left by a grubby break.

Transubstantiation   35 metres   Hard Severe 4b   (27.12.72)
A line up the right-hand flanking buttress of South Gully. First ascent details
are sparse and the line described has optional variations. Start from the
platform to the right of the base of South Gully, at a greasy niche. Climb a
chimney with a knobbly vein running up it. At 5 metres, follow a crack up
and left to a ledge on the arête. Continue in a more or less direct line up
the buttress.

Red Horizon   20 metres   Hard Very Severe 5a   (30.3.97)
Start at the base of a thin crack in the slab to the right. Climb the slab to
an overhang, which is turned on its right. Step back left onto the lip and
climb the rib.

Deceptive   15 metres   Hard Severe 4b   (1970)
Start below the recessed slabby wall. Climb a leftward-slanting crack that
leads below the overhang to reach the area of loose rock in the grubby
corner. Finish direct.

Prima Donna   35 metres   Very Difficult   (29.12.72)
Start as for *Deceptive*.
1 20m. Climb rightwards to the arête, which is followed to a point level
with the overhang. Step up left onto the lip of the overhang and then climb
the upper arête to large spike belays.
2 15m. Follow the arête to its top.

The next route starts down to the right of the recessed slabby wall on
wave-worn ledges.

Laminaria   35 metres   Very Difficult   (9.70)
Start below a small overhang at 3 metres.
1 10m. Climb a wide crack to pass the overhang on its left. Move right,
and cross the slabs to climb a wall.
2 10m. Move left to follow a deep groove up and right to a jammed
block belay. Alternatively, climb direct from the stance at a slightly harder
grade.
3 15m. Climb the groove above to finish up the lichenous right-hand
arête.

From the start of *Laminaria*, stepped ribs lead up to the right to a triangular
ledge below a corner-crack/chimney.

Beta   30 metres   Very Difficult   (31.8.69)
A sunny little route that mixes in with *Laminaria* in places but pre-dates it.
Start at the left edge of the triangular ledge.
1 20m. Climb the edge of the wall and then follow the line of the arête to
a ledge below the lichenous upper section of the arête.
2 10m. The arête merges into a lichen-covered rib, which is followed to
its top.

Iapetus   40 metres   Very Severe   (27.12.71)
Start below the centre of the crack-seamed wall left of the
corner-crack/chimney.
1 20m. 4c. Climb the wall trending up and rightwards to gain the slabs
above. Continue to a ledge that leads rightwards to an easy groove.
Follow the groove and then the right edge of a steep slab to a ledge.
2 20m. Move right to the arête; then climb a short smooth slab to a
ledge. Finish easily up a lichenous slab.

The Pit   30 metres   Severe 4a   (14.9.70)
This takes the corner-crack at the back of the triangular ledge. Climb the
right-hand crack for 10 metres, and then move into the chimney on the
left, which is followed via some awkward moves to the top.

Porth Loe Cove: Towers of Deception
(Granite) OS Ref 365 220

Outlook: West.
Non-tidal except in very high spring-tides. The starts of the climbs may be
affected by heavy swell under some conditions.
Coastguard Identity: Porth Loe.

Approach from Porthgwarra car-park by walking up the coastguard road
until it bends sharply to the left on the open cliff-top. From this point, follow the
path that runs downhill towards an obvious low point on the coast. The path
skirts an area of reedy marsh to join the coast path above the eroded lip of Porth
Loe Cove. An easy descent of a gravelly break leads to the boulder beach. The
Towers lie about 100 metres along the beach to the left (facing out).

Much of the rock in Porth Loe Cove is grim, in decay, and with a high erosion
count. The front faces of the towers and buttresses present somewhat better
rock, however, and there are some striking features offering climbs for the
adventurous only. The towers are about 25 metres high. They stand proud of
the main cliff and are separated by a wide break containing a lower block
which forms chimneys to either side. To seaward of the Towers, across a
bouldery gap, is a smaller isolated pinnacle.

Left of the Towers (facing in) is a depression with slabby black rock in its lower
half and a jutting prow of rock with an impressive mid-height overhang on
its left.

Scandals (25 metres E5 6b † 1989) climbed through the overhang. It had
three bolt runners, a lower-off bolt, and a man-made hold. The bolts have
been removed and the grade merely reflects the line's former state.

There is a groove-system on the right side of the big overhang.

☆Magical Motions 35 metres E4 6a † (1989)
The lower groove is climbed to finish up the groove in the upper wall.
Quite likely to be damp.

The twin towers are climbed by a number of routes. Stainless steel drilled peg
belays are fixed on the summit of the towers for an abseil descent. The tops of the
towers are separated from the edge of the main cliff by a bouldery break and a
5-metre gritty wall. It **may** be possible and indeed preferable to **preplace a
rope** from good blocks on top of the cliff opposite the towers if a direct escape is
sought, and in case the drilled pegs have corroded or been removed.

☆A Broken Mirror 25 metres E1 5b † (1989)
Climb the jamming-crack in the lower front face of the left-hand tower and
continue up cracks until a move right is made around the edge of the
tower to finish up the right wall.

Two of a Kind 25 metres Very Severe 4b † (1989)
Climb the left-hand chimney of the central break to a ledge; then follow
cracks and finish up the back of the tower.

The following routes are on the right-hand tower.

Jack the Ripper 25 metres E2 (1989)
An interesting line with a committing top pitch up a remarkable hanging
flake in the gold-lichened right wall of the second tower. However it is
spoilt by the shattered nature of the rock. Start at the base of the break that
separates the towers.
1 10m. 5a. Climb the block in the lower half of the break and move
right to gain a ledge.
2 15m. 5b. Climb the exposed flake in the wall above, past many
detached sections, moving right at its top to a beaked block. Finish up the
short wall to the earthy top of the tower.
Variation
2a 5a. Move left at the top of the flake to finish up to the left.

Sweeney Todd 25 metres E3 5c (1989)
A dramatic pitch up the heavily-cleaned arête of the tower. Start in an
alcove at the right-hand base of the break between the towers. Gain the
arête by a move up and right past a peg, and continue in a direct line up
the arête, passing another peg.

Kellogg's Crack 25 metres E2 5c † (1989)
A line up the right-hand arête of the tower's right-flanking wall. Start
around to the right of the front face of the tower. Climb the overhanging
wall to a ledge; then climb the flaky crack in the arête to another ledge
and on to the top of the tower.

Immediately right of the towers is a deep recess of very poor rock. The right wall of the recess leads around into a shallow bay, the black-faced right arête of which gives three routes on slightly more solid rock.

Just above the edge of the cliff and the shared finish of these three routes, a bolt-and-chain belay in a small boulder was installed by the first ascensionists. The bolt and chain have been removed, but ample block belays for use with a **preplaced rope** are available a short distance up the slope.

Star Touch   35 metres   E2 5b   (1989)
This takes the obvious rightward-snaking crack at half height on the left side of the arête. Climb a greasy groove to gain the crack, which is followed to the upper crest of the arête. Finish up the arête.

☆**The Shining**   35 metres   E2 5c †   (1989)
A direct line up cracks in the black wall right of *Star Touch* to join that route on the crest of the arête.

Into a Looking-Glass   35 metres   E2 5c   (1989)
Climb the crest of the black arête direct past two pegs.

Carn Guthensbrâs (Granite)   OS Ref 364 217

Outlook: South-west.
Tidal: accessible for about three hours either side of low water. Affected at all states of the tide by swell and rough sea.
Coastguard Identity: Carn Guthensbrâs.

Carn Guthensbrâs [diagram page 106] is the small promontory lying at the north-west end of Chair Ladder. It has a great deal of charm; a secluded annexe to its formidable neighbour, yet with a strong identity of its own. There are some excellent short pitches at all grades.

Approach as for Chair Ladder (page 100). From the coastguard lookout at Gwennep Head, walk westwards across the rim of Zawn Rinny. Follow the path that curves round the western edge of the zawn and eventually leads down to Chair Ladder's Bulging Wall area. Just before the point where steeper rock begins, branch off to the right (facing out) and go across the grassy rock-studded slopes, gradually descending between small buttresses to a point above a rocky bay on the western side of Carn Guthensbrâs Promontory.

Descent. Go down into the bay and then left (facing out) towards a dark rift. The black wall on its left holds one route, *Livinbrâs*. For the main climbing

Mean Street (E4), Carn Barra
Climbers: Sven Scholz and Heike Arnold Photo: Nick Hancock

Grande Plage (E2), Carn Barra
Climber: Nick Hancock   Photo: Simon Blagdon

area, scramble to seaward down short grooves and slabs and then traverse up and round to the left to the seaward face of the headland. Lowish tide required.

The seaward face has an open first section, with the distinctive flake of *Hairy Cornflake* being an obvious feature. On its right side (facing in) is the clean-cut groove of *Cleavage*. Beyond *Cleavage*, a narrow squeeze between the face and a large seaward block leads to a cosy little square-cut zawn with huge jammed blocks in its base. A number of fine routes start from the zawn.

At high tide and in calm seas the zawn-bed is generally above sea-level, although it is then cut off from the descent as described. However, the zawn can be reached by abseil down *Cinnamon* from jumbled boulders directly above. These abseil boulders can be reached by diverting to seaward half-way along the approach line across the top of the promontory.

The first route is on the left wall of the dark rift at the beginning of the descent.

Livinbrâs 20 metres Hard Severe 4b (25.10.80)
Start below the black left-hand wall of the dark rift. Climb difficult cracks in the short wall to reach the slab. Climb a crack to a good ledge and finish up the groove on the right.

White Rib 24 metres Hard Severe 4b (3.73)
The arête opposite *Livinbrâs*. Start on a triangular ledge at the left side of the arête. After an awkward start, follow the obvious crackline in the arête; some crumbly rock.

Dagger in the Back 30 metres Very Severe 5a (13.10.91)
Start below twin cracks about 10 metres right of *White Rib*. Climb the cracks; then go straight up to the base of the hanging flake of *Hairy Cornflake*. Climb diagonally leftwards and finish up an awkward off-width groove.

The next routes lie on the seaward face of the promontory.

Tooth Decay 24 metres Hard Severe 4b † (29.3.84)
Climb the groove and overhang just left of the hanging flake high on the face.

Hairy Cornflake 24 metres Very Severe 4c (1982)
A striking line centred on the hanging flake high in the face. Climb the lower wall and then the flake itself.

Draculus 18 metres Severe (6.3.69)
A pleasant pitch, which takes the narrow slab that forms the left arm of the V-groove of *Cleavage*. Climb the narrow slab, traverse left onto the arête, and finish through blocks.

Cleavage   15 metres   Hard Severe 4b   (9.11.80)
Neat climbing up the distinctive V-groove. Some looseness at the top.

John Peel   24 metres   Hard Very Severe 4c   (17.3.84)
Climb the wide crack right of *Cleavage*.

Black and Tan   20 metres   Very Severe 4c   (5.73)
A line up the arête overlooking the junction of the squeeze rift and the
square-cut zawn. Start at the foot of the arête, below a small roof. Climb
to the roof and clear it on the right. Continue up the arête, moving left
near the top.

The following routes start from the square-cut zawn.

☆☆**Urban Spaceman**   27 metres   E4 6a †   (26.2.87)
Power-packed climbing up the steep crack in the impending back wall of
the zawn to finish up the steep wall at its top.

★**Graculus**   24 metres   Severe 4a   (6.3.69)
A fine pitch up the back corner of the zawn. Climb easily to a ledge and
then go up the steep corner. Reach a ledge where the crack widens; then
climb diagonally right past bulges to the top.

Cinnamon   24 metres   Hard Very Severe 5a   (5.73)
Delicate, tense climbing on small holds up the wall right of the
corner-crack of *Graculus*. Poor protection.

Barbacus   18 metres   Hard Severe 4b   (5.69)
The rounded crack in the right wall of the zawn is taken direct. Start on a
ledge just to the left of the foot of the crack. Make a hard move into the
crack, which is climbed for 10 metres to where it widens. Continue
strenuously to the top.

Rodney the REMF   20 metres   E3 6a   (25.9.94)
Start to the right of *Barbacus* and climb the centre of the steep slab to
good breaks and protection. Continue up the slab and at the final break
move right and step up into a small groove (hard). Follow the groove to
the crux at the top, a good 4 metres above protection.

Pirouette   20 metres   Hard Very Severe 5a   (5.90)
The crack in the wall to the right of *Barbacus*, gained by stepping off the
huge block in the base of the zawn and then traversing along a foot-ledge.
Follow the crack to the horizontal break, climb up a few metres, and make
an awkward move to reach the arête on the right. Finish easily up the arête.

Across   80 metres   Very Severe 4b   (1.9.86)
An interesting exploratory traverse from right to left around the seaward
face of the headland, starting from the zawn and taking the easiest line.

The following routes lie on the wall to the right of the square-cut zawn and are in full view of the Bulging Wall area of Chair Ladder. They are reached by traversing along the foot-ledge from the huge block in the zawn to reach ledges below the face.

A Clean Breast 23 metres Hard Severe 4b (30.3.91)
Start at the left end of the ledges. Climb the pleasant arête to a ledge and then continue direct through the bulge.

Gypsum Johnny 24 metres Very Severe 4c (5.73)
Nicely strenuous. Just above a step down in the ledge below the face is a good crack; climb this to a series of flakes trending up rightwards. Make an awkward move through an overhang, after which easier climbing leads to a finishing ledge. Scramble off round to the left.

☆**Local Martians** 27 metres E3 5c † (5.90)
An intriguing pitch taking a strenuous line into the narrow zawn on the right of the wall. Climb the thin crack in the wall (3 metres right of the crack of *Gypsum Johnny*) and gain a horizontal break. Move right and then up to reach a ledge. Climb the narrow ramp on the edge of the zawn to the capping roof and then move right round the arête to a point below a flake. Climb the flake to a bulge and continue direct with minimal protection via a line of shallow flakes to the finishing-ledge. Scramble off around to the left.

For the following routes, scramble towards Chair Ladder and jump the small zawn to the foot of a black 10-metre wall with obvious cracks. **Judgement Day** (Moderate †) takes the left-to-right diagonal crack. **Here's Laughing at You** (Difficult †) goes up the centre of the wall. **Two Big Clean Breasts** (Very Difficult †) climbs the right-to-left diagonal crack. **Aren't Chickens Mad, Uncle Hen?** (Hard Very Severe †) is a good route up the unprotected arête at the right end of the wall. All are 10 metres long and were climbed on 25.9.94.

Chair Ladder (Granite)   OS Ref 365 216

'Now round the corner is the Chair Ladder cliff – the finest in Cornwall...'
(A W Andrews, 1950.)

Outlook South-south-west.
Tidal. The base of the main areas of cliff can be reached for about three hours either side of low water, although for less than this during neap-tides. Bishop Buttress and the sea-level climbs on The Pinnacle are accessible for up to four hours either side of low water but only in calm seas without swell.

Coliseum Wall and Coliseum Buttress are accessible for two hours either side of low water, although for less during neap-tides. All the sea-level climbs at Chair Ladder may be affected by swell and rough seas at any state of the tide, with potentially lethal effect. At high tide or in rough seas, many routes can be reached above their first pitches. Ways of doing so are described in the relevant sections below.

Coastguard Identity: Gwennap Head. The lookout at Gwennap Head is staffed by volunteers of the National Coastwatch Institution during daylight hours, every day of the year, provided volunteers are available. Rescue services can be contacted from the lookout when the facility is open and staffed. When the lookout is closed, the nearest public telephone is at Porthgwarra.

Environmental issues: Kittiwakes, Herring Gulls, Great Black-backed Gulls, Fulmars, and Jackdaws all breed in this SSSI: please be careful not to disturb nesting birds. Please avoid damaging the good lichen growth on the upper cliffs. Descent paths are all showing signs of wear, so tread carefully.

For many, Chair Ladder is the epitome of West Penwith climbing. On a sunny, blue day, with a sparkling Atlantic surging restlessly around the foot of the cliff and the Isles of Scilly visible on the horizon, there are few better places to be. It is the most southerly point of Penwith and more naturally the 'end of the land' in a maritime sense, being known as the 'Fisherman's Land's End'. Viewed from seaward it is one of the finest pieces of cliff architecture in Cornwall. From its eastern end, undersea reefs run for a mile southwards to the Runnelstone Buoy, which can often be heard moaning and belling dolefully. The two painted cone-shaped structures on the cliff-top are 'leading' marks, once used by offshore vessels for clearing the reefs before technology reduced reliance on visual navigation. The name Chair Ladder comes from a local legend of a witch, Maggie Figgen, who sat on a rocky throne and lured ships to their doom.

Chair Ladder provides some of the best middle-grade climbing in Cornwall on solid, golden granite seamed with cracks and well endowed with holds and comfortable belays. Routes like *Pegasus, Pendulum Chimney, South Face Direct, Flannel Avenue, Diocese, Bishop's Rib*, and *Terrier's Tooth* are among the finest Penwith has to offer.

Approach. There is adequate (paying) parking at Porthgwarra Cove, although the car-park there can become very busy in the holiday months from mid-morning onwards. From the car-park, follow the flanking lane that runs uphill. This leads past granite buildings on the left (ex-coastguard houses). Follow the road in a loop round to the left above the houses; then take the convenient path leading up rightwards across the heathland to Gwennap Head coastguard lookout, which stands commandingly on the highest and central part of Chair Ladder. Rucksacks can be left at various places just below the level of the cliff-top.

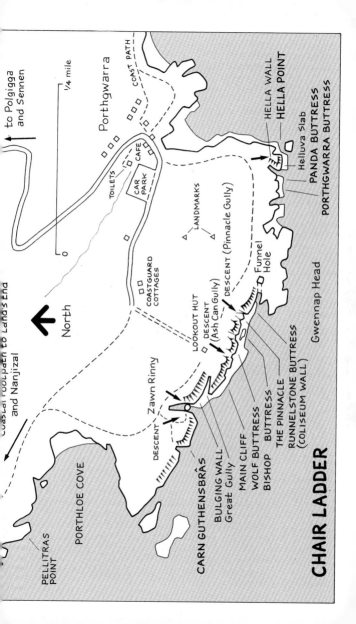

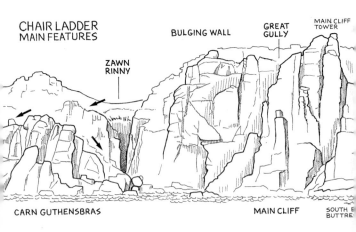

Cliff layout. Only the summits of the buttresses and the tops of their flanking gullies can be seen from the bare rounded top of Chair Ladder. The main features of the cliff are best taken in sequence running from right to left (looking out to sea). They are Zawn Rinny, Bulging Wall, Great Gully, Main Cliff, Ash Can Gully, Wolf Buttress, Bishop's Buttress, Pinnacle Gully, The Pinnacle, and Runnelstone Buttress (Coliseum Wall).

As one looks out to sea from in front of the coastguard lookout, the lichen-covered tower of Main Cliff is a prominent feature. Behind and to the right of the lichen-covered tower is the bottomless couloir of Great Gully, which divides Main Cliff from Bulging Wall. Beyond Bulging Wall is Zawn Rinny, the western boundary of Chair Ladder.

Immediately left of the lichen-covered tower of Main Cliff is the wide amphitheatre of Ash Can Gully, one of the key descent routes to the base of the cliff. The impressive Wolf Buttress lies on the left side of Ash Can Gully with Bishop Buttress further left again. About 20 metres along the cliff edge to the east of the coastguard lookout is the access to Pinnacle Gully, with the striking feature of The Pinnacle rising from its lower reaches. Beyond Pinnacle Gully is Runnelstone Buttress (Coliseum Wall/Buttress) terminating in Funnel Zawn with its famous blow-hole, which gives Chair Ladder its wonderfully unromantic Cornish name of Tol-pedn-Penwith, 'the holed headland of Penwith'.

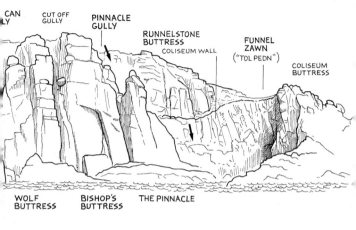

CAN
LY

CUT OFF
GULLY

PINNACLE
GULLY

RUNNELSTONE
BUTTRESS

COLISEUM WALL

FUNNEL
ZAWN
("TOL PEDN")

COLISEUM
BUTTRESS

WOLF
BUTTRESS

BISHOP'S
BUTTRESS

THE PINNACLE

Descents. There are three main descents to sea-level, although variations
are available.
1 Zawn Rinny for access to Bulging Wall and the western section of Main
Cliff. This is the easiest of the descent-lines and is reached by walking 20
metres right from the coastguard lookout to a grassy depression, which lies
above the dark cleft of Zawn Rinny. Continue across the top of the grassy
depression and follow a path that leads down the right-hand side of the
zawn. Scramble down rocky ledges (some fragile rock) to a vast jammed
boulder at the zawn's mouth. The boulder is crossed to reach the sea-level
ledges below Bulging Wall. An alternative but more complex approach is
made by descending the grassy left-hand rim of Zawn Rinny. This leads to
steeper rock, which is down-climbed at Difficult standard for about 12
metres, where a move right (facing in) gains a short vein, which leads to the
sea-level ledges as above.

2 Ash Can Gully for access to Main Cliff, South East Buttress, Wolf
Buttress; also Bishop Buttress when tide allows. Ash Can Gully is the obvious
wide break just left of the coastguard lookout. A well-worn path leads down
from the rim of the cliff between narrowed walls to a wide amphitheatre lying
between the high tower of Main Cliff to the right and a remarkable perched
block on an upper ledge of Wolf Buttress to the left. An important strategic
feature is the top of East Chimney. This lies tucked in at the base of the Main
Cliff tower on the right edge of the amphitheatre. It is a useful climbing

descent (Difficult) or abseil line for a number of routes, including *South Face Direct*, which can be joined well above the tide. For access to the base of the cliff, however, continue down the direct descent line of Ash Can Gully on its right-hand side and then descend the final steep section to sea-level ledges. Care should be taken with potentially loose rock.

3 Pinnacle Gully for access to Bishop Buttress, The Pinnacle (seaward face), Runnelstone Buttress, Coliseum Wall, and Coliseum Buttress. Walk left from the coastguard lookout for about 20 metres to the top of a grassy gully, which leads easily to the base of the short, inland wall of The Pinnacle. Traverse left (facing out) from here to cross the top of an earthy gully with care. Continue left past jumbled blocks until just past the bottom of a deep chimney that splits the upper cliff. The chimney is the second pitch of *Dodger's Chimney*. Climb down the break below the chimney (novices may require a rope here) to reach a rocky ledge with a pool of water in a scooped hollow. Coliseum Wall and Coliseum Buttress are reached from the left end of this ledge. For Bishop Buttress and The Pinnacle, descend rightwards from the rocky ledge to reach sea-level ledges.

Zawn Rinny

This is the deeply incut zawn at the extreme western end of Chair Ladder, reached by walking to the right (facing out) for 20 metres from the coastguard lookout to a grassy depression above the zawn. The zawn is a contradiction of Chair Ladder's open sunny aspect but it contains some good rock. Dry conditions are needed.

Descent to the bed of the zawn is by abseil over the eastern rim, which is reached by diverting from the main access path where it crosses the grassy depression.

Consolation Climb 54 metres Very Difficult (5.4.79)
This rather unconsoling route lies on the west side of the zawn. Start at the foot of a steep black chimney at the base of the way down to the jammed boulder at the mouth of Zawn Rinny.
1 20m. Move up; then traverse onto the right wall to reach the foot of a steep incut scoop.
2 10m. Climb into the scoop and onto a ledge.
3 12m. Climb the left-hand face of the pinnacle.
4 12m. A series of steep chimney/cracks lead to the summit pinnacle.

☆☆☆**The Human Skewer** 30 metres E9 6c † (8.98)
The overhanging wall on the west side of the zawn gives an extremely serious route, partly on account of a large spike below its crux. The rock is suspect in places. Climb up a short chimney and rightwards along a ramp to the spike. From the spike, climb with difficulty up two thin parallel cracks, with poor *RP* placements in the left-hand crack, to a small ledge. Continue up well-protected overhanging cracks to the top.

A prominent feature on the east wall of the zawn is a big groove taken by, appropriately enough, *The Groove*.

The Naked Edge (53 metres E5 5a,6a,6b † 5.9.87) was a three-pitch route which had peg and bolt belays at the second stance. It climbed the depression to the left of the big groove, and the crack in the slab to the small roof on the left. After a traverse left it took a steep corner to a roof, moved rightwards to the edge, and climbed a crack to a sloping ledge. This was followed by a corner on the left, a roof, and a traverse rightwards to the arête. A steep wall (peg) and a slab on the left (peg) led to a niche and the top.

The following three routes start from the base of a depression beneath the big groove.

★**The Groove** 53 metres E2   (1976)
Fine climbing when dry. A preplaced belay rope may be useful.
1 27m. 4b. Climb the wall just left of the right-hand depression; then go up to the foot of the big groove. Peg belay.
2 26m. 5c. Climb the pinnacle on the left and follow the obvious line rightwards and back into the groove. Climb this to the roof and pull over onto the slabs above. Follow these to steep grass; traverse left along ledges and then up the steep grass, with care, to belays.

Aquiline 50 metres E1   (1976)
Poor protection.
1 15m. 4b. Climb the depression to ledges, and belay below the arête right of *The Groove*.
2 35m. 5a. Pull over the roof on good holds and continue up the slabby arête, passing a good runner half-way, to a preplaced rope belay as for *The Groove*.

Rinny Wall 52 metres Hard Very Severe   (1976)
Poorly-protected climbing.
1 15m. 4b. *Aquiline* pitch 1.
2 37m. 4c. Follow the ramp/crack rightwards to gain the centre of the steep slab, and follow a faint depression in this to grass, where a traverse left leads to a preplaced rope belay.

Illusion 40 metres Very Severe 5a   (1976)
Climb the chimney and groove right of *Rinny Wall* and left of a prominent pillar.

Also on the east side of the zawn, but closer to its mouth, is a wall with a mid-height overhang on its left side. The wall has two routes.

Black Orchid 30 metres E5 6a †   (1997)
Start on the left-hand side of the wall. Climb the corner-crack, the arête, and two bulges to the top.

CARN GUTHENSBRÂS

1	Cleavage	HS
2	Urban Spaceman	E4
3	Graculus	S
4	Cinnamon	HVS
5	Barbacus	HS
6	Pirouette	HVS
7	Clean Breast	HS

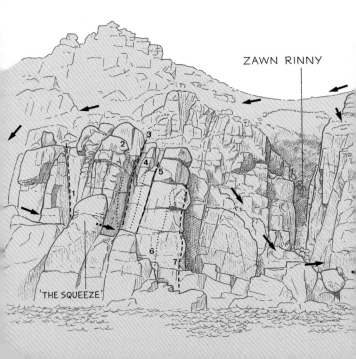

ZAWN RINNY

'THE SQUEEZE'

CHAIR LADDER ~ WEST

BULGING WALL

1	Maureen	VS
2	The Gingerbread Crack	E2
3	Overhanging Chimney	VS
4	Kittiwake	HVS
5	Seal Slab	VS
6	Great Slab Route	D
7	Pegasus	HS
8	West Face Direct	E2
9	Rake's Progress	VD
10	Kaleidoscope	VS

MAIN CLIFF

11	Western Arete	HS
12	Great Western Arete	HVS
13	Western Chimneys	D
14	The Thin Red Line	E2
15	Beaujolais	E1

GREAT GULLY

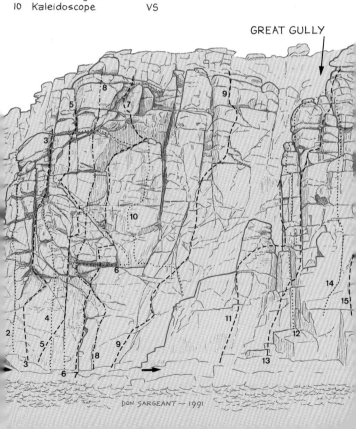

DON SARGEANT ~ 1991

Black Narcissus   30 metres   E6 6b †   (1997)
Low tide required. Climb the centre of the wall to the top.

Bulging Wall

This is the first of Chair Ladder's seaward faces. It is pleasant and amenable, with a rare character of its own. The wall lies between Zawn Rinny and Great Gully and is set back from the main line of the cliff. It is made up of slabs and steep walls split by numerous cracks providing a number of excellent climbs in the middle grades.

Descent. Follow the main Zawn Rinny descent (see page 104). Seen from the jammed boulder, the dank black cleft of Great Gully is strikingly obvious where it divides Bulging Wall from the towering Main Cliff. The first feature of Bulging Wall is a pock-marked slab running up to overhangs. This is Seal Slab (the route of this name takes the steep right-hand corner of the slab). On the right of the slab is the grooved arête of the first pitch of *Pegasus*. Right again is a smooth wall running back into the dark cleft of Great Gully. The wall is broken by the obvious ramp-line of *Rake's Progress*. The tidal ledges at the base of Bulging Wall can be very slippery and are vulnerable to large waves.

The ledges can be reached from the Zawn Rinny descent for two to three hours either side of low water, although swell may reduce such access. At high tide, the routes on the right side of the wall can be reached by traversing from the upper part of Great Gully to the large ledge above their first pitches. The Seal Slab routes (including *Great Slab*) can be approached by traversing across the upper part of Seal Slab from the descent-line of the east side of Zawn Rinny. (This last approach is **not advised** if there is a big swell running.)

Maureen   52 metres   Very Severe   (9.8.66)
A line up the left-hand edge of Bulging Wall. Start on a sea-level ledge 5 metres right of the jammed boulder at the foot of Zawn Rinny.
1 20m. Climb the wall above the ledge to a platform with a black triangular recess. Continue up the wall on the right to a ledge beneath a steep wall with a blackish overhang.
2 20m. 4c. Climb the steep wall above by cracks and on rounded holds. Continue up a slab to belay on top of a pinnacle.
3 12m. 4a. Descend the slab for 3 metres to where it is possible to make an interesting step across onto a traverse-line on the black-streaked wall. Follow this line to the left for 3 metres; then climb a steep groove to the top.

★The Gingerbread Crack   50 metres   E2   (15.3.81)
Tasty crack-climbing to the left of *Overhanging Chimney*. Start at the base of the slab, by a boulder on the right.
1 23m. 5c. Climb direct to the thin crack that splits the narrow buttress left of *Overhanging Chimney*. Climb the crack to a good ledge.

2 24m. 4b. Climb the crack in the wall behind the belay and continue up the slab and block above.

3 3m. Follow the chimney on the right to the top.

Variation

The Great Beast Unleashed E2 † (7.4.98)
Below the start of *Maureen* is a step down on the sea-level platform. Just past this is a thin right-to-left crack in the lower wall.

1a 25m. 6a. Climb the crack by a series of technical moves to a ledge system. Move right and climb a wall until it is possible to step up and right to a rounded ledge (left of *The Gingerbread Crack*). Move up to a line of holds, which lead up and diagonally left to a large ledge (common with the end of *Maureen* pitch 1).

Overhanging Chimney 42 metres Very Severe (10.55)
A strenuous first pitch with tough moves to surmount the block. Start below the left side of the slab.

1 24m. 4c. Climb the left edge of the slab for 10 metres and follow a rippling crack running diagonally right to beneath the overhang. Move left below this to a block at the foot of the chimney. Climb strenuously over the block and follow the chimney more easily to a good stance.

2 18m. Take the easy continuation chimney to the top.

★Kittiwake 48 metres Hard Very Severe (23.5.68)
Committing and exposed and at the top of its grade, this fine route takes the centre of the overhang left of the impending corner of *Seal Slab*. Protection is good, but awkward to arrange in places. Start below the centre of the slab.

1 30m. 5a. Climb direct to the overhang and gain a diagonal ramp trending left. Continue up the wall, on good holds at first, to a small overhang. Climb this on its right-hand side by difficult moves to gain a diagonal crack, which leads up left to a stance shared with *Overhanging Chimney*.

2 18m. *Overhanging Chimney* pitch 2.

★Seal Slab 55 metres Very Severe (1955)
[Photo p.160a.] An enjoyable climb taking the steep corner right of the slab and then the buttress above. Start below the centre of the slab.

1 23m. 4c. Climb diagonally right into the corner, which is climbed with increasing difficulty to a ledge on the easy-angled ramp slanting up to the left.

2 23m. 4b. Climb the short layback crack in the steep wall above the ramp and then a steep, narrow slab to a ledge. Move right and climb a short chimney/groove to a large ledge.

3 9m. Climb the steep lichenous wall on the left and then easy slabs to the top.

Variation

1a Watch Hunt 18m. 4c (1985). A bold one. Climb *Great Slab Route* to the foot of the arête. From here, follow the arête to join pitch 1 at the ledge below its final corner.

Great Slab Route 60 metres Difficult (c.1930)
Happy climbing through good scenery, taking the easy lower corner of
Seal Slab before traversing steeply right to gain the upper wall. Start below
the corner.
1 18m. Climb the corner to a ledge on the right before the corner (of
Seal Slab pitch 1) steepens.
2 18m. From the right-hand end of the ledge, descend slightly and
traverse steeply right on good holds to a large ledge. Climb to the big
ledge that cuts across the right-hand section of the face at half height.
3 14m. Follow the broken slabs up to the left to the foot of a chimney.
4 10m. Climb the easy chimney.
Variation
4a 12m. Very Difficult. Climb the layback crack 6 metres right of the final
chimney and finish via a groove.

★★Pegasus 57 metres Hard Severe (6.52)
Intricate and intriguing pitches weaving a natural line up Bulging Wall.
Start at the far right edge of *Seal Slab* below a bulging corner-crack in the
arête.
1 12m. 4b. At the top of its grade. Climb the corner, moving right at its
top to a ledge.
2 10m. 4a. Climb to the roof and swing over on spanking holds.
Continue to the big half-way ledge.
3 10m. 4a. Move right and climb the black wall easily to a ledge below
the delightful curving corner flanked by a wall on its left.
4 10m. 4a. Follow the curving corner and the slab on the right to a large
block.
5 15m. 4b. Move back left onto the black wall and make an awkward
mantelshelf onto a small ledge. Climb leftwards to a large ledge, move
right, and finish up easier slabs.

★West Face Direct 63 metres E2 (10.9.80)
Fine climbing that seeks out the hardest moves on a direct line up Bulging
Wall. Start at the tempting crackline just round to the right of the *Pegasus*
arête and above a narrow tidal channel.
1 18m. 5c. Climb the crack, which is quite high in the grade, and follow
the steep ramp to the left to a belay ledge.
2 10m. 5c. Climb up to cracks in the bulging rock above. Climb the
cracks and continue to belays by a triangular slab.
3 23m. 5b. Move up and climb a steep arête right of *Seal Slab* pitch 2
rightwards to a good ledge. Make an awkward move onto the slab on the
left and continue airily up this to belays below a steep wall.
4 12m. 5a. Climb to the crack in the roof above and pull over to a good
ledge. Continue up the steep wall to the top.
Variation
3a 23m. 5a. Climb the steep crack half-way up the curving corner of
Pegasus pitch 4 on strenuous jams.

Fat Boy   20 metres   E6 6a †   (7.98)
A bold climb up the thin seam above the start of *Rake's Progress*.

Rake's Progress   66 metres   Very Difficult   (27.6.52)
A ramble; but fun, and with a rakish first pitch. Start 6 metres right of the
corner of *Seal Slab*, below the rake leading up to the right.
1 18m. Follow the rake with increasing difficulty to a large ledge. High in
the grade.
2 10m. Move right and climb a large flake to a ledge.
3 23m. The slabs above lead to a shallow gully; follow this, moving right
to a chockstone. Belay on the huge blocks above.
4 15m. Climb the crack above and move left to a ledge. A short corner
on the right leads to the top.

Altered Images   56 metres   E1   (1983)
Start 6 metres right of the base of the ramp of *Rake's Progress*, below a
shallow slanting groove and crack just left of a more definite crack
(*Kaleidoscope*). Often wet and greasy.
1 15m. 5b. Climb the groove and crack with difficulty to its top. Step left
onto the slab and climb to a large ledge.
2 15m. Climb onto a flake and follow the left edge of the slab. Belay
below a buttress in the centre of the gully.
3 20m. 4b. Climb the left arête of the buttress using a shallow crack;
then pull onto the slab above, which is climbed to a belay ledge.
4 6m. 4c. Climb the slab directly to its top. Poor protection.

Kaleidoscope   67 metres   Very Severe   (27.9.61)
Varied climbing, starting up a steep, often greasy crack in the left wall of
Great Gully and then weaving a slanting line leftwards up the upper wall.
Start below the steep crack 10 metres right of the rake of *Rake's Progress*.
1 14m. 4c. Climb a greasy scoop to enter the steep crack. Jam up the
crack to gain a ledge on the left; then follow the open groove to the large
ledge.
2 15m. 4b. Walk left for 6 metres to a cracked red wall. Climb the cracks
to a small flake; then move delicately right and up to a stance below a
black wall.
3 12m. 4b. Climb the black wall to make an awkward move that leads
onto slabs right of the curving corner of *Pegasus*. Climb easily to the block
belay of that climb.
4 12m. 4b. Descend the curving crack to the left for 6 metres until an
awkward move can be made across the black wall on the left to a ledge.
Continue left to a belay shared with *Seal Slab*.
5 17m. 4a. Move right up a short ramp and then climb to a ledge.
Continue up the wall on the left, before following easy slabs to the top.

Medusa (42 metres Very Severe 4b 8.8.84) takes the upper slabs right of
Rake's Progress, gained from the first pitch of that route or by traversing in to
the half-way ledge.

CHAIR LADDER

MAIN CLIFF

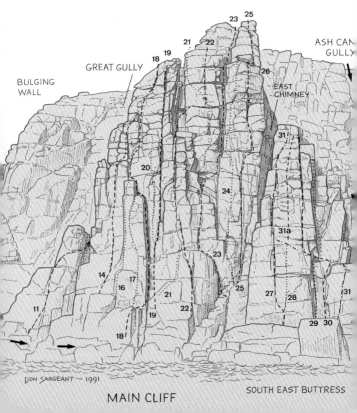

GREAT GULLY

BULGING
WALL

ASH CAN
GULLY

EAST
CHIMNEY

DON SARGEANT ~ 1991

MAIN CLIFF

SOUTH EAST BUTTRESS

WOLF BUTTRESS

32	Wolverine Chimney	VD
33	Giant Steps	S
34	Corporal's Route	HS
35	Aerial	VS
36	Animated Wall	E5
37	Caliban	E3
38	The Tempest	E6
39	Rats in a Rage	E6
40	Cut-Off	S
41	Laceration	HVS

BISHOP BUTTRESS

| 42 | Flannel Avenue | HS |
| 43 | Mine Climb | HVS |

44	Diocese	VS
45	Surfboard	HVS
46	The Steeple	E3
47	The Spire	E3
48	Bishop's Rib	E1
49	Cardinal Sin	E5
50	The Mitre	VS

THE PINNACLE

52	Fat City	E1
53	Expresso Bonzo	E1
54	Terrier's Tooth	HS
a/b	" " variation starts	

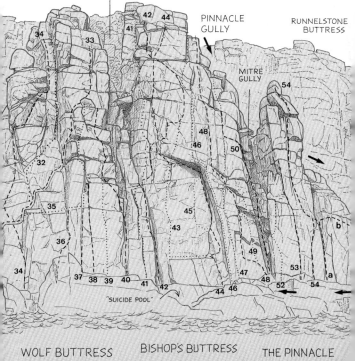

CUT OFF GULLY

PINNACLE GULLY

RUNNELSTONE BUTTRESS

MITRE GULLY

"SUICIDE POOL"

WOLF BUTTRESS   BISHOP'S BUTTRESS   THE PINNACLE

Main Cliff

The large and complex Main Cliff offers excellent steep climbing in splendid positions. The easier lines take the chimneys and cracks, while the walls between provide harder pitches with tough climbing on fingery holds. The right-hand section (facing in) is well used by nesting birds and can be mucky in places: their privilege. The left-hand section leads round from the lower depths of Great Gully by a series of large ledges and steep walls onto the true seaward face. This face is split on its left by a series of flaky chimneys, which give the original route on Chair Ladder, *Western Chimneys*. To the right of *Western Chimneys* is an impressively steep, flat-topped buttress, The Red Tower. It rises above a stepped lower buttress that drops to sea-level. It is flanked on its right by a key feature of the cliff, a square-cut recess within which the starts of a number of high-quality routes are found, including *Red Wall*. To the right of this recess is a big complex face split by *Pendulum Chimney*. On the right-hand side of this face is *East Chimney*, with South-East Buttress on its lower right and Ash Can Gully to the right again marking the end of Main Cliff.

Descend by the main Zawn Rinny Descent for the climbs on the left side of the cliff as far as the Red Tower area (see page 104). The sea-level ledges below this area are the least likely to be free from tide or swell even at low water and should be negotiated carefully. For the climbs on the right-hand side of Main Cliff, descent is by Ash Can Gully. When tidal conditions prevent access to the foot of Chair Ladder it may still be possible to approach the climbs on the right-hand side of Main Cliff either by descending *East Chimney* or by following the first pitch of *Original Route* (Very Difficult) from the large ledge in Ash Can Gully 15 metres above the sea.

The first climb starts inside the cleft of Great Gully.

Free Ride   65 metres   Hard Very Severe   (1983)
Start at the foot of a steep crack and groove in the left edge of the large pillar at the extreme left-hand side of the Main Cliff, opposite *Rake's Progress*.
1 8m. 4a. Climb the groove to a large ledge.
2 12m. 4a. Climb the centre of the slab to the top of the pillar, and descend to the stance of *Western Arête*.
3 20m. 5a. Move left and follow a wide crack to an overhang. Move right onto the face and climb cracks to a large ledge.
4 12m. Climb the wall behind the belay to a ledge. Take the corner to another ledge at the foot of a steep wall.
5 8m. 4a. Climb the steep broken fault up the centre of the wall to its top.
6 5m. Step across the gap to the large platform.

Western Arête   47 metres   Hard Severe   (21.8.66)
The stepped left arête of the Main Cliff. Start right of Great Gully, on large ledges below the prominent detached pinnacle which forms the first step in

the arête. The short crack at the start of pitch 3 is much harder than any other part of the route.

1 6m. Climb easily to the large platform beneath the western face of the pinnacle.

2 6m. Traverse right around the seaward face of the pinnacle and cross the gap to a ledge on the main buttress.

3 17m. 4c. Climb a short, hard crack above the left edge of the ledge. Go easily over blocks to a wide corner-crack. Climb this and move left onto the edge of the arête to a stance. (The hard crack can be avoided by climbing down into the gap mentioned in pitch 2. A traverse to the right past a vertical corner-crack leads to easy climbing on the left-hand wall of *Western Chimneys*. Stepping left after 6 metres gains the base of the wide corner-crack of pitch 3.)

4 18m. 4a. Climb two bulges to a ledge on the arête and finish up cracks.

★Great Western Arête 75 metres   Hard Very Severe   (16.4.84)
Start on a square-cut ledge at the base of the flaky breaks of *Western Chimneys*, at the foot of a steep wall with two cracks in it.

1 6m. 5a. Climb either crack to a ledge below a steep corner.

2 14m. 4a. Climb the corner. Traverse right and follow the arête to a ledge below twin cracks.

3 20m. 5b. Climb the cracks to the second horizontal break. Traverse left to the arête and follow it to a large ledge.

4 35m. 4a. Follow the arête to the top.

Western Chimneys 48 metres   Difficult   (c.1910)
This original 'first course' on Chair Ladder takes an obvious line of deep flaky chimneys in the left-hand side of the cliff. Start from the square-cut ledge at the base of the chimneys.

1 30m. Follow the chimneys to a large broken platform. The pitch can be split.

2 18m. Traverse left for 6 metres and climb the broken chimney to the top. (The cliff in the area of *Western Chimneys* is broken and provides a number of variations to the parent route, generally at a slightly harder standard.)

The following routes are on The Red Tower buttress and can be started from generous ledges below the Tower's left side.

The Thin Red Line 45 metres   E2   (30.12.84)
This takes the steep crack in the fine wall left of the left corner of *The Red Tower*. Start from a good ledge directly below the wall.

1 25m. 5c. Climb the crack and wall to ledges.

2 20m. Finish up the central grooves and crack in the bay above.

Beaujolais 45 metres   E1   (30.12.84)
Start below the wide crumbly corner on the left side of The Red Tower.

1 25m. 5b. Climb the corner and continue to a belay on top of the tower.

2 20m. 5b. Climb the steep wall on the right and finish up the cracks in the right side of the bay.

★★Scarlet Pimpernel   52 metres   E2   (25.3.84)
A finger-testing first pitch on excellent rock, taking the steep left arête of
The Red Tower. Start at the base of the arête.
1 35m. 5c. Climb onto the left arête and follow it to a small ledge. Climb
the wall on the right to a larger ledge; then climb the short wall to a ledge
below a chimney (*Red Wall*, pitch 3). Climb the chimney to another large
ledge and belay.
2 17m. 4c. Climb the crack in the buttress on the left, passing breaks
and keeping to the right of the final block. Finish up the broken arête on
the left.

★The Red Tower   60 metres   E5   (4.76)
The second pitch up the front face of The Red Tower is bold and striking.
Start directly below the tower on a sloping ledge just above the sea. Pitch 2
can be reached easily from left or right to avoid the tide. Protection is blind
and hard to place on the main pitch.
1 15m. 4b. Climb grooves and corners to a good ledge at the foot of the
tower.
2 15m. 6a. Climb the right side of the front face of the tower to a strange
little thread at 6 metres. Move up and then left into the centre of the face
and continue straight to the top of the tower.
3 30m. 4b. Pitches 3 and 4 of *Red Wall*.

The Town and Country Boyz   15 metres   E4 5c †   (7.98)
The right arête of the seaward face of the tower.

★Red Wall   60 metres   Hard Severe   (1947)
A pleasant route at the heart of the Main Cliff. It starts up the narrow red
wall which forms the left side of the square-cut recess. Start left of the
shallow gully that leads to the recess.
1 18m. Climb to the foot of the square pinnacle left of the recess. Move
right to a ledge below the recess and belay below the red wall on the left.
2 12m. 4b. Climb the red wall on good holds near its left edge to a
ledge at its top.
3 12m. 4b. Gain the top of the pinnacle and make a long step from the
left end of the ledge to enter a short chimney, which leads to the vast ledge
above.
4 18m. 4a. Climb steep cracks in the rib on the right to another large
ledge. Climb easier cracks on the right side of the lichenous face.
Variation
2a Suicide Crack 12m. Severe 4b (21.8.36). Climb the crack right of
the red wall. Strenuous and less pleasant than the normal way.

★Centre Piece   25 metres   E2 5c   (3.1.84)
Steep and strenuous but on good holds. Follow *Central Route* for about 6
metres and then move left to take the crack in the steep wall above the
square-cut recess. Follow this over a roof to a break and continue up the
steep wall to a large ledge.

★Central Route 40 metres   Hard Very Severe   (9.59)
The soaring crackline in the back right-hand corner of the square-cut recess. A tough and committing route near the top end of the grade. Start by scrambling up the shallow gully and into the recess.
1 22m. 5a. Climb the crack to a niche at 18 metres and continue more easily to a ledge.
2 18m. Follow the easy continuation chimney to the top.

Central Buttress Chimneys 63 metres   Very Difficult   (27.8.35)
A wandering line taking the easiest way up the front of the Main Cliff. Start below the shallow gully leading up to the square recess.
1 18m. Follow the gully easily to the ledge at the foot of the recess.
2 15m. Climb the chimney on the right to a ledge below the two prominent pinnacles at the top of the central buttress.
3 10m. Climb the inner pinnacle; then move up and left to a ledge.
4 20m. Climb into the recess above and take its left corner, moving left onto a rib. Follow the easy chimney of *Central Route* to the top.
Variation
1a Halfway House 18 metres   Very Severe 4c   (6.87)
Start below the steep crack just below the right arête of *Central Buttress Chimneys*. Climb the crack, then the cracks and bulges up the arête to belay as for *Central Buttress Chimneys*.

The Shadows 53 metres   Very Severe   (23.12.83)
Start just right of the gully leading up to the square-cut recess of *Red Wall*.
1 6m. Scramble over steps to a boat-shaped ledge at the foot of a steep crack.
2 6m. 4b. Climb the crack and move right across a steep wall to a good belay ledge below an obvious V-chimney (*Pendulum Chimney*).
3 12m. 4a. Climb the groove right of the V-chimney and continue up the crack in the wall to a ledge.
4 12m. 4b. Climb the wall left of the chimney.
5 17m. 5a. Traverse right and climb a steep groove over an overhang to finish.

★Neptune 50 metres   Very Severe   (10.6.57)
A route-finding challenge following the easiest line up the steep face left of *Pendulum Chimney*. Start below the shallow gully leading up to the square recess.
1 10m. 4a. Move right to climb a steep corner leading to a platform below an obvious V-chimney (*Pendulum Chimney*).
2 12m. 4a. Climb to and follow the V-chimney until a move right gains the large ledge below a chockstone.
3 20m. 4c. Climb onto the chockstone and step right onto the steep wall. Climb the wall, bearing right at the top to gain a ledge. From the left end of the ledge, continue diagonally left to a niche.
4 8m. 4a. Follow the right-hand crack out of the niche to the top.

★★Excelsior   60 metres   E1   (25.10.59/29.9.61)
A rising scale of first-class pitches, with the final pitch calling for a bold lead. Start at the base of the flat-topped pinnacle to the right of the *Red Wall* gully.
1 15m. Climb the groove to the top of the pinnacle.
2 15m. 5a. There are twin cracks in the left side of the wall above the ledge. Follow these, moving smartly left at mid height into the continuation crack. Continue to a good stance.
3 10m. Climb over easy ground to a large recess capped by an overhang.
4 10m. 5a. Take the right-hand corner of the recess to the overhang and make an awkward leg-swinging move out right to gain the left-hand end of a ledge.
5 10m. 5b. Serious, especially when wet. Gain the black scooped groove in the wall above from the left, and continue with increasing difficulty to an undercut groove above a break. A hard move up the groove leads to better finishing holds.

Mind the Step (15 metres E4 6b † 1990s) takes the system of thin cracks left of the second pitch of *Excelsior* – apparently contrived.

☆☆☆Digit Do It on Sight?   60 metres   E5 6b †   (1993)
The hardest line up the Main Cliff of Chair Ladder starts below the thin crackline left of *Pendulum Chimney*.
1 10m. 6b/c. Step left into the crack and follow it to the wider crack above. Belay on a large ledge.
2 13m. 5a. Climb the right arête on its left-hand side. Belay on the left of a wide ledge.
3 13m. 6a. Move left onto the exposed seaward face of the tower. Follow a vague crack to the top of the tower. Step over a gap and belay.
4 28m. 5c. Surmount blocks and climb a steep wall with two horizontal breaks to an optional belay (of *Excelsior*). Climb the wall above (left of *Excelsior*) to a ledge. Finish up a short wall.

★★Pendulum Chimney   50 metres   Severe   (1947)
One of Chair Ladder's classic climbs, with an interesting chimney pitch which is a touch noxious and noisy during the nesting season. Start at the base of the flat-topped pinnacle to the right of the *Red Wall* gully. The wide base of *East Chimney* is to the right.
1 8m. 4a. Move left and climb the wall of the flat-topped pinnacle to gain the ledge on its top. Belay below the V-chimney.
2 12m. 4a. Climb to the V-chimney and follow it to where a move right gains ledges.
3 12m. 4a. Descend slightly to the right and climb the steep crack on the right to easier ground in the gully above. Continue to a block belay on the right.
4 12m. 4b. Climb the chimney via a niche, from which the original chockstone 'pendulum' has long since swung into the sea. Harder moves above the niche lead to a belay in the corner above.
5 6m. 4a. The steep wall on the left leads to the top.

★Detergent Wall   45 metres   Hard Very Severe   (25.10.59)
A fine, nervy climb with slight protection on the crux pitch. Start in the wide
lower reaches of *East Chimney* about 15 metres above the sea.
1 12m. 4b. Climb to a niche in the left wall via a reddish-black vein.
Continue straight up to a horizontal break and belay at the base of a
lime-streaked crack on *South Face Direct*.
2 15m. 5a. Climb the bubbly wall left of the crack to a layback crack,
which leads to a block belay in *Pendulum Chimney*.
3 12m. 4c. Climb the steep wall right of *Pendulum Chimney*, at first on
the left and then on the right, until harder moves gain the ledge above.
4 6m. 4a. Finish up the short wall on the right.

★South Face Direct   52 metres   Very Severe   (1948)
[Photo p.160b.] Exceptional style and character. Start in the wide lower
reaches of *East Chimney*, below a crack and about 15 metres above the sea.
1 10m. 4a. Climb the crack to a square ledge below a lime-streaked
crack. This point can be reached by down-climbing *East Chimney* or by
abseil if tide or sea conditions are difficult.
2 18m. 4c. A mouth-watering pitch. Step into the shallow crack by a
difficult move, and climb to a niche. Continue up the crack above, and
move right in a fine position via a welcome saddle-horn boss to beneath a
short V-shaped crack, which is climbed to a good stance.
3 14m. 4c. Climb the steep crack above the stance to an awkward
overhang and then continue up an easier corner on the right to a large
ledge below the summit block.
4 10m. 4a. Finish up the slab above by a crack and a niche on the right.

Southern Arête   53 metres   E4   (10.6.85)
Start below the narrow, wedge-shaped buttress on the right of pitch 1 of
South Face Direct.
1 12m. 6a. Climb the steep slabby wall and pull over the left side of the
small roof.
2 18m. 5a. Climb the cracks right of *South Face Direct* and the groove
above to a belay.
3 23m. 4c. Traverse right onto the arête and follow steep cracks and a
groove to a good ledge. Belay or continue up the tower to the top.

Cleft Route   55 metres   Difficult   (c.1930)
The scenic route across Main Cliff, and a pleasant jaunt taking a diagonal
line from right to left. Start on the square block right of the foot of *East
Chimney*, about 10 metres above the sea.
1 10m. Climb *East Chimney* until it is possible to move left onto a square
ledge.
2 10m. Traverse left along rounded ledges and climb to a belay below
the large capstone.
3 15m. Climb over the capstone to the top of the inner pinnacle. Climb
to and then squeeze through the cleft to gain ledges below the large
square recess; then traverse left for 6 metres to a large area of ledges.

4 20m. Climb the corner on the right for 5 metres (as for *Central Route*) and move left along a long flat ledge. Traverse left to the centre of the ledge and then climb a broken crack in the lichen-covered face up to the right to finish.

East Chimney   37 metres   Difficult   (c.1930)
The deep chimney separating the Main Cliff from South-East Buttress. Climb the chimney via a stance on the left after 10 metres.

South-East Buttress

This is the small compact buttress between *East Chimney* and the base of Ash Can Gully. There is a narrow tidal channel beneath it which is fringed by rocky reefs to seaward. A ledge splits the face of the buttress at half height. The first five routes are on the wall below this. Two other routes take the corners of the recessed gully right of the lower face.

Almost   35 metres   Very Difficult   (14.6.74)
Start at the foot of *East Chimney*, below the central crack in the right-bounding wall.
1 15m. Climb the crack to a large ledge on the left.
2 10m. From the left-hand end of the ledge, climb the bulging crack to another large ledge.
3 10m. Climb the steep crack in the wall to the top.

Jenny's Surprise   40 metres   Very Severe †   (29.4.2000)
Start in a narrow tidal channel below the left-hand arête of South-East Buttress.
1 20m. 4c. Climb the arête to the half-height ledge.
2 20m. 4b. Continue up, staying close to the arête, and finish on top of the buttress.

★South-East Face Direct   15 metres   Hard Very Severe 5a (1968)
A sustained pitch taking the crack that splits the lower seaward face of the buttress. Climb a scoop and crack 5 metres right of the main crack. Move left into the main crack and follow it to the half-height ledge.

Love 30   15 metres   E1 5a   (1982)
Bold with slight gear. Start as for *South-East Face Direct* and climb the subsidiary crack. Instead of stepping left, climb the pocketed wall to the break. Continue to the half-height ledge.

★Hysterical Hamsters   15 metres   E4 6b   (26.8.90)
A bold, technical line up the right-hand side of the buttress. Start in the trench and make very hard moves to a sloping foot-ledge on the arête. Climb boldly to reach good holds in the horizontal break. Continue to a flake and gain the next horizontal break strenuously. Move right and climb over the roof on good holds to the half-height ledge.

★The Buccaneer   30 metres   Very Severe   (1.5.56)
Entertaining. Start below the recessed gully on the right of the lower face.
1 12m. 4c. Climb the left-hand corner of the gully, using a flake on the
left near the top. Move right onto the large ledge leading into Ash Can
Gully.
2 18m. 4b. Climb easily to the narrow chimney that runs up the east wall
of the buttress. Make an awkward entry into the chimney and then follow
easier cracks to the top.

Dexter Crack   30 metres   Severe   (26.8.37)
Start as for *The Buccaneer*, below the recessed gully.
1 12m. 4a. Climb the right-hand corner of the gully to the overhang,
and pass it on the right to gain the large ledge above.
2 18m. Step across the gully and move up and left to gain the half-height
break in the seaward face. Climb the chimney/crack above to the top.

★Mermaid's Route   42 metres   Very Difficult   (10.46)
A pleasant, wandering line, starting up the small buttress right of the
recessed gully climbs of *The Buccaneer* and *Dexter Crack*. It then crosses
onto the seaward face to finish up the left side of South-East Buttress. Start
below the slab right of the recessed gully.
1 18m. Climb the slab to a crack and follow this to a large ledge leading
round into Ash Can Gully.
2 6m. Step awkwardly across the recessed gully and move left to the
half-height break in the seaward face. Traverse left along the break to a
ledge and thread belay.
3 18m. Climb the break above on walloping holds.

Original Route   24 metres   Very Difficult   (7.8.38)
Start on the large ledge above the recessed gully of *The Buccaneer* and
Dexter Crack, gained from Ash Can Gully.
1 6m. *Mermaid's Route* pitch 2.
2 18m. Move back right and climb the exposed wall above the break on
huge holds to the top.

Ash Can Gully Area
On the lichen-covered tower which flanks the mid-height amphitheatre of
Ash Can Gully (the top right-hand section of the Main Cliff) there are some
routes which can be used as logical continuations of the climbs on the lower
South-East Buttress. They are also far enough above sea-level to be safe
from tide and swell unless a genuine 'freak wave' hits Cornwall.

★Nearly   31 metres   Hard Very Severe   (31.5.53/1962)
The challenging crack in the left face of the tower. Start in *East Chimney*, 5
metres below the jammed boulder at its top.
1 23m. 4c. Climb the deep crack to the large ledge with a perched
block, below the summit block.

2 8m. 5a. Traverse right onto the face and make an awkward move into the first crack, which is followed to the top.

Not Right   34 metres   Very Severe   (1981)
Start above the jammed boulder at the top of *East Chimney*.
1 10m. Climb a short crack and then a short slab on the right to a block belay.
2 24m. 5a. Step into the groove on the left and climb to a horizontal break. Traverse left into the crack just right of the arête. Follow the crack, joining *Nearly* at the top.

Just About   27 metres   E1 5b   (1987)
From the jammed boulder at the top of *East Chimney*, climb the yellow-lichened crack that zigzags up the face to join *Not Right*.

Not Quite   28 metres   Hard Severe   (13.8.66)
This takes the groove on the right-hand side of the tower. Start above the jammed boulder at the top of *East Chimney*.
1 10m. Climb a short slab to a block belay.
2 18m. 4c. Climb the crack below the small overhang for 3 metres, move left awkwardly into the groove, and follow it to the top.

Legoland   15 metres   E4 5c   (1989)
Climb the right-hand side of the tower of *Not Quite*.

There are several climbs on the right-hand walls of Ash Can Gully (the top right-hand side of Wolf Buttress).

Lizzy's Folly   26 metres   Very Difficult   (1976)
This takes an obviously cleaned line up the lichenous wall high up on the right (facing in) of the point where the Ash Can Gully descent path leads into the mid-height amphitheatre.

Cave Route   24 metres   Hard Severe 4b   (9.8.66)
The left-hand crack with the cave feature in the impressive seaward wall of the lower half of the amphitheatre. Climb into the chimney and move awkwardly – or painfully – into the back of the cave. Follow the chimney to a large ledge below the perched block.

The Lobster   25 metres   E6 6b   (1989)
Climb the shallow hanging crack just right of *Cave Route*.

★Sea Horse   27 metres   Hard Very Severe 5b   (13.8.66)
Tough climbing up the striking off-width crack in the gully wall to the right of *Cave Route*. Something of a classic if you like that sort of thing. Climb the first crack and the bulges above to the foot of the wall. Climb steeply to make a hard move into the undercut crack. Follow this with difficulty to the top.

Wolf Buttress

Wolf Buttress lies to the right of Ash Can Gully and extends to the bottomless Cut-Off Gully, beyond which lies the elegant Bishop Buttress. The upper left-hand section of Wolf Buttress adjoining Ash Can Gully is in the form of a large bay, the base of which is marked by a broken triangular slab. The upper central feature of the bay is the large leftward-facing corner of *Wolverine Chimney*. On its left is the bulging gangway of *Corporal's Route* and on its right the leaning chimney of *Giant Steps*. Right again, the upper section of the buttress rises directly from the steep lower wall and is climbed by *Aerial* and *Cut-Off*, which traverse onto the wall from the left and right respectively. The steep impeccable wall below the bay has a number of highly technical climbs.

Descent is by the Ash Can Gully or Pinnacle Gully Descent. When tide and sea are awkward, the top pitches on the left side (facing in) of Wolf Buttress can be reached safely from Ash Can Gully.

Wolverine Chimney   55 metres   Very Difficult   (1940s)
Open and friendly. Start at the base of Ash Can Gully, at a tidal pool.
1 10m. Climb the gully to a stance on the slab on the left.
2 25m. Step across the gully and follow two 3-metre-high steps to the right. From the top of the second step, move left onto the slab and follow a shallow groove to the foot of the obvious corner/chimney. (The shallow groove can be avoided by climbing to its left.)
3 8m. Climb the chimney on reassuring holds to a recess.
4 12m. Climb the crack in the right-hand side of the gully to the top. An easier finish can be made up the left-hand crack.

Aero Dynamics   8 metres   E6 7a †   (7.12.95)
The fairly steep arête between the third pitches of *Wolverine Chimney* and *Giant Steps*. Relatively easy (6a) moves lead to a break and good protection. From here, a big dyno gains a jug at the top.

Giant Steps   62 metres   Severe   (1949)
This takes the obvious line of left-to-right steps across the bay, finishing by an awkward chimney in the right-hand section of the buttress. Start at the base of Ash Can Gully, at a tidal pool.
1 10m. Climb the gully to a stance on the slab on the left (*Wolverine Chimney* pitch 1).
2 20m. Step right over the gully and climb the line of obvious steps to a belay at the foot of the leaning chimney in the right wall.
3 12m. Climb the leaning chimney to the vast ledges on the front of the buttress.
4 20m. Follow the easiest line up the left side of the rock above.
Variation
3a 14m. Climb to the foot of the corner of *Wolverine Chimney*, and follow the flake crack on the right wall to the large ledge above the leaning chimney.

★Corporal's Route   53 metres   Hard Severe   (1955)
Worthwhile, with a testing first pitch and a pleasantly exposed third, which
takes the bulging wall left of *Wolverine Chimney*. Start about 10 metres
right of the base of Ash Can Gully, at the foot of a thin crack and just left
of a shallow corner.
1 14m. 4b. Climb the crack and move awkwardly left to a ledge.
Continue to a belay on the ledge above.
2 15m. Go diagonally left up the slab above; then continue straight up to
a large block at the foot of a steep, vertical, off-width crack.
3 12m. 4b. Climb the wall left of the crack and move right onto a ledge.
Follow a diagonal crack up to the right to a wide ledge just left of
Wolverine Chimney.
4 12m. 4a. Climb the narrow slab in the gully to the top.
Variation
4a 12m. Traverse left on the lip of an overhang and then climb to a small
slab. Move right and take a narrow slab to the top.

★Aerial   68 metres   Very Severe   (25.5.56/14.11.62)
An elegant climb, which edges towards the great golden heart of the
buttress by a natural line. Start about 10 metres right of the base of Ash
Can Gully, at the foot of a thin crack and just left of a shallow corner.
1 11m. 4b. Climb the crack and move awkwardly left to a ledge (as for
Corporal's Route). This point can be reached at high tide by traversing in
from Ash Can Gully.
2 20m. 4c. Move up, traverse delicately rightwards around the arête to
the foot of a step, and mantelshelf awkwardly onto it. Continue more
easily rightwards and climb the right-hand of twin cracks to a large ledge.
3 17m. 4c. From the left end of the ledge, climb a wide crack and make
a delicate move left under an overhang. Follow the steep crack above to a
good ledge. Continue up a steep wall on the right to a vast platform.
4 20m. Follow the easiest line over the blocks above.
Variation
Other Spirits   40 metres   E1 †   (2.96)
2a 15m. 5b. Follow *Aerial* pitch 2 but continue traversing along the
obvious line to the arête.
3a 25m. 5b. Continue up the arête to easy ground.

The following five routes all have hard, technical lower pitches leading to the
easier upper section of Wolf Buttress. They are described as separate entities;
finishing-pitches are optional.

Insularism   20 metres   E7 6b †   (7.98)
Climb a direct line between *Aerial* and *Animated Wall*: thin and bold.

★★Animated Wall   30 metres   E5   (14.4.87/1990s)
Intense and fingery. Small wires are useful but poor. Start at the base of the
steep clean wall just below a thin rightward-facing, black-streaked flake.

1 20m. 6a. Climb the wall to the flake. Traverse right using an underling to another shallow flake/groove (peg). Climb slightly left; then move back right to reach a blind crack and follow this to ledges on pitch 2 of *Aerial*.
2 10m. 6a. Climb the arête above.
Variation
2a Crash, Boom, Bang 10m. E8 6c † (29.12.95). Climb the arête on its right-hand side and move left to finish.

★Caliban 20 metres E3 6a (1975/18.4.81)
The first attempt at prising Wolf Buttress apart, which takes the thin crack running up the lower wall above a sharp-pointed pinnacle flake. Neatly technical for one or two moves. Step off the pinnacle and climb the crack with increasing difficulty, passing two old pegs. Continue up a short groove and climb the left-hand of the twin cracks above to a large ledge (second belay of *Aerial*).

★The Tempest 20 metres E6 6b (2.2.87)
The E-grade has risen a notch as the two pegs are in a poor state. Start 3 metres right of *Caliban* and climb the wall to reach a small flake. Continue direct to the large belay ledge of *Aerial*.

A highly technical and intense pitch took the swooping wall right of *The Tempest* using two drilled pegs and a bolt (**Rats in a Rage** 20 metres E6 6c 7.87). It climbed the middle of the smooth wall past a drilled peg to a flake crack, which led past a drilled peg and bolt to a horizontal break. The thin crack and wall above, a small roof, and the right arête were taken to finish. The first ascensionist believes the route may well be impossible following the loss of certain holds due to sea action.

Lobos 20 metres E6 6b † (1990s)
A sparsely-protected line up the right-hand side of the smooth wall.

Cut-Off 60 metres Severe (25.3.51)
Start below the corner which forms the right-hand end of the lower wall of the buttress.
1 20m. Climb the corner to a ledge at 5 metres and continue up the easier gully to a ledge on the left.
2 20m. Move left onto a flake on the face and climb it to a ledge. Follow the corner above to a huge block, and then traverse left. The right side of the steep wall above leads to a vast platform.
3 20m. Follow the easiest line up the blocks above to the top.

To the right of *Cut-Off* there is a small buttress flanked by a chimney above a distinctive tidal pool. The pool is known gruesomely as 'Suicide Pool' because of its inviting presence as viewed between the legs from the higher pitches above. On the right edge of the buttress is a tight crack.

Laceration   58 metres   Hard Very Severe   (28.5.56)
Well named for its ripping first pitch, which is worthwhile all the same. Start beneath the crack at the right edge of the small buttress.
1 10m. 5a. Climb the crack to a ledge.
2 20m. 4a. Gain the large ledge above and move right onto the buttress. Climb the wall above on good holds to a niche.
3 20m. 4a. Pass the overhang above on its left and climb to an extensive ledge below the final wall. Large block belay.
4 8m. 4a. From the left end of the block, step left and climb the wall to the top.

Face Marks   20 metres   E4 6b   (1995)
Climb the face and crack just right of *Laceration* to a good ledge.

Bishop Buttress
This is the striking area of rock between Cut-Off Gully and Mitre Gully. It is Chair Ladder's finest section of cliff, offering classic lines on exquisite granite, with golden rock on its lower half and a green and saffron dusting of lichen on the upper walls. The main feature is the magnificent overhung corner of *Diocese*, which is drawn out leftwards to the soaring edge of the face and the amenable line of *Flannel Avenue*. To the right of *Diocese* is the slim and elegant buttress that frames *The Spire* and *Bishop's Rib* before the cliff falls away into the dank contradiction of Mitre Gully.

Descent is by Ash Can Gully or Pinnacle Gully.

Raider's Route   37 metres   Difficult   (1949)
An unprepossessing route up the handsome left edge of Bishop Buttress. Start by climbing down from the bottom of Cut-Off Gully to a ledge about 9 metres below the end of the *Diocese* overhang. From here, climb steep rock on comfortable holds past the stance at the end of the *Diocese* traverse. Continue just left of the arête above to a ledge below the final wall, from where an escape left can be made.

★★Flannel Avenue   56 metres   Hard Severe   (1949)
A Cornish classic that draws the climber onto the exhilarating golden wall above the overhang of *Diocese* at a reasonable grade, although it is quite strong in places. Start below a deep chimney on the left side of Bishop Buttress, above Suicide Pool.
1 18m. 4b. Harder than the rest of the route. Climb the chimney by bridging for 15 metres, move left onto the rib, and climb to a good stance.
2 10m. Move right onto the main buttress and climb steeply but on comfortable holds to a niche.
3 20m. 4a. Delicious exposure. Go up right and then traverse above the overhang to a flat-topped block. Take the steep slab directly above on tidy holds and wink at Suicide Pool on the way; then bear slightly left near the top to an extensive ledge and block belay.

4 8m. 4a. Quite stiff. From the right-hand end of the block, step onto the steep wall and climb strenuously on good holds to the top.
Variation
1a 24m. 4a. An easier alternative start can be used if the tide is overflowing the Suicide Pool. Start below the corner of *Diocese*. Climb up to the right end of the ledge and move along this to its left end. Climb steeply up to the left and make a long move into the chimney, before continuing as for pitch 1.

Mine Climb   62 metres   Hard Very Severe   (3.11.66)
A contrived but direct line up the left-hand side of the buttress, taking the left end of the *Diocese* overhang. Start below the corner of *Diocese*.
1 30m. 4b. Climb to the right end of the ledge and move along it to its left end. Climb steeply up to the left and join the start of *Flannel Avenue* by continuing up the steep wall and then moving right to a ledge. Climb past the stance at the end of the traverse of *Diocese* to a niche below the overhang.
2 20m. 5a. Climb to and surmount the overhang strenuously, using a large hold over the lip. Climb the steep slab above, trending rightwards to the extensive ledge below the final wall. Belay in the chimney to the right of the wall.
3 12m. 4a. Climb the chimney and cracks to the top.

Splash   50 metres   E4 †   (1995)
Start between *Mine Climb* and *Diocese*, at a crack.
1 10m. 5b. Follow the crack to a ledge.
2 20m. 6b. Move slightly left and then follow the slabby wall, trending gradually right, to the first stance of *Diocese*.
3 20m. 5b. Break through the roof and follow cracks to a large ledge.

★Diocese   61 metres   Very Severe   (1951)
[Photos p.192a.] A magnificent route at the top of the grade taking the corner below the overhang and then traversing airily left to reach the golden wall above. Start from the long ledge below the corner.
1 20m. 4c. Climb either the wide crack or, more pleasantly, the slab on its right, to rejoin the crack after 6 metres. Continue trickily to a delightful cave stance.
2 10m. 5a. A memorable pitch. Traverse left by using the rising crack beneath the roof or by a lower more subtle line across the face to make a final exposed move round the nose and onto a good stance.
3 23m. 4a. Move left, and climb the rib above in fine positions to where a short slab leads to the extensive ledge and huge block belay.
4 8m. 4b. Climb the shallow groove in the steep wall 3 metres right of the block.

The Surfboard   60 metres   Hard Very Severe   (1981)
Start from the long ledge below the corner of *Diocese*.
1 25m. 5b. Climb the wide crack or its flanking slab. At the top of the slab, move left onto the wall and take the wrinkled crack in its centre, which leads back right to the cave stance.

2 35m. 5b. Move out left and pull over the roof to finish up *The Steeple* or *Flannel Avenue*.
Variation
Thruster (E1 5a 1986) takes the roof right of pitch 2.

★**Bishop's Arête**   60 metres   Hard Very Severe   (18.10.81)
An interesting connector, starting as for *Diocese*, crossing *Bishop's Rib*, and taking in parts of *The Mitre*.
1 14m. 4b. Climb the narrow slab as for *Diocese* until it nearly peters out, and move right around the arête. Traverse right across the wall to the belay of *Bishop's Rib*.
2 23m. 5a. Climb the roof on the right to another roof. Traverse right and climb the arête, a wide crack, and the arête again to the knob on *The Mitre*. Continue up the arête to a shallow crack on the left. Climb just left of the arête to a good ledge.
3 23m. *Bishop's Rib* pitch 3.

The Crusader   60 metres   Hard Very Severe   (1985)
Start as for *Diocese*.
1 20m. 5a. Climb the narrow slab as for *Diocese* to where it peters out and move right around the arête. Climb the wall just right of the arête and continue up a steep shallow corner to move left to a restricted stance.
2 40m. 4b. Move up into the crack on the right and then bear left up less well-defined cracks to the left of *Bishop's Rib* to a good ledge. Continue easily to the top.

★**The Steeple**   60 metres   E3   (4.76)
A strong eliminate line, E4 or harder if done without a side runner in *Diocese*. Start at the base of the steep arête at the left edge of the slim buttress of *Bishop's Rib*.
1 40m. 6a. Climb the arête until nearly level with the lip of the *Diocese* overhang. (Some sting can be taken out of this serious lower pitch by placing a runner in the crack on the left to protect a hard move at half height.) Step up, and then break out left to traverse along the lip of the overhang for 5 metres to gain a good crack, which leads to a ledge.
2 20m. 4a. Follow corners and cracks to the top.

★★**The Spire**   50 metres   E3   (4.7.71)
Fine, technical climbing on an irresistible line up the thin cracks on the left side of *Bishop's Rib*. Micros especially useful on pitch 1. Start below the faint crackline 3 metres right of the steep arête.
1 20m. 5c. Move up to an obvious finger-slot, and make a series of difficult moves to a small ledge at 8 metres. Step left and follow cracks to a resting-place. Continue up a steep shallow corner and move left to a restricted stance.
2 30m. 4b. Move up into the crack on the right (above the overhang of *Bishop's Rib*). Follow the crack and continue easily to the top.

Marisco Striptease (E2), Carn Barra
Climber: David Hope   Photo: David Hope col.
Fine and Dandy (HVS), Carn Barra
Climber: Paul Robertson   Photo: Dave Turnbull

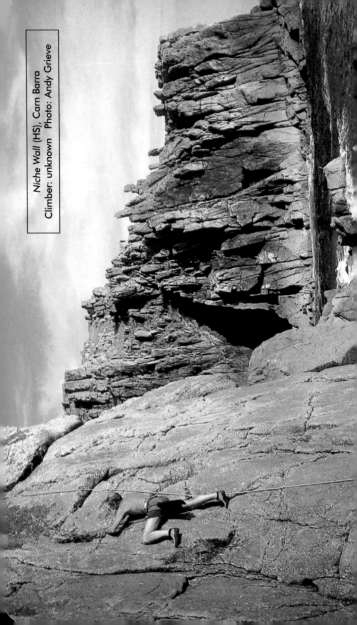

Niche Wall (HS), Carn Barra   Climber: unknown   Photo: Andy Grieve

★Bishop's Rib   58 metres   E1   (1956/21.7.63)
[Photo p.192b.] One of Cornwall's great classics: delicate, strenuous, and independent. Small wires needed. Start below the dank corner of Mitre Gully.
1 15m. 5b. Step up and make a rising traverse leftwards on small holds to a small ledge below the overhang. (A direct E2 5b approach can be made from the trench below the crack.) Move back right and climb the overhang. Continue on better holds to a stance below an overhang on the right.
2 20m. 5a. Climb the wall on the left to gain a diagonal crack running up left beneath the overhang. Follow the crack up and left and then climb through the overhang to a sloping ledge beneath the golden face above. Move left to climb a steep crack on magnificent holds to a recessed ledge.
3 23m. Follow the easiest line up the lichen-covered rock above to the top.

☆Cardinal Sin   46 metres   E5 †   (12.1.85)
Start as for *Bishop's Rib*.
1 14m. 6b. Climb the smooth wall to the roof and make hard moves to clear it. Continue up and belay beneath an overhang as for *Bishop's Rib*.
2 12m. 5a. Climb the roof on the right to another roof (as for *Bishop's Arête* pitch 2). Traverse right to the arête and continue into the gully.
3 20m. 5b. Climb the wall just left of the arête and move rightwards to a large roof. Climb into the overhung groove above the roof and go up to another roof. Pull right onto the steep wall, which is climbed on good holds to the top.

Space Chase   24 metres   Hard Very Severe 5b †   (12.1.85)
The wall and roof right of the top pitch of *Cardinal Sin*.

The steep greasy recess of Mitre Gully divides Bishop Buttress from The Pinnacle.

★The Mitre   59 metres   Very Severe   (1954)
The second pitch of this route has startling exposure in a dramatic position.
1 18m. 4c. Climb the left-hand corner of Mitre Gully, and make a hard move onto the right wall to gain the easy-angled upper gully: this is usually wet and greasy.
2 18m. 4c. Gripping. Climb cracks in the left wall of the gully near its left arête to a gargoyle knob at the foot of a deep crack. Make a difficult move left around the arête into instant exposure, and gain a crack 3 metres further left. Climb the crack to the good recessed ledge above.
3 23m. Follow the easiest line to the top.
Variation
2a 18m. 4c. The exposure cover-up. Start just right of the normal pitch and climb the wall of the gully on good holds to a cave (belay possible). Make an awkward belly crawl beneath the overhang to the left and gain the ledge above the normal pitch.

A rockfall has altered the right-hand side of Mitre Gully. The first pitches of two routes, **Gullible** (27.6.52) and **The Orb** (7.72), have been destroyed. The upper pitches of these routes shared parts of *The Mitre* and *Terrier's Tooth*. Since they have lost their key pitches, these routes are no longer worth describing.

The Pawn   64 metres   Very Severe   (3.4.72)
The first pitch of *The Pawn* climbs the seaward section of the right wall of Mitre Gully. Start at the base of the narrow seaward wall.
1 18m. 4c. Climb the reddish quartzy wall diagonally right past a spike to a break in the arête. Climb for a few metres, move right onto the seaward face, and climb a crack to easy ground. Traverse left to belay in the easy upper gully.
2 23m. 4c. The left wall of the gully has a wide slanting crack on its right-hand side. Climb the crack to a prominent block on the right, below an overhang with a flaky outside edge. Climb over the block and stomach-traverse awkwardly left to the recessed ledge on *The Mitre*.
3 23m. Follow the easiest line to the top.
Variation
2a 25m. Hard Very Severe 5a (1978). Climb the right-hand, slanting crack; then go up directly to the V-shaped roof-crack that slices deeply into the wall above. Climb this and continue directly to the top.

Ratcatcher   20 metres   E2 5b   (14.8.87)
A bold eliminate between the variations of *The Pawn*. Start at the base of   ·
upper Mitre Gully. Climb the central crackline in the left-hand wall to the first overhang. Pull over and climb past wide crack to the second overhang. Use a flake in the wall above to reach some pocketed holds and a spike, and climb onto a large sloping ledge stained with orange-coloured lichen.

The Pinnacle
The next major feature is The Pinnacle, which lies to the right of Mitre Gully. This is a handsome section of cliff rising to a height of 45 metres. It has a steep lower wall leading to an easier-angled mid section crowned by an upper section of large blocks. The base of The Pinnacle is best approached from Pinnacle Gully. To escape from the top of The Pinnacle, climb down a short awkward wall on the left side (facing in) of the summit blocks. This leads to a ledge which runs back into the grassy upper reaches of Pinnacle Gully. The first climbs described are on the lower wall, starting from sea-level ledges.

Fat City   20 metres   E1 6a   (5.85)
The scoop in the wall just right of the lower left arête of The Pinnacle. Start just right of Mitre Gully. The scoop is gained by a hard move which can be rather ingeniously protected by 'lassoing' the spike 5 metres up on the arête of *The Pawn*. Finish by the upper variation of *The Pawn*.

Blockbuster   20 metres   E5 6a   (5.5.84)
Climb a wandering yet hard line up the poorly-protected wall just right of
Fat City.

The Golden Rabbit   40 metres   E3 †   (1996)
1 18m. 5b. From the groove on *Expresso Bonzo*, climb to the first belay
of *The Pawn* in the upper gully.
2 22m. 5b. Climb the left arête of *Terrier's Tooth* pitch 2 to easy ground.

★Expresso Bonzo   40 metres   E1   (28.5.71)
An attractive and delicate first pitch taking the shallow angular groove in
the centre of the left-hand wall of The Pinnacle, just right of *Blockbuster*.
1 20m. 5b. Climb the groove and then follow smooth cracks to a large
ledge.
2 20m. Continue easily up the arête to the top of The Pinnacle.

★★Terrier's Tooth   39 metres   Hard Severe   (24.3.40/25.8.40)
[Photos p.224a.] One of Cornwall's finest. A classic V Diff for many years,
it has been upgraded for the daunting first pitch, which requires some
commitment. For the V Diff leader, the variation starts are safer but less
atmospheric. Start at the foot of the narrow quartz vein, central to the face
and about 10 metres right of Mitre Gully.
1 18m. 4b. Slight protection. Climb the vein to a small ledge on the left,
and make an awkward move up and right onto a sloping gangway. Climb
up the centre of the steep slab above to a ledge right of a crack in the face
above.
2 9m. Climb the steep crack to a good ledge.
3 12m. Climb to the right to a narrow ledge below the slab. Make a
high-stepping move into the crack by using a small hold out on the right,
and continue pleasantly to the top of The Pinnacle. (Descent is leftwards
into the gully with care.)
Variations
1a 20m. 4a. Climb the groove and corner some 6 metres right of the
quartz vein. This leads to the sloping gangway on the normal pitch, and is
better protected than the quartz vein.
1b 30m. A useful option at high tide. Climb the steep corner 18 metres
right of the quartz vein and just left of the easy way down. Traverse left,
passing a corner, to reach the upper slab of pitch 1.

★Grit Exiles   40 metres   E2   (1978)
A good first pitch up the smooth crack between the variation starts to
Terrier's Tooth.
1 20m. 5b. Climb the crack to ledges below The Pinnacle.
2 20m. Climb the hanging flake left of a chimney to a ledge; then go
down right and climb cracks to the top.

Masquerade   24 metres   E2 5c   (1989)
Climb the crack right of *Grit Exiles*, or take the undercling flake to its left.

CHAIR LADDER ~ EAST

THE PINNACLE

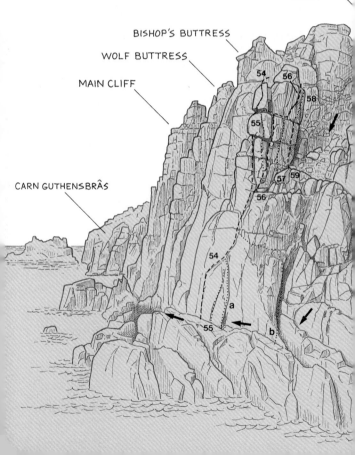

PINNACLE GULLY

BISHOP'S BUTTRESS

WOLF BUTTRESS

MAIN CLIFF

CARN GUTHENSBRÂS

RUNNELSTONE BUTTRESS ~ COLISEUM WALL

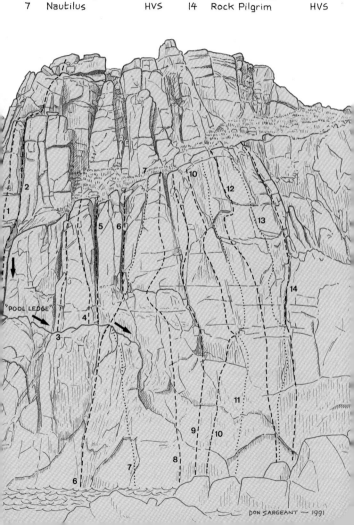

DON SARGEANT ~ 1991

Toothache   50 metres   Very Severe   (14.4.79)
1 35m. 4c. Climb the first variation start to *Terrier's Tooth*. Continue up
the right-hand side of a tower, and climb an arête until the overhanging
chimney to its right can be followed to a ledge.
2 15m. 4c. Traverse right along the ledge to the foot of steep twin cracks.
Climb the left-hand crack.

The following pitches are on the right-hand, lichen-stained wall of the upper
Pinnacle and are useful exercises when sea and tide prevent access to the
base of the cliff.

Asterix in Cornwall   23 metres   Very Severe 5a   (4.83)
Take the crack just right of *Toothache's* final pitch to a ledge. Step right and
climb the left-hand crack/groove-line to its top.

Dangle and Mangle   14 metres   Very Severe 5a   (26.5.84)
Climb the crack on the left side of the wall through a small triangular niche
to a ledge. Step right, and climb the right-hand crack in the wall above.

The crack right of *Dangle and Mangle* gives **Nutcracker** (10 metres Very
Severe 4c 26.5.84). The right-hand crack on the face is **The Mauler** (10
metres Hard Very Severe 5a 26.5.84). The impressively steep wall on the
back of The Pinnacle is climbed via a rightward-slanting crack to give
Dracula the Undead (10 metres E7 6b 24.8.86), and the rounded arête
to the right is **Toothmark** (10 metres E6 6c † 1995).

Girdle Traverses
The two recorded girdle traverses of Chair Ladder are enjoyable, though
disjointed because of the stepped nature of the cliff. They offer first-class
outings, however, especially when adverse sea conditions cut off the lower
faces of the cliff. Both girdles can be highly atmospheric if sea conditions are
lively. But a strong warning holds good about such conditions, since hard
seas and swell can send storm waves 30 metres or more up the face of the
cliff, pushing explosive air-pressure waves ahead of them. It is air-pressure
ahead of storm waves that cracks off overhangs on sea-cliffs. Most of the
pitches described are part of established routes.

The Girdle Traverse   240 metres approx   Severe   (14.4.52)
Start either from the eastern side of Zawn Rinny or from the sea-level
ledges below Bulging Wall's *Seal Slab*, depending on sea conditions. A
third approach is by reversing the top two pitches of *Great Slab Route* to
reach the big ledge at half height. The traverse is sub-divided into pitches,
although belays can be taken at several other points and many variations
are possible. Although taking, for the most part, a high line, it should be
treated with great caution if big seas are running.
1 Take a diagonal line up to the right-hand corner of the slab to gain the
ledge on the right at the top of *Great Slab Route* pitch 1.

2 From the right-hand end of the ledge, descend slightly and traverse steeply right on good holds to a large ledge. Climb to the big ledge that cuts across the right-hand section of the face at half height and follow it into Great Gully.

3 Gain the upper part of *Cleft Route* and reverse that route to a square ledge just left of *East Chimney*.

4 Cross *East Chimney* to the ledges that traverse South-East Buttress at half height. Follow these, and then cross the gully wall to the large ledge in Ash Can Gully (*Mermaid's Route* pitch 2 in reverse).

5 Step right over the gully and climb the line of obvious steps. Belay at the foot of the leaning chimney in the right wall (*Giant Steps* pitch 2).

6 Climb the leaning chimney to the vast ledges on the front of the buttress (*Giant Steps* pitch 3); then cross Cut-Off Gully to gain a niche (top of *Flannel Avenue* Pitch 2).

7 Go up right and traverse above the overhang to a flat-topped block (as for *Flannel Avenue* pitch 2). Climb diagonally to the right on neat holds to the recessed ledge above pitch 2 of *Bishop's Rib*; then follow cracks above, and finish by traversing into Pinnacle Gully.

The Bishop's Chain   240 metres approx Very Severe   (1.6.63)
A more technically challenging right-to-left girdle, which takes a lower line than its companion. Good judgement on the state of the sea is called for. The pitches described and belays can be taken at various points, especially in the latter part of the traverse.

1 Start half-way down Pinnacle Gully and cross The Pinnacle at half height to gain the easy upper section of Mitre Gully.

2 Gain a traverse-line onto *Bishop's Rib* and belay in the niche at the top of its first pitch.

3 Continue leftwards at the same level before descending slightly and moving into the chimney of *Diocese*.

4 Follow the traverse of *Diocese* beneath the roof and continue across Cut-Off Gully onto Wolf Buttress.

5 Reverse pitch 2 of *Aerial* and then traverse into Ash Can Gully.

6 Easier climbing leads across South-East Buttress (*Mermaid's Route* pitch 2). The easiest line is then followed leftwards across Main Face to where Bulging Wall is reached at the wide ledge above the smooth black wall of Great Gully.

7 Finish up the top pitches of *Kaleidoscope*.

Runnelstone Buttress

This is the final feature of Chair Ladder. It lies to the east of Pinnacle Gully and extends to Funnel Zawn and the vast open-topped cavern of Tol-pedn-Penwith. The area is less appealing than the main part of Chair Ladder. The main buttress is broken at half height by a grassy terrace, above which lichen-covered rock provides the main pitch of *Dodger's Chimney*. Pitches have been climbed to either side of the chimney and on the left-hand side of the buttress from ledges just above the sea. Coliseum Wall lies below and to the right of the terrace.

Descend Pinnacle Gully as for *Terrier's Tooth* to reach the obvious pool ledge, where five routes start.

Lies, Lies, Lies   10 metres   Very Severe 4c †   (1990s)
Start 3 metres left of the pool. Step off a block and climb the slab above.

The Young Pretender   10 metres   E5 6c †   (1990s)
From just left of the pool, climb the wall to a rightward-slanting crack. Follow this and its vertical continuation.

Offensively Named   10 metres   E6 6c †   (1990s)
Start at the left end of the pool. Climb the wall just left of the right arête of the buttress. No protection.

Dodge City   15 metres   Hard Very Severe 5a   (c.1960s)
Climb the wall and crack just left of *Dodger's Chimney* pitch 2 on the buttress above the terrace.

Dodger's Chimney   40 metres   Difficult   (1940s)
Start just to the right of the pool.
1 10m. Climb either of two cracks to the grassy terrace.
2 15m. Climb the elegant chimney above, although not necessarily by elegant means, to where a thrutchy exit to a ledge is made either directly or via a narrower chimney on the right.
3 15m. Climb easily over blocks to the top.

Coliseum Wall

Coliseum Wall forms the substantial right-hand side of Runnelstone Buttress below the grassy terrace. It is flanked on its right by Tol-pedn-Penwith Cavern. The wall is nicely angled and covered with little holds, but the rock is brittle in places and protection can be sparse. The starts of all routes are affected by swell at most states of the tide. Reasonable access to the upper pitches is possible by traversing in from the approach ledge.

Descent. Continue right (facing in) along the pool ledge from the start of *Dodger's Chimney* until the ledge fades away. Above the end of the ledge are two 12-metre chimneys: *Mini Minx Chimney* and to its right, the top chimney of *Iron Maiden*, which has a jammed block at its top. To reach the base of the wall, either climb down a shaky rake with care at about Very Difficult standard, or abseil. There is an abseil spike about 5 metres up and right of the ledge. The generous belay ledge in the lower centre of the face can be reached at high tide by traversing past the abseil spike and then descending crumbling ledges with care.

The following routes start from the approach ledge.

Close to the Edge 12 metres Hard Very Severe 5a (29.4.84)
The left side of the buttress left of *Mini Minx Chimney*. Poor protection.

La Speciale 12 metres Hard Very Severe 5a (29.4.84)
Climb the stubbly arête left of *Mini Minx Chimney* to finish up cracks. Poor protection.

Mini Minx Chimney 12 metres Very Difficult (29.4.84)
Thrutch. Climb the short wall and the earthy left-hand chimney above the end of the ledge.

The following routes start from the boulders in the bed of the zawn, which are reached by descending the rake. When the boulders are awash, all the top pitches can be climbed by traversing in.

Iron Maiden 50 metres Very Severe 4c † (4.7.86)
Start from the zawn-bed, directly below the end of the ledge. Climb a groove to the ledge and then continue up the chimney with the jammed block.

Nautilus 43 metres Hard Very Severe † (29.4.84)
Start 6 metres left of the base of the descent rake.
1 23m. 4a. Climb the pocketed wall to the approach ledge.
2 20m. 4c. Traverse up and rightwards to the chimney of *Iron Maiden* and then climb the cracks on the right wall.

Moon Dog 42 metres Hard Very Severe (29.4.84)
Start at the foot of the descent rake.
1 27m. 4c. Climb up to the abseil spike.
2 15m. 5a. Climb the edge of the buttress right of the deep chimney with the jammed block to move up and rightwards by a thin crack.

The first pitches of the next six routes converge on a ledge at 15 metres and use a common belay peg in the floor of the ledge.

Softly Softly 45 metres Hard Very Severe † (29.4.84)
Start at the bottom of the descent rake.
1 15m. 4a. Climb a short wall to the belay ledge below the main face.
2 30m. 4c. Climb right of a shallow depression before following a groove to finish.

The Great Divide 50 metres E2 (29.4.84)
Slight protection. Start a few metres right of the descent rake.
1 15m. 5a. Climb the overlap and slab to the belay ledge.
2 35m. 5c. Climb the smooth wall direct to a 'sticky-out' peg. Move left and then up to a comfortable spike below and left of the small overlap that is the focus of the main face. Climb the thin crack on the left to the top.

Private Performance   50 metres   Hard Very Severe   (29.4.84)
A pleasant climb. Start below the middle of the belay ledge.
1 15m. 4a. Climb direct to the belay ledge.
2 35m. 5a. From the mid-point of the ledge, climb up and then trend left to the spike below the central overlap. Move up and over; then take a thin crack to the top.

★Midnight Runner   50 metres   E1   (29.4.84)
Quite bold, with a stylish and exposed second pitch. Start below the right-hand end of the central belay ledge.
1 15m. 5a. Climb an overlap to a faultline, which is followed to a sloping ledge. Climb the short wall above to the belay ledge.
2 35m. 5b. From a point about 3 metres left of the right-hand end of the ledge, climb up the wall and trend left to the spike below the central overlap. Move right on delightful finger-pockets and swing up and round the overlap to a resting-foothold. Finish up a shallow crack.

The Gladiator   50 metres   Hard Very Severe †   (29.4.84)
Start below the right-hand end of the central belay ledge.
1 15m. 4c. Climb to a rightward-slanting crack and use it to gain the belay ledge.
2 35m. 5a. Climb the wall about 3 metres left of the right-hand end of the ledge, trending rightwards, and climb a thin crack to the top.

Rock Pilgrim   50 metres   Hard Very Severe   (29.4.84)
Start just right of the previous two routes.
1 15m. 4c. Climb the wall and thin crack to the belay ledge.
2 35m. Climb the groove on the right to a small overhang and follow the crack above.

Coliseum Buttress

Chair Ladder's eastern equivalent of Zawn Rinny, with three powerful lines.

Descend as for Coliseum Wall and then continue down the rake. From the boulder-filled zawn that leads into the gaping mouth of Tol-pedn-Penwith Cavern, cross over a small rib of decaying rock below the black right-hand headwall to reach a steep slab to the right of a deep cave.

★★Super Vision   52 metres   E3   (12.5.84)
A challenging piece of rock architecture.
1 34m. 5c. Climb the slab to a flake on the left. Move over the roof onto another slab (peg); then move left into steep cracks and grooves and follow these to a steep crack, which is climbed to a belay ledge.
2 18m. 5b. Climb the rake on the right to the edge of a loose chimney. Follow the buttress left of the chimney.

The next two climbs were graded before their bolt was removed.

Fury of Atlanta (54 metres E4 6a † 2.6.84) started below the slab to the right. Loose. Climb the slab to a ledge and a slab above to another ledge. Bolt belay no longer in place. Descend to the left and traverse below the overlaps (two pegs). Cross the roof via a V-groove and belay on a ledge on the left as for *Super Vision*. Climb rightwards onto the slab, move up, and finish up the headwall (peg).

Master of Disaster (50 metres E4 5b † 9.6.84) followed *Fury of Atlanta* pitch 1. Take the depression on the right and the steep slab (peg) before moving left and climbing another slab (peg). Finish up the headwall (peg).

Polostoc Point (Granite)   OS Ref 367 216

Outlook: South.
Just tidal but affected by swell and rough sea.
Coastguard Identity: Polostoc Zawn.

The point is the seaward face of Polostoc Zawn, the dark cleft of decomposing rock which lies midway between the holed cavern of Tol-pedn-Penwith and Porthgwarra Buttress. The rock is gritty and loose in places, but the outlook is delightful.

Approach from Porthgwarra Cove by following the coast path from where it runs south above the edge of the cove. The path starts from the roadside just down to the left of the car-park. Follow the path for 400 metres keeping left where it branches. Continue along the path as it leads on towards an isolated buttress of golden granite on the slope ahead. The gruesome black wall of Polostoc Zawn is clearly visible down left. Veer down towards the zawn and go over the right edge (facing out) of the headland to open ledges above the sea. The climbs are reached by scrambling easily down to the left to tidal ledges.

The first climb is on the left-hand section (facing in) of the face, which juts out from the rest of the cliff.

Wee Jammer   18 metres   Very Severe 5a   (13.5.92)
Start below a pock-marked wall, which is climbed to a big ledge. A less sporting start can be made up the corner round to the right of the pock-marked wall. Step into the ragged crack above the corner and climb it to easier ground.

The cliff falls back to the right into a slightly chossy corner, which is flanked on the right by an impressive wall with a central slabby section.

SOUTH COAST
CHAIR LADDER TO LAMORNA

0   MILE   1

North

St Buryan

B 3283

B 3315 to Sennen and Land's End

Polgigga

B 3315

Treverv (CAMPING

Porthcurno

Treen

Penberth

PARKING (LIMITED)

CAR PARK

St Levan

CAR PARK

Minack Theatre

Porthgwarra

CAR PARK

PO

PEN

CRIBBA HEAD

LOGAN ROCK (Treryn D

PEDNVOUNDER

LITTLE ZAWN

PORTHCURNO

PEDN-MÊN-AN-MERE

LEVAN'S WALL

VESSACKS

HELLA POINT

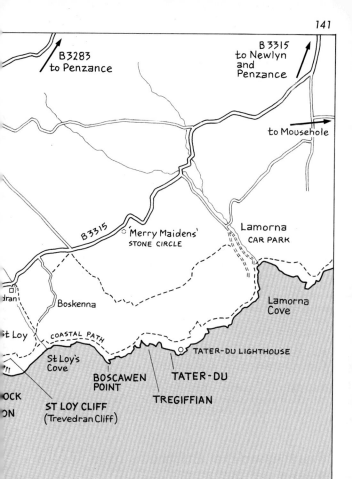

B3283
to Penzance

B3315
to Newlyn
and
Penzance

to Mousehole

B3315

'Merry Maidens'
STONE CIRCLE

Lamorna
CAR PARK

dran

Boskenna

Lamorna
Cove

St Loy

COASTAL PATH

St Loy's
Cove

BOSCAWEN
POINT

TATER-DU LIGHTHOUSE

TATER-DU

OCK
ON

ST LOY CLIFF
(Trevedran Cliff)

TREGIFFIAN

Polo   20 metres   Very Difficult   (13.5.92)
Climb the corner-crack and flanking pillar of rippled rock. Loose near the top.

Stock   20 metres   Severe 4a   (13.5.92)
Start just right of *Polo*. Climb onto a triangular ledge and continue up
dark-coloured rock, keeping right of a block with a serrated edge and
some loose flakes at its top. Finish up the gritty crack in the headwall.

The Amazing Thing   10 metres   E4 6a   (23.12.94)
The obvious central arête with a thin crack up its lower section.

Remember Eileen   27 metres   Severe 4a   (13.5.92)
A nice line. Start at a ledge below a short crack on the right of the steep
brown-stained wall that lies below the central slab. Climb the short crack
to a ledge (optional belay). Step up and round left onto the central slab.
Climb the edge of the slab to the short headwall. Step up and follow the
leftward-slanting break to the highest point of the wall.

The Simmo Way   18 metres   Hard Very Severe 4c †   (23.12.94)
Climb broken ground and make steep moves onto the slab. Climb the
middle of the central slab to a horizontal break. Continue up slabs above
and take a leftward-slanting crack to the top.

Misguided Pixies   12 metres   E3 5c †   (23.12.94)
Start at a pillar to the right of the slabby section. Climb the pillar, past an
overhang at 5 metres, to the slabs above.

Polo Crack   12 metres   Severe 4a †   (22.4.2000)
Climb the obvious corner-crack just right of *Misguided Pixies*.

Polo Solo   12 metres   Hard Very Severe 5b †   (22.4.2000)
Start 5 metres to the right of the corner-crack. Make hard moves up a thin
crack on the right-hand side of the wall to finish up the right arête.

Porthgwarra Buttress and Hella Point (Granite)

OS Ref 371 215

Outlook: South on Porthgwarra Buttress and the seaward face of Hella
Point; north-west on Hella Wall.
Tidal on left section of Porthgwarra Buttress, although all climbs here are
affected by rough sea and swell, as is Helluva Slab. The Hella Wall climbs are well
above the sea, although the entry pitch can be affected by rough sea and swell.
Coastguard Identity: Hella Point/Porthgwarra.

A delightful area with climbing of quality in the lower grades and some impressive harder routes, but a lack of routes in the middle grades.

Approach from Porthgwarra Cove by following the coast path for 400 metres from where it runs south above the edge of the cove. The path starts from the roadside just down to the left of the car-park. Follow the path, keeping left where it branches. The path leads to an area of rocky towers and wide breaks.

On the left (facing out) is the handsome, castle-like mass of Hella Point. On its west side, the dark wrinkled Hella Wall drops steeply into a narrow zawn. This zawn is flanked on its west by Panda Buttress, a small ridge that runs to seaward. To the west of the ridge is a wide broken depression. West of this depression is the striking Porthgwarra Buttress with its splendid piled towers of rounded blocks and fluted chimneys. West again is the impressive, solitary Galactic Boulder and finally Yawn Zawn.

Yawn Zawn

Descent is by climbing down rock on the right side of the zawn. Low tide and calm seas needed for the seaward routes. The climbs are on the well-featured, overhanging left face of the zawn.

Tiger   15 metres   E5 6a †   (9.97)
The vertical crackline and off-width crack above. Bold, unless very large cams are used.

Yosemite Sam   15 metres   E1 5b †   (9.97)
The striking crack/groove and off-width crack, finishing up right.

Dream, Cream, and Scream!   15 metres   E5 6b †   (9.97)
The overhanging arête. A pocketed crack leads to increasingly steep and hard climbing. A painful black finger-pocket between the horizontal breaks is the key to success. Finish up easier ground.

Siesta   15 metres   Hard Very Severe 5a †   (9.97)
The right-to-left slanting crack, with perfect, wave-washed rock.

The Enchanted Lights of Summer 15 metres Very Difficult † (8.97)
Takes the right-hand groove and the wide crack-system above.

Between Yawn Zawn and The Galactic Boulder, just above sea-level, is a short steep arête.

Prayer for the Raven   7 metres   E7 6c   (1990s)
Climb the rounded arête into the obvious finishing groove.

The Galactic Boulder

Asteroid Storm   8 metres   E4 5c   (9.97)
Start at the seaward side of the boulder's sharp left arête. Climb the arête and the shallow scoop/groove. Unprotectable, the possible fall being twice the length of the route, down a deep chimney. Not recommended.

Death Pulse   8 metres   E6 6b   (9.97)
The centre of the face just right of *Asteroid Storm*. Bold, technical climbing with a nasty landing.

Galactic Cruise   8 metres   E4 6a   (9.97)
The best of the three routes on the boulder starts on the right-hand side of its seaward face. Climb the breaks and finish up the rounded arête. Bold higher up.

Porthgwarra Buttress

Descent is via a grubby water-course that leads down the wide broken depression and through an entertaining maze of huge boulders. At the base of the boulders, traverse leftwards (facing in) along narrow ledges until opposite a big recess with a sloping floor. The recess is flanked on either side by chimney cracks. Left of the recess is a broken face flanked on its left by a prominent rounded arête with massive piled blocks and a large distinctive summit block. The following routes start at sea-level at the base of the broken face.

Joshua Tree   27 metres   E2 5c   (1985)
Take the short but striking crackline in the poised boulder at the top of the prominent arête. From the left, climb slabs to the eroded neck of the perched boulder, move right, and climb the crack to the top.

Porthcrawl   40 metres   Very Difficult   (10.4.71)
Start at the lowest point of the scooped starting-ledge, below the arête.
1 12m. Climb a shallow crack between a block on the left and the rounded arête and then continue up a corner to a belay on the right.
2 16m. Follow the chimney above to a cave belay.
3 12m. Traverse left out of the cave and down to a short crack. Climb the crack and then squirm along a diagonal break to the right until an airy finish is possible up a short wall.

★Dowser's Route/Porthgwarra Face   33 metres   Very Difficult   (7.8.38)
A charming route that seems to have lived a double life for years. Start at low tide on a scooped ledge to the right of the base of the prominent arête, and at the foot of a bubbly crack that runs up the face.
1 16m. Follow the crack to a ledge.
2 11m. Continue up the crack on the left to a ledge. The crack in the wall on the right of this pitch is a much harder (4a) alternative, with poor protection.
3 6m. Finish up a short groove on the left.

Variation
3a 12m. (25.5.56). Traverse left through a needle's eye into a cave behind the block. Climb up and squeeze through a skylight.

Jordanaire 36 metres Difficult (19.9.82)
Start 4 metres right of *Dowser's Route/Porthgwarra Face*, at the base of the arête.
1 20m. Climb a series of grooves to a belay by a large jammed block.
2 16m. Move left round the arête and follow cracks to the top.

Porthgwarra Crack 35 metres Very Difficult (9.8.38)
This follows the narrow chimney crack running up the left corner of the big recess. Start below the corner. Climb a short wall (sometimes greasy) and then follow the crack to the final overhang, where the rock should be treated with care. Move up to the right and squeeze under a block to finish.

Shawangunk 36 metres Hard Severe (5.66)
This takes a line up the middle of the slab in the back of the recess.
1 12m. 4b. Go straight up the slab and over a small roof at 5 metres. Move left and then up to reach a line of ledges and a belay.
2 24m. Continue up a short crack, via a slab, to a ledge. Finish up the easier chimney on the right.
Variation
2a Very Severe 4c (30.6.82). From the ledges at the top of pitch 1, climb the corner and the one above. Move left slightly to a bottomless groove and take this, moving left again to a layback; finish up a V-chimney.

★Porthgwarra Chimney 37 metres Severe 4a (9.56)
A pleasant route taking the right-hand corner of the recess and the deep chimney above. Climb the right corner of the recess until below the rounded entrance to the upper chimney (belay possible). An awkward entry into the chimney leads more steadily to the top.

Kilroy Wasn't Here 37 metres Hard Severe (16.8.83)
Start in the corner right of *Porthgwarra Chimney*.
1 10m. Climb an easy break to a ledge on the right.
2 27m. 4b. Above are twin cracks. Climb them past a small overhang to reach a slab. Move up and right into the groove to the right of the tottering pinnacle. Finish up this with care.

Panda Buttress
This is the small ridge running to seaward between Porthgwarra Buttress and Hella Point. For routes on its west side, descend as for Porthgwarra Buttress.

Games Surfers Play 23 metres Severe 4a (19.9.82)
Start just below the blocks on the descent, next to a huge monolithic block.

Step across a deep crack and traverse beneath an overhang to a chimney (optional thread belay). Follow the chimney and continuation groove to the top.

Panda Chimneys   12 metres   Severe 4a   (1978)
The prominent chimney-system on the left side of the face.

Panda Wall   10 metres   Hard Very Severe 5a   (1981)
The slabby wall 8 metres right of *Panda Chimneys*.

Panda Crawl   10 metres   Severe   (1978)
Start in the corner right of *Panda Wall*. Take the diagonal flake-line out rightwards and follow the arête to the top.

Front Piece   10 metres   Difficult   (1979)
The buttress to the right of *Panda Crawl*.

The next routes are gained by scrambling down left from the inland neck of Panda Buttress over crumbling rakes to reach the ledges between Panda Buttress and the narrow zawn below Hella Wall.

Child of the Moon   15 metres   E3 6a   (29.10.85)
The thin crack on the seaward face of the buttress.

Panda   22 metres   Severe   (9.6.63)
Start on a sea-level ledge left of two short chimneys.
1 10m. Climb an open corner.
2 12m. 4a. Climb over blocks into a chimney on the right and follow this for a few metres. Swing left onto a flake and then finish directly up the fluted nose above by a difficult move using prominent black knobs. (The standard is reduced to Very Difficult if the final moves are avoided by continuing up the easy chimney.)

Hella Wall

Hella Point is gained by scrambling down to the east from the inland neck of Panda Buttress over crumbling rakes and then crossing a boulder bridge to climb a slab on the left. Continue through a maze of boulders to reach the top of a long chimney/groove that drops down the seaward face of the Point to the narrow channel between the face and the offlying rock island. Descend the chimney/groove with care until it is possible to move right (facing out) to a good ledge above the sea. Round the corner to the left (facing in) is Helluva Slab. Hella Wall forms the north-west side of Hella Point and is an impressive feature of dark solid rock seamed with cracklines.

To the left of Hella Wall is a deep overhung cleft with a jammed boulder at the top. The next route takes the rib to the left of the cleft and is reached by descending rightwards into the back of the zawn from the boulder bridge.

HELLA POINT

PANDA BUTTRESS

1. Panda Chimneys S
2. Panda (top pitch) S
3. Panda Wall HVS
4. Panda Crawl S

HELLA WALL

5. Ebony Crack E2
5A variation finish E3
6. Fluid Connections HVS
7. Sun Shadow HVS
8. Finger Stretcher E3
9. Helluva Slab S

Merde del Buffalino   27 metres   Very Severe   (1985)
1 17m. 4c. Climb the rib to the jammed boulder and step beneath it across the cleft into a short groove. Climb this to a stance.
2 10m. 4c. Climb the painful crack passing a huge spike.

All the routes on Hella Wall proper start with an entry via Helluva Slab.

★★**Ebony Crack**   47 metres   E2   (30.7.82)
An excellent, exposed top pitch. Start from the good ledge above the sea.
1 12m. 4b. Cross the base of the Slab and continue up the left arête to a traverse-line leading onto Hella Wall. Follow this to belay at the first wide crack.
2 15m. 5b. Move left to the end of the ledge and climb a crack in the arête to a sloping belay ledge.
3 20m. 5c. Climb the leftward-slanting crack on the left. Traverse left to gain another crack leading up right to a wider crack to finish.
Variation
3a 18m. E3 5c. Climb the slanting crack and then the crack directly above.

Fluid Connections   44 metres   Hard Very Severe   (30.7.82)
1 12m. 4b. *Ebony Crack* pitch 1.
2 15m. 5a. Climb the crack to the first horizontal break. Traverse left to the arête and climb it to the belay ledge of *Ebony Crack*.
3 17m. 4b. Climb straight up the crack above.

★**Sun Shadow**   36 metres   Hard Very Severe   (30.7.82)
1 12m. 4b. *Ebony Crack* pitch 1.
2 10m. 5a. Climb the crack to a large flake.
3 14m. 4c. Move left to climb a slanting groove to the top.

Finger Stretcher   32 metres   E3   (30.7.82)
1 20m. 6a. Follow *Ebony Crack* to a slanting crack going up to the left. Climb the crack to the large ledge.
2 12m. 5a. Climb the crack on the left of the steep wall.

★**Helluva Slab**   42 metres   Severe   (25.5.56)
A delightful climb in fine surroundings. Start from the good ledge just above the sea.
1 17m. 4a. Step onto the slab and climb its centre or its left edge. Near the top of the slab, move right and then move delicately onto a fine ledge. (The right-hand corner of the slab is much easier but misses out the best climbing.)
2 15m. Continue up the grooved chimney on the right and then go over large boulders to a big ledge.
3 10m. 4b. Climb the short wall above on small holds and finish via a chimney/cleft, which leads to a trough. Escape by scrambling down left and traversing back round to the boulder-bridge.

Sammy's Slab   37metres   Severe   (1.11.87)
Start from a ledge just up and right of the start of *Helluva Slab*.
1 27m. 4a. Climb the steep slab to a large ledge to the left of a black
knob. Continue over juggy rock then a smooth slab. Make a thin move
around an overhang to a ledge and finish up the steep slab to a big ledge.
2 10m. 4b. *Helluva Slab* pitch 3.

The next route is approached by descending the boulder slope on the east of
the boulder bridge to a large, suspended, flat-topped boulder.

Son of Satan   12 metres   E8 6c   (8.97)
This sequency climb is very committing from the start. It is very strenuous to
place the first protection, and the climb is run out in the upper reaches.
Step off the boulder, climb the short overhanging wall to the small roof,
and arrange protection. Pull through the roof and make long reaches on
small edges to gain a pocket. Move past the pocket and reach back down
to place a vital *Friend 1*. Climb the wall above, moving right to the vein,
and take the wall on the left to the top.

Vessacks West (Granite)   OS Ref 377 217

Outlook: South-west.
Tidal. Accessible for three hours either side of low tide or for longer if
approached by abseil, but can be affected by swell.
Coastguard Identity: Vessacks.

A secluded little cliff with excellent rock and some fine climbs on the
seaward-facing Rockpool Buttress.

Approach from the car-park at Porthgwarra. Follow the coast path east for
about a kilometre until it turns south-east and heads out to the promontory
of Vessacks itself. At the footpath signpost, follow the right fork for 100
metres and turn seaward through a gap in the gorse next to a balanced
boulder. Follow the faint path leftwards down grass slopes to the top of the
cliff. Keep heading left (facing out) until it is possible to scramble down to
sea-level and cut back right beneath Rockpool Buttress.

The most obvious feature is the big heart-shaped back wall streaked with
black stains, but unfortunately the quality of the rock does not match its
appearance. To the left is an undercut buttress and to the right the seawashed
Rockpool Buttress, split centrally by a dark corner.

★Elizabeth   20 metres   Hard Very Severe 5a   (15.9.96)
An elegant line up the stepped overhangs on the left side of the undercut
buttress. Start at a faint vertical crack in the seaward face and climb this
delicately to a niche. Pull strenuously through the overhangs to gain
another niche and an undercling, where it is possible to rest. Pull out right
onto the wall and climb to good holds right of the arête. Step up and
round to the left and gain the slab, which is followed more easily to a
belay using blocks on the ridge.

★★Madonna of the Waves   20 metres   E2 5c   (1.9.96)
The steep golden wall on the left-hand side of Rockpool Buttress. The
classic of the buttress; sustained and strenuous but well protected. Start
beneath the centre of the wall at a thin rightward-slanting crack, which is
climbed to the horizontal break. Move left to a large incut hold and climb
up and left to reach the slanting crack system. Climb strenuously straight
up the wall on miraculous holds to a flared vertical crack. Dynamic moves
to pass this (crux) lead to jugs above. Finish up the crack and mini-corner
and scramble up to belay using blocks on the ridge.

The Shade of Dora Maar   18 metres   Very Severe 4c   (18.8.96)
The central black corner is more enjoyable and better protected than
appearances might suggest. Start from the top of a large round boulder
and climb to a ledge below the corner proper. Climb the corner using
rounded holds on the right wall until after 12 metres the corner leans back
and leads more easily to the top. Belay to blocks on the ledges above.

Majas   18 metres   Very Severe 4c †   (15.9.96)
The crack and arête right of the corner. Good holds and better rock than
appearances might suggest, but still spooky. Cams useful. Start beneath
the crack and climb to a ledge at 3 metres. Delicate climbing leads to the
crack; follow this until forced out right. Climb the wall to an awkward but
essential thread runner on the arête and continue with care straight up left
of the arête to the top. Belay to blocks on the ledges above.

★Saskia   18 metres   Hard Very Severe 5a   (18.8.96)
The smaller bottomless corner right of *Majas*. Sustained and with an
entertaining start due to the rock-pool beneath the corner. Start 5 metres
right of the corner by stepping across the narrow pool onto smooth rock at
the foot of the buttress. Traverse left to underclings and pull round into the
overhung base of the corner. Climb strenuously into the corner proper and
follow it and the steep crack above to the awkward final moves. Belay to
blocks on the ledges above.

Vessacks (Granite)

OS Ref 378 217

Outlook: South-west.
Tidal on Wassocks Wall, which is accessible for about two hours either side of low tide but can be affected by swell. **Non-tidal** on Vessacks Point, although this area can be affected by swell.
Coastguard Identity: Vessacks.

A number of short but worthwhile climbs are situated in a small zawn on the eastern side of the headland which lies to the west of Porth Chapel Beach below St Levan Church. There are three other climbs on the western side of the headland.

Approach from the public car-park by St Levan Church (OS Ref 381 223), which is a short distance along the road from the entrance to the Minack Theatre. Turn right out of the car-park then immediately left to follow the footpath to Porth Chapel Beach. At the junction with the coast path, and just before St Levan's Well, go west up some granite steps and along the coast path for about 300 metres to where the rocky ridge of the headland comes into view down to the left. This point can also be reached by diverting along a right fork on the early part of the approach path soon after crossing the small stream below the church. This fork leads in 300 metres to the main coast path. Turn back east for 50 metres to reach the headland. A path leads down from the coast path towards the headland.

Wassocks Wall

Descent: Wassocks Wall lies in the narrow clean-cut zawn to the east of the headland. Follow the headland to seaward to where it becomes a rocky crest. Go left down ledges and grassy slopes to reach the rocky back of the zawn.

The climbs are all on the steep eastern wall, which rises from the sand. In some years the zawn bed may be scoured clean of sand and may be under water even at low tide, thus making for interesting traverses to reach seaward pitches. At the left edge of the wall there is a narrow ledge which leads to a layback crack. The ledge can be reached at high tide in calm conditions and with care.

Split Up   15 metres   E1 5b   (30.7.91)
Start from the narrow ledge. Climb the layback crack for 2 metres and then move right to a prominent flake. Traverse rightwards along the flake and climb the widest of the cracks above.

Uncle Peter Goes to the Seaside   15 metres   E3 6a   (1.8.91)
Start from the narrow ledge. Use the layback crack to step down and right onto the black wall. Traverse to an overlap; then move up and right with difficulty to an excellent jug. Finish up the thin cracks above.

Crocodile Tears   15 metres   E1 5c   (30.7.91)
Start at the base of the red vein. Climb direct for 5 metres to a ledge on
the left and continue up the steep crack to finish.

Ledge Climb   15 metres   Hard Very Severe 5a   (1.8.91)
Start 5 metres right of the red vein and make a hard move to gain an
edge leading to the right-hand side of the narrow ledge. Climb to and
follow the vein. Protection is difficult to find.

Daddy's Crack   14 metres   Hard Very Severe 5a   (29.7.91)
Climb the deep crack 10 metres right of the red vein. Good jamming.

Triple Jump   14 metres   Hard Very Severe 5b   (2.8.91)
Start below the crack opposite the green humpbacked boulder. Hard
jamming leads to a small niche and a bridging finish.

Acapulco Corner   12 metres   Very Difficult   (1.8.91)
Start at dead low tide at a narrow ledge. The ledge leads to a prominent
corner at the seaward end of the cliff. Climb the corner.

Vessacks Point

Descent: follow the headland to seaward, continue along the rocky crest,
and descend the right side of a slab which faces the offlying rock pinnacle.
This slab is *Vessacks Original*. From the base of the slab, move round right
(facing out) to sea-level ledges which lead back along the base of the cliff.
The ledges can also be reached by scrambling down to the right (facing out)
from the crest of the headland. The routes are short and steep, but give
pleasant climbing.

West Side Story   27 metres   Very Difficult   (3.69)
Start about 40 metres left of the highest point of the wall. Climb the steep
wall direct.

Vessactomy   18 metres   Severe 4a   (6.7.91)
A direct line from the sea-level ledges to the highest part of the ridge via
bulges and ledges.

Phallus   15 metres   Severe   (6.7.91)
Climb the corner at the seaward end of the ledges, before making
awkward moves over a rudely projecting appendage.

Vessacks Original   27 metres   Difficult   (8.35)
A classic example of quietly anonymous early climbing. Follow a direct line
up the right-hand side (facing in) of the descent slab on the seaward
(south) face of the headland.

Pedn-mên-an-mere (Granite)   OS Ref 385 217

This is the complex area of cliff lying just over a kilometre south-west of Porthcurno. Development throughout the 80s transformed this attractive headland into a popular venue. Levan's Wall in particular has some excellent short routes in the middle to higher grades, with easier routes and some hard problem pitches centred on Carracks Cliff. With Porth Chapel's fine beach to the west and culture to the east in the form of the Minack Theatre, what more could the discerning climber ask for?

Levan's Wall
Outlook: South-west.
Tidal on the Lower Tier and on the seaward end of the Upper Tier. Tidal areas are accessible for three hours either side of low water when calm. All routes are wave-washed in heavy seas.
Coastguard Identity: Pedn-mên-an-mere.

Approach from the public car-park by St Levan Church (OS Ref 381 223), which is a short distance along the road from the entrance to the Minack Theatre. Turn left outside the car-park and walk back up the road for a few hundred metres to the first houses. Take the signposted footpath that leads to the right between the houses and towards the coast path. From the junction with the coast path, turn right and walk a few metres to the large boulders overlooking the sea just left of where the coast path dips steeply to the west. From the large boulders, go left down a slight path to a small through-cave formed by a leaning slab. Levan's Wall lies directly below this.

From the through-cave, follow a grassy trough that drops down to the east across the face of the broken upper cliff. Half-way down the trough, go right and head down towards the sea to reach the rim of a distinctive granite wall with a broad sloping ramp at its base. This is Levan's Wall.

Descent can be made three hours either side of low water by going left (facing out) down the rim of the wall to reach its lowest part. Down-climb a few metres of wet greasy rock to a boulder channel that leads back left (facing in) to the broad ramp below the main wall. An alternative access to the ramp at all states of the tide can be made by going right (facing out) up the rim of the wall until above a right-angled corner. Step across the loose top of the corner **with great care**, and work down left until an airy step leads down onto the broad ramp.

Lower Tier
The lower tier is gained from the base of the broad ramp. Once upon a time there were some nice climbs here, centred on a handsome overhang. But

the ocean spoke and all fell down. The overhang is now the underhang, leaving at least one route with the distinction of starting from where it once finished.

Captain Chaos   15 metres   E4 5c †   (17.8.95)
Scramble leftwards over sea-level boulders to an overhang with a slab above it. Climb up to the overhang, cross it right of centre, and finish up the slab. No protection.

The Minstrel   18 metres   Difficult   (27.8.84)
Start at the left end of the tier at a recess flanked on the left by a hanging nose of decaying rock. Climb the black slab on the right-hand side of the recess to a ledge. Step left and climb the white slab.

Panos   12 metres   Hard Severe 4b   (18.3.84)
Climb a short black-sided V-groove just left of the central wall to a ledge. Continue up the wall on the left.

A route goes up the right edge of the central wall onto a ledge on the right and then up a ramp: **Crawfish** (11 metres Very Severe 5a 3.3.84/1980s).

Buttons   12 metres   Severe 4a   (18.3.84)
The narrow chimney cracks right of the remains of *Crawfish*.

Upper Tier
This is the fine slice of rock rising from the broad ramp. A central feature is the rightward-slanting, black and red vein of *Bermuda Wall*.

The Vein Strain   12 metres   E6 6b †   (1990)
Climb the obvious quartz vein on the overhanging left wall of the right-angled corner. Poorly protected.

Phenocryst   12 metres   Hard Very Severe 5a   (1981)
The cracks and chimney in the right-angled corner at the top of the broad ramp. Cheese-grater granite.

Crack-a-Goo-Goo   18 metres   E2 5b   (1.1.85)
The steep crack just right of the corner is climbed to finish left of a hanging overlap. Apple-crumble rock in the upper half.

Heaven's Snake   20 metres   E3 6a   (1.1.85)
The thin crack just right of the previous route, passing a peg half-way. Grittiness.

Jamaica   20 metres   E3 6a   (1.1.85)
The crack right of the previous route via five staggered overlaps. Also gritty.

Bermuda Wall 20 metres E3 5c (4.83)
A plum line. After hard starting-moves, follow the red and black vein that runs diagonally rightwards across the face.
Direct Finish 6a. Climb direct from the upper undercling on the vein.

Frogs in a Frenzy 20 metres E8 6c † (1992)
A desperately thin and serious route taking an almost imaginary line of weakness 6 metres right of Bermuda Wall to the horizontal break, reached by a leap. Originally led with micros at E7, the runners left *in situ* have since ripped out with possible damage to the placements. Abseil inspection advised.

Triangle 30 metres E3 5c † (1.3.85)
A right-to-left tour of the wall. Climb the crackline of *Devil's Meridian* to the first break at 12 metres. Traverse left for 2 metres and climb a groove and crack to the next break. Traverse left again, crossing *Bermuda Wall*; then move up to an undercling that leads left to a finish up *Jamaica*.

Devil's Meridian 18 metres E2 5c (18.3.84)
Fine climbing up the left-hand of two striking cracklines at the bottom of the broad ramp.

Midnight Express 18 metres E1 5b (3.3.84)
Climb the tasty right-hand crackline.

The climbs to the right of here are accessible for three hours either side of low water.

Geriatric 12 metres Severe 4a (20.8.77)
Climb the pleasant red and black slab above the tidal pool.

Layaway 12 metres Severe 4a (c.1960)
Start as for the last route, but take the rightward-slanting cracks.

Fingerflinger 14 metres E3 5c (8.7.84)
Climb the bottomless crack 6 metres along the boulder channel.

Black Adder 14 metres E5 6a (1989)
Climb the distinctive steep black vein. Serious and very strenuous.

Falls the Shadow 14 metres E3 6a (1989)
Climb the crooked crackline right of *Black Adder*.

Zip 15 metres Very Severe 4c (1981)
Where the boulder channel narrows between the wall and a massive boulder there is a thin crack in a slabby groove. Make a tough move up the crack to a ledge and finish direct.

★Seamstress   14 metres   E2 6a   (8.7.84)
Climb the flaky and knobbly wall 3 metres right of *Zip*.

Redfish   10 metres   Hard Very Severe 5a   (27.8.84)
[Photo p.272d.] The distinctive short corner at the right-hand end of the boulder channel is climbed direct after a hard start.

There are numerous short problem pitches on the maze of walls above and to the right of Levan's Wall. About 25 metres right and above the short descent to the boulder channel of Levan's Wall is a clean white wall about 6 metres high, seamed with cracks. A leftward-rising ramp lies at the foot of the wall. The more obvious cracklines give 5a moves, while the centre of the wall has been climbed at 6a to 6c.

Carracks Cliff
Outlook: South.
Tidal on the Lower Tier. Accessible for three hours either side of low water but affected by swell and rough sea. The upper cliff is clear of tide and sea except in storm conditions.
Coastguard Identity: Pedn-mên-an-mere.

This is the complex, broken area of cliff just east of Levan's Wall. It drops directly from the summit of Pedn-mên-an-mere headland. Just offshore lie two isolated rocks called The Carracks. There are a number of pleasant short routes here, although in places the rock is gritty and mildly loose.

Approach as for Levan's Wall (see page 153) but, at the junction with the coast path, cross directly onto the path that leads out to the crown of the headland of Pedn-mên-an-mere, past a National Trust sign and the iron remnants of a radio mast.

An easy **descent** to the base of the cliff can be made by going down right (facing out) via grassy gullies and ledges.

The foot of Carracks Cliff can also be reached from the through-cave above Levan's Wall by continuing down across the broken cliff face to the east or by traversing east from the easy descent to Levan's Wall.

At the foot of the cliff is a sloping sea-stained platform that runs down to the distinctive Marconi Slab. This is a dark-brown sheet of rock about 20 metres high set at a right-angle to the main cliff. The main cliff rises through a series of big ledges and short walls. On its left flank is a distinctive black slab with a smaller black slab above and another below. The wall right of the black slab is seamed with fluted cracks. There are three tiers on the main cliff, Chicken-Head Wall, Upper Tier, and Lower Tier. Routes are described top down, starting with Chicken-Head Wall.

Chicken-Head Wall

Just below the top of the headland and directly above the distinctive black slab is a short continuous wall characterised by a number of large and small chicken-heads of black schorl. The wall runs rightwards to a broad arête and then bends further right behind a pinnacle of rock and some jammed boulders. It is the first feature reached if approach is made from the top of Pedn-mên-an-mere.

Slab Route   10 metres   Difficult   (29.2.88)
Climb the slab direct.

Bustin' Out   14 metres   Hard Very Severe 5b   (27.1.88)
Climb the wide groove on the right.

Chicken Run   14 metres   E5 6b   (27.1.88)
Start 3 metres right of *Bustin' Out*. Climb the slanting crack up to a roof and a chicken-head, before moving left and up past three more chicken-heads.

The Planter   14 metres   Hard Very Severe   (27.1.88)
From the first chicken-head on *Chicken Run*, follow the slanting fault running up leftwards.

Muscle Buster   14 metres   E4 6c †   (27.1.88)
Start just left of the broad arête at a steep wall. Climb the wall using underclings to a large chicken-head. Finish up the groove on the right.

Smile of a Clown   12 metres   E5 7a †   (27.1.88)
From just right of the broad arête at some boulders, climb a faint crack to a horizontal break (peg). Climb left to some small chicken-heads at the base of a blind crack (peg, removed). Move up to a second chicken-head then left onto the arête to finish.

The Other One   12 metres   E3 6a   (27.1.88)
From the peg at the break on the previous route, step right to a small niche and finish up the knobbly crack above.

False Illusions   12 metres   E2 5c   (27.1.88)
In the centre of the wall opposite the boulders is an obvious black-sided crack. Follow this to the top.

Video Breaks   12 metres   E2 5c   (27.1.88)
From just right of the previous pitch, climb a thin crack and a bulge (peg, removed). Finish direct.

Tea for Two   12 metres   Severe 4b   (27.1.88)
At the right edge of the wall a groove runs up the face. Climb the groove to a ledge. From here, climb a bulge, step left, and finish direct.

The short slabby wall across the grassy bay on the right is also dotted with large chicken-heads. Various easier pitches are possible here.

Upper Tier

The first pitches lie just left of the top of the distinctive black slab. A grassy ramp runs down leftwards from the top of the slab. A short overhanging V-groove rises from the base of the ramp. The upper half of the arête to the left of the V-groove is climbed by moving up a groove on its left and then stepping right on tiny holds. This gives a 10-metre pitch (E4 6a). The V-groove gives a similar length pitch at Very Severe 5a.

Sea Pink Slab   24 metres   Very Difficult   (30.4.67)
A pleasantly airy route. Directly below the main black slab is a smaller one. Start at the base of the smaller slab.
1 18m. Climb a leaning corner and then the right edge of the black slab to a ledge. The slab can also be climbed straight up the middle.
2 6m. Climb the smaller slab above, moving right and up to finish.

The seaward face to the right of the black slabs is seamed with cracks and tormented rock. The following climbs start from a long flat terrace above the 15-metre lower wall that rises from the sea-stained ramp running down to Marconi Slab.

Macbate   24 metres   E2 5b   (30.4.67)
Climb the rough cracks at the far left end of the terrace to a smaller ledge below the fluted upper wall. Climb an overhanging crack to gain the fluted cracks and follow these, trending left and then back right and up.

Jack   20 metres   E1 5b   (16.4.87)
Start by the boulder at the left end of the terrace. Climb twin cracks to a ledge and follow the ripping flake crack above.

The following routes all have some shaky rock in their upper sections.

Nova   24 metres   Hard Very Severe 5b   (17.12.87)
Where the terrace widens, a wide broken crack runs up to the steeper upper face. Climb the thin crack a few metres to the right. Gain the upper wall and move left round the arête to finish up the overhanging arête above.

Pocket Burn   24 metres   E3 6a †   (17.12.87)
Start just right of *Nova* and below an obvious small black pocket at 6 metres. Climb past the pocket and onto the bulging wall above. Move up to knobbly overhangs, which are climbed to finish direct.
Variation 6b (12.88). Climb the wall between *Pocket Burn* and the bulging red vein, and finish up *Pocket Burn*.

Smoked Salmon   20 metres   E1 5b   (1986)
Tough for starters, but tasty. From the centre of the terrace, climb the
bulging red vein to the break. Climb to the right of the continuation vein,
moving right and up to a niche. Finish up to the left.

Lost for Words   24 metres   E2 5c †   (17.12.87)
At the right end of the terrace is another short break running up to the steep
upper face. (The break is taken by pitch 2 of *Gentleman's Relish*.) Climb the
short wall just right of the break to a V-shaped crack. Climb steeply to a
slanting crack and continue up a steep slab or a crack on the right.

Lower Tier
The following routes start from the broad sea-stained ramp running down to
Marconi Slab.

Megaphone Chimney   44 metres   Severe   (22.8.76)
Start by a lighter-coloured patch of rock directly below the starting-terrace
of the Upper Tier.
1 20m. Climb direct from the lighter-coloured rock and then move left to
a long ledge. Make a harder move up a red vein to the starting-terrace
below the Upper Tier.
2 24m. 4a. A few metres to the left of the steep continuation of the red
vein (*Smoked Salmon*) is a knobbly black vein with a wider crack to its left.
Climb the black vein or the wider crack to a ledge. Move right to the foot
of the V-chimney, which is climbed by its right wall past a small niche.
Finish by an airy move below and to the left of the lichenous overhang.

A harder variation climbs the roof left of the V-chimney to finish up the
overhanging prow above. This is **Megaphoney** (Hard Very Severe 5a 1989).

Gentleman's Relish   46 metres   Severe   (27.8.70)
Start below the more continuous wall to the right of the previous route and
directly below a prominent brown disc that resembles the old-style anchovy
paste after which the route was named. Others would argue that the name
fits perfectly the style of the first ascensionists.
1 23m. Climb the steep wall to a ledge. Continue to the left of the brown disc,
step over a chimney, and continue up a small corner to a stance and flake belay.
2 23m. 4a. Step down into a broad groove and climb up into a scoop,
before following steep fluted grooves above to the base of a perched
block. Move left onto the wall and follow the left edge of a sloping groove
to finish below a large boulder.

Falling Apart at the Seams   20 metres   Hard Severe   4b   (29.10.85)
This route has lived up to its name since its first ascent, although it is still
available and now steadier. Start just left of the corner between Marconi
Slab and the main face. Climb the sharp flakes and ledges of
biscuit-coloured rock and then trend rightwards up the steep finishing wall.

Marconi Crack   12 metres   Difficult   (31.8.69)
The corner between Marconi Slab and the main face.

Permanendo   15 metres   Hard Severe   4a   (23.8.73)
The thin crack up the centre of Marconi Slab.

Spot the Difference   15 metres   Hard Severe   4a †   (15.11.98)
The right-hand side of Marconi Slab.

Tina Turner   15 metres   Very Severe   5a   (29.10.85)
Black and bold. Climb the overhang and easier V-groove at the seaward
end of Marconi Slab.

Radio Zawn

East of Marconi Slab the cliff is split by a narrow dripping zawn. This is Radio
Zawn. There are some hard routes here, although dry conditions are
required. Abseil entry down the back wall is necessary. The boulder channel
in the floor of the zawn is rarely dry and can be wave-washed in all but flat
calm conditions.

The Floating Looser   13 metres   E1 5b †   (1990)
The back of the zawn narrows into a gruesome chimney, which is best
avoided.

A Drop in the Ocean   37 metres   E2 5b †   (1990)
This is centred on the crack right of the chimney. Start at low tide and in
calm conditions from ledges at the back of the zawn. The crack is climbed
to where an escape can be made onto the overhanging buttress in the
centre of the back wall. The lower part of the crack may be greasy.

Navigator to Heaven   40 metres   E4 6a †   (1990)
A line up the centre of the west-facing wall. Start from ledges at the back of
the zawn or from the base of the centre of the wall, tide and sea permitting.
Climb the wall direct to finish strenuously up the bulging upper wall.

On the stepped face beyond Radio Zawn are two routes. The face is best
reached from the same level as Chicken-Head Wall, where descent can be
made over ledges, with the stepped face on their left, until below some
biscuit-coloured rock.

Pig and Chips   20 metres   Hard Very Severe   5a   (1986)
Climb the biscuit-coloured rock past a crumbling flake on the left and
make a thin move right to a ledge. Climb the short crack above.

All Fools Flake Out   20 metres   Hard Very Severe   5b   (1986)
Further down the base of the stepped face, beyond an area of fluted rock,
a flake and crack are climbed direct.

Seal Slab (VS), Chair Ladder
Climbers: Sam Salmon and Barrie Simpson   Photo: Des Hannigan

South Face Direct (VS),
Chair Ladder
Climber: Steve Gibson
Photo: Rich Mayfield

Porthcurno Bay Area (Granite)

'The beach at Porthcurno has a number of short buttresses most of which are nail-marked by Commando traffic...' (V N Stevenson, 1966.)

Outlook: Mainly south.
Tidal at Green Bay and Pednvounder, with little time to spare during neap-tides.
Coastguard Identity: Porthcurno Bay.

The sweeping bay between Minack Point at Porthcurno and Logan Rock is fringed by one of the finest coastal landscapes in Britain. There is no large stretch of cliff but there are numerous broken buttresses and short walls of excellent granite. For years, climbing has been enjoyed throughout the area. Many hard problems were climbed, and several longer pitches established in the Pednvounder beach area, where J E Littlewood and L S Powell climbed at least seven routes in the 30s. Others have probably repeated these and have certainly climbed new ground over the years. Few lines have been named or recorded. However, recent activity has led to the reporting of a number of routes in the area and these are described. As always, full acknowledgement is due to those who may have gone before.

Porthcurno   OS Ref 386 223
Porthcurno's splendid beach outshines its climbing potential. There are a number of short problem pitches on the small buttresses on the eastern side of the beach.

Green Bay   OS Ref 388 223
This is the small bay lying just east of Porthcurno beyond the rocky ridge of Percella Point. It can be pleasantly sandy in some years, but expect a bare boulder-beach in others. Green Bay is gained from Porthcurno Beach by scrambling over the base of the Point or by walking round on sand at dead low water. The Bay can also be reached from Porthcurno car-park by following the coast path steeply eastwards to reach a painted wooden navigation mast beside an old war-time pill-box. Follow a path down to seaward from the pill-box to a point above the rocky western side of Green Bay. Descend with care to the beach. The next routes are on the eastern wall of the cove where it narrows and cuts into the land.

Missile Man   20 metres   E2 5c   (1983)
Climb an obvious deep chimney/crack for 10 metres to a chockstone, move left, and climb a steep crack in the wall. Gritty in places.

Deep Cruise   20 metres   E1 5b   (1983)
Climb the chimney/crack in its entirety: thrutchy.

A Green Thought in a Green Shade   15 metres   E2 6b †(1990s)
Just to the right of the chimney/crack is an arête. Climb the vein to the
right of it.

Whispering Sands   15 metres   E1 5b †   (1990s)
The striking off-width crack.

Little Cracker   15 metres   E2 5b †   (7.87)
On the seaward face of the east wall is an overhanging crack. Climb the
crack and finish up the overhanging off-width crack above.

Pednvounder – Upper West Buttress   OS Ref 393 224
A secluded little crag situated well above the sea.

Approach from the car-park at the village of Treen (OS Ref 395 230). Turn
left out of the car-park and follow the lane to where it turns sharply left past a
summer campsite and joins the coast path after 300 metres. Cross the coast
path and follow a path which winds down towards Pednvounder Beach.
Follow this path keeping to the right for some distance. After a path that
leads down left by a rock outcrop. Instead, continue rightwards; then veer
down left beneath ribs and buttresses. Continue along the path until the
descent becomes rocky. From this point, a small path leads up left into a
wide grassy gully with a broken-faced buttress at its head. The left side of the
buttress (facing in) has two distinctive grassy breaks. The right-hand break
runs up to a dark-brown, triangular-shaped headwall.

Route I   20 metres   Difficult   (9.88)
Climb the slab on the left of the left-hand grassy break and finish up
broken rock. This line can be used as a descent.

Septimus   25 metres   Very Difficult   (1.1.89)
Climb the clean grey rib between the grassy breaks to a ledge. Step right
across the break and climb the facing wall to finish on top of a blunt
pinnacle.

Horam's Horror   25 metres   Very Difficult   (9.88)
Start at a block at the base of the right-hand grassy break. Climb the
break towards the dark-brown headwall; then go up the slab on the left to
a ledge (on *Septimus*). Make an awkward step onto the slabby rib above
and continue to a large jammed block.

Burning Bridge   20 metres   Very Severe 5a   (6.11.88)
An interesting pitch with some stiff moves. Start at the block at the base of
the right-hand grassy break. Climb the break to below the dark-brown
headwall. Gain the smooth corner on the right and swing up onto the
headwall to make strenuous moves into a small niche. Climb the hollow
flake above the niche to finish direct. There are some loose blocks at the top.

Codicil   15 metres   Severe 4a   (9.10.88)
From the block at the foot of the right-hand break, climb the first grassy groove and step up onto the slab on the right. Move up right to the edge of the slab and continue up the overlapping slab above to a good ledge.

Green Fingers   20 metres   Severe 4a   (20.11.88)
A pleasant, direct route up the front face of the buttress. Start below a steep groove at the lowest point of the buttress. Climb the groove and step up left to a ledge. Continue to another ledge, move right, and finish direct.

Perfidy   20 metres   Very Difficult   (6.11.88)
Start as for *Green Fingers*. Climb the groove and move right beneath a bulge to reach a niche beneath an overhang. Continue up the short left-hand wall to break left onto the front of the buttress, and then finish direct.
Variation 10 metres Hard Severe 4b. From the niche, climb the overhang direct on good holds.

Pednvounder Beach Area   OS Ref 394 224
The beach is reached as for Pednvounder Upper West Buttress as far as the point where the descent to the beach becomes rocky. From this point, scramble easily down rocks to the sand. There are many potential problem pitches and longer climbs on the pinnacles, walls, and buttresses rising from the sand. Mid-beach, there is a narrow break in the cliff running back to a cave. This is Charlie's Chank. On its left is a steep, quartz-studded wall. Treen Buttress lies midway along the beach. At the right-hand end of the beach there is a cave, and then Shady Wall with its three cracklines, the left-hand one being more of a chimney.

Charlie's Chank
★Reach   10 metres   E1 5c   (1974)
Climb the obvious vertical crack at the seaward end of the left-hand wall. Hard to start but finishing on better holds.

★Stranger in a Strange Land   20 metres   E4 6a   (31.12.89)
A fine steep pitch on glassy granite. Start 7 metres right of *Reach* and gain a smooth bottomless finger-crack. Follow the crack to where it widens at 15 metres; first chance of protection. Continue up the crack, moving slightly to the right to finish on better holds.

Exile   30 metres   E2 5a   (31.12.89)
A dank route right at the back of the Chank. Climb the corner-slab to the base of the corner-crack. Follow the crack for 10 metres, break left to the base of a wide jamming crack, and climb it to the top.

Treen Buttress

Half-way along the beach is a high buttress set back from the beach and vegetated in its upper half. A deep trench runs off rightwards to end at a chimney.

★Central Highway   50 metres   Hard Very Severe   (3.1.84)
1 20m. 4c. Climb a flaky groove to a grassy ledge.
2 20m. 5a. Continue up a steep lichen-fringed crack to a ledge.
3 10m. 5b. Climb the overhanging chimney above.

Interceptor   50 metres   E2   (3.1.84)
Start 10 metres up the rightward-rising trench.
1 25m. 5b. Climb an overhanging groove to a ledge.
2 25m. 5c. Take the lichen-covered wall above.

Shady Wall

Sophie's Choice   20 metres   Hard Very Severe 5a   (28.7.89)
Climb the thin crackline to the right of the obvious chimney crack.

Family Meet   20 metres   Very Severe 4b   (24.7.89)
The central crackline, which is easier than it looks. The first half is the hardest.

Barbecue   20 metres   Hard Very Severe 5a   (28.7.89)
Follow the blunt rib right of the crackline of *Family Meet*.

Egyptian House Wall

Further along the bay, about half-way between Shady Wall and the headland of Logan Rock, is a black zawn with a large roof just beyond. **Approach** by descending from the cliff-top north of the zawn.

Too Sexy for Mike   10 metres   Very Severe 4c †   (30.8.92)
The obvious stepped groove below the large roof. Climb the groove to the roof and traverse right to finish up another groove.

Egyptian Roof   15 metres   A3 †   (1.9.92)
Climb the same groove to the roof and aid across it on a variety of pegs ranging from thin blades to angles.

Sticky Fingers   10 metres   E4 6b †   (1.9.92)
Climb the blunt arête just right of the stepped groove and finish up the top groove of *Too Sexy for Mike*.

To the right is a more definite arête, with a large boulder to its right in the mouth of a zawn. The next two routes take cracks just to the left of the arête.

Beaver Fever   10 metres   E2 6a †   (30.8.92)
Climb the left-hand crackline, finishing over the overlap.

Gay Capri   10 metres   E1 5b †   (7.8.92)
The right-hand crack, finishing to the right of the overhang.

Big Jugs   10 metres   E2 5b †   (1.9.92)
Start two metres right of the arête by a big boulder in the zawn. Climb the obvious crack with increasing difficulty, to finish on good holds.

Logan Rock (Treen Castle)
(Granite) OS Ref 397 220

Outlook: All points.
Tidal on starts of all routes on the seaward faces.
Coastguard Identity: Logan Rock. (There is an emergency telephone on the headland.)

Treen Castle (Treryn Dinas) is the magnificent rocky headland that makes up the eastern arm of Porthcurno Bay. It is a classic example of a cliff castle of the early Iron Age. Remains are vestigial apart from the massive earth ramparts on the neck of the headland close to the coast path. Logan Rock is the popular name given to the Headland, although the 'rock' itself or 'loggan stone' is simply the enormous boulder perched on top of the inner tower of the headland. Loggan stones are huge perched blocks, which can be rocked or 'logged' by a light push. Treen Castle's loggan rock was a famous Victorian tourist attraction, but fell victim to an early 'trundle' of mammoth proportions when the 65-ton rock was dislodged in 1824 by a group of sailors under Lieutenant Hugh Goldsmith, nephew of the poet Oliver Goldsmith. Faced with a public outcry, young Goldsmith undertook to replace the rock, and succeeded, with some impressive engineering and a cast of hundreds. The number of routes, boulder-problems and scrambling undertaken from this period to the present day is vast though generally unrecorded. We do know that Logan Rock was used extensively for commando training, and that J E Littlewood and L S Powell climbed twenty-two routes here in the thirties.

Approach from Treen car-park by turning left on leaving the car-park and sharp left within metres, to follow a path past a house and over a stone stile opposite the small Methodist chapel. Follow a signposted path alongside and through fields to the coast path. Treen Castle lies directly to seaward and is gained by a path that leads through a break in the earth ramparts.

Bar Castle Cove
Descend by turning right just before the ramparts of Treen Castle. There is a deep cleft worn into the cliff by the path leading to the cove, which can be an idyllic sun trap, with a sandy beach exposed at low tide. The climbing is on the landward side of the cove, where a number of routes have been recorded on the distinctive boulder and the wall behind it.

After passing through the earth ramparts a choice of paths meander toward the centre of Treen Castle and the 'Logan Rock'. Here the view opens out, revealing a plethora of short walls, chimneys, cracks, and arêtes, with the sea directly ahead.

The West Face
Two recorded routes made up of variations on a theme that has been played out for years lie on the West Face of the headland. They are approached from the col between the two main towers, where a descent can be made to a small rock platform just above the sea.

Time Out   25 metres   Very Severe 5a   (1983)
Drop down to sea-level and move round the arête on the left. Climb a slanting crack.

Deep Think   35 metres   Very Severe 4b   (1983)
Traverse left round the arête to cross the wall. Climb a corner over a jammed block. Descend into a gully until below another jammed block. Climb onto the block and then follow the chimney above to a crack on the left, which leads to the top. Belays can be taken at several points.

At the southern end of the West Face is a hanging slab. **Slap and Happy** (8 metres E1 5c † 8.96) climbs the right-hand side of the slab, while the direct line is taken by **Winter Fun** (8 metres E5 6b † 10.96).

It is not possible to continue scrambling round southwards from the West Face. Instead, from the col between the two towers, take a path on the right (as you descend) to a narrow cleft in the cliff. From here, a short down-climb leads to the top of *The Grassman*. An abseil leads to a tidal platform and two excellent routes.

Omicron   12 metres   E1 5b   (8.96)
Following the obvious crack rightwards and make a committing move left to a leftward-leading flake. Climb the flake past a hidden ledge to join cracks which lead strenuously to the top.

The Grassman   15 metres   E7 6b †   (1.97)
Start just right of the obvious corner at a horizontal break above the sea. Climb onto the slab, which is split by a wide crack that peters out as height

is gained. Climb steadily up the slab above and move boldly right at the top to join a slight groove.

Granite Grater   35 metres   E4 †   (8.96)
Start some 10 metres inland of *The Grassman* and just right of a chimney.
1 20m. 5c. Climb a series of cracks to a belay ledge with a huge perched boulder above.
2 15m. 6a. Climb the boulder by the second crack from the left.

The Logan Rock
On the descent from the col, the inland wall below the Logan Rock proper is immediately to the left. Here there are a number of steep chimney cracks well used in their time by Marine trainees and post-Victorian gents before them. Below and left of the metal plaque signposting Logan Rock is a thin, overhanging crack leading to a break with a wide crack above, the testing *Jack Yer Body*.

Ten metres left of *Jack Yer Body* is a large spike which can be climbed to an excellent hand-jamming crack: **Blondie Jams with Sepultura** (10 metres Hard Very Severe 5a 16.8.98).

Jack Yer Body   20 metres   E4 5c   (15.4.90)
Climb the crack to the break and struggle up the continuation crack, where a car-jack was used for a runner on the first ascent. No need to call out the fourth emergency service, use a huge cam instead.

Down towards the sea from the grassy knoll below *Jack Yer Body*, a rocky spit with a shallow zawn to its right gives an excellent view of Castle Boot Zawn and its surrounding climbs. Immediately below and left of this vantage point is a short wall reached by scrambling. On this wall is **Normal Route** (8 metres E4 6a † 1.97), which climbs a short crack to a chicken-head on the left and another short crack. To the right are **Crack Two** and **Crack One** (both 8 metres Hard Severe 4b 8.96), taking the central diverging left and right cracks respectively. **Laugh Now, Cry Later** (8 metres E1 5b † 8.96) takes the crack at the back of the overhanging groove.

Continue along the ledge to reach Castle Boot Zawn.

Castle Boot Zawn
There are a number of routes on the west side of the zawn, the best being *The Crying Game*. Castle Boot Zawn can be entered by following ledges until a low-tide boulder-hop leads to the east face of the zawn. Alternatively, an abseil approach can be made. The zawn offers some excellent climbing around HVS standard, with the distinctive *Lightning Crack* being particularly worthwhile.

The Crying Game   15 metres   E6 6a †   (8.96)
The central line up the most continuous wall on the west side of the zawn.
From the ledge, follow a thin crack leftwards until it is possible to mantel
onto a sloping ledge below a large horizontal break. Step slightly right
before trending left to join the black-stained crack leading to hard climbing
and eventually the top.

The cracks leading into the chimney to the right of *The Crying Game* are
taken by the loose **NitroCellulose** (15 metres Hard Very Severe 5a † 8.96).

Starting at the lowest point of the zawn is **Photonic Travel** (12 metres Very
Severe 4c 8.96), which climbs a big groove before using a chicken-head
and finishing up more grooves. Sharing the same start is **Lightning Crack**
(15 metres Hard Very Severe 5a 8.96): gain and climb the big groove and
the crack above, whereupon the 'lightning crack' leads to the top. **Jo Says
Why?** (15 metres Hard Very Severe 5a 8.96) climbs the widening crack up
the back of a large pedestal. **Maxim's Crack** (15 metres Very Difficult
10.96) takes the knobbly chimney at the back of the zawn.

Not So Big Slab
Above the east face of Castle Boot Zawn, and set slightly back, is a slab
offering four superb routes. Approached from the lower (seaward) end of
the slab, the first route, **Psycho Su** (10 metres E4 5c 8.96), climbs the twin
veins at the base of the slab. **Beautiful Dreams** (10 metres E4 6a 8.96)
takes the large crack in the centre of the slab. The second crack positioned
slightly higher on the slab is climbed by **The Project** (10 metres E5 6b †
4.98) to a horizontal break. One then moves up a thin crack to make a hard
move to a hidden hold in the central triangle. **Phobia** (10 metres E7 6c †
8.96) climbs the left-hand side of a rounded nose before stepping right onto
a chicken-head and finishing by moving rightwards.

Once on top of Not So Big Slab it is possible to continue scrambling in an
easterly direction immediately passing a small zawn which has an obvious
square-cut corner midway along its eastern side. This is climbed by the
unprotected **Escape Route** (8 metres E2 5b 8.96). Continue along the
eastern side of the zawn to reach a steep wall marked by a distinctive black
hole. **Wet Dreams** (10 metres E7 6b † 8.96) climbs into the hole before
striking a direct and bold upward path to finish.

The East Face
A mass of short walls and zawns make up the East Face, and although not
very high it offers many high quality climbs between Difficult and Very
Severe.

Shark Zawn

At the southern end of the East Face is a large zawn featuring a meandering line up its back wall. **Slash Has a Crash** (14 metres Hard Very Severe 5a 8.96) climbs up on the left-hand side, traverses right at mid height, and finishes strenuously. There are two other routes on the east wall. From sea-level, **Teaspoon Tom** (10 metres Hard Severe 4c 8.96) climbs the ramp to the bulge and groove, before stepping right to finish. **Slash** (10 metres Very Severe 4c 8.96) starts 5 metres left of *Teaspoon Tom*. It climbs a series of flakes and bulges just right of a blank-looking wall before an exposed finish through an awkward bulge.

Lad Cove

There is a distinctive black slab in Lad Cove, where the climbing is excellent, as is the cliff jumping. The ledge at the base of the slab is free of the sea at low tide; it is best approached by abseil. From the sea-level ledge, **Cliff Jumpers** (15 metres Very Severe 5a 8.96) climbs through the overlap to another ledge, after which a steep crack is followed to the top. **Mothver** (10 metres Very Difficult 8.96) starts from the same ledge before taking the easiest line up the knobbly black slab. Finally, **99 Lead Balloons** (10 metres E1 5b 8.96) starts from the lowest point of the slab and then climbs straight up to a hard move and an easy finish.

By scrambling down a short distance north of Lad Cove, another little zawn can be found which has a small rounded arête at its back. A good route called **The Space Cowboy** (10 metres E3 5c † 8.96) climbs directly up the arête.

Next is Cripps's Cove, which has little to interest the climber. Further east of Logan Rock is a small bay fringed by low slabby cliffs. An area of slabs lying well above the sea offers pleasant balancy climbing at Very Severe standard. It is reached by following the path out onto the Logan Rock headland for about 100 metres and then contouring down to the left (facing out).

Cribba Head (Granite)   OS Ref 402 222

Outlook: South-west.
Non-tidal.
Coastguard Identity: Cribba Head.

This delightful area lies to the east of Logan Rock across a small bay. It is split by a narrow zawn with a wide upper amphitheatre. There are two main climbing areas. The West Buttress is the striking square-cut 'coxcomb' block that crowns the Head's western flank and faces across to Logan Rock. It is easily seen from the approach path across the fields. The East Buttress lies on the far eastern edge of the Head. Cribba Head is a National Trust site and an SSSI.

Approach from Treen car-park as for Logan Rock (see page 165). On reaching the coast path, walk east for 200 metres to the top of a slope. Continue on the flat for 50 metres before following sketchy paths through thick gorse and grass down towards the broad top of the headland. West Buttress is reached by scrambling awkwardly down to the right (facing out) or, easier, by descending the upper part of the headland's central zawn and walking round grassy ledges on the right (facing out) to the front face of the buttress.

West Buttress

West Buttress is a handsome block of granite about 20 metres high. Its west face is split by cracklines, corners, and arêtes, which give excellent climbing. The left side of the buttress (facing in) is split by a deep cleft with jammed boulders at its top. Right of the cleft is a sweeping grey wall split by the splendid crescent-shaped crack of *Pass the Pigs*. To the right of the wall is a steep corner with a small block at 5 metres. This is *Kernyck*.

On the far left of the buttress is a poorly-protected chunky black vein, **Etron Fou** (10 metres Hard Severe 4b 21.6.90).

Bottleneck   25 metres   Very Severe 5a   (1986)
Five metres to the right of the chunky black vein is a groove leading to a chimney. Climb the groove and the tough chimney above; then traverse out right and climb directly up the face.

Back to the Grind   15 metres   E3 6a †   (1989)
Start at the break in the low-level roof. Climb up to the higher roof, turn it on the right, and continue more easily to the top.
Variation Start 15 metres E4/5 6a † (1989). Climb the blunt arête past a small roof split by a crack to join *Back to the Grind* at two-thirds height.

Reluctance   15 metres   E1 5c †   (1990s)
This line does not look possible at the grade supplied. Start as for the variation start to *Back to the Grind*. Climb the rightward-slanting crackline on the left-hand side of the chimney.

The deep cleft offers the easiest way to the top of the crag at Difficult standard.

Unlike Siobhan   18 metres   Hard Very Severe 4c †   (16.4.95)
To the left of *Pass the Pigs* is a round arête consisting of four downward-pointing lobes. Climb these on their left-hand side. (Bridging to the adjacent wall of the chimney reduces the grade to Severe). Exit up the thin groove in the main face. Protection is good but well-spaced.

New Sensation   15 metres   Hard Very Severe 5a †   (1989)
Similar in nature to *Unlike Siobhan*. Enter the obvious groove and climb the rounded arête consisting of four downward-pointing lobes on the right-hand side.

★Pass the Pigs 15 metres E4 6a (30.12.88)
Climb the tough but stylish line up the strenuous crescent-shaped crack in the grey wall to a hard finish on chicken-heads.

★Lovely, Lovely, Lovely 15 metres E5 6b (2.9.89)
Exactly named. Climb the striking flake near the right-hand arête of the grey wall and make a very hard move rightwards to a second undercut flake, which is followed up rightwards to a break. Move slightly left to a chicken-head and finish direct.

★Question Mark 15 metres E8 6c (1994)
[Photo p.256b.] An intense experience, harder than *Pre-Marital Tension*. Start in the corner of *Kernyck* and follow the rising flake leftwards to join the arête at half height. Using the arête and small crimps on the wall, make a series of desperate moves to reach the break. Finish more easily.

★Kernyck 15 metres Hard Severe 4b (9.5.65)
Climb the steep corner past a small block at 5 metres to a harder finish.

Kernack 15 metres E1 5b (14.8.85)
Start below the centre of the wall right of *Kernyck*. Hard moves gain the wall, which is climbed direct until a thin move up and right gains the top. Sparse protection.

★Boysen's Groove 15 metres E2 5c (1981)
This is the slim, handsome groove slicing up the face to the right of *Kernack*. Make a hard start into the groove, which is followed past the impressive upper flake.

★Pre-Marital Tension 15 metres E8 6c (1990)
[Photos: rear cover insert and p.272a.] Pure style and boldness. Climb the left side of the soaring arête to the right of *Boysen's Groove*. If you reach the second break, move left and finish more easily. Sky hook protection.

Pre-Marital Tension Right-hand 15 metres E8 6c † (1994)
The right-hand side of the arête is climbed past a peg (removed) in the upper break.

Harder 12 metres Very Severe 4c (9.5.65)
The next corner on the right gives quite tough climbing. Move strenuously up into a niche, which is exited up its right wall.

Mary 12 metres E6 6b (8.9.98)
Climb the centre of the wall between *Harder* and *Storms Over Africa*, before moving left at three-quarters height and finishing up the corner.

★Storms over Africa   12 metres   E6 6b   (1990)
The arête is sustained and very bold. Climb the slanting crack to join the arête. Layback directly up using small crystals on the left to stay in balance. (It is possible to use a thin crack just left of the next route to finish; this reduces the grade to E5 6a.)

Boysen's Cracks   12 metres   E2 5c   (1981)
Climb the nicely strenuous cracks in the buttress's seaward face.

The lower west-facing section of Cribba Head is made up of smooth, easy-angled slabs which make for pleasant bouldering. These slabs give way to steeper rock on the seaward point of the head. There are variable lines here, mainly at Very Difficult to Severe standard. The best of these is described. The start is affected by tide and swell: the state of the sea should be judged carefully.

Sunny Slab   30 metres   Very Difficult   (c.1980s)
A pleasant route, near the top of the grade and with a fine sea atmosphere. The start is reached by descending an easy gully below the seaward edge of West Buttress and then traversing to the right (facing in) to a tidal ledge beneath a slab. Climb a steep pedestal; then traverse to the right onto the slab, which is climbed near its right edge. Finish up a steeper headwall.

Immediately around from the West Buttress there is a zawn which splits the head; there is much rock, but little of it is continuous. A number of good-quality, albeit very short, routes have been climbed on the lowest walls of the east side of the zawn. One route has been recorded on the east wall of the upper amphitheatre. It is reached along grassy ledges.

The wall is seamed with rounded cracks. At the seaward end of the wall is a deep crack next to a large detached block. **Stanstead** (18 metres Severe 4a 5.87) climbs the crack and its wider continuation to a slabby finish.

To the east of the zawn is Cropper Buttress Amphitheatre, a fine place to escape strong westerlies. There are several short, easy routes here, notably a V-groove and a chimney (which provides the best approach) on the left-hand side. Left of the V-groove is a fine line equipped with more than adequate flakes – this can be climbed direct at Very Difficult. Just right of the chimney is a blunt, black arête with a tantalising flake crack going part-way up its right-hand side: **Armadillo** (10 metres Very Severe 4c † 13.3.94).

East Buttress
This is the north-east wall of Cribba Head. It lies about 30 metres north-east of West Buttress and beyond the central zawn. It can be damp in winter but has some good lines which dry quickly in the summer. Below the left side of the wall the ground drops steeply away.

★Skin Graft   24 metres   E2 5c   (6.5.91)
A sporty piece of jamming up the hanging crack on the upper left side of
the face. Start some way down the grassy ramp, below a series of curving
cracks. Climb the cracks to below the rounded overhang. Step left to make
hard moves onto a ledge (belay possible). Climb the crack above with
difficulty to make wild finishing moves.

Mink de Ville   27 metres   Very Severe 5a   (19.8.85)
Start down to the left, just above where the ground falls away. Use a
narrow flake to gain a steep crack and climb this to a grassy ledge (belay
possible). Move easily up and right for about 5 metres to a narrow
chimney, which is climbed with a struggle.

★Geologist's Route   20 metres   E2 5c   (6.8.85)
A neat pitch. Start at a groove about 3 metres in from the right edge of the
face. Climb the groove; then continue up a thin crack that slants to the left.
Pass a small overhang and then climb the steep crack above with
increasing difficulty to finish.

Crag X   20 metres   Hard Very Severe 5a   (6.8.85)
Start at the right end of the face. Climb thin cracks to a horizontal break.
Move left into a large niche; then continue up the groove above to finish.

How Much Longer?   17 metres   Very Difficult   (22.7.85)
Start round to the right of the right-hand edge of the face, at the base of a
grassy break. Climb easily to a break and then continue up a groove on
the right.

Cropper Buttress

Cropper Buttress is the amphitheatre down to the left (facing in) of East
Buttress. It has a grassy ledge at half height, and on the left-hand side is a
wall split by two fine cracks. Scramble stiffly down or abseil to the base of the
wall.

The Apostle   18 metres   E1 5b †   (10.93)
Climb the thin cracks to a good spike on the rounded break. Move
diagonally right to climb the superb flake crack.

The Harvest   18 metres   Hard Very Severe 5a †   (10.93)
Climb the right-hand crack, using a good layaway hold to pass a blank
section. Climb the rounded crack in the arête above (left of a corner).

At sea-level is a fine, black, overhanging wall with two extended problems.
The central line is **Heavy Gravity** (5c), and the right-hand line is **The
Chicken Run** (5c), which continues up a fine corner directly above to a
large belay ledge.

Opposite the East Buttress and virtually down at sea-level are some fine, sunny walls. Most of the climbing is short and easy, though delightful and in a wonderful setting. A distinctive feature is a fine flake crack with a square-cut corner and some slabby walls between 6 and 10 metres high. It looks especially attractive when viewed from the rather sombre East Buttress. A number of routes have been climbed in this area.

Penberth (Granite)   OS Ref 405 417

Outlook: South.
Tidal. Accessible for three hours either side of low water, although the two described routes can be gained at high tide provided the sea is calm.
Coastguard Identity: Penberth.

The crag is a sheltered spot which is suitable for beginners. Although a large number of climbs graded from Difficult to Very Severe have been reported here, they lack stature and have been left for the curious to rediscover.

Approach. There is limited parking on the roadside just above the cove, but this becomes very busy in the summer months. Walk down to the cove and follow the coast path eastwards to the crown of the headland. Go down the right-hand side of the headland (facing out) and scramble down to sea-level. Traverse back right (facing in) below short walls and corners to reach the base of a continuous 20-metre tower of delightful ochre-coloured rock. Rightward-slanting cracks seam the lower face above an overhang.

Thirty Something   20 metres   E1 5b   (16.8.91)
Gain the left-hand crack from the left, and follow it. Make difficult moves where the crack fades and continue up the chimney.

★**They Do at That Age**   20 metres   Hard Very Severe 5a (30.7.81)
A testing little line at the top end of the grade. Climb the right-hand crack and move left into the central crack above the overhang. Climb this crack to a horizontal break, move left , and take the chimney to the top.

Porthguarnon Cove (Granite)   OS Ref 409 229

Approach from Penberth Cove, where there is limited parking. Follow the coast path eastwards for a kilometre until the path drops steeply to Porthguarnon Cove. Porthguarnon West lies on the western arm of the cove. The handsome, three-tiered cliff of Porthguarnon East dominates the eastern side of the cove. Approach to Porthguarnon Cove can also be made via the right-of-way through Treverven Farm, although it is not permitted to park there (see St Loy approach details on page 175). On this approach, a steep descent of the coast path into the cove is necessary to reach Porthguarnon West.

Porthguarnon Cove has a marvellously open atmosphere. There are no major climbs but there are several easier rambles on Porthguarnon West and numerous short pitches on good granite on Porthguarnon East. The latter rises to a height of 60 metres straight from the sea, but in three tiers separated by wide terraces. Chance could have made it a major rock-face. As it is, the area has a persuasive charm without seriousness.

Porthguarnon West
Outlook: East.
Non-Tidal but the bases of most routes are affected by swell.
Coastguard Identity: Porthguarnon.

When approaching Porthguarnon West from Penberth, go half-way down the steep section of the coast path that leads down into Porthguarnon Cove; then strike seawards. Keep high, and reach grass slopes below a short, steep wall with a striking 15-metre faultline at its right-hand end. This is *Last Day's Flier*. The grass slopes fall away into a deep zawn lying between a broken east-facing wall and a rocky spur leading out to an island on the left (facing out). The main climbing lies on the broken east-facing wall.

Separate but often duplicated development of routes has caused some confusion here. Minor realignments have been made in the following descriptions. The whole face of the cliff is generous and allows for variations of all the routes mentioned. 'Follow your nose' is the name of the game here.

The first route starts from the seaward end of the cliff and is reached by descending the broad ridge that runs down to the sea from the top of *Last Day's Flier*.

Giant's Crawl   51 metres   Very Difficult   (12.1.80)
Start at the base of the broad ridge just above the sea.
1 8m. Move rightwards around the arête to the foot of an angled ramp.
2 15m. Continue diagonally left to an easy-angled slab, which is climbed to a corner.
3 10m. Climb the corner to the first groove on the right, and follow the groove to belays on the wall.
4 18m. Take the slab slanting rightwards. Move right past a rounded bollard and finish steeply.

The next four routes start from a narrow ledge at the base of the broken, east-facing cliff below and left of *Last Day's Flier*. The floor of the zawn is littered with vast jammed boulders.

Descent. From the grassy slopes below *Last Day's Flier*, scramble down the rocky spur leading out to the island and then descend, awkwardly in places, via grooves to the zawn-bed. Cross to a narrow ledge between the base of the steep, right-hand section of the cliff and a huge rectangular boulder. A rope may be needed by beginners.

Penny Lane 85 metres   Difficult   (18.10.70)
A wandering right-to-left traverse along the base of the cliff and round the small rocky islet to seaward. Variations exist.
1 10m. Move down from the left end of the ledge and continue to a 5-metre pillar.
2 25m. Continue left to reach the next (higher) pillar.
3 25m. Continue along the base of the cliff towards the small islet, and belay just before the crossing-point.
4 25m. Island-hop, and girdle above the tide.

Devax 38 metres   Hard Severe   (1983)
1 10m. *Penny Lane* pitch 1.
2 12m. Climb the slanting crack on the right to a broad, sloping slab below a corner-crack.
3 10m. 4b. Climb the crack to a ledge.
4 6m. 4b. Finish up the centre of the wall left of the corner.

Sennifer 34 metres   Very Difficult   (15.11.70)
1 15m. From the left end of the ledge, move down left for a short distance; then climb a short chimney to the wide, sloping ledge in the middle of the cliff.
2 5m. From the right-hand edge of the ledge, take a short groove to a large grassy ledge leading off rightwards.
3 14m. Walk rightwards to the far end of the grassy ledge and climb a crack to the grass slopes above the zawn.

Gulliver's Route 39 metres   Severe   (12.1.80)
1 12m. From the left end of the ledge, traverse leftwards to a wide crack and climb it to the broad, sloping ledge.
2 12m. Climb a groove in the right-hand wall to a ledge.
3 15m. 4a. Move up and right to the foot of a steep crack and climb it, traversing left to finish.

★Last Day's Flier 15 metres   E1 5b   (31.12.79)
This short, positive pitch is a biceps-buster at the top of its grade. Start at the upper right-hand wall of the cliff above the arrival slopes. Climb the steep knobbly crack at the right-hand edge of the wall, and exit awkwardly up the groove above.

Porthguarnon East

Outlook: South-west.

Non-tidal on Upper and Middle Tier. **Tidal** on Lower Tier, which is accessible for three hours either side of low water but can be wave-swept by swell and rough sea at all states of the tide.

Coastguard Identity: Porthguarnon.

Approach from Penberth as above, or via Treverven Farm (no public parking here). If approaching from Penberth, follow the coast path down into the cove and then go right along a faint path through dense vegetation to reach the terrace at the base of the Upper Tier. Alternatively, continue steeply uphill on the coast path to where the path from Treverven Farm comes in from the left. Continue east along the coast path for 100 metres through a rocky break and then go right from the coast path for a few metres to grassy ledges. Scramble down an earthy break to the top of the Upper Tier, where an abseil descent can be made to its base. Thick, prickly vegetation makes a scrambling descent of the easy-angled left side of the buttress unpleasant. The base of the Middle Tier can be reached by a further abseil or by scrambling down its left-hand side (facing out). The Lower (Sea-Level) Tier can be reached by a further abseil or by down-climbing *Kelly's Eye*, the prominent chimney/gully splitting the middle of the face.

It is also possible to traverse in to the lower tier: before the coast path rises steeply to go around the top of the cliff, follow a faint path down to sea-level. Boulder-hop and traverse for 200 metres to reach the left-hand side of the Lower Tier at a pair of black left-facing hanging corners.

Lower (Sea-Level) Tier

The main feature is the chimney/gully of *Kelly's Eye*, situated directly below the left-hand end (facing in) of the Middle Tier. The gully has a distinctive black vein running down its centre. The clean walls of the Lower Tier give several pleasant pitches. Care should be taken with the sea.

The main feature on the left-hand side of the Lower Tier is a pair of black hanging corners at 5 metres, above a small easy slab. Just to their left is a small cave.

Undertaker's Crack   30 metres   Very Severe   (5.3.2000)
Start beneath the cave, on a boulder at sea-level.
1 10m. 4c. Climb a slab to the cave, follow a crack out right, and continue more easily to a ledge and good belays beneath a short leaning wall.
2 20m. 5a. Strenuous moves up the leaning wall gain a good flake at the base of a crack. Climb the crack to a ledge and continue in a direct line to a prickly finish and poor belays. Escape easily rightwards to the broad sloping ledge beneath the Middle Tier.

The Hearse   20 metres   Very Difficult †   (30.1.2000)
Start below the larger (right-hand) black hanging corner. Climb up and
follow the corner for a few metres before moving out right onto a rib.
Climb the rib to ledges, and continue rightwards up flakes to the ledge.

Near the left-hand side of the Lower Tier, a narrow ramp leads down to a
step up and a second ramp sloping down towards the sea. *Toy Story* starts a
few metres down the first ramp.

Toy Story   20 metres   Very Severe 5a   (5.7.97)
Start just left of the corner. Make hard moves up two thin cracks to a spike.
Finish easily up the cracks above.

Fences   22 metres   Hard Severe 4b   (10.9.88)
Start at the step between the ramps. Step up onto a sloping ledge, climb
the corner, move left, and follow cracks to the top.

The Fixit   20 metres   Very Severe 5a   (10.9.88)
Climb the cracks a metre right of *Fences* and the continuation cracks to
finish.

Eternity's Few   20 metres   Very Severe 5a   (5.7.97)
Start below a small overhang that caps a niche at 3 metres. Layback up
the crack on the right-hand side of the overhang to reach a ledge. Climb
the corner to the top.

Ridiculous Thoughts   20 metres   E1 5b †   (15.6.97)
Start a metre right of *Eternity's Few*. Climb a crack for 5 metres and move
boldly rightwards along thin cracks to an overhang (crux). Turn the
overhang on its left and finish up the crack above.

Iron Bells   20 metres   Hard Severe 4b   (10.9.88)
Climb the layback crack to two overhangs. Move up between the
overhangs and follow the slight corner to the top.

Moaning Minnie   20 metres   Very Difficult   (10.9.88)
Climb the thin black vein at the right-hand edge of the sloping ledge to a
niche. Finish up the crack above.

The Way Outside   20 metres   Very Difficult   (10.9.88)
Just left of *Kelly's Eye* are a series of open corners, the longest at the top.
Climb the corners, trending left near the top to climb the final corner.

The gully-cum-chimney is **Kelly's Eye** (18 metres Difficult 3.4.70): take the
easiest line up the gully to finish past a hollow-sounding block.

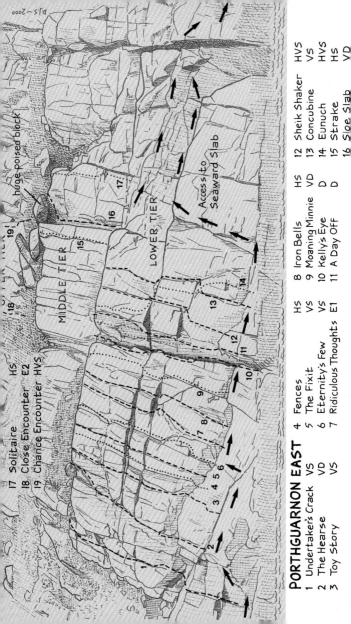

PORTHGUARNON EAST

1 Undertaker's Crack	VS	8 Iron Bells	HS	12 Sheik Shaker	HVS
2 The Hearse	VD	9 Moaning Minnie	VD	13 Concubine	VS
3 Toy Story	VS	10 Kelly's Eye	D	14 Eunuch	HVS
4 Fences	HS	11 A Day Off	D	15 Strake	HS
5 The Fixit	VS			16 Sloe Slab	VD
6 Eternity's Few	VD			
7 Ridiculous Thoughts	E1			
17 Solitaire	VS			
18 Close Encounter	E2			
19 Chance Encounter	HVS			

DJS ~2000

A Day Off   18 metres   Difficult †   (9.10.88)
Start at the foot of *Kelly's Eye* at the high-water mark. Climb the slab just
right of the gully until level with the second overhang. Follow the slanting
crack on the right and finish up the arête.
Variation Severe † (12.3.2000). At the start of the slanting crack, climb
the steep crack and pull over onto a slab. Move slightly up and right and
follow the continuation of the crack to the ledge.

Sheik Shaker   18 metres   Hard Very Severe 5a   (15.6.97)
Three metres right of the gully is a black vein. Start just right of the vein.
Climb directly up the slab to a small ledge. Move rightwards to parallel
cracks and climb these to the top, passing to the left of a protruding fin.

★**Concubine**   18 metres   Very Severe 5a   (19.3.2000)
A good route. Start at a rightward-leading crack. Climb the crack to a
ledge and continue up the pleasant corner-crack above to another ledge.
Step left and climb a well-protected rightward-leaning ramp to a final
steep move.

☆**Eunuch**   20 metres   Hard Very Severe 5a †   (12.3.2000)
Start just right of the rightward-leading crack, at low water. Step across to
surmount an overlap, and climb a slab to a good ledge. Continue left of
the corner-crack of *Concubine* to another ledge. Step left and move up
onto a slab, where technical moves lead to the top left-hand edge and an
unprotected finish.

A scramble across the 30-metre-wide bay on the right leads to a small tidal
slab, which is crossed by a convenient approach ledge just above high-water
mark.

Neptune   10 metres   Very Difficult †   (5.3.2000)
Start at the left end of the approach ledge. Climb thin cracks and then
move left to better holds. Continue up more positive cracks to an abrupt
finish. Block belay to the right.

Fill Yer Pants   14 metres   E2 5b †   (19.3.2000)
Low water and a dead calm sea are required, as the start is from a lower
ledge. Move left into the centre of the lower section of slab and climb
barnacled rock to the approach ledge. Fix protection in a thin crack to the
left before moving up the steep slab to a central sloping ledge. Climb up
and then leftwards to an obvious hold and make a careful reach for the
top. A bold lead with poor protection where it matters and a hungry sea
below!

Flake Crack   15 metres   Severe †   (19.3.2000)
Start just to the right of a step down in the approach ledge. Climb the
leftward-leading flake/crack that splits the slab.

Ocean   12 metres   Hard Very Severe 4c †   (19.3.2000)
Start as for *Flake Crack*. Climb the vertical crack past a horizontal break to
the final slab. Move up this delicately to a rock-over and a long reach for
the top. Poorly protected.

Middle Tier

The Middle Tier is an amenable little slice of rock. On its right-hand side it
falls back sharply into a slabby bay. The centre of the wall is split by a
distinctive groove, *Keelson*, which runs up to boulders on the top edge of the
wall. The cracklines to the left of *Keelson* give pleasant pitches, although they
can be a touch damp.

Cat's Paw   12 metres   Very Severe 4c   (1970s)
Climb twin cracks above a rock step at the left edge of the wall.

Messenger   12 metres   Very Severe 5a   (1970s)
Just right of the twin cracks, climb a steepish slab and finish up a thin
crack.

Cringle   13 metres   Hard Severe 4b   (1970s)
Climb the next crack from a dimpled hole at the base of the wall.

Keelson   13 metres   Severe 4a   (1970s)
Climb a thin crack to a small ledge at half height. Either finish up the
central groove or move left and climb a slab.

Gimbals   13 metres   Severe 4a   (1970s)
Climb the crack just right of *Keelson*.

Fleeting Lights   13 metres   E1 5a   (22.11.98)
Start 3 metres right of the crack of *Gimbals*. Climb the steep slab via
sloping ledges and finish up a faint crack. Poorly protected.

Silicone Chips   13 metres   Severe 4a   (22.11.88)
Start just right of a shallow corner in the middle of the slab, below a thin
crack. Climb to the crack and follow it to the top.

The right side of the wall has a distinctive deep crack running up to finish just
right of a protruding capstone. Left of the deep crack is a thin bottomless
crack starting at half height.

Hound's Band   14 metres   Very Severe 5a   (1970s)
Climb ledges to the thin crack. Follow the crack and step right beneath the
capstone to reach the finishing ledge.

Strake   13 metres   Hard Severe 4b   (1970s)
The deep crack running up to the capstone ledge is climbed direct.

F-Nose (13 metres E1 5a 3.4.70) is an interesting ramble but has been superseded by its neighbours. Start below the edge of the wall where it falls away into a slabby bay. Move up a series of steps, which lead leftwards to the deep crack. Climb the crack for a short way and move right to a ledge. Make difficult, poorly-protected moves up the wall above.

Ask to Risk   13 metres   E2 5b   (21.11.88)
Climb the right arête direct. Protection may be arranged at the half-height break, but a bold and technical finish awaits.

Hi-Ten   13 metres   Very Severe 5a   (3.4.70)
The left wall of the slabby bay on the right of the main wall is split by a dour-looking crack. Climb a short corner to a ledge at the base of the crack, and then the strenuous crack itself.

Sloe Slab   15 metres   Very Difficult   (3.4.70)
Climb the slabby corner of the bay, finishing up to the right or, better, through a hole beneath the huge capstone. A Severe variation can be climbed straight up the middle of the slab.

Solitaire   12 metres   Severe 4b †   (30.1.2000)
Start 6 metres right of *Sloe Slab*. Climb the slab to a bulge, make a hard pull over on the right, and follow easier cracks up the slab to finish right of the huge block.

Upper Tier

The Upper Tier is more broken than the other two tiers. Its far left-hand section has a distinctive glossy black slab with a flanking right wall running up to overhangs. This wall gives the lines of *Wicked Ways* and *Byegone Days*. To the right, the cliff is broken and vegetated, with a distinctive feature being a chunky vein snaking up the face. Beyond is an area of smooth slabs with huge blocks leaning against them.

Wicked Ways   30 metres   Very Severe 4c   (8.4.87)
A worthwhile pitch with a big feel to it and a jungle approach. Climb the groove at the junction of the glossy black slab and its flanking wall past two ancient pegs. Turn the first roof on its left and climb a good crack leftwards to clear the second roof. Continue left and finish up the arête.

Byegone Days   25 metres   Very Severe 4c   (8.4.87)
Follow the groove of *Wicked Ways* to the first roof. Climb rightwards round the roof to the right and continue up the groove above to the top.

The slabs and cracks above the huge leaning blocks have a number of pleasant pitches and combinations at Very Difficult to Severe standard. There are three more substantial routes here, however.

☆**Close Encounter** 21 metres E2 † (9.4.2000)
Start 6 metres left of *Chance Encounter*, where a huge block leans against
the main cliff, at a small ivy-filled groove.
1 14m. 5b. Climb steeply leftwards to a good foothold at 4 metres on
the arête. Follow the arete delicately to easier but unprotected climbing up
a narrow slab. Belay on top of the block.
2 7m. 5b. Step onto the main cliff and fix protection on the right. Climb
with difficulty straight up the slab to finish left of a triangular overhang.
Block belay.

★**Chance Encounter** 18 metres Hard Very Severe 5a (7.85)
On the right edge of the slabs is a pile of boulders sprouting from a
mini-jungle of thorn bushes. The rounded arête above the boulders is
gained by a long step. Move left and climb the thin crack to a ledge. Step
up, move out right in an exposed position, and climb a thin line of
weakness past a small flake to the top.
Variation E2 6a (12.5.94). Start 2 metres left of the rounded arête, just
right of a short corner. Climb up onto the wall and move up delicately to
gain the thin crack. Bold.

Brief Encounter 18 metres E2 6a (7.85)
Above and right of *Chance Encounter* is a distinctive shallow crack in the
scooped wall above an overhang. Make a long step from the depression
on the right and climb the crack to the top.

Fifty metres to the right of Upper Tier, and slightly lower, there is an area of
slabby rock which offers some good pitches from Very Difficult to Hard Severe.

Coffin Cove (Granite) OS Ref 414 228

Outlook: West.
Tidal at the base of the cliff with access for three hours either side of low
water.
Coastguard Identity: Trevedran Cliff.

This is the east-facing wall of the narrow cove lying to the west of St Loy Main
Cliff. There are some pleasant short pitches and two longer climbs.

Approach along the coast path from Penberth or from the B3315 through
Treverven Farm (note that there is no public parking at the farm). The cliff lies
about 200 metres east of the junction of the Treverven Farm track and the
coast path. It is easily seen when looking down from the coast path as a
stepped tower of orange rock rising from the sea. The distinctive dark groove
on the left side of the tower is the first pitch of *Wreckage*.

Descent. A grassy spur runs out from the coast path and merges into a ridge that runs down to the top of the cliff. Scramble down the ridge to the top of the cliff. Descend rightwards (facing out) via a short gully and then steep grass, and trend rightwards to scramble down a short wall to a sloping ramp. At the base of the ramp is the dark groove of *Wreckage*. For *The Seventh Wave*, drop down from the base of the ramp and traverse left (facing in) to sea-level ledges below a short wall.

The Seventh Wave   17 metres   E1 5b   (15.4.90)
Boldly climb the obvious black knobbly fault and finish on better holds.

Manslaughter   17 metres   E7 6b †   (30.3.96)
Between *The Seventh Wave* and *Wreckage* is a narrow wall with a thin crack at its base. Follow the crack past a good but small nut placement to a diagonal crack running right to left. Arrange small wires here before stepping boldly right to the thin seam, where suspect lichenous rock leads to the top.

Wreckage   47 metres   Very Severe   (9.7.88)
A pleasant though escapable line. Start at the bottom of the sloping ramp.
1 15m. 4c. Climb the poorly-protected dark groove to a ledge.
2 12m. 4a. Take the crack on the left to a belay.
3 10m. Scramble over blocks and pinnacles to belay in a gap.
4 10m. 5a. Across the gap on the left is a V-crack, which is climbed past a loose chockstone.

The following routes can be gained from the *Wreckage* ramp by traversing round to the right above the sea. Alternatively, from the top of the cliff, descend its left-hand side (facing out) to sea-level ledges. *Heelstone* starts below the broken V-groove at the left end (facing in) of the ledges.

Heelstone   42 metres   Very Difficult (13.1.80)
1 15m. Climb up and follow the V-groove and the crack above to a ledge.
2 27m. Climb direct over blocks and pinnacles, cross a gap, and climb the right edge of the chimney.
Variation
1a 15m. Severe 4a (15.4.90). Climb the arête right of *Heelstone* to a horizontal break. Continue direct to the belay ledge.

To the right is an obvious hanging slab.

Powerslide   10 metres   E1 5a †   (30.3.96)
Climb the hanging slab using the distinctive arête on the right.

There is a beautiful slab a little further round to the right, where three unprotected lines of about 7 metres can be found. **Mike's Red Party Piece** (E1 5a †) climbs the left-hand side of the slab, the central line is taken by **Jolly Holly** (E1 5a †), and **Who Dares Wins** (E1 5a †) follows the right-hand line. (All three climbed on 30.3.96.)

To the right and set further back from the slab is a short clean wall with three pitches of about 8 metres. The thin crack left of the central flake/corner is E1 5c; the flake/corner, Severe 4a; and the shallow groove at the right end of the wall, a bold Hard Very Severe 5a.

St Loy Cliff (Granite)   OS Ref 416 228

Outlook: South.
Non-Tidal.
Coastguard Identity: Merthen Point.
Enviromental Issues: This area is very rich in flora, lichens, mosses and liverworts. There are Bluebell patches and widespread shrub communities of Sallow, Wild Privet, Blackthorn and Willow between the isolated pinnacles and smaller cliffs. The whole area is susceptible to trampling damage. Birds of prey breed in the area. The St Loy descent path is suffering some wear. Please keep to the existing paths. Care should be taken not to trample the dense vegetation between the subsidiary buttresses. Please avoid damage to lichen.

This distinctive area is one of the most delightful of West Penwith's climbing venues. South-facing, non-tidal, and nicely built, it has the added attraction of being relatively remote. The area offers climbs of the highest quality on flawless granite. These range from the well-protected lower and middle grade routes to serious but excellent extremes on the impressive Main Face.

Bold climbing without recourse to fixed gear was established on hard routes at St Loy in the early Seventies, which says something about ethical precedent. Modern development has remained refreshingly within that challenging tradition.

Approach. The crag lies on Trevedran Cliff between Porthguarnon Cove and St Loy Cove. Car-parking presents some difficulties as there is no convenient off-road parking along the main road, which itself lies nearly three-quarters of a mile inland. There is no convenient parking to the east for several miles and only limited parking at Penberth Cove, which is about a mile west of St Loy along the coastal footpath.

From the main road, there is a right-of-way to the coast path through Treverven Farm (where there is an excellent campsite, but no parking for non-campers). If approached by the Treverven Farm footpath, the coast path is reached at a point above the steep-sided Porthguarnon Cove to the west. If approached from Penberth Cove, this point is reached after a hard hike up the steep eastern side of Porthguarnon Cove.)

ST. LOY CRAG ~ MAIN FACE

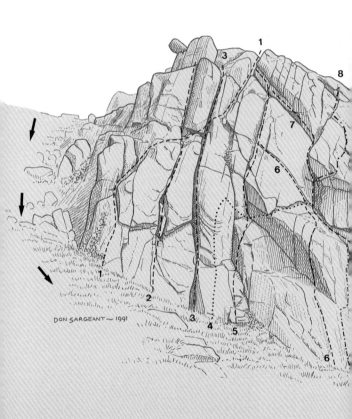

DON SARGEANT ~ 1991

1	Ivy Incorporated	VD	9	Chlorophyll Cluster	E1
2	Chicory Chock	HS	10	The Baldest	E4
3	Chicory Check	VS	11	The Damned	E5
4	The Snip	E3	12	Finesse	E4
5	Harmony	HVS	13	The Barber	E4
6	The Hairiest	E1	14	Sloe Steel	VS
7	Cress Cendo	VS	15	Monochrome Men	E1
8	Old Fools	E3	16	Scarlet Women	E1
			17	The Flying Fakir	E2
			18	Raindance	E1
			19	Slapstick	E3
			20	Margin	E1

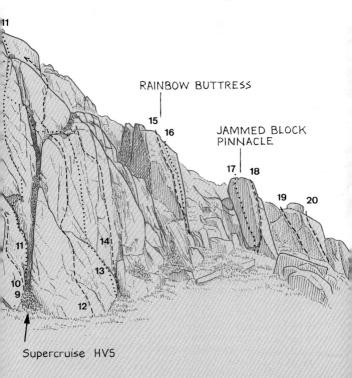

RAINBOW BUTTRESS

JAMMED BLOCK
PINNACLE

Supercruise HVS

A pleasant walk of about half a mile eastwards from here leads to the top of St Loy Main Face, which lies discreetly embedded in an area of grassy cliff-land scattered with granite buttresses and isolated pinnacles: a Cornish 'Easter Island'. The base of the Main Face is reached easily down its western side.

The left side of the cliff (facing in) is made up of broken walls, cracklines, and overhung niches, while the right side features a compact, smooth-faced buttress, up which hard, serious pitches like *The Baldest* and *The Damned* trace elegant lines. Right of these, the distinctive slanting break of *Supercruise* runs steeply rightwards up the cliff. It is flanked on its right by *Finesse*.

To the east of the Main Face there are a number of short pitches on the many smaller buttresses and pinnacles. A useful identifying feature for these is the distinctive Jammed Block Pinnacle, a 15-metre tower with a huge boulder jammed behind it that lies just east of the Main Face.

The first routes lie to the west of the descent route, on two buttresses separated by a narrow gully.

Parents, Priests, and Politicians   10 metres   E6 6a   (1.96
This climb lies 10 metres left of Co-*Extensive Space*. It is best approached from above, however, on account of the brambles between the two routes. Follow the ridge to the right (facing out) of the ordinary descent and then abseil to the base of the route. Climb a groove and the triangular slab above.

The next two routes lie on a small buttress on the right as one descends the path. They are reached by contouring across the hillside for 30 metres from half-way down the path.

Co-Extensive Space   15 metres   E1 5c   (6.93
Climb the thin crack in the right-hand wall of the narrow gully on the left side of the buttress.

The Unclaimed Crack   10 metres   E2 5c †   (1990s
To the right of Co-*Extensive Space*, a crack splits the right arête of the buttress. The crack is easily seen from the foot of the main cliff. Climb the crack and belay on a sloping ledge. Exit to the left.

The Main Face
The next few pitches are on the small buttress forming the left edge of the Main Face.

Ivy Incorporated   30 metres   Very Difficult   (20.4.69
Pleasant climbing up the left edge of the buttress, then up an easy but exposed groove running steeply rightwards. Start a metre from the left edge of the buttress.

1 10m. Climb steeply to an overhang and turn it on its left; then climb a crack in the arête to a large ledge.
2 20m. Traverse right for 3 metres, crossing above two cracklines to climb the deep groove running up to the right.

Chicory Chock   22 metres   Hard Severe 4b   (27.4.69)
The left-hand crack on the buttress gives an interesting pitch. Follow the crack to a good ledge (optional belay). Climb the wide chimney crack above by traditional thrutch or bold layback moves to start. Poor protection.

Chicory Check   23 metres   Very Severe 4b   (27.4.69)
Strenuous and with slight protection. Climb the wide crack right of *Chicory Chock* and follow the continuation corner.
The next two routes start at the slim steep buttress with thin overlaps right of *Chicory Check*.

Checkmate   25 metres   E3 6a   (6.90)
Climb directly up the front of the buttress to a thin crack. Swing round to the right to place protection. Move back left onto the wall and make committing moves to a small ledge. Continue boldly up the centre of the narrow pillar above to reach better holds. Finish more easily.

The Snip   43 metres   E3   (6.5.90)
A stylish left-to-right girdle mixing all the delights of St Loy climbing.
1 18m. 6a. Climb directly up the front of the buttress to a thin crack as for *Checkmate*. Move up with difficulty and then make hard moves round to the right to the sloping floor of the lower niche. Traverse awkwardly round the corner into the higher niche.
2 25m. 5c. Climb the overhang on the right (*Old Fools*); then step right into a crackline, and right again into the deeper crack of *Chlorophyll Cluster*. Continue rightwards, rising slightly at first, with thin subtle moves to reach the slanting break that splits the cliff. Cross the break and finish up cracks.

Harmony   30 metres   Hard Very Severe 5b   (1979)
Nice variety. Start right of *Chicory Check* and climb into a short but steep corner. Make a difficult move up and right onto a slab below an overhung niche (sometimes wet). Climb the rough crack leading up to the left (strenuous) to gain twin cracks in the upper face. Continue up the cracks and then bear leftwards to finish up the deep groove of *Ivy Incorporated*.

Snotter   30 metres   E3 6a   (19.7.94)
Climb the centre of the slab to the left of the black streak of *The Hairiest* to reach the overhanging off-width crack, which is followed to a sloping ledge. Technical climbing for 6 metres up a steep wall leads to an easy finish.

The Hairiest   30 metres   E1   (26.7.81)
Disjointed but with some testing moves. Start below a smooth
black-streaked slab where the base of the cliff levels off.
1 15m. 5b. Climb the black streak to the overhung niche on *Harmony*;
then take the short but steep crack and continuation flake in the right wall
to a higher niche.
2 15m. 5c. Finger-traverse the rising crack leading up and leftwards out
of the niche to finish more easily up cracks.

★Old Fools   30 metres   E3   (1.4.90)
A fine second pitch taking the overhang to the right of the niche of *Cress
Cendo*. Start just right of the black streak on the first pitch of *The Hairiest*.
1 15m. 5b. Climb the short wall to a thin ramp running up left. Step up
right and then make a bold move up and right to gain a scooped crack,
which is followed to the overhung niche on *Cress Cendo*.
2 15m. 5c. Move up and make committing moves out right on the line of
weakness in the roof to reach good flake holds above. Step right to reach
a crack, which leads up and left to the arête and an easier finish.

★Cress Cendo   30 metres   Very Severe   (1970)
An unthreatening line up to and out of the highest overhung niche on the
left side of the face. Start just left of a vegetated niche.
1 12m. 4c. Climb the wall into the niche and follow a disjointed layback
crack on the right, moving left at its top to gain the upper niche. Belay at its
left end.
2 18m. 5a. Move up steeply to enter the deep crack above by an awkward
move. Follow the slab up and left to finish up the deep groove on the right.

★★Chlorophyll Cluster   30 metres   E1 5b   (14.6.70)
Delightful, exposed climbing up the diagonal crack on the left of the
smooth upper face. Start below a large flake, just left of the break of
Supercruise that runs up to the right. Climb a wall and follow the crack
formed by the right side of the flake to ledges (belay possible). Take the
steep wall above (sometimes wet) and enter the slanting crackline above.
Follow the crackline (cams useful) to where it fades and then finish slightly
left. The upper crack gathers some vegetation at times but, since it was first
climbed ungardened, there's no excuse for shunning an on-sight effort.

★★★The Baldest   30 metres   E4 6a   (7.4.74)
A bold and striking pitch, quite low in the technical grade but with slight
protection on the upper slab. Start below a large flake just left of the slanting
break of *Supercruise*. Climb a wall to gain the crack on the right side of the
flake and follow this to ledges, as for *Chlorophyll Cluster* (belay possible).
Climb the short, slanting crack that starts below and to the right. Where it
fades, step right and move up to reach a thin crack formed by an overlap.
Continue direct on minimal holds until it is possible to step right into the faint
beginnings of a rightward-slanting crack. Move up this, step up to a large
foothold, and pull left to a shallow crack. Follow this to the top.

The Damned   30 metres   E5 5c   (8.4.90)
Exquisite climbing on a committing line that takes the fluted wall between *The Baldest* and *Supercruise* and then slices across the unprotected upper slab. Start at the foot of *Supercruise* and climb to the overlap. (A runner can be placed in the initial crack of *The Baldest*.) Step up right onto the wall, follow the shallow flakes until they fade, and move left to a foothold. Make thin moves up to gain another flake before stepping up and right to a resting-ledge, where bold climbing leads rightwards up a shallow depression to the top.

Supercruise   30 metres   Hard Very Severe 4c   (3.11.90)
A sustained pitch. Climb the distinctive break that slices diagonally rightwards up the face.

Finesse   36 metres   E4   (5.4.74)
Well named. Elegant, balancy moves with a lack of protection on pitch 2, although a side-runner on *Supercruise* reduces the grade to E3. Start at the lowest point of the crag, beneath a line of thin cracks in the steep wall. Safer climbed in one pitch.
1 18m. 5c. A satisfying pitch. Climb the thin cracks for 10 metres and follow more cracks diagonally right to reach a stance at the end of a wide ledge.
2 18m. 5c. Step up and climb rightwards along a line of small scoops in the slab. Traverse further right on sloping holds and make a thin move up to a good flake. Mantel onto the flake and finish in more relaxed mode up a crack on the left (it is possible to climb straight up the wall above at E6 6a). Unprotected, although there is a notional placement half-way along the scoops where a wire loop can be 'hitched' on a small nub of quartz.
Variations
1a 18m. 5c (18.3.90). A bold start straight up the wall just to the right of the first pitch via a horizontal crack and small flake hold, followed by thin moves to the belay ledge.
2a 18m. E6 6a (8.95). After making the thin move up to the good hold, continue traversing right towards an obvious spike. Climb the spike and the slab above.

The Barber   36 metres   E4   (1983)
A flanking attack on the unprotected upper wall. Start just right of *Finesse*, below and left of an obvious rightward-slanting crack (*Sloe Steel*).
1 18m. 5b. Climb the flake crack just left of *Sloe Steel* and continue direct to the ledge of *Finesse*.
2 18m. 5c. Climb up and then left across the steep scoop to the left of the ledge, and continue across the unprotected upper wall to cross *The Baldest*.

The Barbary Coast   66 metres   E3 5c   (9.87)
An imaginative right-to-left traverse of the upper section of the Main Face. Bold on the second pitch. Start as for *The Barber*.

1 18m. 5b. Start up the flake crack of *The Barber* and continue along the rising diagonal crack to the break of *Supercruise*.
2 24m. 5c. Move up for a metre (a cam higher in the break is useful). Make a rising leftwards traverse across the smooth unprotected upper wall to cross *The Baldest* and *Chlorophyll Cluster* and belay in a niche 3 metres beyond the crackline of the latter.
3 24m. Descend the groove directly below, and traverse horizontally leftwards to finish either up the final crack of *Chicory Chock* or to its right.

Sloe Steel   12 metres   Very Severe 5a   (28.3.70)
Start below and left of an obvious rightward-slanting crack. Quite intense for the grade, but pleasant. Climb the slanting crack until below a final, deeper crack. Make a long reach up left to a good flake. Move up onto the flake and finish direct.

Mushroom Medley   12 metres   Very Difficult   (14.4.69)
The line of steps in the right-hand side of the cliff leads to a flat, broken area below the narrow chimney of *Broccoli Bucket* pitch 2.

Broccoli Bucket (22 metres Very Difficult 13.4.69) is a line up the right-hand bounding gully of the main face with a scrappy first pitch leading to the flat broken area. Pitch 2 takes the narrow chimney on the left.

Cat Follows Mouse   30 metres   Very Severe   (1991)
Start below the rounded cracks right of *Broccoli Bucket*.
1 20m. 4c. Climb the rounded cracks (quite hard) and then scramble over easy ground to the upper tier just right of the chimney of *Broccoli Bucket*.
2 10m. 4a. Climb the corner above to an awkward move through a neck.

Suede Squeeze   12 metres   Severe 4a   (19.4.69)
Start on the upper terrace to the right of the main face and just right of the second pitch of *Broccoli Bucket*. Climb the cracked wall to a harder exit through the neck, as for the previous route.

Loytering   22 metres   E1 5c   (10.90)
To the right of the *Broccoli Bucket* chimney is a buttress with a prominent flake rising for about 6 metres. Climb the wall left of the flake, trending right and then back left, to a diagonal fault. Step left and climb the obvious crack to the top.

With Intent   12 metres   Hard Very Severe 5a †   (3.92)
Climb the bottomless off-width crack on the right of the face.

Sing Fling   10 metres   E4 5c †   (27.11.94)
Climb the crack just right of the off-width crack, cross the left-hand side of the overhang, and finish up the arête on the right.

Diocese (VS), Chair Ladder
Climbers: Rob Smith (main) and Steve Bunston (inset)
Photo: David Wilkinson

Bishops Rib (E1), Chair Ladder
Climber: Jim Rubery Photo: Chris Craggs

Eastern Buttresses

A number of pitches and pegged lines were climbed on the buttresses and pinnacles east of the Main Face in the late 60s, and several good pitches have been added since. The first of these is on the dome-shaped undercut buttress up to the right of the eastern end of the Main Face and just above and to the left (facing in) of the Jammed Block Pinnacle.

Rainbow Buttress

Monochrome Men   20 metres   E1 5b   (18.3.90)

A fine, open pitch. Start from a cramped ledge a few metres up the left side of the buttress. Climb overhanging cracks leading up and right onto the face to reach easier-angled but still steep rock. Follow the thin crack and then step right to a wider crack, which is climbed to finish.

Scarlet Women   20 metres   E1 5c   (16.4.90)

A fitting partner for the Men. Start up *Monochrome Men*'s overhanging cracks, move rightwards for 5 metres, and follow the crack leading up to the right.

Variation Start E2 5c (28.3.92). Start below the undercut centre of the face. Climb flakes to bigger holds at 6 metres and follow the upper crack.

Jammed Block Pinnacle

The Flying Fakir   12 metres   E2 6a   (16.6.91)

A tough line up the west face of the Jammed Block Pinnacle. Pull over a bulge and then make hard moves trending right to reach the arête at 5 metres. Move up to the start of the obvious crack and follow it to its top. A harder variation climbs the wall direct using a short crack at half height (E3 6a 28.3.92).

Raindance   15 metres   E1 5c   (16.4.90)

From the left base of the seaward face of the Jammed Block Pinnacle, climb a difficult groove to better holds. Move up left and follow a steep crack to finish.

Erectile Zone   20 metres   E3 6a †   (11.12.94)

Start beneath the seaward face of the pinnacle. Climb up to a distinctive knob and move right to place *RPs*. Move left and then right up a crack and continue straight to the top.

Ten metres to the right of the Jammed Block Pinnacle, and on the same level, is another small buttress crowned with a square-cut boulder.

Slapstick   12 metres   E3 6b   (28.4.91)

Climb the strenuous but well-protected crack that splits the side-wall of the buttress.

Margin   12 metres   E1   5c   (7.4.91)
At least it has a grassy landing! The left arête of the front face is climbed
on the left to a jug at 6 metres. Move onto the front face to finish.

Ibis   12 metres   E1   5c   (6.5.90)
Climb the thin crack near the left edge of the face, transfer strenuously to
the right-hand crack, and climb it to the top.

On the same level as the top of this buttress but 20 metres further right is a
short steep slab with a thin, short-lived flake in the middle.

Ripple Blocker   8 metres   Hard Very Severe   6a   (10.8.96)
Climb the left-hand side of the slab to a horizontal break and the top.

High up to the right of the Jammed Block Pinnacle is a small isolated
buttress.

Foxbite   12 metres   Very Severe   5a   (20.5.90)
Climb the slanting crack in the face of the buttress, moving right at
two-thirds height to finish direct.

Rabid   12 metres   Hard Very Severe   5c   (6.93)
Just right of the slanting crack is an edge leading to a flat-topped flake.
Make technical moves to the flake and follow a crack to the top.

Gloy Buttress

The following climbs are on a sturdy little buttress about 100 metres east and
slightly below the Jammed Block Pinnacle. On the west-facing wall are two
good cracklines.

Yardang   12 metres   Very Severe   5a   (1.4.90)
Neat climbing up the left-hand crack after a difficult but interesting start.

Sulcus   12 metres   Very Severe   5a   (18.3.90)
The right-hand crack. Fine climbing to match *Yardang*.

Just right of the previous routes is a distinctive corner with an impending left
wall containing a rust-stained crack. This gave the line of **Gloy** (A2 1.1.70).

Cenopod Corner   12 metres   Hard Severe   4b   (25.1.70)
A good strenuous pitch up the corner-crack.
Variation Very Severe 5a (8.4.90). Climb the corner to where a move left
can be made onto a sloping ledge on the left wall. Finish up the thin crack
above.

Tingaloy   12 metres   Hard Severe   4b   (1.3.70)
Just right of the corner is a thin crack, which is followed to the top.

Test Piece Buttress

Above and to the right of Gloy Buttress is a long 15-metre wall with a distinctive shallow corner leading to an overhang. There are three good pitches here.

★Sabre Dance 12 metres E1 5c (8.4.90)

Intense, technical climbing up the thin twisting crackline in the wall to the left of the shallow corner.

★Test Piece 13 metres E2 5c (8.4.90)

An absorbing pitch; climb the shallow corner to the roof, which is cleared by strenuous laybacking.

Smear Fear 13 metres E2 5c (6.90)

Climb the slight arête 3 metres right of *Test Piece* to a flake. Make difficult moves to stand on the flake and climb the smooth wall above.

About 200 metres east of the Eastern Buttresses there is a small offshore island accessible at low tide. A short route goes up the seaward face of the island.

Fluke 15 metres Very Severe 5a (16.9.90)

Climb a chimney to a roof; then move out and up to the left to reach a triangular shelf. Finish up the right-hand of the V-cracks above.

Boscawen Point (Granite) OS Ref 431 229

Outlook: South.
Non-tidal.
Coastguard Identity: Boscawen Point.

Boscawen Point lies just east of St Loy Bay, which is reputed to be the warmest place in England. The outlook is magnificent, with views westward to Logan Rock. Rock formations and small buttresses of good granite offer bouldering potential while there are some worthwhile longer pitches on a central wall.

The route names reflected the black and brave humour of the principal first ascensionist, who made the ascents between bouts of punishing chemotherapy.

Approach. There is no convenient right-of-way to Boscawen Point from directly inland. The Point can be reached from Lamorna or via the approach from St Loy, although the latter is much longer. Walk west from the car-park at Lamorna for two kilometres. Continue past the top of the entrance steps down to Tater-du Lighthouse and pass a distinctive isolated house with well laid-out gardens on the right. Continue along the coast path for nearly a kilometre to where it rises steeply over slabby rocks. Just beyond here the path levels off where it overlooks St Loy Bay. Turn left off the coast path and go through a low stone wall. Follow an intricate path down past some striking rock formations, including a detached 'Easter Island' pillar/archway, to reach an overgrown depression above a 15-metre wall. (The path becomes heavily vegetated in summer and there are one or two hidden holes underfoot.) The wall is crowned with large blocks, which make ideal belay and abseil points.

Descent. Abseil from blocks or climb down a vegetated break on the right (facing out) beneath a block with two rusty spikes protruding from it, courtesy of 19th century smugglers/fishermen, who quite sensibly believed that the best way to get up and down cliffs was by bolt(ed) ladders. Eat your hearts out, sportsmen!

All the climbs bar one are concentrated on the fine little wall situated below the arrival point. There is also one climb on an independent buttress below and to the right (facing out) of the main wall. The base of the buttress is reached by scrambling down a break on its left-hand side.

★Lucretia   18 metres   Very Severe 5a   (26.4.91)
A fine, exposed pitch. Climb twin cracks into a niche; then make committing layback moves up the final crack.

The main wall offers some short pitches.

Lucylastic   12 metres   Hard Very Severe 5b   (19.5.91)
On the extreme left side of the cliff is a small overhang with a distinctive black knob on the wall above. Start at the base of a rising ramp. Climb diagonally leftwards to the overhang, which is taken direct by bold moves. Move up to the top of the curving flake on the right and finish up a short crack.

Lucy   14 metres   Very Difficult   (15.4.91)
High in the grade. Climb to the obvious leftward-curving flake and gain its crest by bold moves. Finish up a short crack.

Lucozade   14 metres   Hard Severe 4b   (15.4.91)
Climb the crack below a deep upper niche, which is exited by some tricky moves.

By Stealth   15 metres   E4 6b   (4.6.91)
Technical climbing up the smooth wall right of *Lucozade*. Start directly below the wall. Climb for 5 metres and then drift rightwards to fix gear in the crack of *Looking-Glass War*. Move back left onto the face and climb diagonally leftwards; then finish direct by some thin moves.

★Looking-Glass War 15 metres E1 5b (21.4.91)
A pleasant pitch. A thin crackline above a light-brown water-streak splits the upper part of the central wall. Climb small edges leading up from the left to gain the base of the crack and protection possibilities. Climb the crack on good holds.

★Luke Lively 15 metres Very Severe 5a (21.4.91)
This fine, fingery little climb takes the steep crack in the upper part of the face right of the previous route. Start below the light-brown water-streak. Make difficult moves up rightwards over a small overlap to reach the base of the upper crack. Climb direct past a horizontal crack to finish boldly up the wide crack above.

Luke Back in Anger 15 metres Hard Severe 4c (17.4.91)
A slightly contrived line following the left-hand of three cracks that split the face right of *Luke Lively*. Start at the break below and slightly left of the cracks. Climb to a small ledge and then follow the left-hand crack to the top. The harder finishing moves can be avoided by climbing the next crack to the right.

Luke Skywalker 15 metres Severe 4a (21.4.91)
Start as for the previous route. Make a rising rightwards traverse to reach the base of the two right-hand cracks splitting the upper face. Finish up the cracks.

Fluke 15 metres E1 5c (1.8.93)
Start just to the right of the last route below the obvious chicken-heads. Climb straight up past the chicken-heads to a ledge. Make a delicate move out to the right. Climb up, then to a niche, and up easier ground to the top.

★Lord Lucan 15 metres E2 6a (19.5.91)
A pitch of strong character with a hard start. About 5 metres up the right edge of the face is a bottomless slanting crack with two small black edges below it. Thin climbing gains the crack, which is followed to its top. Move left using an undercling to climb the overlap. Finish up the short wall above near its right side. (Side runners on the right are available in the top section.)

Leucal Hero 17 metres Severe 4a (26.4.91)
A worthwhile pitch. Start at the lowest point on the right side of the wall. Climb a flake to a ledge at 3 metres. Continue up cracks; then move left to mantelshelf into a bay. Exit by a tricky move up the crack on the right. A harder direct start can be made to the first ledge.

Tregiffian (Granite)   OS Ref 436 232

Outlook: South.
Tidal at the base of the main slab. Routes on the left-hand side of the cliff (facing in) are also affected by tide but can be reached above their starts by traversing in from the right. The whole area is affected by swell and rough sea.
Coastguard Identity: Tater-du West.

This is a delightful climbing area with a wide selection of short lower-grade routes, especially in Tregiffian Cove itself. The climbing is not strenuous generally, and there is a great deal of enjoyable slab work.

Approach. There is no convenient right-of-way to Tregiffian Cove from directly inland. The Cove can be reached from Lamorna or via the approach from St Loy, although the latter is much longer. Walk west from the car-park at Lamorna for two kilometres. Continue past the top of the entrance steps down to Tater-du Lighthouse and pass a distinctive isolated house with well laid-out gardens on the right.

Continue along the coast path for 100 metres to where an indistinct path goes off left into an overgrown meadow. In summer there can be a lot of nettles here – bare legs, beware. The meadow is flanked by a granite wall with a fringe of elder trees. Follow the path alongside the wall to cross a low wall onto the open cliff. Caution underfoot: there are nasty holes. Tregiffian Cove with its central sweep of slabs is directly below. Veer down right to a boulder ridge that runs to seaward.

To the west of Tregiffian Cove and separated from it by the boulder ridge is Union Star Cove. This was where the Penlee (Mousehole) lifeboat, *The Solomon Browne*, was lost with all hands in December 1981 during an astonishingly courageous bid to rescue the crew of the coaster *Union Star*. The coaster had been driven ashore in savage south-easterly gales gusting to Force 12. All eight aboard the *Union Star*, including two children, were also lost. At dead low tide and in calm weather, the boulder-strewn bed of the cove is smothered with blood-red seaweed and still meshed with the torn and twisted wreckage of the *Union Star*. Climbs have been recorded here.

Union Star Cove
Descent is by scrambling down the western side of the boulder ridge and then traversing back into the cove at sea-level, or by climbing down at various other points.

Wind in the Willows   25 metres   E4 6a †   (10.97)
Serious. Right at the back of the cove is a pillar with a crack running leftwards up it. Climb the crack and the wall above, placing plenty of gear

before the 'false summit'. Continue with difficulty up 3 metres of vertical earth. Belay on bushes before escaping along animal runs in the thick gorse.

The following routes lie on the inner walls of the broken, west-facing wall of the cove. A distinctive mark is a black quartz-tourmaline vein in the shape of an arrow.

Black Adder   15 metres   Very Severe 4c †   (1986)
Climb the quartz-streaked wall direct.

Fish out of Water   12 metres   Hard Very Severe 5a †   (1986)
Climb the deep hanging chimney 6 metres to the right of *Black Adder*.

Black Adder II   15 metres   Very Severe 4c †   (1986)
Start 3 metres right of the previous route. Climb the rightward-leaning corner crack.

After Burner   25 metres   E1 5b †   (1986)
Climb strenuously up a black-marked hanging arête to a ledge at 5 metres, before traversing round into a deep niche to finish up an overhanging corner.

The following routes are on a level above and to the right of the first four. They start from a sloping ledge below a steep wall split by good cracks. The starts are above high-tide level but may be affected by swell or rough sea.

Eliminator   20 metres   Very Severe 4c   (1986)
Climb the diagonal cracks at the left edge of the wall.

Stone   20 metres   Very Severe 4c   (1986)
Climb the vertical crack to the overhang, traverse left, and finish upwards. The direct finish is 5a.

Hail   20 metres   E2 5c   (1986)
The crack on the right of the wall is at the top of its grade.

14 Lives, 13 Souls   20 metres   E7 6c †   (24.3.96)
The central line up the steep slab right of *Hail* was climbed with preplaced protection.

Tregiffian Cove
Descend by scrambling half-way down the boulder ridge on the western side of the cove and traversing back east through a remarkable wave-sculpted cave, which is part of a raised beach. More scrambling leads to the base of the cove.

The main feature of the cove is a handsome 20-metre sweep of slab, flanked on its right by a buttress jutting out to sea. To the left of the slab is a break with a wide green streak of water-weed running down the upper cliff, just right of a shield of black rock. Left again is a series of leftward-leaning arêtes, slabs, and cracks terminating in a shallow recessed zawn.

The first climb is on the west wall of the cove and to seaward of the through-cave on the descent. A narrow black vein runs up the wall from a wide ledge into a triangular-shaped niche. Below and to the right of this is a 6-metre groove.

Prior Claim 20 metres Severe 4a   (10.6.90)
Start at the base of the groove and climb to the wide ledge. Move left, gain the niche via a rightward-slanting crack, and follow its continuation out of the niche. A considerably harder entry to the niche can be made up the black vein on the right.

The recessed zawn at the back left-hand side of the cove has a distinctive black vein which runs in a zigzag and X-shape through the granite. The following route starts up the left leg of the vein at the entrance to the zawn.

Thea 17 metres Severe 4a   (6.5.90)
[Photo p.272b.] Climb the black vein to an awkward step left. Follow the pleasant slab above on good holds to belay on the pinnacle. Scramble through blocks to finish.

Sleeping Chimney 18 metres Difficult   (24.10.87)
At the back of the recessed zawn above a pointed boulder is an obvious chimney crack, which is climbed direct.

Exit 25 metres Very Difficult   (3.5.83)
A pitch centred on the junction of the distinctive black veins. Start to the right of the right-hand edge of the recessed zawn and climb a nose to a platform below a black wall. Move left and traverse to the junction of two black veins. Follow the vein running vertically up the arête above.
Variation Hard Severe 4b. From the vertical black vein, finish up to the left.

Scab 15 metres Hard Very Severe 5a   (11.7.90)
The result of a powerful rockfall. A good line, but care is advised owing to some shaky rock. Start below a curving groove below a gritty orange wall to the right of the arête of *Exit*. Climb the lower groove and then make harder moves into the final groove to finish. Cams and large hexes useful.

★Acid Test 18 metres Very Severe 4c   (30.3.86)
A fine, stylish pitch up the clean wall right of the groove of *Scab*. Climb the crack running up the wall; then move right where the crack ends at a wide black vein.

Little Frankie   18 metres   Very Difficult   (10.6.90)
Climb the leftward-leaning, wide break parallel to and 5 metres right of
Acid Test.

The next feature is the smooth, cupped slab taken by *Gravity Slab*, flanked
on its left by an arête and groove running up to a small overhang.

Anaphylactic Reaction   15 metres   Very Severe 5a   (7.6.96)
Climb the sharp arête left of *Gravity Slab* direct from its cut-away base.
Climb the easy wall above.

Gravity Slab   15 metres   Very Severe 4c   (26.8.87)
Good, delicate climbing up the slab and shallow corner to the roof, where
a thin traverse right gains the easy upper slab.
Variation 4c. Instead of traversing right at the top of the shallow corner,
climb straight over the roof to gain the upper slab.

Deception Groove   12 metres   Severe   (8.7.87)
Just round to the right from *Gravity Slab* is a deep break with a broad
streak of green weed running down the upper wall. The deep groove on
the outside edge of the left wall of the break is climbed to a finish up slabs.

Green Streaks   30 metres   Very Severe   (1.10.88)
Aptly-named, with a good first pitch. Start at the left edge of the main slab,
just right of a pool.
1 15m. 4c. Climb a thin leftward-trending crack to the edge of the slab,
and then go up steeply to a large ledge.
2 15m. Step up and traverse easily left, crossing the green streak, to the
corner below the shield of black rock. Move up right and follow the dark
groove to finish on shaky rock.
Variation 12 metres Very Difficult. Pitch 1 can be avoided by climbing the
gully to the left of the slabs to reach the end of the traverse on pitch 2.

Famished Five   20 metres   Very Severe 5a   (5.9.93)
Start from the base of *Green Streaks*. Climb directly up the slab to a ledge.
Continue up a narrow seam (thin) to join *Loose Limpet Crack* where that
route moves left. Climb a short wall to a large ledge and finish up the wall
above.

The main slab is criss-crossed with several pleasant lines. The first few moves
of the slab may be coated with seaweed at times. Improves footwork.

Zebra   27 metres   Very Severe 4c   (29.8.87)
Delicate climbing. Start 2 metres right of *Green Streaks* and follow a
tenuous rightward-rising line to cross deep cracks. Finish direct on good
holds.

Little Bear I Do Love Thee of Esmaduna
                               20 metres   Very Difficult   (2.4.83)
Great name: more substantial than the climb, which is nevertheless
pleasant after a deceptively hard start. Start 5 metres right of *Green
Streaks* at a slanting crack. Climb the crack for 8 metres and move around
a bulge to a small ledge. Continue up a cracked wall to a large ledge.

Jeans Genius   27 metres   Very Severe 4c   (29.8.87)
Delicate climbing. Start about 2 metres right of the crack of *Little Bear...* at
the left end of a tidal pool. Take a rightward-rising line to follow a thin vein
across deeper cracks and finish up flakes at the top right-hand corner of
the main slab.

★Loose Limpet Crack   27 metres   Hard Severe 4b   (12.7.87)
An engaging line. Step across the tidal pool to gain the leftward-sloping
crack, preferably with dry feet. Climb the crack to a point just before it
peters out and step right into a higher crack. Continue up this for 2 metres
to a junction with a deeper crack. Gain the beginning of a crack on the left
by a high approach or by a more difficult lower move, and then follow it to
a ledge. Finish up a cracked wall on the left.

At the right-hand end of the main slab is a deep cleft formed between the
slab and a blocky buttress lying to seaward. The following routes start from
the foot of the cleft.

★Solomon Browne   27 metres   Very Difficult   (2.4.83)
Another pleasant pitch. Start at the foot of the cleft. Take the good crack
leading diagonally left for 5 metres; then gain a ledge on the right. Move
back into the crack and step into the second crack on the left, which leads
to a ledge. Follow the line of knobs straight up the block above.

Direct Approach   20 metres   Very Severe 4c   (24.10.87)
From the foot of the cleft, climb a thin vertical crack, move slightly left, and
then finish up the steep, sharp crackline in the wall above.

The Great Gonzo   20 metres   Very Difficult   (3.4.83)
Good steady climbing. Go up the cleft to a small flake ledge on the slab
on the left. Continue up flakes above via ledges to a platform. Finish up
the short corner above.

Down Under   20 metres   Hard Severe 4b   (2.4.83)
Climb the cleft for 3 metres and then move onto the main slab. Traverse
diagonally rightwards along thin cracks and flakes, finishing direct on
small holds to reach a large ledge.

Not Quite So Ordinary Route   12 metres   Difficult   (8.7.87)
The narrow buttress immediately right of the cleft is climbed direct to the
top via a crack and slab.

On the front face of the blocky buttress right of the cleft is an obvious left-trending ramp above a very deep and tempting natural swimming-pool.

All the Fours   18 metres   Hard Severe 4b   (24.10.87)
Climb the left-trending ramp to a ledge at half height; then move out right onto a short slab and cross it towards a recess. Step down from the edge of the slab into the recess and climb a groove to finish.

Tater-du (Greenstone)   OS Ref 439 231

Outlook: South.
Tidal at the base of the Main Face and in the Sentry-Box area. Accessible for three hours either side of low water. Wave-washed by swell and rough seas.
Non-tidal in the *Gully Route* area, while most second pitches on the Main Face can be easily reached by a mid-height traverse at Difficult standard.
Coastguard Identity: Tater-du.
Environmental Issues: SSSI. There are good crevice plant communities here, some wet flushes, and lichen cover on the upper walls, so tread (and climb) carefully. Although there is no formal restriction, protected birds nest in the area and climbers are asked to avoid climbing here during the nesting season.

Tater-du is the only greenstone cliff on Penwith's south coast; a cool relief after all those miles of sun-baked granite. It has a long and firmly established tradition of climbing and was a great favourite of the Marines and Commando Cliff Assault Wing, who pioneered many of the routes in the Fifties and left their mark in name also. The climbing is generous, with most routes at the middle grades, although several hard pitches are concentrated in the Lamorna Wall area. Tater-du can be a splendid sun-trap. The rock is more solid than killas and there are excellent belays and adequate protection.

An unexpected and startling intrusion at Tater-du can be the sudden ear-shattering fog-horn blasts from the nearby lighthouse, which is automatically controlled. The fog-horn is sometimes activated even in clear weather and the decibel count from its seventy-odd speakers can be diverting, especially on crux moves.

Approach. The cliff lies to the west of Lamorna Cove (OS Ref 450 238), where there is good car-parking, although the cove is extremely busy at the height of the season. From Lamorna, two kilometres of coastal path lead pleasantly, if a little steeply in places, to a point above the cliff. Approach can also be made via St Loy but this is substantially longer than the Lamorna approach. There is no right-of-way to Tater-du from any convenient point inland. The cliff lies just west of the lighthouse.

LAMORNA : TATER DU

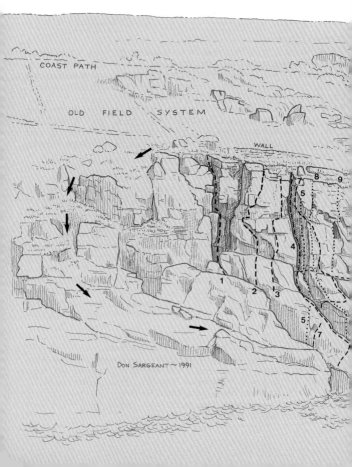

DON SARGEANT ~ 1991

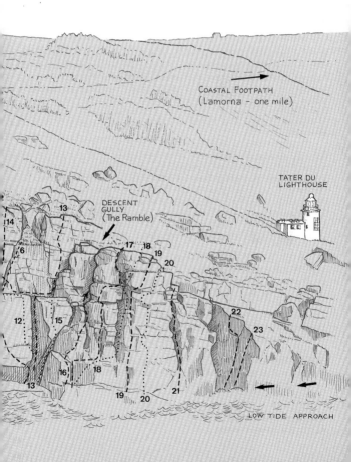

Descent. The convenient way to the cliff down the approach steps to the unmanned lighthouse is not allowed, so continue west and upwards along the coast path for 200 metres. Grassy slopes followed by a series of rocky steps lead down leftwards to a large tidal platform below the Main Face. Once one is established on the cliff, other lines of descent are traditionally available.

Routes at the shorter, eastern end of Tater-du can be reached from the top of the cliff just west of the lighthouse by walking down the substantial ledges that run to the sea below the lighthouse. From the base of the ledges just above sea-level, a traverse westwards over barnacle-encrusted tidal rocks gives access to the *Dorna* and *The Sentry-Box* area. This approach also leads on to beneath the Main Face but is tidal and subject to swell. It should be treated with care.

A more convenient descent to the base of the Main Face is by a wide gully with some jammed blocks that lies just west of the lighthouse. The gully leads to a wide ledge, the narrow continuation of which (*Western National*) runs right across the Main Face at half height. From the wide ledge, a descent at about Difficult standard of an easy-angled buttress (the first pitch of *The Ramble*) leads to the large tidal platform at the base of the Main Face. This platform is accessible for three hours either side of low water when there is no swell.

Tater-du develops in height from left to right (facing in). Up on the left, above a series of leftward-leading stepped ledges known as The Gangway, are three short routes. Right of these is the first substantial buttress flanked by the distinctive *Gully Route*. Right again lies the impressive Main Face, the left flank of which is taken by the *Crow's Nest* routes. The lower half of the Main Face is made up of a jet-black undercut wall which is bounded on its right by the corner/chimney of *Eric's Route*. The Main Face is broken at half height by a line of ledges, which is followed by *Western National*.

At right-angles to the Main Face, and separated from it by the descent gully and the lower slab of *The Ramble*, is a steep, narrow buttress with blocky overhangs which *Willie's Way* runs up direct. The cliff then turns east across the wall of *The Sentry-Box* and ends at the west-facing *Dorna* wall.

The first three routes high on the left of the cliff are all near an obvious corner between two black walls. The left wall overhangs a little, and further left the wall becomes more broken and grassy.

Sitting Tenant   18 metres   Very Difficult   (2.5.83)
Left of the overhanging wall is a leaning buttress, to the left of which is a distinct groove. From below the groove, follow a zigzag line up ledges to the top.

Sitting Comfortably   12 metres   Difficult   (2.5.83)
Climb the obvious corner.

Taking It Easy 15 metres Hard Severe 4b (2.4.83)
Start at the right edge of the right wall. Climb diagonally left into the centre of the wall. Move up to a horizontal break; then climb up to the roof and through at the obvious gap. A vegetated groove leads to the top.

Bedrock Chimney 23 metres Very Difficult (9.9.73)
The first substantial buttress left of the Main Face is flanked on its left by a chimney which is capped by an overhang. Climb the chimney for 5 metres to where a chimney on the left can be climbed to a large ledge. Continue up the chimney above and finish up the steep wall keeping left.

Knight's Move 24 metres Very Severe 4c (30.8.88)
Climb *Knight's Pillar* for about 8 metres. Traverse left onto the left wall and make a right-to-left rising traverse to the top.

Knight's Pillar 20 metres Very Severe 4c (11.60)
Start above a sentry-box below the left edge of the buttress. Climb a short corner and traverse left across a groove to a slight rib. Follow the rib to a ledge and climb the nose above by the groove on its left.
Direct Finish
Checkmate 20 metres Hard Very Severe 5a † (1995)
Climb the short corner and continue straight up to the top.

Just Du It 20 metres Very Severe 4c (1985)
Climb the wall between *Knight's Pillar* and *Pericles*.

Pericles 20 metres Hard Very Severe 5a (8.79)
Pleasant climbing up cracks in the centre of the buttress. Follow the cracks to a good ledge; then move right and climb direct to the top.

Lysander 43 metres E1 5b (8.79)
A fine upper section. Start below a short steep wall to the left of The Gangway. Climb directly up the wall to a ledge. Move left for 5 metres; then take the steep wall just right of *Gully Route* on satisfying holds.

Western National 36 metres Difficult (1950s)
An exposed but easy traverse along the ledge-system which runs across the Main Face at half height. It finishes on the large ledge below the wide gully used as an easy way down from the east. Start half-way up the left side of the Main Face below the start of *Gully Route*'s second pitch.
1 18m. Move right onto the face and continue easily along the broad ledge to belay in a recess at the foot of a chimney in the centre of the face.
2 18m. Continue pleasantly along the ledges to the foot of a deep slanting groove. Traverse right in the same line to the large ledge at the foot of the broad gully, which leads to the top. A more interesting finish is to climb the deep slanting groove.

A series of ledges runs diagonally leftwards up the lower left flank of the Main Face. This is The Gangway, the start of which provides a reference point for several of the following routes.

★Commando Special   35 metres   Very Severe   (1950s)
A nicely exposed route with a good top pitch to the right of the Crow's Nest routes. Start 10 metres to the left of the start of The Gangway.
1 20m. Climb the short wall on good holds to The Gangway; then move right and climb the slab to the broad ledge of *Western National*.
2 15m. 4c. Climb the corner above to an overhang, where a bold swing right leads to a large ledge. Climb the wall above to finish.

Rook's Folly   35 metres   Hard Very Severe 5a †   (1979)
Start just left of the base of The Gangway. Climb onto The Gangway and up the steep, fingery wall, just left of *Crow's Nest Direct*, to a belay on the ledge of *Western National*. Climb the wall above, move leftwards between the roofs near the top of the cliff, and finish straight up.

★Crow's Nest Ordinary   48 metres   Hard Severe   (1950s)
A fine, exposed climb up the left side of the Main Face. Start below a short wall just to the left of the start of The Gangway.
1 24m. Climb the wall and then follow The Gangway left to climb a break leading onto the slab. Climb the slab to the broad ledge of *Western National*.
2 24m. 4b. Climb diagonally left to a hollow on the edge of the face and traverse left around the edge on good holds. Make an exposed step left; then climb the steep wall above on juggy holds.

Gully Route   38 metres   Severe   (1950s)
Start at the foot of The Gangway.
1 20m. Follow The Gangway to the foot of the gully.
2 18m. 4a. Climb a chimney for a few moves; then make quite an awkward move left to climb the rib into the gully. Move left again and climb the edge to the top.

★Crow's Nest Direct   37 metres   Hard Very Severe   (6.11.62)
Bold and exposed. Start at the foot of The Gangway.
1 20m. 5b. Climb easily onto The Gangway; then climb the overhanging wall left of the arête on fingery holds and mantelshelf onto a ledge. Continue more easily up the arête to the broad ledge of *Western National*.
2 17m. 4b. Climb to the hollow on the left edge of the face as for *Crow's Nest Ordinary*; then bridge up to make a very exposed move to the right by mantelshelfing into a recess, which leads to the top.

The following routes start from a low wave-worn ledge with two rock-pools on it.

★Martell Slab   48 metres   Very Severe   (1957)

Full of character, with a fine first pitch and an exhilarating optional finish. Start behind the left-hand rock-pool, below the slabby wall at the left end of the undercut section of the Main Face.

1 20m. 4c. Top end of the grade and sustained. Climb an awkward scoop and slab into a depression below the upper slab. Either make a long step left and then move up to a slanting crack, or climb direct for a metre or so and then move left to the slanting crack. Climb the centre of the slab to just below its top. Step up right to make a balancy move across left, using good holds in the short wall above to gain a fine stance and belay.

2 10m. Climb easily to the ledge-system of *Western National* and move right a short distance to a distinctive recess below a steep chimney.

3 18m. 4b. Climb the chimney; then trend up and left to climb a corner-crack leading to an overhang. Turn this airily on its left and finish direct.

Variations

1a Superdirect 18m. E1 5a †. Start behind the left-hand rock-pool at a low-level short wide crack. Climb boldly up to join the parent route below the diagonal crack.

1b Direct 18m. E1 5a. Start behind the left-hand rock-pool beneath a nose at 3 metres. Gain a scoop on the left-hand side of the undercut slab and move up to join the parent route.

2a 18 metres E1 5a (8.79). Strenuous, with healthy exposure. Climb directly from the belay at the end of the first pitch to a roof. Pull up into a groove and follow it to the top.

Martell Groove   20 metres   Hard Very Severe 4c

Follow *Martell Slab* to the depression and continue up the corner above to belay as for that route.

★The Tram Line   35 metres   E2   (15.9.91)

Two good contrasting pitches.

1 15m. 5c. Sparse protection. Start from the block below *Lamorna Wall* and above the tidal pool. Gain a small niche on the arête at 2 metres by climbing a diagonal crackline. Make hard moves up and left on small holds to gain the horizontal break. Continue up and leftwards across the wall on better holds to a good stance on the lip of the overhang.

2 20m. 4c. Climb directly to the ledge-system of *Western National* by the corner on the left of the huge rib. Continue direct to make exhilarating moves through small roofs. Pass a large hole; then climb vertical cracks and make exposed moves up and left to clear an overhang.

★Lamorna Wall   37 metres   E2   (6.59/1978)

Sustained and steep on the first pitch. Start on the block below the corner/chimney at the right-hand end of the Main Face.

1 20m. 5c. Climb leftwards from the foot of the chimney to the overhang, which is cleared by hard moves to gain a small ledge. Climb direct to the half-way ledge and a recess below a steep chimney.

2 17m. Move right for a metre or so and climb the wall to a good ledge. Finish up the lichen-covered face above.

Variations

1a 23m. Hard Very Severe 5a (1976). Climb *Martell Slab* to the depression below the upper slab; then traverse right strenuously along a break in the overhangs to gain a good ledge on the arête. Continue to the half-way ledge.

1b The Water Margin 20m. E4 6b (4.5.87). A steep, strenuous line that starts at a thin rightward-slanting crack just left of the right-hand rock-pool. Climb the crack and the leftward-curving flake above before climbing leftwards to the ledge as for *The Tram Line*.

1c 20m. Hard Very Severe 5a (1976). Climb the original line to the overhang; then continue traversing left below the overhang to a foothold. Climb direct to join pitch 1a.

The Veil   42 metres   E1   (11.60)
A steep second pitch, where protection is sparse. Start below the corner/chimney at the right-hand end of the Main Face.
1 10m. *Eric's Route* pitch 1.
2 15m. 5a. Make a few moves up the chimney and traverse left for 2 metres. Climb the steep wall direct on small holds to the half-way ledge and belay just to the left of a slanting groove.
3 17m. 4b. Climb straight up the wall above.
Direct Start E1 5b (8.84). Climb direct to join pitch 2, starting 3 metres out from the chimney.

Eric's Route   39 metres   Very Difficult   (1950s)
An open, generous route taking the corner/chimney on the right of the Main Face and then the steep wall above. Start below the corner/chimney.
1 10m. Climb easily to the foot of the chimney.
2 12m. Continue up the chimney to the large ledge at the end of the *Western National* traverse.
3 17m. Walk across the ledge to the foot of the reddish wall tucked in on the left. The wall can be started on either the left or the right, the former being slightly harder. Keep to the left until a ledge is reached; then go diagonally right, past a niche, to the top.

The Rabbit Run   30 metres   Very Difficult   (1950s)
An exposed but technically easy climb, which starts on the ledge at the end of the *Western National* traverse. The start can be reached by descending the broad gully at the east end of the Main Face.
1 18m. Traverse left along the ledge to reach a short chimney. Climb the chimney and step left across a deep slanting groove. Move up to a belay in the corner.
2 12m. Move right and climb a short corner to a ledge. Finish direct.

Fat Panda 20 metres Severe 4a (25.4.81)
A few metres right of the initial corner of *Eric's Route* is a deeper chimney.
Start below the square-cut groove in the left wall of the chimney. Climb the
groove to a ledge; then finish up the arête on the left.

The Ramble 34 metres Very Difficult (1950s)
Start at the base of the easy-angled buttress right of *Fat Panda*.
1 20m. Climb the left edge of the buttress to the large ledge at the foot of
the wide gully.
2 14m. From the foot of the gully, step right, and climb the shallow
chimney to the top.

The next two climbs lie on the steep buttress right of the easy-angled buttress
taken by *The Ramble*.

★Willie's Way 31 metres Hard Very Severe (6.60)
A direct line with a tough third pitch. Start below the left-hand side of the
buttress below a slab. There is a corner on the left capped by an
overhang.
1 10m. Climb the corner to a ledge, move up, and traverse right between
two large overhangs to a belay.
2 14m. 4a. Climb the wall directly above the belay to a good ledge.
Continue over the small overhang above to a large ledge at the foot of an
undercut V-chimney.
3 7m. 5a. Climb the chimney, with some difficult moves, to finish over
blocks.

Bus Route 34 metres Very Difficult (1950s)
Start as for *Willie's Way*.
1 20m. Traverse right across a slab below the small overhang to a
shallow chimney. Climb the chimney to a belay in a good niche.
2 6m. Move right onto the protruding block; then traverse back left over it
to a large corner ledge. Belay below the undercut chimney of *Willie's Way*.
3 8m. Climb the short slab on the right to the top.

The following two routes take the arêtes either side of the chimney of *Bus
Route*.

Flaky Wall 30 metres Very Severe † (1995)
1 20m. 4a. Start 2 metres right of *Bus Route*, at the right-hand side of the
slab. Climb the left-hand side of the arête above and belay in a niche.
2 10m. 4c. Climb up and then leftwards, and cross the blocky overhang
to gain the top.

Raven's Nest Direct 30 metres E1 † (1995)
1 18m. Climb a short wall to the blunt right-hand arête of the *Bus Route*
chimney, and follow the arête to a small ledge.
2 12m. 5b. Climb straight up through overhangs to the top.

Marine Parade   27 metres   Very Difficult   (1950s)
Start below the right side of the steep buttress, at the foot of a small groove
capped by an overhang. Climb the groove, surmount the overhang, and
continue up a rib to a ledge below the final overhangs. Move right through
the overhang and climb easily to the top.

Up to the right of the starting point for the previous routes is a broad ledge
with a 12-metre corner above its right end, which gives *Pregnant Pause*. The
west-facing wall beyond is taken by *Dorna*.

Final Touch   25 metres   Hard Very Severe 5a †   (1995)
Start at the left-hand end of the ledge. Climb up, pass to the left of an
overhang at 5 metres, and continue up to the right side of the roof above.
Cross the roof and gain the top.

★**The Sentry-box**   24 metres   Severe   (1950s)
A neat little climb with good moves. Start in the middle of the broad ledge.
Climb a steep wall to enter the 'Sentry-box'. Exit more easily to the right before
traversing left and climbing through the overhang to finish up an easier groove.

Pregnant Pause   20 metres   Severe   (7.12.80)
Climb the 12-metre corner past a square overhang to just below a large
ledge (belay possible). Move left for a metre or so above the large overhang
and make an exposed move into the hanging groove on the left to finish.

Dorna   18 metres   Hard Severe 4b   (1950s)
A persuasive pitch. Start below a crack running up the centre of the
west-facing wall to the right of the previous routes. Climb the crack on
good holds and move left onto a ledge. Traverse left under the overhang
for 3 metres and finish up the steep wall above by mantelshelf moves.
Alternatively, instead of traversing, crack-climb direct at the same grade.

Head Hunter   18 metres   E1 5a   (8.84)
Climb straight up the unprotected wall right of *Dorna*.

Andy's Route   18 metres   Hard Very Severe 4c   (20.4.81)
Climb the crackline near the right edge of the wall. Slight gear.

Lamorna Cove (Granite)   OS Ref 450 240
At Lamorna Cove there is one recorded route on the quarried rock lying just
above the coast path to the west of the car-park.

Cardiac Arête   40 metres   E2 5a   (18.10.89)
Climb the obvious prow of rock on the lower left-hand side of the upper
amphitheatre.

The quarry to the east of the cove is a sensitive wildlife habitat that is monitored
by the Cornish Wildlife Trust, who request that no climbing takes place there.

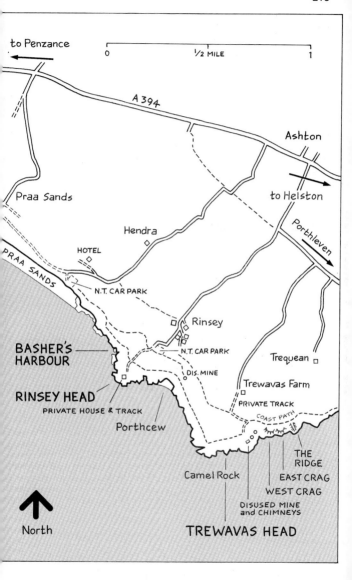

to Penzance

0   ½ MILE   1

A 394

Ashton

to Helston

Porthleven

Praa Sands

Hendra

HOTEL

N.T. CAR PARK

PRAA SANDS

Rinsey

N.T. CAR PARK

BASHER'S HARBOUR

DIS. MINE

Trequean

Trewavas Farm

PRIVATE TRACK

COAST PATH

RINSEY HEAD

PRIVATE HOUSE & TRACK

Porthcew

THE RIDGE

EAST CRAG

WEST CRAG

Camel Rock

DISUSED MINE and CHIMNEYS

North

TREWAVAS HEAD

Trewavas Area

'Beware Adders.' (Sign next to approach path)

The stretch of coastline from Basher's Harbour to Trewavas Main Cliff is formed by the Tregonning granite, a small granite body which is separate from the Land's End granite. The rock is finer-grained and more compact than most of the Land's End granite. The area remains emphatically Penwithian in style, however. The area, particularly Trewavas Main Cliff, has long been a favourite with locals; as with Culdrose trainee pilots who do impressive things with Sea Kings along the cliff-edges outside the climbing area.

Basher's Harbour (Granite) OS Ref 588 272

Outlook: South-west.
Tidal throughout. Accessible for about three hours either side of low water. **The flood tide works rapidly here** and can cut off the base of the main area of cliff with impressive speed. Escape back west to Praa Sands is also a diminishing option as the flood increases. The whole area is affected by swell and rough sea.
Coastguard Identity: Rinsey Head.
Access Advice: Basher's Harbour lies just to the west of the distinctive Rinsey Head with its solitary cliff-top house. The area of cliff which includes Basher's Harbour, Rinsey Head and Rinsey Zawn is privately owned. The owners are happy for climbing to continue at Basher's Harbour, but have expressed a desire that **Rinsey Head and Rinsey Zawn are not used for climbing**, as they lie directly below their house and garden and there is no public access.

Basher's Harbour was named after the formidable Basher family, who were *not* early exponents of the bolt, chip, and chisel method of winning infamy, although they left plenty of rusting metal and bolt-holes in the rock. In the early 1900s, the Bashers worked a small fishing-boat during quiet summers from the rock channel at the south-eastern end of the cliffs. They raised and lowered the boat to and from a narrow ledge by means of a cleverly rigged pulley system. They were genuine hard men who would have considered climbing utterly pointless.

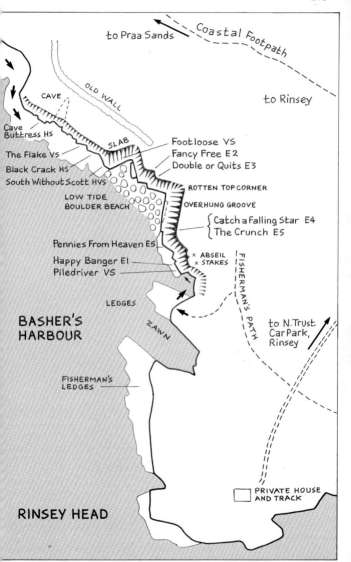

to Praa Sands Coastal Footpath

OLD WALL

to Rinsey

CAVE

Cave Buttress HS

The Flake VS

Black Crack HS

South Without Scott HVS

SLAB

LOW TIDE BOULDER BEACH

Footloose VS
Fancy Free E2
Double or Quits E3

ROTTEN TOP CORNER

OVERHUNG GROOVE

Catch a Falling Star E4
The Crunch E5

Pennies From Heaven E5

Happy Banger E1

Piledriver VS

× ABSEIL
× STAKES

FISHERMAN'S PATH

LEDGES

BASHER'S HARBOUR

ZAWN

to N.Trust Car Park, Rinsey

FISHERMAN'S LEDGES

PRIVATE HOUSE AND TRACK

RINSEY HEAD

Approach.

1 On a first visit, the cliff is best approached from the west. From the A394 Penzance to Helston road at Ashton, take the narrow lane signposted Hendra (OS Ref 604 287). The lane leads down to a car-park above the eastern end of Praa Sands beach. The cliff can then be approached along the shoreline from the end of the beach below the car-park for two to three hours either side of low water through a fascinating maze of sea-polished boulders and swathes of sand. Alternatively, walk east from the car-park along the coast path for 400 metres to where a wall marks the boundary of National Trust property. Continue along the path for some distance until the junction with the well-marked path leading to Rinsey Head house is reached. Continue as described below.

2 The National Trust car-park below Rinsey Farm (OS Ref 592 272) is gained from the A394 Penzance to Helston road by turning off south at Ashton and keeping straight ahead at a sharp left bend. Continue through the hamlet of Rinsey and follow signs to the car-park, the final stretch being along rough track. From the car-park, follow the coast path westwards, crossing a stream in a shallow valley, to a junction with a well-marked path which leads back eastwards towards Rinsey Head house. Follow this until a faint path to seaward leads to the east end of the cliff top, next to a trio of bleached granite blocks. Go back west along the grassy cliff edge to locate a dry-stone wall which lies directly above the *Footloose* area.

Descent. The cliff at Basher's Harbour has no easy descent points and the top of the cliff is often loose and indeterminate. The best descent is from the area of the dry-stone wall, where an abseil or a down-climb of *Mince Pie Problem* can be made (Difficult). The top of *Mince Pie Problem* is located by following the grassy edge of the cliff down to seaward from the dry-stone wall almost to the point where the cliff edge turns to the west again. Slabby rock leads down to a break followed by a ramp, which leads to the bouldery base of the cliff. If abseil or down-climbing are not employed, then a lengthy detour to the west, above short walls and across wet ground, is required to regain sea-level rocks.

The rock at Basher's Harbour gives fine climbing on the lower sections, although there is variable looseness on the upper part of the cliff. Rubble and grassy finishes and a lack of final belay points in some places demand careful thought. Belay stakes are in place above a few routes though these may have deteriorated due to the salty atmosphere. Their position and condition should be established prior to descending to climb. A number of routes have been climbed at Basher's Harbour by Rowland Edwards. He has not supplied details of them as he is concerned about possible damage to the cliff-top flora.

The first feature at the western end of the cliff on approach along the beach is a short orange-coloured wall above a boulder-filled trench. About fifty metres beyond lies an X-shaped tidal channel. The walls above can be wet in places and are streaked with white kaolin and mineral stains. East of the short walls lies a boulder-filled beach beneath the main cliff. The first big feature lying just round to the right of the short approach walls is Cave Buttress, with an obvious cave on its right-hand side.

From the cave, the cliff runs across broken walls and then turns sharply inward across the distinctive black slab of *Footloose*. From the slab, an impressive area of rock made up of hanging grooves, overhangs, and the striking 'double arête' of *Double or Quits* then runs east to a rippled, crack-seamed wall. Beyond here, the cliff falls away into the narrow channel of 'Basher's Harbour'.

The first routes are on the short approach walls, which give a variety of boulder problems and a few more substantial pitches. At the left end of the approach walls are some distinctive white streaks of kaolin. Just right of these, a short ragged crack leads to a slab. Climb the crack, make an awkward move to gain the slab, and finish off to the right (10 metres Severe 4a). Twelve metres to the right is a distinctive narrow V-groove above a short wall. The wall and the groove are climbed (8 metres Very Difficult): adder country above! Five metres right of this pitch is an elegantly brutal little overhang, which leads to a flaky crackline (10 metres Hard Very Severe 5a).

Ten metres round to the right of the previous pitches is a leftward-slanting ramp and crackline at the left side of Cave Buttress.

Mince Pie Problem   15 metres   Difficult   (17.7.88)
Climb the ramp via a tricky move; then finish up easier rock.

Cave Buttress   20 metres   Hard Severe 4b   (1982)
The centre of Cave Buttress is split by thin cracks. Climb the cracks, moving right at half height and then back left to finish.

The Sea for Breakfast   18 metres   Severe 4a   (17.7.88)
Climb the right arête of Cave Buttress overlooking the cave, taking the overhang as it comes. Escapable.

From the cave, the cliff runs across a wall to a sloping recess at half height with a diagonal crack splitting its left wall.

The Flake   20 metres   Very Severe 4c   (1982)
This route climbs the triangular-shaped flake at the base of the centre of the wall and to the left of the recess. Gain the recess by a short overhanging groove and finish up the corner above.

Just right of the half-height recess, a steep leftward-rising fault runs up the face. At its base a small black slab abuts the cliff.

Black Crack   25 metres   Hard Severe 4b   (7.86)
Climb the short black slab and the fault above to finish up the steeper headwall.

About 20 metres to the right the cliff turns sharply inward across the *Footloose* slab.

South without Scott   25 metres   Hard Very Severe 5a   (1982)
A line up the broad left arête of the *Footloose* slab. Climb to a shallow recess at 10 metres, just left of the arête; then gain a ledge on the arête by a difficult move. Finish up the arête.

★Footloose   30 metres   Very Severe 4c   (10.8.82)
[Photo p.272c.] A good slab route. Start at the bottom of a groove at the right-hand side of the distinctive black-coated slab. Climb the groove to reach the right-to-left diagonal crack, which is followed awkwardly to more cracks. Trend up and left to the top left-hand edge of the slab. Avoid loose rock by moving round the arête and then climbing left of its edge. Belays are 15 metres higher in the wall.

To the right of the *Footloose* slab is a 10-metre-high pillar leaning against the face. Above and to the right of the pillar there is a line of overhangs at half height breached by hanging grooves and dramatic arêtes.

★Fancy Free   30 metres   E2 5c   (7.86)
A good line linking the two hanging grooves by a short traverse below the overhang. Gain the left-hand, lower, groove from the left (peg runner above). Climb the groove; then traverse right at the roof to finish up the groove above.

☆Double or Quits   37 metres   E3 6a †   (29.3.89)
Challenging positions. Start below the two impressive arêtes to the right of the *Fancy Free* groove. From the right-hand base of the lower arête, gain a sloping ledge at 3 metres. Move up and left to gain the arête and climb it to the junction with *Fancy Free*. Climb into the upper groove and continue for a couple of metres to place good runners in a horizontal break. Descend and make a difficult and exciting traverse rightwards along the lip to gain the second arête. Fix runners up to the right and then climb the arête direct.

Beyond the last two routes, the cliff falls back into a chossy-looking groove topped by a cracked overhang. Right of this a big wall of chaotic, orange-coloured rock with an overhang at mid height leads rightwards to a steep seaward-facing wall of much better rock seamed with cracks.

☆☆Catch a Falling Star   30 metres   E4 6b †   (30.3.89)
A fine, unrelenting line up the left edge of the wall via a cracked rib and a thin weakness in the headwall. Start from boulders at the base of the rounded left arête of the wall and below a ledge at 2 metres. Gain the ledge; then move left up a bronze-coloured ramp and continue straight up. Swing left and then move onto the smooth final wall, which is climbed past a peg runner.

☆**The Crunch**   30 metres   E5 6a †   (31.3.89)
Start below the ledge at 2 metres. Follow *Catch a Falling Star* for 10
metres; then climb the obvious cracks, trending rightwards to reach a
small ledge. Climb the thin cracks above to good finishing holds.

The cliff now leads right across a smooth orange-coloured wall above a
narrow overhang. The continuation of the wall is split centrally by a
handsome crack.

★**Pennies from Heaven**   25 metres   E5 6a   (29.3.89)
Airy crack-climbing. Start from boulder-ledges directly below the crack in
the upper wall. Move up to a bulge. Make a fierce pull up leftwards to
gain the first faint crack before following the main crack to the top.

Sleaze   25 metres   Hard Very Severe 5a †   (31.3.97)
The obvious flake-line up the wall of the buttress to the right. Climb the
steep wall to an awkward exit onto a triangular ledge. Bridge up the short
corner above to a second ledge and finish up the hanging groove to the
right.

☆**Happy Banger**   30 metres   E1 †   (2.11.86)
A breezy first pitch. Start below the vertical crack 3 metres right of *Sleaze*,
at the extreme right-hand end of the cliff.
1 15m. 5b. Climb the crack to a ledge at 12 metres below some
terra-cotta crumble.
2 15m. 4b. Follow cracks that lead right to a ledge. Move back left and
break through the overhangs by a series of steep moves on the right,
taking care with the rock. The stake belays are well back.

Piledriver   30 metres   Very Severe   (2.11.86)
Start just right of *Happy Banger*.
1 15m. 4b. Climb a rightward-slanting groove to a ledge. Follow the
slanting crack above and make an awkward mantelshelf onto a sloping
ramp up on the left. Belay at the left end of the ramp.
2 15m. 4b. *Happy Banger* pitch 2.

Rinsey Head   (Granite)   OS Ref 589 269

Outlook: South.
Non-tidal on Rinsey Head and in Rinsey Zawn but affected by very high
spring-tides and by swell and rough sea. **Non-tidal** in Rinsey Cove for *War
Games* if approached by abseil. **Tidal** at entrance to Rinsey Cove and for *Jilted*.
Coastguard Identity: Rinsey Head.
Access Advice: Both Rinsey Head and Rinsey Zawn lie directly below the
prominent house on the summit of the headland and are on private land.
The landowners have stated that, although they are happy for climbing to
continue at Basher's Harbour, they wish **no climbing to take place at
Rinsey Head or Rinsey Zawn**, as they lie directly below their house and
garden and there is no public access. Details of climbs are included in the
interests of a complete record but it is hoped that climbers will respect the
wishes of the owners.

Rinsey Head
Rinsey Head is distinguished by a large beaked overhang on its seaward
face and by a remarkable through cave which connects to Rinsey Zawn.

Just west of the arête before the main face is an obvious thin crystal
crackline. **Chocolate Log** (15 metres Severe 4a † [PR] 26.12.96) climbed
this to a ledge at 8 metres and followed a loose corner from the left end of
the ledge. On the right, **Rock Cake** (15 metres Hard Severe 4b † [PR]
31.12.96) took the leftward-rising hand-traverse to the same ledge, moved
diagonally right from the right end of the ledge to a stepped corner, and
followed this to the top. At the left edge of the overhang on the seaward face,
Rinse Out (30 metres E2 5c † [PR] 1982) took the crackline to the roof,
stepped left, and continued up another crack.

Rinsey Zawn
The eastern side of Rinsey Head has a distinctive and unappealing zawn
leading out from the through-cave. A sewage pipe with intermittent habits
rakes the walls of the zawn in breezy conditions.

Land of the Living (30 metres Hard Very Severe 4c † [PR] (15.3.87) took
the steep, stepped crack and corner with increasing difficulty. The rock
deteriorates near the top.

Rinsey Cove
Rinsey Cove is not affected by the climbing restriction referred to above.
However, the cove is an important nesting area for sea-birds and most
climbers would not wish to brave the birds during the summer nesting
season. There are two climbs on the east wall of the cove, which is

approached as for Rinsey Zawn. Descent for *War Games* can be made by abseil down the east wall at all states of the tide, although at low water the route can be approached by a scramble, as for *Jilted*.

War Games   25 metres   E1 5b †   (8.8.90)
Near the back of the east wall above some slabs is a good-looking crack with an overhang at mid height. Start by scrambling from the bed of the cove to the top of the slabs. Move up onto a pinnacle with increasing difficulty. Clear the overhang and then continue up the corner above on small holds to finish by a mantelshelf. Belay well back at an outcrop on small nuts.

Jilted   18 metres   Hard Very Severe 5a   (11.9.91)
This climb can be reached for one hour either side of low water. Approach down the east side of the cove; then scramble down to seaward, veering back west and in towards the cove down rocky steps. Start at the base of the obvious off-width crack to the right of the tall cave. Climb the crack; then finish up a short corner on the right.

Trewavas (Granite)

Outlook South.
Non-tidal on Main Cliff.
Tidal on the 'island' climbs at Trewavas Head and on sea-level cliffs below Main Cliff. All sea-level climbs can be affected by swell and rough sea.
Coastguard Identity: Trewavas Head.

The granite here has a rather different character from that in Penwith. Cracklines are disconcertingly blind in places and the rock is generally steep. Protection is ample, however. The climbs are outcrop in nature but can give excellent climbing. The main climbing area is far above the sea and can be tropical on a hot summer's day. There are climbs on the sea-level cliffs, although the rock is loose in places.

Approach. The National Trust car-park below Rinsey Farm (OS Ref 592 272) is gained from the A394 Penzance to Helston road by turning off south at Ashton and keeping straight ahead at a sharp left bend. Continue through the hamlet of Rinsey and follow signs to the car-park, the final stretch being along rough track. Take the coast path eastwards past the massive, handsomely-restored engine-house of Wheal Prosper. Trewavas Head lies 800 metres east of the car-park. Just east of Trewavas Head stands a distinctive pinnacle known as Camel Rock or The Bishop, which has been climbed. Trewavas Main Cliff is 400 metres to the east of Trewavas Head itself and offers a large number of low to middle-grade climbs, along with some harder new additions, on several fine small buttresses.

Trewavas Head

OS Ref 596 264

There are some climbs in the area of the distinctive feature known as The Island, which lies on the west of the Head.

Approach from the National Trust car-park by walking east along the coast path. From the Wheal Prosper engine-house, follow the lower, narrower path towards the western edge of Trewavas Head and locate The Island. This is not a true island, being connected to the headland by a narrow, boulder-filled saddle.

There are a few climbs on a small but distinctive buttress, the so-called Northumbrian Block, which lies a short distance west of The Island. On the steep south-west facing wall, **Posties Run** (10 metres Very Severe 4c † 10.8.95) follows a direct line from the lowest point of the wall. **Corner Stone** (10 metres Very Severe 4c † 10.8.95) climbs the shelved arête to the right, with the crux at the top. Just right again, **Love Handles** (10 metres Severe 4a † 8.8.95) starts at the undercut base of the wall and climbs direct through the stepped overhangs on surprisingly good holds.

Just before The Island there is a small zawn. The following climbs lie on a black wall on the western side of the zawn. Descent is by abseil down shorter walls nearer to the sea to a sloping ledge. The wall is bounded on its right (facing in) by a corner.

Tinker   14 metres   Very Difficult   (4.8.91)
Climb the crack on the left of the wall.

Tailor   14 metres   Very Severe 4b   (4.8.91)
Climb the middle of the wall.

Soldier   14 metres   Hard Very Severe 4c   (4.8.91)
Climb the crack just left of the corner on the right.

Spy   15 metres   Very Severe 4c   (4.8.91)
Nice climbing up the corner.

The following pitches are on The Island. Approach by crossing the saddle and following easy ledges on the landward side.

Low Tide   12 metres   Very Difficult   (1972)
This route is on the seaward side of The Island and can be reached only at dead low tide. Step over a low ridge into a sea-washed V-groove. Step up left and make a hard move into an open chimney, which is climbed.

★★**Serial Killer**   28 metres   E4   (4.8.91)
Start at dead low tide on the seaward face of The Island, to the right of *Low Tide* and below an impressive overhanging corner.

1 8m. 4c. Climb the lower corner boldly to reach a belay below the main corner.

2 20m. 6a. Make difficult moves to an obvious layback hold in the crack. Use it to reach a hold in the middle of the wall. Climb boldly straight to the top of the wall and finish up a rounded crack.

Ridge-Id   25 metres   E3 5b †   (17.7.95)
Delicate climbing up the beautiful arête to the right of *Serial Killer*. Cross over the sea trench and traverse right to the arête. Climb straight up to a poorly-protected crux at the top.

The following route is also on the seaward face, to the right of the arête of *Ridge-Id*, and is not visible from any landward point. To reach the route, abseil from a summit block to a hanging belay on the abseil rope, just above the sea.

Ultramarine   20 metres   Very Severe 4b †   (4.8.91)
A bold pitch. From the hanging belay, follow a line up the middle of the wall to a niche, which is exited on the left to reach a large ledge. Traverse right to a rib and easy finishing slabs.

The seaward face is bounded on its east by a shallow groove (part of *Cliché*) below the large hanging slab, which is easily seen from the rocky platforms opposite. The next two routes are reached by abseiling from the summit block to a small sloping ledge at the high-tide mark.

Metaphor   20 metres   Hard Very Severe 5a †   (4.8.91)
Climb directly from the small sloping ledge to bulging rock. Pull over the bulge and follow an easy slab to finish.

Cliché   20 metres   Very Severe 4c †   (4.8.91)
Climb rightwards from the small sloping ledge to the edge of the wall. Gain the shallow groove by a tenuous move and follow it to the top.

Traverse of the Gods   25 metres   Very Difficult †   (9.93)
Start at the left end of a large ledge on the landward side of The Island, above the seaward end of the boulder-filled saddle. Climb parallel cracks and step onto a slab. Traverse across to the left arête and follow it to the top.

Crack and Slab   12 metres   Very Difficult   (1972)
Follow *Traverse of the Gods* as far as the slab, move right, and continue up the slab to the top.

Blistering Barnacles   25 metres   Hard Very Severe 5b †(10.8.95)
Start at sea-level, below the seaward end of the saddle. A difficult leftwards finger-traverse gains a crumbling shallow groove. Climb the groove until it is possible to traverse left onto a sloping hold. Climb the crack above to a large ledge, move right, and finish up the ridge.

Opposite *Crack and Slab*, on the landward side of the saddle, is a smooth orange wall. **Ex Nihilo** (8 metres E4 6a † 28.7.94) climbs the thin crack just left of centre by dynamic, unprotectable moves. **The End** (12 metres Very Severe 4b † 18.9.93) starts below the undercut arête at the right end of the wall, pulls up strenuously into a groove, and finishes up the steep juggy wall just right. An alternative start (4c) gains the groove by using deep sidecuts to layback onto the lip of the overhang from the left. Right again is **The Tower** (9 metres Difficult 1972). **Niche Route** (14 metres Very Difficult 1972) starts in a corner about 5 metres to the right of *The Tower*. Step up into a short niche; then move right and climb the corner.

The Camel Rock, just east of Trewavas Head, has been assaulted from all sides, Carruthers. As with most camels, the hardest approach is full-frontal; up and over the snout at 5c.

Rainbow Warrior   20 metres   E2 5b †   (25.5.85)
This isolated route lies about 200 metres to the east of Trewavas Head and takes a distinctive green-stained arête. It is reached by descending earthy slopes to the cliff edge and then by abseil. Climb the arête strenuously by a flake crack.

Trewavas Main Cliff   OS Ref 602 266

This area gives the best of Trewavas climbing, mainly on a series of impressive small buttresses rising from grassy slopes above the lower sea-cliffs. The buttresses offer many good routes in the lower grades, though recent additions have started 'upping the numbers'.

The crags are on private property. Access is long established because of the benevolence of the owner. Once the almost exclusive preserve of local climbers, Trewavas has become more widely known in recent years. Certain areas, notably below the east face of Poised Boulder Buttress, are now showing distinct signs of wear due to increased usage. **Please treat this delightful area with respect.**

Approach. Walk east from the National Trust car-park to the Wheal Prosper engine-house. From here, take the higher, wider path continuing beyond Trewavas Head to pass above the two ruined engine-houses of Wheal Trewavas, once a rich copper mine. Just beyond the engine-houses, the top of West Crag lies to seaward of the path. A little further on, the impending west face of East Crag, split by the distinctive cleft of *Bending Chimney*, is clearly seen from the path. East Crag is the most extensive area of rock. Between West and East Crags lies Sea Crag, below the grass. Beyond East Crag lies the independent comb of rock known as The Ridge.

There are routes directly below the two ruined engine-houses passed on the approach path to the main cliffs. To reach them, walk out onto the headland between the mine buildings. From good anchors, abseil steeply for about 30

Terrier's Tooth (HS), Chair Ladder   Climbers: Jack Sargeant,
Matthew Porter, Christine Preis   Photos: Don Sargeant, Egbert Dozekal

A critical audience above Redfish (HVS), Levan's Wall

metres to ledges at the base of a semi-detached pinnacle. The ledges are accessible for about one hour either side of low water and are affected by swell and rough sea. The ledges can also be reached by descending the steep grass slope at the back of the zawn to the left of the headland (facing out).

Roger   27 metres   Very Difficult †   (29.3.92)
A pleasant route. Climb the pinnacle from its right-hand side.

Over and Out   24 metres   Very Severe 5a †   (29.3.92)
From the top of the pinnacle, descend to a col and then move left for 6 metres. Climb the side of the zawn, moving right to an arête; then trend up and right to finish.

Brown Sugar   26 metres   E2 5b †   (2.5.93)
Takes the central crack on the main face right of the pinnacle. Climb the crack past a bulge at 8 metres. Move left at the top of the crack, then right to finish with care.

Dennis   14 metres   Severe 4a   (24.6.73)
From the foot of the grassy slope, go left round a corner to a brownish slab. Climb the left edge of the slab; then surmount an overhang to a steep grassy finish.

West Crag

This sunny little buttress is best approached from its top by a path down the right-hand side (facing out) of the west face through prickly undergrowth. Wreaks havoc with tights.

Mantelshelf Wall   11 metres   Severe 4a   (24.2.74)
On the extreme left of the west face is a wall with two slabs beneath it. Step onto the first slab then left onto the higher slab; finish up the steep wall.

Rucsac   9 metres   Very Difficult   (18.2.73)
The corner chimney right of *Mantelshelf Wall*.

Triple Fugue   11 metres   Severe 4a   (22.1.78)
Contrapuntal. Start at the good crack in the middle of the west-facing wall. Step up onto a ledge at 2 metres and then move up, using the crack to reach a ledge. Finish up the harder corner on the left, using holds on the right wall.

Per Ardua   11 metres   Very Severe 4c   (5.3.78)
A hard little problem. Start a metre or so to the right of *Triple Fugue*. Climb the fault to a niche; then make a thoughtful move up right to reach the edge on the left. Finish up the wall above.

Sunshine Wall   17 metres   Very Difficult   (11.3.73)
Start on a ground-level slab at the right edge of the west face. Move up the
corner to a large flake. Keep left and go up to a ledge before ascending
the wall above.

Campion   12 metres   Very Difficult   (14.7.74)
On the seaward face of the crag is an obvious gully; to its left is a large
block. Start at the right-hand corner of the block and climb to a platform.
Move up the short steep wall and then climb diagonally right to the top.

Last Resort   12 metres   Very Difficult   (1973)
Climb the lichenous gully in the centre of the south face.

No Gear, No Fear   12 metres   Hard Severe 4b   (1985)
Climb the bubbly brown wall in the centre of the face.

Pennywort   14 metres   Very Difficult   (1974)
Start at the right-hand end of the face below a grooved corner. Ascend the
grooved corner via a flake to a ledge; then climb the wall above.

★**Wild Mountain Thyme**   18 metres   E1 5a   (6.5.90)
A challenging pitch. Start just in from the extreme right edge of the face.
Climb a hard groove to ledges. Climb the steep wall above on large holds
'of proven infidelity'.

☆**The East Tower**   17 metres   E1 5b †   (8.10.92)
A fine pitch. Start directly below the obvious vertical crackline on the
left-hand side of the east-facing wall, to the right of *Wild Mountain Thyme*.
Climb up left, then back right by a hard move. Climb into the groove at
the start of the crack. Follow the crack past a horizontal break to easier but
quite committing finishing moves.

Sea Crag
This lies at sea-level below West Crag. Approach via the descent to West
Crag and then follow a low wall (now getting rather overgrown) westward
for about 30 metres. Descend past a deep square hole to sea-level. Traverse
left (facing in) for 20 metres to a square chimney with black and red
markings. Continue left to an amphitheatre with a backing wall of orange-
coloured granite. There are twin cracks on the left side of the wall.

Sidewinder   20 metres   Hard Severe   (17.3.82)
Good climbing. Start below a groove below and to the left of the twin
cracks. Climb the groove to a niche; then traverse left, using holds on a
black slab, to the foot of another groove. Follow this groove to a large
ledge and finish up a short overhung wall. Scramble carefully to block
belays.

Fran's Route   24 metres   Very Severe 4c   (17.6.90)
Start to the right of *Sidewinder*. Climb a short wall to a flake block and
surmount the overhang above via a clean crack. Follow a slab and then
cracks to a loose finish. .

Hot Cross Bun   18 metres   Severe 4a   (4.4.80)
Start at a corner just left of the square chimney with black and red
markings. Move up and traverse left until it is possible to mantelshelf onto
a ledge. Traverse back right into the corner. Climb to a platform and finish
up the corner.

Air Sea Rescue   18 metres   Severe 4a   (26.10.78)
Start in the left corner of the square chimney. Move right and up to a
sloping stance at 8 metres (often wet). Move up and left; then climb the
corner to the top.

The Mocker   10 metres   Difficult   (8.2.82)
From the base of the way down, traverse right (facing in) to below a
narrow slab. Climb the short chimney to the left of the slab and finish up
cracks above.

East Crag
East Crag is the extensive area of rock that starts 100 metres across the
vegetated slopes from West Crag. The top of East Crag is conveniently flat and
grassy and easily reached from the coast path. It is divided into three sections:
Bending Chimney Buttress, Avalanche Buttress, and Poised Boulder Buttress.

Bending Chimney Buttress is the steep west-facing buttress and its south-
facing extension. It is best reached from above by a path down its right-hand
side (facing out).

Cornel   12 metres   Hard Severe 4b   (20.10.74)
This tricky pitch takes the obvious corner on the left side (facing in) of the
west face.

Flanker Direct   14 metres   E1 5b †   (13.6.93)
Climb the shallow groove just right of the easy lower section of *Cornel* to
ledges. Finish direct up the right-hand side of the arête.

Flanker   20 metres   Hard Very Severe 5a   (1980s)
Good climbing. Climb the shallow groove to ledges, traverse rightwards
along the faultline, and finish up the steep crack. (This is *Sam's Indirect
Finish to Bending Chimney*.)

Spanker   15 metres   E3 6a   (2.5.93)
Sustained with good moves and protection. Start 3 metres right of *Flanker*.
Climb the centre of the wall, finishing to the left of the steep crack.

Sam's Indirect Finish to Bending Chimney
                              18 metres   Very Severe 5a (8.3.82)
Bold and brash. Follow *Bending Chimney* to the foot of the upper chimney.
Move left for a couple of metres and climb the steep crack that splits the
upper wall – by jamming if you're a real climber, youth, or by effete
laybacking if you're not.

★Bending Chimney 17 metres   Very Difficult   (1920)
Climb the obvious central cleft with classical finesse.

Sidestep 17 metres   Hard Severe 4b   (28.7.74)
A neat upper section. Start as for *Bending Chimney*. Follow the chimney for
about 8 metres before stepping right onto a ledge. Traverse right a little
before moving up to another narrow ledge at the base of the upper wall.
Climb the vertical crack in the short wall above.

Sidestep Direct 17 metres   E1 5c   (1975)
Start just right of *Bending Chimney* and climb directly up the wall to the
mid-height ledges. Finish up the final crack of *Side Step*.

★Harvey Proctor 20 metres   E2 5c   (22.4.90)
Sustained and perverse. Start on the right side of the wall. Climb a slanting
groove and then move right to a jamming crack. Make hard moves to
gain the mid-height ledges. Climb to the base of the final wall; then move
right along a diagonally rising crack to make a difficult finish onto a ledge.

The overhanging front face has two routes, and its fine right-hand arête is
taken by a third, *Debut Arête*.

The Prow 20 metres   E1 5b †   (19.1.2000)
Start at the lowest point of the face. Climb bulging slabs and gain the wall
left of the central crackline. Move up to a good hold level with the top
horizontal break. Swing strenuously up and right to a flat block, and finish
though the wide fissure above.

The Bowsprit 20 metres   E2 5c †   (13.2.2000)
Climb the central crackline. Gain the short wall beneath the roof by taking
the overlap on the right. Move left under the roof and finish though the
wide fissure above.

Debut Arête 12 metres   E4 6a †   (16.1.94)
Climb the arête on its right-hand side.

The following routes are on the next small buttress to the east, past a gully.

Simon 12 metres   Very Severe 4c   (1975)
Start in the gully at the left edge of the seaward face. Climb cracks in the
right wall to a small groove at 3 metres. Gain a small sloping ledge. Trend
up and left to make some hard moves on sloping holds to the top.

Green Crack   12 metres   Very Severe 4c   (4.3.82)
Start 3 metres right of Simon, below a diagonal crack. Climb a short wall to a ledge, make an awkward move into the crack, and climb it to the top.

Slight   12 metres   Difficult   (27.8.74)
Climb directly up the front of the buttress, just right of the gully.

Gaffer's Revenge   12 metres   Severe 4a   (9.2.75)
There is a slim buttress with a small overhang at its base a couple of metres right of Slight. Make a hard move to clear the overhang and climb the front of the buttress.

The Tiercel   10 metres   Hard Severe 4b   (1985)
Start below the left wall of the next gully. Climb to the small overhang and surmount it boldly but on good holds.

Gaffer's Wall   10 metres   Severe 4a   (5.1.75)
The next buttress has an overhanging corner on its left wall. Climb the corner to reach a ledge at 6 metres. Step left onto a block; then move up right to an open groove and the top.

The Pillar   14 metres   Very Difficult   (1974)
To the right is a slim buttress. Follow its front face to the top.

Short 'n' Sweet   12 metres   Severe 4a   (23.3.75)
Well named. About 10 metres right of The Pillar and left of a grassy descent gully there is a small outcrop with a white wall. Below and left is a short arête. Climb the arête easily and step down to a grassy ledge at the base of the white wall. Climb the wall, trending rightwards to finish.

Avalanche Buttress is the area of rock lying to the right of the grassy descent gully. This leads down from the right (facing out) of the grassy depression and flat ledges at the top of the crag.

Mouseproof   14 metres   Severe 4b   (2.9.81)
Start below a wide, shallow groove to the right of the easy way down. Climb the groove to a ledge. Go up right to a smaller ledge below a thin flake crack on the slab above. Make a hard move onto the slab; move up and right and finish awkwardly up the arête.

Bramble   15 metres   Very Difficult   (1973)
A pleasant pitch. Start about 4 metres down to the right of Mouseproof. Move up and left before stepping onto a small overhang and into a groove. Climb the groove, traverse left, and climb a short slab to a short wall. Climb the wall boldly.

TREWAVAS HEAD
EAST CRAG ~ SOUTH FACE

AVALANCHE BUTTRESS

1	Mouseproof	S
2	Bramble	VD
3	Avalanche Direct	VS
4	Avalanche	VS
5	Easy Gully	D
6	Carrivick	VS
7	Ivy Chimney	VD
8	South Groove	E1

POISED
BOULDER
BUTTRESS

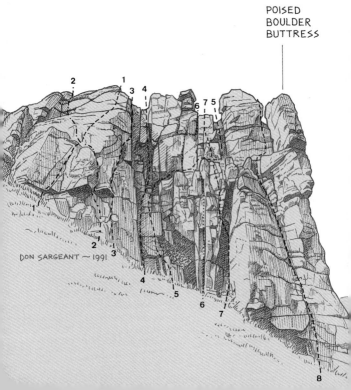

DON SARGEANT ~ 1991

TREWAVAS HEAD
EAST CRAG ~ EAST FACE

POISED BOULDER BUTTRESS

1	Colomen	VS
2	" direct start	5a
3	Williams's Chimney	HVS
4	The Banner Variation	E1
5	Mascara	VS
6	Crossover	HVS
7	Joy Direct	VS
8	Nephew's Variation	VS
9	Joy	S
10	Sancho	VD
11	The Groove	D
12	Hesitation Cracks	VS
13	Mexicano	HS

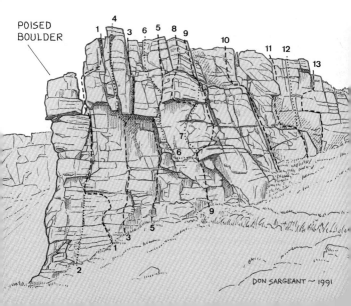

POISED
BOULDER

DON SARGEANT ~ 1991

Glissade   18 metres   E2 5c/6a   (3.5.92)
Start as for *Bramble* and climb the right edge of the wall for about 6
metres to a little roof with a niche above it. Continue directly and boldly up
the arête.

Avalanche Direct   12 metres   Very Severe 5a   (1975)
Stylish, then strenuous. Follow *Glissade* to the niche and then traverse right
to the recessed wall of *Avalanche*. Climb the beetling crack on the right of
the recessed wall to finish.

Avalanche   12 metres   Very Severe 5a   (15.9.74)
Strenuous but well protected. Start as for *Easy Gully*. Climb over the blocks
to the ledge below the steep recessed wall. Climb the beetling crack.

Giggle Wiggle   12 metres   E3 6a †   (21.5.95)
Climb over blocks in the left-hand side of the central recess to a grassy
ledge, as for *Easy Gully*. On the right of the recess make a thin move up
and follow the steep diagonal crack rightwards to the top.

Easy Gully   15 metres   Difficult   (4.2.73)
Climb over blocks in the left side of the central recess to a grassy ledge;
then move right along a ledge to finish up the left wall of a wide break.

Carrivick   14 metres   Very Severe 4c   (10.76)
Subtle moves to start. Start by a V-groove a couple of metres or so right of
Easy Gully. Climb the arête on the right of the groove and then the broken
area above to the ledge. Climb the straight-edged crack on the left by
awkward initial moves; then traverse right into the niche and move up to
finish.

Ivy Chimney   14 metres   Very Difficult   (4.2.73)
The corner/chimney where the central wall turns to seaward. Climb the
chimney until forced out left onto the wall. Continue up the wall to the grassy
ledge. Finish via the steep niche in the wall just left of the wide break.

The central wall merges on its right into an impressive tower of rock with a
huge square-cut boulder resting on its top. This gives the name to Poised
Boulder Buttress, which constitutes the remainder of the crag, including the
impressive east face.

Dis Lichen   14 metres   Severe †   (19.1.94)
The arête between *Ivy Chimney* and *South Groove*.

★South Groove   15 metres   E1 5c   (1976)
A surprising pitch up the deceptive groove on the seaward face of Poised
Boulder Buttress. An initial mantelshelf takes the smile off your face just in
time for some tricky, poorly-protected climbing up the groove to the ledge
left of an airy cleft.

West Wing   17 metres   E2 5c   (19.1.94)
Follow *South Groove* to where it eases. Swing out right on a large flake to
the arête. Climb over a small roof and up the narrow headwall.

The Serpent   27 metres   E5 6a   (5.95)
A much-tried line up the big, leaning arête of Poised Boulder Buttress. Start
at the toe of the buttress, by a detached block and below a niche. Make a
very difficult and bold mantelshelf and then climb boldly up the steep slab
to the niche. Pull out right from the niche, make a couple of moves up the
east face (as for *Colomen*), and hand-traverse (thin) back left to the arête.
Climb the hanging V-groove with difficulty to join *West Wing* and some
welcome runners. The small roof and headwall of *West Wing* provides a
magnificent finish.

Colomen   21 metres   Very Severe   (1974)
Nicely compact, quite intense, and at the top end of the VS grade. This is
the groove leading up to the cleft on the left edge of the east face of Poised
Boulder Buttress. Start below and to the right of the groove, at a shallow
crack going up left.
1 15m. 4c. Climb the crack and gain a ledge at 3 metres. Traverse
delicately left to a small ledge at the bottom of the groove (crux). Climb the
groove and cracks to exit airily through the 'window'.
2 6m. 4c. Climb the wall on the right to a ledge and then finish up a
corner. Not well protected.
Direct Start 5a. Climb direct from the lowest point of the face to the small
ledge at the base of the groove. Technical and unprotected.
Direct Finish Hard Very Severe 5a † (5.95). From the 'window', swing
left and climb the headwall.

Single Blondes   20 metres   E4 6a †   (1990s)
A bold eliminate which starts between *Colomen* and *Williams's Chimney*.
Climb straight up to the roof, pull through, and finish easily.

Williams's Chimney   20 metres   Hard Very Severe 5a   (7.9.74)
A good, testing pitch at the top end of the grade. Start about 2 metres right
of *Colomen*. Climb to a small ledge; then make thin moves up the groove
to a resting-place at 10 metres. Move up right to the overhang beneath
the rippled chimney. Enter the chimney and then continue up the groove
above.
Variations
The Banner Variation   20 metres   E1 5b   (12.8.76)
A tough alternative finish. Move left from the resting-place below the
overhang and then climb through the steep break above.
Slade's Pillar   20 metres   E3 5c †   (16.9.98)
Even tougher is to cross the overhang and climb the surprisingly
independent pillar above. Strenuous but well protected.

★Mascara   20 metres   Very Severe 4c   (6.7.70)
Another good pitch. Start below the black corner running up to the
right-hand end of the overhang. Climb to a ledge and then move right
and up into the corner below the overhang. Move out right, and make a
strenuous and airy move to gain a ledge. Continue up the corners above.

Crossover   20 metres   Hard Very Severe 5a   (1975)
Start at the crest of the old wall beneath the right-hand end of the main
face. Climb to an overhang and then move left along a thin hand-traverse
to step up left onto a small ledge on the arête. Quite tricky. Climb the steep
groove in the arête to the small ledge above the overhang of *Mascara*.
Follow the corner of *Mascara* for about 3 metres, and then step left onto
the wall and continue to the top.

Joy Direct   18 metres   Very Severe 4c   (1974)
Some looseness. Start from the old wall and move up to stand on a flake
under the overhang. Step up left round the overhang and climb a hollow
flake to within 3 metres of the higher overhang. Traverse right into a
groove; then step up left to climb a steep short wall. **Nephew's
Variation** (4c) traverses left below the higher overhang to clear it on the
left. Finish direct.

Joy   18 metres   Severe 4a   (21.4.74)
A pleasant pitch. Climb *Joy Direct* until beneath the overhang. Step up left
before making bold moves to reach good holds and gain the ledge on the
right. Follow the groove above; then step left to finish up a short steep wall.

Sancho   18 metres   Very Difficult   (4.12.69)
Start about 5 metres right of the old wall, below a triangular niche. Climb
the cracks in the face above to a grassy ledge. Finish up the short wall
above.

The right-facing corner just to the right gives a rather scrappy 15-metre
Difficult.

Hubble Drekt   15 metres   Severe   (16.7.93)
The wall left of *The Groove*. Start about 6 metres right of *Sancho* at a short
wall. Climb the wall on its right edge to a ledge. Continue up the wall
above to finish up a vertical crack.

The Groove   12 metres   Difficult   (1974)
There is an overhanging nose high on the right. Climb a leaning block to
a grassy ledge; then go right under the nose and finish up the groove.

Hesitation Cracks   12 metres   Very Severe 5a   (1974)
A nice little test-piece up the wall to the right of *The Groove*. Climb the
leaning block to the grassy ledge. Step right onto the wall and climb it
direct with hard moves up the thin crack.

Mexicano 12 metres   Hard Severe 4b   (1970s)
Climb the steep crack in the far right wall to the horizontal break; move
left, then up and right to finish.

The Girdle 39 metres   Hard Very Severe   (4.75)
Start at the right-hand end of the east face.
1 12m. 4b. Move left across the wall of *Hesitation Cracks* with feet in the
horizontal cracks. Step left onto the nose of *The Groove* and continue left
to reach the top of the groove of *Joy*. Descend the groove to the ledge
above the overhang.
2 15m. 5a. Descend the overhang and follow the thin hand-traverse of
Crossover to the small ledge on the arête. Climb the groove above to the
next ledge and then descend the overhang of *Mascara* leftwards into the
corner. The next section across the face is near the top end of the grade.
Climb left across the steep wall to the resting-place under the overhang of
Williams's Chimney. Continue left under the overhang and then through
the 'window' slot to the ledge at the top of the first pitch of *Colomen*. (The
last section, starting as for *Mascara*, gives an excellent independent pitch –
Hard Very Severe 5a.)
3 12m. Step down *South Groove* for a couple of metres and then traverse
across *Ivy Chimney* and *Easy Gully* to the wall left of the beetling crack of
Avalanche. Step up onto the wall; then move left round the corner.
Traverse across the small slab to climb the wall as for *Bramble*.

There is one route on the sea walls below the east face of the Poised Boulder
Buttress. It is reached by descending the grass slopes below the seaward
edge of the east face to some large boulders, from where an abseil leads to
non-tidal ledges (abseil rope is best left in place to serve as belay). The
ledges are subject to swell and rough sea.

Struth 37 metres   E1 5b †   (22.3.92)
Start to the left of a distinctive pinnacle block, below an overhanging crack.
Climb the crack to a slab, then a V-groove to a ledge on the right. Step left
and down, and traverse boldly left for 10 metres to the arête. Make a
nerve-wracking mantelshelf in an exposed position; then climb back
rightwards to reach the top of the pinnacle block.

The Ridge
Across grassy slopes to the east is the curving comb of The Ridge. The climbs
are all on the west-facing wall.

Approach by walking a short distance east along the cliff path until abreast
of the top of The Ridge. From here, descend grass slopes on the west side.
An alternative approach can be made from the base of the east face of
Poised Boulder Buttress by walking along the grassy cliff edge. The left side of
the crag is made up of a short wall at right-angles to the rest of the face.

Nerth   12 metres   Very Severe 4b   (20.6.74)
A little devil. On the left of the short wall is a shallow chimney which leads
to a large ledge. Climb a short slab and step right into the chimney, which
is climbed awkwardly. Move right near its top to gain the ledge. Finish up
the corner on the right.

Trimsaran   12 metres   Severe 4a   (24.3.74)
Tidy climbing up the corner-crack to the right of *Nerth*.

Nosey   12 metres   Hard Severe 4b   (25.9.77)
Tricky first moves. To the right of *Trimsaran* is a nose of rock. Step onto the
nose on its seaward side and climb to a ledge, which leads left to the
corner of *Trimsaran*. Climb the corner to the big ledge on the left. Gain the
ledge and then climb the wall above to finish.

White Light, White Heat   12 metres   E1 5b   (7.87)
A central line up the wall to the right of *Trimsaran*. A move left into
Trimsaran to arrange protection was made on the first ascent before the
hard final moves were tackled.

★★Turning Up the Heat   18 metres   E2 5b   (7.9.91)
A powerful line directly up the wall to the right of *White Light, White Heat*.
Climb a steep line of flakes and cracks near the right arête of the wall to
the roof. Move up; then use undercuts and layaways to make a long reach
up and right to good holds. Finish direct.

Colenzo   14 metres   Very Difficult   (29.9.73)
Climb the narrow chimney on the left of the main faultline in the centre of
the face.

Eyeful Tower   14 metres   E1 5b †   (3.94)
Climb the front face of the buttress between *Colenzo* and *Wee-Nutcracker*.

★Wee-Nutcracker   14 metres   Very Severe 5a   (20.6.76)
Harder than it looks. Climb the sustained corner-crack right of *Colenzo* to
a ledge; then finish up the wall on the right.

☆Fast Furious Drive North   14 metres   E3 5c †   (3.94)
Climbs the wall right of *Wee-Nutcracker*.

Afterthought   15 metres   Very Difficult   (28.10.73)
Start about 5 metres right of the narrow chimney of *Colenzo*. Make
awkward moves up a short wall and then climb diagonally right to the top
of the ridge.

The Traverse   30 metres   Very Severe 4c   (16.1.77)
Start about 6 metres right of *Afterthought*.
1 12m. 4c. Climb 3 metres to a ledge and then traverse left for 6 metres.
Step up and left awkwardly to get onto the ledge above the first pitch of
Wee-Nutcracker.
2 18m. 4c. From the ledge, climb the short wall on the left and then
continue, to step down into the chimney of *Colenzo*. Climb to the top of the
chimney, step across, and then move left round the corner to traverse
across the wall, finishing at the top of *Trimsaran*.

Below The Ridge is a 12-metre-high amphitheatre, reached by descending
grassy slopes and easy rock to sea-level. Twelve metres to the right (facing
out) are two parallel vertical cracks, between which are good ledges just
above the sea.

Microseconds Crack   12 metres   Severe 4a †   (5.1.97)
Climb the left-hand crack with increasing difficulty. Belay on blocks 10
metres back.

The Lizard

'I was supported almost entirely by the muscular strength of my fingers, and a mass of loose stone projected over my head. These I must surmount; but how?' (Reverend C A Johns in A Week at the Lizard, 1848.)

Despite its relatively recent discovery and development, The Lizard has much in common with the traditional granite areas of neighbouring West Penwith. Most of the cliffs face south or west and thus catch any sunlight available, whilst the hills of the Lands End peninsula take some of the bite out of westerly gales. The majority of the routes described have little seriously loose rock and there are no mind-blowing abseil descents or long committing sea-level traverses to reach the foot of the crags. All the climbs are located on the stretch of coast between Mullion and Bass Point. Three main rock types are of relevance: Mica Schist, Amphibolite (originally known as Hornblende Schist), and the unique Serpentine, or soapstone. The first two lend themselves to steep, often overhanging, juggy walls. In contrast, Serpentine has a schizophrenic quality, varying from a gabbro-like excellence to the most treacherous material possible, fully deserving its comparison with dry, crumbling soap, in textural, structural and frictional properties.

Another, more general, advantage of this area is its relative unpopularity as a tourist centre, which means that campsites are often uncrowded, even in high season. There is a good basic site at Predannack Wollas, well-situated for Vellan and Predannack Heads. The home-baked bread from the farm is recommended, as are the pasties from Anne's Famous Pasty Shop in Lizard village. Helston is famous for its annual Floral, or Furry, Dance, and for a remarkably potent beer, Spingo, brewed and sold at the Blue Anchor pub, after a few pints of which even the most dedicated crag rats may find themselves skipping through the streets with flowers in their hair. As an added bonus, any day-after downfalls on the crag are within a minute's flight time from the search and rescue naval air station at RNAS Culdrose.

Although The Lizard cannot compete with its illustrious neighbour, Penwith, in numbers of quality climbs, the best here do compare favourably with any in the region and the situations offer a superb and refreshing contrast.

Environmental Issues: The Lizard area is noted internationally for its flora and is home to over twenty very rare flowering plants. A very high number of plants, animals, and insects here are notified in the Red Data Book of rare and endangered species. The climbing areas of The Lizard are all category A sites of great importance for mosses and liverworts. The coast from Mullion Cove to Vellan Head is one of the most outstanding stretches of vegetation in the United Kingdom. The cliffs stretching for 800 metres from the harbour at Mullion Cove to Predannack Head are part of The Lizard

National Nature Reserve and climbing is not allowed. A single climb (**One in a Mullion** E1 4c † 7.87) pre-dated this designation. The extent of the reserve is clearly signposted on the coast path. See The Diamond Wall, Hidden Buttress, and The Hollywood Walls for further environmental considerations.

Predannack Head Amphibolite

Outlook: South-west.
Coastguard Identity: Predannack Head.

This broad headland consists of a complex series of rocky ridges and buttresses divided by steep-sided zawns and grass slopes. The described routes are situated on the more substantial areas of rock but there is also scope for climbing of an exploratory nature, most of which is left to the inclination of the individual. The sea-level traverse of the entire headland would make an excellent expedition.

Approach: From the National Trust car-park at Predannack Wollas Farm (OS Ref 669 162), a signposted path leads south at first then south-west to join the main coast path near Ogo-dour Cove. Follow the footpath westwards to the individual cliffs.

Pedn-Crifton   OS Ref 660 165

The small headland of Pedn-Crifton is on the northern side of Predannack Head, and lies to the south of The Lizard National Nature Reserve. The headland is easily seen from the coast path and an easy descent leads to it.

The following two climbs are on a compact wall which faces west.

Pollock   20 metres   Hard Very Severe 5a †   (5.88)
Climb the groove and arête bounding the wall on the left-hand side.

Rothko   20 metres   E3 6a †   (5.88)
A bold climb with sparse protection. Climb the middle of the wall on small ncuts and edges.

The next route takes an obvious groove half-way along the headland proper. Abseil down the groove to ledges at the high-tide mark.

Klein   18 metres   Very Severe 4b †   (5.88)
Climb the groove, passing an overlap near the top.

The first zawn south of the headland has a slabby wall at its back. Descend the northern side of the zawn to ledges which lead into the zawn.

Whiplash 40 metres Hard Severe 4b †   (5.88)
Climb the slabby wall up and diagonally right until it is possible to break right up a groove, which leads to the top. The pitch can be split at mid height.

Predannack Head South   OS Ref 661 163

The north shore of Ogo-dour Cove contains three zawns and a conspicuous diamond-shaped buttress, 20 metres high: The Diamond Wall. About 100 metres to the north is a wide zawn, easy-angled on its west side, with the line of *Secret Squirrel* on the opposite face. Further north again is a similarly shaped zawn containing two routes, and approximately 100 metres before Predannack Head itself, hidden from above, is a small square pillar with a conspicuous slanting break on its overhanging north face. Immediately to the south is a steep wall above a deep trench, broken by a vertical, ragged crack: *Compensation*.

Compensation 42 metres Hard Very Severe †   (23.4.84)
Start at the base of the crack.
1 30m. 5a. Climb the steep crack on solid holds to a large platform beneath an overhanging recess on the right.
2 12m. 4b. Go up into the recess and pull out over the roof on good holds to reach grassy slopes and belays.

The following routes are found in the northernmost of the wide zawns, roughly 200 metres from the Diamond Wall. Descend easy-angled slabs on the north side to a traverse-line leading back into the zawn beneath a steeper wall.

Sesame Street 25 metres Very Severe 5a †   (6.84)
Start in the cleft to the right of the wall, at the bottom left-hand edge of the slab forming the back of the zawn. Climb diagonally leftwards on small holds to a crack, which is followed with a slight rightward deviation to the top.

Easy Street 55 metres Severe †   (6.84)
This takes the obvious overhung groove just left of centre of the slab.
1 15m. Climb up and over the first overlap.
2 40m. Move up and right into the groove and from its top, go rightwards for 3 metres before pulling over onto the steep wall. This leads to the top via an easier groove.

There is one route in the first of the large zawns north of the Diamond Wall. Descend the easy slabs on the north side and cross the bed of the zawn, which is littered with huge boulders.

Secret Squirrel   35 metres   Very Severe 4c †   (23.4.84)
This climbs the fine flake in the blunt arête on the south side of the zawn.
Unfortunately, the top section is extremely loose and a preplaced rope
might be a wise precaution for the final 10 metres. Scramble up easily to
steeper rock, where a committing move left leads to a short groove. Climb
the groove and gain the flake crack, which is followed to its top. Step right
into a crack leading to a wall and the final arête. Belay well back on a
small bluff of rock.

Approach the next four routes by descending easy slabs just west of
Diamond Wall.

Juggling Tortoises   10 metres   Hard Severe 4b †   (27.5.97)
Climb the left-hand corner, which is easier than it appears.

☆**Dogs Befriend the Inventor of the Sausage Lottery**
                            15 metres   E3 5c †   (26.5.97)
The superb overhanging groove in the arête is awkward to enter; climb it
strenuously and urgently.

☆**Small Pets Rejoice on Tufty's Birthday** 20 metres E1 5b† (27.5.97)
Start as for *Dogs...* Climb to the base of the groove and traverse
rightwards below the overhang in a fine position before escaping up an
easy corner to the break. Step right, pull over a small exposed overhang,
and climb slightly leftwards up the final wall.

Seagulls Draw the Line at Four Bhajis 15 metres E1 5c † (27.5.97)
Start at a quartz vein 4 metres to the right of *Dogs...* Make technical
moves up the deceptively steep wall, following the vein to the overhang.
Pull through at a notch and continue to the top.

The Diamond Wall   OS Ref 665 158
This steep, distinctive buttress is easily identified on the approach from
Predannack Wollas.

Approach from the wire fence above the wall by descending a grassy
slope, keeping to the left-hand side, to reach a rock platform. Go left (facing
out) along ledges to the top of The Diamond Wall. From here, the two routes
on the wall proper are reached by abseil to a hanging stance as close to the
waves as the second will permit, although at dead low water it *may* be
possible to climb from the base of the wall.

Environmental Issues: There are excellent plant crevice communities
here and Golden Samphire, Sea Aster, Sea Beet, and Sea Spleenwort are
vulnerable. Heed the approach advice given above. The area below The
Diamond Wall is a Grey Seal breeding site; they are especially vulnerable in
September and October.

Left of the wall are two routes approached by descending easy rock on the seaward side of The Diamond Wall, and then traversing back to a large groove. This is taken by **Forever** (25 metres Difficult 4.83). Also starting in the groove is another route.

First Water   25 metres   Hard Severe   4a   (4.83)
From the groove, make steep moves up to a fault that takes you right to the arête. Step around the arête to good holds leading to the top.

★Koh-i-Nor   25 metres   E2 5b   (6.84)
A fine technical climb. The centre of the Diamond Wall is split by a crack. Start from the hanging stance near the base of the crack and climb out left to gain an indistinct line of holds. Follow these until it is possible to move right by a strange hole to gain better holds. Make a series of strenuous moves, up and left, to the upper slab and easier climbing.

★★Girl's Best Friend   25 metres   Hard Severe   4a   (4.83)
A miniature classic, taking the obvious crack in the centre of the wall.

To the left (facing out) of Diamond Wall is an impressive overhanging wall with a flat rock platform at its top. Abseil to the base of the wall: a ledge just above the sea can be reached by swinging on the rope.

★★★Total Body Wag   25 metres   E4 5c †   (10.97)
Belay below the centre of the wall by a distinctive flake. Climb a gentle slab to the overhanging wall and pull around a bulge to gain some holds and a good rest. From the left-hand end of the holes, climb the thin crack to the top.

Hot Black Dog   25 metres   Hard Very Severe   5a †   (10.97)
A rightward escape route in case one is feeling totally wagged. From the ledge, climb up to the break below the overhanging wall. Traverse rightwards along the junction between the vertical and the overhanging to reach chockstones in the gully.

Diamond Wall Zawn

From the Diamond Wall, scramble over rocks 50 metres to the left (facing out) to a narrow zawn with a steep bubbly wall. Climb down the seaward arm of the zawn, over chockstones, and down a rib to arrive at the fine crack of *Treloar*.

Dizzy Spells   15 metres   E3 5c †   (4.95)
Climbs the fine bubbly wall to the left of *Treloar*. Start at the base of *Treloar* and hand-traverse left until standing on a narrow spike. Climb straight up for 5 metres and step right to a good foot-ledge. Climb straight up to finish in a shallow scoop.

Treloar   15 metres   E3 6a †   (4.95)
Climb the crack.

Vellan Head Amphibolite and Serpentine OS Ref 667149

Outlook: South-west.
Tidal unless the V Diff descent is taken. Affected by heavy seas.
Coastguard Identity: Vellan Head.

This prominent, rocky headland lies at the centre of the most dramatic section of the Lizard coastline. **Approach** from either Predannack Wollas or Kynance Cove (a useful place to deposit the family). The former is the shorter and flatter route. From the National Trust car park at Predannack Wollas (OS Ref 669 162), follow the coastal path south until a wide marshy plateau is reached. Vellan Head itself is to the right but offers only short scrambles. For the Chameleon Slabs and Hidden Buttress it is better to continue directly over the plateau on a muddy path which rejoins the cliff path at the top of the Chameleon Slabs, a broad, rolling expanse of rock, much vegetated on its right-hand side. Immediately north of the slabs is an area of steep grass and short broken buttresses. Approximately 100 metres north again, the crest of a more substantial tower-like buttress is joined to the cliff-top by a small grassy col. This is the summit of the aptly named Hidden Buttress.

Hidden Buttress
Descend the grassy gully on the south side of the buttress on its left-hand side (facing out) to blocks on the slopes above *Going Places*. Abseil from the blocks. Alternatively, from the top, descend the gully bearing left over rocky ribs towards an obvious grass-topped pillar. Continue down corners and gullies on its south side.

Environmental Issues: The area forms part of The Lizard National Nature Reserve managed by English Nature. The descent gully harbours some extremely vulnerable (and fascinating) plants amidst its important general vegetation. Prostrate Broom, Thyme Broomrape, and Carline Thistle are all vulnerable here. Please try to use the first (abseil) approach option outlined above, treading lightly and keeping on rock as much as possible. Also tread carefully when topping out on the climbs.

A traverse-line just above high water extends northwards around the pillar and across a greasy corner (below half tide only) to a wide, easy-angled slab below the seaward face of the buttress. Adjoining the slab is a deep overhung recess, above which is a complex face of steep grooves, overhangs, and ramps. The bottomless V-groove of *True North* is a prominent feature above the right-hand side of the recess, and to its left, the leftward-slanting ramp-line of *Dead Reckoning* ends on a large stance beneath a much steeper headwall. Left again is an overhung corner whose steep left rib is taken by *The Fix*. Across a narrow trench a reef runs out to sea and at low tide provides an excellent viewpoint of the cliff. To the right of the central area are further slabs and ledges beneath a shorter steep wall with the open corner of *Alpharatz* in the middle. These slabs slant rightwards towards the top of the pillar passed on descent and once their position is established, provide easy access to, or escape from, the main area at any state of the tide.

★**The Fix**   85 metres   E2   (20.5.85/10.5.86)

A good route giving intricate climbing up the stepped rib 10 metres left of the deep overhung recess. Protection is sparse, small wires being essential. Overhanging rock to the left and the right lend a certain inescapability to the route.

1 40m. 5b. Climb the rib, either direct, or if wet, by moving right onto an easy-angled slab, and then bearing left to regain the rib where it steepens. Continue direct to a poor peg in a short corner. Pull over onto the subsidiary slab, which has good protection opportunities. Move right under the impending wall to an obvious exposed foot-ledge. Climb the open corner above and step left to a small overhung ledge. Pull steeply onto the glacis to gain peg and nut belays.

2 45m. 4a. Escape by climbing easier slabby rock up to the left. Alternatively, climb the top pitch of *Dead Reckoning* for a variation more in keeping with the first pitch.

☆**The Elderly Brothers**   57 metres   E5 †   (16.4.95)

A series of contrasting pitches culminating in a spectacularly wild finale up the thin cracks in the yellow headwall between *Dead Reckoning* and *Beauty and the Beast*. Start below a leaning corner 5 metres right of *The Fix*.

1 .30m. 6a. Ascend a slabby groove to the leftward-leaning corner. Climb the corner with increasing difficulty to ledges at the top. Cross the traverse of *The Fix* and climb a slight yellow groove to a small blocky pinnacle. Pull over onto the large glacis above and walk right to the *Dead Reckoning* stance.

2 15m. 5b. Traverse right across a black gangway and enter a narrow groove via a short thin crack. Follow the groove with interest to a good ledge below a yellow headwall.

3 12m. 6b. Do the obvious: take the awesome crackline straight to the top. Very steep.

☆**Obseam**   30 metres   E7 6c †   (16.4.95)

The leftward-rising seam in the blank shield of rock left of the top pitch of *Dead Reckoning*. A hyper-tense lead, technically and psychologically without let-up from start to finish. The pegs will help to avoid unidirectional wire placements (mainly RP2s and Rock 1s) lifting out. Start on the glacis, 3 metres left of the *Dead Reckoning* belay. Boldly link a series of fingerholds left of the seam to clip the first peg at 6 metres. Follow the seam (peg) to an incipient horizontal break. Step left to the obvious foothold and climb diagonally left past a third (hard to clip) peg into a bottomless groove (peg). Take the groove to finishing holds whereupon an easy, loose groove leads rightwards to the top.

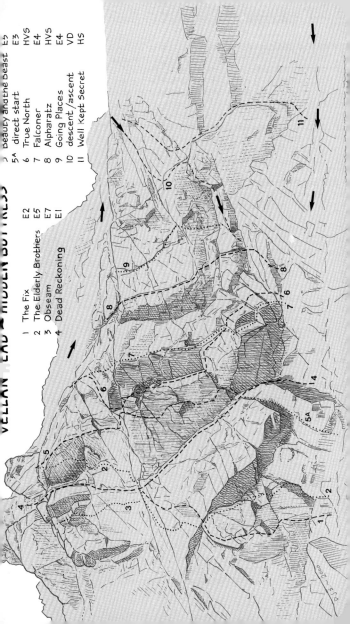

YELLAN HEAD – EAST & HIDDEN BUTTRESS

1 The Fix   E2
2 The Elderly Brothers   E5
3 Obseam   E7
4 Dead Reckoning   E1

3 Beauty and the Beast   E5
5A direct start   E3
6 True North   HVS
7 Falconer   E4
8 Alpharatz   HVS
9 Going Places   E4
10 descent/ascent   VD
11 Well Kept Secret   HS

★★**Dead Reckoning**   70 metres   E1 (20.10.85)

A good route, marred slightly by the ease of escape at the glacis, though this enables the surprisingly amenable, though poorly-protected first pitch to be appreciated in its own right. Start at the back of the deep overhung recess.

1 35m. 5a. Climb the often-wet left wall on good holds until it is possible to swing out left to gain the slab below the capping overhang. Go up and left and follow the straightforward diagonal ramp in a position of comfortable exposure for about 20 metres to peg and nut belays on the right edge of the glacis, beneath a much steeper wall.

2 35m. 5b. Above the belay are twin cracks. Climb these (crux) to a large corner, which is followed to a slab leading to the top.

★★**Beauty and the Beast**   60 metres   E5 (15.4.87)

A magnificent route which takes the overhang and steep open rock between *Dead Reckoning* and *True North*. Fairly easy to escape on the left throughout the first pitch. Start as for *Dead Reckoning*, in the deep overhung recess.

1 35m. 6a. Climb the wide crack, moving left as for *Dead Reckoning*, to fix protection on the slab; then move back right to the overhang at the top of the cleft. Take the bulging crackline above to a ledge and continue up the cracks on the right to a bay with an impressive crack splitting its overhanging back wall. Gain the crack from the left and follow it strenuously to a ledge after 6 metres. Nut and medium cam belays.

2 25m. 6b. Step up left to the slender black groove in the crest of the buttress and climb this with difficulty to escape via a smooth, leftward-sloping yellow ramp.

Variation Start

1a E3 5c (15.4.95). Climb the obvious but deceptive corner 8 metres left of the *Dead Reckoning* entry.

★★★**True North**   60 metres   Hard Very Severe (29.5.83)

Another impressive line, centred on the exposed V-groove above the lip of the cave. Start 20 metres right of the cave at a wide crack.

1 25m. 4b. Climb the crack for a short distance and traverse left on slabby rock to a ledge. Move up and left to another ledge overlooking the base of the corner. Step left to a small exposed stance in the corner itself.

2 15m. 5a. Climb the corner on excellent holds, moving left at the top to gain cracks beside a pedestal. Continue to a large ledge. Step left then back right to belay on a sloping shelf.

3 20m. 4c. Traverse rightwards along the shelf, with increasing exposure, to reach the arête. Steep moves up its right-hand side allow easy ground to be reached. Belay on the grassy slopes above.

☆☆**The Falconer**   47 metres   E4 † (31.3.89)

Fine, open, and exposed climbing up the buttress to the right of *True North*, although one starts 2 metres left of the wide crack of that route..

1 12m. 5c. Move up past an overlap and climb a short smooth slab to a ledge. Move down left into a steep groove and climb it to a stance in a bay.

2 35m. 6a. Climb the steepening face to a point overlooking the groove of *True North*. Step right and make steep moves to a ledge. Follow the flake crack above and continue direct to big holds beneath a steep final crack, which leads to easy ground.

To the right of the cave and above the left side of the slab are two parallel chimney/groove lines. Right again is an open-book corner.

Alpharatz   35 metres   Hard Very Severe 5a   (15.5.83)
Below the open-book corner is an area of steep broken rock. Numerous ways, some easier than others, can be taken up this to gain a large ledge beneath the corner. Climb the corner and scramble up the slabs on the right.

The right wall of *Alpharatz* is overhanging and contains a fine leftward-slanting crack.

Going Places   25 metres   E4 6a   (31.3.89)
Climb up easy rock to the foot of the crack; launch out leftwards along it to finish with an awkward pull onto the easy slab above.

Beneath the right wall of *Alpharatz* is an area of slabby rock leading towards a rib on the right. These slabs provide an easy escape from the cliff with one awkward step right around the rib (Very Difficult). Once discovered, this route provides an easy way in above the tides. To the right of the rib is another open corner.

Well Kept Secret   27 metres   Hard Severe 4b   (4.83)
Start below the corner at a short slab. Climb the slab and a steeper section above. Move right into the corner crack, which is followed to a finish on the right.

Above the finishes of *Going Places* and *Well Kept Secret* is the summit buttress. It has one climb.

Mirror Lady   25 metres   Very Severe 4c †   (13.7.97)
From the lowest point of the buttress, climb steep cracks up the wall (strenuous) and follow the broken upper arête to the top.

Mirror Wall and Chameleon Slabs
Non-tidal apart from the traverse.

Chameleon Slabs are the unmistakable, high, rolling slabs half-way between Vellan Head and Soap Gully. They are heavily vegetated in the area of the right-hand bounding rib and gradually steepen to a 20-metre-high headwall. Left of the slabs is a wide gully of scree and huge poised blocks beneath a steep face of black and white rock (Mirror Wall). Descent to the foot of the slabs is by abseil from good anchors down Mirror Wall to gain the gully.

Mirror Wall

Despite the large expanse of rock there is only one route, a good example of the more reprehensible qualities of serpentine.

Rattlesnake   40 metres   E2   5a/b †   (23.4.84)
A serious route with illusory protection; holds should be pushed rather than pulled. Start on a large square boulder approximately a third of the way down the gully 15 metres up from the base of the gully. Climb the open slab to a narrow ramp at 8 metres. Move right and up past two peg runners (not *in situ*; inserted by hammer, extracted by hand). Step left using an obvious flake. Continue direct to ledges beneath the overlap (another self-extracting peg runner). Move left and climb through the overlap to finish.

The next two routes tackle the main slabs and are better than initial appearances would suggest.

Chameleon Slabs

Kimodo Dragon   82 metres   E2 †   (1.4.83)
This takes a natural line up the left-hand side of the slabs. Start in the scree gully 15 metres up from the base of the slabs.
1 45m. 5a. Climb diagonally right to a sloping turf ledge in a corner. Go up and left to gain steeper cracks in the slab above. Follow these to easier ground and peg belays (removed).
2 12m. Step right and climb easily to peg belays (removed) below the headwall.
3 25m. 5b/c. Climb the thin crack above the belay to a poor peg runner (removed). Make a difficult move to gain the horizontal break and continue up the crack above to a broad sloping shelf. Finish easily on the right.

Salamander   85 metres   E1 †   (8.8.81)
Combining the top pitch of this route with the first pitch of *Kimodo Dragon* gives the best climbing on the slabs. At the base of the slabs are a number of large white-topped boulders. Opposite these is a gully/chimney. Start at the foot of the reddish coloured wall immediately right of the gully.
1 35m. 4b. Climb the centre of the wall, moving left at 15 metres to a crack. Go up this to easy-angled slabs and peg belays on the left (removed).
2 25m. 4c. Move left onto a ramp below a faint crack in the steepening slab. This is climbed with little protection to peg and nut belays on the narrow grass ledge beneath the headwall.
3 25m. 5a/b. Climb the flake crack behind the stance to a small broken ledge. Step up right to another incut ledge and take the diagonal line of weakness on the left (good thin blade peg, removed). Continue leftwards to the top. A fine sustained pitch.

The rib on the right of the slabs gives a pleasantly exposed scramble that could be used as a descent: **Chameleon Rib** (80 metres Difficult 3.4.83).

The Sea Traverse from Soap Gully to Vellan Head
                    1000 metres   Very Severe   (2.4.83)
A fine example of the genre. Best started on a falling tide. The first half as
far as the Hidden Buttress is mostly scrambling in very impressive
surroundings but from this point on the climbing is continuous. It follows a
natural line between 3 and 10 metres above the high-water mark, and
has a number of 4c pitches. The rock is sea-washed and very solid and
obvious escape routes are passed at intervals.

Serpent's Buttress

The next gully north of Soap Gully is an unappetising mixture of steep grass
and loose rock. However, its right (facing out) wall is much more attractive,
easily identified by a curious smooth white V-corner above and to the right of
a slender leftward-sloping pillar. Beyond the pillar is a magnificent and
unclimbed headwall above a large complex buttress. The following route
climbs up into the V-corner. Abseil down the line rather than descending the
gully, which is not advised.

The Serpent's Tail   40 metres   Hard Very Severe   (15.4.87)
An unusual and worthwhile climb, though the rock in the lower section
requires careful treatment, making the climb fairly serious. Start at the base
of a crack leading up to the V-corner.
1 30m. 5a. Climb the crack, which is more of a line of weakness at first,
to better rock where it steepens and deepens. A small ledge with an *in-situ*
peg at the base of the corner provides a poor stance; it may be safer to
continue.
2 10m. 4c. Climb the V-corner; a classic example of soapstone
slipperiness, but highly interesting.
Variation
1a 30m. 5a. Climb a crackline further left up to a deep corner on the
apex of the buttress below the pillar (possible stance). Steep moves right
are then made to reach the original crack above its lower loose section.

Soap Rock to Kynance Cove
                    OS Ref 675 145 to 685 134

Outlook: South-west.
Coastguard Identity: Soap Rock to Kynance Cove.

There is an impressive amount of rock in this area, but much of it is of very
indifferent quality. There are a handful of routes on the narrow promontory
of The Horse whilst Kynance Cove has a sandy beach in spectacular
surroundings which is very popular in summer.

Pigeon Ogo
OS Ref 673 143

One of the Cornish coast's more memorable natural features. By comparison, Bosigran's Great Zawn is a pleasant sunny spot, ideal for family picnics. Ogo is Cornish for cave and this is a vast example whose roof has long since disappeared. Overhanging sides festooned with bilious green slime and liberal quantities of guano do not encourage an atmosphere of light-hearted anticipation. The north face is marginally the less repellent and provides the only route so far.

Loose Change   85 metres   E3 †   (8.79)

An oppressive experience. The second pitch is a serious lead on rock that is much looser than it appears. Abseil down the middle of the north face from spikes and pegs (removed) to sloping ledges just above high water.
1 30m. 5a. Traverse left, following a horizontal line of weakness to a ledge below a steep groove capped by a roof.
2 35m. 5b. Surmount the roof and follow the shallow corner above on disintegrating holds until it is possible to traverse left to an exposed ledge on the rib. Continue the traverse across more solid rock to a slab. Peg and nut belays.
3 20m. 4a. Go easily left on the slab till a final steeper move up and right gains mixed ground. Scrambling for a further 20 metres ensures salvation and block belays.

The Horse
OS Ref 672 139

The rock on this narrow promontory tends to be more solid than elsewhere in the immediate area. The south side of The Horse consists of rough easy-angled slabs, whilst the north face is much steeper. The seaward point is split by an impressive narrow zawn and through-cave. The next three routes are situated on the rock north of the cave.

Descend by abseil down a slabby wall on the right (facing out as one stands above the steep yellow slab). This leads to high-tide ledges. The next two routes start from the left end of the ledges.

Yip Yip Coyote   27 metres   Very Severe 5a †   (4.84)

Move left into a short steep groove, which is climbed to the yellow slab. Finish direct up the middle of the slab.

☆**The Amazing Mr Ed**   30 metres   Very Severe 4c †   (4.84)

A good route. Move up right to a short steep wall, which is climbed until a step right gains the foot of a fine groove in the arête. Follow the groove to finish on ledges on the left.

The seaward west-facing wall at the end of the point is characterised by a steep crack in its mid section.

Tie that Crittur Down   45 metres   Very Severe †   (4.84)
An excellent route in a fine position. Start at a chimney/crack low down at
the extreme left end of the wall. The rock on the second pitch requires
careful handling.
1 25m. 4c. Climb the chimney/crack to a broad ledge, move right, and
climb the steep crack to an overhung recess. Exit right onto a narrow edge
below an impending wall.
2 20m. 4c. Move right and climb the arête direct until the wall steepens.
Continue up and to the right to a belay ledge. Scramble left to finish.

Kynance Cove   OS Ref 685 134
Park at the National Trust car-park and enjoy the beach, which is preferable
to the climbing here. However, the pinnacles provide many scrambles and
short problem pitches, but beware of nesting seagulls. Two hundred metres
north of the cove the footpath crosses the top of a featureless 25-metre-high
slab. The one route on this slab can be reached down a grass slope and
scree a little further north.

Potemkin   25 metres   Very Severe 4c †   (31.12.83)
Climb the middle of the slab until it steepens (a wire nut may still be *in situ*
from the first ascent). Make a bold move up and finish on looser rock.

Lizard Point   Mica Schist and Amphibolite   OS Ref 694 115

Outlook: South.
Non-tidal for the most part.
Coastguard Identity: Lizard Head.

The area immediately surrounding Lizard Point contains the highest
concentration of routes in this section. Generally the cliffs are lower than at
Vellan Head, but relative ease of access, sound rock, and an even
distribution of good climbs throughout the grades more than compensate
for this lack of length. Cars can be parked for a small payment in the field
next to the lighthouse or in the centre of the village. A short stroll whets the
appetite and warms up tired muscles after the long drive from those
Sheffield cellars. The nearest emergency telephone is in the village.

Coastguard Cliff   OS Ref 695 116
There is a bench seat at the top, 50 metres beyond a drystone wall leading out
to the crest of the buttress, which is very steep on its seaward side. This is Tower
Buttress, bounded on its east side by a wide fan of scree and earth above a
narrow, dark zawn. Left of this (facing out) is a smaller buttress whose lower
half forms the Hollywood Walls. The coastguard lookout which gave the crag
its name was demolished shortly after the crag photo was taken!

Tower Buttress
Non-tidal apart from the first and the last two routes.

An impressive feature; most of the climbs here force their way through overhangs of all shapes and sizes. Luckily the holds are accommodating and the rock, a mica schist, is reliable. The **descent** is on the west side of the buttress; ledges and ramps lead down and across an easy-angled corner to a narrow continuation ramp, which opens onto sloping slabs at the foot of the buttress, well above high-water mark. Strikingly obvious is the line of overhangs guarding the base of the buttress. Near their left-hand side, a diagonal flake crack leads out to the left to a fang on the lip. Further right, an exposed vertical corner marks the transition from the overhanging central routes to less overhanging but more bulging rock. Hidden beyond the rib is a wide gully-system running the full height of the cliff, bounded by a slender buttress above a sea-cave. Further right again is a narrow black zawn.

The first route is in the deep zawn just north of the Tower Buttress descent route.

Pulling Out the Boat   45 metres   Very Difficult †   (10.5.98)
Follow the descent ramp to the first arrow in the crag diagram! From here, abseil down a groove capped by an overhang to the top of a pedestal. Continue down the seaward face to a slab. Belay above the high-tide mark at the seaward end of the south wall of the zawn.
1 30m. Drop down easily and traverse left below overhangs into the zawn. At their end, climb up to the top of the pedestal that was passed in descent.
2 15m. Follow the groove and corner to the overhang and pass it on big jugs on its left to reach the top.

Blink   30 metres   Severe †   (10.5.98)
Follow the descent ramp to the step across the easy-angled corner. Start at the base of the groove that leads to overhangs on the north face of Tower Buttress. Climb easily up the groove, to the right of a crack, to the roof. Traverse rightwards across slabs (protected by cams in holes) to the right edge of the face. Continue around onto the west face and finish up a chimney.

★★Aboriginal Sin   48 metres   E3   (28.12.85)
A spectacular route taking the compelling flake crack out across the roof. Start directly beneath the crack at an overhang and undercut block.
1 33m. 5c. Pull steeply onto the block, from which a series of strenuous moves lead out and left to welcome relief at the obvious fang on the lip. Climb the crack above to a niche and move right out of this to better holds leading to a commodious ledge.
2 15m. Climb steeply over more broken rock to the summit of the buttress. (Alternatively, traverse easily left for 30 metres to gain the descent ledge.)

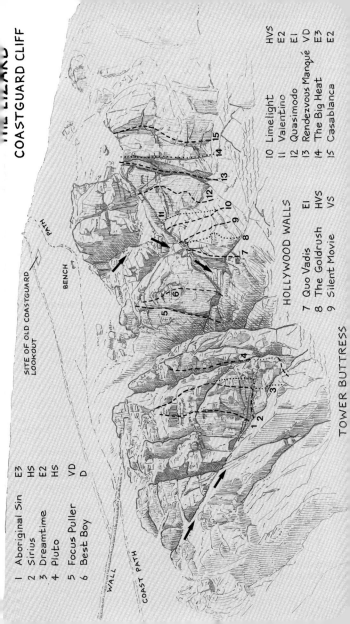

COASTGUARD CLIFF

1	Aboriginal Sin	E3
2	Sirius	HS
3	Dreamtime	E2
4	Pluto	HS
5	Focus Puller	VD
6	Best Boy	D

10	Limelight	HVS
11	Valentino	E2
12	Quasimodo	E1
13	Rendezvous Manqué	VD
14	The Big Heat	E3
15	Casablanca	E2

HOLLYWOOD WALLS

7	Quo Vadis	E1
8	The Goldrush	HVS
9	Silent Movie	VS

SITE OF OLD COASTGUARD
LOOKOUT

BENCH

PATH

TOWER BUTTRESS

WALL

COAST PATH

★**Sirius**   45 metres   Hard Severe   (5.5.85)
[Photo p.272d.] The first pitch is a pleasant blend of huge holds and surprising exposure, but the route is high in its grade as the protection is not all it might be. Start below the central section of the overhangs at a square-cut ledge beneath a vertical corner.
1 20m. 4a. Traverse right and pull steeply up into the corner. Massive arm sinkers lead to a stance on a diagonal ramp.
2 25m. 4b. Above is a shallow corner left of the arête. Climb to its capping roof, which is avoided on the left. Continue in a direct line to a grass-covered ledge and thread belay.

Dreamtime   50 metres   E2   (8.6.86)
Although in effect this is merely a harder variation to *Sirius* the climbing is good and the situations most spectacular. Start in a cleft further down to the right of the corner of *Sirius*.
1 25m. 5c. Climb up to an overlap at 3 metres, which is crossed to reach a ledge leading leftwards to a point directly below an S-shaped fault. Climb the fault steeply to an overhung pillar. Move right in an amazing position on superb holds to gain a ledge. Go back left onto the line of *Sirius* and follow it to the stance on the ramp.
2 25m. 4b. *Sirius* pitch 2.

Pluto   56 metres   Hard Severe   (6.5.85)
A wandering line up to and across the main fault to gain the slender buttress on the right. Start in a niche below the right-hand side of the main overhangs.
1 20m. 4a. Traverse right to a corner well endowed with holds. Climb up the corner and then rightwards to a stance in the main gully.
2 30m. 4b. Traverse right to a groove in the face of the slender buttress, which is climbed on good rock to a ledge overlooking the widest part of the gully. Traverse steeply right to grassy ledges.
3 6m. Climb the easy groove above the belay to a grassy finish.

Southern Cross   93 metres   Hard Very Severe   (11.5.85)
A fine girdle following the natural traverse-line just above the main overhangs. Exposed, but safe with cams. Start 5 metres right of the cave at the foot of a short rib (half tide or lower).
1 33m. 4c. Climb the rib to a shallow corner, which is followed to a horizontal break beneath the roof. Continue steeply past the left side of the roof to an open corner. Move left across the deep crack splitting the roof of the cave and carry on leftwards on good holds to a small stance above the corner of *Pluto*.
2 20m. 4b. Continue left along the natural faultline past an obvious thread just before the rib. Go up and left to a belay above the initial groove of *Sirius*.
3 40m. 5a. Parallel horizontal cracks lead left across the wall above the main roof to a niche. Move down slightly onto the exposed rib. Bridge across the corner to gain a good hold. Carry on leftwards to belay just above the descent ramp.

The left wall of the black zawn consists of a series of diagonal roofs. At low tide it is possible to traverse rightwards from the sea-cave to a subsidiary corner leading up to these roofs.

The Zawn Escape   35 metres   Very Difficult   (7.7.85)
Start on a ledge above the corner beside an undercut slab. Pull across onto the slab and traverse left to an open corner. (The traverse can be continued to join the first pitch of *Southern Cross*.) Climb the corner and exit left onto an easy-angled slab. Follow this to grass slopes.

The Hollywood Walls
Non-tidal, but heavy seas can provide unwanted excitement.

The buttress to the east of the scree slopes, immediately below the site of the old coastguard lookout, is broken on its west side by a broad platform (a sun trap on a summer's day) beneath a large square-cut roof. The platform is reached by easy scrambling down the left side (facing out) of the scree fan. The platform overlooks the central section of the Walls. Continue down to the right in a wide gully until a narrow ramp leads back to the left, ending on ledges running across slabby rock beneath the Walls.

Environmental Issues: This area is very rich in general plant life and crevice communities. English Stonecrop, Fringed Rupturewort, and Thyme Broomrape are vulnerable. Please descend on rock where possible and tread very carefully when exiting from climbs.

The left-hand section of the cliff, a fine open wall of reddish rock, is undercut at its base. Right of this is a triangular slab with a slanting overhung groove on its left side and the deep chimney/groove of *Rendezvous Manqué* on its right. Beyond is a deceptively steep wall split by a ragged crack. The wall also has a prominent slanting corner near its right edge. The cliff continues steeply but lower towards the tidal rocks and reefs known as The Quadrant. The climbing, like the cliff's namesake, has an exhilarating, uninhibited atmosphere.

Overlooking the central zawn is a slabby buttress above a narrow ledge-system about 15 metres above the bed of the zawn. A route has been done up a crack system to the left of the crack which splits the buttress: **True Lies** (30 metres Very Difficult 6.96). The crack splitting the buttress gives **Focus Puller** (33 metres Very Difficult 26.5.85). The rounded right arête is **Best Boy** (25 metres Difficult 26.5.85).

From the foot of the approach ramp, a line of weakness splits the overhanging wall right of the arête.

Quo Vadis   20 metres   E1   5a   (26.5.85)
Climb the line of weakness on large holds until a long reach allows the upper wall to be gained. Follow the crack near the left edge to the top.

★The Goldrush   25 metres   Hard Very Severe 5a   (11.5.85)
Steep climbing on excellent rock. Start 10 metres right of the arête,
beneath the overhanging wall. Pull up steeply on good holds and climb
diagonally right between the overhangs to an exposed foot-ledge at the
base of the red face. Climb the face direct on finger-pockets, moving left
near the top past larger pockets.

★Silent Movie   25 metres   Very Severe 4b   (31.8.84)
Another fine route. The central slab is bounded on its left by a groove.
Start a short distance left of the groove at a large thin flake. Pull up onto
the flake and continue steeply to the open face above. Go slightly left and
climb the vague depression on good finger-holds to the top.

★Limelight   30 metres   Hard Very Severe 5a   (7.7.85)
Continues the general theme of the left-hand side of the Hollywood Walls.
Start at the base of the slanting groove beneath a flake crack. Pull steeply
left and climb direct to a shallow corner (the left-hand of two). Steeper
moves on widely spaced holds lead up and then back left to finish up the
open slab above.

★Valentino   28 metres   E2 5c   (1.9.85)
This takes the right-hand corner/scoop. Start as for *Limelight*, but instead
of pulling left, climb direct up a steep crack to the scoop. Break out right
and surmount the roof. Continue up the obvious line to the top.

★Mae West   30 metres   Hard Very Severe 5a   (1.9.85)
As exposed as she would have liked and steep too. Climb the
right-slanting groove formed by the junction of the wall and the central
slab for 8 metres. Move left across the roof to a crack. Steep climbing
leads up to another roof, which is taken on large holds. Continue to a third
roof, traverse right to the rounded arête, and finish direct.

An inferior variation of the last climb, **Lizard of Oz** (25 metres Hard Severe
4b 31.8.84), continues leftwards from the first roof at 8 metres to finish on
the left skyline.

★Quasimodo   30 metres   E1 5b   (1.9.85)
Above the apex of the slab is a steep right-to-left diagonal crack. Climb
the centre of the slab on an obvious line of weakness to gain the crack,
which leads with more difficulty to a pancake of rock and a groove. Finish
direct.

Rendezvous Manqué   33 metres   Very Difficult   (9.6.84)
Climb the obvious chimney/groove at the right-hand side of the slab.

To the right of the chimney/groove the rock changes texture and is deceptively
steep.

Bouldering at Cripps Cove, Logan Rock
Climber: Shane Ohly Photo: Norman Lomax

Question Mark (E8), Cribba Head
Climber: Ken Palmer   Photo: Nick Hancock

The Big Heat 33 metres E3 5c (7.7.85)

A steep and exciting route of great character, which takes the rugged crack 5 metres right of *Rendezvous Manqué*. Climb the crack, which is on the wrong side of vertical, and move left into a niche. Continue up over a bulge to ledges and gain the overhanging corner above. Climb this until it is possible to swing left to the arête and finish up the slabby groove above. Peg belay in a block 5 metres back.

Casablanca 35 metres E2 (26.5.85)

Fifteen metres right of *Rendezvous Manqué* is a prominent slanting corner leading to a wide sloping ramp. Start on a wide sloping ledge directly beneath the corner.

1 25m. 5a. Move right and climb steeply to the corner, and follow it strenuously until the ramp on the right can be reached. Large nut belays half-way up the ramp.

2 10m. 5c. Continue up the ramp to the impending V-corner, which is climbed with difficulty. Peg belay 5 metres back in a large block. A lesser alternative to pitch 2 is to traverse right from the top of the ramp and climb the wall just beyond the arête. This reduces the overall grade to Hard Very Severe.

Chorus Line 45 metres Very Severe (26.5.85)

Start as for the previous route on a sloping ledge near the right-hand edge of the grey wall.

1 30m. 4a. Traverse the horizontal break rightwards (exposed) to a small stance and belay below a thin steep crack.

2 15m. 4c. Climb the crack to easy ground. Belays well back.

The coast east of Lizard Point appears to offer little of any interest to the climber. However, from the lighthouse to Bass Point there is a concentration of enjoyable shorter routes in all grades, and at Pen Olver and Bass Point there are some very impressive walls with powerful climbs at the top of the grades. The first area is easily reached from the Lizard Point car-park.

Lighthouse Cliff OS Ref 707 115

There is a wooden bench on the footpath below the lighthouse. From here, a grassy path leads down to a series of small zawns and walls with two small tidal islands. On the easternmost of these is the prominent pinnacle of Bumble Rock. The climbs here are located in two zawns.

A small open zawn can be seen on the descent to Bumble Rock from the coast path beneath the lighthouse. The east wall of the zawn is home to three routes.

Wonderwall 12 metres E3 5c † (1995)

A poorly-protected, loose route. Climb a crack for 3 metres before trending right and back left to avoid blocks.

It's the Next Day Tomorrow   10 metres   E4 5c †   (1995)
Climb straight up the unprotected wall 2 metres right of the crack.

Bow Wall   10 metres   Severe †   (1995)
Climb the bow-shaped crack situated 4 metres right of the *Wonderwall* crack.

The second group of climbs is in a zawn just to the west of the channel which
separates the western island from the mainland. This narrow zawn has a
smooth wave-washed platform below a slab. **Far South** (25 metres Difficult
9.3.86), climbs this slab. Just to seaward is a boulder-choked gully beneath
a steep black wall.

Pharos   20 metres   E1 5a   (9.3.86)
Start at the right side of the wall by a short corner. Climb up for 3 metres
and trend left to a pocket. Move up and then step up and left to a
diagonal crack. This is followed leftwards to the top.

Polarized   12 metres   E1 5b †   (1995)
Climb the east wall of the narrow zawn, starting a couple of metres from
its entrance.

Eclipsed   12 metres   E3 5c †   (1995)
Climb the seaward arête of the east wall of the zawn.

Housel Bay to Bass Point   Amphibolite

Approach. From Lizard village, walk east down the road past Anne's
Famous Pasty Shop and turn right at the school. Continue down the lane to
Housel Bay Hotel and join the coast path.

Bumble Rock   OS Ref 707 115
Tidal.

A distinctive feature on the western edge of Housel Bay, the pinnacle is only
approachable at low tide, by descending easy slabs and scrambling over
boulders. Descent from the pinnacle is down the easy-angled landward slab
at Difficult standard. Careful timing is essential to avoid the embarrassment
of being marooned in full view of passing tourists.

Buzzed   20 metres   E3 5b †   (1995)
Start on the left-hand side of the overhanging south face. Climb up to the
prominent horizontal crack at half height and traverse rightwards to its
end. From here, climb boldly to the top.

Buzzin' 20 metres Hard Very Severe 4c † (5.4.86)
Start at the south-east arête and climb diagonally right to the rib, which is followed to the top.

Buzz 15 metres Very Severe 4c † (1995)
Start at the west face. Climb a groove and the crack above.

Housel Bay Buttress OS Ref 708 121
This is the nearest buttress to the Housel Bay Hotel. Follow the path along the edge of the hotel grounds to the coast path, turn right, and continue until another path leads down into the bay. At low tide it is possible to walk back east to the foot of the buttress.

Raffles 30 metres Hard Very Severe 4c (29.5.86)
On the left-hand side of the buttress is a wide crack. Start just to its right at a thinner crack, which is climbed curving right to a pillar. Move up to a vertical crack leading to the top of the slab and belays. Climb off into a gully on the right and follow this with care to the top.

Pen Olver OS Ref 712 117
Outlook: South-west.
Tidal: Accessible at mid to low tide.

Approach: On reaching the coast path, turn left (east) and continue for 200 metres to the Marconi Wireless Station, where a faint path veers off right to the Pen Olver headland. For Pen Olver Slab Wall, take the faint path towards the headland until a rock with a precariously-balanced summit block comes into view on the right. Do not walk to it, but turn right and descend grassy slopes until they narrow between two rock bluffs. Descend the rocks on the right until it is possible to traverse left to a slabby area. Down-climb to the right of the cleft (of *Bod*) beneath the jumbled boulders.

A less obvious descent, used for the north-west end of the cliff, is to follow the faint path into the dip, turn right, and walk down to a grassy spur. Descend to the left of the spur and slant down rightwards to ledges above the right-hand (facing out) end of the cliff. Descend the cliff by a ramp, which is initially hard to locate from above.

This is a rarity of a crag, since it has simple access and a large number of good-quality easy routes. It is in a lovely position for families and picnics, and even has its own mini bathing tub.

The left-hand end of the cliff is marked by a black stump of rock, reached by a jammed boulder. Beside it in the wave-cut platform is a large pothole filled with water that serves as a cooling dip on a hot day. Directly above the pothole is a steep crack running up a black wall, just left of a steep corner.

Let Her Children Play   20 metres   Very Severe 4c   (6.9.97)
Climb the crack to a bulge, step left and then back right to the crack, and reach a ledge below the final headwall. Step right around the arête and pull up a steep little wall and lichenous ramp on the left. Multiple belays.

Slanting up rightwards from the corner is a ramp with steps cut in it, providing an easy escape or descent route.

★The Womb Tomb   15 metres   Severe   (16.6.96)
Ten metres to the right of the base of the ramp is a tomb-like chimney at the back of a corner. Climb the widening chimney to its top before finishing by an exposed rightward traverse to the arête. (Very Difficult if the direct exit is taken.)

To the right is an overhanging prow and immediately right of it are three vague cracks.

Sails   15 metres   Hard Very Severe 4c   (25.7.96)
Strenuous. Climb the central crack to the overhang at 3 metres, move left, and use the left and central cracks to continue to the top.

Butterfly   15 metres   Hard Severe 4b   (25.7.96)
Climb the right-hand crack.

Silent Minute (12 metres Difficult 7.9.97) follows the curving line of broken, stepped rock just to the right of *Butterfly*. Step left (crux) onto slabs and climb leftwards to the top. Close by on the same section of broken, stepped rock is **Descent Route** (12 metres Difficult 16.6.96), which finishes up the short yellow corner.

★Bilson's Fowl Play   15 metres   Very Difficult   (16.6.96)
Climb a short wall and take the steep two-part corner to the top.

Grieving   15 metres   Severe   (6.9.97)
Climb the middle of the right wall of the corner by following a vague crackline to bigger finishing holds.

Dolphin Surprise   15 metres   Hard Severe 4b   (16.6.96)
Climb the awkward steep crack 2 metres right of *Grieving*, and finish up the continuation groove.

To the right is a deep-cut inset bay with an obvious chimney/crack at the back. The left-hand side of the bay has a triangular platform at 3 metres with three grooves above it. The right-hand groove is the longer of the three.

★The People's Queen   25 metres   Very Severe 4c   (6.9.97)
Climb a short groove in the left wall of the bay to the triangular platform. Follow the right-hand groove and finish up its continuation crack.

PEN OLVER

1 Let Her Children Play   VS
2 The Womb Tomb   S
3 Lying Eyes   S
4 Songs from a Broken Heart   VS
5 Letting Go   HVS
6 Great Slanting   VD
7 Saltheart   VD
8 Mile End   M
9 Blind Pew   VD
10 A Little Gemma   VD
11 Love is Blind   VD
12 Family Affair   VD

PEN OLVER TOWER

AMNESTY WALL

PINNACLES

PEN OLVER SLAB WALL

FLAT-TOPPED PINNACLE

BLACK STUMP

DON SARGEANT ~ 2000

★Ocean of Tears　25 metres　Difficult　(6.9.97)
Although it often looks damp and unpleasant, the chimney provides a high-quality climb, giving bridging more often encountered in grooves than the graunch associated with chimneys, and at an amenable grade.

★Songs from a Gentle Man　25 metres　Very Severe 4c　(16.6.96)
Three metres right of the chimney is a fine-looking arête giving delicate climbing.

To the right is a small pinnacle, behind which, on the main cliff, is a large open-book corner.

Vumba　20 metres　Very Difficult　(22.6.86)
Climb the corner.

The pinnacle has a collection of attractive climbs. The first three start to seaward of the pinnacle from barnacle-encrusted ledges. Descend from the pinnacle by the landward face.

Lying Eyes　15 metres　Severe　(16.6.96)
Climb the obvious left-slanting ramp to reach an overlap. Pull over and follow the left edge to the summit.

★Songs from a Broken Heart　15 metres　Very Severe 4c　(25.7.96)
Start 2 metres right of *Lying Eyes*. Climb a steep broken crack to a large platform. Climb the arête to the small overhang on the left and pull up the cracks immediately right of the arête to finish.

Pilot's Song　15 metres　Very Severe 4c　(16.6.96)
The seaward upper face of the pinnacle has an obvious central crack. Climb just left of an undercut prow to the large ledge. Take the crack above, steeply at first, to the top.

Flowers for a Lady　20 metres　Very Difficult　(7.9.97)
On the main cliff behind the east face of the pinnacle is a steep groove. Climb the groove using a series of nicely placed jugs to reach a large ledge. Walk 3 metres right, climb an open corner to another ledge, and finish up another groove.

To the right of the pinnacle is a broken bay choked with huge boulders.

Sesame Street　15 metres　Very Difficult　(25.7.96)
On the left of the boulder-choked bay is an obvious corner with a bow-shaped crack in its right wall. Climb the crack and finish up the short corner above.

Pen Olver Slab Wall

Pen Olver Slab Wall is the large slabby wall to the right of the boulder-choked bay. The ledge beneath the wall is flooded at high tide. The first route here is the left arête of the wall.

Letting Go   20 metres   Hard Very Severe   (7.9.97)
Climb up the crack on the left side of the arête for 2 metres. Swing right on two good jugs and pull steeply up onto the slabby yellow face above. Continue up this direct to the main belay ledge.

Great Slanting   15 metres   Very Difficult   (15.6.96)
Start 5 metres right of the arête at a prominent, left-slanting flake crack. Climb the flake crack to the arête and make an awkward step to reach the belay ledge above. There is also a mantelshelf start 2 metres to the left.

Saltheart   15 metres   Very Difficult   (15.6.96)
A couple of metres right is a steep wall leading to an open groove. Follow the groove to the belay ledge below the upper broken walls.

Mule   15 metres   Hard Very Severe 5a   (25.7.96)
Start 2 metres right again at a thin crack running up a steep wall and the slab above. Pull strenuously up the crack to gain the slab and continue to a small overlap. Cross the overlap and continue delicately up the centre of the final wall to reach the ledge.

Mile End   15 metres   Moderate   (15.6.96)
An ideal beginner's route, up the rightward-slanting wide crack in the centre of the wall. The high crux is protected by a sling round a chockstone.

Blind Pew   25 metres   Very Difficult   (15.6.96)
Five metres right of the start of *Mile End* is a groove beginning 3 metres up. Climb the short slab to reach the groove and follow it to the belay ledge. From here, go up, step right to avoid the overhangs, and finish up the final break.

A Little Gemma   20 metres   Very Difficult   (15.6.96)
Two metres to the right is a slim, vague groove-line which starts 3 metres up. Climb the slab to reach the groove-line and follow it until it fades into the upper slab. Continue direct, before finishing up a short V-groove just above a horizontal break.

Love is Blind   15 metres   Very Difficult   (15.6.96)
Two metres right again is a flake/groove. Follow the left-facing flake and then climb up the slab to a right-facing flake, finishing at the base of the summit pinnacle.

Umbrella Groove   22 metres   Difficult   (25.7.96)
1 12m. Follow the right-slanting crack on the right-hand side of Pen Olver Slab Wall to the left arête. Step left and climb the slab to a belay ledge.
2 10m. Climb the groove above.

Redruth   12 metres   Difficult   (25.7.96)
Climb the broken corner-crack and broken chimney above to a belay platform at the top.

A descent or escape can be made via grooves in the short arête to the left (facing in) of the chimney taken by *Bod*.

Bod   12 metres   Difficult   (25.7.96)
Climb the short rightward-slanting chimney to ledges, move left, and climb the stepped arête to the top.

A short steep wall follows, being the easternmost section of the Pen Olver Slab Wall.

Family Affair   10 metres   Very Difficult   (25.7.96)
Climb the large central widening crack.

To the east, the cliff deteriorates into broken rocks before rearing up again into an impressive square-cut buttress with two through-caves. **Approach** as for the north-western section of Pen Olver (page 259) but carry on to the rocks of the Pen Olver headland. Walk down to the right for 50 metres to reach broad rock ledges close to the square-cut buttress. Scramble down to ledges below the imposing west face of the buttress at low tide, otherwise abseil in.

West Face (Amnesty Wall)
Raindance   33 metres   Hard Very Severe 5a   (3.95)
This climbs the left arête of the West Face. Start next to the chasm. Climb up for 3 metres and traverse left until it is possible to climb up to a good ledge. Above the ledge, surmount the bulge on the left and traverse right to an exposed finish up the arête.

★★★International   25 metres   E4 5c   (3.95)
A brilliant route up the centre of the West Face. Start in the centre of the wall, at a shallow leftward-facing corner. Climb the corner to a slanting crack. Step up to reach a flat-topped spike and move right on finger edges to good holds. Step up and reach left for good pockets. Continue straight up steep rock to the top.

★★★Amnesty   25 metres   E3 5c   (22.6.86)
A superb route following the line of weakness which splits the right side of the impending face, just left of a line of overhangs. Start at the foot of the diagonal crack running from right to left. Climb the crack for 5 metres and

move right to a ledge. Move right again to a rounded flake and go up with difficulty to a deep horizontal slot (*Friend 4* useful). Follow the crack up to the left to a peg runner and continue to the top on improving holds.

South Face
Low tide is required for the routes on the South Face.

Stay Pretty, Die Young   25 metres   E4 6a †   (4.95)
Start just left of the arch of Prisoner of Zenda. The route climbs the narrow face through stepped overhangs. Climb boldly to the first overhang. Swing right to a rest and good gear. Go diagonally leftwards to the blunt arête. Step back right and finish up the bold but easier headwall.

The Prisoner of Zenda   25 metres   Hard Very Severe 4c(29.5.86)
Start below the inset slab in the huge arch on the seaward face and climb direct to the roof. A series of very exposed moves leads out under the roof to gain a chimneying position at the seaward end of the crack. Finish direct.

Gweek   25 metres   E6 6b †   (8.95)
Start right of Prisoner of Zenda. Climb a leftward-curving overlap, a shallow hanging groove, and the headwall. A serious climb.

Beyond the leaning block is a tower containing a curved crackline on its west face. On the opposite face are two parallel cracks. Descent is by abseil. The first climb lies on the west face.

Galileo   15 metres   Hard Very Severe 5a   (9.3.86)
A good little route. Start in a niche below the curving crack and go up to an overlap. Bold moves gain large flakes and the top.

An easier way to reach the summit is by the obvious wide crack right of the last route.

The Beach   15 metres   E4 5c †   (8.95)
Loose and poorly protected but escapable to the right. Tidal. Climb the seaward arête of the tower, which is initially very steep.

On the east side of the tower, gentle slabs lead down to sea-level.

Down the Welly   15 metres   E1 5a †   (8.87)
[Photo p.288a.] Climb the wall and steep crack on the east face of the pinnacle.

Leaning Tower   20 metres   Hard Very Severe 5b †   (23.3.86)
This route could not be identified and is included in case the reader would like to do some guidebook research. On the south-east arête is an obvious groove. Start at the base of the groove, where back-and-footing gains a ledge on the arête. The crack above leads to the top.

East of the tower is a dramatic zawn, which is easily reached at lowish tide.

Pisapis   25 metres   Severe 4a   (5.4.86)
From a large ledge on the left, traverse into the zawn, on rock that looks brittle but is in fact quite solid, to reach a crack. Climb the crack until it widens and finish up the slab on the right.

The Black Hole   25 metres   Very Severe 4c   (11.7.86)
At the western end of the buttress taken by *Meteorite* is a zawn/cave approached easily down the rocky ridge just to the west. Step across the cleft and then make bold moves up and right to gain a deep crack. Climb the wall just left of this to the top.

Prison Zawn
To the west of the Pen Olver headland is a zawn with a narrow entrance: Prison Zawn. Above the back of the zawn, and easily reached, is an overhanging diamond-shaped wall. **T Rex Corner** (12 metres Hard Very Severe 4c † 1990s) follows the corner on the left-hand side of the wall. **Snap, Crackle, and Pop** (15 metres E3 5b † 1990s) is a loose, poorly-protected proposition which starts as for *T Rex Corner*. It then traverses rightwards onto the crumbly overhanging wall before continuing to the top.

Bass Point   OS Ref 717 118
Outlook: South.

This is the next headland east of Pen Olver and comprises an area of steep walls and small zawns. The outstanding feature, easily recognized, is a superb overhanging wall rising about 35 metres from sea-level ledges just to the west of the coastguard station. On the left side of the wall is an off-width crack, to the left of which is an obvious corner-crack. **Descent** to the sea-level platform is possible at lowish tides by following easy-angled rock to the right of the cliff (facing out). Routes close to *The Cull* are more commonly approached by abseil.

The first route is on the steep buttress on the right (facing out), which rises straight from the sea. Cross a small cleft to reach a commodious ledge on the edge of the buttress.

Meteorite   25 metres   Very Severe 4c   (5.4.86)
A good route but deceptively steep. From the ledges on the edge of the buttress, descend a short crack and traverse above the high-water mark into an overhung niche. Move out of this on the left and climb the steep wall up and to the right to an overhung ledge. Belay on the ledge on the left.

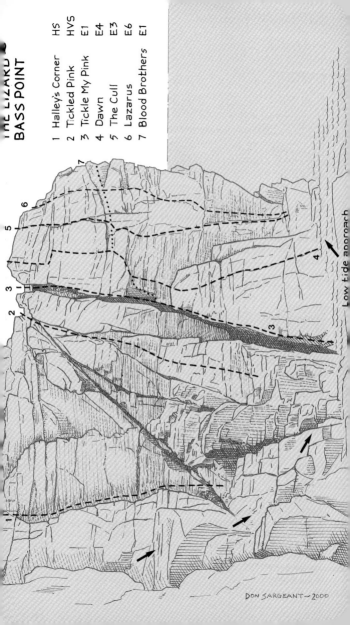

THE LIZARD
BASS POINT

1	Halley's Corner	HS
2	Tickled Pink	HVS
3	Tickle My Pink	E1
4	Dawn	E4
5	The Cull	E3
6	Lazarus	E6
7	Blood Brothers	E1

Low tide approach

DON SARGEANT ~ 2000

Ford Prefect   20 metres   E1 5b   (1995)
Climb the obvious steep crack in the descent gully.

To the left of the main face is an obvious corner with a short buttress to its left.

Walk Out   17 metres   Difficult †   (17.7.2000)
Climb the short groove on the left to a ledge. Finish up a corner at the left end of the ledge.

Three Tiers   18 metres   Very Severe 5a †   (17.7.2000)
Climb the short groove of *Walk Out* to the ledge. Take the thin seam in the centre of the wall above to a second ledge. The centre of the top wall gives a fine finish.

Comet   23 metres   Very Severe 4b   (16.3.86)
Climb the obvious line of weakness on the front face of the buttress.

Blade   17 metres   Severe 4a †   (17.7.2000)
Climb the left-hand side of the arête and finish up the narrow V-groove on the right-hand side.

★Halley's Corner   25 metres   Hard Severe 4a   (16.3.86)
A fine route. Climb the corner.

Tickled Pink   25 metres   Hard Very Severe 5a   (16.3.86)
Start on ledges left of the off-width crack, and climb with difficulty onto a short pillar. Finish direct on steep rock.

Tickle My Pink   30 metres   E1 5a   (16.3.86)
The off-width crack is climbed on a variety of rock types. Bold.

★Blood Brothers   50 metres   E1 5a   (5.86)
This left-to-right girdle is a great, dramatic pitch for its grade. From the rib below *Tickle My Pink*, climb to the belay ledges of *Dawn*. Follow *Dawn* to large pockets and continue rightwards, crossing *The Cull*, to reach the arête. Step around onto ledges and climb straight up to finish.

★★Dawn   40 metres   E4   (5.4.86)
A brilliant second pitch up the steep wall right of the off-width crack. Start on sea-level ledges at the bottom right-hand end of the face.
1 20m. 4b. Move left to an obvious crack in the slab, which is climbed to ledges at the base of the impending wall.
2 20m. 5c. Climb steeply to a horizontal break before traversing right into the centre of the wall and a horizontal slot. Continue in a direct line past a pocket to another horizontal crack. Move left and finish on good holds.
Variation
1a 20m. 5c (1990s). Start left of the crack. Climb the centre of the slab to the ledges.

Dawn Direct 37 metres E5 6a † (1.11.97)
Climb a crack just to the right of the slab to a ledge in a small corner (below and right of the parent route's belay ledges). Climb straight up the wall above, past the horizontal slots of the parent route, and continue to the top. The last few moves are not easy, but protection is excellent.

The Cull 33 metres E3 5b (16.3.86/10.87)
A stunning route of the highest calibre, taking the obvious crackline just right of the centre of the face. Climb the flake crack right of the corner for 15 metres to conspicuous flakes and horizontal breaks. Move right into the crack and follow it strenuously past a difficult section just below the top.

Lazarus 30 metres E6 6b/c (20.5.88)
A very fingery, bold and sustained pitch taking the obvious challenge of the right-hand section of *The Cull* wall. Start below a thin leftward-slanting flake crack to the right of the line of flakes taken by *The Cull*. Follow the crack to the thin horizontal break where it ends, traverse right, and move up with difficulty to a poor peg. More hard climbing leads to a large hold 5 metres higher, before good holds lead to a superb thread beneath a small roof. Move up and left, and climb an obvious crack to the top.

The only details for **Seal** (E6/7 6b † 1993) are as follows: 'Climb the line of flakes above the traverse on *Lazarus*. The peg on *Lazarus* and small wires protect. The wide crack above is followed to join *The Cull*.'

To the right of the main face is an evil cleft, which is only accessible at low tide.

Seal Chop Chimney 25 metres Difficult (16.3.86)
A classic of sorts. Climb the greasy chimney until sufficiently deterred by the green slime at 10 metres, when it is possible to move right to a short crack. Step left across the cleft and climb the obvious crack above.

Dirty Ice 20 metres Very Severe 4b (16.3.86)
To the right of the cleft is a diagonal crack leading to some large shaky flakes. Surmount these and continue to the top via a groove, which is loose to the point of brazen promiscuity.

Dingo Buttress
Immediately to the east of this buttress is a zawn with a slabby west wall and a steep front face. Descend to the east of the buttress down steep but easy rock.

Bingo 25 metres Severe (8.6.86)
Climb the centre of the slabby west wall.

★Dingo   20 metres   E2 5c   (8.6.86)
[Photo p.288b.] Climb the central crack in the front face.

By Jingo   20 metres   Hard Very Severe 5b   (4.7.86)
Climb the right-hand crack until it widens near the top. Swing right onto
the arête and finish up this.

Spingo   20 metres   Severe 4a   (8.6.86)
Right again is a groove. Climb this and the obvious flake on the left to
finish up a steep wall.

Bass Point East
Directly beneath the coastguard station on the east side of the Point is a small
bay. On the back wall is an obvious vertical crack 3 metres left of a long
corner.

☆Giotto   30 metres   E1 †   (16.3.86)
1 20m. 5a. Climb the crack direct to a ledge.
2 10m. 4c. Move up and left into the corner. Climb steeply to the top.

Green Lanes Cliff
Approach. From the red and white wall below the Coastguard lookout hut
at Bass Point, take a faint path down to a grassy gully. Descend the gully to a
blocky outcrop and scramble down the landward side of the block under two
arches to reach the seaward face.
Tidal and affected by rough seas.

This newly developed crag lies 150 metres east of Bass Point. It is has two
faces with an arch between them. Another arch links the crag to the main
cliff.

The first two routes are on the left-hand face.

You're In Crack   10 metres   Hard Very Severe 5a †   (9.98)
Climb the leftmost crack to a horizontal break at 8 metres. Follow the
widening crack rightwards to the top. The direct finish is E2 5b (6.2000).

Incestuous Crack   10 metres   Very Severe 4c †   (6.97)
Climb the next crack to a widening groove and the top.

☆☆Make the Break   10 metres   E2 5a †   (7.99)
The right-hand side of the arch. From the left end of the right-hand face,
climb to a good flake at 3 metres, swing into the arch, and make a long
move to a half-height break. Finish up the arête.

You'll Never Take Me Alive   10 metres   E2 5b †   (6.2000)
Climb the left-hand of two parallel finger-cracks to half height. Move right
to the other crack and a slabby finish.

Lonesome Lizard   10 metres   E2 5c †   (6.2000)
Climb straight up the centre of the face, follow a rightward-leading
diagonal crack, and make a hard move to gain the crack of the next
route. Finish up the crack.

On the right side of the face, three cracks splay out diagonally leftwards,
straight up, and diagonally rightwards.

A Clean Getaway   12 metres   E1 5b †   (6.2000)
Climb the leftward-leading diagonal crack.

Looning the Lizard   10 metres   Hard Very Severe 5a † (6.2000)
Take the vertical crack to the top.

A Criminal Lifestyle   12 metres   Very Severe 4c †   (5.2000)
No prizes for guessing… the rightward-leading diagonal crack.

Black Head Peridotite   OS Ref 779 162

Outlook: East.
Non-tidal apart from some routes on the Wall of Holds. A low spring-tide is
needed to reach the boulder-beach on the far west side of the cliff beyond
the Wall of Holds. All routes are affected by heavy seas and swell. Most
routes provide good climbing but the top pitches are often contrived and
disproportionately easy.

South-west of Coverack is a small outcrop. The rock is Peridotite, a coarse-
grained, greenish-black igneous rock, which here is also streaked with
serpentine veins. It is hard and sound where it is sea-washed but initially
alarmingly loose in the upper reaches, where Romanis noted, *'Not absolutely
reliable but is considerably better than the kind of stuff met with on Nare Head
and by careful inspection of foot and handholds, danger may be eliminated.'*
This loose rock will eventually disappear as the climbs have more ascents. The
head itself is precipitous and has an impressive amphitheatre of rock right at
its tip, the Black Amphitheatre. Since its last appearance in a guidebook it has
been extensively developed. It has also been documented in *An Interim Guide
for Black Head* by Toni and Barnaby Carver, on which this text is based.

Approach from Coverack on the coast path, heading south for approximately
three kilometres to the derelict coastguard lookout on Black Head. (Take the

uphill path just after a stone seat to avoid a detour towards Chynhalls Point.) The shorter route is from roadside parking at the hamlet of Trewillis. Continue along the lane until it becomes a metalled farm lane and then a track which turns left, following the field wall to a stile. From here, a footpath leads to the coast path about a kilometre from the Head. From the derelict lookout, a path leads further onto the Head and down the north-east side of the crag to ledges at sea-level. The Black Amphitheatre is easily visible to the right when facing south.

The Black Amphitheatre dominates the lower part of Black Head. Assuming calm weather, the routes here, and the approach traverse, are accessible at all states of the tide. From the high-water mark or above, a traverse left leads to the very slippery runnel named the Water Slide at the bottom of The Black Amphitheatre. The obvious corner-crack above is the line of *Archangel*, the impending wall to the right, Rebel Wall, and the large slab on the left, which attracts vast quantities of guano during the nesting season, White Slab. The leftward-rising fault which bisects White Slab is the first pitch of *Black Dyke*. At the apex of White Slab the fault meets a gully. This gully, which can be reached from the cliff-top, is the easy way down to the ledges at the base of The Wall of Holds. Calm sea and a falling tide are useful here. At low tide the ledges lead to the boulder-beach, beyond which is Dinas Cove.

The Wall of Holds
This is the 25-metre-high south-facing wall just around the edge of White Slab. Approach by descending grass slopes on the western side of the ridge until a rock ledge with a large square block on it is reached. This is the top of the wall. From here, follow the grass ledges eastwards to a steep gully. The gully leads down to ledges just above sea-level. The top of the gully can also be reached by climbing pitch 1 of *Black Dyke*.

Falling Gull   25 metres   Very Difficult   (14.7.96)
Climb a direct route up the centre of the wall, a metre or so left of the fault of *Happy Landings*. Finish on the large grassy ledge of the descent. Steep climbing on good holds.

Happy Landings   25 metres   Very Difficult   (14.7.96)
Interesting bridging up a large diamond-shaped fault leads to a wall, which is climbed to a seagull nesting-ledge. Climb leftwards over more ledges to the block on top of the wall.

The Rib   20 metres   Very Difficult †   (9.6.2000)
Climb straight up the rib between the fault of *Happy Landings* and the small corner. Finish up the descent gully.

Disputed Ground   70 metres   Very Severe   (15.6.96)
Start at an obvious corner just right of the diamond-shaped fault.
1 20m. 4c. Climb the corner to an overhang, which is taken on its left. Continue up the wall until a large ledge is reached.

Thea (S), Tregiffian Cove
Climber: Steve Bunston   Photo: David Wilkinson

Footloose (VS, first ascent), Basher's Harbour. Climber: Mike Freeman. Photo: David Hillebrandt

Sirius (HS), Lizard Point
Climber: Pete O'Sullivan   Photo: Don Sargeant

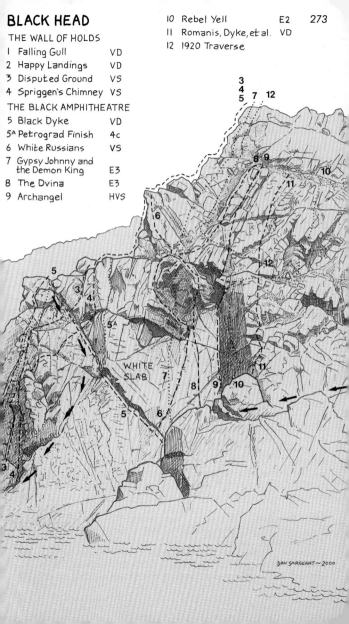

BLACK HEAD

THE WALL OF HOLDS

1	Falling Gull	VD
2	Happy Landings	VD
3	Disputed Ground	VS
4	Spriggen's Chimney	VS

THE BLACK AMPHITHEATRE

5	Black Dyke	VD
5ᴬ	Petrograd Finish	4c
6	White Russians	VS
7	Gypsy Johnny and the Demon King	E3
8	The Dvina	E3
9	Archangel	HVS
10	Rebel Yell	E2	273
11	Romanis, Dyke, et al.	VD
12	1920 Traverse	

WHITE SLAB

DON SARGEANT ~ 2000

2 25m. 4a. Left of the wall of pitch 2 of *Spriggen's Chimney* is another shorter wall. Climb this wall then the left edge of the wall above.
3 25m. Scramble up the ridge to finish.

Black Crack   20 metres   Very Difficult †   (9.6.2000)
Climb the crack just right of the small corner of *Disputed Ground*. Finish up the gully.

Spriggen's Chimney   70 metres   Very Severe   (14.7.96)
Five metres right of the corner of *Disputed Ground* is a deep chimney with a chockstone near the top.
1 20m. 4b. Step down into the base of the chimney and climb it to the large vegetated ledge above.
2 25m. 4c. Climb the 6-metre wall just right of the ledge, steeply but on good holds. Climb the wall above and the small overhang on good jugs.
3 25m. Scramble up the ridge to finish.

White Crack   55 metres   Severe †   (9.6.2000)
A pleasant route, which starts at the base of the descent gully and then disappears around the arête into The Black Amphitheatre.
1 30m. 4a. Move around to the right onto White Slab and traverse 10 metres further to a crack, which is followed to the diagonal fault of *Black Dyke*. Make an interesting step to cross the small overlap. Climb a fine finger-crack and then a short groove on the right to flake belays.
2 25m. Move up leftwards and follow the ridge to the top.

The Black Amphitheatre
The remaining routes all start from a belay at the Water Slide, the low-angled but extremely slippery runnel where White Slab meets Rebel Wall.

Black Dyke   55 metres   Very Difficult   (30.7.95)
1 25m. 4a. Take the diagonal fault below the overlap across the slab and around the corner to belay. A good pitch.
2 30m. Scramble up the gully and move up right to gain the main ridge, which is followed to the top of the crag.
Variation
2a The Petrograd Finish 4c (15.6.96). From the belay, move back round onto the upper slab and climb the crack and corner above to join the ridge.

White Russians   55 metres   Very Severe †   (15.6.96)
This takes the crack in the centre of White Slab, which leads to the ramp on the headwall.
1 30m. 4c. Move along the fault of *Black Dyke* to a slight corner, where the crack starts. Follow the crack up the slab to the headwall. Climb leftwards up the ramp on the headwall and step up and around onto the

arête (crux). Climb the arête to a good belay.
2 25m. Move up left to the ridge, which is followed easily to the top.

Gypsy Johnny and the Demon King   45 metres   E3 †   (22.9.96)
This takes a direct line up the centre of the headwall. A committing but well-protected route with its crux in a fine position.
1 25m. 5c. Move a little way up the fault of *Black Dyke* and surmount the overlap to gain the upper slab, to the left of the crackline of *The Dvina*. Climb the slab, crossing the crack of *White Russians*, to the base of the headwall below the left end of the ramp. Steep moves up the wall gain the ramp (beware inhaling guano dust on the mantelshelf). Spectacular moves up the central crack of the headwall lead to the best 'thank God' holds in the world. Block and thread belays in the gully.
2 20m. Variable. Climb the left-hand side of the gully, picking the most interesting sections of rock.

The Dvina   40 metres   E3 †   (8.88)
Start at the Water Slide belay, from which a diagonal line of serpentine leads to a thin blind crack running up the White Slab.
1 25m. 5c. Climb along the serpentine line to gain the crack and follow it to the headwall, 2 metres left of the corner-crack. Climb the overhanging wall above, making a difficult move to gain a small ledge, and exit up the groove on the right to gain the gully above. Move up a short distance to block and thread belays.
2 15m. 4a. Cross the gully and take a direct line up the slab and groove to the left of pitch 2 of *Archangel*.

★Archangel   40 metres   Hard Very Severe   (1980s)
A three-star first pitch leads to disappointing but pleasantly situated climbing above.
1 25m. 5a. Climb the well-protected corner-crack and then hand-traverse rightwards above Rebel Wall to a ledge. Good block and nut belays.
2 15m. 4a. Move back left above the hand-traverse to gain a steep crack, which gives some interesting moves up to the slab above. Trend left up the slab to finish on the terrace.

★Rebel Yell   45 metres   E2   (14.7.96)
Fine steady wall climbing straight up Rebel Wall. Pumpy, if not climbed carefully. Start at the Water Slide.
1 25m. 5b. Climb a faint depression on the left of the wall up smooth rock, trending slightly right until better friction and holds are reached at 5 metres. Climb past the vague horizontal fault at half height, trending left to the vertical crack that leads exhilaratingly up the centre of the wall to the top. Good block and nut belays as for *Archangel*.
2 20m. 5a. Scramble rightwards along the terrace for nearly 10 metres to the edge of the slab, a slightly impending prow. Climb straight up, and finish easily up the slab above.

Romanis, Dyke, et al.   26 metres   Very Difficult   (4.8.20)
Pleasant climbing right of the Black Amphitheatre, giving a good
introduction to the nature of the climbing on Black Head. Start in the
Amphitheatre at the Water Slide.
1 6m. 4a. Climb the wide crack right of Rebel Wall to large ledges.
2 20m. Take the easy stairway just right of the arête of Rebel Wall to the
large terrace. Belay here if required. The slab above is more interesting
and is taken direct to a much larger second terrace, where the climb
finishes and the descent path is easily reached.
Variation
2a 1920 Traverse 35 metres (4.8.20). Take the easy stairway to the
first terrace, where, 'a difficult and sensational traverse may be made to
the left into the grassy gully above the Amphitheatre.' Climb the walls of
the gully and the pinnacle ridge on the left.

The Isles of Scilly (Granite)

The climbing potential of The Isles of Scilly cannot match that of Penwith's great cliffs or of Lundy or the Channel Isles. There is good granite, however, with some small Sennen-style crags and a wealth of boulders and small carns.

Climbing on Scilly's rocks has been recorded from at least the 1940s and probably before then. Ted Pyatt's seminal book *A Climber in the West Country*, published in 1968, gave a good outline of climbing potential on the islands, where locals have scrambled, bouldered, and climbed extensively through the years both in the natural way of islanders and in the formal climbing sense. At least two parties have climbed the same routes independently and there have even been reports of well-documented local guidebooks, although none has been found. The easier routes recorded here should be seen as possibly post-dating the achievements of many earlier pioneers.

Environmental Issues. The Scillies are immensely important nesting and passage sites. Large numbers of migratory birds stop off on the Islands during spring and autumn, while many important species nest on the island rocks. The cliff areas with recorded climbs as described here are not known to have protected species nesting on them.

Climbing has been recorded on a number of offlying stacks. The following islands and rock stacks have official restrictions on landing. Such restrictions are crucial to the principle of sanctuary as well as being legally enforced.

Islands closed from April 15th to August 20th: Annet, Gorregan, Green Island (Samson), Melledgan, Men-a-vaur, Norrard Rocks (including Castle Bryher, Illiswilgig, Maiden Bower, Mincarlo, and Scilly Rock), Stony Island, and Western Rocks (including Daisy, Great and Little Crebawethan, and Rosevear).

The Scillies in general also come under several environmental protection designations, while there is strong local vigilance and influence over conservation. Climbers are advised to act with restraint; the nature of the climbing potential on the islands tends to encourage this.

The only camping permitted on the Scillies is at the authorized sites on St Mary's, St Agnes, St Martin's, and Bryher.

St Mary's

St Mary's is the largest of the islands and is also the busiest. Its harbour community of Hughtown is the arrival point for the mainland ferry. St Mary's is about 15 kilometres in circumference and the coastline provides some fine short pitches on headlands and in zawns; good bouldering is also available.

Peninnis Head   OS Ref 911 092

Outlook: East on the Inner Head. East and west on the Monk's Cowl.
Tidal on Inner Head and at the base of the east face of the Monk's Cowl. The starting-ledges at the base of the south face of the Monk's Cowl are affected by swell and rough sea.
Coastguard Identity: Peninnis Head, St Mary's.

The most southerly point of St Mary's is the wind-sculpted headland of Peninnis. It is crowned with a lighthouse and is an obvious feature as one arrives at the Scillies by boat via St Mary's Sound. The rock is excellent clean granite. Peninnis is famous for its beautifully formed boulders and pinnacles with such names as Laughing Man, Old Witch, Walrus, and Sleeping Bear. Around the lighthouse lie clusters of fantastically shaped rocks with large rock basins. They are known as the Kettles and Pans. The many blowholes, caves, and rock inlets that fringe the headland boast names like Izzicumpucca and Sleep's Abode.

Approach by walking south along the coast path from Hughtown's Porthcressa Beach or from Buzza Tower above Hughtown.

The Head rises from the sea to a height of about 25 metres. There are three features offering routes: the Inner Head, the Outer Head, and The Monk's Cowl.

The Inner Head is a 20-metre pinnacle rising from the sea to the west of the main headland. It has four recorded routes and there are some boulder-problem pitches on its island side. The pinnacle is reached at about half tide across a connecting reef.

The Alien   8 metres   E4 6a †   (10.7.97)
A very obvious 'alien head' feature is reached shortly after crossing onto the Inner Head. Rounded cracks lead up to the 'alien', which is climbed to the top. (A cunning 'lasso' over a rounded ledge provides protection.)

Robin Bastard   10 metres   E1 5c †   (11.9.96)
Start 6 metres right of *The Alien*, at a clean slabby wall. Climb the wall and follow a thin (but widening) crack to the top.

Trident   20 metres   Hard Severe 4b   (1977)
A rewarding pitch. From the approach reef, move left and scramble down a boulder-filled gully to a ledge. Start here. Step down leftwards onto the arête; quite tricky. Traverse across the face to a wide crack, which is climbed with a finish to the left.

Curving Crack   20 metres   Hard Very Severe 5a †   (11.7.97)
Start beneath the obvious black slab split by a curving crack, which faces
The Monk's Cowl. Climb the crack and the lighter-coloured block above to
the very top of the Inner Head.

The more substantial Monk's Cowl is the highest rock feature of Peninnis
and lies south-west of the lighthouse. It is the first obvious feature reached on
the approach from Porthcressa Beach. It has north, south, and west faces.
The north face is non-tidal and is deeply seamed with fluted cracks. There
are half a dozen recorded routes on this face. The south face has an
impressive overhang at two-thirds height. The base of the south face is tidal
and routes towards its seaward end require an above-tide approach
traverse.

The north face of the Monk's Cowl is marked by deeply-fluted vertical
cracks. A striking feature at the top left edge of the face is an isolated,
tapering pinnacle called the Tooth Rock or Elephant's Tusk (or other
anatomical part). Near the left end of the wall (facing in) is a distinctive
chimney. This is *Peninnis Chimbley*.

Zest   15 metres   Hard Severe 4b   (1977)
Five metres left of *Peninnis Chimbley* a line of flakes runs up the wall.
Climb for 3 metres and then make an interesting move rightwards to finish
using large flakes.

Gone Fishing   10 metres   Very Severe 4c †   (11.9.96)
Climb cracks and flakes midway between *Zest* and *Peninnis Chimbley*.

Peninnis Chimbley   10 metres   Severe 4a   (1977)
Make awkward moves to enter the chimbley, sorry, chimney, which leads
more easily to the top.

Rock Hard Peninnis   15 metres   E4 6b †   (10.7.97)
An excellent climb which starts at the twin cracks between *Peninnis
Chimbley* and *Sean's Cleft*. Follow the pair of steep cracks to horizontal
breaks. Climb faint continuation cracks and make steep, dynamic,
layaway moves to finish.

Sean's Cleft   15 metres   Hard Very Severe 5a †   (9.9.96)
Climb the deep chimney near the right-hand side of the face.

Time and Motion   20 metres   E4 6a †   (10.9.96)
The seaward arête. Start below an 'hourglass' feature, at a shallow black
groove. Follow the groove to the 'hourglass', which takes a sling. Continue
up rounded cracks and flakes to the top.

✩✩**Fear of the Furnace**   25 metres   E2 5c   (1990s)
The narrow west face rises straight from the sea, so at high tide and in
good conditions this route can be tackled as a deep-water solo. Climb the
crackline and the flake above to the top.

The south face is a handsome feature with an impressive capping overhang
dominating its right-hand side. This lies above an easy-angled ledge at mid
height called The Gangway. Below The Gangway is a crack-seamed wall
with a distinctive crescent-shaped depression; this wall rises from the narrow
channel.

Starting-ledges at the base of the south face of the Head are gained by
descending cracked slabs running down from a saddle to the left of The
Tooth.

✩✩**Sunk Without Trace**   25 metres   E3 6a †   (10.7.97)
A fine line up the striking undercut crack on the left-hand side of the face.
Traverse left along the base of the wall and belay below *Britannia*'s lower
corner. Make a rising traverse leftwards to the deep crack and follow it past
a large block to the roof. Cross the roof and finish up the crack above.

Island Life   25 metres   E2 5c †   (10.9.96)
From the *Sunk Without Trace* belay, climb the shallow crack just to the left
and step into the corner at its top. There are two cracks splitting the roof
above; gain the left-hand crack and follow it with difficulty to the top.

★**Britannia**   30 metres   Very Severe   (1977)
This takes a line up the seaward wall just left of the left edge of the
overhang and The Gangway. From the ledges, traverse leftwards along a
narrow ledge, passing below a sickle-shaped depression, to reach the
base of twin cracks.
1 5m. Traverse left from the approach ledge to reach a square ledge.
2 15m. 4b. Climb the wall above, skirting an overhang on its left to
follow a slabby corner, which leads to a small ledge below the left edge of
the upper overhang.
3 10m. 5a. Climb an overhanging groove to finish.

★**Excalibur**   25 metres   Very Severe   (1977)
From the ledges, traverse leftwards along a narrow ledge, passing below
the sickle-shaped depression, to reach the base of the twin cracks.
1 10m. Climb the rounded left-hand crack to a stance below a corner.
2 15m. 4c. Climb the corner to a pedestal below the left edge of the
upper overhang (belay possible) and finish up the upper corner.

Neptune   15 metres   Severe 4a   (1977)
Climb the steep, rounded crack just right of the sickle-shaped depression
to finish on the The Gangway. Traverse off to the right to reach the descent
break.

The descent break has a smooth central slab.

Rigs   27 metres   Difficult   (1977)
Climb the crack on the left of the smooth slab to reach the higher, triangular-shaped slab below the base of The Tooth. Finish up either side of the slab.

Creepy Crawly   35 metres   Very Difficult   (17.5.80)
An eccentric route.
1 20m. Climb the centre of the smooth slab, with delicate moves midway, to belay in a corner on the left of the base of The Tooth.
2 15m. Climb a crack in the steep left wall of the notch between The Tooth and the main bulk of the Head. Reasonable if the notch is chimneyed; much harder if the crack is climbed direct. Reach a rounded ledge, from where a move right around an arête is followed by a worming crawl to reach a belay. Descent is by cracks via a grassy ledge in the landward edge of the north face.

Kings Road   27 metres   Difficult   (1977)
Climb the crack on the right of the smooth slab. Finish to the right of the base of The Tooth, past a poised block.

There are a number of pitches up the lower wall to the right of the starting-ledges. Only one has been recorded.

Diced Carrots   25 metres   Very Difficult   (17.5.80)
Near the base of the descent slabs is a short gully breaching the right wall. Climb the gully to a ledge (belay possible); then continue up the chimney between the huge block and a narrower block.

There are many bouldering possibilities and short problem pitches on Peninnis's Outer Head to the south-east of the Monk's Cowl; two are described. They start from a non-tidal ramp beneath a compact wall of good rock.

Caravan Convert   8 metres   Hard Very Severe 5c †   (12.9.96)
The left-to-right diagonal crack near the left-hand end of the wall.

Fantasy Island   8 metres   E3 6a †   (12.9.96)
The staggered rounded cracks which start 5 metres right of *Caravan Convert* succumb to a good traditional tussle.

Giant's Castle   OS Ref 925 100
Outlook: South-west.
Non-tidal on the one recorded climb.
Coastguard Identity: Giant's Castle, St Mary's.

One and a half kilometres east of Peninnis Head is the striking promontory of Giant's Castle, the site of an ancient cliff castle like those of Gurnard's Head and Logan Rock on the mainland. There is one recorded route.

Approach by walking east along the coast path from Old Town, which itself is reached by road from Hughtown.

The cliff rises through a series of steps to layered overhangs from a huge platform well above the sea. The final overhang has a distinctive crimped edge like a giant Cornish pasty.

Bastille   30 metres   Hard Very Severe   (4.81)
A steep orange-coloured wall rises from the huge platform. Start at the left side of the wall.
1 18m. Climb to the first ledge and then trend up and rightwards via walls and ledges to below a break on the right of the overhangs. (There are much harder starts up the initial wall via cracks.)
2 12m. 5a. Make hard moves through the break in the overhang; then climb more easily rightwards to finish.

St Martin's
There is potential for bouldering and for short problem pitches, but only one route has been recorded. This lies on the third headland north-east of New Quay, beneath Chapel Down and close to Mullet Pool.

Fantasia   15 metres   E2 5c †   (6.7.95)
Half tide required. Climb the obvious overhanging groove in the middle of the wall to a finely positioned finish. Block belays.

Bryher
Bryher has long excited climbers' interest, which has been focused on Shipman Head at the island's north end. The Head is a beautiful and remote place. It is separated from the main island by a narrow rock channel containing a jammed boulder which almost seems to keep Head and Island prised apart.

The Head is not a restricted area, although many birds nest on its northern and eastern sides. It has a great deal of rock, yet surprisingly there are no continuous faces to give anything other than short problem pitches. Access is tightly controlled by tide and weather.

There are some short pitches and bouldering possibilities in the area of The Horse on the north-east shoulder of Bryher itself.

St Agnes
St Agnes has many short and not-so-short problem pitches along its south-western shore from Long Point to Wingletang Bay.

First Ascents

This list is as comprehensive as possible. Due regard should be paid to early pioneers – and some contemporary ones – who made ascents with a healthy distaste for posterity and left no record.

A number of route duplications have been noted. Some involve routes climbed and recorded many years ago, omitted from previous guidebooks and then subsequently climbed and claimed with good intent. Where possible the subsequent ascent is mentioned. It is hoped that first ascent vanity does not produce too much quibbling. In some cases, the authors have had to make judgements on routes which have questionable independence over existing ones. Again the initial line has taken precedence.

The policy of retaining the original name of an aid route that has been totally free-climbed is followed even when variations in line or combinations have been established. Where a free ascent has produced a recorded new name this is mentioned.

AL and VL in brackets indicate alternate and varied leads respectively. The number of any points of aid known to have been used on a first ascent is given in brackets after the name of the climb; the word Aid indicates that the climb was originally climbed as an aid route or with an aid section.

No details for:	**Helmet Ridge, Carn Boel Cleft, Martell Groove**
c.1910	**Western Chimneys** A W Andrews and J E Littlewood *Climbed separately and unaware of each other's activities.* *Andrews descended the chimneys; Littlewood ascended. Both rose* *into the Pantheon.*
1920 Aug 4	**Romanis, Dyke, et al.** D G Romanis, C B Jerram *Rediscovered and named by J Dyke, S Reynolds on 30 July 1995.* *1920 Traverse climbed on 4 August 1920 by D G Romanis,* *C B Jerram.*
1920	**Northside Chimney, Southside Chimney, Southside Traverse, Chockstone Chimney, Pinnacle Traverse** A W Andrews
1920	**Bending Chimney** D G Romanis, C B Jerram *Other climbs at Trewavas and elsewhere in West Penwith were* *probably climbed by Romanis and Jerram, who pioneered at a* *time when there was less emphasis on claiming routes.*
c.1930	**Cleft Route, East Chimney, Great Slab Route** J E Littlewood and party
1935 Aug 27	**Central Buttress Chimneys** L S Powell, E M Mitchell, G Streatfield, J F Littlewood *Halfway House variation by R Edwards (solo) in June 1987.*
1935 Aug	**Vessack's Original** F W T James, R E F James
1937 Aug 26	**Dexter Crack** L S Powell
1938 Aug 7	**Porthgwarra Face** C F Kirkus, P S Fallows *Climbed on 25 May 1956 by C Fishwick, R W Fishwick and claimed*

in good faith as Dowser's Route owing to misleading location details. Dowser's Route has one independent section: pitch 3a.

1938 Aug 7	**Original Route** C F Kirkus, W J Fallows, P S Fallows	
1938 Aug 9	**Porthgwarra Crack** C F Kirkus, P S Fallows	
1938 Sept 12	**North Wall Climb** A G Potter, C A Acheson, J C Acheson	
1939	**Southside Crack** J A Smalley, C Bechgard	
1940 March 24	**Terrier's Tooth** J Mallory, M A Roster	

*By the easier right hand start. The Direct and far right starts:
J E Q Barford, F Feilden on 25 August 1940.*

1946 Oct	**Mermaid's Route** (upper pitches only) A J Smyth
1947	**Pendulum Chimney** J Courtlandt-Simpson, E Stones

The eponymous pendulum stone finally plummeted. The upper chimney had been climbed by J E Littlewood in the early 1930s.

1947	**Red Wall** J Courtlandt-Simpson, E Stones

Suicide Crack variation had already been climbed by L S Powell on 21 August 1936.

1948	**South Face Direct** J Courtlandt-Simpson, E Stones

A Penwith classic. Chair Ladder's answer, and Simpson's answer, to his own Bosigran classic, Zig Zag.

1949	**Flannel Avenue** Royal Marines
1949	**Raider's Route, Giant Steps** (Chair Ladder) M E B Banks, J Flint
c.1940s	**Whisky** A W Andrews

Malt, of course.

c.1940s	**Economist's Climb, Nut Route, The Green Face Wolverine Chimney, Dodger's Chimney** Royal Marines
1950 Oct	**Hampshire Zigzag** A J Imrie

1950	***Cornwall* by Arther Andrews and Ted Pyatt**

1951 March 25	**Cut-Off** M J Ridges, J F Lilly
1951 March 27	**Folly Corner** M J Ridges, J F Lilly (AL)
1951 March 27	**Zawn Face Climb** (Fox Promontory) M J Ridges, J F Lilly

*The Outside Start by V N Stevenson and R Rochester on
16 September 1962.*

1951	**Diocese** M J Ridges, J F Lilly

One of Chair Ladder's sainted lines. A prior claim to a first ascent rests with R Hanley and E Phillips, while H T H Peck is said to have top-roped the definitive line in the late Forties using a shunt device. They should all be blessed.

1951	**Muscle Chimney** M J Ridges, J F Lilly
1952 March 31	**Edge Climb, Recessed Slab Climb** A J Imrie, R Goodier
1952 April 14	**The Girdle Traverse** (Chair Ladder) M J Ridges, A E Simpson, R Morden (AL)

*An east-to-west girdle of the main face had been followed by
J E Littlewood, L S Powell in 1902.*

1952 June 27	**Gullible, Rake's Progress** R Handley, A J Hallam, V Phillips

The main pitch of Gullible was destroyed by rockfall.

1952 June	**Pegasus** R Handley, E Phillips

The top pitch was added by J Deacon in June 1952.

1952 Sept 16	**The Grooves** (Carn Lês Boel) Mrs N E Morin

The Direct Start: D Kemp on 1 June 1953.

1953 May 31	**Nearly** J M Edwards, N Albon, Mrs N E Morin

*The upper pitch was added by M B McDermott, D W Bateman in
1962.*

1954 Nov	**Helmet Ridge Direct**	R Fleming, A G Mitchell
1954	**The Mitre**	J Deacon, J W Kinnaird
1955 May 22	**Wrist Climb**	R Goodier, R L Shepton, R E Bisley
1955 May 26	**Criss**	R Goodier, A J Imrie
1955 June 29	**Socket Wall**	R Goodier, F A B Peel, J H Deacon, M E B Banks
1955 July 2	**Peel Crack**	F A B Peel, R Fleming, R Goodier
1955 July 4	**Zeke's Route**	J Deacon, R Goodier
1955 July 5	**Slant Crack**	R Goodier, R L Shepton
1955 July 7	**Niche Wall**	R Goodier, J Lawton

1955 Aug 12 — Amen Corner R Goodier, J Deacon (AL)
A challenging climb for its day and a fitting conclusion to Goodier's Carn Barra development.

1955 Aug 22	**Sea Fury** (2 pts aid)	B M Biven, H T H Peck, P H Biven
1955 Oct	**Overhanging Chimney**	J Deacon
1955	**Corporal's Route**	J Deacon, M E B Banks (AL)
1955	**Seal Slab**	G Smith, J Deacon (AL)

Watch Hunt variation climbed on 6 August 1985 by M Edwards, J Cooke.

1955 — *Climbing in Cornwall (New Climbs supplement)* by Rawdon Goodier, Peter Biven, Barrie Biven, et al.

1956 May 1	**The Buccaneer**	H T H Peck, P H Biven
1956 May 20	**The Muzzle**	A Blackshaw, J Deacon (AL)
1956 May 20	**Sunshine Cracks**	J Deacon, A Blackshaw
1956 May 25	**Aerial**	H T H Peck, P H Biven

After pitch 2, Cut-Off was followed. Pitch 3 as described: V N Stevenson, E T Rook on 14 November 1962. Other Spirits variation: N Hancock, R Meek in February 1996.

1956 May 25	**Helluva Slab**	C Fishwick, R W Fishwick
1956 May 28	**Laceration**	H T H Peck, P H Biven
1956 May	**Reveille**	J Deacon, A Blackshaw
1956 May	**Sinister** (Fox Promontory)	J Deacon, D M Holroyd, A Blackshaw

1956 Sept — Porthgwarra Chimney C W F Noyce
Wilfred Noyce climbing where his cousin Colin Kirkus had made first ascents nearly twenty years before.

1956 — Bishop's Rib J Deacon, J W Oakes
Gained from Diocese by a fine unprotected lead. The start as described: M B McDermott, R A P Mellor, D W Bateman on 21 July 1963.

1956 — Swiss Route H B Grey
Pitch 2 climbed by S Westmacott, B Seiffert in June 1973. Towerful variation climbed by M Edwards and party in 1980.

1957 April 15	**Mild and Bitter**	M B McDermott, M E B Banks, J Deacon
1957 April 16	**Seal Passage**	J Deacon, M E B Banks

Variation: P Gordon, G Morgan on 15 July 1973.

1957 June 10	**Neptune** (Chair Ladder)	J A Dennis, W Broome
1957	**Excalibur** (Carn Lês Boel)	J Deacon, D M Holroyd
1957	**Martell Slab**	J Deacon, D M Holroyd

Direct Finish: P O'Sullivan, Ms C Woodhead in August 1979. This may have been climbed in 1976 by P Livesey, R Fawcett, P Botterill.

1959 May 16	**Bitter End**	E H Marriott, O H Barnard

1959 June	**Lamorna Wall** (Aid)	J Deacon, M B McDermott

Free-climbed by R Edwards in 1978. Pitch 1a: R Fawcett in 1976; pitch 1b The Water Margin: K Palmer, A Grieve, P Saunders on 4 May 1987; pitch 1c: P Livesey in 1976.

1959 Sept   **Central Route**   P C F Cullinan, A Blackshaw
1959 Oct 25   **Detergent Wall**   V N Stevenson, J Deacon (AL)
1959 Oct 25   **Excelsior**   V N Stevenson, J Deacon (AL)

The top pitch as described: V N Stevenson, B Wake on 29 September 1961.

1950s   **Dorna, Marine Parade, Bus Route, The Ramble, The Rabbit Run, Eric's Route, Commando Special, Crow's Nest Ordinary, Western National, Gully Route, The Sentry-Box**   Royal Marines

Direct Finish to Dorna climbed by M Edwards (solo) in August 1984.

1950s   **Great Chimney**   J Deacon, R Goodier
1950s   **Longships Ridge**   Mrs N E Morin, J M Edwards
1960 June   **Willie's Way**   W H Morrow
1960 Nov   **The Veil, Knight's Pillar**   J Deacon, D R Knights

Direct Start to The Veil climbed by M Edwards (solo) in August 1984. Direct Finish to Knight's Pillar climbed by R Edwards in 1995 as Checkmate.

c.1960   **Layaway**   R E F James
1961 Aug   **King Crab Crack**   H I Banner, R G Wilson, J B Sanders
1961 Sept 27   **Kaleidoscope**   V N Stevenson, R Todd
1961 Sept   **Biceps Wall**   V N Stevenson, B Wake
1961 Sept   **Gringo**   B Wake, V N Stevenson (AL)
1962 June 11   **Pygmalion**   P W Vaughan, E H Herbert (AL)
1962 Nov 6   **Crow's Nest Direct**   V N Stevenson, G B Wilson
1962   **The Pyg Track**   E Whittacker, N Mann
1963 June 1   **The Bishop's Chain**   M B McDermott, R A P Meller (AL)
1963 June 9   **Panda**   V N Stevenson, J M G Sheridan
1963 Aug 12   **Dour Cracks**   V N Stevenson, P Stevenson
1963 Aug 12   **Pandour Grooves**   V N Stevenson

The Cut direct start climbed in 1989 by R Edwards, M Edwards.

1963 Aug 15   **Cuboid Corner**   V N Stevenson, D W Bateman

Direct Start: P W Vaughan, E H Herbert on 1 June 1966.

1963 Aug 15   **Pullover, The Illusion**   V N Stevenson, D W Bateman
1963 Aug 18   **The Vixen's Embrace** (2 pts aid)   V N Stevenson, D W Bateman
1963 Aug 19   **Pollyvia**   V N Stevenson
1963 Aug 20   **Stackolee**   V N Stevenson, P Stevenson
1963 Aug 21   **The Whisker, The Curtain Raiser**   V N Stevenson, D W Bateman, D Brown

A fine conclusion to Stevenson's impressive contributions to the South Coast, followed in 1966 by his excellent guidebook.

1965 May 9   **Kernyck, Harder**   M B McDermott, D W Bateman, V N Stevenson
1965 June 8   **Nothing Much**   D Wiggett, A G Smythe

Nothing quite like it. The name was a fierce understatement for many years until it was upgraded. Variation: I F Duckworth, G Morgan in January 1971.

1966 March 6   **Birthday Route** (Aid)   M B McDermott, D W Bateman

FFA by R Edwards, M Edwards on 8 June 1980 as Powerflex.

1966 May	**Shawangunk**	M Westmacott, S Westmacott, R Chorley
		Variation climbed by R Edwards on 30 June 1982.
1966 June 1	**Reynard's Revenge**	P W Vaughan, E H Herbert
1966 Aug 9	**Cave Route, Maureen**	H I Banner, D W Bateman
1966 Aug 13	**Not Quite, Sea Horse**	H I Banner, D W Bateman
1966 Aug 21	**Western Arête**	H I Banner, D W Bateman
1966 Nov 3	**Mine Climb** (1 pt aid)	M Springett, M Beacham
		Originally called Parishioner but later excommunicated.
1966	**Veedy**	D Wiggett, A G Smythe

1966   *Cornwall Volume 2 by Vivian Stevenson*

1967 March 5	**Gandalf**	P Gordon, M Springett
1967 March 5	**Saruman**	M Springett, P Gordon
1967 March 31	**Eileen**	D W Bateman, J Armitage
1967 April 30	**Macbate**	M McDermott, D W Bateman
1967 April 30	**Sea Pink Slab**	D W Bateman, M McDermott
1967 May 25	**The Scabbard** (2 pts aid)	M Springett, R Hodgson

Climbed free by H I Banner, W O R Hill on 1 July 1967. This was a significant early piece of true 'free-climbing' in Penwith, reflecting the calibre of the climbers. The Direct Start: M Edwards, R Edwards on 5 August 1981.

1967 May 31	**Pendragon** (1 pt aid)	H I Banner, D W Bateman
1967 June 17	**Bosistow Chimney**	H I Banner, N Horne, W O R Hill
1967 June 24	**The Crack**	H I Banner, N Horne, W O R Hill, K Rhodes
1967 June 27	**Anna's Climb**	N Horn, H I Banner, W O R Hill (AL)
1967 July 2	**The Cut**	H I Banner, W O R Hill, K Rhodes, N Horne
1967 July 3	**Cinecs**	K Rhodes, N Horne, W O R Hill, H I Banner
1967 July 3	**Easy Way Down**	H I Banner, N Horne, K Rhodes
1967 July 18	**The Ramp**	W O R Hill, N Horne, H I Banner (AL)
1968 Jan 10	**Phiz**	S Young, R Coates
1968 May 23	**Kittiwake**	M Springett, J Cooke
1968 July	**Octopus**	P Pasquil, G Penketh
1968 Aug 15	**Samphire Wall**	D W Bateman, G Morgan
1968	**South-East Face Direct**	P R Littlejohn (solo)

1968   *Cornwall Volume 1 by Peter Biven and Mike McDermott*

1969 Feb 2	**Claire**	D W Bateman, C Andrews
1969 Feb 16	**Pedantics, Sea Fox**	D W Bateman, G Morgan, D Brown
1969 March 6	**Graculus, Draculus**	S Young, N Barnes
1969 March	**West Side Story**	R E F James (solo)
1969 April 13	**Broccoli Bucket**	D Brown, G Morgan, B Lessister
		First moves on St Loy after jungle warfare to get there.
1969 April 14	**Mushroom Medley**	G Morgan, B Lessiter
1969 April 19	**Suede Squeeze**	B Lessiter, D Brown, G Morgan
1969 April 20	**Ivy Incoporated**	D Brown, J Atherton

The start was originally a separate climb named Turnip Twostep climbed by J Street, D W Bateman.

1969 April 27	**Chicory Chock, Chicory Check**	D Brown, G Cooper, B Lessiter, G Morgan (VL)
1969 May	**Barbacus**	S Young, R Coates
1969 Aug 31	**Beta**	P Jose, T Newbury
1969 Aug 31	**Marconi Crack**	R E F James, T R F James
1969 Dec 4	**Sancho**	S R Young, R D Hodgson

The start of modern development at Trewavas, where Romanis and Jerram had climbed in the 20s.

c.1960s	**Dodge City** Unknown	
1970 Jan 1	**Gloy (Aid)** G Morgan, D Brown	
1970 Jan 25	**Cenopod Corner** G Morgan, D Brown	
	Variation: M Dunning, N Crowhurst on 8 April 1990.	
1970 March 1	**Tingaloy** P Gordon (solo)	
1970 March 28	**Sloe Steel** D Steel, I F Duckworth	
1970 April 3	**F-Nose** C Cooper, D Brown, G Morgan	
	'Why did you go so far without any gear?'	
1970 April 3	**Hi-Ten** G Morgan, D Brown, C Cooper	
	As an aid climb. Free-climbed subsequently by a number of parties.	
1970 April 3	**Sloe Slab, Kelly's Eye** D Brown, G Morgan	
1970 June 14	**Chlorophyll Cluster** P Gordon	
1970 July 6	**Mascara** S R Young, K D A Peterson	
1970 Aug 27	**Gentleman's Relish** R E F James, D W Bateman	
1970 Sept 14	**The Pit** R Crossley, K D Lyne, P Gross	
1970 Sept 16	**The Beak** R Crossley, K D Lyne, P Gross (AL)	
1970 Sept	**Laminaria** P Gross, R Crossley, K D Lyne	
1970 Oct 18	**Penny Lane** S R Young, N S Barnes (AL)	
1970 Nov 15	**Sennifer** S R Young, N S Barnes	
1970	**Cress Cendo** P Gordon, G Morgan	
1970	**Deceptive** T Newbury, M Dawson	
1970	**Hay Fever** G Morgan, D W Bateman, D Brown	
1971 April 10	**Porthcrawl** R Bennet, J Brennan (AL)	
1971 April 11	**The Sigh (1 pt aid)** B R E Wilkinson, D Gregson	
	FFA in 1985 by T Carver, P Johnstone, D Hannigan. Variation finish by N White, S Thorpe in 1984.	
1971 April 14	**The Lurch** P Livesey (solo)	
1971 May 28	**Expresso Bonzo** P R Littlejohn	
1971 July 4	**The Spire** P R Littlejohn, W A Carver	
1971 Oct 25	**Teacher's Pet** S B Jones, P R Littlejohn (AL)	
1971 Dec 27	**Iapetus** J Brennan, R Bennett	
1972 April 3	**The Pawn** C Milford, M Putnam	
	Pitch 2a: A Freen, J Hart 1978.	
1972 July 23	**Ra** P de Mengel, C Bartlett, B Hocken	
1972 July	**The Orb** P Rigg, W Birch	
	The main pitch was destroyed by rockfall.	
1972 Aug 30	**Axis** A McFarlane, I F Duckworth, B Hocken	
1972 Aug 30	**Dialectic (2 pts aid)** I F Duckworth, A McFarlane	
	Left-hand variation: C Nicholson, A Gallagher in May 1979. Right-hand variation: R Edwards, M Edwards in 1978. Original line free-climbed by R Edwards, M Edwards in May 1980.	
1972 Oct 22	**Siân** C Bartlett, A Mahony	
1972 Dec 27	**Transubstantiation, Tobacco Road** R Bennett, J Brennan (AL), D Irons	
1972 Dec 29	**Prima Donna** R Bennett, J Brennan (Al), D Irons	
1972	**The Tower, Niche Route, Low Tide** L Williams, D W Bateman	
1972	**Crack and Slab** D W Bateman, L Williams	
1973 Feb 4	**Easy Gully** L Williams, D W Bateman	
1973 Feb 4	**Ivy Chimney** D W Bateman, L Williams	
1973 Feb 18	**Rucsac** L Williams, D W Bateman	
1973 March 11	**Sunshine Wall** L Williams, D W Bateman	
1973 March	**White Rib** . W Chapple, O Smith	

Down the Welly (E1, first ascent), Pen Olver
Climber: Dave Turnbull   Photo: Ken Palmer

Dingo (E2, first ascent),
Bass Point
Climber: Pete O'Sullivan
Photo: Don Sargeant

1973 May 6	**Times Remembered**	D W Bateman, J Atherton
1973 May	**Black and Tan**	M White, P Rigg
1973 May	**Gypsum Johnny, Cinnamon**	M White, O Smith
1973 June 24	**Dennis**	L Williams, D W Bateman
1973 July 15	**Xenolith**	R Bennet, J Brennan, K Hipkess (VL)

Variation 1a: S Young, R Mitchell on 20 June 1987.

1973 Aug 23	**Permanendo**	R E F James (solo)
1973 Sept 9	**Bedrock Chimney**	D W Bateman
1973 Sept 29	**Colenzo**	D W Bateman, J Colenzo
1973 Oct 28	**Afterthought**	L Williams, D W Bateman
1973	**Last Resort**	D W Bateman, L Williams
1973	**Bramble**	L Williams, D W Bateman
1974	**Reach**	J Cotton and party

Climbed in good faith and named by P Craggs on 31 December 1989.

1973   *Great Zawn* by Frank Cannings and Pat Littlejohn

1973   *Chair Ladder: an Interim Guide* by Roger Gook and Mike White

1973   *Climbing in Cornwall* by Toni Carver, Peter Stanier, and Pat Littlejohn

1974 Feb	**Mexican Pete**	I F Duckworth
1974 Feb 24	**Mantelshelf Wall**	L Williams, R Frith
1974 March 24	**Trimsaran**	L Williams, D W Bateman
1974 April 5	**Finesse**	P R Littlejohn, S B Jones

St Loy resurrected, with finesse. Variation 1a climbed by P O'Sullivan, M Dunning on 18 March 1990. Variation 2a climbed by S Ohly, G Slade in August 1995.

1974 April 7	**The Baldest**	P R Littlejohn, S P Jones

'I felt that if the Almighty had provided one crystal less I was going to break my neck.'

1974 April 21	**Joy**	L Williams, D W Bateman
1974 April	**Sweet and Sour**	M E B Banks, M Pickup
1974 June 14	**Almost**	Unknown
1974 June 20	**Nerth**	L Williams, D W Bateman
1974 July 14	**Campion**	L Williams, D W Bateman
1974 July 28	**Sidestep**	L Williams, D W Bateman
1974 Aug 27	**Slight**	L Williams, D W Bateman
1974 Sept 7	**Williams's Chimney**	L Williams, D W Bateman, P Murray

Banner Variation climbed by H Banner, D W Bateman on 12 August 1976. Slade's Pillar variation climbed by G Slade, S Ohly on 16 September 1998.

1974 Sept 15	**Avalanche**	L Williams, D W Bateman
1974 Oct 20	**Cornel**	L Williams, D W Bateman
1974	**The Groove** (Trewavas Head)	D W Bateman, L Williams
1974	**Hesitation Cracks**	L Williams, D W Bateman
1974	**Pennywort**	L Williams, D W Bateman
1974	**Joy Direct**	L Williams, D W Bateman
1974	**The Pillar**	D W Bateman, L Williams
1974	**Colomen**	L Williams, D W Bateman, P Murray

Direct Finish climbed in May 1995 by J Ford, S Elliott.

1975 Jan 5	**Gaffer's Wall**	P Murray, D W Bateman
1975 Feb 9	**Gaffer's Revenge**	L Williams, P Murray, D W Bateman

1975 March 23	**Short 'n' Sweet** L Williams, D W Bateman
1975 April	**The Girdle** (Trewavas Head) D W Bateman, L Williams, R Pryor
1975 Oct 5	**Iron Cross** B R E Wilkinson, J Wilkinson
1975	**Caliban** (aid) R Abbas, N Cotton
	Free-climbed by J de Montjoye, A C Whitehouse on 18 April 1981.
1975	**Razor** B R E Wilkinson, C French
1975	**Sidestep Direct** P Gordon, G Morgan
1975	**Simon** S Trathan, P Murray
1975	**Avalanche Direct** G Geanelli
1975	**Crossover** L Williams, D W Bateman

1975   ***Chair Ladder and the South Coast by Bob Moulton and Terry Thompson***

1976 April 16	**Demelza** M Vallance, K J Vickers
1976 April 16	**Weasle** B R E Wilkinson, G F Hollyman
	Touchstone variation climbed on 26 May 1982 by S Salmon, R Hall.
1976 April 17	**Foxblood** B R E Wilkinson, G F Hollyman
1976 April	**The Red Tower, The Steeple** P Livesey, A Evans
	Characteristically hard additions to Chair Ladder.
1976 June 20	**Wee-Nutcracker** R Pryor, P Murray
1976 Aug 22	**Megaphone Chimney** R E F James, T R F James
	Megaphoney variation: R Edwards, 1989.
1976 Oct 2	**Camelot** J Barry, D V Nicholls (AL)
1976 Oct	**Carrivick** D Carrivick, R Pryor
1976	**South Groove** R Pryor
1976	**Lizzy's Folly** D Connor, K Evans
1976	**Aquiline, Illusion, Rinny Wall, The Groove** (Chair Ladder) R Edwards, F Smith
	Edwards's first foray on Penwith's South Coast.
1977 Jan 16	**The Traverse** D W Bateman, L Williams
1977 Aug 8	**Cumbelloe** B R E Wilkinson, A Gallager
1977 Aug 20	**Geriatric** R E F James, A Skinner
1977 Sept 25	**Nosey** L Williams, P Murray
1977 Oct	**Chopper Chimney** S Salmon, J Pearce, R Hall, S Ferguson
1977 Oct	**Lesser Known Tunisians** J Pearce, S Salmon
1977	**Trident, Zest, Peninnis Chimbley, Britannia (The Isles of Scilly), Excalibur, Neptune, Rigs, Kings Road** D Bassett, J Bassett
	Imaginitive development onThe Isles of Scilly. Some routes may have been climbed previously.
1978 Jan 8	**Blind Spring** D W Bateman, D Atherton
1978 Jan 22	**Triple Fugue** P Murray, L Williams, D W Bateman
1978 March 5	**Per Ardua** G Geanelli, L Williams
1978 May 21	**Burning Gold** P R Littlejohn, C King
	A first great climb on Paradise Wall. A similar line had been aided several years before by unknown climbers who used some bolts. Burning Gold was free-climbed in its entirety and no bolts were placed by its first ascensionist.
1978 Oct 26	**Air Sea Rescue** P Murray, J Twigg
1978 Oct 28	**The Huntsman** A Gallagher, B R E Wilkinson
1978	**Panda Chimneys, Panda Crawl** R Edwards and party
1978	**Cain** P R Littlejohn
	A powerful addition to Pordenack.

1978	**Grit Exiles** R Fawcett, S Foster	

1978	***Bosigran and the North Coast* by Ed Hart**

1979 April 5   **Aquastat**   D W Bateman, D Bolton, R Prager
1979 April 5   **Consolation Climb**   C D Boston, D Dawson, P King
1979 April 14   **Toothache**   S M Richardson, J Knifton
1979 July 29   **Foot Loose**   R W Lanchbury, P Murray, R Brenchley
1979 July 29   **Bloody Finger**   R W Lanchbury, P Murray
1979 Aug   **Loose Change**   P O'Sullivan, I Peters (AL)
An unwise choice as a first foray on The Lizard.
1979 Aug   **Pericles, Lysander**   P O'Sullivan, Ms C Woodhead
1979 Sept 9   **Club Route**   Members of Land's End CC
1979 Oct 22   **Exodus**   R Edwards, M Edwards
1979 Oct 23   **Illustrated Man**   R Edwards, M Edwards
1979 Dec 31   **Last Day's Flier**   R Edwards, M Edwards
1979   **Front Piece**   R Edwards and party
1979   **Harmony**   I Lonsdale, A Hartnett
1979   **Rook's Folly**   R Edwards and party
1979   **Little Trapeze, Little Trapeze Right-hand, Exit Climb, Halfway House, Full House, Big Ned, Teetotal**
R Edwards and party
1970s   **Cat's Paw, Messenger, Cringle, Keelson, Gimbals, Hound's Band, Strake, Mexicano**
Climbed by a number of parties
1970s   **Dago**   A McFarlane
1980 Jan 2   **Atlantic Crossing**   R Edwards, M Edwards
1980 Jan 12   **Giant's Crawl**   R Edwards, M Edwards
1980 Jan 12   **Gulliver's Route**   R Edwards, M Edwards, S Peplow
1980 Jan 13   **Heelstone**   D W Bateman, R Harvey, A Harvey (AL)
Variation: P O'Sullivan, D Hannigan 15 April 1990.
1980 March 16   **Stone Boom**   R Edwards, R Perriment
Telegraph Road variation climbed by R Edwards, M Edwards in 1983. Cable Highway variation climbed in August 1998 by M Edwards, I Blake.
1980 March 30   **American Dream**   R Edwards, C Bryan
A fine start to a worthwhile development.
1980 April 4   **Hot Cross Bun**   P Murray, J Twigg
1980 April 18   **The Arch**   R Edwards, M Edwards, M Peplow
1980 May 10   **Crack in the Sky**   R Edwards, M Edwards, C Bryan
1980 May 10   **Fine and Dandy**   C Bryan, R Edwards, M Edwards
1980 May 17   **Creepy Crawly, Diced Carrots**   S Salmon, D Hannigan
1980 May 23   **Sunny Corner Lane**   R Edwards, M Edwards
1980 May 23   **Grande Plage**   R Edwards, M Edwards
Variation Start climbed by R Edwards, M Edwards on 10 May 1984.
1980 May 24   **52nd Street, Geireagle II**   R Edwards, M Edwards
1980 June 6   **The Screw**   R Edwards, M Edwards
1980 Aug 27   **Four Directions**   R Edwards, I S Hunter, S Ghulamali
1980 Sept 3   **The Immaculate Crack, Immaculate Groove**   R Edwards, M Edwards
1980 Sept 3   **Kari, Wandering Worlds**   R Edwards, M Edwards, K Harrison
1980 Sept 10   **West Face Direct** (Chair Ladder)   R Edwards, M Edwards, A Shearder (AL)
1980 Oct 5   **Dark Denizen**   R Bennet, M Dunning
1980 Oct 25   **Livinbrâs**   S Salmon, D Hannigan

1980 Nov 9	**Cleavage** S Salmon, D Hannigan
1980 Nov 26	**Tower Direct** M Edwards, Members of Plymouth College
1980 Dec 7	**Pregnant Pause** S Salmon, D Hannigan
1980	**Little Cracker** (Pordenack) R Edwards and party

1980   ***Trewavas Head, A Climbing Guide* by Dennis Bateman and Les Williams**

1981 Jan 7	**Gig in the Sky** M Edwards, R Edwards
1981 Jan 10	**Immaculate Arête** R Edwards, M Edwards
	An excellent climb. It also featured the first bolt to be placed on a modern route of significance in Penwith. The bolt was subsequently removed. Direct Start: R Edwards, C Edwards 24 May 1987.
1981 Feb 13	**Friends** M Edwards, S Peplow
	Pitch 2: G A Jenkin, F E R Cannings 24 May 1981. The return of old friends.
1981 March 15	**The Gingerbread Crack** R Edwards, M Edwards (AL)
	The Great Beast Unleashed variation by P O'Sullivan, C Griffiths on 7 April 1998.
1981 April 18	**Sports Plan** R Edwards, M Edwards, F Smith, R Barker
	The direct start via the pinnacle was climbed as a direct start to The Muzzle by G M Gravina, H G Nicol on 11 May 1959.
1981 April 20	**Andy's Route** A Trevorrow, R Harvey
	Retrospectively claimed by M Edwards and the Peplow brothers in 1997 as Kalahari (1980).
1981 April 25	**Fat Panda** S Salmon, D Hannigan
1981 April	**Bastille** D Bassett, J Bassett
1981 June 21	**Folly Groove, Hallucinations** M Edwards, R Edwards
	Hallucinations (Fox Promontory) has since been destroyed by rockfall.
1981 July 26	**The Hairiest** C Nicholson, S Salmon
1981 July 30	**They Do at That Age** D Cook, S Shimitzu, N Freemantle
1981 July	**The Immaculate Grovel** C Nicholson, S Salmon
	Possibly climbed before.
1981 Aug 8	**Salamander** I Peters, P Buttrick (AL), A Clark
1981 Sept 2	**Mouseproof** S Salmon, M Crayton
1981 Sept 19	**Lovely Cruise** (Aid) S Salmon, B Warburton, P Thompson
1981 Oct 18	**Bishop's Arête** R Edwards, M Edwards, N Wharton
1981	**Phenocryst** J Milton, J Hooper
1981	**Zip** J Hooper
1981	**Dexter's Groove** R Edwards, M Edwards
1981	**Boysen's Groove, Boysen's Cracks** M Boysen, A Hubbard
1981	**Not Right** J Knifton, B Hawkes
1981	**The Surfboard** A Pollitt, P Bailey, H Clover
	Pitch 1 had been climbed many years before as Diocese Direct. Thruster variation climbed by M Edwards, I Blake in 1986.
1981	**Panda Wall** M Edwards (solo)
1981	**Air Tripper** R Edwards
1981	**The Hog from Camborne** J Hooper (solo)
1982 Feb 8	**The Mocker** S Salmon, D Hannigan, R Lewis
1982 Feb 23	**Touchwood** S Salmon, M Crayton
1982 Feb 25	**A Little S and M** S Salmon, M Crayton
1982 March 4	**Green Crack** S Salmon, M Crayton
1982 March 8	**Sam's Indirect Finish to Bending Chimney** S Salmon, M Crayton

1982 March 17	**Sidewinder** S Salmon, M Crayton	
1982 April 11	**One Way Ticket** R Edwards, M Edwards	
1982 April 18	**White Eagle** R Edwards, M Edwards	

The Edwardses begin a major development of Paradise Wall.

1982 May 15	**Fantasy Crack** R Edwards, M Edwards
1982 May 15	**Modern Images** M Edwards, R Edwards
1982 June 26	**Interspace** R Edwards, M Edwards
1982 June 30	**Cool Diamonds** R Edwards, M Edwards

Edwards's finest contribution to Paradise Wall.

1982 July 5	**The Badlands** M Edwards, R Edwards
1982 July 9	**No Place for Cowboys** R Edwards, M Edwards
1982 July 14	**The Greek's Knees** S Salmon, J Pearce (AL)
1982 July 22	**Vietnamerica** G Gibson, D Beetlestone, M J Brown

Retrospectively claimed by M Edwards, The Peplow brothers (1981).

1982 July 30	**Ebony Crack, Fluid Connections, Finger Stretcher, Sun Shadow** R Edwards, M Edwards (VL)
1982 Aug 8	**Zero, Second and Penultimate** S Salmon, J Pearce
1982 Aug 10	**Footloose** D Hillebrandt, M Freeman
1982 Aug 14	**Hot Line** M Edwards, R Edwards
1982 Sept 19	**Games Surfers Play, Jordanaire** S Salmon, J Pearce
1982 Sept	**Hiroshima Mon Amour** C Parker, J Matthews
1982 Sept	**A Pocket Full of Crystals** M Edwards
1982	**Pitches on approach walls to Bashers Harbour** M Freeman
1982	**Blue (Pordenack)** S Cardy, A Bunning

Retrospectively claimed by R Edwards and party in 1997 as Thin Highway (1979).

1982	**Fourteen Fathoms, Love 30, Wet Barnacle** G Gibson
1982	**Golden Brown** G Gibson, P Gibson
1982	**Hairy Cornflake** N Hancock, A Grieve
1982	**Kooky Crack, Blue Kazoo** M Edwards, R Edwards (VL)
1982	**Cave Butress, The Flake** M Freeman, J Parker
1982	**South without Scott, Rinse Out** P Sykes, M Freeman
1982	**Pendower Direct** R Edwards, M Edwards

1982	***North Cornwall and West Penwith New Climbs* by Pete O'Sullivan and Bob Moulton**

1983 March 21	**Swot Crack** M Edwards, R Edwards
1983 April 1	**Kimodo Dragon** R Croft, I Peters (AL), P O'Sullivan
1983 April 2	**The Sea Traverse from Soap Gully to Vellan Head** R Croft, I Peters (AL)
1983 April 2	**Down Under, Little Bear I Do Love Thee of Esmeduna, Taking It Easy** I Duncan, S Wilkey (VL)
1983 April 2	**The Runner, Launch** M Learoyd, L Foulkes
1983 April 2	**Solomon Browne** K Vickery, J Eales
1983 April 3	**The Great Gonzo** K Vickery, R Freeborn, J Eales
1983 April 3	**Immaculate Conception** (1 pt aid) M Learoyd, L Foulkes
1983 April 3	**Chameleon Rib** I Peters, P O'Sullivan
1983 April 21	**Top of the Class, Late Developer** R Edwards, M Edwards
1983 April	**Asterix in Cornwall** P Harrison, N Harrison
1983 April	**Bermuda Wall** M Doyle, J Hooper
1983 April	**Forever, First Water** P O'Sullivan, R Croft
1983 April	**Girl's Best Friend** R Croft, P O'Sullivan

1983 April	**Well Kept Secret** P O'Sullivan, R Croft, I Peters
1983 May 2	**Sitting Comfortably, Sitting Tenant** K Vickery, J Eales, R Freeborn
1983 May 3	**Exit** K Vickery, J Eales
1983 May 15	**Alpharatz** I Peters, A Clark, P O'Sullivan
1983 May 29	**True North** P O'Sullivan, R Croft, I Peters, C Robins
1983 Aug 16	**Kilroy Wasn't Here** S Salmon, R Tewson, P Thompson
	Retrospectively claimed by R Edwards and party in 1997 as No Chatter (1979).
1983 Aug 28	**Weekend Treat** S Salmon, S Richards
	Variation: M Edwards, A N Other April 1984.
1983 Sept 1	**Smash and Grab, A Touch of Glass, Glass Arête** R Edwards, M Edwards
1983 Nov 6	**Curtain Call** R Edwards, M Edwards
1983 Dec 23	**The Shadows** R Edwards, M Edwards
1983 Dec 31	**Potemkin** P O'Sullivan, K Tole
1983	**Sea Wolf** R Edwards
	The original route traversed right around the arête from the good ledge to finish up Weasle. The route described is more logical.
1983	**Socket Arête, Sea Wolf, Time Out** R Edwards
1983	**Altered Images, The Barber, Free Ride, Omega Man, Second Skin** R Edwards, M Edwards (VL)
1983	**Devax** R Edwards, B Humphery, A Noble
1983	**Deep Think** R Edwards, B Humphery, B Cooper
1983	**Deep Cruise** R Edwards, M Edwards
1983	**Missile Man, The Last Stand** M Edwards, R Edwards
1983	**Bosistow Island North Face** R Edwards, M Edwards, P Rogers
1983	**Weekend Retreat** M Edwards (solo)
1983	**Loose Feelings** M Edwards (solo)
1983	**The Groove** (Pellitras Point) Unknown
1984 Jan 3	**Centre Piece** R Edwards, M Edwards
1984 Jan 3	**Central Highway** R Edwards, M Edwards (AL)
1984 Jan 3	**Interceptor** M Edwards, R Edwards (AL)
1984 Feb 28	**Immaculate Off-Width, Memento, Shaky Fashion, Mina** P O'Sullivan, H Baumgart
1984 March 2	**Mean Street** R Edwards, M Edwards
1984 March 3	**Midnight Express** A Trevorrow, D Hannigan
1984 March 3	**Crawfish** D Hannigan, M Crayton, S Wright
	Reclimbed in the 1980s, after the rockfall.
1984 March 17	**John Peel** A Grieve, N Hancock
1984 March 18	**Devil's Meridian** A Trevorrow, P O'Sullivan
1984 March 18	**Panos** R Cope, J Hooper
1984 March 18	**Buttons** S Wright, D Hannigan
1984 March 25	**Scarlet Pimpernel** R Edwards, M Edwards
1984 March 29	**Tooth Decay** N Hancock, A Grieve
1984 March	**Dog Town** M Edwards, R Edwards
1984 April 16	**Great Western Arête** R Edwards, M Edwards
1984 April 23	**Compensation** R Croft, I Peters (AL)
1984 April 23	**Rattlesnake** I Peters, R Croft
1984 April 23	**Secret Squirrel** P O'Sullivan, D Sargeant, K Tole
1984 April 29	**Rock Pilgrim, The Gladiator, Private Performance, The Great Divide** R Edwards, M Edwards

| 984 April 29 | **Midnight Runner, Softly Softly, Moon Dog, La Speciale, Close to the Edge, Nautilus** M Edwards, R Edwards |
| 984 April 29 | **Mini Minx Chimney** M Edwards (solo) |

An exhaustive and exhausting day. Eleven new routes with tidal starts, involving over 400 metres of climbing. Let's hope they kept their feet dry.

984 April	**The Amazing Mr Ed** K Tole, P O'Sullivan
984 April	**Yip Yip Coyote, Tie That Crittur Down** P O'Sullivan, K Tole (AL)
984 May 2	**Grande Paradiso** M Edwards, R Edwards
984 May 5	**Blockbuster** M Edwards (solo)
984 May 12	**Super Vision** R Edwards, M Edwards
984 May 26	**The Mauler, Nutcracker** R Edwards, M Edwards
984 May 26	**Dangle and Mangle** M Edwards, R Edwards
984 June 2	**Fury of Atlanta** R Edwards, M Edwards
984 June 9	**Master of Disaster** M Edwards, R Edwards
984 June 9	**Rendezvous Manqué** I Peters, K Tole
984 June	**Cruisin' for a Bruisin'** P Rogers, K Rogers

Black Eye for a Guidebook Writer variation climbed in August 1998 by M Edwards, R Bath.

984 June	**Easy Street** P O'Sullivan, M Doyle
984 June	**Koh-i-Nor, Sesame Street** M Doyle, P O'Sullivan
984 July 8	**Fingerflinger, Seamstress** C Nicholson
984 July 16	**Slagroom, The Harp** R Edwards, A N Other
984 Aug 1	**Funeral for a Friend** M Edwards, R Edwards
984 Aug 5	**Marisco Striptease** P Harrison, S Boyden
984 Aug 8	**Medusa** R Edwards, A N Other
984 Aug 25	**Broad Street** R Edwards, M Edwards, E Stone
984 Aug 27	**The Minstrel** S Salmon, S Richards
984 Aug 27	**Redfish** S Salmon
984 Aug 31	**Silent Movie, Lizard of Oz** I Peters, A Martin, K Tole
984 Aug	**Head Hunter** M Edwards, A N Other
984 Sept 10	**One Inch Rock** S Salmon, S Richards
984 Dec 30	**The Thin Red Line, Beaujolais** M Edwards, R Edwards
984	**Arc of a Diver** S Boyden, P Harrison, S Wilkie

Also claimed as Psychosis (1984) by M Edwards, R Edwards.

| 984 | **Vive la Difference** M Edwards, A N Other |
| 984 | **The Sewing Machine Man** M Saunders, P Hayes, P Rogers, G Pearson. |

After top-rope practice. Four honest men.

| 984 | **Motivator** R Edwards, M Edwards |
| 984 | **Amigos** M Edwards (on-sight solo) |

| **984** | **Cornwall – West Penwith** by Pete O'Sullivan |

985 Jan 1	**Crack-a-Goo-Goo, Heaven's Snake** M Edwards, R Edwards
985 Jan 1	**Jamaica** R Edwards, M Edwards
985 Jan 12	**Cardinal Sin, Space Chase** M Edwards, R Edwards (AL)
985 March 1	**Triangle** R Edwards, M Edwards
985 May 5	**Sirius** I Peters, P O'Sullivan (AL)
985 May 6	**Pluto** I Peters, P O'Sullivan (AL)
985 May 11	**Southern Cross** I Peters, P O'Sullivan (AL)
985 May 11	**The Goldrush** I Peters, P O'Sullivan
985 May 25	**Worried Warrior** R Edwards, M Edwards

1985 May 25	**Rainbow Warrior** K Palmer, N Hancock
1985 May 26	**Best Boy** R Cope, P O'Sullivan
1985 May 26	**Casablanca** I Peters, K Tole
1985 May 26	**Chorus Line** K Tole, I Peters (AL)
1985 May 26	**Focus Puller, Quo Vadis** P O'Sullivan, R Cope
1985 May	**Fat City** M Lynden, S Fenwick, B Craig
1985 June 10	**Reflections on the Sea** R Edwards, M Edwards, R Greaves
1985 June 10	**Southern Arête** R Edwards, C Edwards
1985 June 15	**Crazy from the Heat** M Edwards, R Edwards, R Greaves
1985 June 27	**Silent Sleeper** R Edwards, M Edwards
1985 July 6	**Footless Madness** M Edwards, R Edwards, R Greaves
1985 July 7	**Limelight** I Peters, P O'Sullivan
1985 July 7	**The Big Heat** P O'Sullivan, I Peters

The substance of the route was climbed on 26 April 1985 by P O'Sullivan and R Cope. Loose rock forced a detour.

1985 July 7	**The Zawn Escape** P O'Sullivan, I Peters
1985 July 20	**Carmen** M Edwards, R Edwards
1985 July 20	**The Consul** R Edwards, M Edwards
1985 July 22	**How Much Longer?** S Salmon (solo)
1985 July 24	**Aggressive Edge** M Edwards, R Edwards, R Greaves

Destroyed by rockfall.

1985 July 26	**A Pocket Full of Quartz** M Edwards
1985 July 26	**Love Drives Me Crazy** M Edwards, C Heyl
1985 July	**Twisting by the Pool** P Rogers, K Rogers
1985 July	**Chance Encounter** R Cope, P O'Sullivan, I Thomas, P Johnstone

Variation Start climbed on 12 May 1994 by P O'Sullivan, C Griffiths.

1985 July	**Brief Encounter** P O'Sullivan, R Cope, I Thomas, P Johnstone
1985 Aug 6	**Crag X, Geologist's Route** S Salmon, P Thompson
1985 Aug 9	**Blood on the Rocks** M Edwards, M Adams, J Cooke, J Mas
1985 Aug 9	**Dépêchez-Vous** M Edwards, M Adams, J Cooke, J Mas
1985 Aug 10	**Sock It to Me** M Edwards, R Edwards, D Allport
1985 Aug 10	**Holiday Tripper** R Edwards, M Edwards, D Allport
1985 Aug 14	**Kernack** S Salmon
1985 Aug 16	**Mr Haggis** M Edwards, M McMahon, I Graydon, L O'Callaghan
1985 Aug 16	**Mr Married Goes for a Hike** M Edwards, S Woolard, M McMahon
1985 Aug 16	**Twist Again like Moira Did Last Summer** M Edwards, S Woolard
1985 Aug 19	**Mink de Ville** S Salmon
1985 Sept 1	**Valentino, Mae West, Quasimodo** P O'Sullivan, J Barber
1985 Oct 20	**Dead Reckoning** P O'Sullivan, K Hosie (AL)

The first pitch had been climbed on 29 May 1983 by I Peters, P O'Sullivan, R Croft.

1985 Oct 29	**Child of the Moon** M Edwards

The first known deep-water solo in the area.

1985 Oct 29	**Tina Turner, Falling Apart at the Seams** D Hannigan, M Crayton
1985 Nov 10	**Howlin' Wolf** D Hannigan, P Johnstone, R Pryor, T Carver

Retrospectively claimed by M Edwards in 1997 as Sabre (1982).

1985 Dec 28	**Aboriginal Sin** P O'Sullivan, I Peters, J Barber
1985	**The Crusader** R Edwards, B Cooper

1985	**Joshua Tree** R Edwards, I Blake
1985	**Merde del Buffalino** D Cook, P Devine
1985	**The Armed Knight** R Edwards, M Edwards
1985	**Bottle Throttle** C Nicholson, B Wilkinson
1985	**The Immaculate Runner** P Johnstone, J Hooper
1985	**Just Du It** A Grieve and party
1985	**No Gear, No Fear** E Ford, M Crayton, D Hannigan
1985	**The Tiercel** E Ford, D Hannigan
1986 Feb 6	**Isis** M Edwards, R Edwards
	'Felt very hard. I was sick on top.' (Ben Bransby aged 13)
1986 March 4	**Solitaire (Folly Cove)** R Edwards, C Gearon
1986 March 9	**Far South** K Hosie, P O'Sullivan
1986 March 9	**Pharos, Galileo** P O'Sullivan, K Hosie
1986 March 16	**Comet** P Buttrick, K Hosie
1986 March 16	**Tickled Pink** S Bishop, S Bell, P O'Sullivan
1986 March 16	**Tickle My Pink** P O'Sullivan, S Bell
1986 March 16	**Dirty Ice, Giotto, Halley's Corner** K Hosie, P Buttrick
1986 March 16	**Seal Chop Chimney** S Bell (solo)
1986 March 16	**The Cull** S Bell, P O'Sullivan, S Bishop
	Bell rested on gear, but returned in October 1987 and free-climbed the route.
1986 March 19	**Easy Touch** R Edwards, M Edwards
1986 March 19	**Simplicity City** M Edwards, R Edwards
1986 March 23	**Leaning Tower** P O'Sullivan, P Rodgers
1986 March 30	**Acid Test** I Barnard, C Anderson, S Geake
1986 April 4	**Sky Highway** R Edwards, C Gearon
1986 April 5	**Dawn** P O'Sullivan, S Bell
	A superb find. Variation Start: N White in the 1990s.
1986 April 5	**Pisapis, Buzzin', Meteorite** P O'Sullivan, J Barber
1986 April 10	**Space Cruiser** R Edwards, M Edwards
1986 May 10	**The Fix** I Peters, R Croft
	Pitch 2 previously climbed by I Peters, K Hosie, P Buttrick on 26 May 1985.
1986 May 20	**Reflections on a Mirror** R Edwards, M Edwards
1986 May 24	**Time Starts Now** R Edwards, M Edwards
1986 May 29	**The Prisoner of Zenda, Raffles** P O'Sullivan, C Pretty
1986 May	**Blood Brothers** P O'Sullivan, S Bell
1986 June 5	**Droplove, Tiptoe, Pilgrims, Rough Rider** R Edwards, A Timmer, E Timmer, R Meyer
1986 June 6	**Shadow on a Wall** R Edwards, M Edwards
1986 June 8	**Dreamtime** P O'Sullivan, D Sargeant
1986 June 8	**Dingo, Bingo** (both at Bass Point) P O'Sullivan, D Sargeant, D Condor
1986 June 8	**Spingo** D Sargeant, P O'Sullivan
1986 June 12	**A Leap in the Dark** R Edwards, C Gearon
1986 June 22	**Amnesty** P O'Sullivan, C Pretty
1986 June 22	**Vumba** C Pretty, D Pretty, P O'Sullivan
1986 June 25	**The Blade** R Edwards, C Munsch, C Baron
	The (Bogus) Blade variation climbed on 16 July 1995 by S Ohly, thinking it was the original line.
1986 June 25	**Second Blood, Vixen's Crack** R Edwards, C Baron, C Munsch
1986 July 4	**Iron Maiden** M Edwards, A N Other
1986 July 4	**By Jingo** I Day, P O'Sullivan

1986 July 11	**The Black Hole** P O'Sullivan, A Watt, J Barber
1986 July 12	**Technicolour Dream** R Edwards, M Edwards
1986 July	**Crystal Voyager** P Rogers, K Rogers
1986 July	**Black Crack** (Basher's Harbour), **Fancy Free** P Sykes, M Freeman
1986 Aug 1	**His Nibs** M Edwards, A N Other
1986 Aug 1	**Fiddler** R Edwards, A N Other
1986 Aug 1	**Initiation** (Folly Cove) R Edwards, C Gearon
1986 Aug 5	**Waiting for the Sun** R Edwards, C Gearon
1986 Aug 11	**Moon Child** R Edwards, C Gearon
1986 Aug 24	**Dracula the Undead** M Edwards (solo)
1986 Aug 30	**Total Eclipse** R Edwards, C Gearon
	This bolted route marked the start of a long drawn out controversy
1986 Sept 1	**Across** T Carver, P Johnstone
1986 Sept 25	**The Music Man** R Edwards, S Masters, C Gearon
1986 Oct 2	**Computer Commuter** R Edwards, M Edwards
1986 Oct 2	**Dream Machine** R Edwards
1986 Oct 16	**The Bush Man, Sun Lord** R Edwards, S Masters
1986 Nov 2	**Happy Banger** D Milward, D Hillebrandt, D Hannigan
1986 Nov 2	**Piledriver** D Milward, D Hillebrandt, M Freeman
1986	**Bottleneck** P Thompson, S Salmon
1986	**Wild Oscillations** K Palmer, A Grieve
	Retrospectively claimed by R Edwards in 1997 as Rapido (1982). After rockfall, R Edwards reclimbed the route in 1990.
	Miss Selfridge G Butler, N Hancock
	Retrospectively claimed by M Edwards in 1997 as Life's Moments (1982). After rockfall, M Edwards reclimbed the route in 1990.
1986	**Joy Rider** R Edwards, C Gearon
1986	**Smoked Salmon** P Johnstone, G Hobbs, D Hannigan
1986	**Pig and Chips** D Hannigan, G Hobbs, P Johnstone
1986	**All Fools Flake Out** P Johnstone, J Matthews
1986	**Hail, After Burner** A Simcock, D Soles
1986	**Stone, Fish out of Water** P Boon, M Andrews
1986	**Black Adder** (Tregiffian) D Soles, A Simcock
1986	**Black Adder II, Eliminator** M Andrews, P Boon
1987 Feb 2	**The Tempest** M Edwards, R Edwards
1987 Feb 26	**Urban Spaceman** R Edwards, M Edwards
1987 March 15	**Land of the Living** D Hillebrandt, C Stripp
1987 March	**At Home** N Dixon (solo)
	The upper arête was added in May 1987 by M Edwards, R Edwards as Pig City.
1987 March	**Spring Squill Salad** A Popp, A Mutter, N Dixon
1987 April 8	**Wicked Ways, Bygone Days** P R Littlejohn, J Davies
1987 April 14	**Animated Wall** R Edwards, M Edwards
	Pitch 2 added by M Edwards (solo after abseil inspection) in the 1990s. Crash, Boom, Bang variation climbed by S Ohly on 29 December 1995.
1987 April 15	**Beauty and the Beast** P R Littlejohn, F Ramsay
	Variation Start: 15 April 1995 by M J Crocker, R Chappell.
1987 April 15	**The Serpent's Tale** F Ramsay, P R Littlejohn
1987 April 16	**Jack** H I Banner, D Pritchard
1987 April 17	**Second Time Around** R Edwards, D Body
	Mid-century, and the remarkable Edwards threatens to start all over again.

1987 April 25	**Five Year Itch**	M Edwards
1987 April 26	**A Hollow Man**	R Edwards, M Edwards, D Body
1987 April 26	**The Inquisition, Hidden Glories**	R Edwards (solo)
1987 May 4	**Lunatic Owl**	M Edwards, Mrs E Edwards
1987 May 5	**A Walk on the Dark Side**	R Edwards, M Edwards
1987 May 11	**On the Loose** (Pordenack)	R Edwards, C Edwards
1987 May 15	**Bubble Wall**	R Edwards, C Edwards

The direct start was climbed by M Edwards in 1987.

1987 May 20	**Eat 'Em and Smile**	M Edwards, R Edwards, I Blake

A major effort. 'This route involved a certain amount of hangdogging, mainly because of holds coming off (30-foot fliers) and the advance of the tide, which was slowly drowning Mark's second (myself). The route was finally led clean.' (Rowland Edwards, Mountain 1988.)

1987 May 29	**A Job for Life, A Question of Time**	R Edwards, C Edwards
1987 May	**Stanstead**	S Elliott, R Banaster
1987 June 5	**Rack and Ruin**	R Edwards, M Edwards
1987 July 8	**Not Quite So Ordinary Route, Deception Groove**	
	S Young, R Mitchell	
1987 July 12	**Loose Limpet Crack**	S Young, R Mitchell
1987 July 24	**Walking on the Light Side**	R Edwards, M Edwards
1987 July 21	**Nelson's Eye**	A Newton, K Griffith, A Renshaw
1987 July 22	**Kicking Steps**	A Newton, I Clarke
1987 July	**Rats in a Rage**	M Edwards, I Blake

An immensely technical climb, which brought the bolt and drilled peg controversy to Chair Ladder's traditional cliff.

1987 July	**White Light, White Heat**	W A Carver, J Ford
1987 July	**Little Cracker** (Porthcurno Bay)	M Edwards (solo)
1987 July	**One in a Mullion**	D Turnbull (solo)

Situated in what is now a nature reserve.

1987 Aug 14	**Ratcatcher**	J Shaw, J Willson
1987 Aug 26	**Gravity Slab**	S Young, R Mitchell
1987 Aug 29	**Jeans Genius, Zebra**	S Young, R Mitchell, D Hannigan
1987 Aug	**Down the Welly**	D Turnbull, G Butler, N Hancock, A Grieve
1987 Sept 5	**The Naked Edge**	R Edwards, I Blake
1987 Sept 12	**Mister Fixit, Water-Man**	R Edwards, Mrs E Edwards
1987 Sept 12	**Sandman**	R Edwards
1987 Sept	**The Barbary Coast**	T Carver, J Ford
1987 Oct 1	**Big Bad Blues**	R Edwards, M Edwards
1987 Oct 24	**All the Fours**	S Young, R Mitchell
1987 Oct 24	**Direct Approach**	S Young, R Mitchell
1987 Oct 24	**Sleeping Chimney**	S Young (solo)
1987 Nov 1	**Sammy's Slab**	S Young, R Mitchell
1987 Dec 17	**Nova**	R Edwards (solo)
1987 Dec 17	**Lost for Words, Pocket Burn**	M Edwards, R Edwards

Variation to Pocket Burn climbed by M Edwards (solo) in December 1988.

1987 Dec	**Short pitches between Levan's Wall and Pedn-mên-an-mere**	M Edwards
1987	**Just About**	M Edwards (solo)
1987	**Relax**	J Hooper, T Benfield
1987	**Pop!**	M Edwards

1988 Jan 27	**Bustin' Out, Chicken Run, The Planter, Muscle Buster, Smile of a Clown, The Other One, False Illusions, Video Breaks, Tea for Two** R Edwards, Mrs E Edwards
1988 Feb 29	**Ruby Nails** R Edwards
1988 Feb 29	**Rubber Neck** R Edwards, Mrs E Edwards
1988 Feb 29	**Slab Route** Mrs E Edwards R Edwards
1988 April 4	**Journey to the Stones** M Edwards (solo)
1988 May 10	**The Bitts** D Hannigan
	Retrospectively claimed by R Edwards, Mrs E Edwards in 2000 as Tall Ships Wall (1985).
1988 May 20	**Lazarus** P R Littlejohn
1988 May 23	**London's Burning** M Edwards, C Brooks, D Dickenson
1988 May	**Pollock, Rothko, Whiplash** P O'Sullivan, M Lacey
1988 May	**Klein** M Lacey, P O'Sullivan
1988 July 9	**Wreckage** D Hannigan, D W Bateman
1988 July 17	**Hampshire Bypass** S R Young, J R Mitchell
1988 July 17	**Mince Pie Problem** D E Hope (solo)
1988 July 17	**The Sea for Breakfast** D E Hope, A Milburn
1988 July	**The Wall** S R Young, J R Mitchell
1988 Aug 2	**Boulder Buttress** R Edwards, N Mooney
1988 Aug 30	**Knight's Move** J Frankiss, T Dennell
1988 Aug	**The Dvina** P O'Sullivan, J Barber
	Unknowingly reascended as 'Bomb' Berlin by W A Carver, B Carver on 7 September 1996.
1988 Sept 10	**Sunshine Slab** M Edwards, C Johns
1988 Sept 10	**Fences, The Fixit, Iron Bells, Moaning Minnie** R Edwards
1988 Sept 10	**The Way Outside** R Edwards, Mrs E Edwards, C Johns
1988 Sept	**Route I** J Dyke, C Irwin, P Irwin, C Scholes
1988 Sept	**Horam's Horror** J Dyke, P Irwin, C Irwin
1988 Oct 1	**Green Streaks** S R Young, J R Mitchell
1988 Oct 9	**Codicil** J Dyke, R Banaster
1988 Oct 9	**A Day Off** R Edwards, Mrs E Edwards
	Variation climbed by J Hooper, P Oak on 12 March 2000.
1988 Nov 6	**Burning Bridge** R Banaster, J Dyke
1988 Nov 6	**Perfidy** J Dyke, R Banaster
1988 Nov 20	**Green Fingers** R Banaster, J Dyke, N Barnes
1988 Nov 21	**Ask to Risk** R Edwards
1988 Nov 22	**Fleeting Lights, Silicone Chips** R Edwards
1988 Dec 30	**Pass the Pigs** A Grieve, N Hancock
1988	**The Lost Arrow** M Edwards, S Anson
1988	**Empty Spaces** M Edwards, R Edwards
1988	**Mental Breakdown, Hidden Gems** R Edwards, M Edwards
1988	**Scary Route** M Edwards
	An impressive piece of climbing not reported for nearly ten years!
1988	***North Devon and Cornwall by Iain Peters***
1989 Jan 1	**Septimus** J Dyke, R Banaster
1989 March 29	**Double or Quits, Pennies from Heaven** E Cooper, P R Littlejohn
1989 March 30	**Catch a Falling Star** P R Littlejohn, E Cooper
1989 March 31	**The Crunch, The Falconer** P R Littlejohn, E Cooper
1989 March 31	**Going Places** E Cooper, P R Littlejohn
1989 July 23	**Who Knows Where the Nose Goes** C Jones, S Viejtoris
1989 July 24	**The Big Easy** C Jones, S Viejtoris

1989 July 24	**Family Meet**	A Evans, G Exley
1989 July 28	**Barbecue**	A Evans (solo)
1989 July 28	**Sophie's Choice**	A Evans, S Milner
1989 Aug 6	**Hare Krishna**	C Jones, 'Nelson Mandela'
1989 Sept 2	**Lovely, Lovely, Lovely**	N Hancock, A Grieve, G Butler
1989 Oct 18	**Cardiac Arête**	P Craggs, D Woolhouse
1989 Dec 31	**Stranger in a Strange Land, Exile**	P Craggs, S Johnson, P Kavanagh

1989 **New Editions** (Pordenack)   R Edwards
The direct start (R Edwards, C Edwards 2 April 1987) and variation finish (29 February 1988) of Cain linked to give a virtually independent route, the only shared climbing being in a different direction!

1989 **Black Adder** (Pedn-mên-an-mere), **Falls the Shadow, Last Gasp**   M Edwards, R Edwards

1989 **Legoland, The Lobster, Masquerade, Sunburst Crack**
M Edwards
The Lobster climbed without its bolt by the same climber the same year.

1989 **Magical Motions, Return Ticket, Sabre Cut, In Touch**
R Edwards, M Edwards

1989	**Scandals**	M Edwards, S Anson
1989	**A Broken Mirror**	R Edwards, S Anson, N Mooney
1989	**Two of a Kind**	R Edwards, N Mooney
1989	**Jack the Ripper, The Shining**	R Edwards, C Baron
1989	**Sweeney Todd, Into a Looking-Glass**	R Edwards, S Anson
1989	**Kellogg's Crack**	R Edwards, M Edwards (AL)
1989	**Star Touch**	R Edwards, S Anson, M Edwards

1989 **Seal Chimney, Time Tavern, Demelza's Arête**
M Edwards, R Edwards

1989 **New Sensation**   N Mooney and party

1989 **Back to the Grind**   A Grieve, N Hancock
Also claimed by M Edwards in 1989. The direct start was soloed by M Edwards in the same year.

1989 **Fragile Earth**   M Edwards

1980s **Archangel**   I Peters
The ascent was not recorded by Peters. The climbing and naming of the route by W A Carver, B Carver, T Carver on 2 June 1996 was the catalyst for the intensive development of Black Head.

1980s	**Flanker**	Various climbers
c.1980s	**Sunny Slab**	Various parties
1990 March 18	**Monochrome Men**	P O'Sullivan, K Hosie, M Dunning
1990 March 18	**Sulcus**	N Crowhurst, M Dunning
1990 April 1	**Old Fools**	P O'Sullivan, D Hannigan
1990 April 1	**Yardang**	M Dunning, N Crowhurst, D Hannigan, P O'Sullivan
1990 April 8	**Sabre Dance**	P O'Sullivan, D Hannigan
1990 April 8	**Test Piece**	P O'Sullivan, D Hannigan, M Dunning, N Crowhurst

1990 April 8 **The Damned**   P O'Sullivan, M Dunning, D Hannigan, N Crowhurst
Climax to a fresh burst of activity at St Loy.

1990 April 15 **Jack Yer Body**   K Palmer, A Grieve, N Hancock, G Butler

1990 April 15 **The Seventh Wave and short pitches at Coffin Cove**
P O'Sullivan, D Hannigan

1990 April 16	**Scarlet Women** P O'Sullivan, S Elliott	

Variation Start by M J Crocker, P Oxley on 28 March 1992.

1990 April 16	**Raindance** (St Loy) N Hancock, A Grieve
1990 April 22	**Harvey Proctor** P O' Sullivan, D Hannigan, N Crowhurst
1990 May 6	**Wild Mountain Thyme** N Crowhurst, Mrs S Crowhurst
1990 May 6	**The Snip, Ibis** P O'Sullivan, D Hannigan, J Barber
1990 May 6	**Thea** G Hobbs, J Hobbs
1990 May 20	**Foxbite** D Hannigan, N Crowhurst
1990 May	**Local Martians, Pirouette** P O'Sullivan, D Hannigan
1990 June 10	**Prior Claim** K Talbot
1990 June 10	**Little Frankie** J Hobbs, G Hobbs
1990 June 17	**Fran's Route** F Wells, R Banaster
1990 June 21	**Etron Fou** S Law, P Sobczyk
1990 June	**Smear Fear, Checkmate** P O'Sullivan, M Lacey
1990 July 11	**Scab** R Bennett, J R Mitchell
1990 Aug 8	**War Games** J Ford, S Elliott
1990 Aug 26	**Hysterical Hamsters** P O'Sullivan, N Crowhurst
1990 Sept 16	**Fluke** (St Loy) L Pavey, F Wells
1990 Oct	**Loytering** P O'Sullivan
1990 Nov 3	**Supercruise** K Menadue, S Menadue, D Menadue

Rather overgardened.

1990	**Wolf at the Door** M Edwards
1990	**Pre-Marital Tension** N Dixon, T Reseigh

A fine route well ahead of its time. Climbed with a high side-runner in the crack to the left.

1990	**Storms over Africa** M Edwards

Originally lead with a drilled peg runner in the upper part of the crack. S Ohly on-sight soloed the route and subsequently removed the peg on 31 May 1995. C Waddy climbed a variation using the other side of the arête in 1994.

1990	**Spirit of Summer** M Edwards, R Edwards
1990	**Adios Kernow** M Edwards, S Jones
1990	**Rock Citadel** R Edwards, S Jones
1990	**The Cornishman** M Edwards, R Edwards

Cerberus variation climbed by M Edwards in the same year.

1990	**The Floating Looser, A Drop in the Ocean** R Edwards, M Edwards
1990	**Navigator to Heaven** R Edwards, C Baron
1990	**Rapido** R Edwards (See Wild Oscillations, 1986).
1990	**Life's Moments** M Edwards (See Miss Selfridge, 1986).
1990	**The Vein Stain** M Edwards, C Baron
1991 March 30	**A Clean Breast** S Salmon, B Simpson, C H Perrin
1991 April 7	**Margin** A Hall, B Hannon
1991 April 15	**Lucy** J Hobbs, G Hobbs
1991 April 15	**Lucozade** G Hobbs, J Hobbs
1991 April 17	**Luke Back in Anger** G Hobbs, J Hobbs, D Hannigan
1991 April 21	**Luke Skywalker** J Hobbs, G Hobbs, D Hannigan
1991 April 21	**Looking-Glass War** D Hannigan, J Hobbs, G Hobbs
1991 April 21	**Luke Lively** G Hobbs, J Hobbs, D Hannigan, P F Hannigan, W G E Matthews
1991 April 26	**Leucal Hero** G Hobbs, J Hobbs
1991 April 26	**Lucretia** G Hobbs, J Hobbs, D Hannigan
1991 April 28	**Slapstick** B Hannon, A Hall
1991 May 6	**Skin Graft** P O'Sullivan, M Dunning

1991 May 19	**Lord Lucan** G Hobbs, D Hannigan	
1991 May 19	**Lucylastic** G Hobbs, D Hannigan	
1991 June 4	**By Stealth** P O'Sullivan, A MacFarlane	
1991 June 16	**The Flying Fakir** A Hall, B Hannon	
	Variation by M J Crocker, P Oxley on 28 March 1992.	
1991 July 6	**Vessactomy** G Hobbs, J Hobbs	
1991 July 6	**Phallus** J Hobbs, G Hobbs	
1991 July 29	**Daddy's Crack** A Morley, G Hobbs, J Hobbs	
1991 July 30	**Split Up** A Morley, G Hobbs	
1991 July 30	**Crocodile Tears** A Morley, G Hobbs, J Hobbs	
1991 Aug 1	**Acapulco Corner** J Hobbs, G Hobbs	
1991 Aug 1	**Ledge Climb** A Morley, J Hobbs, P O'Sullivan, G Hobbs	
1991 Aug 1	**Uncle Peter Goes to the Seaside** P O'Sullivan, G Hobbs, A Morley	
1991 Aug 2	**Triple Jump** A Morley, J Hobbs, G Hobbs	
1991 Aug 4	**Tinker** P O'Sullivan (solo)	
1991 Aug 4	**Tailor, Cliché** B R E Wilkinson, P O'Sullivan	
1991 Aug 4	**Soldier, Spy, Serial Killer, Ultra Marine, Metaphor** P O'Sullivan, B Wilkinson	
1991 Aug 16	**Thirty Something** P Harrison, A Piercey, N Jonett	
1991 Sep 7	**Turning Up the Heat** P O'Sullivan, A Wade	
1991 Sep 11	**Jilted** J Ford, S Elliott	
1991 Sep 15	**The Tram Line** J Ford, S Elliott	
	Retrospectively claimed by R Edwards, M Edwards in 1997 as Lighthouse Arête (1978).	
1991 Oct 13	**Dagger in the Back** K Menadue (solo)	
1991	**Awskberg, Fatal Attractions, Seal Crack, The Edge, Right Edge** R Edwards, N Mooney, J Blake	
1991	**Broken Hearts, Glass of Sweet Wine, Between the Sheets** M Edwards, R Edwards	
1991	**Cat Follows Mouse** J Ford (pitch 1 only)	
	Pitch 2 previously climbed as Follow the Mouse by S Young, R Mitchell on 10 May 1987.	

1991 *Bosigran and the North Coast by Des Hannigan*

1992 March 22	**Struth** K Menadue, S Menadue, D Menadue	
1992 March 29	**Roger, Over and Out** K Menadue, S Menadue, D Menadue	
1992 March	**With Intent** K Menadue	
1992 April 22	**Great Western** M E B Banks, R I Thompson	
1992 April 23	**Sou'wester** M E B Banks, R I Thompson	
	Forty-three years since Mike Banks's first Penwith route, and still going strong.	
1992 May 3	**Glissade** P O'Sullivan, K Hosie	
1992 May 13	**Wee Jammer, Polo, Stock, Remember Eileen** D Hannigan, D W Bateman	
1992 Aug 7	**Gay Capri** M Barnes, R Skelsey	
1992 Aug 30	**Beaver Fever, Too Sexy for Mike** M Edwards, M Barnes	
1992 Sept 1	**Egyptian Roof (Aid), Sticky Fingers, Big Jugs** M Edwards, M Barnes	
1992 Oct 8	**The East Tower** J Ford, S Elliott	
1992	**Comedy of Errors, Big Guns** M Edwards, R Edwards, M Barnes	
1992	**Raindancer, Hot Wire Fire** M Edwards, M Barnes	
1992	**Just Another Inquisition** M Edwards, C Bryan	

1992	**Eye of the Crystal** M Edwards
1992	**Frogs in a Frenzy** M Edwards
1992	**Howling at the Moon** M Edwards, M Barnes

| **1992** | ***Chair Ladder and the South Coast by Des Hannigan*** |

1993 May 2	**Brown Sugar, Spanker** B Hannon, P Jones
1993 June 13	**Flanker Direct** B Hannon
1993 June	**Co-Extensive Space** P O'Sullivan, M Dunning, F Gilbert
1993 June	**Rabid** P O'Sullivan, C Griffiths
1993 July 16	**Hubble Drekt** G Hobbs, R Hardwick
1993 Aug 1	**Fluke** (Boscawen Point) P O'Sullivan, D Hannigan, A Hall
1993 Sept 5	**Famished Five** D Hannigan, J Hobbs, N Pascoe, R Mitchell, K Talbot
1993 Sept 18	**The End** H Mullen (solo)
1993 Sept	**Traverse of the Gods** P Mullen (solo)
1993 Oct	**The Apostle, The Harvest** M Raine, M Crayton
1993	**Farewell to Stone** M Edwards
1993	**A Nightmare of Nightmaidens** M Edwards, P Williams, J Fisher
1993	**Digit Do It on Sight?** M Edwards, S Rourke
1993	**Seal** O Hayward
1993	**On the Loose** (Sloose Zawn) M Edwards (solo)
1993	**Through the Looking-Glass** R Edwards (solo)
1993	**Smear on Sight** M Edwards, R Edwards
1993	**Step on a Cloud, Empty City, Star Turn** R Edwards, M Edwards
1993	**Eye of the Owl** R Edwards, N Mooney
1994 Jan 16	**Debut Arête** S Ohly, M Raine
1994 Jan 19	**West Wing** S Ohly, M Bell, G Slade
1994 Jan 19	**Dis Lichen** M Bell, I Coleman
1994 March 13	**Armadillo** M Raine (solo)
1994 March 16	**Ella-phant** S Ohly
1994 March	**Who Ya Gonna Call** M Raine, S Ohly
1994 March	**Eyeful Tower, Fast Furious Drive North** M Raine, I Harper
1994 July 19	**Snotter** S Ohly, G Slade
1994 July 28	**Ex Nihilo** H Mullen (solo after top-rope practice)
1994 Aug 28	**Rejoice the Luddites** M Raine, S Ohly, G Slade (on sight)
1994 Aug 28	**Wavedodgers** G Slade, S Ohly
1994 Sept 25	**Rodney the REMF** S Ohly, G Slade
1994 Sept 25	**Judgement Day, Here's Laughing at You, Two Big Clean Breasts, Aren't Chickens Mad, Uncle Hen?** S Ohly, G Slade (all soloed by the pair) *Some of these had been climbed before but not claimed.*
1994 Nov 27	**Sing Fling** S Ohly, G Slade
1994 Dec 11	**Erectile Zone** S Ohly, G Slade
1994 Dec 23	**The Amazing Thing** S Ohly, M Raine, G Slade *Climbed with some preplaced protection.*
1994 Dec 23	**Misguided Pixies** S Ohly, G Slade, M Raine
1994 Dec 23	**The Simmo Way** G Slade, S Ohly
1994	**Anglo-American Nightmare** A Cotton, D Lacey. *A similar line to A Nightmare of Nightmaidens.*
1994	**Disappointment Arête, Second Class Slab** R Edwards
1994	**Winged Victory** R Edwards
1994	**Question Mark** M Edwards

1994 **Pre-Marital Tension Right-Hand** M Edwards
Responsibility for the two mystery drill holes on the right side of the Pre-Marital Tension arête were eventually revealed in 1997 by Cornish Rock to have been used for a bolt placement by M Edwards; he was reported in Cornish Rock to have climbed the right side of the arête using the bolt for protection. He had left the route unclaimed and no date was given, although he later recorded a bolt-free ascent in 1994.

1994 **Beelzebub's Boobs** S Ohly
Probably climbed before.

1995 March **Raindance** (Pen Olver), **International** M Raine, S Ohly (on sight)
1995 April 16 **The Elderly Brothers, Obseam** M J Crocker, R Chappell
1995 April 16 **Unlike Siobhan** C Arthur, R Stephenson
1995 April **Dizzy Spells** S Ohly, M Raine
1995 April **Treloar** M Raine, S Ohly (on sight)
1995 April **Stay Pretty, Die Young** S Ohly, M Raine
1995 May 21 **Giggle Wiggle** S Ohly (solo)
1995 May **The Serpent** S Ohly, M Raine
1995 July 2 **Racing Line** S Ohly, G Slade (preplaced protection)
1995 July 6 **Fantasia** B Winston
1995 July 16 **Baby Bouncer, Thrutched Up** S Ohly, G Slade
1995 July 17 **Ridge-Id** H Mullen, L Pavey
1995 July 27 **Three Seals Watching** M Kemball, M Vigg
1995 July 30 **Black Dyke** J Dyke, S Reynolds
The Petrograd Finish climbed by T Carver, Miss R Densham on 15 June 1996.

1995 Aug 8 **Love Handles, Corner Stone** H Mullen (solo)
1995 Aug 10 **Blistering Barnacles, Posties Run** H Mullen (solo)
1995 Aug 17 **Captain Chaos** S Ohly, G Slade
Retrospectively claimed by M Edwards, J L Fisher in 2000 as Edwards/Fisher Slab (1990s)

1995 Aug **Gweek** S Ohly, L Houlding
1995 Aug **The Beach** S Ohly, G Slade
1995 Dec 7 **Aero Dynamics** S Ohly
1995 Dec 29 **Crash, Boom, Bang** S Ohly (solo)
1995 **Wonderwall** G Slade, M Raine
1995 **It's the Next Day Tomorrow, Eclipsed, Buzzed** S Ohly, G Slade
1995 **Bow Wall** (The Lizard), **Buzz, Polarized** G Slade, S Ohly
1995 **Ford Prefect** J Ford, S Elliott
1995 **Face Marks, Splash** M Edwards, R Edwards
1995 **Toothmark** M Edwards (solo)
1995 **Flick It, Lick It, Lil' Bitty Gritty, Lil' Bitty Groove, Paul's One Liners, Pick It, Roll It, Williams Formula One** M Edwards, T Dennell
1995 **Flaky Wall, Raven's Nest Direct, Final Touch** R Edwards (solo)
1996 Jan **Parents, Priests, and Politicians** S Ohly, M Lush
1996 March 24 **14 Lives, 13 Souls** S Ohly, G Slade (preplaced protection)
1996 March 30 **Manslaughter** S Ohly, G Slade (on sight)
1996 March 30 **Mike's Red Party Piece, Jolly Holly, Who Dares Wins, Powerslide** S Ohly, G Slade (all soloed by the pair)
1996 June 7 **Anaphylactic Reaction** P Longley, P Birchell
1996 June 15 **Disputed Ground** W A Carver, B Carver
1996 June 15 **White Russians** W A Carver, Miss R Densham, T Carver (AL)

1996 June 15	**Great Slanting, Saltheart, Blind Pew, A Little Gemma, Love Is Blind** D E Hope, D Issitt
1996 June 15	**Mile End** D Issitt, D E Hope
1996 June 16	**The Womb Tomb, Dolphin Surprise, Songs from a Gentle Man, Pilot's Song** D E Hope, D Issitt
1996 June 16	**Lying Eyes** D E Hope, D Issitt
1996 June 16	**Descent Route, Bilson's Fowl Play** D Issitt, D E Hope
1996 June 22	**Blood, Sweat, and Fears** D Viggers, B Bransby
1996 June 23	**Loco Parentis** D Viggers, B Bransby
1996 June	**True Lies** D Issitt
1996 July 14	**Falling Gull** W A Carver (solo)
1996 July 14	**Happy Landings** B Carver (solo)
1996 July 14	**Spriggen's Chimney** T Carver, M Meardon (AL)
1996 July 14	**Rebel Yell** W A Carver, B Carver (on sight)
1996 July 17	**Audacity** S Ohly (after top-rope inspection)
1996 July 25	**Sails, Butterfly, Sesame Street** J McShea, D Issitt
1996 July 25	**Umbrella Groove** E Hope, B Hope, R Hope
1996 July 25	**Redruth** R Hope, B Hope, E Hope
1996 July 25	**Bod** B Hope, R Hope, E Hope
1996 July 25	**Songs from a Broken Heart** D E Hope, R Hope, E Hope, B Hope *But full of hope?*
1996 July 25	**Mule** J McShea, B Hope, E Hope, R Hope, D E Hope
1996 July 25	**Family Affair** D E Hope, B Hope, E Hope, R Hope *A productive day on the CC Family Meet.*
1996 Aug 10	**Ripple Blocker** P O'Sullivan, C Griffiths
1996 Aug 18	**Saskia, The Shade of Dora Maar** B R E Wilkinson, M A Grapes
1996 Aug	**Slap and Happy, Omicron, Crack One, NitroCellulose, Lightning Crack, Photonic Travel, Beautiful Dreams** G Slade, S Ohly
1996 Aug	**Granite Grater, Crack Two, The Crying Game, Jo Says Why?** S Ohly, G Slade
1996 Aug	**Laugh Now, Cry Later** M Raine, G Slade (on sight)
1996 Aug	**Psycho Su** S Ohly, G Slade (solo)
1996 Aug	**Phobia** S Ohly (on-sight solo)
1996 Aug	**Escape Route** S Ohly (solo)
1996 Aug	**Wet Dreams** S Ohly, M Raine
1996 Aug	**Teaspoon Tom, Slash, Mothver** G Slade, T Harrison
1996 Aug	**Cliff Jumpers** G Slade, S Ohly, T Harrison, A Sanders
1996 Aug	**Slash Has a Crash, 99 Lead Balloons, The Space Cowboy** S Ohly, A Sanders
1996 Sept 1	**Madonna of the Waves** (1 rest pt) B R E Wilkinson, M A Grapes
1996 Sept 9	**Sean's Cleft** S Hawkin, A Grieve
1996 Sept 10	**Time and Motion** S Hawkin, A Grieve
1996 Sept 10	**Island Life** A Grieve, S Hawkin
1996 Sept 11	**Robin Bastard** A Grieve, S Hawkin, R Plymouth
1996 Sept 11	**Gone Fishing** R Plymouth, S Hawkin, A Grieve
1996 Sept 12	**Caravan Convert** R Plymouth, S Hawkin, A Grieve
1996 Sept 12	**Fantasy Island** A Grieve, S Hawkin, R Plymouth
1996 Sept 15	**Elizabeth, Majas** B R E Wilkinson, M A Grapes
1996 Sept 22	**Gypsy Johnny and the Demon King** W A Carver, B Carver (AL, on sight)

1996 Oct	**Winter Fun** S Ohly, J Kelly
1996 Oct	**Maxim's Crack** D Huges, T Loxely
1996 Dec 26	**Chocolate Log** P A J Oak, S Wilson
1996 Dec 31	**Rock Cake** P A J Oak, S Wilson
1996	**Scratchmarks, The Soloist's Mist** M Edwards (both solo)
1996	**The Golden Rabbit** M Edwards, W Perrin
1996	**Sundogs** D Viggers, D Carroll, P Twomey, B Bransby
	Retrospectively claimed by M Edwards, C Edwards in 2000 as Sock Shock (1991).

| **1996** | ***An Interim Guide for Black Head* by Toni and Barnaby Carver** |

1997 Jan	**The Grassman** S Ohly
1997 Jan	**Normal Route** S Ohly, S Tailing
1997 Jan 5	**Microseconds Crack** P A J Oak, S Wilson
1997 March 30	**Red Horizon** B Carver, M Berriman, T Carver
1997 March 31	**Sleaze** J Bradley, R Feurst
1997 May 26	**Dogs Befriend the Inventor of the Sausage Lottery** N Taylor
1997 May 27	**Juggling Tortoises, Seagulls Draw the Line at Four Bhajis, Small Pets Rejoice on Tufty's Birthday** N Taylor
1997 June 15	**Sheik Shaker** B Carver, M Berriman, T Carver
1997 June 15	**Ridiculous Thoughts** T Carver, B Carver, M Berriman
1997 June	**Incestuous Crack** M Burgoyne, T Wells
1997 July 5	**Toy Story** K Zolkiewicz, M Berriman, B Carver
1997 July 5	**Eternity's Few** T Carver, W A Carver
1997 July 10	**The Alien** S Hawkin, A Grieve
1997 July 10	**Rock Hard Peninnis, Sunk Without Trace** A Grieve, S Hawkin
1997 July 11	**Curving Crack** S Hawkin, A Grieve
1997 July 13	**Mirror Lady** D E Hope, D Issitt
1997 Aug	**Son of Satan** M Edwards, I Blake
1997 Aug	**The Enchanted Lights of Summer** M Edwards (solo)
1997 Sept 6	**Let Her Children Play, Grieving, The People's Queen, Ocean of Tears** D E Hope, D Issitt
1997 Sept 7	**Silent Minute** D E Hope (solo)
1997 Sept 7	**Flowers for a Lady, Letting Go** D E Hope, D Issitt
	Tributes for Diana, Princess of Wales, on the weekend of her funeral.
1997 Sept	**Siesta, Dream, Cream, and Scream!, Tiger** M Edwards, I Blake (on sight)
1997 Sept	**Galactic Cruise, Death Pulse, Asteroid Storm** M Edwards (solo)
1997 Sept	**Yosemite Sam** I Blake, M Edwards (on sight)
1997 Oct	**Wind in the Willows** S Ohly, G Slade
1997 Oct	**Total Body Wag** M Raine, S Ohly (on sight)
1997 Oct	**Hot Black Dog** M Raine, G Slade (on sight)
1997 Nov 1	**Dawn Direct** A C Whitehouse, S M Whitehouse
	The finish had been climbed by M J Crocker, P Oxley on 21 March1992.
1997	**Black Narcissus, Black Orchid** M Edwards

| **1997** | ***Cornish Rock* by Rowland Edwards and Tim Dennell** |

| 1998 April | **The Project** M Gibson, S Ohly |

1998 May 10	**Pulling Out the Boat** D Hillebrandt, C Griffiths (AL)
1998 May 10	**Blink** C Griffiths, D Hillebrandt
1998 May 24	**The Crack (Fox Pronotory), The Arête** M Hammill (both solo)
1998 May 24	**The Wall and Bulge** M Hammill, M Raine
1998 May 24	**Put the Red Card Out for the Correspondent** D Henderson (solo after top-rope inspection)
1998 July	**Fat Boy** M Edwards, Ms S Nuttall
1998 July	**The Town and Country Boyz** M Edwards, I Blake
1998 July	**Insularism** M Edwards (solo)
1998 Aug 15	**Las Meninas** P O'Sullivan, C Griffiths
1998 Aug 16	**Blondie Jams with Sepultura** B Carver, M J Frith
1998 Aug	**The Human Skewer** M Edwards
1998 Aug	**Far North Crack** M Edwards, R Bath
1998 Sept 8	**Mary** D Birkett (solo)
	Climbed during a BMC-organised exchange with South African climbers.
1998 Sept	**You're In Crack** T Wells, M Sullivan
	Direct finish: J Fletcher, T Wells in June 2000
1998 Nov 15	**Spot the Difference** B Carver, T Carver, M Berriman
1998	**Solar Explorer** M Edwards, Ms S Nuttall, E Dozekal
1999 July	**Make the Break** T Wells, A Humby
1990s	**A Green Thought in a Green Shade, Whispering Sands** M Edwards (both on-sight solo)
1990s	**The Unclaimed Crack** Unclaimed by A Trevorrow, and later emphatically unclaimed by A March.
1990s	**Mind the Step** M Edwards, W Perrin
1990s	**Lies, Lies, Lies, Offensively Named, The Young Pretender, Lobos, Prayer for the Raven** M Edwards (the first three on-sight solo, the last solo after top-rope practice)
1990s	**Reluctance** T Rainbow, K Hoskings
1990s	**Single Blondes, Snap, Crackle, and Pop** S Ohly, G Slade
1990s	**T Rex Corner** G Slade, S Ohly
1990s	**Fear of the Furnace** 'Azzy'
1990s	**Bingo** (Pordenack Point) M Edwards
2000 Jan 19	**The Prow** J Ford, D R Semmens
2000 Jan 30	**Solitaire (Porthguarnon Cove), The Hearse** J Hooper (solo)
2000 Feb 13	**The Bowsprit** J Ford, R Banaster
2000 March 5	**Neptune, Undertaker's Crack** J Hooper, P Oak
2000 March 12	**Eunuch** J Hooper, P Oak
2000 March 19	**Concubine, Flake Crack, Fill Yer Pants, Ocean** J Hooper, P Oak
2000 April 9	**Close Encounter** (Porthguarnon Cove) J Hooper, P Oak
2000 April 22	**Polo Crack, Polo Solo** B Carver (both on-sight solo)
2000 April 29	**Jenny's Surprise** K Döring, R Brownsword, D Cowley
2000 May	**A Criminal Lifestyle** T Wells, J Whiston
2000 June 9	**The Rib** M J Frith (on-sight solo)
2000 June 9	**Black Crack** (Black Head) B Carver (on-sight solo)
2000 June 9	**White Crack** B Carver, M J Frith (AL)
2000 June	**You'll Never Take Me Alive** T Wells, J Fletcher
2000 June	**Lonesome Lizard** S Purvis, P Robson
2000 June	**A Clean Getaway** T Wells, B Carver
2000 June	**Looning the Lizard** P Robson, S Purvis
2000 July 17	**Walk Out, Three Tiers, Blade** B Carver (on-sight solo)

Addendum

The following routes were received after the book had been typeset and are unchecked.

Carn Barra

Left of the *Criss Cross* face is a clean-cut wall with a sharp, square-cut arête on its upper right-hand side. There are two routes on this wall.

Sunset Bathing 16 metres E1 5a †   (2000)
Bold. Climb directly up the centre of the wall.
F.A. M Edwards (on-sight solo)

Miss Cellaneous 16 metres E1 5a †   (2000)
A bold line with scant protection below half height. Climb up right of centre, moving diagonally right to finish up the left-hand side of the upper arête.
F.A. M Edwards, H Lee

Ferret in Wolf's Clothing 25 metres E1 5c †   (2000)
Climb *Sea Wolf* to the horizontal break. Foot-traverse the break – a delicate set of moves – before joining and finishing up *The Weasle*'s upper slanting crack.
F.A. M Edwards, H Lee

Vamos! E2 5a †   (2000)
A bold, unprotected pitch. Climb the wall left of *Rapido* to finish up the obvious upper crack.
F.A. M Edwards (on-sight solo)

Spotted by a Nurse 8 metres E6 6b †   (2000)
A very bold, unprotected climb. A fall could result in a trip down the dark chimney. Step off the boulder in the recess left of the *Rapido* face, and climb the short but bold and difficult arête on its left side.
F.A. M Edwards (on-sight solo)

Levan's Wall, Lower Marconi Slab Area

Raiders from a Distant Dawn Very Severe 4a †   (2000)
Climb straight up the centre of the slab right of *Permanendo*.
Unprotectable.
F.A. M Edwards, H Lee

Left of *Falling Apart at the Seams* is an overhanging wall, and 10 metres left again is a buttress. An open, right-facing groove with a small flake/crack at its top is taken by the next route.

Two Tins, One String...   15 metres   E1 5b †   (2000)
Climb from blocks to the groove, enter the upper right-facing
groove/crack, and climb it to the top.
F.A. M Edwards (on-sight solo)

On the overhanging wall left of *Falling Apart at the Seams* are several short
harder routes, all unprotectable. The wall is undercut by a head-height roof
and has a sharp left-facing groove at each end.

Hazy Groove   13 metres   Very Severe 4c †   (2000)
Climb the left-hand groove, finishing up the overhanging wall.
F.A. M Edwards, H Lee

Cadmium Dusk   10 metres   E3 6a †   (2000)
Pull over the left edge of the roof and climb the right arete of the left-hand
groove.
F.A. M Edwards (on-sight solo)

Lightning and Thunder   10 metres   E3 6a †   (2000)
A variation on *Starlight and Storm*. Pull through the roof to join *Starlight
and Storm*, and break left to climb the upper wall.
F.A. M Edwards (on-sight solo)

Starlight and Storm   10 metres   E3 5c †   (2000)
Boldly climb straight up the wall to the left of the right-hand groove, and
finish up the leftward-slanting flake crack.
F.A. M Edwards (on-sight solo)

Treen Cliff
At the extreme end of Penvounder Beach, and just before the Logan Rock
promontory, is a short, south-facing wall at sea-level. Approach at low-to-half
tide from the Logan Rock footpath.

Bryn's Crack   23 metres   E2 5c †   (19.8.2000)
In the centre of the wall are two thin cracklines. Climb the left-hand
crackline with difficult moves centred around the horizontal break at
two-thirds height. Finish leftwards up the slab above.
F.A. P Harrison, B Lucas

Harrison's Crack   20 metres   E3 6a †   (19.8.2000)
The tougher, right-hand crack.
F.A. P Harrison

Index

New Climbs

Accident Procedure

First Aid

If spinal or head injuries are suspected, do not move the patient without skilled help, except to maintain breathing or if this is essential for further protection. Do not remove the patient's helmet.

If breathing has stopped, clear the airways and start artificial respiration. Do not stop until expert opinion has diagnosed death.

Stop bleeding by applying direct pressure.

Summon help as quickly as is compatible with safety. Do not delay.

Rescue

In the event of an accident where further assistance is required, dial 999 and ask for the Coastguard. The Coastguards are responsible for the co-ordination of all sea-cliff rescues, and will co-ordinate other services such as helicopters, lifeboats, cliff rescue teams, etc.

It is important to report the exact location and details of the accident and also to have someone meet the rescue team to guide them to the spot. Use the Coastguard Identity and OS Reference of the cliff; these are given at the start of each section of the guide.

Nearest Phone Points

Bosigran – There is a pay-phone in the Count House, the Climbers' Club bunkhouse immediately to the north of the National Trust car-park. However, the bunkhouse is often locked.

Chair Ladder – There is a phone at the lookout at Gwennap Head, above the cliff. If the lookout is closed use the public phone box at Porthgwarra.

Logan Rock, Cribba Head – There is a 999-only phone near the Logan Rock headland.

Helicopter

In the event of a Helicopter evacuation all climbers on or off the cliff should take heed. A helicopter flying close to the cliff will make verbal communication very difficult and small stones will be dislodged by the rotor down-draught. All loose equipment should be secured and climbers in precarious positions should try to make themselves safe.

he people with the injured person should try to identify their location. No
ttempt should be made to throw a rope at the helicopter, but assistance
hould be given to the helicopter crew if requested. Do not touch the lowered
rew member or his winch wire until the trailing wire has earthed the
elicopter's static electricity.

Local Hospitals

he walking wounded can receive treatment in the casualty departments of
he following hospitals:

West Cornwall Hospital, St Clare Street, Penzance.
Phone number 01736 874000.

Royal Cornwall Hospital, Treliske, Truro.
Phone number 01872 250000.

Follow-Up

After an accident, a report has to be compiled. Normally the details will be
ollated at the scene by the Coastguard or rescue team, who will then pass
he information to the Mountain Rescue Council Statistics Olfficer.

f unreasonable equipment failure is suspected then the British Mountaineering
Council's technical committee may wish to investigate; contact the BMC at
177-179 Burton Road, West Didsbury, Manchester, M20 2BB.

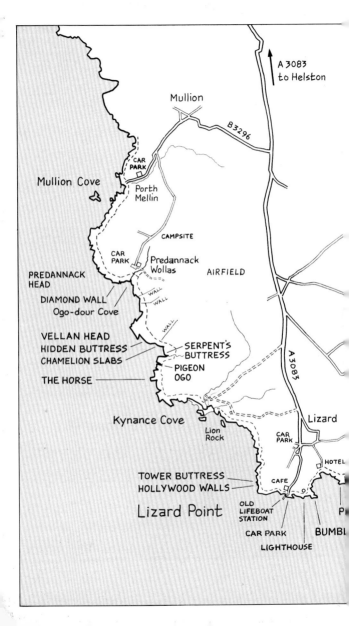